*Child Health
and the
Community*

# Child Health and the Community

*Second Edition, Updated and Expanded*

ROBERT J. HAGGERTY
KLAUS J. ROGHMANN
IVAN B. PLESS

Transaction Publishers
New Brunswick (U.S.A.) and London (U.K.)

New material this edition copyright © 1993 by Transaction
Publishers, New Brunswick, New Jersey 08903.
Originally published in 1975 by John Wiley & Sons, Inc.

Library of Congress Catalog Number: 91-828
ISBN: 1-56000-036-8
Printed in the United States of America

**Library of Congress Cataloging-in-Publication Data**

Child health and the community / [edited by] Robert J. Haggerty, Klaus
  J. Roghmann, Ivan B. Pless.—2nd expanded ed.
    p.  cm.
  Includes index.
  ISBN 1-56000-036-8
  1. Children—Health and hygiene—United States.  I. Haggerty,
Robert J.  II. Roghmann, Klaus, J.  III. Pless, Ivan B. (Ivan
Barry), 1932–
  [DNLM: 1. Child Health Services—United States.  2. Comprehensive
Health Care—United States.  WA 320 C5345]
RJ42.U5C48  1993
362.1'9892'000973—dc20
DNLM/DLC
for Library of Congress                          91-828
                                          CIP

# Contents

PART ONE: THE SETTING AND THE PROBLEMS

# Illustrations

# Tables

# Preface

## to the

## Second Edition

*Child Health and the Community*, published in 1975, was a case study of the service and research program of the University of Rochester's Department of Pediatrics during the decade beginning in 1965. It was not intended as a textbook on community pediatrics, nor was it a monograph on our health services research, although it touched on both. Textbooks can be revised and monographs can be followed by additional volumes, but case studies can only be updated.

The flavor of this update is along the lines of "Community Pediatrics Revisited." Its structure follows the three-part structure of the original: a factual outline of the setting and its changes; an examination of new utilization patterns; and an evaluation of old and new programs. The section "Facts and Figures" examines demographic, economic, and health system changes in the Rochester community over the last 20 years. The setting and its problems are revisited. The section "The New Health Care Market" describes new ways in which services for children are organized. Health services for children, and models for their study, are reexamined. The theoretical orientation shifted from medical sociology to clinical epidemiology. The section "Analysis and Assessment" reviews professional and institutional changes from the perspective of the survival of once-novel approaches. It attempts to determine what was only a fashion and what was the beginning of a long-term trend. Finally, "Summary and Implications" again reviews the previous and present values and visions that guide pediatric care programs and research. The format for this new edition is a reprint of the 1975 edition with its three parts followed by "Part Four: Update 20 Years Later." Sections like the Preface and Acknowledgements that appear in duplicate are subtitled "to the original Edition" or "to the Second Edition."

Medicine, in its clinical perspective, is applied natural science, while the organization of health care is applied social and management science. We never had any illusions that such applications are value-free, nor that our research approach was value-free. The openness of community pediatrics, its willingness to form links across disciplines, to be an applied science, and to become involved both locally and nationally, remain the key ingredients for the successful development of this approach to health service delivery for children. The audience addressed by the 1975 edition is also the audience for which the second edition was written. For academicians in the medical and social sciences, this is meant as a case study to be seen in the larger national context. For those engaged in primary care delivery, public health or health planning, it may serve as a guide for community action. The integration of the theoretical and academic with the practical and feasible in addressing specific problems was a key challenge to our approach.

*William T. Grant Foundation*          ROBERT J. HAGGERTY, M.D.
*515 Madison Avenue*                    *President*
*New York, New York*

*University of Rochester*               KLAUS J. ROGHMANN, PH.D.
*Department of Pediatrics*              *Professor of Pediatrics, Nursing and Preventive Medicine*
*School of Medicine and*
*Dentistry*
*Rochester, New York*

*McGill University*                     IVAN B. PLESS, M.D.
*Montreal Children's Hospital*          *Professor of Pediatrics,*
*Montreal, Quebec*                      *Epidemiology and Biostatistics*
*Canada*

# Preface
## to the
## Original Edition

Health is affected by environmental and social processes as well as by biological factors. The community in which a child lives is a major determinant of his health. Although such statements are widely accepted intellectually today, they are not yet reflected in our health care institutions.

This book describes how the commitment of one department of pediatrics to this expanded idea of child health was translated into research projects and program developments to move medical care, in one community, toward a greater orientation to health for all children. The book presents a diagnosis of health care needs, describes how most of these are now met, and shows how those that remain unfulfilled can be satisfied. Though at times the book has elements of a research monograph, and at times elements of a textbook on community pediatrics, our main objective has been to describe what can be done to promote child health. As many of the methodological details as possible have been relegated to the appendices in order to keep the narrative flowing.

This book is intended for everyone who has an interest in the better functioning of children in the context of their families, the broader community, and its institutions. It should be of equal interest to doctors in private practice and to those in public health, to nurses and social workers, to health planners and health administrators, and to all persons involved in the study of community medicine. Its intended audience is not confined to health professionals working exclusively with children, however, but extends to those in family medicine, obstetrics, and preventive medicine. We often forget that children are members of a family. Nor is the book of exclusive interest to those in the health field: social scientists will find that it contains information of unusual breadth and depth on many topics relative to their disciplines.

The major part of our program reflects the efforts of a team of investigators who have worked together in one community for more than seven years. It covers a program of activities beginning in the late

1960s and extending into the mid-1970s—a period of major social change in American life. It is, accordingly, unusual with respect to the degree to which it reflects these changes while at the same time being the product of a group whose members have shared a common vision and a common goal. It should therefore be of interest to all those whose lives and work affect the well-being of children and to all those whose lives are touched by children.

*The University of Rochester*                 ROBERT J. HAGGERTY, M.D.
*School of Medicine & Dentistry*              *Professor and Chairman*
*Rochester, New York*                         *Department of Pediatrics*

*The University of Rochester*                 KLAUS J. ROGHMANN, PH.D.
*College of Arts and Science*                 *Associate Professor of Sociology and Pediatrics*
*Rochester, New York*

*The University of Rochester*                 IVAN B. PLESS, M.D.
*School of Medicine and Dentistry*            *Associate Professor of Pediatrics,*
*Rochester, New York*                         *Preventive Medicine, and Community Health*

# Acknowledgements
## to the
## Second Edition

The Second Edition was drafted by one of the editors (K.J.R.) when he was on sabbatical leave from the University of Rochester. Support for typing and editorial consultations was received from the William T. Grant Foundation (89-1264-89). Patricia Lester, an instructor in English at the Rochester Institute of Technology at the time and now a medical student at the University of California (SF), served as consultant, preparing and editing our drafts. We gratefully acknowledge this support.

Data collection involved several knowledgeables in the academic and community setting. We want specifically to acknowledge interviews and correspondence with Loretta Ford and Harriet Kitzman from the School of Nursing, Matthew J. Barlow, Thomas K. McInerney, and James P. Goetz as pediatricians in the community; and Betty Satterwhite and Robert Hoekelman in the Department of Pediatrics. James Perrin reported on his experience while at one of the local health centers. Staff at the Finger Lakes Health Systems Agency and at the Anthony Jordan Health Center provided many insights. We greatly appreciate the time they generously provided.

Finally, we contacted many of our earlier contributors to obtain their assessments. We want to thank Evan Charney, Robert Chamberlin, Stan Friedman, Robert Hoekelman, and Philip Nader for their generous feedback.

Much of the research reported on was supported by federal grants as well as by local agencies. We want to specifically acknowledge Maternal and Child Health Grant (MCR-36051) National Center for Health Services Research Grant (IF32 HS 00018), and local support from Rochester Blue Cross. The draft was circulated widely among faculty and fellows at Rochester and elsewhere. Many conference calls and meetings were needed to bring it into the present form. The final version is a reflection of the input of too many to list separately. It should be attributed to a group of scholars rather than any one individual editor.

R.J.H.
K.J.R.
I.B.P.

# Acknowledgments
## to the
## Original Edition

Research of the kind reported here cannot be done without the help of many people. Each of the investigators acknowledges the assistance of teams of interviewers and coders too numerous to list individually. As editors, we wish to thank in particular the field supervisors of the Rochester Child Health Studies. Sonia Halik and Betty Satterwhite; the programmers, Jane Annechiarico and Rosalie Pratt; the secretaries, Patricia Bartle, Patricia Corbett, and Norma Skinner; and our editorial assistant, Sydney Sutherland, who put the manuscript into its final shape. We are particularly grateful to the thousands of parents and children who gave generously of their time, to the physicians of this community who contributed vital assistance and cooperation, and to researchers and staff at other institutions such as the Genesee Region Health Planning Council and the Monroe County Health Department.

The research has been supported by several grants. Initial seed money was provided by the Children's Bureau (Grants H-104 and H-148), as well as by a Markle Foundation grant awarded to Dr. Haggerty. Dr. Pless received support from the Milbank Memorial Fund and through a Career Development Award (HS-47,255). Dr. Roghmann was also supported by a Career Development Award (HS-47,266).

The bulk of the research was funded by the U.S. Public Health Service. Specific grants were HS-467 (Rochester Child Health Studies), HS-294, NU-751, K3-MH-18,542, and MG-103C. A Demonstration Teaching Project in Family Medicine and Adolescent Care as funded by the Maternal and Child Health Service (MCT-148). An Office of Economic Opportunity grant (CG-8771-D), although primarily covering services, included a research component.

Local support was received from the Genesee Region Health Planning Council, the Monroe County Department of Health, the Townsend Pediatric Research Foundation, and the John F. Wegman Foundation.

To all financial supporters we express our appreciation. To all those who helped in our endeavor we express our gratitude.

R. J. H.
K. J. R.
I. B. P.

# Collaborating
# Authors

Robert W. Chamberlin, M.D., M.P.H. Developmental Pediatrician and Consultant in Maternal and Child Health, Exceptional Family Member Program, United States Army, 2nd General Hospital, Lanstuhl, Germany

Evan Charney, M.D. Professor, Department of Pediatrics, Massachusetts University Medical School, Worcester, Massachusetts

Stanford B. Friedman, M.D. Professor, Department of Pediatrics, North Shore University Hospital/Cornell University Medical College, Manhasset, New York

Pamela Hecht, Ph.D., Research Associate, University of Chicago

James T. Heriot, Ph.D.

Robert A. Hoekelman, M.D. Professor, Department of Pediatrics, University of Rochester School of Medicine and Dentistry, Rochester, New York

Harriet J. Kitzman, R.N., Ph.D. Associate Professor, School of Nursing, University of Rochester, Rochester, New York

Michael C. Klein, M.D. Professor of Family Medicine, McGill University Medical School, Montreal, Quebec, Canada

Philip R. Nader, M.D. Professor, Child and Family Health Studies, University of California, San Diego, LaJolla, California

Betty B. Satterwhite, M.A. Instructor, Department of Pediatrics, University of Rochester School of Medicine and Dentistry, Rochester, New York

Ralph R. Sell, Ph.D. Director of Demography and Social Research, Center for Governmental Research, Rochester, New York

Peter G. Szilagyi, M.D., M.S. Assistant Professor, Department of Pediatrics, University of Rochester School of Medicine and Dentistry, Rochester, New York

Irving B. Weiner, Ph.D. Professor, Department of Psychology, Case Western Reserve University, Cleveland, Ohio

Anne W. Zimmer, M.S. Administrator, Manor Care Nursing Center, Hemet, California

*Child Health*
*and the*
*Community*

# INTRODUCTION:
## Community Pediatrics

A good predictor of a country's future vigor and effectiveness is the state of health of its children. Most societies have devoted an increasingly large proportion of their resources to services for children because this represents an "investment in the future." The United States, however, is an exception. In 1940 1 out of every 2 federal dollars spent on health was for children; by 1970 the ratio had fallen to 1 in 17. In a so-called child-oriented society this meager amount is surprising, particularly since the need for improved health services may be greater in the United States than in many other developed countries.

It has long been recognized that the level of child health is due largely to social factors such as the quality of family life, education, nutrition, housing, and recreation, plus, of course, genetic predisposition. Health services to individuals can only soften the impact of these factors. Unfortunately, in America today, this softening is often not achieved because of our failure to provide equal access to services for all children, nor do we have a national policy to improve the underlying social factors. Some children do not receive valuable preventive health services (e.g., immunizations), and too many receive services of dubious value (e.g., tonsillectomy). In short, a country that takes pride in its development of medical knowledge, expertise, and technology has not been able to claim similar advances in the social organization of medical services.

The problems in our organization of medical care include inequities in the distribution of health resources, rapidly rising health care costs, changing health problems, inefficient and ineffective care delivery systems, and lack of comprehensive monitoring systems.

The current "system" of delivery of health care has demanded a larger and larger proportion of our gross national product (although most of this increase is not for children's services). But this system remains inadequate in coping with the major health problems facing our society. New ways of financing medical care for the poor (e.g., Title XIX of the Social Security Act) and proposed national health insurance plans may have major undesirable secondary effects (e.g., increased medical care prices)

1

without achieving their primary goals, such as an increase in quality and redistribution of services. Although current concerns for cost controls may delude us into thinking that changes will ensue from different incentives, the present problem of lack of access to high-quality care will not be solved by changes in financing alone.

It is clear that the major health problems of children today are not the same ones which led to the present organization of services. A "new morbidity" exemplified by children's behavioral and learning problems and family stress has replaced the concern of parents over infectious disease. Faced with these problems, how can we best organize health services for children and train health science students to meet the challenge of the future? And how can we contribute to rational decision-making in this field? This book presents one possible answer.

Decisions about any sizable investment in the future, and about the efficient management of such an investment, require a reliable and continuing data base (HEW, 1972). This is especially true for a health care system that is experiencing rapid changes. Yet no comprehensive monitoring or surveillance system exists for child health care. With a growing awareness of inequities in the distribution of health resources and rapidly rising costs of care, it becomes obvious that a "laissez-faire" approach toward child health cannot continue. Recent attempts to develop a Cooperative Federal-State-Local Health Statistics System, and pending proposals for a health insurance system with built-in control and evaluation components, have been the first responses to this situation.

A lengthy consideration of these various problems led us to develop a conceptual model of "community pediatrics" (Haggerty, 1968). This model includes a research program to explore the dimensions of "community pediatrics"; a health care monitoring system and research paradigm that is in many ways similar to the Cooperative Health Statistics System (HEW, 1972); development and implementation of new services to meet identified needs; and a variety of evaluation procedures. This book describes our experiences. Although it is the story of one community, we believe that it has lessons for many other communities equally committed to improving child health services.

## The Concept of Community Pediatrics

The term "community pediatrics" indicates our concern with the health and medical care of *all* children in a specific community; this community is Monroe County and its chief city, Rochester, New York. The family was our initial focus of study since now, as in the past, the quality of family life is the most important factor in the health of children. Originally we had planned to call our book "Child Health and Family Life," as a sequel to the classic thousand family study in Newcastle-upon-Tyne (Spence et al., 1954; Miller et al., 1960). During the research, however, our focus shifted to the community as a whole as the larger social unit encompassing the family. This shift reflects a theoretical move from "family focused pediatrics" to "community pediatrics." A key difference in the latter approach is that it includes *all* children in a defined area, not merely those with the initiative and resources to seek help. Planning of health services, we now feel, can be done most effectively at the community level.

Though the family is still the basic social unit in our society, it is delegating more and more of its original functions to the community. It increasingly turns over to institutions the care of children with mental retardation, and to day-care centers and preschool and Head Start programs the responsibilities for child rearing and early education. The cost of major illness has become too great to be borne by the family alone. The organization of services at the community level is likely to continue to increase in importance. The present welfare system does not contribute to the maintenance of family stability among the poor. Furthermore, the black household cannot be viewed from the same perspective as that for middle-class whites with the nuclear family as the central unit.

When the economic system fails to provide for those on the bottom rung of the ladder, and they cannot fall back on an extended family for support, community agencies are the last resort. People, especially children, have their social roots in small neighborhoods. Whereas friendship groups, church affiliations, social clubs, or voluntary associations provide emotional support for adults, peer groups and school friends are the major sources of support for children.

Providing new institutions at the community level appears to be a promising way to reach people and to help solve some of today's health problems. Health centers in poverty areas may initiate contact with families (thereby reaching many persons who will not seek aid on their own initiative), assist them with welfare problems, register them in Medicaid programs, provide comprehensive health services, and promote better school performance. Schools already provide breakfast and hot lunch programs and are increasingly addressing themselves to a broader range of needs. Frequently attached to schools or health centers are day care centers for the children of working mothers.

While sociological analysis can help us to understand these changes, the social psychology of help-seeking and of helping can provide some theoretical insights for designing better intervention systems. The practical translation of such knowledge into new programs for children is our goal. Those at the medical school in this community are in a strong position, possessing the manpower and the expertise to apply the knowledge we now have and to seek out the knowledge we need to develop such services in a rational fashion.

## The Research Program

Concern about health care in Monroe County led us to initiate a long-term research program in the mid-1960s. A team representing several disciplines (pediatrics, nursing, sociology, and psychology) was assembled, office space was rented, and the group began to meet for regular seminars. Fellows in training for academic positions in community pediatrics attended these seminars and contributed to the research. In spite of the range of skills represented, several gaps in the group—economics, business administration, and political science—were apparent, each having an important contribution to make to the study of community health services. These disciplines were, however, represented elsewhere in the community; thus the services of qualified persons were obtained.

A sequence of surveys,[1] using standardized interviews and random samples of families, provided the core of the information. We measured the level of child health, identified gaps in the system of health services, tried to account for the failures, and evaluated new programs (Project I). Collaborative research with pediatricians in private practice (Project II) helped us in the development of new ways of delivering comprehensive health care through pediatric nurse practitioner programs. Problems of the chronically ill became the objective of one project and later led to a special manpower program of family counselors which, when expanded, received funding through the local Regional Medical Program (Project III). Determinants of children's behavior were studied in the preschool age group (Project IV). And, lastly, a suburban adolescent study (Project V) was part of the program in the earlier years.

This book presents as much of the research as possible, as well as several descriptions of new programs which resulted from that research. Although we sympathize with those who are impatient for "instant" action and who argue that society cannot afford the time or the cost of research, we believe that "intuitive brilliance, unless substantiated and supported by objective evidence, is soon dissipated like any other fra-

---

[1] A set of questionnaires, code books, and lists of variables are available from the authors. Secondary analysis of the edited master files is welcome (Roghmann and Haggerty, 1972).

grance" (Cleghorn et al., 1971). Hopefully, more useful child health services will result from this research.

There is a difference between the single, controlled research project (even if done in the community) and this "series" of studies. Our designs are more like the survey type—developing a system of data collection and then regrouping the data to answer many different questions. This has allowed us to measure the effects of unplanned changes in the health care system as well as planned ones. Such an approach, although less likely to lead to clear-cut inferences about causal relationships, as are possible with more controlled experiments in their necessarily artificial settings, has the advantage of showing relationships in their natural settings.

Problems of design in health services research arise repeatedly. One problem of crucial importance is the generalizability of findings. Most of the data presented were collected in interviews with over 3000 families, as well as from several other sources, including Medicaid payment files, birth and death statistics, manpower inventories, and census summary tapes. Our focus on the total "system" makes this research quite accurate for the community under study. The question then must be asked, "To what extent is this community atypical?" On the one hand, Monroe County has many of the problems characteristic of urban America: large poverty areas, a heavy migration of blacks during the postwar years, early racial tensions, and far from adequate health and other services for some parts of the population. On the other hand, this community may be atypical in its approach to solving these problems. It has a good record of success among voluntary agencies and a long history of effective planning in the health field. Because of its well-known medical school, the community is medically self-sufficient. Moreover, a stable industrial base provides an average income well above the national level. At times there is progressive leadership. As a result Monroe County may have had a head start in developing solutions which have spread across the country during recent years. By studying this rapidly changing community and, in particular, evaluating the effectiveness of innovations in medical care, information has been obtained that should help in attacking these same problems in other communities.

## The Research Paradigm

All sciences aim at the systematic, comprehensive, and objective exploration of their fields of study. Some theoretical model or paradigm guides the research in order to build, in a cumulative fashion, a body of knowledge to be passed on. Health services research, too, should be guided by some framework or paradigm to ensure balanced and cumulative growth. Doubts may exist about the necessity and feasibility of such an extensive research program in a clinical department of a medical school because the skills and conceptual tools for analyses of this kind are not part of the traditional repertoire of physicians. On the other hand, medicine as a profession is problem oriented, and the incorporation of social science knowledge and research skills may be exactly what is required to meet the challenges that exist in the organization of medical care, much as the skills of biochemistry needed to be incorporated in the past. Most doctors cannot compete with social scientists in the development of theories, but they can apply their concepts, experiences, and techniques to medical problems. Economics, sociology, and social psychology have proved most helpful to us, and it is from these disciplines that techniques were adapted for our research.

From economics we took the comprehensive systems approach of looking at health services as a market and then examining the operating forces. From sociology we took a focus on patient behavior, and from social psychology the emphasis on stress, attitudes, and short-term response patterns. As a result, our unit of analysis varies from chapter to chapter, dealing on occasion with illness episodes, and at other times with encounters, individuals, families, neighborhoods, or the community as a whole. Various "types" of theories are employed, ranging from the pure logic of systems analysis, concerned with the consequences of specific designs, to the strictly behavioral learning and socialization models of children as patients.

Our present structure of health services has developed over the past decades through trial and error. This natural growth of medical care according to the "laissez-faire" principle has had two major consequences: first, services are unevenly distributed in the population in the same way as are other valuable but scarce commodities; second, armchair planning is of limited value. A system in which unlimited needs compete for limited resources may be efficient, but results in "casualties" that traditionally have been cared for by charitable organizations. Implicit in this form of allocating resources is the idea that those who failed in the competition "deserved" to fail. Our concept of community pediatrics implies a concern for *all* children in the community, not merely those who seek medical care or those who have succeeded in the system.

Criticism of structural imperfections inherent in the health services market is growing. There are local monopolies of providers, since services cannot be stored or shipped but have to be rendered locally at short notice. Consumer information is limited, as providers do not advertise or compete. The supply of physicians is relatively inflexible because of licensing and long training periods. Moreover, external factors affecting demand exist, such as outbreaks of contagious disease (Lave et al., 1971). These vital imperfections of the free market mechanism have led a growing number of citizens to assert that health, like primary education or national defense, is a matter of public interest. Accordingly, better ways of allocating scarce resources to needs must be found. Whatever form is finally chosen by our nation, the strict market place allocation process will almost certainly be modified. Some form of rational planning will be required, although the tools for this process have not been fully developed. Planning and evaluation procedures have to make assumptions about the behavior of doctors and patients. Systems analysis and economic theories may delineate the consequences of various alternative assumptions explicitly, but only empirical behavioral studies can determine which assumptions are correct! This reasoning guided our selective use of skills from several different disciplines.

If there are rising expectations about the role of health services in improving the nation's health and general welfare, and these expectations are to be met, changes in the present system are inevitable. New ways of organizing services will have to be designed and tested.

Research will be required on the care system at the national, regional, and local level. Our research involves the microsystems or local level of care—hospitals, physicians' offices, health centers, cities, counties, and regions—and, for this type, university medical centers are in a strategic position. If changes are to be made, providers must be involved in assessing current defects and in devising and evaluating possible solutions. If the challenge inherent in the term "community pediatrics" can be met at all, the effort must involve the medical schools as well as other providers of care, rather than being implemented entirely by national planners or by nonproviders.

Figure 1 illustrates how the exchange of professional services through the medical care system was conceptualized. The model depicts the quality and quantity of services delivered as a function of how the demand for services can be matched by the supply. A flow diagram with feedback loops is an appropriate way to view the model—for example, states of health have to be perceived by the population before they present as health needs. The perceived needs have then to be translated into actual demand or attempts to reach services, and these in turn encounter barriers such as space, time, finances, and emotional stress. Gaps exist whenever the services available do not match "reasonable" demand under certain conditions. There may be a demand that cannot be met because the conditions attached are not acceptable to the supplier (frequent night calls), or the offering of services may not be acceptable to the consumer under the

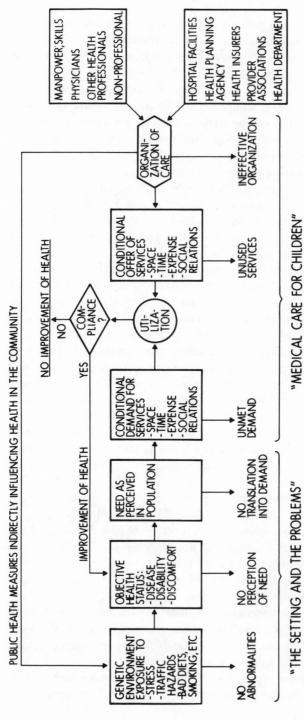

Figure 1.   Model of the community health system.

8

price conditions attached by the supplier. The quantity of service (output) is measurable, and so is the health status of the population (outcome). The cost of the service can be calculated as well as the benefits estimated for the child and for society.

The details of such computations are outside the range of our competence, but their importance is recognized and the research oriented accordingly. It is from this model that many concepts are derived. When reference is made to "medical needs," professional judgments are involved, whereas "perceived needs" are those reported by patients. Both types of needs may be "unmet" by the health system. If medical needs are unmet, professionals speak of "underutilization." If a perceived need is not judged to be a medical need, but is met nevertheless, the term "overutilization" is used. Both over- and underutilization can be indicative of gaps in health education, or of the existence of barriers to the care of some children and of incentives for the care of others.

The left part of Figure 1, "The Setting and the Problems," is covered in Part I of the text, which deals with studies of the base population and its medical and perceived needs. The right part of Figure 1, "Medical Care for Children," is described in Part II, in which studies of facilities, manpower, and utilization of services dominate. Changes in the system and evaluations of them are presented in Part III. Our book is guided by this paradigm and is focused on children, their needs, and the care they receive.

## REFERENCES

CLEGHORN, R. A., CLEGHORN, J. M., and LOWY, F. H.

1971 "Contributions of Behavioral Sciences to Health Care: An Historical Perspective." *The Milbank Memorial Fund Quarterly*, XLIX(2), April, Part I, 158–174.

HAGGERTY, R.J.

1968 "Community Pediatrics." *New England Journal of Medicine*, 278:15–21.

HEALTH, EDUCATION, AND WELFARE, DEPARTMENT OF

1972 *The Cooperative Federal-State-Local Health Statistics System*. Publication No. (HSM) 72–1209. Washington, D.C.: Government Printing Office.

LAVE, J., LAVE, L., and LEINHARDT, S.

1971 *A Model for Delivering Medical Services to the Urban Poor*. Pittsburgh: Carnegie-Mellon University (working paper).

MILLER, F. J. W., COURT, S. D. M., WALTON, W. S., and KNOX, E. G.

1960 *Growing Up in Newcastle-upon-Tyne*. London: Oxford University Press.

ROGHMANN, KLAUS J., and HAGGERTY, ROBERT J.

1972 "Mini Data Archives: The Rochester Child Health Studies Masterfiles."
*Inquiry*, IX:66–71.

SPENCE, J., WALTON, W. S., MILLER, F. J. W., and COURT, S. D. M.

1954 *A Thousand Families in Newcastle-upon-Tyne*. London: Oxford University
Press.

PART ONE

# The Setting
# and the Problems

This part sets the stage for what is to follow. It describes the setting in which children and their families live, and documents their needs for health care. Our approach throughout combines the perspective of the social scientist with that of the epidemiologist and tries to link the two with that of health planners, who are charged with the responsibility of trying to improve medical care.

The three chapters in this part move from a global description of the community in question—its evolution to the present social and political structure, and its health resources and their organization—to a picture of the families studied, and finally to a specific examination of the health problems of the children in the community. Thus the focus is progressively narrowed, enabling us to view the health needs of children within a meaningful context and not in isolation from the major environmental factors that generate and interact with these needs.

Chapter 1 begins with an analysis of the county. The present political, economic, and educational structures are examined against a historical perspective, and several important recent changes in the social structure are highlighted. The basic population data are provided in relation to social areas within the county, and account is taken of shifts in population growth that affect health care. These constantly shifting populations must be understood in order to evaluate changes in utilization described in subsequent sections. Likewise, the probability that "political" decisions will be accepted can best be predicted by knowing the past history of decision-making in the community and understanding the present distribution of power and influence.

In the second part of Chapter 1, the present health care facilities, manpower, and financing are presented against a backdrop of comprehensive health planning activities. The accomplishments of health planning in relation to such factors as the availability of hospital beds are contrasted with the continuing problems that result from the maldistribution of health care manpower.

Finally, we suggest that the reader turn to the Appendix to Chapter 1, which describes the way we obtained most of the data presented in subsequent sections. The principal procedure employed was a survey of a random sample of the childhood population, repeated at two-year intervals. Epidemiological studies of this kind are important tools of health planners, provided that adequate attention is paid to the quality of sampling and fieldwork. Knowledge of the frequency with which illnesses occur in a well-defined population is necessary before rational planning for health services can be accomplished. Sufficient details about the manner in which the surveys were conducted are given to allow the reader to judge the validity of the findings as well as to provide some guidelines for conducting similar studies elsewhere.

In Chapter 2, both qualitative and quantitative approaches are used to provide a better understanding of the composition and functioning of the families studied. We suggest a method for assessing the quality of family life and describe the impact on the family created by major illness in a child. In addition, we describe the levels of stress experienced in families and the manner in which stress interacts with illness. The effects of such interactions on the use of health services are important factors for organizing health care.

Childhood illnesses can be categorized in several ways. In Chapter 3 we examine traditional child health problems (e.g., infant mortality and both acute and chronic physical illnesses), as well as providing evidence of a "new morbidity" attributable to problems of behavior and development, schooling, and the adjustment difficulties experienced during adolescence. In this chapter we leave the community level to deal with the illnesses of individual children. The focus is initially on vital statistics and then on problems associated with each age group during childhood. One section is devoted to the frequency of acute, episodic illness; a second, to the frequency and consequences of chronic physical disorders. Each is described separately because each imposes a different set of demands on the health resources of the community.

The implications of the findings reported in this section are considered only in summary fashion. It remains for Part II to show how these needs are being met, and for Part III to demonstrate some of the ways in which we have tried to improve services in response to these findings.

CHAPTER ONE

# The Community

## A. SMUGTOWN OR MASTER MODEL?[1]

KLAUS J. ROGHMANN

[There are] two pressing needs in the fields of health and social work. [First], social planning, in all of its phases, can be done intelligently only when the basic population data of the area are taken into account . . . Secondly, the environment in which the individual (or family) operates is recognized as important in any consideration of the problems that beset the individual. The fields of medicine, education and social work are increasingly devoting attention to this "social background" in their treatment of health and social problems.[2]

Earl Lomon Koos, 1942

This statement is as relevant now as it was over 30 years ago. Accordingly, this opening chapter provides the "basic population data" of the area and describes the community as part of the "environment" in which the children, their families, and their doctors live. It describes the setting in which the studies reported in the rest of the book were carried out. Monroe County, as was pointed out in the Introduction to this book, is in numerous ways typical of many American communities. Knowledge gained from this setting should, therefore, have wide applicability.

An increasing awareness of Koos's "two pressing needs" in the field of health has, over the years, been the moving force behind the growth of social and community medicine. Major contributions to this new discipline have come equally from social scientists and physicians. Koos himself was one of the pioneers, and it is interesting that his first major publication—*The Health of Regionville* (1954), now widely regarded as a

---

[1] The preparation of this chapter was aided by Pamela Hecht, graduate student in sociology.

[2] This quotation comes from the Introduction to "Rochester, New York, 1940" (Research Department, Council of Social Agencies, 1942). The Department of Sociology of the University of Rochester and the Council of Social Agencies edited this series of publications to make census data more readily accessible to the public.

"classic" in this field—was based on research carried out in a town 50 miles south of Rochester.

Even before Koos, the groundwork was being laid for this work. Luther Fry of the Department of Sociology at the University of Rochester was instrumental in having Rochester accepted by the Bureau of the Census as a tract city as early as 1935. These and other early efforts, using the community as a research laboratory, have left a strong tradition of community interest and involvement in many departments of the university. We believe they are examples of the kind of role that modern universities must play in relation to their communities in the future (Haggerty, 1969).

This section has two subdivisions. The first places the community in a historical context and deals with what Koos called "the social environment." It describes the development of the social structure and the restraints and opportunities that presented themselves during the period of the study. The second describes the population base, its structure and trends, and offers an analysis of social areas that permits the grouping of census tracts according to their health needs and health care provisions.

## *The Social Environment*

Rochester and its surrounding towns are relatively young. The last year of our study period, 1971, marked Monroe County's sesquicentennial celebration. The Rochester community's first 100 years were characterized by an initially rapid, frontier type expansion, followed by swift industrialization and heavy European immigration. The last 50 years have been a period of consolidation.

The area was inhabited initially by Seneca Indians of the Iroquois tribe. Rivalry between French and English trading posts was settled in 1759 when Fort Niagara was conquered by the British. After this victory, the Genesee Valley was reserved as Indian territory and most trading continued to be with Canada. In 1783 the British recognized the area south of the Great Lakes as U.S. territory, and by 1790 grist mills were being built by the first settlers from New England.

In 1810 Colonel Nathaniel Rochester moved to Genesee Country from Maryland and vigorously promoted its development. In 1817 the area became incorporated as a village with the name of Rochesterville, and four years later the county was created in its present form from parts of the neighboring counties of Ontario and Genesee.

The Erie Canal was opened in 1825, carrying a constant stream of migration westward. The early economy was based on wheat production and used the Genesee River as a source of power for the flour mills. Both wheat and flour were transported on the canal. It was only in the second half of the nineteenth century that the industrialization of the city began, attracting mainly light industry and especially the manufacturing of photographic, optical, electrical, and other precision instruments.

From 1830 to 1920 the city population increased from 8000 to 300,000, but the rural population in the surrounding areas remained relatively stable. Since then, expansion has been limited chiefly to the neighboring towns and villages, which have lost their rural character and have become a belt of suburbs.

## The Political Structure

Monroe County was initially governed by a board of supervisors, first established in 1821. When the Home Rule Article (1925) gave counties, cities, towns, and villages power to adopt their own laws, a new charter was developed calling for 29 districts in the county, each having a population of about 21,500. This charter was accepted in 1928 and now forms the basis for a strong county government.

A county manager form of government was adopted in 1935. The executive branch under the county manager provides coordination of essential services in health and social welfare. The countywide Department of Health provides a number of personal services, such as tuberculosis control, well-child care, immunizations, and school health. It also includes an Office of Vital Statistics and a Department of Social Services, which administers the local welfare and Medicaid programs. In addition the county runs (with the university responsible for professional staffing) the Monroe Community Hospital (a chronic disease facility) and the Monroe County Home (a residential care facility for the elderly).

The city of Rochester was governed until 1928 by a mayor and councilmen. In that year, a city manager form of government was adopted which has remained to the present. City and county affairs overlap; county problems are often city problems as well, as in the building of cross-county highways or in the provision of health care facilities. But the interests of the two are not necessarily the same, and countywide management leads to many conflicts about the allocation of resources. Until recently, the Republicans traditionally held control over both city and county legislatures. In the 1960s, however, the Democrats gained strength in the city and assumed control of the school board and city hall in 1964; they have remained in power except for a brief period from 1971 to 1973, when the Republicans temporarily regained sway in the city.

The Economic Structure

After the frontier boom of Rochester as a trading and flour city with a large agricultural hinterland had ended, and the nursery boom with its vast mail order business had faded, Rochester's economy prospered on industry. The clothing industry developed in the 1840s and has remained about fifth in size among U.S. clothing markets. At about the same time, a number of shoe manufacturers opened up and remained important until the closing of several factories in the 1920s (Hosmer, 1971:13, 115).

At present, Rochester's industry is characterized by highly skilled mechanical, electronic, and optical enterprises. The best known Rochester firms in this field are Eastman Kodak, Xerox, and Bausch and Lomb, which together employ 68,000 people. The giants among Rochester industry, Kodak and Xerox, have significantly affected the total economic development of the county.

George Eastman greatly influenced the affairs of Rochester for the first 40 years of this century (Schulman, 1969). The continued expansion of Eastman Kodak through the Great Depression helped Rochester to endure those difficult years, and Eastman's personal philanthropies made it possible to create or expand a number of outstanding institutions that enriched the cultural, educational, health, and civic life of the community. His generosity leaves deep traces even into the present.

In the 1960s, the expansion of Xerox became the success story of U.S. industry. The involvement of Xerox's board chairman, Joseph C. Wilson, in the community was not of the same length and direct influence as that of George Eastman, but he stands out as the one person who most affected post-World War II development in this county. His sudden death in 1971, at the age of 61, shocked the community as the loss of no other local figure could have done. It became evident that he symbolized the values and hopes of this community in a unique way.

One remarkable feature of the economy of Monroe County is the absence of heavy industry like steel production or coal mining, or of large-scale assembly work, as in the automobile industry. Since there was little need for unskilled labor except in service work, Rochester did not have the heavy, later immigration that characterized, for example, Buffalo, New York, with its Polish influx. This particular economic focus also delayed the arrival of black Americans from the south. Furthermore, the highly technical production of Rochester is less affected by the business cycle of the nation. The unemployment rate has generally been about 2 percentage points below the national level; median family income, about 25% above the U.S. average.

The Educational Structure

The educational system in New York is state regulated. As the costs of education increased, the state encouraged union free districts in rural and suburban areas to combine into central school districts (League of Women Voters, 1971: 106). As a result, there are now 16 central school districts and 1 union free district in the 19 towns of Monroe County. The school district boundaries are independent of town and county lines. The Rochester City school district, because of its large size, was excluded from the centralization process. It is run by a seven-member board of education but is fiscally dependent on the City Council. In contrast, the school boards in suburban districts determine tax rates, raise the necessary funds, and have financial responsibility for their districts.

Two Boards of Cooperative Educational Services (BOCES) have been established for the suburban districts, one for the east and one for the west of the county. These provide psychological testing, social workers, and special education programs for their respective areas.

Of the over 200,000 students enrolled in the county's elementary and high schools in 1970, 177,000 were in the public school system and about 35,000 in parochial and private schools. Further public education is offered by a two-year community college and a four-year state college. The Rochester Institute of Technology and the University of Rochester, as well as three smaller church-affiliated colleges, comprise the major private educational institutions of the area. Graduate education at the Ph.D. level is provided only at the University of Rochester, including its medical school.

Recent Change in Social Structure

During the study period, two crises involving Rochester made headlines in the national press as well as local newspapers. The first was the racial crisis triggered by the riots in 1964, followed by a series of efforts to integrate the black population into the labor force of the community. The second was a school reorganization crisis in the city in 1970, and the ensuing antibusing campaign.

These two events destroyed Rochester's earlier confidence and general feeling of well-being so amusingly described in "Smugtown, U.S.A." (Gerling, 1957, 1958). They also raised doubts about the high ranking on "moral integration" that Rochester had been given by Angell (1951). The changes went deeper than a simple adjustment in self-perception; larger and more important trends were exposed. The political power structure changed toward less influence for the established business elite and more power for grass roots organizations like neighborhood associations. Federal programs had succeeded in modifying the traditional local "charity approach" to social ills, while industry had become more cosmopolitan in its orientation and generally aloof from the local deprived community. Work training programs developed slowly, and many firms chose, because of high labor costs and high taxes, to look for other localities in which to expand. The somewhat unique position that Rochester had enjoyed through the consistent control of the county and city government by the Republicans, and through some outstanding leaders, became a thing of the past.

The social "climate" that now prevails is different from that of the mid-1960s, when our studies began. It is reflected in declining birthrates, lower school enrollments, fewer student registrations at private colleges, and a general reorientation from an expanding to a "steady state" community, where "quality of life" has usurped the role that "growth at any price" played before.

The racial crisis of the mid-1960s in Rochester triggered a number of organizational innovations (e.g., Rochester Jobs Inc. as a branch of the National Alliance of Businessmen) to cope with the problem of job discrimination in the big firms. The industrial elite had a history of creating committees and institutions, often with retired business executives in charge, to attack community evils. But such an approach was of little use in dealing with industry's own structural deficiencies, and after the riots of 1964 many important changes occurred. It has been argued that these changes were only halfhearted reactions in response to pressure from outside the establishment (Schulman, 1969). The Council of Churches took the initiative by bringing in Saul Alinsky, a nationally known and experienced minority organizer, to form a black community group—FIGHT. This acronym initially stood for Freedom, Integration, God, Honor, Today, but after a long internal debate Integration was replaced by Independence. FIGHT was supported by a white organization, Friends of FIGHT, which later changed its name to Metro-Act. Schulman argues that only the confrontation of FIGHT with Kodak, and the national (and international) publicity created by this dramatic demonstration of the job discrimination that prevailed in the established industries, led to the nationally acclaimed "innovations" that ensued. Needless to say, this critical view is not universally accepted in the community (McKelvey, 1972).

A similar situation arose later from the highly segregated housing pattern. Black families, priced out of the suburban home markets, became increasingly crowded in the deteriorating houses of Rochester's two oldest neighborhoods, while the flight of young white families into the suburbs continued. Neighborhoods changed rapidly. The polarizing effects occurred swiftly and were most visible in the school system. Frequent reports of disciplinary problems and low academic performance appeared in the newspapers. Several plans for reform were drawn up, and a progressive school board ultimately reorganized the schools to diminish de facto segregation and improve the quality of education. Inevitably this involved increased busing, and formerly all-white schools suddenly received substantial numbers of black pupils. The result was emotional opposition, leading to an aggressive antibusing campaign that in 1971 ousted the former school board. The reorganization plan was rescinded by the new board, and segregation has returned to the previous level. The underlying conflicts remain, however, and financial, racial, and academic problems are likely to plague the city schools as long as the present philosophy prevails.

There have been other crises and new programs, most of which show a similar pattern of innovation through conflict, pressure tactics, or confrontations. They represent a definite change from the conservative "business as usual" style. Tensions exist and are aired but without exploding into riots. Political involvement has widened; minority participation is a fact. No matter how these changes may be ultimately evaluated, a pattern has been set that should increase the speed of social change in the future. Moreover, national events in the health field, in social legislation, and in economic development will have stronger impacts on Rochester than would have been possible before. The community is ready for these changes.

## Basic Population Data

### Social Area Analysis

The Rochester Child Health Studies started in 1966 and continue to date. It is for the period until 1972 that we report the population base, its composition, and geographic distribution. The community and its neighborhoods are spatially defined. To allocate individuals, facilities, needs, and services to specified areas, coding by census tract is of great value. These tracts also serve a unique function as units for linking aggregate data from various files. They can be grouped to describe existing service areas or to help plan for future services (Roghmann, 1972).

Monroe County covers a compact, roughly square area of a size typical of American counties. The distance from the east to the west boundary is about 30 miles; that from Lake Ontario in the north to the south boundary, about 25 miles. The Genesee River, flowing from the south to the north into Lake Ontario, divides the county into an eastern and a western part.

Three types of grouping will be used. The first is a *sociopolitical* one that distinguishes the two black poverty areas, the remaining, largely white city area, and the suburbs. The second classification adds finer geographic distinctions and is referred to as *sociogeographical*. The third grouping is by *socioeconomic* ranking (Wagenfeld, 1966).

The sociopolitical classification focuses on the two inner city poverty areas (Figure 1A.1), each of which is defined by eight contiguous census tracts. They are separated by the Genesee River and cover two old city wards (the Third and the Seventh), though they are not precisely identical with these. The tracts were selected to include over 80% of the total black population, with each tract preferably more than 50% black. Initially the selected 16 tracts met these conditions (1964 census), containing 81% of all blacks and averaging 54% black per census tract. By 1970, however, they contained only 60% of all blacks in the county, but averaged 75% black per census tract. As is shown in Figure 1A.2, the trend toward segregated living has markedly increased over the last decade. Today the two areas can no longer house the rapidly expanding black population, which consequently has moved into adjacent census tracts. Only 25,000 blacks lived in the county in 1960; by 1970 the figure had risen to over 56,000.

With respect to age, the white suburban population is considerably younger than the white city population. On the average, white city residents are about five years older than suburbanites, while the black population is even younger than the suburban whites. Thus the city has a bimodal age distribution, with a rather old, white population remaining and a very young, black population moving in.

Suburban family income in 1960 was nearly twice as high as the income of blacks in the two inner city areas; 10 years later, the difference was even larger. The suburban white population had about three years' more education than the blacks. The mobility of the black population was very high, reaching nearly 60% over the five-year period from 1955 to 1960, compared with only 45% for the total county. However, the mobility of the black population was due mainly to migration from one part of the city to another.

About 25% of the housing units in the two inner city areas were officially listed as deteriorating, compared with 10% for the rest of the city. Moreover, 7% were dilapidated versus less than 2% for the rest of the city. Only 30% of the houses were owner occupied, compared with over 50% elsewhere, and the average house value was one-third below the level for the rest of the city—$8000 versus $13,500 (1960 census). Overcrowded

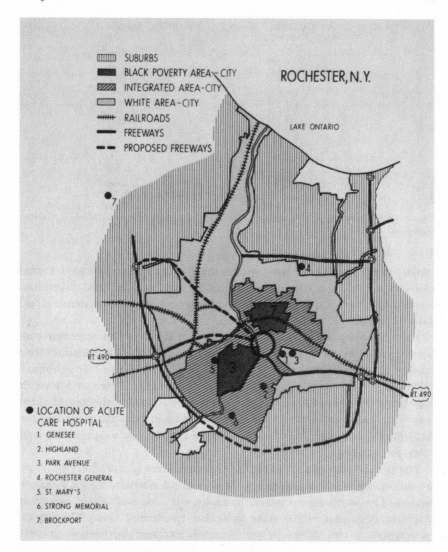

SUBURBS
BLACK POVERTY AREA–CITY
INTEGRATED AREA–CITY
WHITE AREA–CITY
RAILROADS
FREEWAYS
PROPOSED FREEWAYS

ROCHESTER, N.Y.

LAKE ONTARIO

RT 490

RT 490

● LOCATION OF ACUTE
CARE HOSPITAL
1. GENESEE
2. HIGHLAND
3. PARK AVENUE
4. ROCHESTER GENERAL
5. ST. MARY'S
6. STRONG MEMORIAL
7. BROCKPORT

*Figure 1A.1. Sociopolitical areas of Monroe County.*

conditions existed in 13% of the black housing units, compared with 4% elsewhere.

The second grouping of census tracts, by sociogeographic area, was developed when we first analyzed the results of the 1967 surveys. To contrast the inner city with the rest of the city and the suburban areas, we had assumed that the latter areas were homogeneous. It is clear that this is not accurate, and the second classification better reflects the hetero-

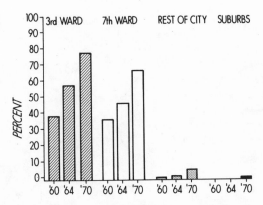

*Figure 1A.2. Location and percentage of nonwhite population in Monroe County, 1960–1970.*

geneity of the residential areas within the city, as well as that of the areas surrounding it. Also, the classification is more detailed and takes into account factors like distance from the city center, population density, and natural barriers (Figure 1A.3).

The sociogeographic grouping in Figure 1A.3 shows three major concentric areas. At the center is the city, surrounded by a residential circle labeled "close suburbs," which is in turn enclosed by the "far suburbs." Within the city, the two nonwhite poverty areas, the Third and Seventh Wards, are combined into "black poverty areas," with the rest divided into "integrated areas" and "white areas." Within both the close and the far suburbs, three divisions are given: the northeastern, southeastern, and western.

The part of the county east of the Genesee River is more heavily populated than the western part and is divided into a northern and a southern section. The southeastern section contains the old, established suburban neighborhoods and is the most desirable residential area. The northeastern part is very different; the terrain is flat, and this section consists of working class suburbs and fruit growing areas. The less populated western part of the county is industrial close in, but flat and rural in character farther out.

The third grouping of census tracts is by socioeconomic area (SEA) and is included here because of its wide use by other local researchers. The SEA index of a census tract is frequently used as a substitute for the socioeconomic standing of its residents. When no information on a family's income, occupation, or education is available, the SEA rating of the tract in which the family lives may provide a rough indication of its socio-

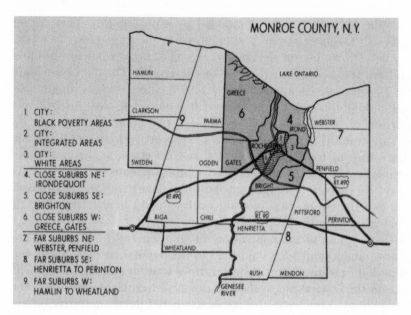

*Figure 1A.3. Sociogeographic areas of Monroe County.*

economic standing, although large errors are involved because of wide variation within tracts.

### Population Structure and Distribution

Over the first seven years of our studies the county population increased by nearly 100,000 from 645,000 to about 735,000. The child population rose by 30,000 from 220,000 to 250,000, and the black population nearly doubled from 37,000 to 65,000. The white population increase occurred mainly in the suburbs, whereas the increase in the black population was almost exclusively in the city. Such major population changes have a large impact on the health care system.

The changes occurred so rapidly that using previous census figures as a base to compute rates would distort the results. Base figures were, therefore, computed for each year, using compounded annual growth rates to estimate the development of the white and the nonwhite population separately. These two estimates were then added to obtain the "total" figure.

The speed with which changes occurred is indeed impressive. The white population of the two poverty areas decreased from 18,000 in 1966 to 10,000 in 1971, while the black population increased from 28,000 to 36,000. Thus these areas went from 61% black to 77% black in five years. If the present trend continues, the city will be over 50% black in the early 1980s, but will remain surrounded by white suburbs. These racial changes will become even more pronounced in the younger age brackets.

The western sections of the county, as well as other rural surrounding areas, have few blacks listed in the census reports. On the census date (April 1), however, the approximately 1000 migrant workers usually employed in these areas during the summer had not yet arrived. A significant proportion of our community's nonwhite population come to upstate New York initially as migrant workers. They arrive from the South for the harvesting of fruits and vegetables, and for many, at the end of the harvesting season, there is no alternative but to remain in Rochester. As early as 1949 concern was expressed about the poor living and health conditions experienced by these migrant workers, and Chapter 10 is devoted to problems concerning their health care.

This description of the population distribution and its changes is important to understand what happened to the population base during the study period. It is insufficient, however, if we want to anticipate what will happen in the years ahead so that we can plan health care properly. For this we need to know the age-sex composition and the reproductive behavior in each area of the community.

The age-sex composition of the total community is presented in Figure 1A.4. The population pyramid shows a young and growing population. The "coke bottle" waistline in the 30–40 year age group is the result of the recession of the 1930s. The average cohort of adults is about 8000. The school age cohorts who will enter the labor force over the next 10 years number about 14,000. By comparison, the number of preschoolers is declining, and school enrollment in the years ahead will be down by about 2000 per cohort. This drop occurs, interestingly enough, while the number of women in the childbearing age is increasing rapidly.

There are, of course, major differences by areas and population group. The population pyramid of the *black* population has the flat, bottom-heavy shape of a young and rapidly expanding group. Because there are few old people and few deaths, about 90% of each cohort of newborns represent a net population increase. Similarly, the number of women in the childbearing age is growing from year to year. Thus school enrollment of blacks, especially at high school age, will increase rapidly. In contrast, the population pyramid of the city's *white* population looks like a very slim "coke bottle." The white child population is stable at all age levels, including the preschool group. The number of women of childbearing age will also remain the same in the decade ahead.

As a result of these analyses, we predict that the major increase in child health needs and school enrollments in the city will come from the black population. More precise predictions are premature since they require a

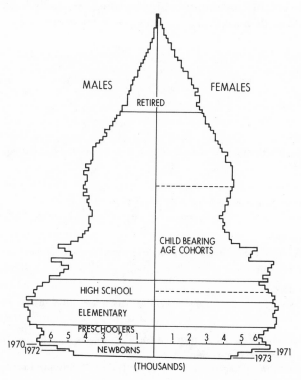

*Figure 1A.4. Age-sex population pyramid, total population, Monroe County, 1970.*

closer examination of changes in reproductive behavior (see Section 3.A and Chapter 8) and of migration patterns. It is safe to assume, however, that the increase of blacks in the city will take the form of a more even spread over age categories, economic positions, and residential areas. As their economic situation improves, more and more black families will leave the poverty areas and settle in the integrated middle-class neighborhoods. The previous correlation between poverty and blackness will, therefore, become progressively weaker and eventually disappear.

Changes in the suburbs may prove equally dramatic. The population pyramid for the suburbs shows a big bulge at the school age level and a shrinking base of preschoolers. Accordingly, child health needs and school enrollment will decline in striking proportions—age cohorts of 9000 each will fall to cohorts of 6000. This decline is due to both a change in reproductive behavior and a reduction of in-migration of young families. How permanent these changes are is difficult to say, but a reversal to the old growth pattern is unlikely.

This, then, is the community setting in which we studied the child population, its health needs, and the care provided between the years 1966 and 1972.

## REFERENCES

ANGELL, ROBERT C.

1951 "The Moral Integration of American Cities." *American Journal of Sociology,* 51:1–140.

GERLING, CURT

1957 *Smugtown, U.S.A.* Webster, New York: Plaza Publishers.

1958 *Good Enough for Grandpa* . . . Webster, New York: Plaza Publishers.

HAGGERTY, ROBERT J.

1969 "The University and Primary Medical Care." *New England Journal of Medicine,* 281:416–422.

HOSMER, HOWARD C.

1971 *Monroe County, 1821–1971.* Rochester: Rochester Museum and Science Center.

KOOS, EARL L.

1942 "Rochester, New York, 1940." Rochester: The Research Department of the Council of Social Agencies.

1954 *The Health of Regionville.* New York: Hafner Publishing Company.

LEAGUE OF WOMEN VOTERS OF THE ROCHESTER METROPOLITAN AREA

1971 *Local Government: Rochester, New York—Monroe County.*

MC KELVEY, BLAKE

1972 *The Rochester Riots: A Crisis in Civil Rights or Cityatrics?* (mimeographed).

ROGHMANN, KLAUS J.

1972 *Community Fact Book, Monroe County, New York.* (Version of February 15, 1972). 1545 Mt. Hope Avenue, Rochester, New York.

SCHULMAN, JAY

1969 "The Study of a Local Power Elite" (unpublished manuscript.)

WAGENFELD, MORTON O.

1966 *Calculation of Socio-Economic Areas of Rochester and Monroe County, New York* (mimeographed).

## B. FACILITIES, MANPOWER, PLANNING, AND FINANCING[1]

ROBERT J. HAGGERTY
AND
KLAUS J. ROGHMANN

In addition to the relative affluence described in the preceding section, Monroe County is also well endowed with medical resources. It has a prestigious medical school and a long and successful history of community health planning activities (Lembcke, 1949; Rosenfeld and Makover, 1956). A very high proportion of the population is covered by the local Blue Cross, and there is a wealth of voluntary health agencies.

As in most metropolitan areas, however, bleak spots mar an otherwise rosy picture. Physicians and hospitals are concentrated in certain areas and are almost totally absent in others. Not only is there a relative lack of primary care physicians in comparison to subspecialists and surgeons, but also the financing of primary care is deficient and uncoordinated.

### Facilities and Health Planning

Some time ago it would have been agreed that the more hospital beds an area had, the better. In the past decade, however, the opposite viewpoint has become more generally accepted. Hospitals are the most expensive part of medical care, and, in general, "Roemer's law" seems to hold— a hospital bed built will be filled even if there is no apparent need, thus increasing cost with no proven benefits after a certain basic level is achieved (Roemer, 1961:36). Certainly there is agreement among pediatricians that overutilization of the hospital for the care of children is undesirable. In general, it appears that (as long as essential needs are met) the smaller the number of hospital beds to population, the better the cost/benefit ratio. In Chapter 9 some alternatives to hospitalization are described. Until recently, however, the major method of controlling hospital bed use in Rochester was to restrict new construction.

[1] Richard Wersinger, M.A., from the Genesee Region Health Planning Council, has been most helpful in checking various figures reported, supplying background material, and commenting on an earlier draft of this chapter. Hyman J.V. Goldberg, D.D.S., Dental Director of the Rochester Neighborhood Health Center, provided us with details on the dental care system in the community, especially on the Eastman Dental Center. Ms. Mady Chalk, Planning Associate of the Genesee Region Health Planning Council, contributed the data on mental health facilities for children.

Acute Care Facilities

In 1969, seven acute general hospitals in Monroe County had a total of 2366 beds[2] (342/100,000 population). This compares with an average ratio for other parts of the United States of 490/100,000, and for Canada of 680/100,000 (McCracken, 1969; Anderson and Hull, 1969).

The number of children's beds is difficult to determine for the United States; they are not separately listed in many hospitals. In Monroe County, 226 beds were for children—a ratio of 33/100,000 population. In Britain it has been recommended that there be 50 acute care children's hospital beds per 100,000 with an additional 200 pediatric beds per million in the university hospital (Division for Architectural Studies of the Nuffield Foundation, 1963; Symposium for the Nuffield Provincial Hospital Trust, 1965). In Russia, the figure is more than twice as large with 120/100,000 acute care children's beds recommended for somatic conditions alone (Bogatgrev, 1972).

Another way to look at facilities is to examine the number of children discharged per year from acute care hospitals. In Rochester the rate of 517/10,000 (in 1968) is similar to Britain's rate (444–747). Because of the average shorter hospital stay in the United States, however, the total number of children's days spent in hospitals is about 40% less in Rochester. By these standards, therefore, Rochester has a low ratio of hospital beds for children. But the Kaiser Hospital system is lower still. Hospital beds are kept at a minimum, since that system maximizes ambulatory care and employs disincentives to minimize hospital care. As a result Kaiser plans only 18 pediatric beds per 100,000 (i.e., about 45% less than the 33/100,000 in Monroe County) but does not provide as much tertiary care —open heart surgery, neurosurgery, and the like. In Rochester about 20–30% of pediatric beds are used for this purpose; in addition, 11% of all pediatric beds are occupied by children from outside the county. Furthermore, one third of all pediatric admissions in 1968 were for tonsillectomy and adenoidectomy, most of which are generally considered unnecessary. We could, therefore, reduce hospital beds for children in Rochester from the present 226 to between 150 and 175 if this operation alone were limited to the 2–3% of children who require it (Haggerty, 1968).

All except one of the seven hospitals are located in easily accessible parts of Rochester. Pediatric services are maintained in four of these hospitals. Practically all births occur in hospitals.

[2] The figures reported are based on "Health Data Resource Book, 1971" (Genesee Region Health Planning Council, 1971). They varied slightly (2327 to 2387) from year to year, as some beds were discontinued and others added. The 1969 figures were chosen as midpoint data for the study period.

In the near future the need for children's hospital beds will be mainly a function of total births and in-migration (see Section 3A). To a lesser extent the need will reflect, too, the types of procedures developed to care for severe illness such as that requiring an organ transplant. Over the past few years the occupancy rate for all pediatric beds has been falling and in 1971 averaged about 65%. Thus, for the short term, still fewer children's beds are needed, whereas in the long run, as the population increases, about the same number will be required as today.

In summary, the number of hospital beds for children in Monroe County is well below national averages. Also, their use, except for tonsillectomy and adenoidectomy, approaches closely what is considered the irreducible levels of the Kaiser system. As a result, the community spends less for its child health care than most other communities. Individual hospital bills may be large, but the total community bill for hospital care of children is relatively low.

Four possibilities could account for this low number of hospital beds: (1) inadequate numbers of beds with resulting unmet needs; (2) extensive referrals out of the region; (3) less illness and, therefore, less need; (4) effective planning, efficient use of beds, and an extensive ambulatory program. As there is no evidence for any of the first three factors, we believe that the fourth, planning, is the only possible explanation. In the past the major focus was hospital bed planning, whereas in recent years the combination of a falling birthrate and the extensive development of ambulatory services as alternatives to hospitalization seems the main reason for this success.

## Chronic Disease Facilities

Inpatient services for children with chronic physical disabilities are limited to 12 beds in the Monroe Community Hospital. In addition, there is a large state hospital for children with serious mental disorders and a residential treatment center for those with milder emotional conditions. To date, children with mental retardation who need custodial care have been sent outside the county. A new developmental center for 500 retarded children, whose program will be intimately tied to the university, was completed in 1974.

## Ambulatory Services

The major source of ambulatory services is the physician's office, where 85% of all care is given. Other facilities include emergency rooms at all seven acute care hospitals, the outpatient departments of the three hospitals with full pediatric services, one neighborhood health center before

July 1972 (there are now three), several well-child clinics, and a rehabilitation center where seven agencies are combined to provide services for the physically handicapped and the mentally retarded.

### Comprehensive Health Planning[3]

Health planning has long been regarded as the best solution to such problems as gaps in health services, costly duplications, excessive dependency on the hospital, and a relative lack of adequate ambulatory care facilities. However, most of the planning in Rochester before 1970 was related almost exclusively to hospital beds.

Since 1945 the community has sought to rationalize the number of beds and their location. Rochester had the first hospital planning council in the nation that was administered by a community group, rather than professionals. Over the first 15 years of its existence, hospital bed construction was limited chiefly by voluntary means. But in 1961, when all the hospitals submitted plans for the construction of additional beds worth 35 million dollars, new leverage for control emerged. Marion Folsom, a former Secretary of Health, Education, and Welfare, disagreed with these plans and organized the Patient Care Planning Council. He argued that many inpatients did not really require hospital care, and that the only practical way to curtail bed use was to limit their number. A survey established that 14–18% of hospital patients did not need this level of care.[4] As a consequence the goal of a capital fund drive was reduced from 35 to 10 million dollars, and the number of beds planned was decreased proportionally. Although Mr. Folsom's prestige and his influence with the major donors helped to achieve this reduction locally, the state legislature later passed the Metcalf-McClusky Act, requiring hospital council approval before new beds could be built in any community. This occurred long before the national comprehensive care program issued the same requirement.

Although successful, community health planning in Rochester has largely concentrated on the problems of the aged and on hospital bed

[3] The information of the following parts is based, among other sources, on a lengthy interview with Marion Folsom on May 19, 1972, and publications of the commission for which he was chairman (National Commission on Community Health Services, 1967; Conant, 1968: Chapter III).
[4] The Bed Estimate Study is by now an ongoing effort with a well-developed methodology that provides the basis for planning and review decisions. Every county in the Genesee Region planning area is studied every three years. For some findings, see Berg et al. (1969, 1970).

utilization (Berg et al., 1969, 1970). From the point of view of the pediatrician, it has been too little concerned with facilities and programs for children. The major exception is reflected in the Stokes Report (1965), a study of child health facilities in Monroe County.

In June 1966 the Health Council of Monroe County (HCMC) was organized, and in August 1969 the Genesee Region Health Planning Council (GRHPC) was formed with HCMC and the Health Division of the Council of Social Agencies as its core. The GRHPC functions as the "B" agency of comprehensive health planning (under the Partnership for Health Act) for the 11-county "Genesee Region." This agency has the responsibility to recommend to the New York State Health Commissioner where and when to permit hospital and health facility construction (Article 28: Review Function). Although a wide variety of committees is represented, efforts to develop a child health committee in the Health Planning Council were not successful until 1973. As a result planning for children's services was fragmented among several standing committees such as the Committee on Rural and Inner City Health Care and the Chronic Care Committee.

## Mental Health Services

Planning for children's mental health services is not traditionally a part of a pediatric department's activities, but behavioral problems are so frequent and comprise such a large part of child care that pediatricians must deal with many of these problems. As is discussed later, the boundaries between physical and mental health, and between health and other human services, are becoming increasingly blurred. Therefore several important mental health services have been developed by the Department of Pediatrics of the University of Rochester School of Medicine and Dentistry and are described in later chapters. We have not been much involved, however, in planning for mental health services at the community level. In this chapter justice cannot be given to the long and vigorous efforts of the community as a whole in mental health planning. The following short summary (Chalk, 1972), however, highlights some of the contributions:

> In 1963 a visit by Dr. Robert Felix brought into sharp focus "the diverse sources of mental health service financing and the multiplicity of uncoordinated service and planning efforts." The community had grown weary of "strike as you can" planning by ad hoc committees lodged here and there. The Council of Social Agencies and the County Mental Health Board then formed a Mental Health Council to provide continuous comprehensive planning of these services. This Council, composed of 68

individuals representing more than 40 agencies and bodies, was established as an operating unit of the Health Division of the Council of Social Agencies and later was to become a part of the Regional Health Planning Council.

From its inception the Council's Children's Services Committee identified specific objectives for the development of a full range of mental health programs.

Within the mental retardation field, a coordinating group was organized to develop more adequate preventive and treatment programs for the mentally retarded and other handicapped children. They were in part responsible for the plan to develop a Developmental Center. . . .

In the years between 1966 and 1972, the Community Mental Health Centers Act was passed. Rochester and Monroe County received two of the first five federal grants in the state for mental health centers, and one of the first for a state mental retardation center. As a result a comprehensive community mental health center was developed through a merger of a child guidance clinic, an alcoholism treatment clinic, and the addition of outpatient psychiatric services for adults. The impact of this merger was a major expansion of treatment programs and out-patient services in the mental health center. An additional child guidance clinic was later to become part of the second community mental health center, located at Strong Memorial Hospital. This progress was the result of the community's ability to mobilize itself quickly and to plan in a coordinated fashion.

### Evaluation

We are still undecided as to the merit of planning health services specifically for children. On the one hand, we believe that health services need to be provided on a family basis, and in certain communities children's services—especially children's hospitals—have undoubtedly garnered more than their share of scarce health dollars. On the other hand, an agency that plans for *all* health services is bound to be overwhelmed by the problems of the aged, and to push equally needed children's services, especially broad-gauged preventive services, into the background. Except for the Coordinating Committee on Mental Retardation and the Children's Committee of the Mental Health Council, the only planning for services especially for children until 1973 has come from practicing pediatricians, from the hospital council (the Stokes Report, 1965), and from the Department of Pediatrics itself.

At the state level, a Committee for Children, whose purpose is advocacy, has recently been created. We believe the same is needed in each community. The success of preventive services has lulled the public into believing that child health problems are solved. It is only when teenage drug use, an epidemic of learning disorders, child delinquency, or a high rate of infant mortality intrudes upon a community's conscience that some of the remaining health problems of children achieve a high priority.

In Rochester the planning for children's hospital beds has, however, been generally successful because of the combined action of the Monroe County Pediatric Society and the Hospital Council. In the mid-1960s all the hospitals in the county were facing problems of low occupancy in the children's wards. There were pressures, mainly from pediatricians, to combine all of these services into a single children's hospital to achieve greater efficiency. This situation led to a study of child health facilities in 1965 by Dr. Joseph Stokes, Jr., mentioned previously. Over the year, information from a wide segment of the community was brought together and submitted in a report that has subsequently guided the planning of children's hospital bed facilities in the area. Stokes advocated closing general pediatric services in two of the hospitals and consolidating the services of the three largest hospitals with a single residency program and full-time university faculty at all three hospitals. In addition, he recommended providing some specialization at the two nonuniversity hospitals to avoid duplication and give status to each service.[5]

Accordingly, one hospital that already had a large hemophiliac program was designated to care for all children with coagulation problems, and another, with a vigorous gastroenterology specialty unit in internal medicine, was assigned to develop that specialty in pediatrics. The university hospital was to become the site for the remaining organ subspecialties.

The care of newborns presented a different problem because the five largest hospitals had obstetric services of about equal size. Intensive care newborn nurseries were required at no more than two, and the plan called for each of the other hospitals to have a specially trained pediatrician responsible for policies and the care of newborns. The five newborn services were then to be linked together through regular meetings of these specialists. This has been done. Further consolidation is now needed, however, because of the marked reduction in the birthrate (see Section 3A).

The question of the degree to which this consolidation has worked is answered to some extent in the chapters describing the system as it now operates in the community. Regrettably, no formal evaluation was considered in the initial recommendation. On balance, the plan seems to have been successful: the fact that independent hospitals voluntarily

[5] It is remarkable how similar these recommendations were to those in the Smillie (1941) report of 25 years earlier.

agreed to give up pediatric services is impressive. Probably this was done only because they were losing money on low-occupancy child units which could then be converted to higher-occupancy adult units. Hence enlightened self-interest plus community pressure combined to achieve this result. The two general hospitals with pediatric services other than the university hospital[6] have had, as a result of university recruiting, full complements of high-quality resident and attending staff—an undramatic sounding but relatively unusual achievement for a whole community.

Initially, there was considerable resistance from some house staff members to spending three months of each of their first and second year residencies at community hospitals, but with the build-up of a competent full-time faculty, the integration of attending pediatricians, the availability of professors' rounds, and the special learning experience provided at these hospitals, resistance has diminished. Other problems, however, still exist. Occupancy has generally been lower at the two community hospitals than at the university hospital, and, in general, the fewer the patients, the less happy the residents. Nevertheless, the consolidation seems to be working.

Attempts to consolidate children's emergency room and newborn services have been less successful. In 1970, 28% of the 69,300 children's emergency visits in the county and 40% of deliveries were at hospitals without pediatric house staff. As with the half-filled bottle argument, it must be pointed out that 60% of all newborns and 72% of all emergency visits of children are now in hospitals with full pediatric house staff. Short of creating a single maternity-children's hospital for the county and mandating that all deliveries, emergency room visits, and admissions occur there, we have moved further to raise quality and conserve resources through consolidation of children's hospital services than most other communities. As a result, in an era of rising hospital costs, the expense of hospital care for children in Monroe County has not increased as rapidly as the cost of medical care for the rest of the population. The effectiveness of preventive programs and better living conditions, which reduce the need for hospital care, has also contributed to this happy state of affairs.

Finally, in any review of past efforts in health planning in Rochester, the work of Dr. George Goler must be mentioned. From 1892, when he came to Rochester, until his retirement as health officer in 1932, Goler took many courageous actions that advanced the health of the community: the provision of certified milk, free milk stations for infants, and free smallpox vaccinations; the construction of a contagious disease hospital

6 In regard to the terms "university" and "community" hospital, all hospitals in this community are, properly speaking, community hospitals, but for convenience only those other than the one owned by the University are called "community hospitals."

and later a municipal hospital, together with the new university hospital; the recognition and popularization of the dominant role of poverty in ill health; the institution of adult health education in the public schools; and the establishment of safe garbage disposals and pure waters. This is only a partial list of the accomplishments that can be attributed, in whole or in part, to Goler (McKelvey, 1956).

At first reading there is a temptation to attribute these accomplishments to the clearness of the goals and the ease of their achievement; on closer scrutiny, however, it is evident that the same forces impeded progress in Goler's day as now—lack of scientific knowledge to back up action, inadequate resources, public complacency, and opposition by various political forces. His crusading enthusiasm, therefore, must be given the major credit for his successes and should be an inspiration to those today who seek to improve the health of the community. There is no substitute for committed people to bring about effective community action.

## Manpower

In June 1969 there were 1270 doctors in Monroe County, giving a physician/population ratio of 177/100,000. [This is considerably higher than the national average of 156 (Balfe et al., 1971) and exceeds the figures for many countries of western Europe (Switzerland, 147; Norway, 127; England, 115).] Only 118 physicians were general practitioners, a decline of over 30% from five years earlier. In addition to 67 pediatricians in private practice, there were 32 pediatric house officers who, as well as caring for all hospitalized children, provided about 15% of all ambulatory services to children in the county. The ratio of primary care doctors to children is 80/100,000.[7]

Nevertheless, much anecdotal evidence still exists that the demand for physicians' services for children exceeds the supply. Families moving to the area frequently report calling six or eight practices before finding one that will accept them for routine care. This is due in part to the maldistribution of physicians with few in the outer suburbs or the inner city area. But maldistribution is not entirely responsible for the widely reported shortage. Even in areas with high physician/child ratios, most pediatricians report that they are fully as busy as they can be.

The work loads of pediatricians and of family doctors have been documented in two studies of random samples of these practitioners (Hessel

---

[7] This is based on a calculation which considers each general practitioner as having an average of 25% children in his practice and which excludes house staff.

and Haggerty, 1968; Riley et al., 1969). Such studies give a picture of the provider side of the equation and are necessary in any community that seeks to plan its health services.

The study of pediatricians was conducted by a medical student visiting 19 pediatricians randomly selected from the 51 practices in the county. The same method was used with general practitioners. The data show that Rochester pediatricians report slightly higher numbers of office visits than their counterparts in the West or nationally. This is so in spite of relatively high ratios of doctors to population. Family doctors see nearly one-third more patients per week than pediatricians—indeed, on patient visits alone, one family physician equals the work of one pediatrician plus one internist! Unfortunately, the number of family practitioners has been rapidly declining, though recent developments may succeed in reversing this trend.

In another study of the office work of pediatricians (Hercules and Charney, 1969), it was shown that, although 60% of patients seen are ill, more time is spent per patient in well-child work. The doctor's work was characterized by the type of service provided: promotion of health (James Stage I), preventive services (Stage II), diagnostic and therapeutic services (Stage III), and rehabilitation (Stage IV). The greater emphasis placed by pediatricians on promotion of health and prevention of illnesses (Stages I and II), and the small time spent on chronic illness by these doctors as compared to family physicians, are striking (Hessel and Haggerty, 1968; Riley et al., 1969).

From these studies it is clear that pediatricians and family physicians in this county work an average of 48–52 hours per week. They spend only 10 minutes or less per patient and cannot expand their productivity without working even longer hours. Because of the difficulty in rapidly increasing the number of pediatricians or radically changing their distribution, emphasis has instead been placed on developing other health providers such as the nurse practitioners described in Chapter 11.

In 1969 nonphysician health professionals in Monroe County numbered over 9000. There were 506 dentists and 446 dental hygienists licensed and registered to practice; in addition, there were 5802 registered nurses and 1751 licensed practical nurses in the county, as well as 412 pharmacists, 66 optometrists, and 110 opthalmic dispensers.

## The Financing of Medical Care

No record is kept on the total medical expenditures in Monroe County (nor, indeed, in any other county in the United States). It seems certain, however, that they will reach at least the per capita amounts reported for the nation as a whole.

National figures for "personal health care expenditure" amounted to $280 per capita in 1970 and varied greatly with age. The personal health care expenditure for children was only $123 per capita compared with $790 for senior citizens. This means that the total estimated personal health care expenditure for children amounted to 30 million dollars or 15%[8] of the county's total health care costs, although children represent 34% of the population. What the allocation of resources should be is not clear; but, as we discuss in the summary chapter at the end of the book the current allocation is, in our view, too low. To determine what is appropriate requires careful study of societal values.

Blue Cross and Blue Shield plans provide the main insurance for Monroe County residents. Membership increased by about 5% each year between 1966 and 1969, and then slowed to 2% in 1970, stopping completely in 1971. As a result, about 81% of the total population is now covered by this form of insurance. For the healthy employed population, the coverage is nearly 100%, whereas for those 65 and older it is only about 60%.

In 1971 Blue Cross paid 142,000 claims for hospitalization and 242,000 for outpatient services, amounting to subscriber benefits of 56.0 million dollars against total premium income of 64.6 million dollars. Probably no more than 8 million dollars of the benefits represented children's services.

The main source of medical care funds for those not covered by Blue Cross is Medicaid. The total expenditure for Medicaid rose from 7.3 million dollars in 1966 to over 13 million in 1967, and to an estimated 45 million in 1971. Private practitioners received less than 5% of this expenditure, and all physicians' services totaled no more than 10%. The explosive growth in Medicaid payments greatly changed medical care in this county and across the nation. An attempt to evaluate the program, therefore, was a focal point of our research effort and is described in Chapter 7. The effect that the availability of Medicaid had on the inflation of medical care prices can be only partially assessed. Notwithstanding, vigorous attempts were made to control costs through limiting Medicaid benefits. Before February 1, 1969, Medicaid paid "usual and customary" fees; from February to May, 1969, physicians' fees were paid according to a fixed New York State schedule, lower than most physicians had charged; on June 1, 1969, these fees were cut by a further 20%!

---

[8] This estimate can also be arrived at from the volume of services multiplied by current fees. The 1.1 million doctor visits probably cost some 12 million dollars; the 13,000 hospital admissions, some 12–13 million dollars. Medications, transportation, and specialty care account for the rest.

The inflation of medical care prices was not the only contributor to the soaring costs. The number of people eligible, enrolled, and receiving services fluctuated from month to month but generally increased. In the first three years a monthly payment was made for only 33% of enrolled persons, whereas from 1969 to 1971 45% received payments. Similarly, in the early years of the program, the "welfare" population remained fairly stable between 20,000 and 25,000. From the middle of 1969, however, the number began to climb, averaging 35,000 in 1970 and 48,000 in 1971. Initially the rising cost of Medicaid was due chiefly to an increasing enrollment of people eligible for medical assistance, but not for welfare. In 1967 and 1968 these "medically indigent" represented nearly 60% of all enrollees; but, as a result of changes in eligibility criteria made in 1969, their proportion was down to about 25% in 1971.

Per capita Medicaid costs vary by age even more than overall per capita costs. Thus children comprise about 50% of all persons on the Medicaid rolls, but they account for only 10% of the total cost. The total medical care costs for the some 30,000 children receiving Medicaid in 1970 amounted to 3.5 million dollars. Over 50% of Medicaid costs are for nursing home care of the aged.

The role of the Community Chest (local counterpart of United Fund) in financing medical care in Monroe County has declined but is still important. Of the 9.5 million dollars that the Community Chest contributes, nearly 50% goes to health related activities of which children receive a fair share, but very little of this money is spent for direct hospital or personal health services.

A final word should be said about the development of prices. As elsewhere, the cost for hospital based care has soared in Monroe County. The price of an inpatient day rose at about 12% a year, and the cost of an emergency room visit increased about 15–20% between 1969 and 1971 (Medicaid fee rates). Moreover, these price changes reflect cost increases during a period of economic recession. It is obvious that, if such inflation rates continue and the cost of medical care doubles every five years, none of the programs described could conceivably lead to benefits that would offset such increases. It was the inequalities, gaps, and maldistribution of care noted at the beginning of our study that, with the lifting of financial barriers through Medicaid, led to the short-term inflation. In the years ahead, increased facilities, additional manpower, and declining needs due to lower birthrates should bring price developments in the children's medical care sector into line with the rest of the economy.

## Summary

It appears that successful hospital planning in Monroe County has kept the number of children's beds low; however, in spite of larger numbers of primary care physicians for children than in many other communities, both resources, beds and doctors, are poorly distributed. As a result, needs are not universally well met. For hospital beds this is probably less of a problem because of good transportation facilities. For ambulatory care, however, there still is a need for better distribution in areas of population growth and for some expansion of primary care manpower. Nevertheless, the greatest challenge lies in creating a more efficient means of organizing these existing resources rather than in expanding them.

## REFERENCES

ANDERSEN, R., and HULL, J.T.
  1969   "Hospital Utilization and Cost Trends in Canada and the United States." *Medical Care*, 7:4–22.

BALFE, B.E., LORANT, J.H., and TODD, C. (Eds.)
  1971   "Reference Data on the Profile of Medical Practice." Center for Health Services Research and Development, American Medical Association.

BERG, ROBERT L., BROWNING, FRANCIS E., CRUMP, S. LEE, and WENKERT, WALTER
  1969   "Bed Utilization Studies." *Journal of the American Medical Association*, 207:2411–2413.

BERG, ROBERT L., BROWNING, FRANCIS E., HILL, JOHN G., and WENKERT, WALTER
  1970   "Assessing the Health Care Needs of the Aged." *Health Services Research* (Spring). 5:36–59.

BOGATGREV, I.D.
  1972   "Establishing Standards for Outpatient Care." *International Journal of Health Services*, 2:45–49.

CHALK, MADY
  1972   Personal Communication Regarding Data on Mental Health Facilities for Children from the Planning Associate of the Genesee Region Health Planning Council.

CONANT, RALPH W.
  1968   *The Politics of Community Health*. Washington, D.C.: Public Affairs Press.

DUNCUM, B. (ED.)
  1963   *Children in Hospital: Studies in Planning. A Report of Studies made by the Division for Architectural Studies of the Nuffield Foundation*. New York: Oxford University Press.

GENESEE REGION HEALTH PLANNING COUNCIL/ROCHESTER REGIONAL MEDICAL PROGRAM

1971   *Health Data Resource Book.* Rochester, New York.

HAGGERTY, ROBERT J.

1968   "Diagnosis and Treatment: Tonsils and Adenoids—A Problem Revisited."
       *Pediatrics,* 41:815–817.

HERCULES, COSTAS, and CHARNEY, EVAN

1969   "Availability and Attentiveness: Are These Compatible in Pediatric Practice?"
       *Clinical Pediatrics,* 8 (7):381–388.

HESSEL, SAMUEL J., and HAGGERTY, ROBERT J.

1968   "General Pediatrics: A Study of Practice in the mid-60's." *Journal of Pedia-
       trics,* 73 (2):271–279.

LEMBCKE, P.A.

1949   "The Necessity for Closer Relationships between Small and Large Hospitals:
       Summary of Program of Rochester Regional Council." *The Canadian Hos-
       pital,* 26:29.

MC CRACKEN, G.

1969   "Trends in Facilities, Personnel and Capital Funds in Canada and the
       United States." *Medical Care,* 7:23–28 (Supplement).

MC KELVEY, BLAKE

1956   "The History of Public Health in Rochester, New York." *Rochester History,*
       Vol. XVIII, No. 3.

MC KEOWN, T., DAVIES, L., AND COWEN, P.

1965   *A Balanced Teaching Hospital. A Symposium at Birmingham published for the
       Nuffield Provincial Hospital Trust.* New York: Oxford University Press.

RILEY, GREGORY J., WILLE, CARL R., and HAGGERTY, ROBERT J.

1969   "A Study of Family Medicine in Upstate New York." *Journal of the
       American Medical Association,* 209 (12):2307–2314.

ROEMER, MILTON I.

1961   "Bed Supply and Hospital Utilization: A Natural Experiment." *Hospitals,*
       35:36–42.

ROSENFELD, L.S., and MAKOVER, H.B.

1956   *The Rochester Regional Hospital Council.* Cambridge, Massachusetts: Harvard
       University Press (published for the Commonwealth Fund, New York).

SMILLIE, W.G.

1941   "A Survey of the Facilities for the Care of the Sick of Rochester, New York."
       Rochester Community Chest, Rochester, New York.

STOKES, J.

1965   *Preliminary Report on Pediatric Facilities in Monroe County, New York.*

CHAPTER TWO

# The Families

## A. FAMILY FUNCTIONING AND FAMILY PROBLEMS

IVAN B. PLESS
AND
BETTY B. SATTERWHITE

One of the most important aspects of pediatrics is the emphasis placed on the family unit. Few child health workers would deny that the quality of family life is closely related to the health of children. Nevertheless, remarkably little attention has been paid to the family as an object of systematic study by those interested in medical care research. Typologies of the family proven to be valuable for sociologists or anthropologists have not found their place in medicine, and, to date, very few clinically useful systems for the description or classification of families have been developed. Apart from simple evaluative judgments like "good," "problem," "multiproblem," or "disorganized," clinicians are generally unable to describe objectively the families they see. Furthermore, too little research has been devoted to examining the relationships between the family—its structure and functioning—and the health and development of the child. This section describes one major effort to correct this deficiency—the development of a reliable method of measuring family functioning—and, in addition, provides evidence of the importance of the relation of the family to health.

Our concern is directed predominantly at the child: the relationship between the family and the child, however, is a reciprocal, dynamic one. The nature of the child as a person, his sickness, temperament, attractiveness, and intelligence all have an effect on the family unit. This effect, at times, can be devastatingly disruptive, whereas at others it may be the cohesive force that holds the family together. In the case of children who are physically or mentally handicapped, the impact on the family is, in most cases, a negative one (Holt, 1958; Farber, 1959; McMichael, 1971).

Of equal importance, however, is the effect that the quality of family life may have on the child. It may prove to be the most important deter-

41

minant of his development and of his ability to cope with a major illness. Although this observation has been made repeatedly by experienced clinicians and child psychologists, some means for assessing the family objectively and systematically is needed before it can be substantiated.

Some physicians, after years of experience with a family, acquire a sensitive and accurate appreciation for its dynamics. Nevertheless, it would seem important to enable the doctor to acquire the same level of understanding at a much earlier stage of contact with the family through deliberate inquiry rather than through experience and intuition alone. Haggerty (1965), however, has shown that many of the clinical measures of family diagnosis are relatively unreliable (although no more so than traditional laboratory and radiology tests), while those commonly used by social scientists (Straus, 1969), although of generally greater reliability, are not readily applicable in a clinical situation.

The development of a reliable and valid measure of family functioning was one of the main objectives during the early stages of the special studies on chronic illness (see Section 3C). The Family Functioning Index, described below under "Methods," was not originally intended for clinical application. Rather, it was developed as a research tool to examine questions dealing with the relationship between the family and the psychological adjustment of children with chronic illnesses. Subsequent experience with this measure, however, suggests that there may well be a place for it, or something akin to it, in assisting doctors caring for children, particularly those with chronic illnesses or behavioral problems, to more accurately diagnose the family.

*Methods*

The household interview conducted during the special study of chronic illnesses in 1968 included a sequence of 15 questions asked of parents of both chronically ill and healthy children. These included a series intended to assess marital satisfaction and several questions from the earlier work of Blood and Wolfe (1960) on decision-making patterns in families. A variety of others assessed communication between family members, family activities, frequency of disagreements, and judgments about the family's "closeness" and "happiness" compared with other families known to the respondent. Simple weights of 0, 1, or 2 points were used to score each response in accordance with the extent to which the response was indicative of "good" family functioning.

The range of possible scores of two-parent families for the entire sequence of questions was from 0 to 35 with the higher scores indicating higher levels of functioning. The mean score for these families was 25.4; standard deviation (SD), 4.9; and standard error (SE), 2.61. Families with high scores were those in which the parents appeared to be in agreement on most important aspects of family life, resolved differences satisfactorily through open discussion, frequently engaged in activities involving the whole family, viewed themselves as happier and closer than most other families, and felt that their children related well with each other; also, the mother was well satisfied with the aspects of her marriage that she ranked most important. (Families in which a spouse was absent were analyzed separately, using only the items applicable to their situation.)

The Family Functioning Index (FFI) was developed initially only for use in studying the adjustment of children with chronic illnesses. To minimize any bias and, therefore, to permit valid comparisons between those with chronic illnesses and the healthy controls, the FFI was designed and administered in such a way as to minimize the possible effect of the impact of the illness on the family. The questions were asked in identical fashion of one parent of each of 203 of the 209 children with chronic illnesses as well as one parent of each of 182 of the 190 controls. (Usually the respondent was the mother. There were insufficient data for 14 families.) The mean scores of these two broad groups of families did not differ significantly (25.3 vs. 26.7), nor was there any significant relationship between the index score and the severity of the child's disability. As a result the FFI was used subsequently to examine the relationship between the family's scores and the child's adjustment on the assumption that the family functioning was influencing the adjustment, and not the reverse.

## Applications

Several studies have shown high validity and reliability coefficients for the FFI (see the Appendix to Section 2A), suggesting that it may be of value in clinical settings as well. The measure could be used as a basis for deciding whether families of children with emotional or physical handicaps are likely to require special attention or additional assistance to help prevent secondary psychological or social maladjustment. The questions comprising the FFI can be asked in less than 10 minutes, and scoring requires only a few minutes. The normative data now available enable the clinician to regard as "high risk" any family scoring below 20. The application of the FFI in predicting the likelihood that children with chronic physical disorders will have psychological difficulties is described in Section 3C.

The concept of "high risk" is of considerable importance in planning health services, particularly those that have prevention as their goal. Families whose children are "at risk" for many undesirable, health related outcomes based on family income, race, and structural features are already generally recognized. The FFI is intended to add to this knowledge by making available additional information about the dynamics of family functioning when obvious social risks are not present. If, by taking both the structural and the functional components of family life into account, we can more accurately identify those needing assistance and those most likely to benefit from it, we shall be one step closer to achieving a truly efficient and equitable health service for all.

*Impact of Illness on the Family*

In the special study of children with chronic illnesses, an attempt was made to assess the impact of a child's illness on the other members of the family. Although the way the family reacts to the child is determined chiefly by the style of functioning that normally prevails, the burden imposed on the family through having a child with a chronic illness also influences the way in which the family responds to the child on a day-to-day basis.

It must be emphasized that most of the problems reported by families with sick children are also experienced by families with healthy children. Indeed, it is of interest that the same proportion of families in both groups (80%) reported having at least one major problem in the year preceding the household interview. And while health problems were identified most frequently for those with sick children, the other major problems of family life appeared in the same order in both groups. For all families, apart from health problems, the major difficulties were found chiefly in the area of behavioral problems or financial burdens. Each of these was reported by approximately 10–15% of the families in both groups. Other important areas of difficulty involved schooling, housing, and marital relationships. Similar descriptions of the high frequency of such problems are detailed in Section 2B on coping with stress. Most families described being able to reach some sort of solution to these problems through discussion, though a higher proportion (10% vs. 4%) of those with sick children reported an inability of parents to discuss such problems with one another.

In the case of children with chronic disorders the parent interview included an open-ended question asking if the child's condition had affected the family in any way. The majority of responses given reflected, above all, the amount of worry and concern associated with these illnesses.

One parent noted, "We are always conscious of the problem," while an-·other recalled, "We were all upset and nerves were frayed for several months at a time." Reflecting what must be a very common but rarely admitted attitude, one mother commented, "We watch her [the ill child] more carefully and are a little overprotective of her."

Among the spontaneous replies to this question were indications by some parents of their concern about other children in the family: "Our daughter resented the attention given to her brother and often acted up," and "The other children have lost their patience with him." Also mentioned were the many ways in which the parents' lives were directly affected: "We occasionally cancel plans if he is uncomfortable, and some-times have had to come home in the evening to comfort him." A number of parents noted difficulty in finding baby-sitters who were willing to stay with a child having a disorder that might require special attention, no matter how minor. Although few parents mentioned it in reply to the open-ended question, many comments suggested parental friction as a frequent consequence of having a handicapped child. "The pressures have caused dissent and disagreement between us as parents," was one typical comment; in the words of another, "Both of us are often irritable and nervous."

On the other hand, because the question about the effect of the child's illness on the family was asked in such a way as to include examples of a positive nature, several parents responded by describing ways in which the family appeared to benefit. Some viewed the condition as a unifying force, drawing them closer and motivating them to work together to a greater degree. Others thought that it had increased their sensitivity to the problems of others: "Our children are more tolerant of other people with handicaps"; "They accept other children with some affliction"; "It has helped our children to understand physical defects of others more."

The open-ended question was followed by another in which mothers were asked to describe what they considered the hardest part of caring for children with the condition in question. The most commonly mentioned problem, alone or in combination with others, cited by 90 parents (43%), was "worry." Factors relating to adjustment, finances, physical strain, and a host of others were also identified. When asked what advice they would give other mothers whose children had the same condition, most parents (42%) responded by offering some specific medical pointers. In addition 65 parents offered suggestions of a psychological nature: "Learn to live with the disorder"; "Learn how to accept it"; "Treat him as a normal child." Only 12 parents emphasized the importance of choosing a "good" doctor or the "right" doctor.

A list of specific ways in which families were affected by a child's chronic disorder was then presented, and the parents were asked the extent to which any of these had been a problem for them and whether they had occurred in the past year or previously. These problem areas are shown in Figure 2A.1 in relation to the severity of the child's disability. For the most part it is clear that the more severely disabled children have a greater impact on the family in each of these respects, though there are some notable exceptions. Because these questions could not be asked of the parents of healthy children, only a comparison of the responses by parents of the severely disabled with those by parents of children with little or no disability could be made. For example, nearly 50% of the families with a chronically sick child reported significant financial difficulties as a consequence of the child's condition. For families with severely disabled children the percentage was 66%; for those with only mildly disabled children the percentage was still 44%.

Apart from sheer fatigue, reported by about one quarter of all families, and particularly by the parents of the more severely disabled, the other areas of impact were described by only about 10–15% of families. The ways in which a major illness can affect a family are not mutually exclusive. Consequently some "clustering" of problems was apparent; for example, parents of children with allergies often reported the need to alter both sleeping arrangements and household furnishings, while those who had children with major physical handicaps tended to mention difficulties associated with traveling and embarrassment stemming from the reactions of strangers. The important point, however, is that few families were entirely free of *some* effect of the child's illness. Moreover, any *one* of the areas mentioned could be burdensome in the extreme. The effect on the family's social life, for example, may sound trivial, but could (and did in some cases) mean that the parents had *never* been out together since the child's illness began. The effect on "sleeping arrangements" meant, in some cases, that the child routinely slept in the parents' bedroom, and, in a few instances, shared the same bed so that "attacks" of one kind or another could be identified promptly. The fact that only 10% of respondents cited marital friction as a consequence of the child's illness may seem surprising.[1] Similarly it is likely that the extent to which other children in the family were neglected or resented the attention that was devoted to the sick child is underreported in a study of this kind. In the relatively

---

[1] It is very likely, however, to be an underestimate of the true frequency of this problem and does not take into account the many single-parent families in the sample. There is no way of telling from a study such as this the extent to which divorces or separations are related to a child's illness—it is clear that such an association existed in several well-documented cases.

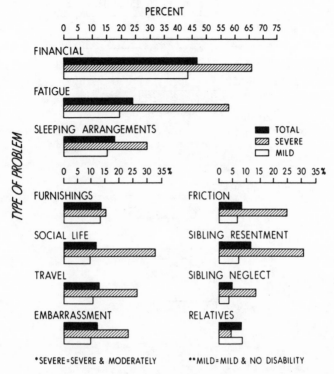

*Figure 2A.1.  Impact of chronic illness on the family: Percentage of families reporting problems in each area by severity of child's illness. Total=209, Severe\*=28, Mild\*\*= 181.*

few cases in which these areas were identified the descriptions given of the degree of neglect or resentment were often striking.

An attempt was made to determine the characteristics of the child's illness and/or of the family that were related to the amount of impact the family experienced. To do so a total impact score was obtained by assigning 1–4 points for each problem area cited, depending on the severity and recency of the problem (e.g., much-recent, 4 points; little-past, 1 point). The total score for each family was found to be related to the severity of the child's illness and to several other factors as shown in Figure 2A.2. It is clear that the relationships between both the severity of the disorder and impact on the child and the total impact on the family are direct ones. Less clear, though significant, relationships exist between family impact and the health of other members of the family and the way in which it functions. One-parent families appear to fare the worst, while

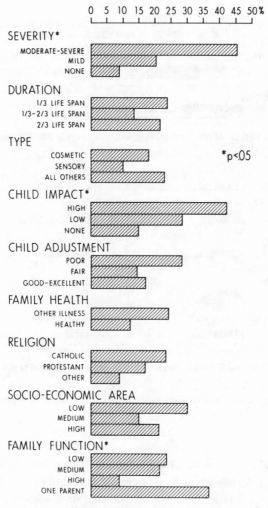

Figure 2A.2. Percentage of children and families who have high impact scores by selected factors (41 high-impact-score families among all 209 families).

families with high family functioning scores are least affected by the child's illness.

What is particularly distressing about these findings is that very few families with major problems in any of these areas had received any significant assistance from health professionals, social workers, public health nurses, or family service agencies. Certainly the physician was rarely mentioned in connection with these problems, presumably because difficulties of this kind are not now seen as part of the doctor's job.

*Discussion*

The study of the family in relation to health and disease is still in its infancy. Some work has been done by social scientists (Sussman, 1959; Chen and Cobb, 1960) and by investigators in the field of child development (Clausen, 1966), but there are still few ways in which these studies can be applied in clinical practice or in the organization of child health services in the community. Both an understanding of family dynamics and its effect on the child and an awareness of the impact of the child's illness on family members are of potential value. More knowledge about the effect that the family has on the child—his growth, development, and responses to illness—is of immediate value in enabling the clinician or health planner to identify families or groups of families that will require special services and attention. More knowledge about the ways in which illness in one member of the family affects others may not only result in the formulation of measures whereby the impact can be reduced, but may also help to minimize the consequences of the illness for the patient. Each of these components will, therefore, be discussed separately.

In the first part of this section an attempt to measure family functioning in an objective fashion is described. Although this area is not well documented, it is doubtful that physicians know a great deal about the families of their patients. Since most children do well in spite of this lack of information, it might be concluded that a detailed knowledge of the family is unnecessary in day-to-day practice. This seems unlikely, but there is no evidence that the quality of care is significantly improved when the doctor's knowledge of the family is increased. Logic dictates, however, that it is difficult to care adequately for a child with chronic illness or one with a behavioral problem without reasonably extensive knowledge about the structure and functioning of the family.

Family structure may not be adequately described simply by distinguishing between "broken" and "intact" families with respect to the presence of both parents (Roghmann et al., 1973). As we move into the mid-1970s, such a simple distinction appears to be increasingly unimportant, particularly when the concept of "family" is changing so rapidly. Nevertheless, it has been shown that some responses to illness depend on such structural features as family size, the type of family unit (i.e., nuclear or extended), and the state of family development. Similarly, the racial, ethnic, religious, and social class characteristics of the family may assist the doctor in understanding and predicting how an illness in a member can best be handled. These structural features are usually known to the doctor, though the information is not routinely recorded in the patient's record (Chamberlin, 1971).

As important as these family characteristics undoubtedly are, it is likely that the "functional" attributes of the family are of even greater potential value. Unfortunately, these attributes are difficult to describe, let alone to measure objectively. Geismar and Ayres (1959) have described a procedure for measuring this dimension of the family. It is intended to evaluate "the social functioning of disorganized families" and is based on the judgments of case workers who have had extensive contact with these families. Because the procedure requires this lengthy contact, its value in large-scale social research or medical practice is limited, in spite of its reliability and validity.

The "functional" aspects of family life include such factors as the way members relate to one another, the manner and ease with which they communicate, the extent to which activities are carried out jointly, the level of marital satisfaction of the spouses, and the happiness and closeness of the unit as a whole. They represent, in short, the pulse and temperature of the family as a group, as contrasted with its external appearance. They tell us something of how the family operates, and what the quality of family life is like. "Functioning" is an aspect that clinicians having long experience with a family appear to recognize almost instinctively, though they would be hard put to describe it other than to say, "This is a 'good' family; they'll cope all right on their own," in contrast to another family for which they know that help will be needed. Because this kind of judgment seems of such great potential importance, and because it is entirely dependent on experience and sensitivity, the FFI or a similar objective measure should help the doctor to develop the basis for making such judgments more quickly and universally.

The relation between various forms of stress and illness in the family will be described in Section 2B. The work of Meyer and Haggerty (1962) showing how stress influenced individual susceptibility to streptococcal infections, and many other studies demonstrating a similar relation between stress and illness (e.g., Holmes and Rahe, 1967), provide models for further examination. The most striking demonstration of the influence of parents on a child's illness is seen in studies in which children with asthma have been removed from the family (Purcell et al., 1969). Both Mattsson and Gross (1966) and Spencer and Behar (1969) have described how family relationships, particularly the role of the father, may influence the coping and adaptation of children with hemophilia. Others have shown similar relationships between parental attitudes and the adjustment of deaf children (Neuhaus, 1969; Gordon, 1959). And, as is shown in Section 3C, functioning as measured by the FFI is an important factor in determining the adjustment of children with chronic disorders generally (Pless et al., 1972).

The reverse half of the picture has been painted in greater detail; much more is known about the consequences of mental or physical illness for the family. Some studies have focused chiefly on the economic impact of disease on the family (McCollum, 1971; McLean et al., 1968). Surprisingly, few describe in any systematic fashion the effect of illness in one child on his siblings (Schreiber and Feeley, 1965; Berggreen, 1971; Tew and Laurence, 1973). In general, the dynamics of the way in which a major handicap affects the family are fairly well understood. The importance of the way in which parents are informed of the diagnosis initially (D'Arcy, 1968; Clifford and Crocker, 1971; Meadow, 1968), and the importance of a sound and accurate understanding of the nature and cause of the child's illness in relation to feelings of guilt about the past and anxiety about the future (Korsch and Barnett, 1961), are each well documented. The effect on mother-child interactions is the focus of reports by Gardiner et al. (1972) and by Kogan and Tyler (1973). Two illnesses—cystic fibrosis and spina bifida—have been used as models for studying the impact of a severe handicap on the family as a whole (Gayton and Friedman, 1973; Walker et al., 1971; Freeston, 1971; Hunt, 1973; Richards and McIntosh, 1973).

The need for intensive, complete, and sustained counseling for many of these families is apparent, yet it is equally evident that such assistance is frequently lacking. The family counselor program, described in Section 11B, has been one response to this shortcoming. It is not a total answer, however, and some means must be found to convince physicians responsible for the care of these children that they have much to contribute in alleviating the tragic burdens borne by their families.

## REFERENCES

BERGGREEN, SHEILA M.
   1971   "A Study of the Mental Health of the Near Relatives of Twenty Multihandicapped Children." *Acta Paediatrica Scandinavica* (Supplement 215).

BLOOD, R.O., and WOLFE, D.M.
   1960   *Husbands and Wives: The Dynamics of Married Living.* New York: The Free Press.

CHAMBERLIN, ROBERT W.
   1971   "Social Data in Evaluation of the Pediatric Patient: Deficits in Outpatient Records." *Journal of Pediatrics*, 78:116.

CHEN, E., and COBB, S.

1960  "Family Structure in Relation to Health and Disease." *Journal of Chronic Diseases*, 12:544–567.

CLAUSEN, J.A.

1966  "Family Structure, Socialization, and Personality." In *Review of Child Development Research*, Vol. 2, edited by M. Hoffman and L. Hoffman. New York: Russell Sage Foundation.

CLIFFORD, EDWARD, and CROCKER, ELEANOR

1971  "Maternal Responses: The Birth of a Normal Child as Compared to the Birth of a Child with Cleft." *The Cleft Palate Journal*, 3:298–306.

D'ARCY, ELIZABETH

1968  "Congenital Defects: Mothers' Reactions to First Information." *British Medical Journal*, 3:796–798.

FARBER, BERNARD

1959  *Effects of a Severely Mentally Retarded Child on Family Integration.* Michigan: University Microfilms.

FREESTON, B.M.

1971  "An Enquiry into the Effect of a Spina Bifida Child upon Family Life." *Developmental Medicine and Child Neurology*, 13:456–461.

GARDINER, A., PORTEOUS, N., and SMITH, J.A.

1972  "The Effect of Coeliac Disease on the Mother-Child Relationship." *Australian Paediatric Journal*, 8:39–43.

GAYTON, WILLIAM F., and FRIEDMAN, STANFORD B.

1973  "Psychosocial Aspects of Cystic Fibrosis: A Review of the Literature." *American Journal of Diseases of Children*, 126(6):856–859.

GEISMAR, L.L., and AYRES, B.

1959  "A Method for Evaluating the Social Functioning of Families under Treatment." *Social Work*, 4:102–108.

GORDON, JESSE E.

1959  "Relationships Among Mothers' *n* Achievement, Independence Training Attitudes, and Handicapped Children's Performance." *Journal of Consulting Psychology*, 23:3:207–212.

HAGGERTY, ROBERT J.

1965  "Family Diagnosis: Research Methods and Their Reliability for Studies of the Medical-Social Unit, the Family." *American Journal of Public Health*, 55:1521–1533.

HOLMES, T.H., and RAHE, R.H.

1967  "Social Readjustment Rating Scale." *Journal of Psychosomatic Research*, 11:213–218.

HOLT, K.S.

1958  "The Home Care of Severely Retarded Children." *Pediatrics*, 22:744–755.

HUNT, GILLIAN M.

1973 "Implications of the Treatment of Myelomeningocele for the Child and His Family." *The Lancet,* December, 1308–1310.

KOGAN, KATE L., and TYLER, NANCY

1973 "Mother-Child Interaction in Young Physically Handicapped Children." *American Journal of Mental Deficiency,* 77 (5):492–497.

KORSCH, BARBARA, and BARNETT, HENRY L.

1961 "The Physician, the Family and the Child with Nephrosis." *The Journal of Pediatrics,* 58 (5): 707–715.

MC COLLUM, AUDREY

1971 "Cystic Fibrosis: Economic Impact upon The Family." *American Journal of Public Health,* 61:1335–1340.

MC LEAN, JAMES, SCHRAGER, JULES, and STOEFFLER, VICTOR

1968 "Severe Asthma in Children." *Michigan Medicine,* 67 (19):1219–1226.

MC MICHAEL, JOAN

1971 *Handicap.* London: Staples Press.

MATTSSON, AKE, and GROSS, SAMUEL

1966 "Social and Behavioral Studies on Hemophiliac Children and Their Families." *The Journal of Pediatrics,* 68:952–964.

MEADOW, KATHRYN

1968 "Parental Response to the Medical Ambiguities of Congenital Deafness." *Journal of Health and Social Behavior,* 9:299–309.

MEYER, ROGER, and HAGGERTY, ROBERT

1962 "Streptococcal Infections in Families—Factors Altering Individual Susceptibility." *Pediatrics,* 29:539–550.

NEUHAUS, MAURY

1969 "Parental Attitudes and the Emotional Adjustment of Deaf Children." *Exceptional Children,* May, p. 721–727.

PLESS, I. BARRY, ROGHMANN, KLAUS J., and HAGGERTY, ROBERT J.

1972 "Chronic Illness, Family Functioning, and Psychological Adjustment: A Model for the Allocation of Preventive Mental Health Services." *International Journal of Epidemiology,* 1(3)271–277.

PURCELL, KENNETH, BRADY, KIRK, CHAI, HYMAN, MUSER, JOAN, MOLK, LEIZER, GORDON, NATHAN, and MEANS, JOHN

1969 "The Effect on Asthma in Children of Experimental Separation from the Family." *Psychosomatic Medicine,* XXXI:144–164.

RICHARDS, I.D. GERALD, and MC INTOSH, HELEN T.

1973 "Spina Bifida Survivors and Their Parents: A Study of Problems and Services." *Developmental Medicine and Child Neurology,* 15:293–304.

ROGHMANN, KLAUS J., HECHT, PAMELA K., and HAGGERTY, ROBERT J.

1973 "Family Coping with Everyday Stress: Self-Reports from a Household Survey." *Journal of Comparative Family Studies,* IV (1):49–62.

SCHREIBER, MEYER, and FEELEY, MARY
    1965   "Siblings of the Retarded." *Children,* 12 (6):221–228.

SPENCER, ROGER, and BEHAR, LEONARD
    1969   "Adaptation in Hemophiliac Adolescents." *Psychosomatics,* 10:304–305.

STRAUS, MURRAY A.
    1969   *Family Measurement Techniques.* Minneapolis: University of Minnesota Press.

SUSSMAN, M.B.
    1959   *Sourcebook in Marriage and the Family.* Boston: Houghton Mifflin Company.

TEW, BRIAN, and LAURENCE, K.M.
    1973   "Mothers, Brothers and Sisters of Patients with Spina Bifida." *Developmental Medicine and Child Neurology* (Supplement 29):69–76.

WALKER, J.H., THOMAS, M., and RUSSELL, I.T.
    1971   "Spina Bifida and the Parents." *Developmental Medicine and Child Neurology,* 13:462–476.

## B. COPING WITH STRESS

KLAUS J. ROGHMANN,
PAMELA HECHT,
AND
ROBERT J. HAGGERTY

Stress and organic illness have been positively correlated in many previous studies (Hinkle, 1958; Holmes et al., 1957; Meyer and Haggerty, 1962; Mechanic, 1962; Skipper and Leonard, 1968), although the physiological mechanisms for this altered host resistance are not yet clear. Easier to understand is the well-documented relation between stress and mental illness (Brown and Birley, 1968; Dohrenwend and Dohrenwend, 1969; Dohrenwend, 1973). More recently, sociologists (Levine and Scotch, 1970; Dodge and Martin, 1970) and psychologists (Lazarus, 1966; McGrath, 1970) have given increasing attention to the sources of stress and to the process of coping with it.

Our focus has been on one specific outcome of family stress: changes in the *use* of health services by mothers and children, and the implications this has for the *organization* of health services. Caplan (1961) postulates that crises are opportune times for intervention because people are more susceptible to changing their coping behavior during such periods. If stress prompts people to seek care earlier and also makes intervention more effective, this could have important implications for the organization of medical care. At present, most care is provided for individuals by their own physicians in spite of the fact that crises and the effects of disease are usually shared by all family members. Similarly, to intervene at the time of a crisis would require easier access to physicians than is now available. Before such drastic changes can be recommended, however, normative data on the frequency of life crises and their relation to the use of health services are required.

One of the objectives of the 1969 survey was to document, for a random sample of families with children under 18, the incidence and course of stressful events, and to determine whether illness is more likely to lead to use of medical services when stress is present than when stress is absent. This section describes the result in regard to the incidence of stressful events and the ways in which families cope with them—data not previously available. Their effect on illness and utilization are presented in Section 4B.

The terms "crisis" and "stress" are used interchangeably in this study, although they are frequently employed to describe separate parts of the same process. "Crisis" or "stressor" usually refers to the external event, and "stress" or "tension" to the individual's response. We defined stress as any upsetting event, *excluding illness*, that affected the family and required some type of coping behavior. Loss of job, marital discord, and divorce are examples of such events. Two types of stress were distinguished: major, chronic stress, for which long time periods have to be studied, and minor, short-term stress, as it occurs on a day-to-day basis. The results of the quantitative analysis will be presented first; a few case studies will be given next to provide a descriptive or qualitative picture of the impact that a stressful life situation can have on families.

*Methods*

A random sample of 512 families was selected in 1969 (see Appendix to Chapter 1). Poorer segments of the population were oversampled, and therefore, weighting factors are used to correct for the underrepresentation of middle-class families, leading to an inflated sample size of 879.

An initial household interview provided demographic data and information about recent illnesses, use of health services, and chronic stress. Various aspects of family life (employment, meeting expenses, housing, transportation, etc.) were systematically screened for situations that might be sources of stress. Acute stressful events like deaths, car accidents, or unwanted pregnancies were inquired about separately. This interview had the effect of sensitizing the mother to the type of events that she would be asked to report. The mother was then asked to keep a diary in which she recorded, for 28 days, the presence or occurrence of three types of events: upsetting events, illnesses, and any use of health services. A nominal fee was paid for keeping these diaries, which were checked periodically for proper recording. These records provided data for the analysis of day-to-day stress. About one year after the initial contact there was a follow-up interview. Coders evaluated the amount of coping required by any special event reported and assigned stress scores accordingly.

*Results*

Quantitative Analysis

Major stress, as identified in the interview, was grouped by chronicity. In the first group, sustained or chronic stress, are such events as unemployment, poor housing, fights on the block, violence in schools, and financial trouble. The second group, short-term or acute stress, includes more dramatic events such as the death of a relative, a major car accident, divorce or separation, or contact with police or courts. The frequency of affirmative responses for the first group of problems is a direct function of annual family income, as shown in Table 2B.1; for example, stress scores for poor housing and school problems showed a direct relation to income. Life in a lower-class situation is, without doubt, more stressful. This is reflected also in the *self-evaluation* of ability to cope with unexpected financial expenses. For example, 11% reported having trouble in paying medical bills; over 12% experience difficulty in making ends meet in general. Again there is a direct linear relation to income.

Table 2B.2. presents the frequencies of major acute stress events. In contrast to the chronic stress variables, these are to a lesser extent and in a less clear-cut fashion related to income, but have a remarkably high incidence. About 40% of the families had a death during the preceding year; about 30% reported a major accident; 20% experienced some other major event such as a divorce or separation.

*Self-evaluation* of relative exposure to such acute stress is also independent of economic status. Overall, 22% of families in our lowest income group rated their lives as having more problems than the average; for all other income groups this proportion was fairly low (5–8%). Generally families tended to be optimistic: four times as many families thought that they had fewer problems than the average, compared with the number who believed that they had more.

Table 2B.1.  *Economic Life Situation as Stressor, by Income: Mothers with Children under 18 Years, Monroe County, New York, 1969*

|  | Income | | | | |
|---|---|---|---|---|---|
| Dependent Variables | Below $6000 | $6000–10,000 | $10,001–14,000 | Above $14,000 | Total |
| 1. Life Situation: | | | | | |
| Percent on welfare (AFDC) | 26.6 | 1.1 | — | — | 3.1 |
| Percent on Medicaid | 55.8 | 7.5 | — | — | 8.0 |
| Percent own house | 20.4 | 68.9 | 89.3 | 98.9 | 78.2 |
| Percent married | 42.7 | 89.5 | 98.5 | 98.9 | 90.2 |
| 2. Coder Evaluation of Stressor: | | | | | |
| Percent of medium or high stress caused by | | | | | |
| housing situation | 34.8 | 20.9 | 12.7 | 8.5 | 16.5 |
| school situation | 15.1 | 11.0 | 3.0 | 2.6 | 6.6 |
| 3. Self-Evaluation of Coping Ability: | | | | | |
| Percent having trouble paying | | | | | |
| rent or mortgage | 16.7 | 12.1 | 2.0 | — | 6.1 |
| installment loans | 14.1 | 9.5 | 4.4 | — | 6.0 |
| medical bills | 20.4 | 16.8 | 10.1 | 1.1 | 11.2 |
| unexpected expenses | 27.1 | 8.4 | 7.4 | 4.2 | 9.0 |
| Percent having trouble making ends meet in general | 34.5 | 16.7 | 9.4 | 1.1 | 12.4 |
| n= | 90 | 261 | 338 | 190 | 879 |

The reports in Tables 2B.3 of short-term stress and daily tension are based on 14,336 family-day descriptions obtained from the mothers' health diaries. The tension rating question ("What kind of day was it for you?") showed that, for the 512 families studied, only about 70% of the days were described as more or less relaxed. Of the remaining 30%, one half were tense or somewhat tense, and about 4% were rated as very tense.

A special event screening question ("Did anything go wrong today, at work, with the children, or with others?") gave an indication of the frequency of difficult situations that might contribute to the tension experienced. These events were assessed by the coder, who assigned stress weights

Table 2B.2.  Special Events as Stressors, by Income (12-Month Period):
Mothers with Children under 18 Years, Monroe County, New York, 1969

| Dependent Variables | Income | | | | |
| --- | --- | --- | --- | --- | --- |
| | Below $6000 | $6,000-10,000 | $10,001-14,000 | Above $14,000 | Total |
| 1. Special Events | | | | | |
| Death of a relative | | | | | |
| Percent with one death | 47.0 | 30.7 | 31.7 | 32.1 | 33.0 |
| Percent with two or more deaths | 5.2 | 10.2 | 9.1 | 9.0 | 9.0 |
| | 52.2 | 40.9 | 40.8 | 41.1 | 42.0 |
| Accidents (car, work, etc.) | | | | | |
| Percent with one accident | 30.7 | 22.0 | 27.8 | 18.9 | 24.5 |
| Percent with two or more accidents | 8.5 | 7.6 | 8.1 | 5.3 | 7.0 |
| | 39.2 | 29.6 | 35.9 | 24.2 | 31.5 |
| Other problems (divorce, police, etc.) | | | | | |
| Percent with one problem | 29.2 | 12.5 | 15.1 | 18.9 | 16.6 |
| Percent with two or more problems | 4.2 | 2.2 | 1.8 | 3.3 | 2.4 |
| | 33.4 | 14.7 | 16.9 | 22.2 | 19.0 |
| 2. Coder Evaluation of Stressor: | | | | | |
| Percent of medium or severe stress caused by | | | | | |
| death of relative | 14.4 | 12.7 | 7.7 | 12.1 | 10.8 |
| accidents | 14.8 | 8.1 | 9.5 | 8.5 | 9.4 |
| other problems | 22.3 | 10.2 | 8.9 | 14.1 | 11.8 |
| 3. Self-Evaluation of Relative Stress Exposure (in percentages): | | | | | |
| Compared with other families, this family has | | | | | |
| more illness | 9.8 | 10.6 | 4.7 | 6.4 | 7.4 |
| less illness | 51.2 | 46.4 | 55.7 | 54.0 | 52.1 |
| more problems | 22.3 | 8.4 | 8.0 | 5.3 | 9.0 |
| less problems | 24.6 | 38.4 | 38.5 | 33.7 | 36.1 |
| $n=$ | 90 | 261 | 338 | 190 | 879 |

Table 2B.3. *Family Well-Being: Tension and Special Events, Rochester Metropolitan Area, 1969*
Family-days, $N = 14,336$; all values in percentages

| Question 1 | | | | | Response Categories | | | Total |
|---|---|---|---|---|---|---|---|---|
| Tension Rating | Very Relaxed | Relaxed | Not So Relaxed | Not Ascertained | Somewhat Tense | Tense | Very Tense | |
| 1.1 "What kind of day was it for you?" | 28.8 | 25.0 | 16.7 | 4.5 | 15.4 | 5.7 | 3.8 | 100.0 |

| Special Events[a] | No (Weight 0) | | Yes Mild Stress (Weight 1) | | Yes Medium Stress (Weight 2) | | Yes Severe Stress (Weight 3) | Total |
|---|---|---|---|---|---|---|---|---|
| 1.2 "Did anything go wrong today.... at work, in the house | 91.4 | | 7.0 | | 1.6 | | 0.0 | 100.0 |
| with the school or the children?" | 90.2 | | 7.4 | | 2.3 | | 0.1 | 100.0 |
| 1.3 "Any trouble with friends, relatives, husband?" | 86.8 | | 11.7 | | 1.4 | | 0.1 | 100.0 |
| 1.4 "Anything else bothering you today?" | 90.3 | | 8.1 | | 1.5 | | 0.2 | 100.0 |

| | No Stress (Score 0) | | Some Stress (Score 1-3) | | High Stress (Score 4-6) | | Very High Stress (Score 7-9) | Total |
|---|---|---|---|---|---|---|---|---|
| Total stress score (sum of weights) | 67.6 | | 29.1 | | 1.6 | | 1.7 | 100.0 |

[a] Excluding health problems.

ranging from 1 to 3.[1] The sum of the stress weights for each day yielded a new variable—"total family-day stress." About 68% of all family days had "no stress," 29% had "some stress," and over 3% had "high stress" or "very high stress." Most days (80-90%), however, were uneventful and relaxed. Only 3-4% of all days presented major problems that required coping responses—the same percentage as had very high tension ratings.

The findings reported in Table 2B.3 were based on family-days as the unit of analysis. If an event continued over three consecutive days, it was reported as three days with a family problem. For some questions, however, it is more adequate to treat such events as one unit or episode. An analysis of episodes (e.g., a set of consecutive days with at least one but not necessarily the same problem to cope with each day) showed that, over the 28 days studied, 10% of families had no episode, 39% had between one and three episodes, 37% had from four to six, and the remaining 14% had seven or more. The average number of episodes was 3.7 per family, and the average length of an episode was 2.3 days. Moving forward or backward in the calendar permits a computation of the probability of illness among family members on days preceding, overlapping, and following a stress episode. The probabilities for specific responses to illness as a function of stress can be established in a similar fashion (Section 4B).

The frequency data on major, chronic stress have implications for a *strategy* of attacking problems of medical care delivery. The data on short-term, minor stress have implications for the *tactics* of daily care. We will return to these points later.

## Qualitative Analysis of Short-Term Stress

The quantification of tension and stress is essential to describe their distribution in the community and to establish causal relations or develop models. But our understanding of the life of the families involved suffers by abstracting scores and computing percentages. A case study approach gives another view of what is happening and allows hypotheses to be generated. It also provides a more human view of families and their problems. The information from 18 families was, therefore, examined qualitatively. The same general outline was used for each of these case reports, including background information (e.g., type of residence, marital status), the health of each family member, problems at school, social-psychological

---

[1] Examples for severe stress (weight 3) are as follows: lost job, child expelled from school, car accident, divorce, unwanted pregnancy, separation, or death in close family. Examples for medium stress (weight 2) are trouble with boss, car broke down, argument with husband, or loan foreclosure. Examples for mild stress (weight 1) are whiny children, complaining neighbors, lack of money, or inability to get along with fellow workers.

information, health diary data, and a summary of each member's problems as illustrated in the following cases (Roghmann et al., 1973):

CASE 1

Mrs. A. is a white, 32-year-old housewife living in a rented duplex house with her husband, 39 years old, and four children, three of whom are girls, ages 4, 10, and 12; the boy is 5 years old. They have lived at their present address for two years, but would like to move to what Mrs. A. calls a "better neighborhood." The house was rated as being in bad condition. They now pay $85 rent per month. Mr. A. works at a local electronics company; the family income is just below $6000.

Mrs. A. rates her general health as poor. In the two weeks before the interview, she experienced back trouble and pain in her hip. She had to spend 3 days in bed and was not feeling well for about 14 days. She has a bone disease for which surgery is required on her hip, and she is worried about the housekeeping during the scheduled hospitalization. One of her legs is shorter than the other, and she must use crutches to walk. Although Mrs. A. can drive a car, she has been in two accidents in the past year because she is slow in braking motions. Mrs. A. also has a heart murmur, diabetes, and frequent pain in her legs. A year and a half ago she was hospitalized because of bladder trouble and diabetes. She last went to a dentist three years ago for emergency treatment.

Mr. A.'s major health problem is chronic skin cancer. Six years ago he had a cancerous growth removed from his face. His teeth sometimes require emergency care. His general health was self-rated as "good."

All the children take vitamins prescribed by a doctor and receive regular dental care every four months. The 4-year-old girl has asthma, which is attended to by a private doctor. Her health is rated as "good." The 12-year-old daughter suffers from sleeplessness, for which she is treated as an outpatient at a hospital. A year and a half ago she caught her foot in a gas lawn mower and was taken to a hospital emergency department. Her health was also rated as "good."

The two middle children have more serious health problems. The boy has suffered from repeated earaches. His adenoids were removed a year ago. He also has hearing and speech problems, the result of brain damage, for which he receives therapy. This 5-year-old boy is allergic to fabric softeners. In the course of the last year he hurt himself at a swimming pool, sustaining leg pains. The mother reports his health rating as "fair."

The remaining child, a girl aged 10, was rated in "poor" health. In the last year she has had asthma, sinus trouble, sleeplessness, dental problems, headaches, and earaches. She also has hearing, sight, and speech problems. Since tubes were placed in her tympanic membranes, the headaches have lessened.

Mrs. A. considers her home happier than most. According to the health diary, 18 out of 25 days were "happy and relaxed." Her major worries seem to be about money, especially since the family had trouble with the car and her husband had to miss a few days of work. He had been attacked on the street, hurt his hand, and had trouble at work. Mrs. A. is also concerned about the consequences of her limited mobility: she has trouble doing the housework and going shopping, and has had two home accidents. During this month, all four children had colds for five days. The boy was not eating properly for about a week. Neighborhood boys kept picking on him. Mrs. A. is concerned about the test he will have to take before he can attend a school; she had trouble getting an appointment for the test.

Mrs. A. spontaneously mentioned the benefits received from being covered by Medicaid. Without Medicaid the entire family's health, in her view, would not be taken care of at all, and she would be dead. With Medicaid this is the first year her children have had extensive dental work done: one had 15 cavities, and one had a speech problem due to teeth, now being corrected with braces. One child got glasses. The health problems of both Mrs. A. and her husband could also be taken care of. Because of the amount of Mr. A.'s salary, they report paying a monthly fee to be allowed to continue on "medically" indigent Medicaid. Also, they are paying a number of medical fees which are not covered. For next year Mrs. A. doubts that they will qualify since her husband's salary is expected to be higher than $120 a week. If this happens, she thinks that the family's health will be totally neglected again, as it was without Medicaid two years ago.

This case, admittedly unusual, was selected to illustrate the relationship between poverty and health and the impact of Medicaid in this setting. Another six case studies will be presented on families chosen because they fell into one of the following two categories: (1) high amount of stress for mother during the 28 diary days; (2) high amount of illness in the family.

1. HIGH-STRESS GROUP. Stress values were calculated from information in the 28-day-diary. The mother's tension ratings and stress scores were summed and totaled over all 28 days. Of the 32 families with stress scores over 35, the 4 families with the highest scores are described in the following abstracts.

CASE 2 (STRESS VALUE = 68)

Mrs. A. is a 24-year-old white housewife. Her husband, age 21, is a truck driver. They have two daughters, ages 4 years and 2½ months. Mrs. A. suffers from impairment of renal functions and may have to undergo a kidney transplant. She also has a perforation of one eardrum which affects her hearing when she has a cold. There were some problems during the birth of the last child because of an old injury to her pelvic bones. Mr. A. does not have any serious health problems. The 4-year-old suffers from asthma and often gets bronchitis. Mrs. A. notes that most days are tiring and tense for her, and she does not feel well at these times. In the diary she listed many events that were stressful for her, mostly because the children were sick and she had to stay inside.

CASE 3 (STRESS VALUE = 69)

Mrs. G. is a 25-year-old white housewife. Her husband, age 24, is a computer supervisor at a bank and holds various seasonal part-time jobs. Mrs. G's major health problem concerns her teeth and gums, and she will have to have a complete upper plate made. Mr. G. is overweight. The children, who are both under 2 years old, do not have any serious health problems. In the diary, Mrs. G. mentions problems related to keeping house, but little about more personal concerns. Her disposition seemed to vary with how her husband felt and whether many stressful events had occurred.

CASE 4 (STRESS VALUE = 77)

Mrs. O., age 24, and her husband, age 39, have one 2-year-old son. The health of this family is generally good. The main health problem is that the boy has amblyopia and must wear an eye patch for six hours each day. This has presented a problem because the child refuses to wear the patch. Mrs. O. is concerned that they might be pushing him too much, and this is causing much tension and strain on the whole family, about which Mrs. O. consults the doctor frequently. She mentioned in the diary that she feels tired and depressed most of the time and is concerned about her relationship with her husband.

CASE 5 (STRESS VALUE = 93)

Mrs. F. is a white, 46-year-old housewife who is separated from her husband. Her two children, ages 17 and 11, live with her. Mrs. F.

is confined to a wheelchair because of multiple sclerosis, and she has a rheumatic heart. Her daughter, age 11, has been absent from school a great deal because of illness such as bronchitis. The 17-year-old son does not attend school, and Mrs. F. is disturbed because he won't settle down. In the health diary more than half of the days, most of which followed the death of her mother, were tense or tiring for Mrs. F. She was also concerned much of the time about her son's unpaid bills and his drinking. Another stressful event was caused by Mr. F. when he suggested that the 11-year-old live with him. Tension and stressful events seem to precede the onset of feeling poorly in this family. Mrs. F.'s main concern, reported in the diary, seems to be the frustration of not being able to solve personal problems.

Three of these families (cases 2, 4, 5) show high amounts of stress which seem to be related to at least one major health problem in the family.

2. HIGH-ILLNESS GROUP.   The amount of illness was expressed as total "sick days"—a weighted total in which illnesses are scored by their seriousness and from which an average illness score is calculated by dividing the total illness scores over family size. Two families with the highest illness scores are described.

CASE 6 (ILLNESS SCORE = 151, NINE PEOPLE IN FAMILY)

Mrs. B. is a 40-year-old housewife. Her husband, age 49, is an unemployed construction worker. They have eight children, ranging in age from 8 to 21 years. Mrs. B. suffers from a chronic hearing problem, asthma, allergies, frequent headaches, and kidney trouble. Mr. B. is an outpatient at a hospital clinic for joint and leg pains. The three youngest children are in fair health, although a 12-year-old girl has a hearing problem. Another daughter, age 15, is mentally retarded and does not attend school. An 18-year-old girl is anemic, and a 20-year-old son has epilepsy. The oldest daughter, age 21, is in good health. According to the health diary Mrs. B. kept, the entire family had the flu for six days, although some members of the family were sick longer. Although this family actually had a great deal of illness during this time, Mrs. B. rated her family as having "less illness" than other families.

CASE 7 (ILLNESS SCORE = 123, SEVEN PEOPLE IN FAMILY)

Mrs. D. is a 48-year-old housewife who lives with her husband, age 51, four children, and a grandchild. She is troubled by leg pains, kidney trouble, heart trouble, and sleeplessness. Although Mrs. D. has a regular doctor, she is looking for another one in case her regular physician is out of town. She has had surgery for ileitis. The 14-year-old son is a source of concern because of his allergies, leg pains, and sleeplessness. The youngest daughter, age 7, is afraid of her brother, who is very rough with her. There is another son, age 20. In the diary, Mrs. D. mentioned some illness-related complaint almost every day for herself and for other members of the family. Many stressful events, mostly concerning interpersonal problems, also occurred during this time. (The stress score for this family was 64. See Case 1.)

These families showed high total amounts of illness during the time the health diaries were kept. However, a distinction must be made between families with acute illness and those in which there is a chronic condition.

## Summary

Family crises are not everyday events, but neither are they rare. Our sample was the size of an average family practitioner's practice. As is common clinically, problems tended to cluster in certain families. This random sample of families for quantitative data, and the short case histories of the families with large numbers of problems, portray one aspect of the "new morbidity" facing the human services system. How the health care component can and should deal with these is a central issue of the future.

## REFERENCES

BROWN, G.W., and BIRLEY, J.L.T.
 1968  "Crises and Life Changes and the Onset of Schizophrenia." *Journal of Health and Social Behavior*, 9:203–214.

CAPLAN, G.
 1961  *An Approach to Community Mental Health*. London: Tavistock Publishers.

DODGE, D.L., and MARTIN, W.T.
 1970  *Social Stress and Chronic Illness*. Notre Dame, Indiana: University of Notre Dame Press.

DOHRENWEND, B.P., and DOHRENWEND, B.S.
 1969  *Social Status and Psychological Disorder: A Causal Inquiry*. New York: Wiley-Interscience.

DOHRENWEND, B.S.

1973   "Life Events as Stressors: A Methodological Inquiry." *Journal of Health and Social Behavior,* 14:167–175.

HINKLE, L.E., ET AL.

1958   "An Investigation of the Relation between Life Experience, Personality Characteristics, and General Susceptibility to Illness." *Psychosomatic Medicine,* 20:278.

HOLMES, T.H., ET AL.

1957   "Psychosocial and Psychophysiologic Studies of Tuberculosis." *Psychosomatic Medicine,* 19:134–143.

LAZARUS, R.S.

1966   *Psychological Stress and the Coping Process.* New York: McGraw-Hill Book Company.

LEVINE, S., and SCOTCH, N.A. (EDS.)

1970   *Social Stress.* Chicago: Aldine Publishing Company.

MC GRATH, J.E. (ED.)

1970   *Social and Psychological Factors in Stress.* New York: Holt, Rinehart and Winston.

MECHANIC, D.

1962   *Students under Stress.* New York: Free Press.

MEYER, R.J., and HAGGERTY, R.J.

1962   "Streptococcal Infections in Families: Factors Altering Individual Susceptibility." *Pediatrics,* 29:539–549.

ROGHMANN, KLAUS J., HECHT, PAMELA, and HAGGERTY, ROBERT J.

1973   "Family Coping with Everyday Illness: Self-Reports from a Household Survey." *Journal of Comparative Family Studies,* IV:I:49–62.

SKIPPER, J.K., and LEONARD, R.C.

1968   "Children, Stress and Hospitalization: A Field Experiment." *Journal of Health and Social Behavior,* 9:275–287.

CHAPTER THREE

# Health and Illness

## A. CHILD HEALTH STATISTICS

KLAUS J. ROGHMANN

I n all modern societies some official agency collects data on births, deaths, and major communicable disease. In Monroe County, the Office of Vital Statistics registers these events, makes summary data available, and reports to other governmental offices.[1] This section describes some of the more important child health statistics for each of the sociopolitical and sociogeographic areas in the county.

Between 1966 and 1970 the annual cohort of white newborns increased slowly but steadily from 10,900 in 1966 to 11,300 in 1970. Births among the nonwhite population also increased, from about 1500 to 1900. But after 1970 a marked decline in live births set in. White births decreased by 1900 (−16.8%) in 1971 and by 1300 (−14.1%) in 1972; black births fell by 100 (−5.0%) in 1971 and by 240 (−13.3%) in 1972.

The small increase in newborns during the early years was due mainly to growth of the population as a whole. If this factor is set aside by examining only the birthrate, a trend toward a decline in births over the five years becomes evident. The dramatic drop in the last two years was due largely to the increased availability of legal abortions, reinforced, perhaps, by the economic recession of the early 1970s. (This phenomenon is discussed in detail in Chapter 8.)

The *birthrate* fell from 19.2/1000 population in 1966 to 18.6 in 1970, and then dropped to 15.3 in 1971 and 12.7 in 1972. This decrease was observable for both the white and nonwhite populations, although the general trend was more striking in the latter. The birthrate for whites decreased from 17.9/1000 population in 1966 to 17.3 in 1970, and then dropped to 14.1 in 1971 and to 11.8 in 1972. The birthrate of the non-

---

[1] During the study period Dr. Margaret Rathbun and Ms. Bonnie DuFresne of the Office of Vital Statistics of the Health Department of Monroe County were helpful whenever we approached them for information, definitions, or data breakdowns.

white population, however, decreased from 39.4/1000 population to 34.2/1000 in 1970, and then dropped to 27.8 in 1971 and to 20.7 in 1972.[2] Compared with national averages, Monroe County had higher birthrates for both the white and nonwhite populations.

There are also striking differences among the social areas of the county, which are, to a large extent, due to their different age structures. For example, the white birthrate in the inner city was very low, ranging from 9 to 16/1000, mainly because of this group's high median age. By comparison, the birthrate for the black population in the same area, ranging from 19 to 40/1000, is also related to age, the median age of the black population being about 10 years lower.

The decrease in the birthrate was observed, however, in all parts of the county, including the inner city. If the present trend continues, racial differences in birthrates will narrow considerably within the next 5–10 years.

The general trend toward lower birthrates over this period reflects a national phenomenon that is best seen in the suburbs of this community. In 1966 the suburban birthrate was 17.0; by 1970 it had fallen to 15.9, and then dropped still further to 13.0 in 1971 and 10.9 in 1972.

Even within the suburbs, however, the rate of birth was uneven. The western areas in both the close suburbs and the far suburbs had relatively high rates, indicating a greater need for maternal and child services in these expanding areas. Ironically, as is so often the case throughout the county, the old established neighborhoods (especially in the southeast) have an abundance of physicians but the lowest need for these services.

The rate of *illegitimate births* increased during the study period. The overall rate rose from 9.5% in 1966 to 13.0% in 1972, well above the national average. The increase could be seen in most areas of the county; and although racial differentials existed within each area, the differences among the areas were usually larger than those among the races. For example, illegitimate births in the white population amounted to about 25% in the inner city, compared with 3% in the suburbs. For the blacks the rate was about 50% in the inner city versus 15% in the suburbs.

The total *deaths at all ages* remained stable at about 5700. The natural growth of the county was, therefore, in the order of 6000–8000 persons per year. Thus half of the annual increase in the county population, described in Section 1A, must be due to in-migration. This applies chiefly

---

[2] These are crude birthrates that need age standardization if comparison as to the effect of race or other variables is desired. No standardization was attempted here because the birthrate is not a dependent variable to be explained; we use volume of births and crude rates as independent variables to explain the need and demand for pediatric services.

to whites; the growth of the black population from migration was much less. Most of the increase in this young population was due to a surplus of live births over deaths.

The number of *childhood deaths* was small except among infants. Infant mortality accounts for about 3% of all deaths in the United States. In this community infant mortality was 18.5/1000 live births in 1969, compared with a national average of 20.8. By 1972 the county's infant mortality rate had fallen slightly to 17.4/1000. In 1969, however, European countries like Finland (13.9), Norway (13.7), Denmark (14.8), Sweden (13.0), the United Kingdom (18.6), and Holland (13.2)—even Japan (15.3)—had infant mortality rates that were even lower; the rate was only 11.7 in Iceland!

Within the county infant mortality rates varied from area to area and from year to year. The large year-to-year variation within each area is due to the small numbers involved. The differences between races, however, are much more stable and more striking. White infant mortality was between 13 and 18/1000—considerably lower than the national average for whites. Nonwhite infant mortality rates, which ranged from 25 to 37/1000 live births, were below the national average for nonwhites.

In the suburban areas rates varied from 10 to 16/1000 over the study period. In general, the southeast suburbs had a remarkably low and fairly stable infant mortality rate of about 12/1000 live births. Western areas, however, had a somewhat higher overall rate with large variations from year to year. Infant mortality as a health index is of limited use, therefore, for short-term evaluation studies of small areas, but is still a major index of child health for populations as large as Monroe County.

Once children have survived their infancy (the first year of life) deaths are rare. In 1971 there were 186 infant deaths, but only 101 child deaths for the entire county. Of the latter, 35 occurred in the 1–4 year group, 17 in the 5–9 year group, and 49 in the 10–17 year group.

The causes of death vary with age. Most (78%) of the 147 neonatal deaths were classed as "*diseases of early infancy*," mainly the risks associated with prematurity. Most of the remaining deaths in the first year were attributed to *congenital malformations*. Deaths between 1 and 17 years were due increasingly to "external causes" (1–9 years, 30%; 10–17 years, 65%). Six children were the victims of homicides, and two adolescents committed suicide. Forty-four children died in accidents—mostly motor vehicle accidents (23); 6 died by drowning, 3 in fires, 3 by falls, 2 by poisoning, and 7 by other accidents.

Over the first five years these statistics were fairly constant. The last two years, however, showed some remarkable differences that will be discussed in Chapter 8. Infant deaths dropped from a high of 250 in 1968 to

170 in 1972. The number of prematures dropped from 1100 in 1969 to 770 in 1972. Most of this decline was due to fewer live births. Infant mortality and the prematurity rate showed only minor drops. Differences by race persisted. Infant mortality for blacks was 30/1000 in 1972, compared to 15/1000 for whites. The prematurity rate in that year was 15% for blacks and 7% for whites.

A traditionally valuable health statistic is the rate of *newly reported tuberculosis* cases. These rates have a social pattern similar to that of infant mortality—but with an even greater variation between areas due to the small numbers. About 100 cases are reported yearly for the 142 census tracts.[3] The rate per 100,000 in the suburbs is only 4–6, compared with an inner city *white* rate between 84 and 142. Clearly tuberculosis is an inner city problem; about half of all new cases come from this area. The yearly figures show only slight improvement from 1966 to 1971.

The tuberculosis rate is one of the few public health measures that differ between the two poverty areas, the Third and the Seventh Wards. Newly reported tuberculosis cases in the Seventh Ward vary between 90 and 140/100,000 population. This is considerably higher than in the Third Ward, where the rate is only 60–90 cases/100,000 population.

## Discussion

The interpretation of health statistics such as these in any community poses problems. As with most analyses of data that were not collected primarily for research purposes, the level of accuracy is difficult to assess. The researcher does not have control over the definitions applied; in fact, during the study period the definition for stillbirth was changed.[4] Some statistics, such as rates for venereal diseases, are so unreliable that it is not meaningful to base comparisons on them.

Other measurement problems are attributable to confusion over classification, as in the case of Puerto Ricans. There were about 12,000 Puerto Ricans[5] in Monroe County at the end of the study period, many of whom

---

[3] Because of the few cases reported, the tabulations at the Department of Health are only by sex, race, and census tract. No separation of "child" and "adult" cases was possible.

[4] The reporting of fetal deaths according to the new definition (all fetal deaths instead of only those with more than 20 weeks' gestation) is considerably less reliable than that based on the old definition.

[5] This is a sample estimate based on the number of Puerto Rican births in 1970 (285) and the birthrate in Puerto Rico (25/1000).

have Negro ancestry.[6] Because of their different cultural background, however, they form a cohesive ethnic group with their own school programs, churches, and community organizations. Consequently, the Office of Vital Statistics maintains a separate social category—Puerto Rican—in addition to white and Negro, but, regrettably, the U.S. Census Bureau does not provide such a category. Puerto Ricans may report themselves as white or Negro as they feel appropriate. This makes it impossible to compute separate Puerto Rican birthrates.

The figures presented here are reasonably comprehensive and accurate. The small size of some absolute figures (e.g., infant deaths and tuberculosis cases), however, limits the interpretation that can be placed on variations between races or areas. Thus the total number of infant deaths varied between 3 and 8 per year in one suburb over the six-year study period, and between 31 and 52 in the inner city. As there is no committee that reviews and evaluates all infant deaths, it is difficult to establish any cause and effect relationships between measures of medical care and these rates. In our assessment of the effects of the new health care programs, therefore, we should use other indices (disability, symptoms, functioning) than those available from simple health statistics.

One way to avoid some of the inherent instability of rates reflecting rare events is to aggregate figures over longer time periods or larger areas (Roghmann and Haggerty, 1970). Three-year averages provide more stable rates, as does grouping of census tracts of equal socioeconomic background. As shown in Figure 3A.1, the use of three-year aggregates pro-

6 Racial breakdowns are no longer reported for Puerto Rico. In the last census (1950) before Puerto Rico became a U.S. commonwealth (1952), 20% of the population was reported as Negro and 80% as white (U.S. Bureau of the Census, 1968:822).

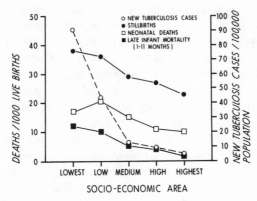

*Figure 3A.1. Major health indicators by socioeconomic area, 1966–1968, Rochester metropolitan area, three-year averages.*

duces a clear picture of the relationship between social class and health. The relative risk of infant and fetal deaths more than doubles from the highest to the lowest socioeconomic areas, and for new tuberculosis cases the risk in the lowest area is about 10 times greater than in the higher areas!

## REFERENCES

ROGHMANN, KLAUS J., and HAGGERTY, ROBERT J.

1970  "Theoretical and Methodological Problems of Medical Care Research: Some Consequences for Secondary Analysis." *Social Science Information* 9:125–154.

U.S. BUREAU OF THE CENSUS

1968  *Statistical Abstracts of the United States.* Washington, D.C.: Government Printing Office.

## B. ACUTE ILLNESS

KLAUS J. ROGHMANN
AND
IVAN B. PLESS

Medical care is sought for many reasons. For most children, acute illness continues to be the main reason for seeing a doctor (44% of all "last" visits in our surveys). Well-child care is the next largest category (43%), whereas the management of chronic illnesses or behavioral disorders represents a relatively small proportion (8%) of all doctor visits.

Over the past few decades, however, more and more acute illness has been prevented. As a result, more attention can now be given to previously neglected areas. Nevertheless, the need for acute illness care will always remain. It appears that different sections of the community receive preventive services to different extents, thus affecting the relative incidence of acute illness. For example, acute illness is still the major reason for seeking medical care among the poor, whereas preventive services now constitute the bulk of all services received by young middle-class children (see Section 6A).

In this section the level of acute illness is described and related to family income, race, and the sociopolitical area in which the family lives. As elsewhere, family income has the largest impact on life opportunities in Monroe County. However, race is still of major importance, independently of income. The combination of race and income determines, for the most part, the neighborhood in which children grow up, and for this reason analyses by sociopolitical area are also included.

*Methods*

The relative decline in the rate of acute illness in childhood is a long-term phenomenon and hence could not be seen over the four-year period covered by our surveys. For clarity the findings are presented for only one point in time. The 1971 survey was chosen because it is the most up to date, it covers *all* family members, and it includes the widest range of illness measures.

Acute illness was never a primary focus of any of the surveys; for example, no questions were asked specifically about colds, coughs, or sore throats. Instead, questions centered on *any* recent illness and about *all* episodes of medical care. Whenever either of these was mentioned, the kind of illness present was sought. The answers to these general questions were classified along three dimensions. First, determination was made simply between "well-child" and "sick-child" care, with the former divided into "check-ups" and "immunizations." Sick-child care was then divided into "acute" and "chronic." Second, for all chronic sick care the affected organ system was classified. And, finally, we coded, when possible, the underlying etiology (e.g., accident or infection).

The interview began with two general illness questions—the first inquired about recent illness, and the second involved a self-rating of general health. Any episode of recent illness was coded along the three dimensions. Additional indications of acute illness came from answers to questions about recent medication or drug use (see Chapter 5).

Most of the answers reflected both the presence of a symptom and some behavioral response to it, such as keeping a child home from school, giving medicine, or calling the doctor. As expected, socioeconomic differentials influenced both the level of perception of symptoms and the behavioral response. As Koos's (1954) study has shown, people may have an accurate perception of symptoms or of their general health, but may not take appropriate action because of their social circumstances.

Strictly speaking, at this point we are concerned only with defining medical needs, not identifying the response to them. Nevertheless, some responses to illness will be described since often the illness itself is identified only through knowing about the response.

*Results*

Parents noted that 23% of the children in the 1971 survey could not "carry on as normal because of illness" on at least one day in the two weeks preceding the interview. The frequency of illness among girls (26%) was greater than among boys (21%). For boys the rate of reported illness fell steadily with increasing age: from 26% in those 2 years of age and under to 16% in those 13–17 years old. For girls the pattern differed slightly—the rate up to 5 years of age remained at about 28% and then fell to 25%, remaining there through age 17. Thus the higher overall rate for girls is due to higher rates of morbidity in later childhood. This pattern can also be seen for taking acute illness medicine (see Chapter 5).

More than 80% of these illnesses were regarded as severe enough to keep the child home from school or from playing with other children. Of those with such illness in the preceding two weeks, 96% were classified as "acute," and only 4% were judged to be "chronic." Most of the acute disorders could not be related to a specific system; that is, 459 of the 552 children with disabilities severe enough to keep them home were judged to have minor, general disorders. Of the remaining 95 for whom a specific system was identified, the majority (43%) of illnesses involved eyes, ears, nose, or throat, and most of the rest were divided equally between disorders involving the urinary tract (15%), the respiratory system (13%), and the musculoskeletal system (11%). Skin, nervous system, and gastrointestinal disorders accounted for the remaining 18%.

As would be expected from the above, the majority of the acute illnesses (77%) were coded as due to infections. Diseases attributable to disorders in specific organs accounted for 15%, and accidents for 3%.

Parents were also asked to make general assessments of their children's health *over the last year* as good, fair, or poor. Approximately 90% of all children were rated as being in "good" health, and between 1 and 2% were judged to be in "poor" health. The proportion of those with a rating of either "fair" or "poor" was slightly greater for boys (9%) than girls (7%) and tended to diminish slightly with age, falling from 10% for those under 3 years of age to 7% for those 12–17 years old.

*Variation by Income, Race, and Sociopolitical Area*

The sequence of questions on "illness in the last two weeks" is not an objective measure of illness as such, but rather constitutes a method for eliciting a behavioral response to illness. Different groups and individuals in these groups have varying thresholds for restricting normal activity and for keeping children at home or in bed. For example, the data show that white mothers report more recent illness for their children; but when black mothers do report an illness for a child, it is likely to be more severe. Blacks seem to have higher thresholds of this kind than do whites; they apparently require more severe illness to keep their children in bed than do whites. Evidence for this comes from the length of reported illnesses. If black children were kept in bed, they had to stay there for about four days, compared with only two and one-half days for white children.

This different response pattern to illness also depends on socioeconomic status. Although the frequency of reported illness does not vary with income, the lower the income the *greater* the severity of illness as measured by length of required bed or home rest. This inverse relationship shows clearly when controlling for race (Table 3B.1). Race affects strongly the level of reported illness; income, the severity of the illness.

The general health rating for the last 12 months was also related to both race and income. Only 7.5% of white children had their health rated as "fair" or "poor," compared with 13.4% of the black children. Most, but not all, of the difference could be attributed to socioeconomic factors (see Figure 3B.1). Among "the poor" (income below $6000), blacks and whites had equally poor health ratings, whereas among those with incomes above $10,000 blacks reported more poor health than whites.

*Table 3B.1.  Income and Illness in the Preceding Two Weeks, Controlling for Race*

| | Income | | | | |
|---|---|---|---|---|---|
| Illness | Below $6,000 | $6,000–10,000 | $10,001-14,000 | Above $14,000 | All Children |
| Whites | | | | | |
| Any illness? (%) | 24.2 | 24.3 | 24.7 | 22.6 | 23.8 |
| Stayed at home? (%) | 21.2 | 20.9 | 18.6 | 18.1 | 19.1 |
| Stayed in bed? (%) | 8.5 | 9.4 | 8.5 | 9.4 | 9.2 |
| Length of stay at home? (days) | 6.8 | 4.6 | 3.8 | 3.2 | 4.1 |
| Length of stay in bed? (days) | 4.8 | 2.8 | 3.1 | 1.6 | 2.6 |
| Blacks | | | | | |
| Any illness? (%) | 17.9 | 18.3 | 13.9 | 23.6 | 17.7 |
| Stayed at home? (%) | 13.7 | 15.9 | 12.9 | 23.6 | 14.8 |
| Stayed in bed? (%) | 5.8 | 8.7 | 4.0 | 9.7 | 6.4 |
| Length of stay at home? (days) | 4.9 | 5.5 | 5.0 | 3.9 | 4.9 |
| Length of stay in bed? (days) | 4.3 | 4.3 | 3.0 | 1.6 | 3.9 |

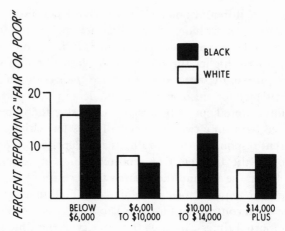

*Figure 3B1.   Health ratings by race and income.*

This interaction of race and income is also reflected in the health ratings of blacks and whites in the various sociopolitical areas (see Figure 3B.2). In the poverty areas, large proportions of black and white children were reportedly in poor health, the white children even more so than the black ones. For the "rest of city" area, the health rating was better for the white, but not the black, children.

*Discussion*

In this section the level of acute illness and its variation by income, race, and sociopolitical areas are examined. Of reported disability days for children, 95% were attributed to acute illness. Clearly, acute illness continues to be the major reason for seeking medical attention for children in most sections of the population. This is certainly the case with children when compared with adults, and applies more to blacks than whites, and more to the poor than the middle class.

These findings are comparable to those of Schach and Starfield (1973), as well as those reported in the periodic U.S. National Health Survey (Jackson, 1971). Schach and Starfield describe the sensitivity and specificity of "short-term specific disability" measures as a consequence of acute illness, defined as problems in eating, sleeping, or behavior, in the two weeks preceding the interview. The results suggest that these child-specific functional measures may be used as alternatives to the "standard" measures of acute illness and disability employed in our survey. For example, in the age group 0–14 years Schach and Starfield report 23% of children

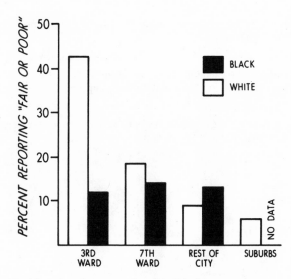

*Figure 3B.2. Health ratings by race and sociopolitical area.*

who were sick in the preceding two weeks, 14% who had restricted activities, and 10% who were confined to bed. These figures correspond closely to those reported in our 1971 survey: 23%, 18%, and 8%, respectively, for both sexes.

There may be little that medicine can do about most of the causes of acute morbidity at present, but any planning or evaluation of health services must consider the differentials described. Improvements are needed in the availability and accessibility of medical care for these acute illnesses, as well as in shifting the pattern of care for the poor toward more prevention. For all classes greater attention must also be paid to the quality of services for the chronically ill. Depending on what is done, some short-term effects may be seen in the use of emergency rooms for acute care. But of greater interest and importance is the extent to which the actions of health planners in providing available services have long-term effects on the functioning and overall health levels of children. Our studies have yet to show such effects, but this issue will be examined in detail in Part III.

## REFERENCES

JACKSON, ANN

1971 *Children and Youth: Selected Health Characteristics, U.S., 1958 and 1968.*
National Center for Health Statistics, Department of Health, Education, and

78  *Health and Illness*

Welfare, Public Health Service, Series 10, No. 62. Washington, D.C.: Government Printing Office.

KOOS, EARL L.

1954 *The Health of Regionville: What the People Thought and Did about It.* New York and London: Hafner Publishing Company.

SCHACH, E., and STARFIELD, B.

1973 "Acute Disability in Childhood: Examination of Agreement between Various Measures." *Medical Care,* 11 (4):299–309.

## C. CHRONIC ILLNESS

IVAN B. PLESS
AND
BETTY B. SATTERWHITE

Modern pediatrics has become increasingly devoted to the care of children with chronic disorders, generally defined as conditions that persist for more than three months. Various estimates suggest that the total cumulative prevalence of these conditions in children under 18 years of age is between 10% and 20% (Pless, 1968). These figures apply only to children with physical disorders; they exclude those who are mentally subnormal, emotionally ill, or who have specific learning disorders, all of which are also chronic.

The growing importance of chronic disorders is, in part, a secondary effect of the changing pattern of acute illness. There has been a marked decline in the frequency of nutritional disorders, accompanied, in the past few decades, by a similar decline in the frequency and seriousness of infectious disease (Pless, 1974). There is also a presumed increase in the survival of many children with chronic conditions (Illingworth, 1964). Thus chronic illnesses are emerging as a focal point for attention, in part because they are apparently increasing in number, but additionally because they continue to present major challenges for the planners and providers of care for these children.

Little progress has been made, for the most part, in dealing with many of the problems these illnesses pose. The problems persist because of the difficulty in providing technically adequate but nonetheless comprehensive care[1] in a health care system oriented primarily toward the care of acute illness.

This section describes the frequency of symptoms of chronic illnesses reported in household interviews with parents of a random sample of children of all ages. It then presents in some detail the characteristics of children of school age found to have definite chronic disorders and highlights problems in their psychological and social functioning. The possible relationship of these problems to the nature of care provided is discussed in the conclusion of the section.

## Methods

Methodological details about the design of the interlocking studies, the questions asked, and the type of tests administered are provided in the Appendix to Section 3C. Briefly, the procedure followed was to use the information obtained in the 1967 1% random sample interview about chronic symptoms as a means of screening the population. The parents of children of school age with symptoms judged to be serious were interviewed again the following year (1968), along with a smaller group of healthy matched controls. The second interview was more detailed, and every child in whom a chronic illness was confirmed, as well as all controls, received a series of tests to assess psychological adjustment.

## Results

### Prevalence of Reported Symptoms

In each of the three survey years (1967, 1969, 1971) asthma, hay fever, and other allergies constituted the single largest diagnostic group of symptoms. The second-ranking group of conditions, comprising approximately one-fifth of the total, involved the special senses—speech, hearing, and vision. Skin disorders, asked about only in the 1967 survey, constituted the third-ranking group of conditions. Many children had more than one symptom, and many of these were not regarded by the parent as serious. When the

---

[1] The term "technically adequate" implies the type of care that is needed to diagnose and treat rare disorders requiring highly specialized diagnostic or therapeutic measures. "Comprehensive care" in this context describes the services required to meet the broader needs of the patient and the family—needs related to psychological support, counseling, and guidance. It thus involves skills that are largely interpersonal and more likely to be found among primary physicians than among disease-oriented subspecialists.

frequency of these symptoms is analyzed by age and sex, they are found to be more often reported for boys than for girls (with the exception of genitourinary disorders). Some are more frequent among younger children (e.g., anemia and speech problems), whereas others, such as arthritis and hay fever, appear to be problems of later childhood or adolescence. (These patterns are supported by the results of a similar analysis of the 1971 data, except that the latter showed proportionately fewer boys than girls with visual difficulties.)

### Prevalence of Chronic Physical Disorders

The special study of chronic illnesses in 1968 provided information that permitted a more definitive diagnosis of "diseases," as opposed to "symptoms." Accordingly, of the 364 children from the 1% sample originally presumed to have chronic illnesses, 209 were established as valid cases. Of the others, 113 failed to meet the criteria for a chronic physical disorder, and the remaining 42 were children whose parents refused to participate or who could not be traced.[2]

The overall total period prevalence rate of chronic illness—137 per 1000—as shown in Table 3C.1 is comparable to rates reported in similar studies (Pless, 1968).

### Clinical Characteristics

Information obtained from physicians and interviews with the parents made it possible to categorize each of the 209 children with chronic illness according to the severity, type, and duration of disability. The measure of *severity* derived principally from questions concerning interference with ordinary daily activities. Although the reliability of this classification has been established (Pless and Graham, 1970), it cannot be ascertained with certainty, from a cross-sectional study such as this, whether what is being assessed is true biological severity or the child's behavioral response to the illness. However, as Figure 3C.1 indicates, less than 10% of those with chronic illnesses were rated as having *moderate* or *severe* disability in the sense that the condition interfered with the performance of "ordi-

---

[2] Of the 364 children with chronic symptoms in 1967, 113 failed to meet the criteria for a chronic disorder established for the special study in 1968 according to the information obtained during the household interview. These were regarded as "secondary" controls, and, after examining their social and demographic characteristics, we added them to the "original" controls for a total of 190 "healthy" controls. The 209 established cases consisted of 170 who came from the 364 with symptoms, 24 who were siblings in the original sample correction estimates, and 15 from the group of "matched" controls. Thus the full number of losses due to refusals, removals, and other causes was 81.

| Diagnosis | N | Rate of 1000[a] | Percent of All Cases |
|---|---|---|---|
| Infective and Parasitic | 1 | 0.7 | 0.5 |
| Endocrine, Nutritional, Metabolic | 6 | | 2.9 |
| Thyroid | 1 | 0.7 | |
| Diabetes mellitus | 3 | 2.0 | |
| Obesity | 2 | 1.3 | |
| Blood and Blood-Forming Organs | 3 | | 1.4 |
| Anemia | 3 | 2.0 | |
| Mental Disorders | 15 | | 7.2 |
| Speech disturbance | 13 | 8.6 | |
| Mental disturbance | 2 | 1.3 | |
| Nervous System and Sense Organs | 43 | | 20.1 |
| Cerebral palsy | 4 | 2.6 | |
| Epilepsy | 4 | 2.6 | |
| Migraine | 6 | 4.0 | |
| Refractive error | 12 | 7.9 | |
| Strabismus | 2 | 1.3 | |
| Deafness | 15 | 9.9 | |
| Circulatory System | 1 | | 0.5 |
| Ill-defined heart disorder | 1 | 0.7 | |
| Respiratory System | 80 | | 38.3 |
| Bronchitis | 4 | 2.6 | |
| Asthma | 13 | 8.6 | |
| Sinusitis | 8 | 5.3 | |
| Hay fever | 55 | 3.6 | |
| Digestive System | 6 | | 2.9 |
| Gastric ulcer | 1 | 0.7 | |
| Ulcerative colitis | 1 | 0.7 | |
| Functional disorder | 3 | 2.0 | |
| Other diseases of intestines | 1 | 0.7 | |
| Genitourinary System | 10 | | 4.8 |
| Chronic nephritis | 3 | 2.0 | |
| Chronic pyelonephritis | 3 | 2.0 | |
| Other disease of urinary tract | 2 | 1.3 | |
| Menstrual disorder | 2 | 1.3 | |
| Skin and Subcutaneous Tissue | 28 | | 13.4 |
| Eczema and dermatitis | 17 | 11.2 | |
| Psoriasis and acne | 11 | 7.2 | |
| Musculoskeletal and Connective Tissue | 6 | | 2.9 |
| Rheumatism | 1 | 0.7 | |
| Osteochondrosis | 2 | 1.3 | |
| Scoliosis | 1 | 0.7 | |
| Flat foot and other deformities | 2 | 1.3 | |
| Congenital Anomolies | 5 | | 2.4 |
| Cardiovascular | 3 | 2.0 | |
| Cleft lip and palate | 1 | 0.7 | |
| Limbs | 1 | 0.7 | |
| Accidents and Ill-Defined Conditions | 5 | | 2.4 |
| Fracture of foot | 1 | 0.7 | |
| Poisoning | 2 | 1.3 | |
| Open wounds | 2 | 1.3 | |
| | 209 | 137.5 | 99.7 |

[a] Based on sample N = 1520.

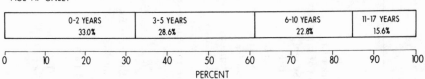

SEVERITY OF DISORDER

| SEVERE | MODERATE | MILD | NO DISABILITY |
|--------|----------|------|---------------|
| 10%    | 11.1%    | 50.5% | 37.4%        |

TYPE OF DISORDER

| MOTOR | SENSORY | COSMETIC |
|-------|---------|----------|
| 66.5% | 20.0%   | 13.5%    |

DURATION: PROPORTION OF LIFE SPAN

| OVER 2/3 | 1/3 TO 2/3 | LESS THAN 1/3 |
|----------|------------|---------------|
| 44.0%    | 29.5%      | 26.5%         |

AGE AT ONSET

| 0-2 YEARS | 3-5 YEARS | 6-10 YEARS | 11-17 YEARS |
|-----------|-----------|------------|-------------|
| 33.0%     | 28.6%     | 22.8%      | 15.6%       |

```
0      10     20     30     40     50     60     70     80     90     100
                                  PERCENT
```

*Figure 3C.1. Clinical characteristics of children with chronic disorders, both sexes, 6-17 years, Monroe County (n = 209).*

nary" daily activities typical for children of that age and sex. This finding is in keeping with the results reported by others (Richardson et al., 1965; Pless and Graham, 1970; Schiffer and Hunt, 1963).

The chronic conditions included in this sample were so varied that it was also necessary to categorize them according to the *type* of disability produced. Because children with cosmetic disorders and those with sensory disorders had been shown by Richardson (1971) and Cowen et al. (1961), respectively, to have higher risks of psychosocial adjustment problems, it was decided to classify each child's major disability into one of three groups: *sensory* (disorders affecting speech, hearing, or vision), *cosmetic* (disorders affecting appearance), and *motor* (all other conditions affecting locomotion, either directly or indirectly). As shown, 20% of the conditions were classified as sensory, 13.5% as cosmetic, and the remaining 66.5% as motor.

The *duration* of the disability was specified in relation to the proportion of the child's life span involved. (A condition that has lasted for three years in a 6-year-old—50% of his life—obviously has different significance than one that has persisted for three years in a 15-year-old.) Nearly one half (44%) of the conditions had been present for more than two thirds of the child's life, whereas about one quarter (27%) were conditions of relatively short duration. A related aspect of duration is the age at which the condition was first diagnosed, since this too has potentially different significance at different ages. Of the disorders, 16% began before 6 months of age (most were congenital); a further 7% began before the age of 2. By the age of 6, nearly 60% of the diagnoses had been made, and in 75% of children the conditions were established by the age of eight.

## Medical History and Medical Care

Because in so many cases the condition was of long duration, in most instances the course of the illness was quite stable. Only a minority of parents (14%) thought the illness had worsened since it began, whereas about one half (53%) believed there had been some improvement. In the remaining third the condition had either remained unchanged or pursued a variable course of "ups and downs."

Most parents thought that the treatment had made the child better, but a small proportion were convinced that it had aggravated the condition. Most frequently, physical factors such as weather, overexertion, or some kind of trauma were thought to be the cause of deterioration. About 1 parent in 10, however, thought that psychological or social factors were often instrumental in aggravating the child's illness.

Although there are many ways in which a chronic illness may affect the life of the child, the most common is the need for frequent, complex, and often unpleasant forms of medical care. Surprisingly, perhaps, only 40 children (20%) had been hospitalized for their illnesses, but of these nearly one half occurred within the first 2 years of life. Most of the hospitalizations were lengthy, about one half being from two to six weeks in duration.

Much more of a burden, for both parents and children however, is the necessity for regular visits to a physician. Because of the chronic illness, 55% of the children had seen a doctor within the preceding year. The converse may be of greater significance: 45% of the children had not seen a doctor for the chronic disorder for more than 12 months. Of the children who had seen physicians in the last year, one quarter had contacts with more than one doctor. Of the parents involved, 11% estimated that they had taken the chronically ill child to a doctor more than 10 times, and about one fifth estimated that they had made more than 20 visits!

In recent years and particularly in urban areas, children with chronic disorders tend increasingly to receive their care exclusively from specialists. This trend was confirmed to some degree by our interviews. Twenty-two percent of parents reported that the child had seen a pediatrician in the past year, and 21% that the child had seen a family doctor. By comparison, however, 32% of the children had seen *only* a specialist, whereas only 16% were receiving care from *both* specialists and primary doctors.

## Parental Knowledge and Attitudes

The knowledge most parents possessed of the medical aspects of the child's illness was, in their own estimation, scanty: 33% judged that they had "very little" understanding of it, and a further 21%, "little." Fewer than one parent in five thought that they understood the condition well, or could describe it in such a way that the interviewer rated the level of understanding as "high."

These findings are of potential importance for several reasons. Various studies have shown a relation between the level of understanding and the patient's compliance with the doctor's instructions (Pratt et al., 1958; Francis et al., 1969). It has also been suggested that understanding may be related to the attitudes and behavior a parent expresses toward the sick child, and that this, in turn, influences the child's response to his illness (Korsch, 1958). Since 50% of the parents thought that the child's illness was the result of some hereditary or congenital cause, it was not surprising that 23% believed the condition could have been prevented. As a result, it was estimated that about one third of parents expressed some unresolved guilt feelings over the child's condition. Clinicians familiar with the care of these children often state that such feelings may be partly responsible for parental overprotection, excessive denial, or rejection of a handicapped child (Mattsson, 1972).

Similarly, the interviews revealed that most parents (74%) had some specific worries about the chronically ill child, many revolving around the question of what would happen in the future. Nevertheless, 66% said that they thought the condition would improve when the child was older; only 6% expected it to worsen; and 22% believed that it would remain unchanged.

Parents were asked about specific ways in which they thought the condition might affect the child's future opportunities. Sixty percent believed there would be no adverse consequences; of those who did identify areas of concern, the most frequently mentioned was employment, followed by social relations in general, and marriage in particular.

Looking back over these questions dealing with knowledge, attitudes, fears for the future, and problem areas, we were impressed with what appeared to be a tendency to minimize or deny some of the realities associated with these illnesses. Although many parents whose children had mild conditions were being realistic, many others with more severely disabled children responded in a similar (but, in these instances, overoptimistic) fashion.

Consequences of Chronic Illness

One of the main purposes of the studies of chronic illness that began with the special survey in 1968 was to examine the secondary effects of these conditions on the child's psychological, social, and scholastic development. We believe that these secondary consequences are largely preventable if comprehensive health care is provided. Knowledge as to which children are most vulnerable, however, is necessary to make these services both effective and efficient.

Impact on Physical Functioning

As indicated in Table 3C.2, very few of the children were sufficiently disabled to require help with washing or dressing (2%), or walking or climbing upstairs (2%). Twenty-one children (12%) required help with injections or other medical treatments, and nearly one half (46%) had taken some kind of medication in the two weeks preceding the interview (not shown in Table 3C.2). Other forms of treatment included physiotherapy (4%), splints or braces (appliances, 4%), hearing aids or glasses (6%), speech therapy (9%), and special diets (10%). Each of these forms of therapy directly or indirectly produces some limitation on the child's activities, if only by virtue of the time and inconvenience involved.

A more direct indication of the extent to which children are "disabled" by their illnesses is that about 37% were thought by their parents to be *unable* to participate in some activities in which they would otherwise have taken part. These included the usual range of athletics and games as well as social activities. In addition, 9% described activities the child was able to do, but which the doctor would *not permit*. More revealing, perhaps, were the 20% who identified activities they chose to help the child with because of his illness (e.g., dressing, homework, or bathing).

On a more subjective level 84% of parents thought the condition had made the child "uncomfortable" in some way; 41% identified the chief "discomfort" as physical in nature, 18% as psychological, and 25% as both.

Impact on School Attendance and Performance

Only 12 of the children (7%) were receiving special education because of their handicaps; the majority of their parents viewed this arrangement positively. Four children (3%) had received special tutoring either at home or in the hospital. In all, 10% had missed some school as a result of their illnesses in the last month, and 27% had done so in the past year.

The likelihood of school absence was directly related to the severity of the condition, as was the frequency of days spent in bed. For the group as

*Table 3C.2.*   *Impact of Illness on Functioning*
All values in percentages

| Area of Impact | All (n = 209) | Moderate-Severe (n = 28) | Mild (n = 104) | Non-disabling (n = 77) |
|---|---|---|---|---|
| Daily Functioning | | | | |
| Physical discomfort | 41 | 29 | 45 | 41 |
| Psychological distress | 18 | 21 | 21 | 11 |
| Both physical and psychological distress | 25 | 43 | 24 | 20 |
| Activities limited | 37 | 71 | 49 | 7 |
| Assistance given | 20 | 58 | 23 | 4 |
| Activities not permitted | 9 | 19 | 11 | 1 |
| Activities decreased | 16 | 39 | 20 | 4 |
| School absence[a] | 27 | 50 | 36 | 7 |
| Bed disability[a] | 21 | 39 | 28 | 5 |
| Aid in washing, dressing | 2 | 9 | 1 | 0 |
| Aid in walking, going up and down stairs | 2 | 13 | 0 | 0 |
| Aid in self-care | 4 | 18 | 2 | 3 |
| Treatment | | | | |
| Aid with injections or other medical treatments | 12 | 13 | 13 | 10 |
| Regular medication | 72 | 74 | 70 | 73 |
| Physiotherapy | 4 | 15 | 3 | 0 |
| Glasses, hearing aid | 6 | 15 | 4 | 4 |
| Appliances | 4 | 12 | 3 | 1 |
| Speech therapy | 9 | 19 | 7 | 7 |
| Diet | 10 | 23 | 8 | 7 |
| Other | 14 | 12 | 17 | 10 |
| Psychosocial Effect | | | | |
| Behavior worsened | 20 | 28 | 23 | 12 |
| Social relations worsened | 15 | 23 | 19 | 7 |
| School work worsened | 10 | 19 | 12 | 3 |

[a] Any absence or disability days in past year due to the illness.

a whole, 8% reported one or more days spent in bed in the last month, and 21% reported one or more days in bed over the past year. In other words, in the month preceding the interview, 16% of the children had decreased their usual pattern of activities, 10% had missed days at school, and 8% had spent at least one day in bed because of the condition.

No attempt was made to match the chronically ill children and the "controls" by intelligence. There were no significant differences between them in IQ, yet the proportion of chronically ill children with achievement test scores *below* their tested abilities is generally greater than the rate for healthy children of the same age. Thus in the group of boys 6–11 years of age 34% were underachieving, compared with 19% of the controls, and for the older boys the figures were 46% versus 32%. For the younger girls there were no significant differences, whereas for the older girls the pattern was reversed—a higher proportion of the healthy were underachieving (46% versus 35%). These findings may be explained to some extent by increased frequency of school absences, but this alone is not a sufficient explanation and suggests that motivational or emotional factors may also exist.

The child's behavior in the classroom and the frequency of referrals for child guidance or to a school psychologist were also examined. Surprisingly, there were no significant differences in the proportions of healthy and sick children referred to psychologists, although the actual percentages are consistently higher among the chronically ill: 12% versus 9% in the older boys and 12% versus 3% in the older girls.

## Impact on Psychological and Social Development

One of the major concerns of this study was to determine the extent to which children with chronic illnesses are troubled by psychological and social problems that may be related to the presence of a physical disorder. Although such an association has been frequently observed (Wright, 1960), it has been difficult to establish conclusively that the problems so often experienced by children with these conditions are a *consequence* of them. There are many theoretical reasons for assuming that a child with a chronic disorder who behaves differently from his peers is likely to experience changes in self-image, self-concept, or self-esteem. Evidence for a causal relationship between these changes and the illness, however, can come only from a longitudinal study. One alternative, followed in this study, is to examine children cross-sectionally, using adequate controls and taking care to minimize bias by conducting the psychological evaluation so that the examiner is unaware of the child's health status.

### Psychological Consequences

Most parents thought that the child's illness had not influenced his behavior one way or another. Only 20% were convinced that it had made the child's behavior worse (i.e., difficult, more unhappy, more aggressive, or more withdrawn). Interestingly, almost twice as many parents (36%) thought the illness had made the child a "better person," that is, more compassionate, conscientious, understanding, sympathetic, or tolerant of others. Many parents were able to identify factors that might have made it easier or more difficult for the child to adjust to his illness, such as personality, intelligence, appearance, or family relationships.

As valuable as these parent observations may be, they are subjective and need substantiation by objective methods. To study this question systematically, a comparison group of healthy children was selected in such a way that the influences of age, sex, social class, and race differences were controlled. It was assumed that by doing so any psychological differences between the groups could, for the most part, be attributed to the chronic disorder, although, as stated previously, in the absence of "before and after" measures such a conclusion can be only tentative.

To minimize difficulties in assessing psychosocial function, this study was limited to children of school age, thereby enabling us to obtain information from teachers and classmates and to administer several "paper and pencil" measures of self-concept.[3]

The results of the psychological tests listed in the Appendix to Section 3C are shown in Table 3C.3, which gives the percentages of children with scores indicative of "maladjustment" for each of the major groups (chronically ill, divided into subgroups according to the severity of the disability, and healthy controls). The pattern of results suggests that proportionately more of those with chronic disorders are maladjusted, although few of the differences are statistically significant. Larger differences are found most often in self-ratings and parent ratings, as contrasted with the ratings of teachers or peers. Only in one half of the measures listed do the results indicate a *direct* relationship between the severity of the disability and the frequency of maladjustment. In most of the others the relationship is curvilinear, maladjustment being more frequent in the severely disabled and the nondisabled groups and less in those with intermediate levels of disability.

This curious finding has been noted in other studies (e.g., McAnarney et al., 1974) and suggests that two different mechanisms may be at work.

---

[3] In spite of the steps described, many difficulties remain in assessing the psychological adjustment of children with chronic illnesses. Tests designed for normal children cannot be applied to those with disorders without some safeguards; tests that are applicable to adolescents may not be appropriate for primary school children (and vice versa). Perhaps of greatest concern is the fact that many of the most popular and useful projective measures cannot be administered by nonprofessional personnel. Although it might have been desirable to have all children assessed by a psychiatrist and all families evaluated by a social worker, this is rarely possible under survey circumstances, especially when "controls" are included.

*Table 3C.3.*   *Psychological Indicators of Maladjustment*
Values in percentages

| Type of Indicator | Moderate–Severe ($n = 28$) | Mild ($n = 104$) | No Disability ($n = 77$) | Healthy Controls ($n = 166$) |
|---|---|---|---|---|
| Self Ratings | | | | |
| Self-esteem—low | 27 | 31 | 25 | 26 |
| Self-test—poor | 28 | 38 | 36 | 29 |
| Picture test—sad | 100[a] | 40 | 67[a] | 35 |
| Sentence completion—negative | 65[a] | 47 | 39 | 37 |
| Individuation—different | 41[a] | 34 | 31 | 22 |
| Manifest anxiety—high | 35[a] | 27 | 31 | 19 |
| California Total Adjustment—low | 81 | 71 | 72 | 68 |
| Peer Ratings | | | | |
| Attention score—low | 57 | 48 | 56 | 47 |
| Evaluation score—low | 50 | 54 | 46 | 50 |
| Parents' Ratings | | | | |
| Emotional health—not excellent | 60 | 65 | 57 | 52 |
| Behavioral symptoms—2 or more | 50[a] | 52[a] | 43[a] | 30 |
| Friends own age—too few | 24[a] | 12 | 10 | 7 |
| Teacher and School Ratings | | | | |
| Behavior symptoms—many | 36 | 27 | 32 | 36 |
| Referral to psychologist—yes | 12 | 13 | 7 | 6 |
| Overall adjustment—poor | 43 | 31 | 23 | 25 |
| Underachievement—yes | 52[a] | 37 | 24 | 31 |
| Adjustment index—low | 46 | 36 | 33 | 28 |

[a] Significance: $p < .05$.

In the case of the severely disabled, maladjustment may represent a direct effect of disability on self-concept, whereas in those having illnesses that produce no obvious disability the maladjustment may reflect the "marginal" nature of their situation and the resultant conflict produced (Barker et al., 1953).

In either case it cannot be proven that the association between maladjustment and chronic illness is causal, since the information was not obtained in a longitudinal fashion. Nevertheless, cautious inferences can be drawn from these findings, suggesting that some children with chronic disorders are indeed more likely to become maladjusted and that this outcome may be preventable (Pless et al., 1972).

Relation Between Adjustment and Other Factors

To simplify the results and permit further analysis, an "adjustment index" was devised. Each child was ranked according to scores on each of the tests in the psychological battery. Points were assigned according to the distribution of scores on each test, were added for each child, and were expressed as a percentage of the total possible score for all the tests completed. Those whose total scores are in the lowest 3 percentiles are assumed to be significantly maladjusted. Thus, as shown at the bottom of Table 3C.3, 46% of children with moderate-severe chronic disabilities had low adjustment index scores, compared with only 28% of healthy controls.

The association of low index scores with other features of the chronic disease and with various characteristics of the child's family is shown in Table 3C.4. These results suggest that maladjustment is more frequent among children whose illnesses begin before the age of six and among adolescents. As might be expected, it is inversely related to intelligence and is directly related to severity. Maladjustment is also found more frequently among those with sensory or cosmetic disorders (46%), but does not appear to be related to the total duration of the disorder.

The relationships between maladjustment and characteristics of the family are somewhat unexpected. Psychological problems do not appear to be significantly related to family size but are much less frequent among sick children living with the mother alone; the reverse is true for healthy children! The less educated, lower social class families more frequently have children with chronic illnesses who have low adjustment index scores; the same holds for healthy children.

The family characteristic of greatest importance appears to be the level of family functioning as assessed by the FFI (see Section 2A). Families with low index scores are almost twice as likely to have children with low adjustment scores than are families that are functioning well (high index scores).

Finally, we also found that the better the parent's knowledge and understanding of the child's illness, the better the child's adjustment. Only 27% of children whose parents had "excellent" knowledge of their illnesses had low adjustment index scores, compared with 43% of those with parents having "poor" understanding.

*Discussion*

The findings described in this section illustrate many of the problems experienced by children with chronic disorders and by their families. For

Table 3C.4. *Relationship between Characteristics of Child and Family and Maladjustment*[a]
Values in percentages

| Child Characteristics | Sick (n = 209) | Family Characteristics | Sick (n = 209) | Controls (n = 166) |
|---|---|---|---|---|
| Age of Onset (years) | | Family Size | | |
| 0–5 | 42 | Only child | 40 | 23 |
| 6–11 | 22 | 1 or 2 | 29 | 35 |
| 12–16 | 33 | 3 or more | 37 | 26 |
| Intelligence quotient | | Marital Status of Mother | | |
| Under 90 | 54 | Married | 37 | 25 |
| 90–110 | 44 | Other | 14 | 60 |
| 111+ | 32 | Educational Level of Mother | | |
| Type of Disability | | Less than high school | 42 | 37 |
| Cosmetic | 46 | High school only | 33 | 28 |
| Sensory | 46 | Beyond high school | 36 | 17 |
| All others | 31 | Social Stratum | | |
| Duration of Disability | | Low | 52 | 33 |
| Less than one third of life | 36 | Middle | 28 | 37 |
| One to two thirds of life | 33 | High | 38 | 19 |
| More than two thirds of life | 37 | Family Functioning | | |
| Severity of Disability | | Low | 44 | 35 |
| Moderate–severe | 46 | Middle | 39 | 25 |
| Mild | 36 | High | 28 | 18 |
| Nondisabling | 33 | | | |

[a] "Maladjustment" = adjustment index scores in the lowest three percentiles.

many children these problems are far from trivial, and for some, such difficulties may be of great significance in influencing their future development. There are only indirect hints in these data of the reasons for some of the problems, though in many instances the explanations are obvious. Illnesses that are disabling and of long duration, that require continuous and complex medical attention, and that disrupt and burden the family financially must take their toll. But it is not only the severely handicapping disorders that create difficulties for these children or their families; in some instances children with relatively minor disorders are also seriously disturbed. This seems particularly likely with children whose families are functioning poorly—where there is dissatisfaction with aspects of the marriage, difficulties in communication, or a lack of cohesiveness and mutual support and understanding.

The importance of these findings for those interested in community child health is the extent to which they may be related to the care provided for these children. Although there is no *direct* evidence that these problems can be prevented through changes in medical care, this possibility merits thorough exploration. Many of the problems are clearly related to an inadequate understanding of the chronic condition and a lack of guidance in day-to-day management. This in turn suggests a deficiency in the amount or kind of support, counseling, and assistance provided by health professionals. Considering that the present system is characterized by excessive demand, by lack of time, by lack of training in behavioral problems, counseling, and health education, and by discontinuity, lack of coordination, and a division of responsibilities between specialists and primary physicians, it would be surprising if no room for improvement can be found.

Beyond possible improvements in the routine care of all children with chronic disorders, these findings suggest that children or families with certain characteristics merit special attention. An appreciation of the particular vulnerability for maladjustment experienced by children with cosmetic and sensory disorders, by those whose parents lack understanding of the condition, and by those in families that function poorly would enable health planners to "target" the population for whom a greater concentration of effort may reap many benefits.

In the years ahead chronic disorders will inevitably occupy a larger place in the spectrum of childhood illnesses. Studies such as those described in this section are but a few examples of the springboards from which a more rational attack on these illnesses can be launched. Efforts must be devoted to replicating these findings, to analyzing these relationships in greater detail using more refined measures, and to conducting experimental trials to evaluate new methods of managing these children.

Among some of the possibilities to be explored are the efficacy of new manpower resources such as family counselors (described in Section 11B); better means of linking the skills of specialists with those of the primary physician; and improved methods for ensuring continuity, coordination, and the delivery of fully comprehensive services when they are required.

## REFERENCES

BARKER, ROGER, WRIGHT, BEATRICE, MEYERSON, LEE, and GONICK, MOLLIE

1953 *Adjustment to Physical Handicap and Illness: A Survey of the Social Psychology of Physique and Disability.* New York: Social Science Research Council.

COWEN, EMORY, UNDERBERG, RITA, VERRILLO, RONALD, and BENHAM, FRANK

1961 *Adjustment to Visual Disability in Adolescence.* New York: American Foundation for the Blind.

FRANCIS, V., KORSCH, B., and MORRIS, M.

1969 "Gaps in Doctor-Patient Communication: Patients' Response to Medical Advice." *New England Journal of Medicine,* 280:535–540.

ILLINGWORTH, R.S.

1964 "The Increasing Challenge of Handicapped Children." *Clinical Pediatrics,* 3:189–190.

KORSCH, BARBARA

1958 "Psychologic Principles: Pediatrician and Sick Child." *Advances in Pediatrics,* 10:30–65.

MATTSSON, AKE

1972 "Long-Term Physical Illness in Childhood: A Challenge to Psychosocial Adaptation." *Pediatrics,* 50(5):801–811.

MC ANARNEY, ELIZABETH, PLESS, I. BARRY, SATTERWHITE, BETTY, and FRIEDMAN, STANFORD

1974 "Psychological Problems of Children with Chronic Juvenile Arthritis." *Pediatrics,* 53:523–528.

PLESS, I. BARRY

1968 "Epidemiology of Chronic Disease." In *Ambulatory Pediatrics,* edited by M. Green and R. Haggerty. p. 760. Philadelphia: W. B. Saunders.

PLESS, I.B. and GRAHAM, P.

1970 "Epidemiology of Physical Disorder." In *Education, Health and Behavior,* edited by M. Rutter, J. Tizard, and K. Whitmore. London: Longman Group Limited. pp. 285–296.

PLESS, I. BARRY, ROGHMANN, KLAUS J., and HAGGERTY, ROBERT J.

1972 "Chronic Illness, Family Functioning, and Psychological Adjustment: A Model for the Allocation of Preventive Mental Health Services." *International Journal of Epidemiology,* 1 (3):271–277.

PLESS, I.B.

1974  "The Changing Face of Primary Pediatrics." *Pediatric Clinics of North America*, 21 (1):223–244.

PRATT, LOIS, SELIGMAN, ARTHUR, and READER, GEORGE

1958  "Physicians' Views on the Level of Medical Information among Patients." In *Patients, Physicians and Illness*, edited by Jaco, Gartley E., pp. 222–229. New York: The Free Press.

RICHARDSON, STEPHEN

1971  "Handicap, Appearance and Stigma." *Social Science and Medicine*, 5:621–628.

RICHARDSON, W.P., HIGGINS, A.C., and AMES, R.G.

1965  *The Handicapped Children of Alamance County, North Carolina: A Medical and Sociological Study*. Wilmington, Delaware: Nemours Foundation.

SCHIFFER, C.G., and HUNT, E.P.

1963  "Illness among Children." Data from U.S. National Health Survey. Washington, D.C.: Government Printing Office.

WRIGHT, BEATRICE A.

1960  *Physical Disability—A Psychological Approach*. New York: Harper and Row.

## D. THE "NEW MORBIDITY"

The traditional concerns of pediatricians involve the diagnosis and treatment of acute and chronic illness and the maintenance of the health of the well child. Some of the major problems related to these concerns have been described in the preceding sections. Pediatricians will continue to devote their energy and attention to the conventional areas of health and illness to ensure that all children with these disorders receive care, and to continually improve the quality of that care. However, because of the advances of medical science, infectious diseases are now much reduced, and serious illness and premature death are no longer the dominant concerns.

A group of new childhood difficulties that we have termed the "new morbidity" is now gaining attention. Many of these difficulties lie beyond the boundaries of traditional medical care. Our household surveys, for instance, included questions relating to problem areas not strictly medical. Parents indicated much dis-ease, dissatisfaction, and unhappiness about such problems as behavior disorders among preschoolers, inadequate functioning in school, and the management of adolescents' adjustment difficulties.

Handling such problems will be important to the future of pediatric practice, and a major shift in the orientation of training programs is required to prepare pediatricians for these tasks. More time at each visit is needed to deal with these problems, which in turn requires changes in the manner of paying for health and social services. If the new morbidity does not become the pediatricians' responsibility, those planning child health services must designate others to provide these services.

The most prominent of the child health problems that have emerged in the past decade or two are behavioral and schooling problems found in children of all ages. Sexual maturation and growing independence from the family add other problems peculiar to the adolescent period. It is to these areas that we will devote most attention in this section. There are, however, other areas of new morbidity that cannot be covered here, such as new environmental hazards, poor dietary habits, or mental health problems. Some of these are actually old problems that always existed but were left unattended as more pressing needs took priority. Others are new and stem from technological "progress"; air pollution, automotive accidents, recreational accidents from minibikes or snowmobiles, household accidents, unsafe toys, and lead paint are examples of new man-made health hazards. Underlying some of the new morbidity are problems arising from modern society such as social and geographic mobility, crowding, high-rise living, and urban decay. Other problems (alcohol, drugs, venereal disease) are old, but their diffusion to younger and younger age groups and the lessening of social controls make them concerns for pediatricians and parents.

The concept of the new morbidity is important not only to alert us to the constantly changing health needs of children, but also to challenge us to find new ways of meeting them.

## Behavioral Problems of Preschoolers

ROBERT W. CHAMBERLIN

Between 20 and 30% of children entering first grade have been identified as having behavioral and emotional problems (Bower, 1969; Cowen et al., 1963). Follow-up studies indicate that these problems tend to persist (Zax et al., 1968) and that there is a shortage of mental health professionals to deal with them (Joint Commission on Mental Illness and Health, 1961). Furthermore, recent reports show that preschool behavioral problems are rarely internalized and often respond to brief intervention techniques (Chamberlin, 1967; Thomas et al., 1968).

The possibility of preventing behavioral and emotional disturbances in school-aged children through a program of early recognition and modification of preschool behavior patterns is certainly appealing. The primary care physician is in a particularly strategic position to coordinate such a program because of his continuing relationship with families having young children.

Before "preventive" programs can be launched on a widespread basis, however, questions regarding the extent of behavioral problems, their persistence, their etiology, the role of the family, and the effectiveness of intervention need to be answered. Pertinent data from the 1969 Rochester survey (the "R" sample, $n = 474$) described in the Appendix to Chapter 1, as well as those from a special interview of parents of 2-year-olds (the "S" sample, $n = 200$) are examined here in an attempt to answer these questions. A broader discussion of the samples used and other methodological considerations are included in the Appendix to Section 3D.

## The Frequency of Behavioral Problems among Preschool Children

Except for a small percentage of children with psychotic disturbances, the difference between problem and "normal" children is one of degree rather than kind. Whether or not a particular behavior becomes labeled as a problem depends as much on who is doing the labeling as on the behavior itself. Our data enable us to examine this question from the viewpoint of the parent, the primary care physician, and the investigator, and to compare these findings with the results of other studies.

### Mothers' Reports

From the two samples it is clear that preschool children display a wide variety of behaviors troublesome to adults. For example, in the "S" sample mothers were asked whether their children displayed any behaviors (a) causing worry or concern or (b) leading to frequent conflicts; 38% answered "yes" to the first question, and 47% responded affirmatively to the second. Table 3D.1 lists the behaviors most commonly identified for each question.

In the "R" sample mothers of 1- to 4-year-olds ($n = 474$ weighted) were asked about five types of behavior (stubbornness, resisting bedtime, awakening at night, temper outbursts, and demanding attention). Sixteen percent indicated concern about one or more of these behaviors.

In spite of these anxieties, however, few mothers discussed them with their physicians. In the "R" sample *all* mothers taking the child to a physician within the two-week period preceding the interview were asked to describe the purpose of the visit. None mentioned discussion of behavioral problems. Similarly, less than 15% of the mothers indicating concern about a child's

Table 3D.1.  Behaviors Mentioned Most Frequently as Causing Conflict
or Concern by Mothers of Two-Year-Olds (Rochester "S" Sample)

| Behaviors Causing Conflict (Rank order of mention) | Behaviors Causing Concern (rank order of mention) |
|---|---|
| 1. Stubbornness | 1. Habits such as nailbiting and thumbsucking |
| 2. High activity level and getting into things | 2. Temper outbursts |
| 3. Temper outbursts | 3. Aggressive behavior with siblings or peers |
| 4. Resistance to bedtime | 4. Dependent-inhibited behaviors such as fears, separation upset, crying too easily, not defending self |
| 5. Reluctance to eat | 5. Delayed speech development |
| 6. Whining, nagging, or demanding attention | 6. Stubbornness |
| 7. Aggressive behavior with siblings or peers | 7. Bedtime and sleep problems |
| 8. Resistance to toilet training | 8. Amount of food intake |

stubbornness, temper, or attention-demanding behavior said that they discussed this with their physicians.

The mother's reluctance to mention her concern is not the only reason for this lack of communication. Physicians may not ask about behavior (Stine, 1962; Miller et al., 1960) or may ignore concerns that are mentioned (Starfield and Barkowe, 1969).

## Physicians' Criteria

At the time of the 2-year-old well-child visits, each "S" sample physician filled out a checklist describing the behavior of the child in the office, his opinion as to whether or not the child had any behavioral problems, and his evaluation of the mother's childrearing approach. Fifteen children (8%) were identified as having behavioral problems.

The rating of the mother's childrearing style was usually based on office observation rather than specific inquiry. A mother was identified as "overpermissive" if her child was misbehaving and she took no steps to set limits. "Overstrict" mothers were those who responded to exploratory behavior with frequent "no's," threats, or hand slaps. An "overprotective" mother was observed to have difficulty in separating from her child and expressed

Table 3D.2. *Physicians' Ratings of Child's Behavior and Mother's Childrearing Style (Rochester "S" Sample)*

| Item Rated | Children Identified as Having Problems (N = 15) | Children Not Identified as Having Problems (N = 183) |
|---|---|---|
| 1. Child's Office Behavior Percent Showing Marked or Moderate | | |
| Resistance to examination | 67 | 23 |
| Mother dependency | 67 | 20 |
| Hyperactivity | 60 | 15 |
| 2. Mother's Childrearing Style Percent Being Marked or Moderate | | |
| Overanxious | 73 | 10 |
| Overpermissive | 33 | 7 |
| Overstrict | 15 | 2 |
| Overprotective | 27 | 2 |

much concern about minor deviations in health. That this brief view of the mother may be misleading is suggested by the fact that some of the mothers identified as "overpermissive" admitted, when interviewed, much use of yelling, scolding, and spanking.

Table 3D.2 compares the ratings of children identified as having behavioral problems with those who had none identified. Although there is a tendency for the physician's diagnosis to be related to his rating of the child's behavior in the office and the mother's childrearing style, it became clear, in talking to four of the physicians doing the rating, that a number of factors influence a diagnosis of "behavioral problem," especially a heavy dose of "gut feelings"[1] or indirect evidence.

### Investigators' Viewpoint

Investigators also have difficulties in defining a "behavioral problem." Most rely on an interview or checklist to indicate whether or not the child displays certain symptoms and, also, the degree to which they manifest (Glidewell et al., 1963; Drillien, 1964; Hornberger et al., 1960; MacFarlane et al., 1962). Individual symptoms are so common in young children that only the total number of symptoms, their duration, or some judgment as to their severity can be used as criteria to establish a diagnosis.

The prevalence of preschool behavioral problems (using different definitions) in various populations varies from 8% to over 50% (Miller et al., 1960; Drillien, 1964; Thomas et al., 1968). Only in the Thomas study was a psychiatric evaluation carried out on each suspect child. By the age of 5, 18% of the children in that selected sample had developed a behavioral disorder of sufficient intensity to warrant some kind of intervention.

### Association of Family Settings with The Development of Behavioral Disorders

If behavioral disorders arise largely in the context of severely disturbed families, the primary physician's main role will be to initiate referral to a skilled mental health professional. On the other hand, if many behavioral disorders originate in relatively stable family settings in which the parents are having difficulty in coping with one particular type of child, the possibilities for modification through brief intervention are good.

In the "S" sample, families known to have serious problems were deliberately excluded from the study. In the "R" sample, a stress index was

---

[1] It appears that the physician diagnoses a behavioral problem when the mother has indicated concern about the child's behavior, and either describes it or is observed to be having difficulty in coping with it. Sometimes this impression is heavily influenced by the physician's knowledge of how this mother has coped with her children in the past. With this group of physicians, it would seem that only rarely, if ever, was a diagnosis based on the child's behavior alone.

obtained by adding one point for each item such as poor housing, single-parent home, frequent marital trouble, mother working full time, and low family income. Thirty percent of the families had a stress score of 1 or more.

The frequency of these problems was correlated with a behavioral problem index computed by counting the presence of the five behaviors mentioned previously (wakes often at night, stays up late, is stubborn, has temper tantrums, demands attention). Forty-seven percent of the families had a score of 1 or more. The Pearson correlation between stress and behavioral problems was $r = .20$, which, although significant for this sample size ($p = <.01$), accounts for less than 5% of the variance of the behavioral problem index score.

In the stable family settings of our sample there are several associations between particular childrearing patterns (see the Appendix to Section 3D) and the development of behavioral disorders which account for nearly 20% of the total variance. Other investigators report similar relationships between childrearing and child behavioral patterns (Yarrow et al., 1968; Thomas et al., 1968). Thomas and his colleagues present considerable evidence to support the thesis that many behavioral differences have their basis in temperament and that emotional disorders arise out of a lack of fit between a particular type of child and the response pattern adopted by the parent.

### The Role of Central Nervous System Dysfunction in the Etiology of Behavioral Problems

Recent studies have identified a higher incidence of abnormal birth histories and/or signs and symptoms of central nervous system (CNS) dysfunction in children manifesting behavioral disturbances than in a control group (Rutter et al., 1970; Drillien, 1964; Rogers et al., 1955). However, these and other studies indicate that (1) the majority of children developing behavioral disturbances do not have evidence of CNS dysfunction (Rutter et al., 1970; Werner et al., 1971); (2) of the children with CNS dysfunction and a behavioral disturbance, no one type of behavioral disorder predominates (Paine et al., 1968; Rutter et al., 1970; Shulman et al., 1965); and (3) within the group of children with CNS dysfunction the same associations between the development of a behavioral disorder and family and social factors are found as exist with children who have no evidence of CNS dysfunction (Rutter et al., 1970).

In the "S" sample, which excluded children with obvious brain damage, there were no significant relationships between the occurrence of such events as bleeding during the pregnancy and the 2-year-old behavioral patterns.

Discussion

Many parents have concerns about the behavior of their preschool child, but frequently do not discuss them with the physician. The relationship between early home behavioral problems and later school problems is not clear. Although the presence of central nervous system dysfunction or an unstable family situation increases the risk for the development of behavioral disorders, many problems develop in children without such findings or histories. Though the development of behavioral problems is associated with childrearing patterns, it appears to be related also to the temperament of the child.

## The Frequency and Nature of School Problems

PHILIP R. NADER

Of all children's problems, those involving school are the ones most frequently identified by parents. This "modern epidemic" includes a nationally estimated 10–30% who experience significant learning problems or behavioral difficulties manifested in poor school achievement or performance (Cowen et al., 1963; Lapouse and Monk, 1958; Glidewell et al., 1963). Health professionals increasingly recognize school functioning as one measure of health. The extent of school-related complaints presented to physicians indicates the need for a documentation of the epidemiology of school problems.

Methods

Repeated random sampling of families by the Rochester Child Health Studies in 1967, 1969, and 1971 (See the Appendix to Chapter 1) provided an opportunity to investigate the extent and nature of school problems. For children 5–17 years of age, we determined what school the child attended, his present grade, and the length of time he had been attending this school, as well as the frequency of absence for reasons other than illness. School functioning was measured by the question, "Has he/she ever had trouble with schoolwork;[2] ever been held back a grade; ever been asked to leave school?" If so, we asked, "What was the reason?"

Details of the coding, response reliability, and category assignment for the verbatim responses given by parents to the above questions are discussed in the Appendix to Section 3D.

[2] The wording was "schoolwork" in 1967 and 1971, but "school" for most of the 1969 survey. The discrepancy was not detected and corrected until halfway through the survey. Trouble with "school" hints at disciplinary problems; trouble with "schoolwork" is aimed more at academic functioning.

Results

Table 3D.3 gives the frequency of school problems reported in each of the three principal areas in the three surveys, and Table 3D.4 provides a breakdown by reported reason. For the group as a whole, "trouble with schoolwork" was attributed mainly to behavioral and academic causes; being "held back," to academic reasons; and being "asked to leave," chiefly to disciplinary problems.

*Table 3D.3.  Frequency of School Problems among Children Age 5–17, Monroe County, New York*
### Values in percentages

| Problem | 1967 | 1969 | 1971 |
|---|---|---|---|
| Trouble with schoolwork? | 23.0 | 13.8 | 21.9 |
| Ever held back? | 16.7 | 16.0 | 14.1 |
| Ever asked to leave? | 1.6 | 3.0 | 5.0 |
| Any of the above? | 27.0 | 22.9 | 28.9 |
| White students | 25.5 | 21.0 | 26.6 |
| Black students | 45.8 | 42.5 | 41.8 |
| $n =$ | 1519 | 1760 | 2048 |

*Table 3D.4.  Reported Reason for School Problems among Children Age 5–17, Monroe County, New York*
### Values in percentages

| Problem | 1967 | 1969 | 1971 |
|---|---|---|---|
| Trouble with Schoolwork? | | | |
| Behavioral | 35.6 | 33.9 | 31.4 |
| Academic | 45.6 | 27.0 | 46.2 |
| Discipline, others[a] | 18.8 | 39.1 | 22.4 |
| Ever Held Back?[b] | | | |
| Behavioral | 23.1 | 22.9 | [b] |
| Academic | 31.1 | 40.5 | |
| Discipline, others[a] | 45.8 | 36.6 | |
| Ever Asked to Leave?[b] | | | |
| Behavioral | 24 | 8 | [b] |
| Academic | — | 5 | |
| Discipline, others[a] | 76 | 87 | |

[a] Includes absenteeism, mobility, language problems, physical handicaps, and teacher-pupil interaction problems.
[b] No coding by *major reason* available for 1971.

The percentage of children aged 5–17 years reported by their parents to have any of these three problems varied from 23 to 29%. About 15% of children had been held back at least once, and 2–5% had been asked to leave school.

TROUBLE WITH SCHOOLWORK.  Of the children reported to be having trouble with schoolwork, about 45% had academic and reading problems (Table 3D.4). Behavioral problems ("immaturity," "motivation," "hyperactivity," and "emotional difficulties") were thought by parents to be the cause of the trouble in about one third of the cases in each of the years.

The 1971 survey also inquired about what action had been taken regarding problems with schoolwork. Teachers were contacted most frequently, and for most children (76%) some remedial action was taken either within the school setting, through special programs, or by change of schools. Less than 1% were referred for help outside the educational system. Parents reported that by the time of the interview the situation had improved for 65% of the affected children.

Boys were seen to have more trouble with schoolwork than girls: in 1967 28% of the boys surveyed were so designated versus 18% of the girls; in 1969 and 1971 both groups had lower rates, but the rate for boys was still higher than that for girls.

Black parents reported that 37% of their children were having trouble with schoolwork in 1967, compared to only 20% in 1969. Controlling for sex showed that the racial difference was concentrated chiefly among girls —white parents identified 10% of their daughters as having trouble with schoolwork versus 26% of daughters of black parents. White girls were reported to be mainly experiencing academic and reading difficulties, whereas black girls' parents reported primarily disciplinary reasons for their daughters' troubles.

EVER HELD BACK A GRADE.  The chance of being held back increases with the age group examined. In 1967 the percentages of each age group that had been held back were as follows: 5–8 years of age, 9%; 9–12 years of age, 17%; 13–15 years of age, 21%; and 16–17 years of age, 26%. The figures for 1969 and 1971 show a similar pattern.

Black children were reported as held back twice as often as white children. The frequencies were 29% to 15% in 1967, 39% to 14% in 1969, and 24% to 12% in 1971. Reading and other academic problems were the main reasons reported. For black girls absenteeism and mobility were also frequently named.

In 1969 parents in the two inner city wards reported the highest rates of children being held back—43% in one and 22% in the other. These figures were significantly greater than those reported by parents residing in the outer parts of the city (18%) or in the suburbs (13%). Similar differences persisted in 1971: the inner city wards had rates of 22% and 28%, compared with 19% for the rest of the city and only 10% for the suburban areas.

ASKED TO LEAVE SCHOOL. The longer a child is in school, the greater the possibility of his being asked to leave, chiefly because of disciplinary and behavioral problems. In 1971 black parents indicated that 11% of their children had, at one time, been asked to leave school, compared with only 4% of white children. City children were asked to leave school most often; the rate for inner city areas (13%) far exceeded that for suburban areas (1%).

ANY SCHOOL PROBLEMS. The presence of any school problem (with schoolwork, being held back, or being asked to leave) for Monroe County children varied little for the three survey years (27% to 29%). Striking racial differences are apparent and have persisted—black children have about twice as many problems as white. For whites those having such problems ranged from 26% to 28%, while for blacks the range was from 42% to 46%.

## Discussion

The main measures utilized in this study are parental reports of the school behavior and adjustment of the child. Possibly teacher reports would have yielded somewhat higher proportions of children with school problems. Several factors suggest, however, that parental perceptions represent a close estimate of the extent of certain difficulties. The greater frequency of problems reported for boys, blacks, inner city dwellers, and city children would be expected from both clinical experience and other reports.

The situation in Monroe County, and especially in the city school district at the time of the surveys, is one factor that might account for some of the results. Over the period of the studies the percentage of black students increased from 22% to 29% in the city high schools, and from 35% to 39% in the city elementary schools. Considerable efforts (and one countereffort) were made toward diminishing de facto segregation. Busing and school violence were the main issues in the school board elections of 1971. According to newspaper accounts, discipline in the city schools deteriorated. Budget problems forced cutbacks in programs and increased the average class size. For a time, especially during the 1969–1970 school year, police were present in the high schools to maintain order (see Section 1A).

In spite of these upheavals, between 1967 and 1971, a number of special education programs and projects such as "Head Start," "Guided Observation," ungraded schools, individualized instruction, and new approaches toward dealing with learning disabilities and behavioral problems were begun. Yet nonacademic areas continued to constitute a large portion of school related difficulties—at least as perceived by parents. It would seem prudent, therefore, to increase efforts to upgrade the skills of both teachers and parents in handling these problems. The high proportion of youths who are unsuccessful in school must be viewed as a failure not just of the school system, but of the community as a whole. Finally, as a part of the community with a special responsibility for the development of children, the pediatrician must assume some role in helping to deal with this major problem in our society.

## Special Problems of Adolescents

STANFORD B. FRIEDMAN
AND
IRVING WEINER

Adolescent medicine, hardly recognized as a special field a decade ago, is attracting nationwide interest; many medical facilities now include an adolescent clinic or ward (Rigg and Fisher, 1970, 1971). It seems unlikely that this trend reflects a sudden increase in the medical needs of teenagers; rather, it appears that increasing numbers of physicians have begun to perceive that adolescents have unmet medical needs. The data that follow support the need for special programs either as independent services or as part of other services for this age group.

Since the belief that adolescence is a period of good health lessens the motivation for creating health services for teenagers, it is critical to examine what little data exist relative to this issue. In a one-year period in Monroe County there were 11,946 hospital admissions of patients under 18 years of age, of whom 2672 were adolescents between the ages of 13 and 18 (see Table 3D.5).[3] Of these, 502 represented deliveries; in addition, 36 girls under 13 years were obstetrical admissions! Thus about one fifth of all hospitalized children will be teenagers distributed among the various pediatric, surgical, medical, and obstetrical services. Of the older girls, approximately half may be expected to be admitted for delivery of a baby (see Section 6B).

[3] Data are from the 1968 Patient Origin Study, Genesee Region Health Planning Council.

Table 3D.5.   Teenage Admissions to Hospital, 1968, Monroe County, New York

| Cause | Boys 13-15 | Boys 16-17 | Girls 13-15 | Girls 16-17 | All Adolescents 13-17 |
|---|---|---|---|---|---|
| Delivery | | | | | |
| Number | — | — | 80 | 422 | 502 |
| Percent | — | — | 13.4 | 46.9 | 18.8 |
| T & A[a] | | | | | |
| Number | 80 | 51 | 116 | 72 | 319 |
| Percent | 12.3 | 9.9 | 19.3 | 8.0 | 11.9 |
| Other surgery | | | | | |
| Number | 340 | 276 | 277 | 288 | 1181 |
| Percent | 52.1 | 53.1 | 46.2 | 32.1 | 44.2 |
| Medical | | | | | |
| Number | 233 | 192 | 127 | 118 | 670 |
| Percent | 35.7 | 37.0 | 21.2 | 13.1 | 25.1 |
| Total | | | | | |
| Number | 653 | 519 | 600 | 900 | 2672 |
| Percent | 100.0 | 100.0 | 100.0 | 100.0 | 100.0 |

[a] Tonsillectomy and adenoidectomy.

Table 3D.6 provides an estimate of the numbers of adolescents with

Table 3D.6.   Chronic Illnesses[a] and Behavior Problems[a] in 617 Adolescents 13–17 Years of Age (1969)

| Chronic Illnesses | | Behavioral Problems | |
|---|---|---|---|
| Condition | Frequency % | Behavior | Frequency % |
| Asthma | 1.8 | Fighting | 4.0 |
| Hay fever | 4.4 | Restless | 5.2 |
| Other allergies | 8.9 | Solitary or withdrawn | 5.3 |
| Sinus trouble | 1.6 | Afraid of things | 2.3 |
| Joint pains | 2.8 | Clumsy | 2.3 |
| Kidney trouble | 1.8 | Sleeplessness | 1.6 |
| Heart trouble | 0.5 | Other problems | 11.7 |
| Frequent earaches | 1.8 | | |
| Hearing loss | 1.6 | | |
| Poor vision (even with glasses) | 3.2 | | |
| Speech problems | 1.1 | | |
| Other problems | 15.1 | | |

[a] Only those considered to be "somewhat" or "very" serious.

symptoms of a chronic illness judged to be "somewhat" or "very" serious in the 1969 survey. Approximately 30% had one or more physical problems, with 9% described as having multiple disorders. (These illnesses were reported by the teenagers' mothers; it is not known how the figures would differ if the adolescents themselves were queried directly.)

Questions were also directed to the identification of behavioral problems. Replies indicated that 130 teenagers had one or more of the six specific problems listed in Table 3D.6, and a further 72 reported "other problems." Thus approximately 18% of this representative sample of adolescents were described as having behavioral problems. This figure may be unrealistic, however, since many of the social and behavioral problems most typical of adolescents were not specifically included in the questionnaire, although many were identified through the open-ended "other problems" question.

There is evidence (Section 3C) that children with chronic physical illnesses have increased incidence of emotional problems. This association holds also for our sample of adolescents, in which a correlation[4] of $g = +.40$ was obtained between the two sets of complaints. This finding does not, of course, prove a causal relationship; nevertheless, it seems of practical importance to recognize its existence. Furthermore, it appears likely that the medical problems listed might interfere with school performance. Indeed, a correlation was noted between physical complaints and "trouble over attendance" ($g = +.47$), "trouble with schoolwork" ($g = +.34$), and "ever held back" ($g = +.26$).

Even greater associations exist between behavioral problems and difficulties at school. Though many of the behavioral problems reported may have occurred in the setting of the school (e.g., "fighting") and thus contributed to these correlations, it appears likely that the association also reflects a more basic relationship.

Thus hospital admission data and the survey findings both suggest that adolescents have traditional physical and behavioral complaints with sufficient frequency to warrant more attention to their needs.

Another, newer concern regarding adolescents is the problems associated with alcohol and drug use. To establish the frequency of these problems, a random sample of approximately 7400 high school students (grades 10–12) in Monroe County was surveyed (Yancy et al., 1972). As shown in Table 3D.7, alcohol continues to be the most commonly used drug, with 85% of the students having "tried it at least once." Comparable figures

---

[4] All correlations in this paragraph are gamma coefficients. Significance was determined by chi square analysis, and all reported probability values are less than .01. Note that the chi square test is conservative as it ignores the direction of the relationship.

Table 3D.7.  High School Students' Reported
Experience with Drugs, Monroe County, New York[a]
(n = 7414)

| Drug | Tried It at Least Once (%) | Tried It More Than 15 Times (%) |
|---|---|---|
| Alcohol | 85.0 | 45.0 |
| Marijuana | 27.7 | 13.2 |
| Barbiturates | 14.9 | 2.9 |
| Amphetamines | 14.2 | 3.0 |
| LSD | 8.6 | 2.7 |
| Mescaline | 8.3 | 1.8 |
| Glue | 7.2 | 1.3 |
| Opium | 6.8 | 1.4 |
| Cocaine | 3.7 | 0.6 |
| Heroin | 2.6[b] | 0.6 |

[a] Adapted from Yancy et al. (1972), p. 740.
[b] Because of the small number of heroin users, a few incorrectly marked responses account for the discrepancy in these essentially equivalent percentages.

for marijuana are 28% "tried at least once," 13% "more than 15 times," and 22% "still using." Some experience with LSD was reported by 9% of the students; nearly 3% claimed to have tried heroin at least once. Three fourths of the students stated that a "drug center" would be beneficial, with 66% believing such a facility would be utilized by students. In a related study of 400 high school sophomores, 50% of the girls and 31% of the boys reported that they would welcome the opportunity of talking to a physician (Yancy and Nader, 1970). These problems are examples of an identified but generally unmet area for services required by adolescents.

In order to acquire a better sense of what "nonpatient" adolescents are like, a study was conducted to provide some data about "normal" adolescents and their families. A random sample of 26 boys and 26 girls from the junior class of a suburban high school was interviewed, as well as their parents.

The first half of the interview was devoted to questions about academic performance and aspirations. It was learned that over 80% were planning to continue some educational training beyond high school, and for this reason the majority considered their schoolwork important. The inquiries yielded two additional findings of interest. First, there was little evidence of conflict between these adolescents and their parents. Over 80% stated that, as far as they know, their parents supported their plans for the future. Second, it was found, surprisingly, that the parents were only minimally involved in their youngsters' study habits.

The second part of the interview concerned social behavior. Here, too, the lack of evidence for the generation gap and family conflicts thought to be widely characteristic of American youth was impressive. For one thing, there were very few disagreements in these families about rules for the teenagers' behavior.

Finally, some interesting social data emerged with regard to communication. The subjects were extremely accurate in describing how their parents actually responded to a question regarding appropriate sexual behavior for high school juniors. Three quarters had a very clear idea of where their parents stood with respect to kissing, necking, petting, and intercourse among the teenage population.

## Discussion

The field of adolescent medicine appears to be gaining a secure place in academic medicine, and this, in turn, should lead to future practitioners having improved skills in managing adolescent patients. It would be remiss, however, not to stress the critical shortage of psychiatrists and mental health workers for this age group. Hopefully, increased exposure of medical students and residents to such problems will lead to better understanding of them, so that earlier detection and more successful intervention may be possible.

Adolescents with chronic physical disabilities represent another group of teenage patients in need of specialized services. Typically such problems are cared for in specialty clinics organized within pediatric departments. Thus young patients with diseases such as diabetes mellitus, cystic fibrosis, hemophilia, and nephrosis are generally cared for in a pediatric specialty clinic through infancy and childhood. The management of adolescents, however, becomes quite diffuse in most situations. At some point, someone decides that the patient is old enough to go to an adult clinic. Unfortunately, the "adult clinic" is no better prepared to deal with adolescent problems compounded by medical illness than the specialty pediatric clinic. Except for the larger medical centers it is difficult for an adolescent clinic to provide the specialized technical services needed by such patients. The only solution to this dilemma is for the physician interested in adolescents to become an integral part of both the pediatric and the adult clinics that care for these patients.

In planning health services for adolescents it must be acknowledged that many of these young people are not integral members of a family unit, and many others are not in a position to obtain medical attention in the traditional fee-for-service health care system. Hence so-called free clinics have attracted many adolescents, though, typically, even these clinics do not meet the medical and psychiatric needs of adolescents from the lower socioeconomic classes. The solution to all these problems is not to argue for a formal "subspecialty" of adolescent medicine, but for existing clinical departments to acknowledge the special needs of patients in this age group. The task then will be to develop more acceptable, creative, and effective ways of offering such services to all adolescents.

## Implications for the Delivery of Care

ROBERT W. CHAMBERLIN

Although the ability of any preventive program to reduce the incidence of behavioral or school problems has yet to be demonstrated, our present state of knowledge indicates that much more can be done to relieve parent concerns in these areas. A program for achieving these goals could include the components described below.

### Prevention through Education

Many parental concerns and conflicts appear to be related to lack of knowledge about typical stage related behaviors. An active program of education in these areas, similar to those of Hill (1960) and Brazelton (1962) based on anticipatory guidance, should be implemented. Referral to books such as that by Ilg and Ames (1960) and parent discussion groups could supplement such a program.

In terms of individual differences, Carey (1970) has developed a questionnaire that can be used in office settings to help mothers identify the temperamental characteristics of their children. Moreover, Cooper and Tapia (1970) have developed a programmed text with a similar goal, although this aid is not yet commercially available. Early recognition of the "difficult" or "slow to warm up" child could help parents avoid needless guilt feelings and may minimize response patterns that accentuate rather than diminish some of these characteristics (Thomas et al., 1968). Books by Brazelton (1969) and Chess et al. (1965) are also available to help parents recognize and cope with individual differences.

Finally, recent knowledge about the effects of "cognitive stimulation" programs on the development of the child could well be included in an education program (Schaeffer, 1972).

### Screening for Behavioral Problems

As discussed earlier, many parents do not spontaneously bring their concerns about behavior to the physician's attention. Data from the "S" sample and the report by Willoughby and Haggerty (1964) indicate that some kind of behavioral checklist will be more economical in time, and more productive in identifying areas of concern, than reliance on a few questions during the well-child visit. Also, since behavioral complaints are often not recorded in the medical record, such a list could serve as a baseline against which to identify, over time, persistent or increasing problem areas.

Since nursery school behavioral patterns have been shown to have predictive value for later school functioning (Chamberlin and Nader, 1971), routine screening procedures should include teacher descriptions of the child's classroom behavior. A checklist like that developed by Eisenberg et al. (1962) or Rutter et al. (1970) could be used for the identification of school related problems in a similar fashion.

### Clarification of the Nature of the Problems

If the screening procedures identify problems in more than one area or if problems persist in spite of advice, the physician should invite both parents to return so that more information can be obtained. The semistructured interview developed by Rose and his associates (Philadelphia Child Guidance Clinic and Health Welfare Council, 1962), and described by Harrington (1965), is one effective way for gathering the information needed.

If it becomes clear that the parents have a marital problem or are attempting to cope with other difficulties on their own, referral to a mental health professional is generally indicated.

If the child shows markedly deviant behavior, slow motor or speech development, or other neurological signs, there should be further evaluation by an appropriate specialist.

If the family is coping well in general, and the problem appears to arise from a "lack of fit" between the type of child and the parents' response pattern, a three- to six-month trial of altering this response pattern should be attempted.

### Modifying Parents' Response Patterns

A number of brief therapy approaches such as "parental" guidance (Chamberlin, 1967; Thomas et al., 1968), behavior modification (Wahler

et al., 1965), and family therapy (Augenbraun et al., 1967) have been ·
found useful in modifying parent handling of the child. As yet, there are
no controlled studies indicating the superiority of one approach over
another. Experience indicates that preschool children who are going to
respond to such an approach generally do so within two to five months
(Chamberlin, 1967). A lack of response after this length of time calls for
a careful re-evaluation.

If the child is in nursery school or kindergarten, such a program needs
to be coordinated with what the teacher is doing in the classroom. The
teacher too may be having difficulty in coping with the child, and modification of his or her response patterns may also be required to change
the child's behavior (Allen et al., 1964; Sloane et al., 1967).

Finally, some highly active children with short attention spans may
benefit from drugs such as Ritalin (Eisenberg et al., 1961).

### Integrating a Mental Health Program into a Medical Setting

There remains the problem of how to integrate a program of prevention
and early recognition into the setting of a busy practitioner's office. One
of the principal characteristics of primary care is high volume, and, in
spite of declining birthrates, this situation is unlikely to change in the
very near future. Although some physicians with special interests and skills
in behavioral pediatrics have been able to make enough time available
to carry out parts of the program outlined, it is unlikely that the majority will choose to do so. Existing fee scales are such that an adequate charge
for the time involved presents a financial problem for most families with
young children. One solution to this dilemma would be to develop a
major role in this area for pediatric nurse practitioners (described in
Section 11A) or lay mental health counselors (Pless and Satterwhite,
1972). Such persons do not take care of the large numbers of sick children that confront the physician daily and hence are often seen as more
accessible by the parents. Also, they can charge a lesser, but adequate,
fee to cover the time spent in counseling or visiting the home and school.

### Conclusions

This discussion of implications for health services goes beyond our
current data but illustrates the importance for child health care of coming to grips with the problem of behavioral disorders. Their frequency
and the demand that parents could make on existing services for help
are justification for careful study of the area. The five types of intervention programs are agendas for the future.

The reason for including data on "new morbidity" is their obvious importance for the way in which child health services are organized for a community—the theme of this book. We have yet to incorporate these ideas fully into our care programs in any systematic way, in part because the data on the effectiveness of such an approach await the completion of ongoing studies. But obtaining data in communities on the prevalence of behavioral problems in child populations has proved useful in generating support for changes in the delivery system, e.g., "physician expanders" skilled in this area, and acceptance by the medical care system that these are in part medical problems with which any comprehensive system must be prepared to cope.

## REFERENCES

ALLEN, F., HART, B., BUELL, J.S., HARRIS, F.R., and WOLF, M.

1964 "Effects of Social Reinforcement on Isolate Behavior of a Nursery School Child." *Child Development,* 35:511–518.

AUGENBRAUN, B., REID, H., and FRIEDMAN, D.

1967 "Brief Intervention as a Preventive Force in Disorders of Early Childhood." *American Journal of Orthopsychiatry,* 37:697–702.

BOWER, E.M.

1969 *Early Identification of Emotionally Handicapped Children in School,* Second Edition. Springfield, Illinois: Charles C Thomas.

BRAZELTON, T.

1962 "A Child Oriented Approach to Toilet Training." *Pediatrics,* 29:121–128.

BRAZELTON, T.

1969 *Infants and Mothers: Differences in Development.* New York: Dell Publishing Company.

CAREY, W.B.

1970 "A Simplified Method for Measuring Infant Temperament." *Journal of Pediatrics,* 77:188–194.

CHAMBERLIN, R.W.

1967 "Early Recognition and Modification of Vicious Circle Parent-Child Relationships." *Clinical Pediatrics,* 6:469–479.

CHAMBERLIN, R.W., and NADER, P.R.

1971 "Relationship between Nursery School Behavior Patterns and Later School Functioning." *American Journal of Orthopsychiatry,* 41:597-601.

CHESS, S., THOMAS, A., and BIRCH, H.

1965 *Your Child Is a Person.* New York: Viking Press.

114                                                         *Health and Illness*

COOPER, B., and TAPIA, F.

1970  *Nine Measurable Qualities of Temperament: A Learning Program.* Columbia, Missouri: Privately printed.

COWEN, E., IZZO, L., MILES, H., TELSCHOW, E., TROST, M., and ZAX, M.

1963  "A Preventive Mental Health Program in the School Setting: Description and Evaluation." *Journal of Psychology,* 54:307–356.

DRILLIEN, C.M.

1964  *The Growth and Development of the Prematurely Born Infant.* Baltimore: Williams and Wilkins Company.

EISENBERG, L., GILBERT, A., CYTRYN, L., and MOLLING, P.A.

1961  "The Effectiveness of Psychotherapy Alone and in Conjunction with Perphenazine or Placebo in the Treatment of Neurotic and Hyperactive Children." *American Journal of Psychiatry,* 117:1088-1093.

EISENBERG, L., LANDOWNE, E., WILNER, D., and IMBER, S.

1962  "The Use of Teacher Ratings in a Mental Health Study: A Method for Measuring the Effectiveness of a Therapeutic Nursery Program." *American Journal of Public Health,* 52:18–28.

GENESEE REGION HEALTH PLANNING COUNCIL

1968  "Patient Origin Study" (unpublished data).

GLIDEWELL, J., DOMKE, H., and KANTOR, M.

1963  "Screening in Schools for Behavior Disorders: Use of Mothers' Reports of Symptoms." *Journal of Education Research,* 56:508–515.

HARRINGTON, E.

1965  "A Major Pitfall: Inadequate Assessment of the Patient's Needs, Resulting in Inappropriate Treatment." *Pediatric Clinics of North America,* 12:156–173.

HILL, L.

1960  "Anticipatory Guidance in Pediatric Practice." *Journal of Pediatrics,* 56:299–307.

HORNBERGER, R, BOWMAN, J., GREENBLATT, H., and CORSA, L.

1960  *Health Supervision of Young Children in California.* Berkeley, California, Bureau of Maternal and Child Health; California Department of Public Health.

ILG, G., and AMES, L.

1960  *Child Behavior.* New York: Dell Publishing Company.

JOINT COMMISSION ON MENTAL ILLNESS AND HEALTH

1961  *Action for Mental Health.* New York: Basic Books.

LAPOUSE, REMA, and MONK, MARY

1958  "An Epidemiologic Study of Behavior Characteristics in Children." *American Journal of Public Health,* 48:1134–1144.

MAC FARLANE, J., ALLEN, L., and HONZIK, M.

1962  *A Developmental Study of the Behavioral Problems of Normal Children* between Twenty-One Months and Fourteen Years. Berkeley and Los Angeles: University of California.

MILLER, F., COURT, S., WALTON, W., and KNOX, E.

1960  Growing Up in Newcastle-upon-Tyne. London: Oxford University Press.

PAINE, R., WERRY, J., and QUAY, H.

1968  "A Study of Minimal Cerebral Dysfunction." *Developmental Medicine and Child Neurology*, 10:505–520.

PHILADELPHIA CHILD GUIDANCE CLINIC AND HEALTH WELFARE COUNCIL, INC., OF PHILADELPHIA

1962  Initial Contact, Interview Manual (privately printed).

PLESS, I.B., and SATTERWHITE, B.

1972  "Chronic Illness in Childhood: Selection, Activities and Evaluation of Non-professional Family Counselors." *Clinical Pediatrics*, 11:(7):403–410.

RIGG, C.A., and FISHER, R.C.

1970  "Some Comments on Current Hospital Medical Services for Adolescents." *American Journal of Diseases of Children*, 120:193–196.

RIGG, C.A., and FISHER, R.C.

1971  "Is a Separate Adolescent Ward Worthwhile?" *American Journal of Diseases of Children*, 122:489–493.

ROGERS, M.E., LILIENFIELD, A.M., and PASAMANICK, B.

1955  "Prenatal and Paranatal Factors in the Development of Childhood Behavior Disorders." *Acta Psychiatrica et Neurologica Scandinavica* (Supplement 102).

RUTTER, M., TIZARD, J., and WHITMORE, K.

1970  Education, Health and Behavior. London: Longman Group Limited.

SCHAEFFER, E.

1972  "Parents as Educators: Evidence from Cross-Sectional Longitudinal and Intervention Research." *Young Children*, 27:227–239.

SCHULMAN, J.L., KASPER, J.C., and THRONE, F.M.

1965  Brain Damage and Behavior. Springfield, Illinois: Charles C Thomas.

SLOANE, H., JOHNSTON, M., and BIJOU, S.

1967  "Successive Modification of Aggressive Behavior and Aggressive Fantasy Play by Management of Contingencies." *Journal of Child Psychology-Psychiatry*, 8:217–226.

STARFIELD, B., and BARKOWE, S.

1969  "Physicians' Recognition of Complaints Made by Parents about Their Children's Health." *Pediatrics*, 43:168–172.

STINE, O.

1962  "Content and Method of Health Supervision by Physicians in Child Health Conferences in Baltimore." *American Journal of Public Health*, 52:1858–1865.

THOMAS, A., CHESS, S., and BIRCH, H.

1968  Temperament and Behavior Disorders in Children. New York: New York University Press.

WAHLER, R., WINKEL, G., PETERSON, R., and MORRISON, D.
  1965  "Mothers as Behavior Therapists for Their Own Children." *Behavior Research and Therapy*, 3:113–124.

WERNER, E., BIERMAN, J., and FRENCH, F.
  1971  *The Children of Kauai.* Honolulu: University of Hawaii Press.

WILLOUGHBY, J., and HAGGERTY, R.
  1964  "A Simple Behavior Questionnaire for Preschool Children." *Pediatrics*, 34:798–805.

YANCY, WILLIAM S., and NADER, PHILIP R.
  1970  "A Survey of Tenth Grade Students in Monroe County, New York, Using a Self-Administered Health Inventory" (unpublished data).

YANCY, WILLIAM S., NADER, PHILIP R., and BURNHAM, KATHERINE L.
  1972  "Drug Use and Attitudes of High School Students." *Pediatrics*, 50:739–745.

YARROW, M.R., CAMPBELL, J.D., and BURTON, R.V.
  1968  *Child Rearing.* San Francisco: Jossey-Bass Inc.

ZAX, M., COWEN, E., RAPPAPART, J., BEACH, D., and LAIRD, J.
  1968  "Follow-up Study of Children Identified Early as Emotionally Disturbed." *Journal of Consulting and Clinical Psychology*, 32:369–374.

# PART TWO

# Health Services
# for Children

T he preceding chapters dealt with the population of children to be served and analyzed their health needs. Part II describes the volume of medical care actually provided for children and the manner in which it is distributed.

Chapter 4 reviews several models that have been proposed to explain patient behavior and tests these models by the use of data from our surveys. A new short-term model is proposed that, in our view, overcomes many of the fundamental problems of earlier ones. In traditional models the focus is on the motivation of patients (what makes them seek health care?) and the concept of barriers (what prevents them from getting it?). The new model is conceptualized as a short-term process that cannot be captured with normal survey techniques. The chapter puts various pieces of the puzzle together, enabling us to see the total picture more clearly. It is important not only in linking many loose ends, but also as a source of knowledge that can be applied and tested in future programs.

Chapter 5 examines the use of prescribed and nonprescribed medications. It draws upon a special source—the household diary—as a better way to collect data on events that, in standard surveys, are usually underreported. The results add to our knowledge about medicine-taking as a special type of utilization and the way in which it relates both to needs and to the availability and accessibility of care.

Chapter 6 deals with the volume of services. It provides statistics on ambulatory care utilization, hospitalization rates, and hospital days per 1000 population by diagnosis and area. These statistics are unusual in that they come from both suppliers and consumers. The two sources are checked against each other to assess their validity. The data permit us to describe patterns of services and to compare these with the distribution of needs described in Part I.

A surprising finding was the decrease in utilization rates for children, from 1967 to 1971, for both ambulatory and inpatient care. Emergency room visits, house calls, and school physical examinations led the decline in ambulatory care; tonsillectomies, the decline in inpatient care. The occupancy rate for pediatric beds dropped below 60%. The shifts in services for special target areas—from emergency rooms and outpatient departments to health centers—were expected, but the degree of change in the private sector was not. Over the study period the proportion of all contacts with pediatricians increased from 40% to 60%. This change seems to have affected admission patterns as well as the way mothers cope with minor problems.

A special problem concerns the provision of well-baby care in indigent families. Even when care is made available to them, only 10% of the babies actually receive the services considered adequate by local pediatric standards. Special follow-up by public health nurses can be shown to improve entry into the well-baby care system. Similar efforts are required to keep patients there.

Thus, although Chapter 6 shows major shifts toward a more equitable distribution of medical services for children, there remain large areas of unmet needs for traditional preventive health services in some population groups which future programs will have to address.

# CHAPTER FOUR

# Models of Health
# and Illness Behavior

## A. AVAILABLE MODELS

### KLAUS J. ROGHMANN

The paradigm described in the Introduction covered most of the components that can be the focal points of health services research. Though arrows in Figure 1 (p. 8) indicated a time ordering of events in the same way as flow charts show the sequence of tasks in a goal-oriented system, the paradigm was meant neither as an organizational chart nor a theoretical model. It served, rather, as an ad hoc checklist so that no major component would be overlooked in our study of one community health care system.

This chapter examines the nature of some of the arrows in the paradigm. A few of these, leading from an independent or input variable to a dependent or outcome variable, may indicate biochemical or disease processes. Most of them, however, stand for relationships indicating psychological or social processes. If we understand a process and can manipulate the input variable, we should also be able to influence the system to achieve a desired outcome. Only arrows standing for behavioral processes will be examined, and only a small number of models describing such processes will be tested. The focus will be on the patient and on his or her use of medical care. Though the reasoning may occasionally appear rather academic, the findings will have major implications for the organization of child health care. If the patient's beliefs and attitudes are decisive factors accounting for the well-known differentials in utilization rates, and not the availability, accessibility or cost of services, then health education efforts may be the appropriate intervention. If not, some restructuring of our system of care may provide an answer to the problem.

Other paradigms or working models for health services research could have been used without affecting the basic findings and conclusions. For example, the model of Starfield (1973) directs attention more toward health status as the ultimate outcome variable of any health care system. She examines the interactions of four main factors—*genetics, environment, behavior,* and *medical practice*—which determine health status. In these terms, this chapter focuses on the behavioral factor. Health status has been examined in earlier chapters, and medical practice will be considered in later chapters. Starfield's model differs from ours chiefly in that it is more *outcome* oriented; we also work toward this goal, but, because of problems in measuring outcome or even influencing it by medical care, we now place greater emphasis on behavior and medical practice.

Another paradigm or framework for viewing health services has been elaborated by Andersen (1968; Andersen and Newman, 1973). This conceptualization, in contrast to Starfield's, is *process* oriented. It was originally developed to account for variation in utilization behavior reported in large, nationwide household surveys. The organization of care, and the effect of utilization on health status, are, therefore, referred to only marginally. Andersen's three main factors influencing utilization are "Societal Determinants," "Health Services System," and "Individual Determinants." Within "Individual Determinants" Andersen distinguishes between predisposing, enabling, and need factors. The further subdivision of these individual determinants, as shown in Figure 4A.1, is probably best known. Though one-directional arrows connect variable groups in this framework, they serve an organizing function similar to that of the arrows in our paradigm. Hence these are variable groupings presented in a logical order and not postulated causal relations. To the extent that Andersen claims specific linkages between health beliefs and utilization behavior, he also presents a substantive model that can be checked against empirical evidence.

Andersen's framework could also have served to organize our findings. Thus we have reported in preceding chapters on the "community," the "families," and their "health status." We have described "health system

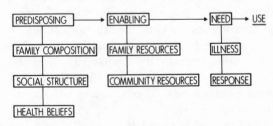

*Figure 4A.1. The general behavioral model of Andersen to explain use or nonuse of health services.*

resources" and their organization. This chapter attempts to link health beliefs and social and family structure to reported utilization.

Three substantive models connected with the names of Suchman, Rosenstock, and Andersen, which are most frequently cited in the literature, will be described and tested in the first section of this chapter. In the second section a conceptualization of our own will be formulated and checked against the data.

*Some Substantive Models of Health and Illness Behavior*

Models are here defined as "theoretical formulations that postulate causal links between a specified set of independent variables and a dependent variable such as medical care utilization." There is usually overlap between the sets of independent variables. Some of these variables, like socioeconomic status or family structure, are deeply rooted in sociological thinking. The groupings are chosen by the researcher because they reflect different theoretical emphases. They also provide convenient ways of presenting the findings.

The type of health care to be accounted for is ambulatory care, as reflected by the frequency of physician contacts and the purpose and place of the last contact. In Chapter 5 we will, in a similar way, account for the use of medicines.

The Suchman Model

The term "Suchman Model" is used to refer to both a specific theoretical approach and to a style of work as expressed in the analysis of a population survey of illness behavior in the Washington Heights district in New York City (Suchman, 1965), and of health behavior among sugar cane cutters in Puerto Rico (Suchman, 1967).

Suchman's style of thinking has the pragmatic character of the applied sociologist. He argues, for instance, that, as long as social scientists cannot agree about basic social processes and the relations between them, there is no reason not to consider all variables at the same time, and see to what extent they account for the variance in the dependent variables. The models or framework he proposes came after a detailed analysis of empirical research, that is, they were inductively developed from specific bodies of survey data. Replication in different surveys is important for testing the theory.

In developing his model of illness behavior, Suchman starts with the well-known fact that health status (illness) and the utilization of health services (medical care) are strongly related to demographic variables, but he claims that these empirical relationships make little theoretical sense unless some linkage mechanism is found. This linking is especially important in finding strategic points for intervention. The linking mechanisms on which he concentrates are of a sociopsychological nature: "Social Group Organization" and "Individual Medical Orientation." His analysis showed that these "intervening" variables are strongly related to social class and only moderately related to health status and source of medical care. (If, however, he controls for his "intervening" variable, the original strong relationships between social class and health variables still persist.) In a sophisticated tabular analysis, looking at as many as five variables at the same time, Suchman demonstrates a complicated network of relationships which is proposed as his model of illness behavior (Figure 4A.2).

In a similar way, he developed a model of preventive health behavior from his study in Puerto Rico. Additional psychological variables were added; more relationships were found. Because of the smaller sample in this study, the analysis was not as detailed as the one in his earlier article. The listed relationships, if they existed independently of each other, would explain an extremely large proportion of the total variance. Like the model of illness behavior, this conceptualization was intended as an exploration of relationships in a new field of study. Our examination of the model is not intended, therefore, as a strict statistical test, but rather as following Suchman's approach to explain a set of data.

"Individual Medical Orientation" was assessed by three variables in our surveys: *Knowledge about Disease* (cognitive); *Skepticism of Medical Care* (affective); and *Dependency in Illness* (behavioral). "Social Group Organization" was assessed by only one variable: *Friendship Solidarity* (social group level). The other two variables—Ethnic Exclusivity (community level) and Family Tradition and Authority Orientation (family level)—could not be included. Instead a related variable was substituted:

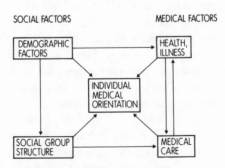

*Figure 4A.2. The Suchman model of illness behavior.*

*Group Support.* The items and the formulas used to compute these independent variables are listed in the Appendix to Section 4A.

Utilization as the dependent variable was measured as "percent of children with a doctor contact in the last two weeks," and, in the absence of such a contact, as "utilization rate over the last 12 months" (see the Appendix to Section 6A for methodology). The last doctor visit, no matter when it occurred, was checked to see whether it was for a preventive or curative purpose, and whether or not the doctor contacted was in private practice. In the absence of a rigorously specified causal model, a simple analysis of variance was considered most appropriate. The results are presented in Table 4A.1.

The $F$ test used here is a conservative test of significance; it ignores the postulated monotonic relationship. Therefore the arithmetic means of the dependent variable for each category of the independent variables are presented to show whether there is a monotonic or possibly a linear relationship. A monotonic but not significant relationship is of greater interest than a significant but erratic one. A monotonic and significant relationship is of greatest interest.

The findings support Suchman's general reasoning about the role of "Individual Medical Orientation" variables as predictors of utilization, but the relationships are weak, frequently nonmonotonic, and mostly lacking in statistical significance. Utilization decreases with Skepticism of Medical Care; that is, those high on Skepticism show less utilization, a higher proportion of illness than preventive care, and greater use of public facilities. Those high on Dependency in Illness are similar to those high on Skepticism. Knowledge about Disease, unlike Skepticism, increases utilization.

The "Social Group Organization" variables were not consistently related to utilization. Most of the relations were nonmonotonic and not significant.

### Rosenstock Model

Rosenstock (1966) reasons somewhat similarly to Suchman. He maintains that the well-established relationship between personal and demographic variables, on the one side, and health and illness behavior, on the other, fails to explain why some people use health services and others do not. He claims (1966:95) that utilization and morbidity studies may be employed for descriptive purposes and the planning of health facilities, but that they have failed to provide hypotheses about *why* services are used or not used. What is needed, in his view, is the identification of linking mechanisms between the personal characteristics and the observed behavior (1966:97). Specifying some of these intervening variables, he believes,

Table 4A.1.  *Medical Care Utilization as a Function of Variables Suggested by Suchman Model*

| Independent Variable | Percent with Doctor Contact in Last 2 Weeks | Utilization Rate over Last 12 Months | Percent with Last Doctor Contact: Preventive | Percent with Last Doctor Contact: Private | Number of Children |
|---|---|---|---|---|---|
| Knowledge about Disease | | | | | |
| 10  Low | 11.2 | 1.78 | 50.0 | 62.7 | 134 |
| 12 | 12.6 | 1.96 | 45.8 | 61.6 | 515 |
| 14 | 13.2 | 2.42 | 49.3 | 73.7 | 750 |
| 16 | 13.1 | 2.35 | 49.5 | 79.8 | 580 |
| 17 | 12.3 | 2.16 | 42.5 | 75.7 | 334 |
| 18  High | 14.7 | 2.30 | 45.2 | 79.5 | 639 |
| | n.s. | n.s. | n.s. | $p<.01$ | |
| Skepticism (Benefits) | | | | | |
| 1  High (Low) | 13.0 | 2.04 | 38.4 | 61.6 | 284 |
| 2 | 10.1 | 2.01 | 45.0 | 70.1 | 535 |
| 3 | 13.6 | 2.29 | 48.6 | 75.8 | 764 |
| 4 | 14.0 | 2.36 | 49.7 | 76.1 | 827 |
| 5  Low (High) | 14.6 | 2.34 | 47.8 | 77.5 | 542 |
| | n.s. | n.s. | n.s. | $p<.05$ | |
| Dependency in Illness | | | | | |
| 1  Low | 11.5 | 2.12 | 47.5 | 74.4 | 1508 |
| 2 | 14.6 | 2.43 | 48.0 | 74.3 | 1287 |
| 3  High | 17.8 | 1.90 | 36.3 | 63.7 | 157 |
| | n.s. | n.s. | n.s. | n.s. | |

Friendship Solidarity

|  |  |  |  |  |  |
|---|---|---|---|---|---|
| 0 Low | 12.8 | 2.14 | 52.0 | 76.8 | 564 |
| 1 | 13.5 | 2.36 | 46.2 | 76.3 | 1042 |
| 2 | 13.3 | 2.13 | 47.2 | 69.9 | 1010 |
| 3 High | 12.8 | 2.36 | 41.7 | 72.6 | 336 |
|  | n.s. | n.s. | n.s. | n.s. |  |

Group Support

|  |  |  |  |  |  |
|---|---|---|---|---|---|
| 1 Low | 17.6 | 2.19 | 39.4 | 72.1 | 147 |
| 2 | 12.9 | 2.32 | 48.1 | 73.2 | 619 |
| 3 | 11.8 | 2.23 | 48.3 | 65.6 | 491 |
| 4 High | 13.3 | 2.22 | 47.1 | 76.5 | 1695 |
|  | n.s. | n.s. | n.s. | $p<.05$ |  |
|  |  |  |  | $r=.05$ |  |

will contribute to an "understanding" of behavior in the health area
(1966:98). In contrast to Suchman, whose intervening mechanisms are
based on social psychology or sociology, Rosenstock relies on individual
psychology.

Three groups of variables (see Figure 4A.3) are considered to be of
greatest relevance: first, factors of *Personal Readiness* to use medical services, such as "perceived vulnerability" and the "perceived consequences"
of certain illnesses; second, the *Perceived Benefits* of various actions and
the *Perceived Barriers* to taking action; and third, the concept of *Cues* or
*Triggers for Action*. The first two groups of variables have been well
measured, and several studies bear evidence on their fruitfulness in adults
(Kegeles, 1963; Kegeles et al., 1965; Kirscht et al., 1966; Rosenstock et al.,
1966; Swinehart and Kirscht, 1966). They seem to be of special relevance
to *health* behavior (preventive actions). The conceptualization of Triggers or Cues for Action is less well developed, but may be of greater relevance for *illness* behavior. The general reasoning of the model is that the
factors of Personal Readiness, balanced against Perceived Benefits and
Barriers, determine who will take health action. Cues and Triggers are
required to turn basic willingness into action. The main reason why the
concept of Triggers for Action has not been tested adequately is methodological—recall and perception in this area are difficult to measure, and
perceived cues are often suppressed. Rosenstock argues that a prospective
study is required to further develop this part of the model. The concept
of Cues and Triggers for health and illness behavior is a very promising
one and will be pursued further in our own model.

All variables of Rosenstock's model could be measured except "per-

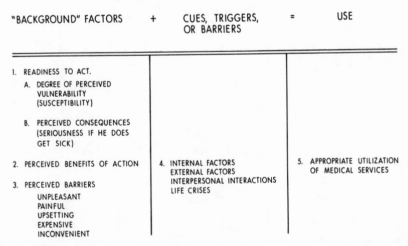

*Figure 4A.3. The health belief model of Rosenstock et al.*

ceived vulnerability." "Perceived consequences" of ill health are captured by a three-item index labeled *Seriousness*. Perceived benefits of medical care are measured by the Suchman index, *Skepticism of Medical Care*. Perceived barriers are measured by an index of *Barriers*, based on statements about cost, accessibility, availability, inconvenience and unpleasantness as reasons "why people do not see a doctor as often as they should." Finally, a generalized *Readiness to Seek Care* index was computed, based on items concerning whether the respondents would seek care for symptoms such as a sore throat without fever, a sore throat with fever over 100° for two days, diarrhea for a week, feeling tired for several weeks, unexplained loss of weight of over 10 pounds, and shortness of breath. (All the items used as well as the scoring procedures for these variables are given in the Appendix to Section 4A.)

Perceived Seriousness did not increase utilization; rather it reduced it (Table 4A.2). The proportion of preventive visits, however, was not affected by this variable. But there was a tendency for those with high perceived seriousness to use clinics and health centers to a greater extent than private practitioners.

The perception of Barriers to care correlated slightly with utilization: the higher the perceived barriers, the lower the utilization rates. There was also a tendency for those seeing many barriers to use clinics and health centers rather than private practitioners.

Readiness to Seek Care correlated moderately with utilization. There was also a slight tendency for people with high readiness scores to use private practitioners rather than clinics and health centers, but these relations were weak and inconsistent.

## The Andersen Model

Andersen (1968; Andersen et al., 1972) attempted to integrate the Rosenstock and the Suchman models, as well as a number of economic models, into a "general behavioral" model of health service use. The adjectives "general" and "behavioral" were used to indicate the incorporation of biological, psychological, social, and economic variables into an overall scheme to account for variation in the use of services. The result is a model that uses the family as a unit of analysis, separates social from economic factors, introduces community characteristics into the analysis, and also considers health beliefs of family members.

These factors were considered, to a large extent, in our initial discussion. *Health beliefs* cover much of what Suchman called "Individual Medical Orientation" (Skepticism of Medical Care). The index Knowledge of Disease was actually taken from the Andersen monograph. The

*Table 4A.2. Medical Care Utilization as a Function of Variables Suggested by the Rosenstock Model*

| Independent Variable | Percent with Doctor Contact in Last 2 Weeks | Utilization Rate over Last 12 Months | Percent with Last Doctor Contact: Preventive | Percent with Last Doctor Contact: Private | Number of Children |
|---|---|---|---|---|---|
| Seriousness | | | | | |
| 1 Not serious | 13.2 | 2.44 | 49.5 | 82.2 | 394 |
| 2 | 13.4 | 2.35 | 45.4 | 76.3 | 1356 |
| 3 Very serious | 13.0 | 2.05 | 48.3 | 68.1 | 1202 |
| | n.s. | n.s. | n.s. | $p<.01$ $r=-.12$ | |
| Benefits (see "Skepticism," Table 4A.1) | | | | | |
| Barriers | | | | | |
| 1 No barriers | 14.8 | 2.39 | 51.6 | 79.6 | 372 |
| 2 | 12.7 | 2.62 | 46.8 | 78.2 | 417 |
| 3 | 12.9 | 2.28 | 42.0 | 79.8 | 603 |
| 4 | 11.0 | 2.06 | 49.0 | 73.8 | 580 |
| 5 | 13.9 | 2.15 | 46.6 | 66.9 | 511 |
| 6 Many barriers | 14.7 | 2.06 | 48.8 | 65.0 | 469 |
| | n.s. | n.s. | n.s. | $p<.05$ $r=-.12$ | |

| Threshold (Readiness to seek care) | | | | | |
|---|---|---|---|---|---|
| 1 Low (high) | 17.0 | 2.92 | 46.4 | 65.2 | 330 |
| 2 | 14.0 | 2.11 | 49.2 | 78.7 | 1164 |
| 3 | 11.6 | 2.20 | 45.2 | 73.4 | 787 |
| 4 | 11.9 | 2.25 | 47.3 | 70.6 | 385 |
| 5 | 12.0 | 2.02 | 49.1 | 74.6 | 175 |
| 6 High (low) | 11.7 | 2.35 | 36.9 | 59.5 | 111 |
| | n.s. | n.s. | n.s. | $p < .05$ $r = -.04$ | |

Readiness or Threshold index from the Rosenstock model is identical with the Attitude toward Physician Use index of Andersen. This index was claimed by Andersen to form a Guttman scale (R = .95). We were unable, however, to replicate this mostly because our simple "agree-disagree" dichotomy did not allow the many different cutting points used by Andersen with his two "agree" and two "disagree" categories. *Social structure* variables are not identical with the "Social Group Organization" variables of Suchman but refer instead to standard social variables such as education, occupation, and race. *Family composition* variables correspond to what Suchman and Rosenstock refer to as "demographic" factors like family size, age and sex of head of household, and marital status of mother. Health beliefs, social structure, and family composition variables form the "predisposing factors," most of which are represented in our variable list. The influence of health beliefs has already been discussed. Tables 4A.3 and 4A.4 present as contrasts the influences of family composition and social structure variables.

The *age of the child* is one of the strongest predictors of the utilization rate, but hardly affects the proportion of preventive or private practice visits. Although *marital status* of the mother affects utilization rates little, it strongly influences the purpose and site of the last visit. *Family size* affects both utilization rates and place of care, but not the reason for the last visit. Compared to the earlier findings for the Suchman and Rosenstock models, these relationships with family composition variables are much stronger and more consistent.

Similar findings can be reported for the social structure variables. *Maternal education* correlates strongly with utilization rates, purpose, and place of care. *Maternal race* is also strongly related to these variables. *Parental occupation*, coded according to the Hollingshead scheme (Hollingshead, 1957, 1958), is a powerful predictor for the place of care. *Maternal religion* failed to show a clear-cut pattern. Overall, the social structure variables are excellent predictors for place of care and utilization rates. The proportion of preventive visits is also affected, but much less so.

Among the enabling factors only the family resources will be examined because the community resources are assumed to be equal for the study area. Table 4A.5 presents the findings for *socioeconomic area, family income, insurance,* and *access to care.* The higher the socioeconomic area, the family income, and the insurance coverage, the higher was the utilization rate. There was no clear-cut relation between the proportion of preventive visits and these variables, but they were strongly related to place of care. Children in the two lowest socioeconomic areas, having annual family incomes below $6000 or covered by Medicaid, received most

*Table 4A.3. Medical Care Utilization as a Function of Family Composition Variables*

| Independent Variable | Percent with Doctor Contact in Last 2 Weeks | Utilization Rate over Last 12 Months | Percent with Last Doctor Contact: Preventive | Percent with Last Doctor Contact: Private | Number of Children |
|---|---|---|---|---|---|
| Age of Child (years) | | | | | |
| 0-4 | 21.4 | 3.84 | 52.3 | 79.0 | 761 |
| 5-9 | 11.4 | 2.18 | 44.6 | 74.8 | 841 |
| 10-14 | 7.8 | 1.44 | 46.3 | 70.3 | 874 |
| 15-17 | 13.2 | 1.62 | 44.7 | 70.2 | 476 |
| | $p<.001$ | $p<.001$ | n.s. | n.s. | |
| | $r=-.11$ | $r=-.28$ | | | |
| Marital Status of Mother | | | | | |
| Married | 13.5 | 2.28 | 48.3 | 78.5 | 2586 |
| Not Married | 11.2 | 1.95 | 38.8 | 40.2 | 366 |
| | n.s. | $p=.05$ | $p<.001$ | $p<.001$ | |
| Number of Children in Family | | | | | |
| One | 19.3 | 2.61 | 49.0 | 82.6 | 357 |
| Two | 17.9 | 2.85 | 47.9 | 81.3 | 797 |
| Three | 12.4 | 2.40 | 46.1 | 82.4 | 716 |
| Four or more | 8.2 | 1.63 | 46.6 | 59.6 | 1082 |
| | $p<.05$ | $p<.01$ | n.s. | $p<.001$ | |
| | $r=-.13$ | $r=-.16$ | | $r=-.20$ | |

Table 4A.4. Medical Care Utilization as a Function of Social Structure Variables

| Independent Variable | Percent with Doctor Contact in Last 2 Weeks | Utilization Rate over Last 12 Months | Percent with Last Doctor Contact: Preventive | Percent with Last Doctor Contact: Private | Number of Children |
|---|---|---|---|---|---|
| Maternal Education | | | | | |
| Up to 11th grade | 11.9 | 1.71 | 42.8 | 50.6 | 893 |
| High school | 12.3 | 2.30 | 48.1 | 79.7 | 1113 |
| Some college | 14.9 | 2.68 | 49.4 | 88.6 | 545 |
| College graduate | 16.9 | 2.73 | 51.1 | 88.8 | 401 |
| | n.s. | $p<.05$ | n.s. | $p<.001$ | |
| | | $r=+.12$ | | $r=+.28$ | |
| Maternal Race | | | | | |
| White | 13.5 | 2.36 | 47.8 | 80.6 | 2952 |
| Black | 11.2 | 1.50 | 42.9 | 29.3 | 392 |
| | n.s. | $p<.01$ | n.s. | $p<.001$ | |
| Parental Occupation | | | | | |
| Higher executive and professional | 15.9 | 2.95 | 45.4 | 90.4 | 271 |
| Lesser executive and professional | 15.7 | 2.25 | 53.1 | 88.2 | 382 |
| Small business | 15.3 | 2.34 | 47.9 | 85.7 | 413 |
| Clerical and sales | 13.0 | 2.58 | 49.6 | 78.9 | 284 |
| Skilled worker | 11.5 | 2.14 | 48.7 | 76.9 | 756 |
| Semiskilled | 11.3 | 2.09 | 41.3 | 60.9 | 470 |

|  |  |  |  |  |  |
|---|---|---|---|---|---|
| Unskilled | 16.3 | 1.43 | 46.5 | 48.8 | 129 |
| Unemployed | 7.8 | 1.98 | 40.4 | 33.5 | 218 |
|  | n.s. | $p=.05$ | n.s. | $p<.001$ | |
|  |  |  |  | $r=-.33$ | |
| **Maternal Religion** |  |  |  |  |  |
| Catholic | 12.8 | 2.22 | 47.9 | 79.8 | 1490 |
| Protestant | 13.7 | 2.23 | 46.1 | 67.1 | 1242 |
| Other | 13.6 | 2.48 | 47.7 | 70.5 | 220 |
|  | n.s. | n.s. | n.s. | $p<.05$ | |
|  |  |  |  | $r=-.10$ | |

*Table 4A.5.  Medical Care Utilization as a Function of Enabling Factors (Andersen Model)*

| Independent Variable | Percent with Doctor Contact in Last 2 Weeks | Utilization Rate over Last 12 Months | Percent with Last Doctor Contact: Preventive | Percent with Last Doctor Contact: Private | Number of Children |
|---|---|---|---|---|---|
| **Socioeconomic Area** | | | | | |
| 1 Highest | 14.8 | 2.61 | 45.9 | 88.5 | 338 |
| 2 | 12.7 | 2.38 | 51.6 | 82.3 | 1017 |
| 3 | 13.6 | 2.20 | 47.3 | 79.9 | 1013 |
| 4 | 12.7 | 2.13 | 37.5 | 44.0 | 400 |
| 5 Lowest | 12.0 | 1.30 | 44.6 | 31.0 | 947 |
| | n.s. | $p<.05$ $r=-.09$ | $p<.05$ $r=-.06$ | $p<.001$ $r=-.34$ | |
| **Family Income** | | | | | |
| Below $6000 | 13.6 | 2.10 | 46.7 | 34.4 | 413 |
| $6001-10,000 | 13.3 | 2.00 | 47.8 | 72.4 | 692 |
| $10,001-14,000 | 13.6 | 2.37 | 44.6 | 82.1 | 900 |
| $14,001 plus | 12.7 | 2.35 | 49.2 | 84.1 | 184 |
| | n.s. | n.s. | n.s. | $p<.001$ $r=+.34$ | |
| **Insurance** | | | | | |
| Private insurance | 13.4 | 2.18 | 51.1 | 84.9 | 186 |
| Blue Cross | 18.1 | 2.31 | 47.9 | 80.6 | 2334 |
| No insurance | 17.0 | 1.46 | 40.4 | 51.1 | 47 |
| Medicaid | 13.5 | 1.94 | 41.6 | 29.6 | 385 |
| | n.s. | n.s. | n.s. | $p<.001$ $r=-.35$ | |

| Access to Care | | | | |
|---|---|---|---|---|
| Two regular M.D.s | 22.4 | 4.35 | 26.7 | 92.5 | 161 |
| One regular M.D. | 12.9 | 2.30 | 49.7 | 86.7 | 2225 |
| No regular source | 5.2 | .94 | 43.2 | 33.9 | 192 |
| Regular place | 15.0 | 1.78 | 42.8 | 9.4 | 374 |
| | $p<.05$ | $p.<01$ | $p<.05$ | $p<.001$ | |
| | | $r=-.15$ | | $r=-.61$ | |

of their medical care at public clinics and health centers. On the other hand, children in the two highest socioeconomic areas, having family incomes over $10,000 or covered by insurance, had more than 80% of their last visits with physicians in private practice.

Regular source of care is, of course, related in the strongest way to utilization. This independent variable is conceptually and operationally so close to the dependent variable that correlations reach the size known for reliability measures. We measure nearly the same phenomenon (last visit at private physician) as regular source of care. Frequency of utilization is highest for those with two regular private physicians, and lowest for those with no regular source of care. Actually, having two regular private physicians is a sign, not of great wealth, but rather of bad health. Such children had three fourths of their last visits for sick care, compared to about one half for those with only one regular doctor.

The need factors in the Andersen model refer to reported illness level (see Table 4A.6). We used two "one-year" measures (the number of major symptoms and the general health rating) and two "last-two-weeks" measures (days kept from school or play, and days in bed). As would be expected, the one-year measures were the best predictors of the 12-month utilization rate, and the two-week measures were the best predictors of two-week utilization. The percentage of last visits made for preventive reasons was also a direct but inverse function of illness level—the more illness, the higher the proportion of sick care. There was also a tendency for children with their health rated as "poor," or having high "two-week" illness forcing them to stay in bed, to be more dependent on public clinics and health centers.

*Discussion*

The three models presented and tested imply very different approaches to accounting for medical care utilization. Rosenstock's approach, based on individual psychology, aimed at decision-making about specific health behaviors like dental check-ups, immunization programs, or "Pap" smears. Our research was not designed to test this theory in relation to specific behaviors, but raised the question whether Rosenstock's categorical approach cannot be expanded in scope to cover health and illness behavior in general. All our measures, such as perceived seriousness, benefits, and barriers, were concerned, not with a specific disease, but with health and care in general. General health beliefs proved weak in predicting either health or illness behavior and cannot be claimed as intervening or independent variables to account for utilization rates or purposes.

Suchman's approach, based on social psychology, was more successful.

"Medical Care Orientation" variables tended to predict utilization behavior, though his "Social Group Organization" variables did not. Suchman's "beliefs" were not individualized as were Rosenstock's, but rather stereotypic expressions of a general trust in medical care and physicians. Our items measured this general trust; thus our data can be seen as providing a valid test of Suchman's model. To the extent that Suchman's variables are claimed to be intervening between "demographic" and medical care variables, there is no support for the model. To be intervening the orientations would have to have correlated more strongly with the medical care variables than do the demographic variables. Group Support and Friendship Solidarity were unrelated to care. If a demographic variable was involved, it was education as influencing degree of stereotyping. The effect of education on utilization, however, seems to be direct and not to operate via generalized attitudes such as popular versus scientific orientation. Other researchers (Reeder and Berkanovic, 1973; Roberts et al., 1973), studying adult populations in California and Texas, were more successful in replicating Suchman's findings, but they too found inconsistencies and only weak correlations.

Andersen's approach, to the extent that it builds on the beliefs of Rosenstock and the attitudes of Suchman, also proves to add little. In so far as Andersen introduces demographic, social structure, and "family resources" variables, however, he covers most of the relevant factors that determine need for and access to medical care. The needs are largely dependent on age, sex, and marital status. Although social structure determines exposure to health hazards, family resources determine which health and illness needs can be taken care of. To predict medium-term health care utilization (one year) in a given population, these are, no doubt, the relevant variables. However, utilization by an individual over a lifetime, utilization for a given chronic illness for the period of that illness, or utilization for preventive measures like dental check-ups or family planning is a different matter. Short-term utilization (two weeks single days) also requires a different model. For the kind of survey data on child care presented here, the Andersen model, so far, fits the data best.

A few additional methodological issues require discussion. Have the proper dependent variables been selected? Has the best analytical technique been used? Utilization of medical services is only a means of keeping in good health (preventive care) or returning to health (sick care). Only "appropriate" utilization is effective. Two estimates for frequency of utilization were provided: percentage of children having a visit within the last two weeks, and rate per year for those without a visit in the last two weeks. The proportions of last visits for preventive or curative services and to private physician or clinic were used to split the vol-

138

Table 4A.6.  Medical Care Utilization as a Function of Need Factors (Andersen Model)

| Independent Variable | Percent with Doctor Contact in Last 2 Weeks | Utilization Rate over Last 12 Months | Percent with Last Doctor Contact: Preventive | Percent with Last Doctor Contact: Private | Number of Children |
|---|---|---|---|---|---|
| Days Lost from School or Play Because of Illness in Last 2 Weeks | | | | | |
| None | 9.8 | 2.22 | 50.4 | 73.9 | 2399 |
| One | 10.8 | 2.19 | 36.9 | 76.4 | 157 |
| Two | 22.1 | 2.28 | 33.6 | 69.7 | 122 |
| Three | 21.2 | 2.04 | 45.5 | 77.3 | 66 |
| Four or more | 46.6 | 2.86 | 26.0 | 71.6 | 208 |
| | $p < .001$ | n.s. | $p < .01$ | n.s. | |
| | $r = .27$ | | $r = -.14$ | | |
| Days in Bed Because of Illness in Last 2 Weeks | | | | | |
| None | 11.8 | 2.27 | 49.0 | 73.9 | 2696 |
| One | 15.3 | 2.15 | 33.9 | 81.4 | 118 |
| Two | 35.3 | 1.77 | 20.6 | 69.1 | 68 |
| Three or more | 46.5 | 1.58 | 20.0 | 61.4 | 70 |
| | $p < .001$ | n.s. | $p < .01$ | n.s. | |
| | $r = .17$ | | $r = -.12$ | | |

Symptom Index over
Last 12 Months

| | | | | | |
|---|---|---|---|---|---|
| 0 | 8.9 | 1.71 | 55.2 | 72.0 | 1394 |
| 1 | 14.5 | 2.19 | 48.6 | 76.7 | 484 |
| 2 | 13.9 | 2.37 | 41.3 | 77.2 | 460 |
| 3 | 17.0 | 3.15 | 34.4 | 76.5 | 247 |
| 4 | 24.8 | 3.23 | 32.0 | 70.6 | 153 |
| 5 | 21.5 | 3.79 | 32.9 | 65.8 | 79 |
| 6-7 | 22.7 | 4.18 | 26.6 | 73.9 | 85 |
| 8-9 | 45.0 | 5.00 | 28.2 | 74.5 | 21 |
| 10 plus | 26.9 | 6.89 | 34.6 | 73.1 | 26 |
| | $p<.001$ | $p<.001$ | $p<.001$ | n.s. | |
| | $r=.15$ | $r=.26$ | $r=-.17$ | | |
| General Health Rating | | | | | |
| 1 Good | 12.3 | 2.03 | 48.9 | 74.2 | 2718 |
| 2 Fair | 22.0 | 4.79 | 29.0 | 71.5 | 200 |
| 3 Poor | 35.3 | 7.09 | 14.7 | 52.9 | 34 |
| | $p<.06$ | $p<.001$ | $p<.05$ | n.s. | |
| | $r=.10$ | $r=.28$ | $r=-.12$ | | |

ume of care accordingly. Although rates for preventive and curative care might have been more meaningful than overall rates, how could "appropriateness" be measured? Unmet need for sick care can be estimated as the proportion of recent illnesses without recent medical contacts, or the number of major symptoms (regarded as somewhat or very serious by the respondent) that did not receive medical attention over the last 12 months. Both these measures are a function of both illness *and* illness response. Significant differences were found, mostly reflecting differences in the incidence of illness rather than differences in response.

Estimates for unmet preventive care are equally difficult. Should standards be set for the desired frequency of preventive visits per age group? Such criteria could be agreed upon for preschoolers and infants, but not for older children. We did not pursue this matter further.

Different analytic techniques like regression or automatic interaction detection could have been used. There is considerable doubt, however, about how to interpret results from high-level analyses when low-level analyses fail to give clear answers for the component relations discussed here. This question will be considered again in the next section after one more model for explaining utilization behavior, our stress model, is examined.

## REFERENCES

ANDERSEN, RONALD A.

    1968 *Behavioral Model of Families' Use of Health Services.* Chicago: Center for Health Administration Studies, Research Series.

ANDERSEN, RONALD A., GREELEY, MC L., KRAVITS, JOANNA, and ANDERSON, ODIN, W.

    1972 *Health Services Use: National Trends and Variations 1953–1971.* Department of Health, Education and Welfare, Publication No. 73–3004. Washington, D.C.: Government Printing Office.

ANDERSEN, RONALD A., and NEWMAN, JOHN F.

    1973 "Societal and Individual Determinants of Medical Care Utilization in the United States." *Milbank Memorial Fund Quarterly,* 51:95–124.

HOLLINGSHEAD, AUGUST B.

    1957 *Two Factor Index of Social Position.* New Haven, Connecticut (mimeographed).

HOLLINGSHEAD, AUGUST B., and REDLICH, FREDERICK C.

    1958 *Social Class and Mental Illness.* New York: John Wiley and Sons.

KEGELES, STEPHEN S.

    1963 "Why People Seek Dental Care: A Test of a Conceptual Model." *Journal of Health and Human Behavior,* 4:166–173.

KEGELES, STEPHEN S., KIRSCHT, J.P., HAEFNER, D.P., and ROSENSTOCK, IRWIN M.

1965 "Survey of Beliefs about Cancer Detection and Taking the Papanicolaou Tests." *Public Health Reports*, 80:815–824.

KIRSCHT, J.P., HAEFNER, D.P., KEGELES, S.S , and ROSENSTOCK, I.M.

1966 "A National Study of Health Beliefs." *Journal of Health and Human Behavior*, 7:248-254.

REEDER, LEO G., and BERKANOVIC, EMIL

1973 "Sociological Concomitants of Health Orientations: A Partial Replication of Suchman." *Journal of Health and Social Behavior*, 14:134–143.

ROBERTS, ROBERT E., FORTHOFER, RONALD F., FABREGA, HORACIO, and MULFORD, CHARLES L.

1973 "Social Patterns of Health Status and Medical Care." University of Texas, School of Public Health (mimeographed).

ROSENSTOCK, IRWIN M.

1966 "Why People Use Health Services." *Milbank Memorial Fund Quarterly*, Part 2, 44:94–127.

ROSENSTOCK, I.M., HAEFNER, D.P., KEGELES, S.S., KIRSCHT, J.P.

1966 "Public Knowledge, Opinion and Action Concerning Three Public Health Issues." *Journal of Health and Human Behavior*, 7:91–98.

STARFIELD, BARBARA

1973 "Health Services Research: A Working Model." *New England Journal of Medicine*, 259:132–136.

SUCHMAN, EDWARD A.

1965 "Social Patterns of Illness and Medical Care." *Journal of Health and Human Behavior*, 6:2–16.

SUCHMAN, EDWARD A.

1967 "Preventive Health Behavior: A Model for Research on Community Health Campaigns." *Journal of Health and Human Behavior*, 8:197–209.

SWINEHART, JAMES W., and KIRSCHT, JOHN P.

1966 "Smoking: A Panel Study of Beliefs and Behavior Following the PHS Report." *Psychological Reports*, 18:519–528.

## B. THE STRESS MODEL
## FOR ILLNESS BEHAVIOR

KLAUS J. ROGHMANN
AND
ROBERT J. HAGGERTY

The three substantive models of health and illness behavior, when used to explain utilization of child health care, were of little help from the viewpoint of therapeutic intervention. Health education would have been the solution to medical care problems if Rosenstock's generalized health belief model had worked, but it did not explain much of the variation. Although Suchman's "Individual Medical Orientation" attitude cluster worked somewhat better, these attitudes are not easily manipulated. The fact that the demographic, socioeconomic, and family resource variables of the Andersen model remained as the variables with the greatest explanatory power meant essentially that the search for modifiable intervening variables had failed. Neither sex, age, nor race can be manipulated. Supplying people with status and resources through some kind of income redistribution may one day be politically feasible, but such therapeutic methods are not now under the physician's or patient's control.

It was thus decided to make another attempt at finding an intervening variable that could possibly be modified. Two factors are at the heart of the conceptualization: stress exposure and coping ability. Stress exposure is known to correlate with socioeconomic background and with illness; coping ability, with family resources. Stress exposure has been shown to decrease the body's resistance to disease, as well as a person's psychic energies to cope with the adversities of life, including illness. There seems to be a two-way or "feedback" process between stress and illness which can be described as a "vicious circle" when a person moves deeper into illness, or as a "virtuous circle" when, after some protective period to "recharge the battery," he recovers and returns to regular functioning.

*Results from the 1971 Survey*

There were a number of indicators in the 1971 survey that could be used to check the implications of this model. *Stress Exposure* over the past year was measured by checking for the occurrence of life crises (deaths, accidents, and housing, job, or school problems) and assessing their severity by assigning weights. *Family Type* (Roghmann et al., 1973) and *Group Support* each measured, with three questions, the backing given mothers through well-functioning family or friendship units. *Coping Ability* was measured by the mothers' self-assessments of how well they could handle illness and other problems and also how well they could manage their disposable income. Finally, degrees of *Tension* and *Feeling Confined* to the house because of the children indicated the extent to which mothers felt powerless. The Appendix to Section 4B presents the items, the scoring scheme, and a detailed table (Table A9) of results.

Stress leads to increased utilization of medical services, mostly for sick care. The higher the stress, the greater is the reliance on clinics and health centers. It was found that children with unhappily married parents show the highest utilization, again mostly for sick care. Children of happily married couples have the highest use of preventive services from physicians in private practice. In addition, the greater the difficulty with coping, the feeling of being confined, and of living under tension, the greater are the proportions of sick care and of care received in clinics and health centers. Though none of these relations was very strong, they all were consistently in the predicted direction. Considering that the independent variables describe family settings and maternal feelings, and the dependent variables reflect children's health care utilization, this finding is encouraging.

*Results from the 1969 Survey*[1]

A more appropriate test of our model is made possible by using the diary data collected in the 1969 survey. These data were chosen because they have greater reliability and validity (Roghmann and Haggerty, 1974), and because they permit the study of short-term processes of health and illness behavior on a daily basis. The conceptualization of the problem is symbolized in Figure 4B.1. For the sake of simplicity, the model deals with only three "types" of events—stress, illness, and utilization—and the presence or absence of each on any given day. It was assumed that the 24-hour day with its rest and work cycle is the most important time unit around which families organize their lives.

To find out how family members, especially mothers and young children, move through the various states of the three variables over a sequence of days, a health calendar was used (Roghmann and Haggerty, 1972a). The mother was asked to record in the calendar for 28 days (giv-

[1] Findings from this survey have been reported before (Roghmann and Haggerty, 1972b, 1973). This presentation is largely based on the earlier of the two articles.

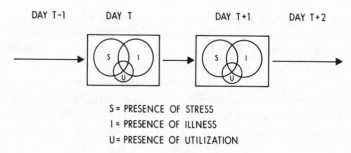

S = PRESENCE OF STRESS
I = PRESENCE OF ILLNESS
U= PRESENCE OF UTILIZATION

*Figure 4B.1. Conceptual model for the study of stress, illness, and utilization (Rogh-mann and Haggerty, 1972b, p. 27).*

ing us four weekly and one monthly cycle) the presence in the family of any upsetting events at work, in the home, with the children, with her husband, and so on. She also recorded the presence of illness and any use of health services for all family members. Coders evaluated the severity of stress: loss of job, a major car accident, or a divorce was coded as *severe* stress; trouble with the boss, argument with husband, or loan fore-closure, as *medium* stress; whiny children, complaints from neighbors, or a broken refrigerator, as *mild* stress. They categorized health complaints by etiology and affected system, and utilization, by place of contact and purpose.

### Static Analysis of Calendar Data

The calendar data provided information on the well-being of 2547 persons for 28 consecutive days. On any given day there was a 30% chance for each family to be in a state of stress. A health complaint was reported for the youngest child[2] on 17% of the days and for the mother on 25%. Med-ical contacts, including telephone calls, were much less frequent than either family stress or child illness, occurring on only 1.8% of child-days and 2.0% of mother-days. Further details on the empirical distributions over the specific states of each of the three variables and their eight com-binations are listed in Table 4B.1, together with the conditional proba-bilities for a medical contact.

The correlations between stress, illness, and utilization were also exam-ined by standard survey methods. Stress correlated moderately with ill-ness, and illness correlated moderately with utilization. But correlation

---

[2] The analysis was limited to the youngest child, instead of all children, for technical reasons: 1) there was always a "youngest" child in each family, even if there was only one child; 2) his or her average age would be relatively low, increasing the probability of illness and of doctor utilization; and 3) taking only one child per family avoided the clustering effects that make statistical interpretations difficult.

Table 4B.1. Distribution of Person-Days: Probabilities for a Medical Contact as a Function of Stress and Illness[a]

| Illness: | No | No | No | Yes | Yes | Yes | Total |
|---|---|---|---|---|---|---|---|
| Stress: | No | Yes | No | No | Yes | Yes | |
| **Total Utilization** | | | | | | | |
| No | 41,760 | 17,771 | 59,531 | 6289 | 4457 | 10,746 | 70,277 |
| Yes | 199 | 152 | 351 | 326 | 362 | 688 | 1,039 |
| $P_{(U)}$[b](%) | 0.47 | 0.85 | 0.59 | 4.93 | 7.51 | 6.02 | 1.46 |
| **Maternal Utilization** | | | | | | | |
| No | 7,943 | 2,734 | 10,677 | 1826 | 1552 | 3,378 | 14,055 |
| Yes | 71 | 32 | 103 | 104 | 74 | 178 | 281 |
| $P_{(U)}$(%) | 0.89 | 1.16 | 0.96 | 5.39 | 4.55 | 5.01 | 1.96 |
| **Youngest Child's Utilization** | | | | | | | |
| No | 8,411 | 3,374 | 11,785 | 1376 | 911 | 2,287 | 14,072 |
| Yes | 59 | 26 | 85 | 98 | 81 | 179 | 264 |
| $P_{(U)}$(%) | 0.70 | 0.76 | 0.72 | 6.65 | 8.17 | 7.26 | 1.84 |
| **Other Members' Utilization** | | | | | | | |
| No | 25,406 | 11,683 | 37,069 | 3087 | 1994 | 5,081 | 42,150 |
| Yes | 69 | 94 | 163 | 124 | 207 | 331 | 494 |
| $P_{(U)}$(%) | 0.27 | 0.80 | 0.44 | 3.86 | 9.40 | 6.12 | 1.16 |

[a] From Roghmann and Haggerty (1972b).
[b] Probability of utilization.

coefficients are poor measures of the strength of the relations in these tables because of unequal marginal distributions and lack of variance in the dependent variable, namely, utilization. It is more useful, therefore, to compare the "risks" of utilization (see the conditional probabilities of Table 4B.1) instead of the sizes of the correlation coefficients. A medical contact was 10 times as likely when illness was present as when illness was absent (6.02% versus 0.59%). With illness held constant, however, stress also had an effect on utilization, but this effect depended on the family member concerned. With illness, the probability for a medical contact was, on the average, about 50% higher with stress. Without illness, the presence of stress increased the chances for a medical contact about 80%. The exception was maternal illness: stress *reduced* the chance of a medical contact by mothers, in the presence of illness, from 5.4% to 4.6%.

How could stress increase utilization? Common sense suggests that stress will increase need and demand through increasing anxiety about an illness, but unless care is easily available, this will have no effect on utilization. Place of contact was used to classify care by availability. Table 4B.2 shows, indeed, that the probability of telephone calls and of visits to emergency and outpatient departments—medical contacts with relatively easy access—is doubled if stress is present, but that there is little change in the probability of office visits. Thus only a certain kind of medical contact is stress sensitive. With a rigid appointment system as one barrier to care, the stress induced demand is kept out of the physician's office, perhaps unwisely. This explains also why the retrospective survey data of 1971 (see the Appendix to Section 4B) did not greatly affect total utilization, but did influence the type and place of contact.

### Dynamic Analysis of Calendar Data

The static analysis used person-days as if each single day were independent of every other. Such an analysis helps to identify basic parameters, but is not of much assistance in making short-term predictions for organizing care. Past experience is usually the best predictor for future experience. It is for this reason that the model focused on the movement of individuals through states. Such dynamic analysis controls for response tendencies[3] (Mechanic and Newton, 1965). Conditional probabilities for

---

[3] Response set tendency can manifest itself in two ways in this context. First, some mothers have different threshhold levels for perceiving, reporting, and treating illness than others. Reported illness differences can reflect objective illness differences, different reporting tendencies, or both. (See the discussion of black/white differentials in Section 3B.) This first "between mothers" manifestation is controlled for in the dynamic analysis as we compare the same mother's reports on different days. Second, the threshhold level of a mother for perceiving and reporting illness can vary over

utilization, illness, or stress were, therefore, computed for any day, given the presence or absence of the same event on previous days (Table 4B.3). Knowing the absence or presence of stress on one, two, or three preceding days makes a great difference for predicting stress today. But the greatest gain comes from knowing the stress state on the immediately preceding day. Going back two or three days does not increase our knowledge much further. Similar findings were obtained for illness and for utilization. The pattern suggests that the clustering of events over time is a stochastic process that may approach the model of a regular Markov chain.[4] Under the assumptions of this mathematical model relatively simple formulas are available to describe minor stress, illnesses, and response patterns over time.

A Markov process is described by its matrix of transition probabilities. The probabilities were computed by averaging the observed 27 transitions contained in the 28-day calendar, which provides an excellent measure of change probabilities. Other panel studies in the social sciences are usually limited to 2 or 3 points in time (instead of 28), with the result that differences may be due to response uncertainty (reliability) or to change. Only small random changes were observed in the transition probabilities from day to day, though a systematic error increased the standard deviation around the mean transition probability. There was a tendency for mothers to report more stress events on the first few days of calendar-keeping than on later days (on 35.0% of all days in the first week; on 29.6% in the second week; on 28.7% in the third week; on 29.1% in the fourth week). The average probability of staying in a stress-free state was .824; the standard deviation around this mean was .172. But this standard deviation was largely due to a systematic increase over time. If the 27 transitions are divided into three groups of nine consecutive days each, the variability in each group is much lower ($X_1 = .795$, $SD_1 = .094$; $X_2 = .830$, $SD_2 = .078$; $X_3 = .846$, $SD_3 = .052$).

time as a function of stress. Mothers may see more illness or attribute more seriousness to symptoms when under stress. Stress may then not increase illness, but only the tendency to perceive and report it. This second "over time" manifestation is not controlled for. Our illness measures reflect only reported illness; it is the perceived and reported illness that influences the demand for medical care and is presented to the physician. Different tendencies to perceive, evaluate, and respond to symptoms are at the heart of such issues as overutilization, the management of the "worried well," and health education. We prefer to discuss these matters under those headings rather than as a methodological issue.

[4] A Markov chain is defined as a sequence of experiments (e.g. days) with a finite number of outcomes (e.g., stress states), in which the probability of a specific outcome (presence or absence of stress) is not necessarily independent of the outcome of the experiment immediately preceding it, but is independent of the outcome of experiments before the one preceding it. (For further details see Kemeny and Snell, 1960.)

Table 4B.2. Percentage of Probability of Utilization by Place of Contact as a Function of Stress and Illness[a]

| Availability | Illness: Stress: | No No | No Yes | Yes No | Yes Yes | Any Day |
|---|---|---|---|---|---|---|
| High: Emergency room | | — | — | 0.36 | 0.89 | 0.10 |
| Phone | | — | — | 1.04 | 2.22 | 0.25 |
| Outpatient department | | 0.05 | 0.17 | 0.89 | 1.62 | 0.27 |
| Other clinics | | 0.05 | 0.12 | 0.18 | 0.21 | 0.09 |
| Low: Office | | 0.37 | 0.55 | 2.45 | 2.57 | 0.75 |
| Total probability (%) | | 0.49 | 0.85 | 4.92 | 7.51 | 1.46 |
| Total number of medical contacts | | 199 | 152 | 326 | 362 | 1,039 |
| Total number of days in each group | | 41,959 | 17,923 | 6615 | 4819 | 71,316 |

[a] From Roghmann and Haggerty (1972b).

148

*Table 4B.3.  Probability of Utilization, Stress, and Illness as a Function of State on Previous Days[a]*

| Type of Event | Values in Percentages. | | | | | | |
| | Number of Event-Free Days Preceding | | | Average Day | Number of Event-Full Days Preceding | | |
| | 3 | 2 | 1 | 0 | 1 | 2 | 3 |
| --- | --- | --- | --- | --- | --- | --- | --- |
| 1. Family Stress | 12.6 | 14.6 | 17.4 | 30.0 | 59.2 | 73.7 | 82.6 |
| 2. Illness | | | | | | | |
|    Mother | 11.3 | 12.5 | 14.1 | 24.4 | 55.7 | 68.3 | 75.9 |
|    Youngest child | 6.7 | 7.2 | 7.9 | 16.8 | 60.0 | 71.6 | 78.3 |
| 3. Utilization | | | | | | | |
|    Mother | [b] | 1.6 | 1.7 | 1.9 | 11.9 | 51.5 | [b] |
|    Youngest child | [b] | 1.7 | 1.7 | 1.8 | 6.8 | 11.8 | [b] |

[a] From Roghmann and Haggerty (1972b).
[b] Insufficient data.

The length of average stress episodes and the frequency of such episodes per month or year for each family can be computed from the transition matrix. In a similar way deductions about illness episodes and medical care episodes can be made. Note that the term "episode" is mathematically defined as a sequence of "event positive" days and not in terms of specific sickness or treatment.

Episodes of stress and illness vary in length, on the average, between two and three days. Maternal illness episodes are shortest (2.24 days), while child illness episodes are longest (2.53) days. For medical contacts the definition gives average episodes of 1.14 days (mother) and 1.07 days (youngest child)—in other words, mostly "one-contact" episodes.

"Event negative" periods vary more than "event positive" ones. The average stress-free period is 5.68 days long; the average maternal "health" period, 6.94 days; and the average child "health" period, 12.66 days. The average medical-contact-free periods are 57.8 days (mother) and 56.8 days (children).

The transition matrices discussed up to now deal with only one type of event at a time. There is no reason, however, why different types of events cannot be combined, especially stress and illness, for which sufficient data exist. It would be of greater theoretical interest to include use of services as well, but the number of reported doctor contacts becomes small in the detailed breakdowns required. An example of such a "combined variable" transition matrix is given in Table A.10. The subgroups of mothers and youngest children were combined for this analysis, but some cells still have low frequencies. Smaller matrices (stress combined with illness, or illness combined with stress) can be derived from this large matrix simply by collapsing various cells. (See Appendix.)

Usually tables only describe the relationship between two or three variables, leaving open assumptions as to which event caused which. The earlier static analysis of person-days was of this type. It was assumed that stress causes illness, and illness causes utilization, and not the reverse. This is reasonable, especially as the events recorded on a page of the calendar occurred in sequence over the 24-hour day, though we did not time each event and, therefore, cannot prove that the cause preceded the presumed consequence. The transition matrix, however, describes the mutual relationships between the three variables with a time lag of one day. If the three letters $S$, $I$, and $U$ stand for stress, illness, and utilization, and they are indexed with 1 for "today" and 2 for "tomorrow," there are nine "one-day time lag" relations to be analyzed: $S_1 \rightarrow I_2$, $S_1 \rightarrow U_2$, $I_1 \rightarrow U_2$, $I_1 \rightarrow S_2$, $U_1 \rightarrow I_2$, $U_1 \rightarrow S_2$, $S_1 \rightarrow S_2$, $I_1 \rightarrow I_2$, $U_1 \rightarrow U_2$. If a vertical line ($|$) represents "holding constant," the expression "$S_1 \rightarrow I_2 \mid I_1$, $U_1$" symbolizes the question: Does stress today lead to increased illness tomorrow, controlling for illness and utilization today? Similarly, the expression "$U_1 \rightarrow U_2 \mid S_1$, $I_1$" symbolizes the question: Does utilization today increase utilization tomorrow, controlling for stress and illness today?

The transition matrix (see Table A.10) contains all the raw data to answer these questions, though up to 16 comparisons are required and some shifting of the matrix rows is needed to make comparisons easier. The matrix is presently arranged to answer the second question above $(U_1 \rightarrow U_2 \mid S_1, I_1)$. It can be shown (wherever there are sufficient data) that today's utilization increases the likelihood of tomorrow's utilization; likewise, today's stress increases the likelihood of stress tomorrow.

Analysis of Calendar Data by Episode

The survey analysis gave the desired frequency data, and the Markov model gave the data especially suited for prediction and management. But how can causal inferences be easily made in the nonexperimental design used here? An earlier study (Meyer and Haggerty, 1962) employed the episode approach, and a combination of the Markov model and the episode approach can solve the problem without recourse to complicated causal models.

In a first analysis of the calendar data a stress episode was defined— in the same way as in the Markov model—as a set of consecutive days presenting at least one problem to cope with. The average number of episodes per family over the 28-day period was 3.7, as predicted by the Markov model. The average length of an episode was 2.3 days. (The figures differ slightly from our prediction because of some assumptions that the computer program had to make about the day immediately preceding the first and following the last calendar day. Lacking information on these days, we assumed that they were free of stress, illness, or utilization.) Indexing forward and backward in the calendar after finding a stress episode permitted a registering of illness in family members on days before, during, and after a stress episode. The average frequency of change in illness states was known from the Markov chain analysis. To the extent that illness onset is observed more frequently during stress episodes than should be expected by chance, conclusions about causal relations can be drawn. Thus, when the observed frequency of onset of illness in mothers on the first day of stress episodes is compared with the expected onset figures, a large increase in reported illness (25% against 10% expected) is seen (Table 4B.4). At the same time the normal return to health is retarded (6% against 10% expected). This is evidence that the general phenomenon of increased illness with stress obtains not only for major diseases and long-term stress but also for minor illness and short-term stress.

The objective of this study, however, was not to study the relation between stress and disease onset, which is already well documented, but the relation between stress and use of health service. The static analysis presented above answered that question only partially. A more complete answer is found by analyzing illness episodes as identified in the calendar data. An episode of illness for any family member was defined as any sequence of health complaint days. The 2547 persons in the sample had

*Table 4B.4. Frequency of Change in Maternal Illness Observed during Stress Episodes*[a]

For 1153 one-day stress episodes; values in percentages.

| Type of change | Maternal Illness | | Expected | Observed |
|---|---|---|---|---|
| | Before | During | | |
| No change | No → No ⎫ | | 78.2 | 68.1 |
| | Yes → Yes ⎭ | | | |
| Onset | No → Yes | | 10.9 | 25.2 |
| End | Yes → No | | 10.9 | 6.8 |

[a] From Roghmann and Haggerty (1972b).

5256 episodes of illness. Mothers had 1643 episodes; the youngest children, 1025 episodes.

In addition to the importance of availability, the combined effects on utilization of stress, length of illness, and person affected can be shown (Table 4B.5). One-day illness episodes, when accompanied by stress, have lower chances of medical contact. (For mothers the probability decreased from 2.1% to 1.5%, and for children, from 6.4% to 4.0%.) The mother seems to accept stress as the cause of these short illnesses and does not expect any help from the physician. For medium-term illness (two to five days) the use of medical services increases with stress for the child (from 9.5% without to 15% with stress), but still decreases for mothers (from 10.4% to 8.4%). For six or more days of illness, stress seems to be less important, but our numbers are too small for definite statements.

*Discussion*

The model of illness behavior presented in this section differs in two respects from the earlier conceptualizations. First, we think of illness behavior as impulsive rather than planned. The recognition that an individual's coping abilities have been exceeded triggers this behavior if care

*Table 4B.5.  Frequency of Medical Contact during Illness Episodes as a Function of Length of Episode and Stress[a]*

| Length of Episode | All Episodes | | No Stress | | With Stress | |
|---|---|---|---|---|---|---|
| | Percent | Number | Percent | Number | Percent | Number |
| Mother Illness Episode | | | | | | |
| 1 day long | 1.8 | 995 | 2.1 | 513 | 1.5 | 482 |
| 2-5 days long | 9.2 | 545 | 10.4 | 222 | 8.4 | 323 |
| 6 or more days | 36.9 | 103 | 36.2 | 47 | 37.5 | 56 |
| All | 6.4 | 1643 | 6.5 | 782 | 6.4 | 861 |
| Youngest Child Illness | | | | | | |
| 1 day long | 5.3 | 582 | 6.4 | 329 | 4.0 | 253 |
| 2-5 days long | 12.5 | 343 | 9.0 | 156 | 15.5 | 187 |
| 6 or more days | 47.0 | 100 | 51.2 | 41 | 44.1 | 59 |
| All | 11.8 | 1025 | 10.6 | 526 | 13.0 | 499 |

[a] From Roghmann and Haggerty (1972b).

is available. Second, illness behavior is perceived of as a short-term process, where timing is of greater importance than the decision itself. This combination of impulsive behavior occurring in a short-term process gives, over the long run, the impression of randomness. Because retrospective interviews scanning long time periods cannot capture the essence of such processes, a special methodology such as the health calendar had to be used to study this phenomenon.

The model of illness behavior sketched here differs fundamentally from our conception of health behavior which is seen as rational, goal directed, and embedded in long-term planning. As such, retrospective survey methods can capture the essentials of this behavior. Dental check-ups, family planning, and immunizations are all actions without immediate gratifications. Appointments can be booked well ahead. Children can be taught proper health habits. Proper health behavior thus fits nicely into the achievement oriented middle-class value system.

In which ways does this model differ from earlier conceptualizations? Suchman's concepts of parochial versus cosmopolitan "Social Group Organization," and his popular versus scientific "Individual Medical Orientation," were appropriate where social structures were changing from those typical of small rural communities or urban neighborhoods to those characteristic of highly mobile, industrial societies. Suchman drew on the old *Gemeinschaft-Gesellschaft* dichotomy, a kind of polarization of subcultures (Gouldner, 1957; Merton, 1957) frequently observed in societies in transition. This distinction is still appropriate for many rural areas of the United States and for most of the developing countries in the world. The Rochester community falls almost exclusively into the scientific and cosmopolitan categories. The old-time *Gemeinschaft* type community has been replaced by new community forms in the same way as the old multigeneration family has given way to the small nuclear family. It is appropriate, in our view, to interpret Suchman as instructing us to watch out for the impact of subcultures, not as claiming that his indices will obtain in all circumstances. The subcultures of our times are organized according to social categories rather than territorial areas, and change more rapidly than the old ones. Youth cultures, alternative life styles, the ecology and the zero-population movements, religious revivals, and the women's liberation movement are examples of such categories. These movements bring about changes in social values and norms that create different needs and demands for medical care. In the long run they may deeply affect existing social structures. It is on such changes that our surveys should focus. It seems inappropriate, therefore, to copy questionnaire items used by Suchman over a decade ago.

The Rosenstock model of health beliefs was developed for categorical preventive care programs. Mass immunizations against polio, mass screening for tuberculosis, and the use of preventive dental check-ups in prepayment plans were the problems with which Rosenstock was concerned. As might perhaps be expected, our extension of this model to cover generalized health behavior was unsuccessful. His concept of cues or triggers was used in a different context, namely, illness behavior under stress. For categorical health education programs directed at child populations, such as automobile safety for children or the prevention of accidental poisonings, the Rosenstock approach may still be valid. Surveys would be a poor design to test such specific programs, however; experimental studies are more efficient and conclusive.

Andersen's behavioral model was interpreted as a framework or paradigm rather than a substantive model like Suchman's or Rosenstock's. Andersen did not intend to identify intervening variables to explain known relationships of health care and demographic variables. Demographic variables like age and sex indicate biological needs or risks; family resources like income and insurance stand for economic factors; and community resources represent the market structure of the health industry in a given community. All these are important aspects of medical care organization influencing utilization, but not theories of patient behavior. Change in the structure of medical care organization is the focal point of Part III of this book. Each single change—a new health center, new legislation (e.g., the abortion law), new ways of financing care for the poor such as the Medicaid program—should be evaluated separately. General trends, such as the decline of general practice, the movement of private practitioners into new medical parks or medical centers in the suburbs, and the trend toward salaried physicians serving inner city populations and working for subsidized care organizations, are evaluated separately in other chapters.

The theories of patient behavior (health and illness behavior) have been examined here from the aspect of what can be learned from them so as to organize medical care and, especially, therapeutic interventions more effectively. The focus has been on the microstructure of care, not the macrostructure. Some implications are already apparent.

First, medical care (or, rather, health care) must become more skilled at the diagnosis and management of situational crises, both to help prevent illness and to assist in the proper management of illness for patients under stress. Caplan's "crisis intervention" theory (1961) postulates that times of family crises are opportune for medical intervention. We must be able to diagnose these when the patient presents himself for medical care. Moreover, it has long been clear to clinicians (Clyne, 1961) that severity of illness alone is not the only reason why people seek help. It seems reasonable that the physician's ability to help his patient will be increased if he learns to deal more effectively with these precipitating causes of medical contacts. Knowledge of where and how often these crisis-related medical contacts are occurring, what types they are, and how far back in time the physician may have to search to identify them, will alert him to their presence and nature. That this is more true in public clinics than in private offices reflects, in part, the greater burden of crises among the segment of the population using public facilities. It remains for an experimental study to show that crisis intervention improves the health of the patient. At least it provides more intellectual interest and possibly some reduction of hostility in the doctor who is asked to see a child with a minor illness if he understands that family stress may be the reason for the visit rather than the illness itself.

Second, since most of these crises are intrafamilial, it is clear that medical care, to manage them effectively, must be family based. Whether this is best done by placing general medical care in the hands of a family physician or in a team of pediatrician-internist-obstetrician with allied professional help is less important than that these intrafamily stresses be diagnosed and considered in illness management. This requires that medical care be accessible at the time of crisis; a more flexible appointment system would be needed for the physician to be available on short notice. It also raises important issues in the current debate over how to manage the "worried well" (Garfield, 1970). It has been proposed that these patients (who, in the public sector at least, are very likely to have stress as a precipitant of contact) be separated by automated multiphasic screening and cared for in a separate health maintenance area. It is doubtful, however, that this mechanical type of care will meet such patients' needs. And since they are more likely to appear in the emergency room or to make contact by telephone, health screening would be difficult.

Finally, there is the philosophic question of how best to deal with such stress induced contacts. It is still an open question whether we should aim to reduce stress or to "immunize" patients against it by strengthening their ability to handle it. As professionals we may be limited to the latter course, although privately we may work for any social policy that helps to reduce external stressors like bad housing or unemployment. Since it seems unlikely that stress will (or even should) ever be eliminated, our goal should be to educate children and families to manage the inevitable stresses of life without a major increase in physical or mental illness. Knowledge of disease processes and their management is important, but knowledge of patient behavior processes and their direction is equally relevant to handle the "new morbidity" of our times and to lead to the new frontier of effective preventive care.

## REFERENCES

CAPLAN, GERALD
1961 *An Approach to Community Mental Health.* London: Tavistock Publishers.

CLYNE, M.D.
1961 *Night Calls: A Study in General Practice.* London: Tavistock Publishers.

GARFIELD, S.
1970 "The Delivery of Medical Care." *Scientific American,* 222:12, 15–23.

GOULDNER, ALWIN W.
1957 "Cosmopolitans and Locals: Toward an Analysis of Latent Social Roles." *Administrative Science Quarterly,* 2:281–306.

KEMENY, J. G., and SNELL, J. L.
1960 *Finite Markov Chains.* Princeton, New Jersey: Van Nostrand.

MECHANIC, DAVID, and NEWTON, M.
1965 "Some Problems in the Analysis of Morbidity Data." *Journal of Chronic Diseases,* 18:569–580.

MERTON, ROBERT K.
1957 "Patterns of Influence: Local and Cosmopolitan Influentials." In *Social Theory and Social Structure.* Glencoe, Illinois: The Free Press, pp. 387–420.

MEYER, R.J., and HAGGERTY, R.J.
1962 "Streptococcal Infections in Families; Factors Altering Susceptibility," *Pediatrics,* 29:539–549.

ROGHMANN, KLAUS J., and HAGGERTY, ROBERT J.
1972a "The Diary as a Research Instrument in the Study of Health and Illness Behavior: Experiences with a Random Sample of Young Families." *Medical Care,* 10:143–163.

ROGHMANN, KLAUS J., and HAGGERTY, ROBERT J.
1972b "Family Stress and the Use of Health Services." *International Journal of Epidemiology,* 1:279–286.

ROGHMANN, KLAUS J., and HAGGERTY, ROBERT J.
1973 "Daily Stress, Illness, and Use of Health Services in Young Families." *Pediatric Research,* 7:520–526.

ROGHMANN, KLAUS J., HECHT, P., and HAGGERTY, ROBERT J.
1973 "Family Coping with Everyday Illness: Self-Reports from a Household Survey." *Journal of Comparative Family Studies,* IV (1):49–62.

ROGHMANN, KLAUS J., and HAGGERTY, ROBERT J.
1974 "Measuring the Use of Health Services by Household Interviews: A Comparison of Procedures Used in Three Child Health Surveys." *International Journal of Epidemiology,* 3:71–81.

# CHAPTER FIVE

# The Use of Medications: A Neglected Aspect of Health and Illness Behavior

KLAUS J. ROGHMANN

Studies on health and illness behavior have, in the past, focused chiefly on doctor utilization. Even then researchers were usually not concerned with utilization rates per se, but with specific kinds of utilization like well-baby care, immunizations, chest x-rays, or "Pap" smears.

Doctor utilization, however, is only one element of a large set of health and illness behaviors. For example, health behavior also covers use of regular medications, home safety measures, the use of safety belts in cars, regular working and sleeping habits, and various aspects of family planning. Illness behavior covers compliance with physician's instructions, use of first aid, bed rest, and consulting the home medical encyclopedia. Some of these behaviors are spontaneous, impulsive, or habitual; others are carefully planned actions requiring rigorous self-control.

This chapter examines the range of medicine-taking among children for acute and chronic conditions or preventive purposes. In contrast to the compliance studies, we will cover nonprescribed medications as well. The chapter also tests whether any of the previously discussed models of health and illness behavior can adequately account for the observed variations. In this respect it differs from descriptive studies on who takes what medicine for which condition, as already well researched in a recent British study of medicine takers (Dunnel and Cartwright, 1972).

## The Extent of Medication Usage among Children

Each of the three surveys (1967, 1969, 1971) inquired about the recent use of medications. For prescribed medications the question was as follows: "Today or yesterday, has (name of child) taken or used any medicine, salves, or pills which were prescribed or suggested by a doctor?" For non-prescribed medications the mother was handed a card on which nine different kinds of medications were listed and was asked about each one: "Has (name of child) taken or used any medicines or salves or anything like that, *not* prescribed or suggested by a doctor, such as ... (interviewer hands card and reads)?" If a nonprescribed medicine was reported, the interviewer inquired whether anyone had suggested it.

The health diary in the 1969 survey also recorded, for each day and each child, whether a medication was taken and whether for preventive or curative purposes. Up to four medications were coded, two under regular preventive care and two under illness-related care.

The findings are presented in Table 5.1. Most remarkable was the stability of the results over the study period. The reporting of medications for *acute* conditions as well as for *chronic* conditions did not change significantly from 1967 to 1971. About 10% of the children took a pain reliever, 8% cold or cough medicines, and 5% some remedies for skin conditions during any two-day period. Medicines taken for the control of chronic illness were reported for 3.5% of the children.

The "one-day" diary data in 1969 reached only about 50% of the level of medicine-taking reported for the "two-day" period for the major acute conditions. For conditions for which several days of medicine-taking were required (antibiotics, chronic conditions), the "one-day" and "two-day" figures are not very different, and the consistency between the calendar and the interview data indicates a high reliability in reporting. On the whole the 1969 figures are somewhat lower than those for 1967 and 1971, probably because of the oversampling of low-income groups, who do not use medicine as much as middle-class children (see "Variations in the Use of Medicines," p. 162).

The only significant increase from 1967 to 1971 was for, presumably, *preventive* medications: vitamins and tonics were reported for 20% of the children in 1967, for 25% in 1969, and for 29% in 1971.

Because of the consistency in the findings over the study period, further analysis will be limited to the 1971 survey. Table 5.2 gives the variation in medicine usage by age, sex, and age-sex combination, as the most important demographic variables.

A child's age is strongly related to the use of medicine for acute illness, for chronic conditions, and for preventive purposes, but in different ways. The relationship is positive for chronic care, negative for preventive care, and curvilinear for acute care. The curvilinearity for acute care is partly due to opposite trends for specific acute conditions and partly to a true curvilinearity. Thus the use of cold and cough medicines decreases with age, the use of skin remedies increases with age, and the use of pain

*Table 5.1.   Use of Medications "Today or Yesterday"*
Values in percentages

| Type of Medication | 1967 Interview | 1969[a] Interview | 1969[a] Calendar | 1971 Interview |
|---|---|---|---|---|
| **For Acute Conditions** | | | | |
| Pain relievers | 11.3 | 8.3 | 3.8 | 10.2 |
| Cold and cough | 7.7 | 6.8 | 3.1 | 8.0 |
| Skin conditions | 4.9 | 2.3 | 1.3 | 4.8 |
| Antibiotics | 1.5 | 2.7 | 2.1 | 2.0 |
| Ear, nose, throat | 1.9 | 1.4 | 0.6 | 1.3 |
| Digestive | 1.3 | 0.6 | 0.5 | 0.9 |
| **For Chronic[b] Conditions** | 2.2 | 3.8 | 2.8 | 3.4 |
| **For Preventive Care** | | | | |
| Vitamins and tonics | 20.0 | 25.6 | 21.1 | 28.8 |
| n = | 2312 Children | 1466 Children | 41,048 Days | 2952 Children |

[a] Oversampling low-income patients.
[b] Not comparable for 1967, when this was restricted to "allergy medicines."

159

Table 5.2.  Use of Medications by Children "Today or Yesterday," 1971 Survey
Values in percentages

| Independent Variable | Selected Acute Care Medications | | | | | Chronic Care Medications | Vitamins, Tonics | Number of Children |
| --- | --- | --- | --- | --- | --- | --- | --- | --- |
| | Pain Relievers | Cold and Cough | Skin Conditions | All Acute Medications | | | | |
| **Age (years)** | | | | | | | | |
| 0–4 | 12.7 | 15.0 | 3.7 | 27.7 | | 2.0 | 44.0 | 761 |
| 5–9 | 8.1 | 9.0 | 1.5 | 18.1 | | 3.8 | 29.8 | 841 |
| 10–14 | 11.0 | 4.0 | 4.8 | 20.4 | | 3.5 | 21.6 | 874 |
| 15–17 | 8.4 | 2.5 | 12.7 | 22.7 | | 4.8 | 15.8 | 476 |
| | $p<.10$ | $p<.01$ | $p<.01$ | $p<.01$ | | $p<.05$ | $p<.01$ | |
| **Sex** | | | | | | | | |
| Boys | 9.2 | 7.1 | 3.8 | 19.1 | | 4.2 | 28.1 | 1486 |
| Girls | 11.2 | 9.0 | 5.8 | 24.9 | | 2.6 | 29.5 | 1466 |
| | $p<.10$ | $p<.05$ | $p<.05$ | $p<.01$ | | $p<.05$ | n.s. | |
| **Age (years)–Sex** | | | | | | | | |
| Boys | | | | | | | | |
| 0–2 | 11.3 | 14.5 | 8.1 | 29.3 | | 1.8 | 39.6 | 283 |
| 3–5 | 9.2 | 11.0 | .4 | 17.5 | | 2.2 | 38.6 | 228 |
| 6–12 | 8.2 | 5.3 | 1.6 | 15.8 | | 4.7 | 26.3 | 620 |
| 13–17 | 9.4 | 2.1 | 7.0 | 18.8 | | 6.3 | 15.6 | 384 |
| Girls | | | | | | | | |
| 0–2 | 15.7 | 16.2 | 2.5 | 30.9 | | 2.0 | 45.1 | 204 |
| 3–5 | 11.5 | 10.8 | 3.8 | 25.0 | | 2.7 | 40.4 | 260 |
| 6–12 | 8.4 | 9.0 | 3.1 | 21.2 | | 2.5 | 25.0 | 608 |
| 13–17 | 13.2 | 3.8 | 12.6 | 27.1 | | 3.3 | 21.4 | 365 |
| | $p<.05$ | $p<.01$ | $p<.01$ | $p<.01$ | | $p<.05$ | $p<.01$ | |
| Total | 10.2 | 8.0 | 4.8 | 22.0 | | 3.4 | 28.8 | 2952 |

relievers declines over the first years of life, increasing again during adolescence.

Sex is strongly related to the use of medicine for acute and chronic conditions, but not for preventive care. Girls used more acute care medicines than boys (25% vs. 19%), but boys took more medicine for chronic illnesses (4.2% vs. 2.6%).

The combined sex-age breakdown replicates many of the earlier findings (vitamins and all acute care, cold and cough medicines), but it also shows important interactions. The increase in chronic care medicine usage with age is a phenomenon only for boys, not for girls. The use of skin medications increases with age for girls, but is related to age in a curvilinear pattern for boys. The overall curvilinear relationship for pain relievers is due to a strong pattern for girls which shows only vaguely for boys.

These findings on the use of medicine are presented to emphasize the high frequency of this type of health and illness behavior. Details as to why the medicine was taken (curative versus preventive usage) and whether it was prescribed or suggested by a doctor have been presented elsewhere (Haggerty and Roghmann, 1972). Purpose and mode of prescription follow closely the type of medicine used. Antibiotic medicines were mainly prescribed and were used for curative purposes. Vitamins and tonics, on the other hand, were taken for preventive purposes, with about half of them prescribed by doctors and half of them not prescribed.

The supplementary question—"Who suggested this medicine?"—used for nonprescribed medicines did not elicit sufficient information for tabular presentation. Pain relievers and cold and cough medications were all self-suggested. Furthermore, the druggist or the nurse was rarely mentioned. For studies of the diffusion of new or specific medicines, or for certain trade names, this question might be very useful, but for the large volume of daily medications self-suggestion and prescription or recommendation by the doctor were the answers given almost exclusively.

The use of sick care medications is obviously a function of illness. Mothers do not make their children take pain relievers or cold and cough medicines when no symptoms are present. Nor are there many symptoms that go untreated. The price of over-the-counter medicines such as aspirin does not present a financial barrier. Our health diary study has shown that on any given day about 14% of the children presented some complaint; only 4%, however, had their normal activities restricted on any given day, and only 2% had their health rated as "poor" for any given day. When a health complaint was reported for a child, the mother judged that for 86% of these complaints some action was needed, and in 97% of all cases for which action was needed, action was also possible. On 93% of all such complaint days with an illness response the therapy was decided by the mother (self-medications, staying home, bed rest, etc.). Only 7% of the illness responses involved a doctor contact.

The differences in the uses of medicines described above reflect, for the most part, different rates of illness, rarely different response patterns to illness. The illness rates reflected in the medicine-taking described in Table 5.2 seem to be due chiefly to biological susceptibility and human development over the childhood years. In contrast to the utilization of doctor services, therefore, the use of medications shows less dependence on "enabling" factors and more on "need" factors (Andersen model). The most remarkable finding from a physician's point of view is the high level of medicine-taking. Nearly 50% of the youngest children in a family had taken a medicine "today or yesterday"! For the next youngest children about 42% had taken a medicine, and for the older children the proportion reached about 33%. Half of these medicines were prescribed by a doctor; two thirds were for preventive purposes.

Research on health and illness behavior has, in the past, focused on hospitalization and doctor utilization. In monetary terms, hospitalizations and doctor visits may indeed be the decisive factors for medical care costs, but they cover only a small proportion of all health and illness behavior. The National Health Survey covered only cost and acquisition of medicines, not daily consumption (Alderman, 1967; Wilder, 1966). If we want to understand patient behavior, the use and nonuse of medicines seem to constitute a more strategic point of entry. In fact, the ample literature on patient compliance with medical regimens (Haggerty and Roghmann, 1972) is as informative about patient behavior as is the literature on ambulatory care utilization.

## Variations in the Use of Medicines

The same problems encountered when explaining the use of physician services arise in explaining the use of medications. Fewer barriers to use are expected, but similar motivations and life styles are relevant factors.

When the variables postulated by the Suchman model were correlated with the use of acute illness, chronic illness, and preventive care medicines, no clear patterns could be observed. The use of preventive medicines increased slightly with Skepticism toward Medical Care and with attitudes of Dependency in Illness ($p < .01$), but the use of sick care medicines did not. Knowledge of Disease and Friendship Solidarity were unrelated to the everyday use of medicines by children, no matter what the medicines were taken for.

The variables postulated by the Rosenstock model—Perceived Serious- ness, Perceived Barriers, and Readiness to Seek Care—were all unre- lated to the everyday use of medicines by children.

The variables specified by the Andersen model, however, did have an impact. The "social structure" variables (see Table 5.3), except for maternal religion, were all significantly related to the use of preventive medicines. The use of chronic illness medicines was also related, but not as strongly. There were no correlations of these variables with the use of acute care medicines.

The higher the social prestige of the parental occupation, and the higher the level of maternal education, the greater was the use of preven-

*Table 5.3.  Usage of Medicines as a Function of "Social Structure" Variables (Andersen Model)*
Values in percentages

| Independent Variable | Acute Care Medicines | Chronic Care Medicines | Vitamins, Tonics | Number of Children |
|---|---|---|---|---|
| **Maternal Education** | | | | |
| Up to 11th grade | 20.3 | 2.5 | 20.7 | 893 |
| High school graduate | 21.6 | 3.9 | 32.1 | 1113 |
| Some college | 26.4 | 5.1 | 31.9 | 545 |
| College graduate | 20.9 | 2.0 | 33.4 | 401 |
| | n.s. | $p<.05$ | $p<.01$ | |
| **Maternal Race** | | | | |
| White | 22.3 | 3.7 | 30.4 | 2560 |
| Black | 20.2 | 1.8 | 18.1 | 392 |
| | n.s. | $p<.05$ | $p<.01$ | |
| **Maternal Religion** | | | | |
| Catholic | 21.4 | 3.2 | 28.4 | 1490 |
| Protestant | 22.7 | 3.8 | 30.0 | 1242 |
| Other | 21.8 | 2.7 | 24.5 | 220 |
| | n.s. | n.s. | n.s. | |
| **Parental[a] Occupation** | | | | |
| Higher executive | 20.7 | 4.4 | 33.2 | 271 |
| Lesser executive | 22.3 | 3.7 | 38.5 | 382 |
| Small business | 26.9 | 4.6 | 31.7 | 413 |
| Clerical | 23.2 | 3.2 | 29.9 | 284 |
| Skilled | 19.7 | 3.2 | 25.3 | 756 |
| Semiskilled | 21.7 | 2.3 | 26.0 | 470 |
| Unskilled | 17.8 | 0.8 | 12.4 | 129 |
| | n.s. | n.s. | $p<.01$ | |

[a] Father's occupation if married; otherwise mother's occupation.

tive and chronic care medicines. Here middle-class values appear to be the underlying factor. This is also reflected in the relation with race: black mothers gave their children only about half as many chronic care and preventive medicines as did white mothers. However, there was no similar significant relation for acute care medicines, though a moderate tendency for white children to take more such medications was evident. This is consistent with the earlier observations (see Section 3B) that blacks have fewer days of restricted activity. As was argued then, the difference in illness behavior may reflect, not actual differences in illness levels, but different threshold levels.[1] A black mother may not see a need to react to a symptom at a point when a white mother has already limited her child's activities and reached into the medicine cabinet.

The enabling factors in Andersen's model were related to the use of all three groups of medicines (see Table 5.4). The higher the socioeconomic standing, the higher was the use of the three groups of medicines. This was also reflected, indirectly, in insurance status, although insurance does not usually cover expenses for medications. In addition, access to care affected the use of medicines. Children with two regular doctors had the highest use of acute care medicines (25%), of chronic care medicines (13%), and of preventive medicines (38%). The lowest proportions of children taking chronic illness medicines (1.6%) and preventive medicines (16%) were those having a regular *place* of care rather than a regular doctor. This pattern is very similar to the one observed for the use of doctor services.

Our stress variables were also moderately related to the utilization of medicines: The Stress Exposure score correlated positively with acute illness medicines; Coping Ability correlated positively with the use of preventive medicines; and Tension correlated negatively with the use of preventive medicines. Though our various measures for illness, stress, and the utilization of doctors and medicines covered different time periods ("today or yesterday" for medicines; "the last 2 weeks" for restricted activity and seeing the doctor; "the last 12 months" for stress and major symptoms) and made it difficult to compute meaningful correlations, the general evidence points to the conclusion that stress and tension not only increase illness, but also decrease preventive behavior and, possibly, coping ability in general.

Evidence for the latter relation comes from the 1969 calendar data. Examination of the relation between stress, illness, and the use of medicines on a daily basis showed that the presence of stress inhibited the use of all three groups of medicines by the mother. The only medicines taken more frequently under stress were sedatives (Haggerty and Roghmann,

---

[1] See footnote 2 of Section 4B for a discussion of different response tendencies.

Table 5.4.   Usage of Medicines as a Function of "Enabling" Variables
(Andersen Model)
                        Values in percentages

| Independent Variable | Acute Care Medicines | Chronic Care Medicines | Vitamins, Tonics | Number of Children |
|---|---|---|---|---|
| Socioeconomic Area |  |  |  |  |
| 1  Highest | 25.4 | 5.9 | 27.8 | 338 |
| 2 | 21.5 | 2.8 | 31.7 | 1017 |
| 3 | 23.8 | 3.8 | 30.0 | 1013 |
| 4 | 18.2 | 2.5 | 23.5 | 400 |
| 5  Lowest | 16.3 | 2.2 | 19.6 | 184 |
|  | $p<.05$ | $p<.05$ | $p<.01$ |  |
| Income |  |  |  |  |
| Under $6000 | 18.6 | 4.1 | 24.0 | 413 |
| $6001-10,000 | 20.4 | 2.9 | 30.2 | 692 |
| 10,001-14,000 | 24.1 | 2.3 | 31.7 | 900 |
| $14,001 Plus | 22.6 | 4.5 | 27.1 | 947 |
|  | n.s. | $p<.05$ | $p<.05$ |  |
| Insurance |  |  |  |  |
| Blue Cross | 22.8 | 3.4 | 30.2 | 2334 |
| Medicaid | 20.3 | 3.6 | 23.1 | 385 |
| Private | 16.7 | 3.8 | 22.0 | 186 |
| None | 19.0 | — | 34.0 | 47 |
|  | n.s. | n.s. | $p<.01$ |  |
| Access to Care |  |  |  |  |
| Two M.D.s | 24.8 | 13.0 | 37.9 | 161 |
| One regular M.D. | 22.1 | 2.7 | 30.6 | 2225 |
| Regular place | 20.9 | 1.6 | 16.3 | 374 |
| No source | 20.3 | 4.3 | 25.0 | 192 |
|  | n.s. | $p<.01$ | $p<.01$ |  |

1972:110). When this relationship was reanalyzed for the youngest child (see Table 5.5), a similar inhibitor effect was found.

Thus the proportions of youngest children taking antibiotics on illness days were 16% with no stress and 10% with stress. The proportion taking vitamins on illness days was 38% with no stress, but only 32% with stress.

This inhibitor effect of stress, of course, had been observed before (Section 4B). Doctor utilization was also reduced in the presence of stress. Although the inhibitor effect had been observed only for short-term illness episodes for mothers and youngest children, this replication for medicine-taking is important as it indicates that a general illness behavior covers both medicine-taking and doctor contacts.

*Table 5.5.   Medicine-Taking as a Function of Stress and Illness
(1969 Diary): Mother and Youngest Child Days*
Values in percentages

| Type of Medication | No Illness | | Illness | | Any Day |
|---|---|---|---|---|---|
| | No Stress | Stress | No Stress | Stress | |
| **For Acute Illness** | | | | | |
| Pain relievers | | | | | |
| Mother | 0.5 | 0.8 | 40.4 | 39.1 | 10.5 |
| Child | 0.0 | 0.0 | 28.3 | 28.4 | 4.9 |
| Cough and cold | | | | | |
| Mother | 0.0 | 0.0 | 10.2 | 6.7 | 2.2 |
| Child | 0.0 | 0.0 | 23.6 | 22.2 | 4.0 |
| Antibiotics | | | | | |
| Mother | 0.0 | 0.0 | 5.7 | 4.2 | 1.3 |
| Child | 0.2 | 0.3 | 15.7 | 10.4 | 2.6 |
| Digestive | | | | | |
| Mother | 0.5 | 0.2 | 5.6 | 3.9 | 1.5 |
| Child | 0.2 | 0.3 | 4.2 | 4.3 | 0.9 |
| **For Chronic Illness** | | | | | |
| Mother | 11.0 | 7.6 | 17.6 | 16.0 | 11.8 |
| Child | 1.8 | 2.8 | 6.6 | 6.0 | 2.8 |
| **Preventive** | | | | | |
| Vitamins, tonics | | | | | |
| Mother | 13.9 | 12.8 | 16.0 | 15.0 | 14.1 |
| Child | 27.0 | 25.8 | 38.1 | 31.7 | 28.2 |
| **Tension Related** | | | | | |
| Sedatives | | | | | |
| Mother | 3.1 | 3.8 | 9.3 | 10.3 | 4.9 |
| Child | 0.3 | 0.5 | 0.3 | 0.8 | 0.4 |
| **Any Medication** | | | | | |
| Mother | 25.8 | 22.6 | 73.8 | 69.1 | 36.8 |
| Child | 28.9 | 28.7 | 78.0 | 71.5 | 36.9 |
| $n=$ Mother Days | 7978 | 2736 | 1967 | 1655 | 14,336 |
| Row percentage | 55.6 | 19.1 | 13.7 | 11.6 | 100.0 |
| $n=$ Child Days | 8456 | 3393 | 1489 | 998 | 14,336 |
| Row percentage | 59.0 | 23.6 | 10.4 | 7.0 | 100.0 |

It is tempting to use Markov models to explain medicine-taking in further detail. Thus the question arose in an epidemiological study (Roghmann and Haggerty, 1973:665) whether taking sedatives by young
mothers follows the pattern of chronic illness medications (regular taking,
i.e., use on preceding days is the best predictor for use today) or of acute

illness medications (irregular taking, i.e., preceding day's use is an unreliable predictor for use today). On any "mother-day," 4.9% of the mothers took a sedative, with 3.7% being regular users (sedatives taken 21 or more out of a possible 28 days). Knowledge of such patterns of medicine-taking is important to estimate the number of women who might accidentally be exposed to a teratogenic substance (e.g., thalidomide) in the early weeks of pregnancy.

Short-term models of illness behavior appear to be more promising than models postulating relatively stable health beliefs and attitudes as the main determinants.

## Discussion

The stress model with its short-term conceptualization of medicine-taking brought us close to specific studies on compliance. Charney et al. (1967) have shown that even the regular doctor of middle-class patients cannot predict which of his patients will be compliant and which will not. Other researchers found the character and quality of the patient-physician relationship to be important (Elling et al., 1960; Korsch et al., 1968). Disappearance of symptoms was the most frequent reason given by patients who discontinued their penicillin against their doctors' instructions (Mohler et al., 1955). Though full of interesting findings, these studies on patient compliance fail to lead in a cumulative way to a theory of patient behavior. Most studies are categorical to specific disease entities, making generalizations to other illness behavior difficult.

Compliance with a regimen, thought necessary for the treatment of disease, requires the regularity and control that were conceptualized for health behavior (Section 4B). If a patient slips back to impulsive, short-term illness behavior, effective therapy is unlikely. Our data suggest that such slipping into "illness behavior" is more likely in stressful situations. A vicious circle is then started: treatment is more difficult, and frustration and hostility on the part of the physician are consequences. Physician overestimation of patient compliance (Davis, 1966) is probably a defense mechanism. When a doctor is confronted with evidence of noncompliance, the cause is often attributed to the patient's "inability to understand" or "uncooperative personality" (Davis, 1966:1043).

These findings have major implications for treatments that require careful patient cooperation in order to assure adequate therapy. The physician should become sympathetic instead of hostile when he encounters noncompliance and should try to think of treatments requiring less patient cooperation or of measures to circumvent resistance.

REFERENCES

ALDERMAN, ALICE J.

1967 *Prescribed and Non-prescribed Medicines—Type and Use of Medicines.* National Center for Health Statistics, Department of Health, Education, and Welfare, Series 10, No. 39. Washington, D.S.: Government Printing Office.

CHARNEY, E., BYNUM, R., ELDREDGE, D., FRANK, D., MAC WHINNEY, J.B., MC NABB, N., SCHEINER, A., SUMPTER, E., and IKER, H.

1967 "How Well Do Patients Take Oral Penicillin?" *Pediatrics*, 40:188–195.

DAVIS, MILTON S.

1966 "Variations in Patients' Compliance with Doctors' Orders: Analysis of Congruence between Survey Responses and Results of Empirical Investigations." *Journal of Medical Education*, 41:1037-1048.

DUNNEL, KAREN, and CARTWRIGHT, ANN

1972 *Medicine Takers, Prescribers and Hoarders.* London: Routledge and Kegan Paul.

ELLING, R., WITTEMORE, R., and GREEN, M.

1960 "Patient Participation in a Pediatric Program." *Journal of Health and Human Behavior*, 1:183–191.

HAGGERTY, ROBERT J., and ROGHMANN, KLAUS J.

1972 "Noncompliance and Self Medication: Two Neglected Aspects of Pediatric Pharmacology." *Pediatric Clinics of North America*, 19:101–115.

KORSCH, B.M., GOZZI, E.K., and FRANCIS, V.

1968 "Gaps in Doctor-Patient Communication. I: Doctor-Patient Interaction and Patient Satisfaction." *Pediatrics*, 42:855-869.

MOHLER, D.N., WALLIN, D.G., and DREYFUS, E.G.

1955 "Studies in the Home Treatment of Streptococcal Disease." *New England Journal of Medicine*, 252: 1116–1118.

ROGHMANN, KLAUS J., and HAGGERTY, ROBERT J.

1973 "Zur Soziologie der Patienten.: Medikamentenkonsum." In *Soziologie*, edited by G. Albrecht, H. Daheim, and F. Sack. Opladen, pp. 648–670.

WILDER, CHARLES S.

1966 *Cost and Acquisition of Prescribed and Non-prescribed Medicines.* National Center for Health Statistics, Department of Health, Education, and Welfare, Series 10, No. 33. Washington, D.C. Government Printing Office.

CHAPTER SIX

# The Utilization of
# Health Services

*A. AMBULATORY CARE: DECREASING UTILIZATION RATES*

KLAUS J. ROGHMANN

tilization, from the perspective of our research paradigm, is the meeting of supply and demand in the health services market. It can be
measured and evaluated from both the supplier and the consumer perspectives. In this section the volume of ambulatory child health services
and their trends during the study period will be assessed from these
perspectives. No attempt will be made in this section to describe and
explain patterns of utilization; they were dealt with in Chapter 4.

*Provider Data*

As a first step an estimate of the volume of services, based on provider data
(hospital and health department statistics, physician's average work load
per week, etc.) for 1967, 1969, and 1971, was prepared (Table 6A.1). The
total volume of medical care contacts with the approximately 250,000
children in the county dropped, according to these estimates, from about
1.6 million to 1.4 million per year. In 1967, the children in our community had about 7.3 contacts per child per year; in 1969 the rate had
dropped to about 6.4, and in 1971 to 5.5. Private practitioners provided
about 90% of all services in 1967, and about 88% in 1969 and 1971.

Whereas the total volume of services provided to children dropped
about 15% over the four years, the child population increased by about
10%. This decreased volume in the face of an increased child population
led to the dramatic drop in rate of services rendered. This unexpected decline needs explanation in view of the increased public financing available
(Medicaid) and the development of a large health center, both designed
to increase services. Was the decline a result of the methods used to meas-

169

ure use, or was it real? Because of the importance of this question, a detailed discussion of the methodology is presented in the Appendix to Section 6A (Note 1). It would be desirable to have actual encounter data rather than estimates derived from household surveys and provider reports. No community in the United States, however, has such data, and those available, even from large populations such as Kaiser enrollees, represent a biased sample of the community: our data, therefore, are the only known large community data available.

*Survey Data*

Information about the last doctor visit and the frequency of doctor visits was collected in our surveys, using the standard recall period for two weeks as recommended in the National Health Survey (NHS).[1] Among the different sources of ambulatory medical care asked for specifically were phone consultations, office visits, and house calls in the private sector, and emergency room, outpatient, and other "clinic" visits (child health conferences, neighborhood health centers, etc.) in the public sector. Schools and "any other place" were checked as a final category.

The survey findings (Table 6A.2), detailed by place of care, and using annual rates, absolute figures, and a percentage breakdown, also show a reduction in total volume of services and rate of use over the study period. The absolute volume as well as the estimated rates are close to the supplier estimates. Even for 1967, for which there is the greatest discrepancy, the relative sampling error of $\pm 7\%$ (95% confidence level) around the aggregate estimate includes the "true" value of the supplier estimate.

The 1000-family samples do not provide enough cases for the necessary detailed breakdowns by source of care. As a rule 15% of respondents reported a physician contact during the preceding two-week period. Therefore, for the 1967 and 1971 surveys, the frequency of doctor visits in the last 12 months was also ascertained in cases where no visit to a doctor was reported in the last two weeks. For children who had no visit to a doctor in either the preceding two weeks or the preceding 12 months, the interviewer asked about the time of the last doctor visit without obtaining details on the frequency of visits occurring more than one year ago.

The results from the questions covering the 12-month period are pre-

---

[1] National Center for Health Statistics: *Health Survey Procedure: Concepts, Questionnaire Development, and Definitions in the Health Interview Survey*. Public Health Service Publication 1000, Series 1, No. 2. Washington, D.C.: Government Printing Office, 1964. (See especially pp. 14–16.)

Table 6A.1.  Estimated Supply of Child Health Services (Excluding Inpatient) by Source of Care, Based on Provider Statistics, Monroe County, New York, 1967, 1969, and 1971[a]

| Source of Care | Estimated Total Volume | | | Rate per Year | | | Percentage | | |
|---|---|---|---|---|---|---|---|---|---|
| | 1967 | 1969 | 1971 | 1967[b] | 1969[c] | 1971[d] | 1967 | 1969 | 1971 |
| Phone consultations | 551,200 | 509,080 | 494,510 | 2.42 | 2.15 | 1.96 | 33.2 | 33.8 | 35.5 |
| Office visits | 885,730 | 766,100 | 690,170 | 3.88 | 3.23 | 2.73 | 53.3 | 50.8 | 49.6 |
| Home visits | 51,370 | 44,640 | 40,440 | 0.23 | 0.19 | 0.16 | 3.1 | 3.0 | 2.9 |
| Total private visits | 1,488,300 | 1,319,820 | 1,225,120 | 6.53 | 5.56 | 4.85 | 89.5 | 87.6 | 88.0 |
| Emergency | 68,430 | 72,940 | 78,150 | 0.30 | 0.31 | 0.31 | 4.1 | 4.8 | 5.6 |
| Outpatient | 53,570 | 55,980 | 38,900 | 0.23 | 0.24 | 0.15 | 3.2 | 3.7 | 2.8 |
| Other clinics | 8,400 | 16,400 | 19,000 | 0.04 | 0.07 | 0.08 | 0.5 | 1.1 | 1.4 |
| Total public visits | 130,400 | 145,320 | 136,050 | 0.57 | 0.62 | 0.54 | 7.8 | 9.6 | 9.8 |
| Other places (school, work) | 43,700 | 42,900 | 30,300 | 0.19 | 0.18 | 0.12 | 2.6 | 2.8 | 2.2 |
| Total visits | 1,662,400 | 1,508,040 | 1,391,470 | 7.29 | 6.35 | 5.51 | 100.0 | 100.0 | 100.0 |

[a] From Roghmann and Haggerty (1973).
[b] 228,000 children up to age 17.
[c] 237,300 children up to age 17.
[d] 252,400 children up to age 17.

Table 6A.2.  *Estimated Rates of Children's Utilization by Source of Care, Based on Two-Week Recall Question in Household Survey, Monroe County, New York, 1967, 1969, and 1971*[a]

| Source of Care | Estimated Rate per Year | | | Implications | | | | | |
|---|---|---|---|---|---|---|---|---|---|
| | | | | Total Volume | | | Percentage | | |
| | 1967 | 1969 | 1971 | 1967 | 1969 | 1971 | 1967 | 1969 | 1971 |
| Phone consultations | 1.45 | 0.76 | 1.24 | 331,000 | 180,350 | 312,980 | 22.0 | 12.5 | 22.3 |
| Office visits | 3.82 | 3.39 | 3.23 | 871,000 | 804,450 | 815,250 | 58.1 | 55.6 | 58.2 |
| Home visits | 0.11 | 0.04 | 0.07 | 25,000 | 9,490 | 17,670 | 1.7 | 0.7 | 1.3 |
| Total private visits | 5.39 | 4.19 | 4.54 | 1,227,000 | 994,290 | 1,145,900 | 81.8 | 68.8 | 81.8 |
| Emergency | 0.55 | 0.46 | 0.31 | 125,400 | 109,160 | 78,240 | 8.3 | 7.6 | 5.6 |
| Outpatient | 0.39 | 0.45 | 0.43 | 88,900 | 106,790 | 108,530 | 5.9 | 7.5 | 7.7 |
| Other clinics | 0.04 | 0.40 | 0.15 | 9,100 | 94,920 | 37,860 | 0.6 | 6.6 | 2.7 |
| Total clinic visits | 0.98 | 1.32 | 0.89 | 223,400 | 310,870 | 224,630 | 14.9 | 21.7 | 16.0 |
| School visits | 0.18 | 0.58 | 0.12 | 41,000 | 137,630 | 30,290 | 2.7 | 9.5 | 2.2 |
| Total visits | 6.56 | 6.09 | 5.55 | 1,491,400 | 1,442,790 | 1,400,820 | 100.0 | 100.0 | 100.0 |

[a] From Roghmann and Haggerty (1973).

Table 6A.3.  Estimated Rates of Children's Utilization by Source of Care, Based on a 12-Month Recall Question Used in Household Interview, Monroe County, New York, 1967, 1969, and 1971[a]

| Source of Care | Estimated Rate per Year | | | Implications | | | | | |
| | | | | Total Volume | | | Percentage | | |
| | 1967[b] | 1969[c] | 1971[b] | 1967 | 1969 | 1971 | 1967 | 1969 | 1971 |
|---|---|---|---|---|---|---|---|---|---|
| Phone consultations | 0.49 | 0.17 | 0.43 | 111,720 | 40,300 | 108,530 | 16.2 | 8.1 | 18.3 |
| Office visits | 1.72 | 1.44 | 1.41 | 392,160 | 341,700 | 355,880 | 56.8 | 68.9 | 60.0 |
| Home visits | 0.07 | 0.01 | 0.01 | 15,960 | 2,300 | 2,520 | 2.3 | 0.5 | 0.4 |
| Total private visits | 2.28 | 1.61 | 1.85 | 519,840 | 384,300 | 466,930 | 75.2 | 77.0 | 78.7 |
| Emergency | 0.19 | 0.13 | 0.15 | 43,320 | 30,850 | 37,860 | 6.3 | 6.2 | 6.3 |
| Outpatient | 0.13 | 0.14 | 0.16 | 29,640 | 33,220 | 40,380 | 4.3 | 6.7 | 6.8 |
| Other clinics | 0.13 | 0.11 | 0.09 | 27,360 | 26,100 | 22,720 | 4.3 | 5.3 | 3.8 |
| Total public visits | 0.45 | 0.38 | 0.40 | 100,320 | 90,170 | 100,960 | 14.5 | 18.2 | 17.0 |
| Other visits | 0.31 | 0.10 | 0.10 | 70,680 | 23,730 | 25,240 | 10.2 | 4.8 | 4.3 |
| Total visits | 3.03 | 2.09 | 2.35 | 690,840 | 498,200 | 593,130 | 100.0 | 100.0 | 100.0 |

[a] From Roghmann and Haggerty (1973).
[b] Based on frequency of visits by the 84% of children who had no visit in last two weeks. The sum of those contacts, divided over the number of children with no visit in the last two weeks, gave the rate.
[c] Retrospective follow-up telephone interview.

173

sented separately in Table 6A.3 for comparison both against the two-week question findings and the supplier estimates.

Using these three sources (provider, two-week, and 12-month population sources), we consistently found a drop in the volume of child health services and in the rates per year from 1967 to 1971. The overall estimates based on the 12-month recall were, however, only about half the size of the supplier estimates and the two-week recall estimates. As for the provider data, methodological problems are also of great importance in interpreting these findings. The possible errors are discussed, in detail, in the Appendix to Section 6A (Note 2).

*Comparison of Provider and Survey Data*

The comparison between the *provider estimate* and the *two-week survey estimate* of the total volume was encouraging (see Figure 6A.1). But if we examine the breakdown by source of care, we find that moderate underreporting in the private sector is largely canceled by large overreporting in the public sector. Three findings stand out:

1. Telephone contacts are 40% lower in the interviewer data than in the provider data. This probably represents underreporting by patients.
2. House calls are 50% lower in the interview estimate than in the provider estimate. However, this does not necessarily denote underreporting, as the number of physicians making house calls has been declining steadily, and the earlier practice data may no longer be appropriate; the supplier data are more likely to be overestimated.[2]

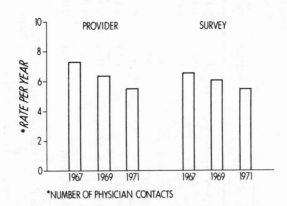

*Figure 6A.1. Overall estimate of children's use of ambulatory care by provider and survey studies (two-week).*

3. Public sector visits were overreported by respondents by about 66% (1961, 1971). These respondents seem to "telescope" their time perspective and to report visits made more than two weeks ago.

The aggregate effect of these errors is a canceling out when it comes to estimating the aggregate figures for the population, and a systematic bias when it comes to a breakdown of utilization by source of care. This systematic bias, especially the overreporting of public sector visits, has, as one consequence, an attenuation of the well-known relation between utilization rate and socioeconomic background. The poorer segments receive *less* services, and the more affluent segments *more* services, than is reflected in these health survey data.

The overall comparison between *provider estimate* and the *12-month survey estimate* was less satisfactory, but only because no cancelation effect occurred. After correction for undersampling high utilizers, the public sector visits are, actually, estimated fairly accurately, though the reporting for the private sector is about 50% too low. Only about 20% of the telephone calls and about 60% of the office visits were reported.

The least measurement error was observed for the 1969 health calendar estimate. The calendar estimate was nearly identical with the supplier estimate as to private doctor visits and emergency room visits, though not a single house call was reported by the 512 families over the 28-day period.

## Discussion

The main finding from our comparison of the volume of child health services and the utilization rate per child per year is a trend toward decreasing utilization. Although some of this decrease may be accounted for by the problems of measurement, we regard this trend as real and significant. Age standardization does not affect the basic finding. The trend, together with the dropping birthrate and the increased training of nurse practitioners, if experienced nationwide, may significantly reduce the future need for more pediatricians. Moreover, there are some indications that this is, indeed, the national trend. For example, a recent publication (Jackson, 1971:34) shows that a rate of 7.0 doctor contacts for children 0–4 years old prevailed in urban areas in 1958, but had dropped to 6.0 in 1968. Similarly, Andersen et al. (1972) report a drop from 4.6 to 4.2 visits

[2] This conclusion is also supported by a 1973 physician survey (Roghmann, 1974) that yielded the following mean values per week: pediatricians—100 phone consultations, 140 office visits, and 2 home visits; general practitioners—68 phone consultations, 133 office visits, and 6 home visits.

for 0–5 year olds and from 2.7 to 2.2 visits for 6–17 year olds between 1958 and 1970.

A more interesting question: "Why the reduced number of visits?" cannot be answered from our data. The reason may be a combination of reduced morbidity (due to measles, mumps, and rubella vaccines or to other advances in therapy), fewer house calls, decreased number of general practitioners, and, in 1971, the economic recession. It is important, however, to point out that this decrease is quite different from the situation for other age groups like the old, for whom services are increasing steadily. In our view this is further opportunity for improving the quality of care for children in order to improve the quality of their lives. Communities can offer better care because they now need to pay for less. These data are also the first of which we are aware to show a "ceiling effect" in utilization in spite of an increase in manpower (providers) and decrease in financial barriers. It has been a common assumption that an increase in providers will increase services rendered, and that a reduction of financial barriers leads to an upsurge in demand. In our community from 1967 to 1971 more pediatricians became available, a neighborhood health center was started, and Medicaid was introduced, yet contacts per child with health care providers decreased. If the same holds in other communities, this decline should provide reassurance about current plans to implement national entitlement to medical care for children. For this age group, at least, we can predict that there will be no upsurge in demand.

REFERENCES

ANDERSEN, RONALD, GREELEY, R. MC L., KRAVITS, J., and ANDERSON, O.W.

1972  Health Services Use: National Trends and Variations, 1953–1971. Department of Health, Education, and Welfare. Publication No. 73-3004. Washington, D.C.: Government Printing Office.

JACKSON, ANN L.

1971  Children and Youth: Selected Health Characteristics, U.S., 1958 and 1968. National Center for Health Statistics, Department of Health, Education and Welfare, Series 10, No. 62. Washington, D.C. Government Printing Office.

NATIONAL CENTER FOR HEALTH STATISTICS

1964  Health Survey Procedure: Concepts, Questionnaire Development and Definitions in the Health Interview Survey. Public Health Service, Publication 1000, Series 1, No. 2. Washington, D.C.: Government Printing Office. (See especially pp. 14–16.)

ROGHMANN, KLAUS J. and HAGGERTY, ROBERT J.
1973   "Measuring the Use of Health Services by Household Interviews: A Comparison
       of Procedures Used in Three Child Health Surveys." *International Journal of
       Epidemiology,* 3:71–81.

ROGHMANN, KLAUS J.
1974   The Volume of Private Practice Care in Monroe County, 1973 (mimeograph).


## B. INPATIENT CARE: DECREASING OCCUPANCY RATES

KLAUS J. ROGHMANN


Data on the hospitalizations of children can be collected from both providers and consumers. A patient origin study, conducted by the Genesee
Region Health Planning Council (1968), collected data from hospitals.
In addition, data from fiscal intermediaries were available for 1972 (Wells,
1974; Annechiarico, 1974); Blue Cross or Medicaid together account for
96% of the total payments for hospital care in Monroe County. Consumer data on child admissions were available from our surveys.


*Provider Data*

The patient origin study abstracted information about age, sex, residence,
diagnosis, and length of stay from the medical records on patient admissions. Residence was coded by the 19 townships for the suburbs and by
eight segments for the city. The seven hospitals in Monroe County reported 79,845 admissions (excluding newborns) for 1968 (admissions of
patients from outside Monroe County, accounting for 11.2% of all hospitalizations, were excluded). Depending on hospital size, the sampling
fraction was 100%, 50%, 20%, or 10%. A computer tape, describing the
actual sample of 14,881 admissions, was made available for secondary
analysis. Weight factors of 1, 2, 5, and 10 were used to arrive at estimates
for the total volume of admissions.

The patient origin study showed that there were about 12,000 child
admissions in 1968, representing a hospitalization rate of 52/1000. Without the 3800 tonsillectomy and adenoidectomy (T & A) admissions, however, the rate would have been only 35/1000. The high proportion of

elective surgery indicates that, on the whole, hospital beds for children were not in short supply.

City children had a higher hospitalization rate (61/1000) than suburban children (46/1000), mostly because of a 70% higher "medical" admission rate, but also because of a relatively high number of teenage deliveries (Table 6B.1). The greater "medical" admission rate for children in the city reflects a higher incidence of diseases due to infections among the city's poor population.

Insurance status has also been shown to be an important determinant of hospitalization rates. The Medicaid covered population had nearly twice the medical admission rate of the Blue Cross covered population (21/1000 compared with 12/1000). For surgical procedures, however, Blue Cross rates were found to be higher than Medicaid rates (15/1000 for Medicaid compared with 20/1000 for Blue Cross). Tonsillectomy and adenoidectomy rates, especially, were higher for Blue Cross subscribers than for Medicaid enrollees—standardized per 1000 children, there were about 7 Medicaid T & As compared with 19 Blue Cross paid T & As. The overall situation by insurance status is also summarized in Table 6B.1.

By 1972 the total number of child hospitalizations had not changed greatly, in spite of an increased child population. Blue Cross records indicate a decrease from the previous 9000 to about 7400 child admissions (Table 6B.2), while Medicaid admissions had risen from 1500 to 2260. Although the number of T & As is not reported separately, the corresponding Blue Cross category for 1972 indicated a drop from the previous level of 3300 to about 2000, explaining most of the decrease in child admissions paid for by Blue Cross. The reported hospital bed occupancy rate for children for all hospitals decreased from 65.5% in 1968 to 58.2% in 1972. Thus there also appears to have been a decrease in pediatric inpatient volume, but this decline seems to have been less than for ambulatory care.

## Survey Data

Each of the three surveys included a question about hospitalization. The first (1967) was the most ambitious. It asked about the *frequency* of admissions in the preceding year and about details of up to three of those admissions—the date, the number of nights spent in hospital, the reasons for the admission, whether there was an operation, who paid for it, what hospital was utilized, and how it was selected. The date of the last admission was inquired about if there was no admission in the preceding year. The two later surveys (1969, 1971) also inquired about how many hospi-

*Table 6B.1. Hospitalizations (Newborns Excluded) by Procedure, 1968, Patients under 18 Years Old Only*

By Insurance

| Procedure | Medicaid | Blue Cross | Commercial Insurance | Others, Self | Total |
|---|---|---|---|---|---|
| Delivery | 277 | 168 | 22 | 71 | 538 |
| T & A[a] | 196 | 3,268 | 347 | 37 | 3,848 |
| Surgical | 437 | 3,523 | 479 | 116 | 4,555 |
| Medical | 592 | 2,015 | 310 | 87 | 3,004 |
| Total | 1,502 | 8,974 | 1,158 | 311 | 11,945 |
| Population | 28,000 | 173,000 | 23,000 | 7,000 | 231,000 |
| Rates/1000 | | | | | |
| Delivery | 9.89 | 0.97 | 0.96 | 10.14 | 2.33 |
| T & A | 7.00 | 18.89 | 15.09 | 5.29 | 16.66 |
| Surgical | 15.61 | 20.36 | 20.83 | 16.57 | 19.72 |
| Medical | 21.14 | 11.65 | 13.48 | 12.43 | 13.00 |
| Total | 53.64 | 51.87 | 50.36 | 44.43 | 51.71 |

By Residence

| Procedure | City | Suburbs | Total |
|---|---|---|---|
| Delivery | 420 | 118 | 538 |
| T & A | 1,592 | 2,256 | 3,848 |
| Surgical | 1,948 | 2,607 | 4,555 |
| Medical | 1,578 | 1,426 | 3,004 |
| Total | 5,538 | 6,407 | 11,945 |
| Population | 91,200 | 139,800 | 231,000 |
| Rates/1000 | | | |
| Delivery | 4.6 | 0.8 | 2.3 |
| T & A | 17.5 | 16.1 | 16.7 |
| Surgical | 21.4 | 18.6 | 19.7 |
| Medical | 17.3 | 10.2 | 13.0 |
| Total | 60.8 | 45.7 | 51.7 |

[a] Tonsillectomy and Adenoidectomy.
*Source:* Roghmann, Klaus J. (1974).

talizations had occurred in the preceding year, but collected detailed information only about the last admission.

The wording of the questions was somewhat more elaborate in the first survey than in the later ones. "Anchor points" in time, such as Labor

*Table 6B.2.  Number of Admissions (Excluding Newborns) of Blue Cross
Patients Aged 0–17 in Seven Acute Care Hospitals, by Age and Diagnosis,
Monroe County,ᵃ New York, 1972*

| Independent Variable | Admissions | Average Number of Patient-Days |
|---|---|---|
| Age (years) | | |
| Under 1 | 370 | 6.6 |
| 1–4 | 1948 | 4.0 |
| 5–9 | 2802 | 3.4 |
| 10–14 | 1767 | 5.8 |
| 15–17 | 1447 | 6.4 |
| Total | 8334 | 4.7 |
| Diagnosis (ICDA Code) | | |
| 1. (500–508) Upper respiratory tract (includes T & A) | 2063 | 1.69 |
| 2. (550–553) Hernia | 537 | 2.39 |
| 3. (780–789) Symptoms and ill-defined conditions | 493 | 4.93 |
| 4. (370–379) Diseases of eye | 435 | 2.49 |
| 5. (590–599) Diseases of urinary tract | 340 | 4.06 |
| 6. (540–543) Appendicitis | 302 | 6.83 |
| 7. (380–389) Diseases of ear | 283 | 1.69 |
| 8. (730–738) Other diseases of musculoskeletal system | 213 | 6.03 |
| 9. (600–607) Diseases of male genitals | 185 | 3.12 |
| 10. (740–749) Congenital anomalies | 179 | 5.45 |
| 11. Other conditions | 3304 | 7.28 |
| Total | 8334 | 4.69 |

ᵃ Includes an estimated 11% out-of-county patients.

Day, Christmas, Easter, and other holidays, or "slightly more than one
year ago," were selected for the questioning, and subjects were asked
whether there had been any hospitalizations since then. If so, the date was
checked to see whether or not the hospitalizations occurred within a one-
year span. In the later surveys, using the same interviewers, the wording
was simplified to read, "Over the last 12 months, that is, since . . . (date one
year ago), has . . . (name of child) been in the hospital for overnight or
longer?" The results are presented in Table 6B.3.

Hospitalizations are relatively rare, and random sample surveys constitute an inefficient way to study them. Only about 5% of all children are
hospitalized each year. At the 95% confidence limits the true percentage

Table 6B.3. *Hospitalizations of Children (Including Deliveries of Teenage Mothers but Excluding Newborns) as Reported in Household Surveys, 1967, 1969, and 1971*

|  | 1967 | 1969 | 1971 |
|---|---|---|---|
| Children in sample | 2,311 | 2,465 | 2,952 |
| Population sampled | 228,000 | 237,300 | 252,400 |
| A. Hospitalized in Last Year |  |  |  |
| Children/1000 | 51 | 63 | 43 |
| Admissions/1000 | 53 | 71 | 49 |
| Average length of stay (days) | 4.38 | 4.97 | 6.13 |
| Estimated Number of Children |  |  |  |
| Admitted | 11,630 | 14,950 | 10,850 |
| Payment for Last Admission (%) |  |  |  |
| Insurance part | 17.4 | 25.3 | 20.3 |
| Insurance all | 65.2 | 52.1 | 54.7 |
| Medicaid | 9.2 | 13.9 | 21.1 |
| Self | 8.2 | 8.7 | 3.9 |
|  | 100.0 | 100.0 | 100.0 |
| B. Not Hospitalized in Last Year (%) |  |  |  |
| When last? (number of years ago) |  |  |  |
| 1–2 | 7.1 | 7.9 | 5.8 |
| 3–4 | 8.2 | 6.9 | 6.7 |
| 5–8 | 5.8 | 12.9 | 9.5 |
| 9 or more | 16.5 | 12.9 | 10.4 |
| Never | 62.4 | 59.4 | 67.6 |
|  | 100.0 | 100.0 | 100.0 |

with our sample size would be within ± 1 percentage point around the estimate; thus the relative sample error is about ± 20%. Our special 1969 sample yielded a rather high hospitalization frequency (6.3%), partly because a list of previous patients, supplied by the largest hospital, was used as a sampling frame for "non-Medicaid, non-Blue Cross" children. But the trend gleaned from provider data is confirmed when using the comparable 1967 and 1971 samples—in 1967, 5.1% of all children were hospitalized, compared with 4.3% in 1971. The average length of hospitalization increased from 4.4 to 6.1 days, suggesting that the decrease in percentage of children admitted occurred among those hospitalized for minor illness or short-term procedures (e.g., T & As).

Private insurance payments covered 83% of all admissions in 1967, but only 75% in 1971. The proportion of admissions paid for by Medicaid increased from 9% to 21%. For children with no admission in the preceding year, the last previous admission was further in the past in the 1971 survey than in the 1967 survey (see Table 6B.3)—another indication of decreasing use of hospital care by children in this county. Measurement error appears to be of minor importance for the hospitalization data. (When asked about the precise month of hospitalization in the preceding year, all of the 12 months before the interview were mentioned with about equal frequency.) Thus the survey data support the trend of decreasing utilization observed in the provider data.

Finally, the data from the three surveys were pooled and analyzed together. Age was the most important factor determining admission rate (Table 6B.4). The probability for hospitalization is highest in the first year of life and drops from then onward until, because of teenage pregnancies, it rises again after the age of 14. Average length of hospitalization is equally affected by age. The shortest hospital stay occurs during the 5–9 year age bracket, when T & As are most frequent. The cumulative effect of admission frequency and length of stay is reflected in the average number of nights per 100 children in each age group. In the 0–4 year group this figure (44.9 nights/100 children) is about three times as high as in the 10–13 age bracket (15.1 nights/100 children). Finally, the cumulative hospitalization experience (the survey question, "When last?") is,

Table 6B.4.   Hospitalizations of Children as Reported in Household Surveys, by Age Group (Surveys 1967, 1969, 1971 Pooled)

|  | Age Group (years) | | | | |
|  | 0–4 | 5–9 | 10–13 | 14–17 | Total |
|---|---|---|---|---|---|
| Children in sample | 1988 | 2329 | 1807 | 1603 | 7728 |
| A. Hospitalized in Last Year | | | | | |
| Children/1000 | 73 | 52 | 32 | 49 | 52 |
| Admissions/1000 | 84 | 54 | 35 | 56 | 58 |
| Average length of stay (days) | 5.34 | 4.24 | 4.32 | 6.96 | 5.17 |
| Nights/100 children | 44.86 | 22.90 | 15.12 | 38.97 | 30.00 |
| B. Not Hospitalized in Last Year (%) | | | | | |
| When last? (number of years ago) | | | | | |
| 1–2 | 7.4 | 10.5 | 4.9 | 4.7 | 6.9 |
| 3–4 | 4.9 | 10.4 | 8.5 | 5.7 | 7.2 |
| 5–8 | — | 10.1 | 17.3 | 10.8 | 9.5 |
| 9 or more | — | — | 18.5 | 34.3 | 13.0 |
| Never | 87.7 | 68.5 | 50.8 | 44.5 | 63.5 |
| | 100.0 | 100.0 | 100.0 | 100.0 | 100.0 |

of course, most age dependent. The rates for "never" hospitalized were as follows: in the youngest (0–4) age group, 88%; in the early school age (5–9 year) group, 68%; in the later school age (10–13 year) group, 51%; and in the high school (14–17 year) group, 45%.

## Discussion

How can this trend toward decreased utilization of child health services in ambulatory and inpatient care be accounted for? First, the age structure of the population can change dramatically, for example, because of a dropping birthrate. If the mean age increases, a shift occurs from young, high utilizers to older, low utilizers. However, direct age standardization of the ambulatory care data, using the 1970 census as the reference point, does not support this argument. As the population pyramid for children (see Section 1A) based on census data indicates, there was a remarkable stability in the age structure from 1967 to 1971. The mean annual cohort of children was about 13,000, with a range of only ±1000 (the sharp decline in births has occurred only since 1971). The group of 17-year-olds was usually of the same size as the group of infants. The mean age was 8.3 years for 1967, 8.5 for 1969, and 8.6 for 1971. The drop in newborns, reported in Section 3A, did not begin until 1971 and had not yet affected the surveys. (A 1973 survey would have been strongly affected because the cohort of infants would have declined 25%, and 1-year-olds 15%, below previous cohorts; also, the mean age would have jumped to 9.7 years.) Age standardization is important for many subgroup comparisons, but for the longitudinal change described here it is insufficient to account for the reduction of child health services.

Second, one could argue that during this period medical care became less available or too costly for families to obtain. But this "medical care crisis" argument is not supported by the data either (Roghmann, 1974). In fact, all the data point in the opposite direction: new facilities, especially for the poor, had opened during the study period; Medicaid had lowered the financial barrier for the very poor; more manpower was provided; the demand for hospital emergency services for children decreased; and pediatric bed occupancy declined. The indications are that the reduction of utilization was not due to reduced manpower or facilities or to increased cost. On the other hand, there has possibly been some increased restraint by physicians, in line with current pediatric teaching, in hospitalizing children without strong reasons. Similarly the reduced T & A rate may be due to peer group pressure among physicians to limit procedures that have uncertain benefits. Even greater future changes in the medical care system are expected in our community through the introduction of prepayment plans, which have generally been shown to decrease hospital use.

Third, it can be argued that consumer demand for pediatric health services has changed—and, in this case, it probably did. Why this is so is not clear. Intense public discussion about the medical care crisis may have reduced expectations. The glorification of the physician has decreased, and greater skepticism toward medical care may have led to a more realistic appraisal of the benefits that can be expected from physician visits. A higher educational level of mothers, better safety measures, improved health of children especially as a result of new vaccines or antibiotics, a better environment, economic recession, and inflation—all these may have contributed to the reduced demand for care in this predominantly middle-class community. Though there are no data as yet to support these hypotheses, impressions indicate that these are plausible explanations. New research is now underway to test this argument.

The trends described in this chapter have major implications for health manpower and facility planning. The development may only be a local one, though some underlying factors, especially the dropping birthrate, can be observed nationwide. But the fact that, at least in one community, the trend toward ever-increasing utilization of health services is being reversed is evidence that the "medical care crisis," at least in respect to children, can be controlled. And what has been observed for Monroe County in recent years may well be the trend for other communities in the years ahead.

## REFERENCES

ANNECHIARICO, JANE P.
1974   *The Medicaid Claims File, 1972* (mimeograph).

GENESEE REGION HEALTH PLANNING COUNCIL
1968   *Patient Origin Study* (unpublished data).

ROGHMANN, KLAUS J.
1974   "Looking for the Medical Care Crisis in Utilization Data." *Inquiry*, XI(4):282–291.

WELLS, SANDRA
1974   *The Blue Cross Enrollment and Claims File, 1972* (mimeograph).

## C. UTILIZATION OF AVAILABLE WELL-BABY CARE BY INDIGENT POPULATION GROUPS

ROBERT A. HOEKELMAN
AND
ANNE ZIMMER

Health care workers are well aware of the difficulties encountered in attempting to deliver well-baby care to indigent families. Although inadequate utilization of available health services by the indigent is not restricted to this type of service, to those concerned with the preventive and maintenance aspects of health care, well-baby care has a high degree of importance.

In Rochester, New York, the five hospitals with active maternity services employ different methods to ensure follow-up in well-baby clinics for babies born to mothers who do not have private physicians. Over 95% of these babies are from low-income families. It became possible to study the effectiveness of a new approach when a public health nurse, employed by the Monroe County Department of Health, was placed, on a full-time basis, in the pediatric clinics of the Strong Memorial and Genesee Hospitals. One function of these nurses was to ensure that each mother without a physician at the time of birth received an appointment at the well-baby clinic of her choice. The public health nurse also assumed responsibility for follow-up if the appointment was not kept.

The three other hospitals (Highland, Rochester General, and St. Mary's) had no one person responsible for ensuring well-baby care visits before or after discharge from the hospital. In some instances (except St. Mary's), mothers were given appointments to the individual hospital's well-baby clinic. In most cases, however, mothers were simply advised to make their own arrangements.

Each hospital effected referrals for home visits by public health nurses in all cases of prematurity and significant neonatal illnesses.

### Purpose of Study

This study was instituted in an attempt to determine (1) what level of well-baby care was received by babies of indigent families, and (2) whether this level depended on the type of referral. If the methods of referral used at the Strong Memorial and Genesee Hospitals produced a higher level of health supervision for babies born there than was received by babies born at the three other hospitals in Rochester, the Monroe County Department of Health would have reason to consider placement of a public health nurse in each of the other hospitals, with expectations of raising the level of well-baby care throughout the city and county for the indigent segments of the population. Other factors, such as the source of well-baby care, residence, race, parity, maternal marital status, and maternal age, that might influence the level of well-baby care received by low-income families were also examined.

*Methodology*

The sample consisted of all 418 babies with a Rochester city address born and discharged without a private physician at each of the five hospitals during three sample months (September and December 1968, and March 1969). Between April 1, 1968, and March 31, 1969, 12,501 babies were born at these hospitals. The 418 babies in the original sample represent 3.3% of all babies born during that year and approximately 25% of those who did not have a private physician.

The records of four of the hospital clinics (St. Mary's Hospital had no well-baby clinic), each of the Monroe County Department of Health sponsored child health conferences, and the Rochester Neighborhood Health Center were reviewed during the summer of 1970 to determine which of the study babies had received care at those facilities. Data concerning each visit were obtained from the individual case records, and a Health Supervision Index (HSI)—a measure of amount and quality of care received in the first year of life—was determined for each baby in the study (Hoekelman and Peters, 1972).

All mothers whose babies had no record of care at these places were followed up by interview. It was found that 28 babies had received the services of a private physician for well-baby care; 16 had moved from Monroe County before their first birthdays; 2 had died during the first year of life; and 23 had no record of well-baby care and could not be located to ascertain whether they might have fallen into one of the first three categories. Although it is recognized that the risk is especially high for the group unable to be located, these and the 46 other babies were excluded from the study. Therefore the final sample numbered 349 babies or 2.8% of all those born during the year studied.

Seventy-one mothers included in our final sample, representative of both high and low users of available well-baby care, were interviewed to determine the extent to which they might have utilized private well-baby care facilities. The number of visits made to private sources in this sample was negligible.

Entry into the well-baby care system and the HSI after entry were the dependent variables in the study. Hospital of birth (and the availability of a public health nurse), primary source of well-baby care, residence, race, mother's marital status, maternal age, and parity were the independent variables.

## Results

### Availability of Public Health Nurse

There were differences in the well-child care obtained by the samples of babies born without a private physician in the five hospitals in the Rochester area (Table 6C.1). These differences, however, involve the proportion of babies who received any well-baby care at all, rather than the average level of such care received.

Of the babies born at Strong Memorial and Genesee Hospitals, 3% were found to have no record of well-baby care, while for Rochester General, Highland, and St. Mary's Hospitals combined, 12% of the babies had no such record. Hospitals without a public health nurse, therefore, had a significantly higher proportion of babies receiving no care than hospitals with a public health nurse ($p < .01$). Whether the relationship would hold should the public health nurses be removed from the hospitals now utilizing their services remains a matter for conjecture. There was no opportunity to study the levels of well-baby care attained by hospital of birth before the introduction of public health nurses.

Analysis of variance of the HSI scores of babies for whom some record of well-baby care was found yielded only insignificant differences among the means for the five hospitals.

The sample populations represented at each hospital of birth were analyzed with respect to similarities in method of payment for maternity and newborn care, race, parity, maternal marital status, and maternal age. There were no significant differences in relation to maternal marital status, maternal age, and parity between the sample populations at each of the five hospitals.

### Level of Well-Baby Care

The study babies tended to receive their care at either the well-baby clinic of the hospital of birth, if there was one, or at the neighborhood well-baby clinic. (The neighborhood clinics include six child health con-

Table 6C.1.   Well-Baby Care Received, According to Hospital of Birth

|  | Strong Memorial | Genesee | Rochester General | Highland | St. Mary's |
|---|---|---|---|---|---|
| Number of babies | 187 | 80 | 41 | 31 | 10 |
| Percent receiving no care | 3.1 | 2.5 | 9.8 | 16.1 | 10.0 |
| Mean HSI of those receiving care | 40.5 | 35.1 | 35.7 | 33.6 | 35.7 |
| Standard deviation (SD) | 23.6 | 25.2 | 19.4 | 25.4 | 17.8 |

ferences run by the Monroe County Department of Health and the Rochester Neighborhood Health Center, funded by the Office of Economic Opportunity.) Babies born at one hospital rarely (less than 1%) attended a well-baby clinic at another hospital.

There were no significant differences among neighborhood well-baby clinics in the mean HSI scores attained by those using them as their primary source of care. Nor were there significant differences between those obtaining their primary care at the various hospital based well-baby clinics. When considered collectively, however, the level of health supervision attained at the neighborhood well-baby clinics ($n = 134$, mean HSI $= 42.0$) was significantly higher ($p < .01$) than that for the hospital based well-baby clinics ($n = 197$, mean HSI $= 35.3$).

The mean HSIs of 36 for the overall sample and of 38 (SD $= 23.9$) for those who received care indicate that this population is receiving considerably less health supervision than is recommended by the American Academy of Pediatrics (AAP), in which case the HSI would be 104. Many pediatricians, however, consider the AAP schedule to be excessive. For instance, private pediatricians in Rochester follow a visit and immunization schedule that would yield a HSI score of 72. The extent to which the HSIs for babies of indigent families in Rochester compare favorably or unfavorably with those for babies of nonindigent Rochester families is not known, as there are no data of this kind for nonindigent babies.

The extent to which the HSIs for babies of indigent families in Rochester compare favorably or unfavorably with the scores for indigent and nonindigent babies elsewhere is revealed to some degree by comparison with data presented by Mindlin and Densen (1971). Their data, derived from a household survey conducted in New York City in 1965 and 1966, compared HSIs during the first year of life for infants living in an interracial poverty area (MH District) and infants living in a predominantly white middle-class neighborhood (W District).

In presenting their HSI data, they utilized a Health Supervision Index

Plane divided into eight zones reflecting the number and timing of well-baby visits made and the number of immunizations administered. These were, in turn, grouped into three categories that roughly reflected "good," "fair," and "poor" amounts of infant health supervision. These schemata lent themselves to tabular and graphic presentation. Their graphic method of presentation has been utilized here for purposes of comparison of our data with theirs. Figure 6C.1 demonstrates that fewer babies received "good" care in our sample than in Mindlin's and Densen's MH District. The other similarities and differences between these two samples and between these and Mindlin's and Densen's W District and the rural community of Hoekelman et al. (1973) are evident in the bar graph presentation. The Mindlin-Densen data may be biased toward higher scores, however, since any visit to a physician or clinic was counted in calculating the HSI, whereas only well-baby visits were included in calculations for our study and in the Hornell, New York, study (Hoekelman et al., 1973).

Only 1 baby in our sample (0.3%) received optimum care as recommended by the AAP, and only 31 (8.9%) received care considered adequate by pediatric practice standards currently accepted in the Rochester community. The distribution of the children over the possible HSI range was bimodal, indicating that a large number of babies entered the health care system partly because of the efforts of public health nurses but, once in the system, were lost to follow-up. It provides evidence that sustained efforts by the public health nurses and others responsible for the delivery of care are needed to keep babies under surveillance. The Rochester Neighborhood Health Center was only beginning its outreach services during the time period covered by this study—its first full year of

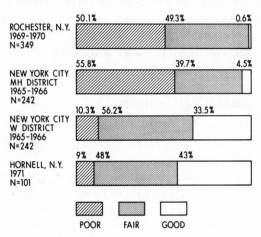

*Figure 6C.1. Percentage distribution of Health Supervision Index in four population samples (Hoekelman et al., 1973).*

operation. Therefore these data can serve only as a baseline and not as an evaluation of its effectiveness.

### The Effects of Race, Parity, Marital Status and Maternal Age

The race of the mother had no effect on the level of well-baby care, but parity did. There was a greater tendency for primipara mothers to enter their babies into the well-baby system than for multiparas, although this difference in proportion of entry only approaches significance ($p<.10$). In addition, babies born to primipara mothers received more health supervision than did babies of multipara mothers once entrance into the well-care system was gained ($p<.05$). Within the multipara mother group there was no relationship between parity and the level of well-care received once a baby entered the system.

Maternal marital status was definitely related to whether or not the child entered the well-baby care delivery system. The babies of 98% of the unmarried mothers gained entrance to the system, in contrast to 92% for the married mothers ($p<.02$). Of infants receiving well-baby care, those born to unmarried mothers received a significantly greater amount (HSI = 40.8) than babies of married mothers (HSI = 35.8) ($p<.05$). Babies of unmarried mothers may have fared better in these areas because their mothers were visited in the home frequently by community based public health nurses to ensure initial and follow-up well-baby care.

Maternal age was also related to getting into the system. The younger the mother, the more likely the child was to receive well-baby care ($p<.001$). However, once entrance into the system was initiated, there was no relationship between maternal age and the level of well-baby care received. Age and marital status are, of course, related, but the relationship between HSI and marital status still holds when controlling for maternal age.

### Other Factors Influencing Utilization

The sample was divided into three groups: 89 "low users" with HSIs of 0–10; 165 "middle users" with HSIs of 11–49; and 95 "high users" with HSIs of 50 or more.

The mothers of the babies in the low-user and high-user groups were interviewed in their homes when their babies were between 27 and 35 months of age. The interview was designed to elicit information about family constellation, parental characteristics, economic status, pregnancy history, neonatal history, well-baby care related history, and health care attitudes and practices of the parents. In general there were few significant differences for the variables investigated between the high-user and low-user groups.

Only 27% of the sample mothers had planned their pregnancy; there was no significant difference between the two groups in this regard. Prenatal care was provided in hospital clinics by house officers for almost all of the mothers. Only 15% of the mothers had had prior contact with the physicians who cared for them; 59% of the high-user and 44% of the low-user mothers were delivered by physicians who had not provided any of their prenatal care. The number of prenatal visits reported by the mothers was similar for both groups with 93% being seen at least five times during the course of the pregnancy. However, only 47% of the low-user mothers made their first prenatal visit during the first trimester, as compared to 64% of the high-user mothers $(p < .005)$—see Table 6C.2.

Knowledge of the appropriate action to take in the management of common acute symptoms in infancy was greater in the high-user than in the low-user group $(p < .05)$.

In the high-user group 92% of the mothers were given a specific appointment for the baby's first well-baby visit, while in the low-user group only 68% of the mothers received such an appointment $(p < .05)$.

Whereas 22% of the low-user fathers were opposed to well-baby care, only 2% of high-user fathers held this opinion $(p < .05)$.

The experience of having obtained well-baby care for their other children positively affected mothers obtaining care for their study baby. Mothers in the high-user group had made well-baby visits and obtained immunizations for 98% of their older children, whereas mothers in the low-user group only made well-baby visits for 61% and obtained immunizations for 76% of their older children $(p < .001)$—see Table 6C.3.

*Table 6C.2.*  *Trimester in Which Prenatal Care Commenced*
Values in percentages

| Trimester | High-User Mothers ($n = 39$) | Low-User Mothers ($n = 32$) |
|---|---|---|
| First | 64 | 47 |
| Second | 36 | 31 |
| Third | 0 | 21 |
| | 100 | 100 |

*Table 6C.3.  Experience of Older Children Receiving Well-Baby Visits and Immunizations*

All values in percentages

|  | High-Users (n = 116) | Low-Users (n = 102) |
|---|---|---|
| Well-Baby Visits |  |  |
| Received | 98 | 61 |
| Did not receive | 2 | 39 |
|  | 100 | 100 |
| Immunizations |  |  |
| Received | 98 | 76 |
| Did not receive | 2 | 24 |
|  | 100 | 100 |

## Discussion

The well-baby care received by the indigent population in Rochester is poor compared to what is considered optimal. Less than 10% of these babies receive a level of health supervision that is considered adequate by Rochester pediatric standards, and less than 1% receive the level recommended by the American Academy of Pediatrics. Periodic physical examinations, advice regarding routine child care, anticipatory guidance concerning physical and emotional development, screening procedures, and preventive immunizations are not being received by a population that, for reasons of socioeconomic deprivation, might benefit more from these services than the well-to-do. Data concerning the level of well-baby care attained by other population groups are scant. Mindlin and Densen (1971) report that only 33.5% of the babies in a white middle-class district of New York City receive adequate health supervision, and Hoekelman et al. (1973) have found that only 43% of babies living in a rural New York community receive such care.

If we are convinced that well-baby care is important and contributes to the physical and psychosocial well-being of our children (something still to be proved), ways must be found to ensure the entry of each baby into the health care system and to continue contact once entry is gained. It has been shown that hospital based public health nurses significantly increase the entry of indigent babies into the well-baby care delivery system. Whether such programs improve the level of well-baby care once entry into the system is attained, however, remains to be determined. It would seem reasonable to assume that persons less highly trained than public health nurses could be equally effective in getting babies into the well-baby care system and keeping them there.

## REFERENCES

HOEKELMAN, ROBERT A., and PETERS, EDWARD N.
1972  "A Health Supervision Index to Measure Standards of Child Care." *Health Services Report*, 87:537–544.

HOEKELMAN, ROBERT A., ZIMMER, ANNE, and KITZMAN, HARRIET
1973  "Pediatric Nurse Practitioners and Well-Baby Care in a Rural Community." In *ANA Clinical Sessions, 1972*. Englewood Cliffs, N.J.: Appleton-Century-Crofts, Publishing Division of Prentice-Hall.

MINDLIN, ROWLAND L., and DENSEN, PAUL M.
1971  "Medical Care of Urban Infants: Health Supervision." *American Journal of Public Health*, 61 (April): 687–697.

PART THREE

# Recent Changes in Child Health Services

A major goal of all our studies is to provide a basis for the rational allocation of health services to fit the needs of children in the community and to experiment with new ways of meeting these needs.

In Part III we describe several changes in health services that occurred during the study period and the effects of these changes, regardless of whether we initiated them or were simply observers of natural social experiments. In all instances these changes have national significance, for, like Medicaid, the liberalized abortion law, neighborhood health centers, or new health manpower programs, they have also occurred in several other areas of the country. Our contribution was possible because we had a data system in place to evaluate the effects more precisely. Part III should appeal especially to those interested in public policy, for data on the effects of these major innovations have been difficult to obtain. At the same time, policy decisions have had to be made, often without conclusive data. Our hope is to show that careful evaluations will permit better decisions in the future.

Different research designs were employed for different programs. Most of the studies were of the evaluation type, in which goals are set and measurements made to determine how closely these goals are achieved. However, we also conducted several planned experiments. The series of household surveys of random samples of families with children living in the county is described in the (see the Appendix to Chapter 1). They, together with vital statistics, provided a baseline of the level of morbidity and the utilization of health services for the entire community before innovations occurred. Repeat surveys carried out after the new programs were initiated allowed us to make before-after comparisons. In the instance of our major innovation to improve care for the poor (the Rochester Neighborhood Health Center), we developed a design that allowed us to compare the changes in the target area with those in a second, similar poverty area where no such new services had been introduced. In Part III we report descriptions of new programs, their internal evaluations, before-after data for the area served, and comparisons with other similar but unserved areas to assess the effectiveness of the innovations.

The first two chapters deal with major changes brought about through statewide legislation—the introduction of the New York State Medicaid (Title XIX) program in 1966 (Chapter 7) and the liberalized abortion law of 1970 (Chapter 8). The goals of the legislation are well documented and can be used as standards for the evaluation. Having a monitoring system in place for child health services for an entire county allowed us to evaluate these changes more precisely than has been done in other settings. As we have emphasized before, Monroe County has most of the social elements present nationwide. The detailed evaluation of these programs is not possible on a national scale, but is most important for policy makers. These two changes—Medicaid and liberalized abortion—as well as changes in the economic and political status have had a larger impact on child health and medical care than anything we could do in specific programs. This is a major lesson learned from health care research.

Chapter 10 describes a program initiated to meet the specific needs of a given target population—seasonal agricultural migrant workers. This community oriented service program has only a rudimentary research component, but it does illustrate another of our major assumptions: health services need to be organized for defined populations—in this case, migrant workers.

Finally, Chapters 9 and 11 describe new programs, each with a strong evaluation component: Chapter 9 deals with a neighborhood health center; Chapter 11, with new manpower programs that can help all physicians to provide more and better care. In two instances a research design was used with either experimental and control or comparison groups. Such designs, essential in sociomedical research, are difficult to execute and are possible only for relatively small populations. The findings on the effects of the neighborhood health center and on the use of the pediatric nurse practitioner, the family counselor, and the psychodiagnostic assistant will interest all who are concerned with improving child health.

# CHAPTER SEVEN

# The Impact of Medicaid

KLAUS J. ROGHMANN

The Medicaid (Title XIX) legislation is not only one of the most important changes that occurred in the medical care system of our community during the study period, but also the change that is best documented because it is a "public" program. The goals that were intended by the legislature are known from public documents; the benefits anticipated by the consumer, from surveys; and the changes that actually took place, from the data generated by the necessary billing procedures as well as from our regular surveys.

The Medicaid program will be examined as one of the social action programs initiated in the 1960s. Such programs can be regarded as large-scale experiments (Greer, 1969) in which an undesirable prior situation is changed to a new and presumably more desirable state. Although health care professionals have no special right (above their roles as citizens) to define what is politically desirable, they should have input into the feasibility considerations of programs and later be involved in investigating their efficacy and effectiveness.

In a previous paper (Tryon et al., 1970) we reported on the anticipated health behavior of families at the time the New York Medicaid program was being established. A detailed question on this issue had been included in our first survey (1967). In the present chapter the extent to which the program was actually effective in reaching some of its objectives concerning the child population is analyzed for the same community. Some of the findings have already been published elsewhere (Roghmann et al., 1971). The stated objectives were to reduce or eliminate differentials regarding the accessibility, availability, and the quality of medical care, by race and socioeconomic status. It was assumed that these objectives could be achieved simply by reducing the financial barriers for low-income families.

Although the data are only for Monroe County, they are given in greater detail than can be obtained for entire states; furthermore, they provide deeper insight into the reasons for changes than less detailed data on New York State as a whole. Local data systems, if already established, can help to evaluate state and federal programs as they become implemented. (See Appendix to Chapter 7, Note 1.)

*Program Implementation: Were the Eligible Persons Enrolled?*

New York was one of the first states to pass Medicaid legislation, early in 1966. This program in Monroe County started in the middle of 1966 by taking the 20,000 persons on welfare into the program (Medicaid A), thus, from the beginning, covering about 3% of the population (Figure 7.1). The welfare population remained rather stable at that level for about three years. At the beginning of the economic slowdown at the end of 1969, however, the figures began a steady climb to reach, one year later, about 50,000 or 6.4% of the population (706,000). It remained at this level through all of 1971 and 1972.

The enrollment of the medically indigent (Medicaid B, above welfare, but under the income ceiling for eligibility in the program) increased steadily after June 1966, reaching a peak by March 1968. The changes in the law in April 1968, and again in 1969, reduced the number of families eligible by about two thirds. Thus the number of people recognized as "medically indigent" (Medicaid B) fell from 40,000 to about 15,000 and remained at approximately that level all through 1971 and 1972. Altogether, the Medicaid enrollment (Medicaid A and B) reached a first peak in early 1968 and a second peak in early 1971, covering about 9% of the population. Because of age-specific eligibility criteria, the coverage for children was, at that time, about 12.5%.

The Medicaid program is so well known in this community, and procedures for enrollment into the program are so well established, that about

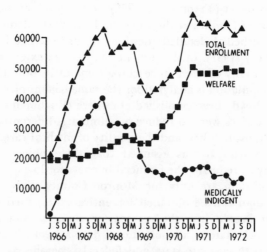

*Figure 7.1.   Enrollment in Medicaid program, 1966–1972.*

90% of eligible children are enrolled. Because of the frequent changes in the eligibility conditions of families and the frequent reviews, people are constantly going on and off the program. The present enrollment percentage for eligible children is probably a ceiling that cannot be raised.

Monroe County's Medicaid expenditure started out at an annual level of 14 million dollars in 1966 and rose to an estimated 32 million dollars in 1971. Of the total estimated personal health expenditure in the county, for all ages per year, of 230 million dollars, the Medicaid budget accounted for about 13%, but only 9% of the population. This was about twice the amount of all Blue Shield payments and nearly as large as the Blue Cross outlay. Nursing homes and the care of the aged took about 50% of all expenditures in 1968, and nearly 60% in 1970. With Medicaid expenses, even more than with other health costs, the aged take a disproportionate amount of all resources. Thus, although children comprise about 50% of all people on the Medicaid roll, they account for only 10% of the total cost. The total medical care outlay for the approximately 30,000 Medicaid children in 1970 amounted to only 3.6 million dollars (or about $120/child/year).

*Greater Accessibility and Availability of Child Care:*
*Results from the 1967, 1969, and 1971 Surveys*

To check the extent to which the goal of greater accessibility had been achieved over the first six years of the program, results from the household surveys were compared (Roghmann and Haggerty, 1970; 1972). The key question is whether socioeconomic differentials in access to health care had been reduced. The evidence shows that they had not, and that, possibly, the opposite had occurred.

In Monroe County in 1967 nearly 90% of the children not on Medicaid had a private practitioner as the usual source of care. Among those enrolled in the Medicaid program, however, only 45% had a private practitioner. In 1969 and 1971 the situation generally changed for the worse. The proportion of Medicaid children with a private physician decreased to 30% in 1969 and 28% in 1971. On the other hand, the percentage of Medicaid children with a "regular place" of care (outpatient clinic or health center) increased from 33% in 1967 to 57% in 1971, whereas the proportion of Medicaid children with no regular source of care decreased from 22% to 15%.

A more specific question was asked about the place of the last immunization for children aged 1–5. In 1967, for 85% of children not on Medicaid a private doctor was given as the place of the last immunization, as compared with 29% of those enrolled on Medicaid. After the Medicaid program had been in operation for three years, the pattern had not changed in the direction of greater accessibility of care in the private sector. In 1969, 88% of the children not on Medicaid reported their last immunization from a private doctor, as compared with only 23% of the Medicaid children. Similar findings were seen for 1971. Hospital outpatient departments continued to be a major source of well-child care for Medicaid children over the study period, but "other clinics" (including health centers) gained ground. In 1967 the latter provided about one third of the well-child care; in 1969 and 1971 their share increased to some 40%. This increase is primarily due to the OEO funded Rochester Neighborhood Health Center (now the Anthony Jordan Health Center), established in late 1968 in one of the two poverty areas. This center was serving 2500 children plus a similar number of adults in 1969, most of whom were on Medicaid.

Socioeconomic differentials noted in 1967 persisted not only for the source of care, but also for the amount of care received. Comparing the rates of utilization of health services per child per year in 1969, we found that children registered for Blue Cross hospital insurance (one measure of middle-class or upper-class status, because at least one parent is employed in the local economy) had, on the average, 5.4 medical contacts per year, nearly all with private practitioners. Children on the Medicaid program had only 3.7 visits per year, of which fewer than half were with private practitioners.

An analysis of these visits by purpose shows that most of the difference between Medicaid and non-Medicaid enrollees lies in the number of preventive visits, but there is also a small difference in the illness related visits. Medicaid enrolled children had 40% fewer preventive visits per year than Blue Cross covered children, and about 20% fewer illness related visits. When dental care rates are analyzed, the differences between the two child populations are even more pronounced: Medicaid enrolled children had only one third as many visits as Blue Cross covered children. These low figures for Medicaid enrolled children for 1969 are probably accentuated because of a 20% dental fee cut in 1968, after which most dentists in this community withdrew from the Medicaid program.

Evidence confirming a failure to achieve greater accessibility to private care comes also from the annual report of the Monroe County Medical Assistance Program for 1969:

We believe that in 1969 physicians began to refuse to accept new Medicaid patients, and as individuals became active on Medicaid, they were unable to find physicians who would care for them privately. These patients presumably went to clinics for care. It is accepted that care in hospital clinics is considerably more expensive than care in a physician's office. Thus the net result of the fee cut on the cost of ambulatory care per capita was to raise the cost of ambulatory care by 31% (Ames et al., 1970).

One year later, the annual report for 1970 read:

Major declines (in expenses) took place in dental services, down 55%, and physician services, down 25%. . . . As long as Medicaid pays below the market rate for these services, professionals will be unwilling to take Medicaid patients on the same basis as they take their regular patients. This inevitably drives patients to the more expensive clinics (Ames et al., 1971).

*Quality of Care Received: Results from the 1967, 1969, and 1971 Surveys*

Although it is difficult to evaluate the quality of care by survey methods, two generally accepted indicators of quality are immunization status and dental check-ups.

Reported immunization for diphtheria-pertussis-tetanus has been quite high in Monroe County—between 81% and 97% in all population groups. There is little difference between Medicaid and non-Medicaid patients, or among the years 1967, 1969, and 1971. Moreover, most of the differences in percentage of affirmative answers are due to different levels of "Can't remember" responses by the Blue Cross and Medicaid populations. Major differences, however, still exist in the reported immunization status against smallpox. The 1967 figures indicate that only 65% of Medicaid enrolled children were immunized, as compared with nearly 90% of other children. There may have been some real improvement in 1969, when 74% of Medicaid enrolled children were immunized, but the 1971 figures do not support this interpretation. Recommendations to discontinue smallpox vaccinations made in 1971 confound this figure, but there probably was no change between 1967 and 1971. A similar statement can be made for poliomyelitis vaccinations. Reported immunization against measles, however, increased for all children between 1967 and 1969, and the 1971 data confirm this trend. For non-Medicaid-registered children, the proportion immunized increased from 70% to about 80%; for Medicaid children the increase was from 30% to 70%.

Thus immunization figures, except for measles, are not encouraging

The second indicator for quality of care, regular dental check-ups, also fails to show improvement. On the contrary, the proportion of Medicaid enrolled children receiving regular dental check-ups declined from about 57% to about 43%.

To summarize, there is no evidence that socioeconomic differentials as to accessibility, availability, or quality have changed in the direction intended by the legislation. Poor families are still more likely to receive less care, to depend more on public clinics, and to have a higher proportion of illness related, rather than preventive, medical contacts. Instead of diminishing socioeconomic differentials as intended by the legislators, better financing of medical care for the poor has led to a solidification of the old two-tiered system. On the whole, however, the quality of care, as measured by these limited indices, has not suffered. The increased use of measles vaccination in both the private and the public sector indicates that acceptance of this innovation was independent of source of care.

The findings presented here may be contrary to the legislators' intentions, but they come as no surprise to researchers in the field. In an earlier emergency room utilization study (Roghmann, 1967) it was found that few Medicaid enrollees had (1) tried to find a private doctor, (2) increased their utilization of medical services, or (3) changed their sources of care. This is exactly what had been predicted by the attitudes observed in the poor before the onset of the program (Tryon et al., 1970). Hence, although the Medicaid program may have been a success in enrolling eligible persons, it was unsuccessful in reaching its declared objectives. Enrolling the poor and paying for their care is one thing; improving either the quality or the availability and accessibility of care is another.

*Analysis of Medicaid Payment Files*[1]

Up to now in this chapter, the household interview surveys have been used to study the impact of the Medicaid program, but other data systems are available which, although maintained for different purposes, can also be employed in this research. For this study the Medicaid payment files, which in many communities form the largest local medical care utilization data system, were examined to study effects of changes within the program. The files cover nearly all the medical expenses of those enrolled and are well maintained because of the public accountability of the program. A detailed description of the files is given in the Appendix to Chapter 7.

1 This is a modified version of an article published in *Medical Care* (Roghmann, 1974).

Some Selected Results on an Aggregate Basis

This discussion is limited to an analysis of physicians' and clinics' claims for Medicaid enrollees up to 17 years of age.

Claims for services delivered by *private physicians* are submitted on an IBM claim card which can cover several visits. In 1968 there were 43,000 physician claims, covering at least 50,000 *visits*. By 1970 the claims had decreased 44%—to 24,000, and the visits had decreased 50%—to 25,000. The cost for *one* physician visit claim remained about the same—$9.70. The cost per *two or more* visit claims, however, increased from $15 to $20, probably because of a shift toward a higher proportion of inpatient services and, perhaps, to physicians scheduling more visits per illness to compensate for the reduced fee for each visit. Such a shift is also reflected in changes in the types of visits reported. The number of emergency treatments (injuries and accidents) increased 25%; the number of teenage deliveries, about 15%. But acute disease treatments decreased an average of 45%, while check-ups and well-baby care declined 56%.

Major differences also existed by area served. Private doctors' services to children from the health center target area declined 21% (from 2300 to 1800 claims), but those to children from the second poverty area (the comparison area) more than doubled between the two years (from 1650 to 3600 claims). The bulk of the reduction in private physician services occurred in the "rest of the city" (−53%), where most of the marginally poor live.

There can be no doubt that drastic changes occurred in the amount of care given by private physicians to children of the poor between the two years studied. These changes reflect at least three factors: first, an increase in the "basic assistance" population, balanced by a decrease in the "medical assistance" population; second, changes in the care facilities of the two poverty areas, such as the new health center in the target area; and, third, changes in the reimbursement from customary fee to a set amount lower than customary (and later cut a further 20%), which led many private practitioners to withdraw from the program.

Claims for services delivered to children at *clinics* are submitted on an IBM Medicaid claim card "for one clinic visit," thus eliminating the distinction between claims and visits that is required for analyzing the private physician claim files. Clinic visits of children increased between the two study years by 23%—from 45,000 to 56,000. The average cost per visit increased 50%, rising from about $14 to $21. This overall picture, so different from that portrayed by the doctors' claim files, is clouded by a number of important changes by providers. Visits to clinics at hospitals, mostly to emergency rooms, declined slightly over the two years, from

Table 7.1.  Clinic Visits of Children under 18 Paid For by Medicaid in 1968 and 1970, by Clinic Facility, Monroe County, New York[a]

|  | 1968 | 1970 | Change % |
|---|---|---|---|
| **Target Area (Seventh Ward)**[b] |  |  |  |
| Strong Memorial Hospital | 5,923 | 4,239 | −28.4 |
| Genesee Hospital | 2,743 | 2,383 | −13.1 |
| Other hospital clinics | 1,576 | 1,556 | − 1.3 |
|  | 10,242 | 8,178 | −20.2 |
| Rochester Neighborhood Health Center | 661 | 10,643 | [c] |
| Eastman Dental Dispensary | 667 | 604 | − 9.4 |
| Rochester Mental Health Center | 38 | 274 | [c] |
| Other nonhospital clinics | 186 | 113 | −39.3 |
|  | 1,552 | 11,634 | [c] |
| **Comparison Area (Third Ward)**[b] |  |  |  |
| Strong Memorial Hospital | 5,806 | 5,500 | − 5.3 |
| Genesee Hospital | 787 | 890 | +13.1 |
| Other hospital clinics | 1,960 | 2,545 | +29.8 |
|  | 8,553 | 8,935 | + 4.5 |
| Rochester Neighborhood Health Center | 23 | 258 | [c] |
| Eastman Dental Dispensary | 803 | 528 | −34.2 |
| Rochester Mental Health Center | 66 | 106 | [c] |
| Other nonhospital clinics | 129 | 747 | + 479 |
|  | 1,021 | 1,639 | + 60 |

| Rest of City and Suburbs[b] | | | |
|---|---:|---:|---:|
| Strong Memorial Hosptial | 8,658 | 8,271 | − 4.4 |
| Genesee Hospital | 4,601 | 4,731 | + 2.8 |
| Other hospital clinics | 5,187 | 6,814 | +31.4 |
| | 18,446 | 19,816 | + 7.4 |
| Rochester Neighborhood Health Center | 184 | 1,776 | c |
| Eastman Dental Dispensary | 1,647 | 1,830 | +11.1 |
| Rochester Mental Health Center | 95 | 917 | c |
| Other nonhospital clinics | 116 | 693 | + 497 |
| | 2,042 | 5,216 | c |

[a] From Roghmann (1974), p. 185.
[b] Census tract coding was successful in the clinic claims file; unmatched services were allocated proportionately.
[c] New facilities—percentage change would be meaningless.

37,200 to 36,900. Strong Memorial Hospital, which traditionally supplies about 50% of all medical care to the poor in Monroe County, had a 12% decrease in visits. For Genesee Hospital, the second largest provider of clinic care, there was a 2% decrease. Visits to other than hospital clinics increased fourfold, from 4500 to 18,500. Most of the increase was due to the availability of the health center. Another large increase was due to expanded mental health services.

Again there were major differences by area served. Visits to hospital clinics from the health center target area decreased by 2000 or 20%; those from the comparison area increased by 400 or 5%. Those from the rest of the community increased by 1400 visits or 7% (see Table 7.1). The various hospitals reflected this change to different extents. Medicaid visits to Strong Memorial Hospital declined no matter where patients came from. The decrease from the target area was 28%, from the comparison area 5%, and from the rest of the community 4%. Genesee Hospital lost 350 visits from the health center target area, but gained 100 from the comparison area.

Most of the increased services given by the nonhospital clinics occurred in the health center target area: the number of nonhospital clinic visits rose from 1500 to 11,500. Services to the second poverty area, however, increased only from 1000 to 1600, chiefly because of an expanded health department clinic.

On first inspection of these results it is remarkable that, with an increase of 10,000 health center visits from the target area, hospital clinic visits were reduced by only 2000. But it should not be forgotten that there was also a decrease of 500 private physician and 300 private dentist claims. And the comparison with the second poverty area is even more important. This comparison area, with about the same number of children, had about 2000 more private physician claims in 1970, about 1000 more private dentist claims, 400 more hospital clinic visits, and 600 more "other clinic" visits. Had there been no health center, a similar increase of about 4000 services from the target area should have been expected. The observed decrease of nearly 3000 services should be seen in relation to this "expected" increase. The 10,000 additional services by the health center probably met 70% of the needs that would otherwise have had to be filled elsewhere, and about 30% of the needs that would have remained unmet. The results are consistent with findings from two earlier studies based on emergency room usage (Hochheiser et al., 1971; Roghmann, 1971). The present study, using information on all ambulatory services, gives a better picture of the total impact, including alternative services.

Exploratory Study of Individual Families

The preceding analysis was limited to the aggregate of claims or visits. This only permits the computation of utilization rates if the base population served is known. What is not revealed is the variation in utilization rates within areas or between individual patients and families. There is no reason, however, why the information from the Medicaid files cannot be sorted by Medicaid number or by individual within a family to provide such information. This also is a convenient way to check for possible errors in the file (see Appendix to Chapter 7, Note 2). An exploratory study based on a small random sample of families was done for this purpose. Medicaid families interviewed in our 1969 household survey were studied as to their children's expenses for hospital admissions, dental care, private physician visits, and clinic services. The average cost per child in 1968 was $82. By 1970 the figure had risen to $98. These costs were somewhat lower than the figure quoted previously (about $120 per child) because expenses for medications and other health services were not included in the present analysis.

To summarize, the analysis of Medicaid claim files provided new insights into the changing pattern of medical care for the poor that could not be gained by other methods. Major shifts occurred in the population base: the number of welfare recipients increased; the number of "medically needy" people was cut by stricter eligibility criteria; and increased unemployment left more families without Blue Cross coverage. The changes in the population base affected the different socioeconomic and sociopolitical areas to different degrees. There were also major shifts in the delivery system: hospitals tended to specialize further in certain areas (e.g., new intensive care nurseries were opened), and payment mechanisms changed. Unless these changes are known and are controlled for in evaluation studies, the pure effects of new medical care programs like the neighborhood health center cannot be assessed accurately.

*Discussion*

The basic question behind this analysis was whether medical care of the poor had been improved. Removing the financial burden was the major approach under Title XIX. In the household interview respondents on Medicaid frequently mentioned the financial relief afforded them by enrollment in the program. However, although they appreciated the help, it did not change their health care patterns. To some extent this was due to satisfaction with the currently used hospital care by poor patients, but another reason was the refusal of many private practitioners to care for the poor. For physicians to be willing to participate, the fees paid for services delivered to Medicaid patients must be equal to those received for care to middle-class patients. A survey of private practitioners in our community showed that they would welcome Medicaid patients if "usual and customary" fees were paid.[2] When such fees were paid in 1967-1968, progress was made in having private physicians involved in the care of the poor.

As stated previously, however, the majority of poor patients did not change their patterns of care. To make the program a success, marketing efforts to bring the consumers and suppliers of services together are required. Expansion of scarce medical manpower, improved transportation, outreach, culturally acceptable personnel and settings, and consumer participation in the working of the program are examples of such efforts. Last, but not least, the consumer and the provider must be given some time to change their attitudes toward each other and to develop a continuous personal relationship. The present Medicaid review procedure leads to a rapid turnover of patients in the program; frequent administrative changes result in a constant turnover of doctors willing to accept new or to serve old Medicaid patients. Our society shows a trend toward more impersonal, one-contact type of relations; the Medicaid program has certainly reinforced this tendency. The passive administration of a constantly changing Medicaid program without involvement of the consumer and the supplier has, in many respects, proved to be a failure. Whether the addition of the suggested components of a comprehensive, long-term program will achieve the goals sought remains to be seen.

[2] Proposal for a Community Health Network, Rochester, New York, Neighborhood Health Centers of Monroe County, Inc., April 15, 1971.

REFERENCES

AMES, W.R., JESMER, J.B., STOCKDALE, D.K., and GREENHUT, J.
  1970  Monroe County Medical Assistance Program 1969: Analysis of Selected Statistics (mimeographed). Rochester, New York: Monroe County Department of Health and Social Services.

AMES, W.R., RUSSO, G. STOCKDALE, D.K., and GREENHUT, J.
  1971  Monroe County Medical Assistance Program 1970: Analysis of Selected Statistics (mimeographed). Rochester, New York: Monroe County Department of Health and Social Services.

The Impact of Medicaid

209

GREER, S.A.

1969  *The Logic of Social Inquiry*. Chicago: Aldine Publishing Company, p. 195.

HOCHHEISER, L.I., WOODWARD, K., and CHARNEY, E.

1971  "Effect of the Neighborhood Health Center on the Use of Pediatric Emergency Departments in Rochester, New York." *New England Journal of Medicine*, 285(3):148–152.

ROGHMANN, KLAUS

1967  *Emergency Room Survey* (mimeographed).

ROGHMANN, K.J., and HAGGERTY, R.J.

1970  "Rochester Child Health Surveys. I: Objectives, Organization and Methods." *Medical Care*, 8:47–59.

ROGHMANN, K.J.

1971  "Looking for the Medical Crisis in Utilization Data." Paper Read at Health Services Research Conference: Factors in Manpower Performance in Delivery of Health Care, Center for Continuing Education. Department of Health, Education, and Welfare, Health Services and Mental Health Administration.

ROGHMANN, K.J., HAGGERTY, R.J., and LORENZ, R.

1971  "Anticipated and Actual Effects of Medicaid on the Medical Care Pattern of Children." *New England Journal of Medicine*, 285:1053–1057.

ROGHMANN, K.J., and HAGGERTY, R.J.

1972  "The Diary as a Research Instrument in the Study of Health and Illness Behavior: Experiences with a Random Sample of Young Families." *Medical Care*, 10(2):143–163.

ROGHMANN, KLAUS J.

1974  "Use of Medicaid Payment Files for Medical Care Research." *Medical Care*, 12:(2):131–137.

TYRON, A.F., POWELL, E., and ROGHMANN, K.J.

1970  "Anticipated Health Behavior of Families in Relation to Medicaid." *Public Health Reports*, 85:1021–1028.

# CHAPTER EIGHT

# The Impact of the New York State Abortion Law

KLAUS J. ROGHMANN

On July 1, 1970, a new law went into effect in New York State, permitting abortions to be performed on consenting women no more than 24 weeks pregnant. There were no restrictions as to residence or facility. Over 7000 abortions were performed in the first two and one-half years under the new law: 1269 legally induced abortions were performed· on Monroe County residents in the last six months of 1970 (93% were done within the county); 2838 in 1971 (76% within the county); and 3016 in 1972 (74% within the county). In spite of family planning counseling efforts, the monthly figures in 1973 show no decline. These legal abortions are reported to the County Office of Vital Statistics in a format similar to that used for births (see Section 3A). Sufficient time has passed since the abortion law went into effect to assess its overall impact.

The new law had a profound effect on the need for health services in our community. About 20% of all pregnancies were terminated in 1971 and about 24% in 1972. The number of live births dropped by 15% in 1971, and by another 14% in 1972. Fetal deaths decreased even more (−35%) in the first year, while premature births and infant deaths reached an all-time low. It will be argued in this chapter that the 1971 drop in live births reflected the true extent of normally unwanted pregnancies, and not a temporary phenomenon due to other factors such as the economic recession; and that the decrease will have a major impact on pediatric manpower needs, pediatric bed needs, and, after a delay of five years, on school enrollments.

Because of the six to seven months' lag time, the number of abortions performed in 1970 had little effect on the number of live births until 1971. Indeed, for 1970, both white and black births reached new peaks (11,356 white births; 1919 black births). But in 1971 white births fell by 1900, black births by 100. A total of 2000 fewer infants were born in

Monroe County in 1971 than in the previous year. The birthrate dropped from 17.3 to 14.1 per 1000 for whites, and from 34.2 to 27.8 for blacks. Illegitimate births declined in all predominantly white areas, reversing the trend of the earlier years of steadily increasing illegitimacy ratios. No such effect occurred, however, for black illegitimate births; ratios as well as absolute figures continued to rise. In the black areas of Rochester, 56% of all children were reported as illegitimate in 1971.

There is good reason to believe that the liberalization of the abortion law will have many other profound effects on child and maternal health needs. Too often, neglect of family planning or ineffective birth control methods lead to unplanned and frequently unwanted pregnancies (Bumpass and Westoff, 1970) characterized by insufficient pre- and post-natal care, a high incidence of prematurity, and high ratios of later child neglect. In New York City, since the passage of the abortion law, a dramatic decrease in maternal morbidity and mortality has been observed (Pakter and Nelson, 1971; *Family Planning Digest*, 1972a). The recent drop in infant mortality has been partly attributed to the availability of legal abortions (*Family Planning Digest*, 1972a, 1972b). Thus the widespread reduction in unwanted children will have long-term effects on the health level of children and on the need for medical care beyond the extent suggested by the reduction of the birthrate. In fact it has been argued that "legalizing abortions [is] one of the most useful and effective social reform measures" (Schwartz, 1972:1335). This chapter attempts to assess the short-term effects in our community by analyzing both aggregate and individual data. Of special interest is the testing of alternative explanations for the drop in births, such as the economic recession of 1970, a factor known to have reduced birthrates in the past.

## Aggregate Analysis by Census Tract

In order to assess the effect of the abortion law on a census tract basis, the abortion ratio[1] in 1971 was computed for each of the 142 census tracts. Only abortions performed inside Monroe County could be considered in this computation, as census tract information was available only for these. A regression analysis was performed to study the effect of the abortion

[1] The terminology follows the convention that measures relating abortions to women or total populations are referred to as *rates*, whereas measures relating abortions to births or pregnancies are *ratios* (World Health Organization, 1970). Our analysis related abortions to live births plus abortions. This type of abortion ratio approximates the ratio per 1000 pregnancies. We will also use the term "termination ratio" when abortions outside Monroe County are considered in estimating total pregnancies.

ratio in 1971, as an independent variable, on the *change* in birthrate, prematurity ratio, illegitimacy ratio and infant mortality during the same year as dependent variables. Other independent variables that affect these dependent variables were controlled in a stepwise fashion[2]: 1) measures of *age structure* (percentage of population under 18, over 65, or being female and 15-44 years of age) were used to control statistically for the different age compositions of the census tracts; 2) *social status* was measured by such indicators as median family income, percentage of male labor force employed, median house value, and median rent; 3) *cultural background* was measured by the percentage of children living in a traditional husband-wife family unit and by the percentage of blacks in the census tract; and 4) *economic change* between 1968 and 1970 was measured by the increase of welfare recipients in each tract.

A second regression analysis used, as dependent variable, *rates* such as the birthrate, illegitimacy ratio, and prematurity ratio for the year 1971. Infant and fetal deathrates, however, were averaged for the five and three years preceding 1971 because the annual absolute numbers were rather small on a census tract basis, and therefore subject to large yearly random fluctuations. Prediction of the yearly *rates* using all of the independent variables was successful: illegitimacy ratio $(R = .95)$, birthrate $(R = .82)$, prematurity ratio $(R = .62)$, infant mortality ratio $(R = .70)$, and fetal deathrate $(R = .49)$. The *changes*, however, could not be predicted to the same extent. The multiple correlation ranged from $R = .29$ (prematurity) to $R = .53$ (illegitimacy).

The correlations between selected independent variables and these dependent variables are of greater interest. Social status (median income in 1970) correlated most strongly with the *rates*, and always in a negative direction: the higher the income, the lower the birthrate $(r = -.63)$ illegitimacy ratio $(r = -.68)$, prematurity ratio $(r = -.34)$, infant mortality ratio $(r = -.54)$, and even fetal deathrate $(r = -.17)$. Income did not, however, correlate as strongly with the *changes*.[3] There was no correlation between income and the abortion ratio. The abortion ratio had the highest correlation with change in white births $(r = -.34)$, change in

---

[2] Only after these independent variables were controlled for in the first 4 steps was the abortion ratio introduced in step 5.

[3] The correlational analysis used a standard statistical package (Nie et al., 1970) that allows weighting. To consider the different sizes of census tracts in the city and suburbs and the different numbers of blacks and whites in each, we used weights in this analysis (1000s of white, nonwhite, or total population). As a result, the standard significance tests cannot be used on the printout. (With an $n = 142$, an $r$ of .15 is required at the $p = .05$ level and an $r$ of .20 at the $p = .01$ level.) Some of the regressions were repeated without a weight factor to examine the effects of the weights. Some changes did occur, but not enough to alter our main conclusions.

white illegitimacy ($r = -.30$), and change in white premature babies ($r = -.12$). These correlations indicate only the direction and strength of the relationships, not the pure effect of each variable controlling for other preceding independent variables.

The proportions of the *explained* variance accounted for by the different independent variable groups, in the order in which they were introduced into the equation by stepwise regression, are more informative. Social status accounted for most of the explained variance in the yearly *rates*, but the economic change and the abortion ratio accounted for more of the explained variance in the *change* measures. It was found that 50% of the explained decline in the birthrate and 25% of the explained reduction in the prematurity ratio were due to abortions. For infant mortality change, however, the abortion ratio was of minor influence. The economic recession, as measured, was of minor importance for determining the drop in birthrates (but possibly contributed to higher prematurity ratios and fetal deathrates)—a finding supported by the fact that economic recovery in 1972 did not bring an increase in live births.

## Analysis of Individual Data

The explorative analysis by census tract answered many questions without a lengthy and expensive prospective study; however, the analysis was limited to the level of aggregate data. Individual data for 1971 and 1972 are also available from birth and abortion certificates. If the live births and the abortions reported by the County Department of Vital Statistics as occurring *in* the county, and the abortions reported by the New York State Health Department for Monroe County residents occurring *outside* the county, are totaled, a comprehensive count of "pregnancies" in the community is found and the number terminated (termination ratio= induced abortions per 1000 pregnancies) can be computed.

There was no difference between the white (202/1000) and the black (195/1000) termination ratios in 1971, consistent with an earlier observation that the abortion ratio did not correlate with income or other status variables. In 1972 the termination ratio for whites increased to 236/1000, and for "non-whites" to 243/1000. The ratio for Puerto Ricans (110/1000 in 1971, 120/1000 in 1972) is lower, as is that for other nonwhites (134/1000 in 1971, 122/1000 in 1972). Black and white women differ to the extent that they go outside Monroe County for their abortions. About 19% of the white women went outside in 1971, as compared with about 10% of the black.

Legitimacy, however, is a major determinant of abortion. In 1971 and

1972 only 9% of married couples' pregnancies were terminated, compared to 54% (1971) and 63% (1972) of pregnancies of unmarried women. Legitimacy has the strongest effects on whites: 73% of illegitimate white pregnancies were terminated in 1971, compared with only 8% of legitimate white pregnancies. For blacks, legitimacy is of less importance. Only 27% of black illegitimate pregnancies were terminated in 1971, compared with 11% of black legitimate pregnancies. For both groups abortion seems to function as a last resort birth control method, but illegitimacy apparently has less social stigma for blacks than for whites.

Pregnancy history is also an important determinant of abortion. Of first pregnancies 23% were terminated in 1971, but of second pregnancies only 9%. The termination ratio increased again after three to five pregnancies (18%) and six or more pregnancies (21%). The 1972 figures show the same pattern, but at a slightly higher level.

For abortion, maternal age is similar in importance to illegitimacy. Pregnancies of women under 15 were terminated in nearly 51% of all cases in 1971. For women 15–19 years old the ratio was 32%. In the 20–29 age group the ratio dropped to 15%. For the 30–39 age group it rose again to 21%, and reached 39% for pregnant women 40 years and older. Again, the 1972 ratios showed the same U-shaped relationship with age as in 1971, but at a slightly higher level (Roghmann, 1975).

Legal abortion in our county is neither a phenomenon of the poor, like infant mortality and illegitimacy, nor a privilege of the suburban middle class. Instead, such abortions seem to be the result of a rational decision based on individual life histories. Pregnancies too early or too late in a woman's life, and first or high-parity pregnancies, are more likely to be terminated. The pregnancy that results from a nonmarital relationship is most likely to be terminated if, as in white society, social stigma or occupational disadvantages are associated with raising children out of wedlock.

*Trend Analysis*

The preceding analyses, on the aggregate and the individual level, ignored time lags and related events occurring in the same year. Looking at events over time provides additional information, and plotting monthly figures (see Figure 8.1) is a first step in this direction. Although there was no abrupt drop in live births, a steady decline started as early as four months after abortions became legal and continued through all of 1971. The monthly live birth figure then stabilized in early 1972.

The monthly figure for abortions performed within the county re-

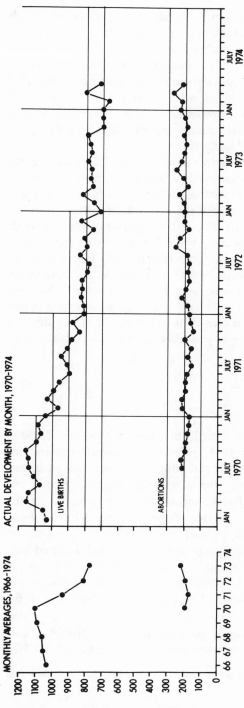

Figure 8.1.  Live births and induced abortions, Monroe County, New York.

The Impact of the New York State Abortion Law

215

mained stable at around 200; the figure for abortions performed outside the county may have risen slightly to about 50 per month.[4]

Fetal deaths[5] not due to induced abortion declined, as did live births. In November and December 1970 they dropped about one third below the previous year's figures. Prematurity ratios also went below the 1969 figures in November 1970 and did not stabilize at the lower level until 12 months later. Neonatal deaths showed large monthly random fluctuations (average number of neonatal deaths per month is only 13 in the county) that prevented any trend analysis.

To summarize, wherever plotting by month was possible, evidence was found that the impact of the abortion law became effective four to six months after July 1970. The monthly level of live births in early 1972 was 300 below the monthly 1970 level; only about two thirds of this drop was probably due to induced abortions. The rest was probably due to a lower number of pregnancies because of more effective conception control methods and changes in desired family size. No evidence was found that economic developments contributed to the drop by temporarily influencing family size or child spacing. Nor was there any evidence for a dramatic technological breakthrough that would have led to an abrupt improvement in conception control methods in late 1970, although the steady drop in birthrates throughout the 1960s was probably due to a modernization of family planning methods.

*Discussion*

The decrease in the number of live births by about 4000—from 13,000 in 1970 to approximately 9000 in 1973—reduced the annual demand for pediatric visits in 1973 by at least 30,000. But this is certainly an underestimate of the real drop in needs, for all evidence indicates that it was the group of children from high-risk mothers that was reduced, not the group of children "planned" by married couples in their twenties. Fetal deaths in 1970-1972 declined 50% (from 890 to 469), while premature births dropped 30% (1094 to 773). Infant deaths, which had declined 20% from 1969 to 1970, fell another 6% in 1971 and 8% in 1972. It is reasonable to expect health indicators like "battered children" or emotional and behavioral problems due to unwanted or neglected children to also de-

---

[4] There was probably underreporting of abortions, particularly from New York City, in the first months after the law became effective. The rise, especially in 1972, may only reflect better reporting.

[5] Fetal deaths in New York State since 1967 include all deaths of recognized conceptions.

cline in the years ahead. Though the pregnancies of highest risk for infant mortality were also those with the greatest chance for an abortion, there are still large high-risk groups of mothers not choosing to have abortions. The infant mortality of children born to teenage mothers is 27/1000; that for children born to mothers aged 25–29, 15/1000. In 1969 about 12% of all live births were to teenage mothers; in 1972, nearly 14%. Thus the temporary decline in infant mortality due to abortions was soon balanced by the relative increase in teenage deliveries.

The statistical analysis, as well as the abruptness of the drop in birthrate from one year to the next, points to the liberalized abortion law as a main causal factor for the change. This local evidence is consistent with statewide (N.Y. State Department of Health, 1972) and nationwide (*Family Planning Perspectives*, 1972:7; Duffy, 1971) figures. No indication was found that the drop in the birthrate is a temporary one due to the economic recession. The existence of an easily available and accessible means to legally end an unwanted pregnancy resulted in the termination of many of the high-risk unwanted pregnancies in our community.

This effect will, of course, be evaluated differently by different people. The view of abortion as "one of the most useful and effective social reform measures" will not be shared by all. To many, abortion as a last means of birth control will remain unacceptable, as have methods of conception control. The benefits of effective family planning in physical, emotional, and economic terms for both individuals and for society, however, are widely accepted by most. The debate concerns the permissible means to achieve this goal, especially the availability of a second chance if conception control proves ineffective. In the past, and even today, methods varying from sexual abstinence to infanticide have been used to control population growth in various cultures. No matter how educators and health planners personally evaluate abortion, they must have knowledge of its short- and long-term effects.

A final point should be made about the interpretation of these data. *Attitudes toward abortion* as a last resort in family planning efforts have been changing during the study period. These changes were not measured in this community, but they probably did not precede the legislation. Acceptance of abortion, in our view, has increased since the legislation was passed because abortions are now legal and part of the regular medical care system. The change in attitude will have a feedback effect in this field of health behavior but was not crucial in bringing about the law. *Attitudes about family size* have also changed, namely, toward smaller families, but this is probably part of a long-term trend and not directly related to the economic developments or the abortion law, either as a cause or an effect (Fine and Pless, 1974). The economic optimism and national pride that accompanied the post-World War II baby boom have been replaced in recent years by a new evaluation of the long-term economic and national outlook.

The main lesson that may be learned from this analysis is that factors beyond the control of the physician and health planner shape the need for conventional child health services, and that the manpower projection of last year may already be outdated this year. The abortion law and dropping birthrate have had a greater impact on the medical care system than have most of the new medical care delivery programs introduced in the past decade. Once some of the immediate demands on pediatricians are reduced, physicians may choose to turn part of their attention to other problems of childhood. The challenge to work for the improvement of the quality of life for children is even greater than the challenge of the past to prevent illness. In our view, the reduction of high-risk births is one step toward the goal of guaranteeing that every child is well born.

## REFERENCES

BUMPASS, LARRY, and WESTOFF, CHARLES F.

1970 "Unwanted Births and U.S. Popuation Growth." *Family Planning Perspectives*, 2(4):9–11.

DUFFY, EDWARD A.

1971 *The Effect of Changes in the State Abortion Laws.* Department of Health, Education, and Welfare, Health Services and Mental Health Administration, Public Health Service, Publication No. 2165. Washington, D.C.: Government Printing Office.

*Family Planning Digest*

1972a "Health, Social Impact of Legalized Abortions." *Family Planning Digest*, 1(4):13–15.

1972b "Family Planning Can Cut Infant Mortality." *Family Planning Digest*, 1(2):7–8.

*Family Planning Perspectives*

1972 "Has Legal Abortion Contributed to U.S. Birth Dearth?" *Family Planning Perspectives*, 4(2):7–8.

FINE, A., and PLESS, I. BARRY

1974 "Family Planning and Population Control." *Social Biology* 20:(4):416–420.

NEW YORK STATE DEPARTMENT OF HEALTH

1972 *Report of Selected Characteristics on Induced Abortions in N.Y. State, January-December 1971* (mimeograph).

NIE, NORMAN, BENT, DALE H., and HULL, C. HADLAI

1970    SPSS—Statistical Package for the Social Sciences. New York: McGraw-Hill Book Company.

PAKTER, JEAN, and NELSON, FRIEDA

1971    "Abortion in New York City: The First Nine Months." Family Planning Perspectives, 3(3):5–12.

ROGHMANN, KLAUS J.

1975    "The Impact of the New York State Abortion Law on Black and White Fertility in Upstate New York." International Journal of Epidemiology, 4(1):(in press).

SCHWARTZ, RICHARD A.

1972    "The Social Effects of Legal Abortion." American Journal of Public Health, 62(10):1331–1335.

WORLD HEALTH ORGANIZATION

1970    Spontaneous and Induced Abortion. Technical Report Series No. 461. Geneva, Switzerland.

# CHAPTER NINE

# The Rochester Neighborhood Health Center

## A. HISTORY AND PHILOSOPHY

ROBERT J. HAGGERTY AND KLAUS J. ROGHMANN

The idea of the Rochester Neighborhood Health Center was conceived to meet two needs: (1) the long-standing lack of medical care in an old Rochester neighborhood (Seventh Ward), and (2) the need for a more realistic setting for teaching primary care at the medical school. It took the combined efforts of many community groups and agencies, as well as financial help from the Office of Economic Opportunity, to translate this idea into actuality. This section describes the history, social setting, and philosophy that led to this innovative health care program. Later sections will examine the extent to which the objectives have been realized.

### The Continuity Clinic Program

A continuity clinic was established in the pediatric clinic of the university hospital (Strong Memorial Hospital) in 1964. The major goal of the program, supported in part by a training grant from the then Children's Bureau (now Maternal and Child Health Services) was to provide better education for the pediatric house staff and medical students and thus prepare them to be more effective primary care physicians. The program offered a small number of patients the now well-agreed-upon components of comprehensive care: continuity by the same house officer or student, care rendered by a team of health professionals, the use of nurse practitioners, outreach by the team to include the hard-to-reach social problem family, combination of preventive and curative care, and a strong family focus.

After the hospital's continuity clinic had operated for two years, it became clear that the program was not achieving all that was desired in optimal patient care, in part because of local factors. The hospital was five miles from the population served and required two bus changes for the typical patient—the black, poor, ghetto resident. There were no geographical boundaries for the dispersed population served, and the ability to reach patients who had never come to the clinic before and who were not receiving care anywhere else was limited because they could not be identified. Bureaucratic barriers existed, as in any large medical institution, starting with an impersonal and time-consuming registration procedure that delayed care, at best, and completely deterred patients, at worst. Family care could not be delivered because members of the same family but of different ages had to go to different clinics at different times and with different records. As a result there were inevitable difficulties of communication between clinics and, perhaps most important, different philosophies of patient care. Unfortunately no organization of consumers was created to inform providers about the consumers' needs.

In addition to the care being inadequate, under these circumstances the education of house staff members, although improved over the past, was inappropriate because they could not experience an effective organization of care. One desirable feature of the continuity clinic in the hospital, however, and one that influenced its continuation as an additional program even after the newer community programs were developed, was the mix of socioeconomic classes for which care was provided. The clinic served, in addition to the black poor, university graduate students—white, highly intellectual, and only temporarily poor. Segregation of the poor in one program is regarded as undesirable, for such separation provides poor education for the medical student, who should see a variety of patients. Unfortunately, the one positive factor of a mixed socioeconomic group in the hospital program was outweighed by all the negative factors.

## The Baden Street Health Center

At the same time that work was being done to improve the continuity clinic at the medical school, other efforts were under way to coordinate various clinic activities at the Baden Street Health Center. The neighborhood served by this center is one of the oldest in the city and for over half a century had been the traditional place where immigrants to Rochester first settled—the Jews in the 1890s, the Italians and East Europeans in the 1910s. Blacks and Puerto Ricans, like their predecessors, settled there as the newest "immigrants" in the 1950-1960s. A fairly extensive network of traditional community services existed through a settlement house and neighborhood organizations, but, for many reasons, social improvement for blacks was slower and less successful than for the previous waves of newcomers. The historical ghetto of former immigrants remained the main residential area for the blacks, and few were able to move elsewhere. Medical care was first made available to this neighborhood through the settlement house on Baden Street. In 1904 a group of nurses started services which, after only a few years, developed into the Baden Street Dispensary, providing an ever increasing volume of care. The growth in number of patient encounters continued through the 1920s and 1930s, reaching about 40,000 visits per year at the beginning of World War II.

At the end of the war the dispensary changed its name to the Baden Street Health Center to indicate a major reorganization. The previous orientation to specific diseases (tuberculosis clinic, venereal disease clinic, and dental clinic) was supplemented by special preventive care clinics (well-baby, cancer detection), but the volume of services dropped, for a number of reasons, to about a quarter of the previous peak. The character of the neighborhood was changing rapidly, and more and more functions of the old private charity services were transferred to separate but competing health department clinics. Various review committees studied what role the clinics at the Baden Street Health Center could take within the health care system of the community. It was finally decided that the health center should no longer be run as a number of different clinics, but should become a family oriented community health center with new staff and a medical coordinator.

In 1965 the medical coordinator was appointed. He also held a clinical faculty position in pediatrics at the medical school and was familiar with the problems of the continuity clinic. The common outlook of both programs and their directors soon led to cooperation in planning for the Rochester Neighborhood Health Center at the site of the old Baden Street Health Center.

*The Design and Establishment of The Rochester*
*Neighborhood Health Center*

There was a long process of involvement with the community—in this case poor people in the inner city—to determine how they saw their health needs, and to begin to develop a consumer group to promote health care. At that time plans for the organization of the Rochester Child Health Surveys, described in preceding chapters, were drawn up to establish the current health needs of children in Rochester, and to provide a baseline against which changes brought about by any new programs could be measured. As is true of all other ghettos, the black poor, living in old sections of the city, were found to have greater morbidity, less utilization of health care, and practically no immediately available health care resources in their area (e.g., at that time there were only two practicing family doctors for nearly 25,000 people).

All these findings led to the planning of a new program for delivering care more effectively to this neighborhood. The Office of Economic Opportunity, then in a rapidly expanding phase of its medical program, contacted us in 1967. Their guidelines seemed to offer the best chances to fund such a program, for they would provide financing for the health care of the entire family, rather than just mothers and children;

*Figure 9A.1. On July 1, 1968, the Rochester Neighborhood Health Center officially opened at this site.*

*Figure 9A.2. The new Anthony Jordan Health Center, officially opened in January 1973.*

mandate involvement of the community in the program; encourage a team effort, with special emphasis on outreach workers, who would be recruited from the community served; and place few restrictions on what was considered to be the boundaries of quality health care. For instance, this flexibility allowed the development, with an adjacent local school, of a new type of school health program and experimentation with other new ways of improving health care. On the other hand, two major drawbacks to OEO financing, from a medical educator's view, were criteria limiting care to poverty group patients, thus restricting the type of population that the student sees, and potential financial instability due to year-to-year funding.

A proposal was hurriedly prepared and accepted, followed by a fairly difficult period of negotiation between grantor (OEO) and subcontractor (the university). The grantee was the local antipoverty agency, Action for a Better Community, which served as a conduit for the funds from OEO to the university. This arrangement was certainly a new type of venture for the latter. The rapidly changing guidelines of the OEO, which were set to overcome institutional rigidities at the local level, were frequently confusing. A long and difficult time was required to carry out these negotiations, and some more or less permanent feelings of estrangement resulted between the university administration, whose members were not convinced that a university should become a major provider of health care and who wanted safeguards against financial risk, the idealistic but naive faculty who were to be the providers, and the poor community who wanted both medical care and power.

The major organizing principle was that one particular multispecialty but family-oriented health care team would see all members of a given family. A typical health care team caring for about 2500 people was to consist of one pediatrician, one-half internist, one-half obstetrician, one-fourth psychiatrist, three public health nurses, and three to five family health aides. The public health nurses would deliver a major portion of the antepartum and well-child care and would be freed of the traditional clinic nurse functions. The family health aides would be recruited from the neighborhood and would serve as "patient advocates," outreach workers, and clinic aides. They would arrange transportation and baby sitting services, recruit patients from the target population, and follow up on all missed appointments. Team physicians would provide continuity of care, admit their health center patients to hospitals as private patients, and remain their personal physicians. One relatively unusual concept was for most of the physicians to be full-time faculty members, dividing their time between fairly large primary care responsibilities and the more traditional faculty responsibilities of teaching and research. In addition, public health nurses in the target area were assigned to the center with concomitant closing of the existing health department clinics in that area.

Thus the concept of health care as planned for the Rochester Neighborhood Health Center went beyond the care traditionally offered either in clinics or in private practice. Although this concept is, today, hardly innovative, in actual practice it is rarely achieved. Whether health care at such a level can ever be achieved in this setting, and whether it can pos-

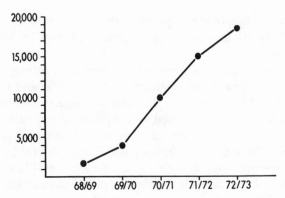

Figure 9A.3.  Patient registration at the Rochester Neighborhood Health Center.

sibly compensate for the relative health disadvantage of the population served, will be examined in the following sections.

The Rochester Neighborhood Health Center officially opened on July 1, 1968, in provisional quarters (see Figure 9A.1) with two health care teams. Another three teams were added in the following years as the patient load increased. A walk-in Saturday clinic and a dental program were added in early 1969, and the school health program opened in September of the same year. Evening clinics and a 24-hour on-call system were in operation from the start. A close cooperation with a community mental health center was also established. A new health center building, designed to eventually serve about 25,000 registered patients, was constructed as permanent quarters (see Figure 9A.2) and opened in early 1973. Figure 9A.3 indicates that the service goal will probably soon be reached; at the end of the fiscal year 1973 over 18,000 patients were registered.

## B. FIVE YEARS IN RETROSPECT

EVAN CHARNEY

Five years after the opening of the Rochester Neighborhood Health Center (RNHC), and some seven years after planning for it began, several elements of the program seem clearly to have been successful. Several others, however, appear, with equal clarity, to have been failures. For a third group it is still not possible to reach a conclusion: either there has been insufficient time to identify their outcomes, or they are at once hopeful and disappointing.

There is no question but that the participants have learned valuable lessons from both the failures and the successes. In this section major elements of the program will be discussed in three categories: "successes," "mixed notices," and "failures." Reasons for such categorizations will be given; however, like all such descriptions, these are subjective and generalized. The successes contain irritating ingredients of failure, while the failures present some distinctly successful aspects. Nevertheless, the descriptions may prove useful to others engaged in similar endeavors.

*Successes*

Replication of the Model

If health services can be considered a subset of the field of biology, we can invoke, as initial evidence, that most demanding indicator of biological success—the ability to grow and reproduce. In fact, the RNHC not only has grown in both size and patient volume, but also has been replicated. Its predecessor, the settlement house sponsored Baden Street Health Center, provided some services to 3000 patients (with 10,000 visits annually) in the early 1960s. As of March 1973 the present program had 18,000 registered patients and reported over 60,000 encounters per year for medical and dental services in the center and in the home. Over two thirds of these registered patients had utilized a health center department during the preceding 18 months.

Evidence of the center's ability to reproduce has been the development of the Rochester Health Network, a community owned nonprofit corporation that now includes the initial health center plus three new centers. The combined registration figure reaches 40,000 in a city that reported only 35,500 persons below the poverty line in the 1970 census. The idea has taken firm root and has spread. A more cynical observer might comment that, unlike a "pure" biological system, this one has required enormous amounts of fertilization in the form of federal dollars. Left to its own devices, the system would never have evolved in the first place and, once removed from this source of sustenance, might soon wither and die. Certainly without the support of the Office of Economic Opportunity the present center and the Rochester Health Network would not be operational. Such outside support is necessary especially during the period when services are initially established. There would seem to be no way in which poor people could themselves amass the required start-up funds for such a program. Moreover, no physician, however idealistic or talented, could by himself sustain the enormous difficulties inherent in establishing comprehensive health care for this number of patients with their pressing health and social problems.

Other health centers have been established in Rochester, and partly on the basis of their criticisms of the initial center's structure and function, have made several changes in the design of their programs. For example, one center is very concerned that a large segment of its clientele be drawn from the middle class, arguing strongly that medical staff recruitment, retainment, and satisfaction cannot long be sustained by serving only the poor. Another center, critical of the large group practice model, argues that the smaller the primary care organization, the more personal and effective it will be for patients, and, accordingly, the more likely it will be to maintain staff satisfaction. Both arguments are pertinent and largely sound. They detract in no way, however, from the validity of the basic thrust of providing planned and integrated health services for a disadvantaged population. The changes made by the other health centers should be seen as evolutionary developments of the program and as logical outgrowths and variations on the original concepts. All modern organizations, including health services, must evolve to survive, and these variations on a theme are seen as essential to the continued health of the model.

A concept basic to *all* of the health centers, however, is that the special needs of poor people must be considered and planned for from the inception of a program and, to some degree, separately from the rest of the population. In this regard these programs vary significantly from other group health programs in the country, which insist that a middle-class clientele first be established to put the program on a firm paying basis, and only later consider extending services to the poor. The Rochester Health Network centers all consider this two-class concept of care, which delays services to those most in need, as unacceptable and even somewhat unethical. In three to five years these "hothouse plants" will be forced to compete more directly with private groups, once altered payment systems become operative. That will be another critical point at which to gauge the validity and vigor of the health center concept.

### Attraction of New Medical and Nursing Manpower and Integration of the Health Center into Education for Primary Care

The majority of the pediatricians, family practitioners, and nurse clinicians in the Network Neighborhood Health centers are recent graduates of the University of Rochester pediatric, family medicine, and nursing programs. One of the successful elements of the program in this community is that the health centers have been able to attract some of the best of these people. Unfortunately, recruitment within internal medicine and psychiatry has been considerably less successful. At the outset serious doubts existed whether it would be possible to attract practitioners of high quality. It was hoped that some kind of affiliation with the university would help in this regard, and this proved to be the case. The Department of Pediatrics and the Division of Family Medicine have been most vigorously involved in community health programs, and the attraction of their graduates to the health centers reflects this orientation. The fact that the other departments have been cooperative but less committed is also evident in the recruitment patterns.

The notion that the health center be staffed by physicians with full-time academic appointments has proved relatively impracticable. Those who wish to practice full time are not as involved with the heavy teaching, research, and committee duties of full-time faculty, and, as a result, face difficulties in competing for academic promotion. At present an alternative has evolved with potential benefit both to the health centers and to the university. The centers are actively involved in medical, nursing, house staff, and postresidency fellowship education as part of an expanded university primary care program. The director of the RNHC is a full-time faculty member; selected practitioners at the health centers are full-time doctors there, but not full-time faculty; and others are part-time salaried clinical faculty in this program. Each has some faculty position. The costs of education within the RNHC remain a subject of debate and concern, but the "special relationship" of the health center to the university has continued to develop both as a concept and as a recruitment mechanism.

### Patient Acceptance

Patient acceptance is a concept that is especially difficult to measure for a low-income population. In 1971 a household interview study (Hillman and Charney, 1972) was conducted to assess health center acceptance among a sample of registered patients.

To gauge the degree of identification that patients have with the RNHC, a random sample of patients was asked to compare it with the services that they had previously received. Table 9B.1 shows their responses to the questions asked, differentiated as to whether or not they knew the names of any of their team physicians. Before the center opened, 75% had used hospital clinic or area clinic and emergency services; 13%, private physicians; and 12%, combinations of these services. Those previ-

*Table 9B.1.   Comparison of Rochester Neighborhood Health Center with Quality of Prior Medical Care, and Use of Provider "If All Care were Free," by Knowledge of their RNHC Physician's name[a]*

|                        | RNHC Physician's Name Known | RNHC Physician's Name Unknown |
|------------------------|-----------------------------|-------------------------------|
| Comparison with Prior Care |                         |                               |
| RNHC better            | 46 (64%)                    | 7 (47%)                       |
| RNHC same              | 21 (29%)                    | 3 (20%)                       |
| RNHC worse             | 5 (7%)                      | 5 (33%)                       |
| If All Care Free, Would Choose: |                    |                               |
| RNHC                   | 51 (65%)                    | 5 (27%)                       |
| Private physician      | 21 (27%)                    | 11 (61%)                      |
| Hospital clinic        | 7 (8%)                      | 2 (12%)                       |

[a] From Hillman and Charney (1972), p. 342.

ously using clinic services tended to be more positive about health center care (41 of 67 rated it better) than those who had had private care (5 of 12 rated it better).

Similar results were found when patients were asked where they would choose to go "if you could go anywhere, and all care were free." Of the patients knowing their doctors' names, 65% would choose RNHC care in the future over private or clinic care, whereas only 27% of those who did not know their doctors' names would prefer center care.

When asked why they chose their hypothetical future site of care, the patients who named the health center cited both factors of easy accessibility and the personal warmth of the staff. Those who would choose a private physician (less than 50% had actually used one) commented largely on the personal care they would anticipate receiving, and the 9% who favored hospital clinics thought that the latter would offer a broader range of services.

An attempt was made to study more closely the characteristics of satisfied and dissatisfied patients. Respondents who considered the RNHC superior to prior sources of care and who also would choose it over private physicians or clinics in the future (32 families in all) were placed in a "satisfied" group. The 19 families who considered the care received equal or inferior to prior care and who would not choose it in the future were considered "dissatisfied." These two subgroups were compared on the basis of various demographic factors and their patterns of actual use of center services during the preceding year. In addition, the team nurse and health assistant were asked, independently, to comment about the family's social problems, such as employment and housing difficulties, internal functioning, and integration into community activities. The family's own response about the RNHC was not revealed to the health workers.

No differences between these two groups were noted in the following variables: number of persons in household, age and educational level of head of household, duration of residence at present address or in the county, and family income. Differences were evident, however, in the frequency of visits to the health center, frequency of home contacts by a team nurse and health assistant, and these persons' estimates of the families' social and medical problems. Somewhat surprisingly it was found that both groups broke appointments equally often (33% for satisfied, 36% for dissatisfied families), and that the satisfied group contained a higher number of families with multiple or complex social problems. It is likely that a satisfying relationship at the RNHC results in increasing use and familiarity, and, to this extent, the results are expected. What is clear is that the "multiproblem family" can be reached by a health center organization, can develop a respectable frequency of contacts (though often continuing to break appointments), and can respond positively and enthusiastically to comprehensive care efforts. Whether or not such families could be equally well engaged with less extensive outreach efforts is uncertain. At least it seems evident that simple demographic factors do not predict with precision which families are likely to be satisfied with neighborhood health center care.

Unfortunately, this basically enthusiastic appraisal is by no means unanimous. Weary house officers who man the hospital emergency rooms are at times cynical about the large numbers of registered RNHC patients who are still going outside the health center system to these emergency rooms for care. As the subsequent discussions of hospitalization and emergency room utilization indicate, acceptance is by no means uniform, and "leaks" to the hospital emergency rooms and clinics continue to plague the center.

On the positive side, the RNHC has never had major or unified community opposition. It has never been picketed, extensively vandalized, or boycotted—to mention some valid though somewhat negative indices of acceptance. To be sure, the community it serves is not a well-organized one, and its most vigorous spokesmen are occupied with more pressing concerns about employment, housing, and education. Articulate neighborhood individuals and groups, however, have increasingly cooperated with the health center's development, and have been important participants in the evolution of the Rochester Health Network. This involvement reflects, in part, their basic satisfaction with the initial model as well as growing realization of the potential influence of this new community institution.

The RNHC has enjoyed generally good relations with the black community and lukewarm acceptance from the Puerto Rican population. On the average, the community's view of the center appears to lie somewhere between tolerance and enthusiasm, with individual opinion ranging from hostile rage to adoration—a spectrum probably not too different from that of most patients in other systems.

### The School Health Program

The RNHC set out rather early to develop a close and intimate relationship between itself and the neighborhood schools. This relationship has been achieved for one school in the community, with enthusiasm on the part of the school administration, teachers, and health center personnel. The development of new health workers (e.g., school health assistants) and of new roles for the school physician and school nurse has been described in detail elsewhere (Nader et al., 1972). The school not only acquires a broad spectrum of health services for its pupils, but also has access to a pediatrician who both advises teachers on health matters and expedites referrals for care. In turn the health center gains another point of contact with its patients, facilitating the implementation of screening and immunization programs, and providing smoother access to and communication with the child's "workday" environment.

This specific program has not, as yet, been replicated by the other health centers and has not spread to junior high schools or high schools in the area. The major reason for this lack of extension and growth is based on a financial rather than a conceptual limitation. Health centers are increasingly reluctant to invest funds in non-income-producing programs such as school health, important as they may be. Equally, the financially hard pressed city school system, under enormous pressure to meet the educational needs of its students, has been unwilling to commit any extra funds to a health program. The plain fact is that new school health programs are more expensive than the traditional ones, and the benefits not that visible. Again, another period of several years will be required to test whether the community will consider these liaisons sufficiently productive and important to fund them.

### The Mental Health Program

The integration of primary mental health and physical health services in one organizational structure can be considered an important conceptual and practical success. The objectives of community mental health centers and "physical" health centers are so interwoven and overlapping that it would seem to be duplicative and wasteful to have these organizationally separate. But how can one categorize this integration as a success? Can it be proved that the mental health of the population involved has been significantly improved by this liaison? The value of psychological services has always been difficult to demonstrate, and, in this regard, the RNHC is no exception. Our conclusions are based, therefore, on the observations and comments of those involved.

Two aspects were most successful: first, improved communication between the medical and psychiatric care systems, and, second, valuable team discussions. The ability to rationally plan the continuity of care for psychiatric patients, and the facility with which physicians and nurses can "get their patients into" the psychological and psychiatric services of the community, are strong points of the program. The fact that mental health professionals are functioning members of both the neighborhood health center and the Rochester Mental Health Center eliminated a major barrier to communication. For example, a patient who requires psychiatric hospitalization can be followed by RNHC personnel, both in the institution and after discharge. Rational plans for after-care are, therefore, improved. The mental health personnel are aware of many psychological services in the community and, more important, have access to them. This greatly multiplies the resources for the general medical staff.

The other valuable element of the program is that each team at the health center has a mental health representative who meets periodically (usually weekly) with the members. This psychiatrist or social worker provides not only advice and guidance in patient management, but also support to the nurses, physicians, and health assistants on the team. Dealing with an enormous volume of multiproblem families, in situations where success is measured, at times, in millimeters, can be an enervating and difficult task for health professionals, and the encouragement provided by the mental health representative enables them to accept limited goals and successes in perspective. This aspect is a vital but hard to document ingredient in sustaining staff morale. The barriers between physical health providers and mental health providers are troublesome and a source of much concern on both sides. For this reason integration of services in one setting and specifically within each team is a promising concept. There seems to be no reason why this model could not be employed equally well in programs oriented toward middle-class families.

### Public Health Nurses

The Monroe County Health Department was involved very early in planning for the RNHC. Probably the most important single idea was to include the public health nurses in the target area as integral team members, along with the physician and family health assistant, rather than have them operate as a separate autonomous unit for the district as they do within the health department. A study conducted during 1971 and 1972 examined the nature of these nurses' jobs and the professional level at which they worked (Charney and Mechaber, 1972). A comparable group of public health nurses employed by the health department in a similar kind of neighborhood was studied for comparison. The results indicated that, although the time allotted to various tasks was similar in the two groups (Table 9B.2), the RNHC nurses worked at a uniformly higher professional level (Figure 9B.1), and did so with approximately 50% more patients (Table 9B.3). These differences are due chiefly to the integration of public health nurses within the primary care system. Communication with doctors, dentists, and other health workers is frequent, informal, and greatly facilitated. The public health nurses have been enabled and encouraged to grow professionally in this kind of atmosphere and have moved easily into the practitioner role. Those who have left the program have uniformly positive attitudes about this integration with medical practice and have sought it in their new jobs.

At an administrative level, the nursing director of the RNHC acts as district supervisor in the Monroe County Health Department and is also a faculty member of the University of Rochester School of Nursing. The fact that all public health nursing staff is recruited through the health department has greatly enhanced communication. The success of this integrated design was largely due to having capable and enthusiastic

*Table 9B.2.   Comparison[a] of Public Health Nurse Activity in Traditional Health Department Role and in Health Center*
Values shown are percentages of time in each

| Health Department | Activity | Health Center |
|---|---|---|
| 35.2 | Patient communication | 30.3 |
| 24.0 | Staff communication | 35.2 |
| 19.2 | Travel | 11.0 |
| 7.7 | Clerical | 9.5 |
| 1.4 | Waiting | 3.8 |
| 3.6 | Other communication | 3.3 |
| 0.1 | Reading | 2.7 |
| 0.8 | Procedures | 1.3 |
| 7.9 | Other | 2.9 |

[a] Based on 200 hours of observation, 20 per nurse for 10 nurses.

*Table 9B.3.* Comparison[a] of Public Health Nurses in Traditional Health Department Role and in Health Center: Patient Encounters and Families Seen in Two-Week Period

|  | Encounters With Own Patients | With Other Patients | Total Encounters $\overline{X}$ (SD) | Total Families $\overline{X}$ (SD) |
|---|---|---|---|---|
| Health Center | 80 | 18 | 98 (34) | 48 (15) |
| Health Department | 39 | 27 | 66 (25) | 37 (22) |

[a] Based on nine nurses in each setting, two separate fortnight sample periods.

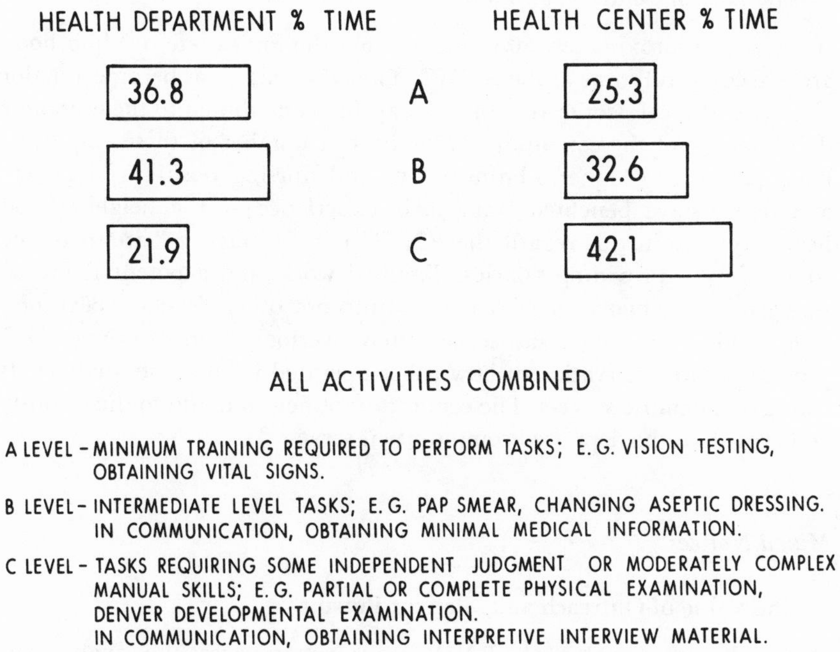

HEALTH DEPARTMENT % TIME          HEALTH CENTER % TIME

| 36.8 | A | 25.3 |
|------|---|------|
| 41.3 | B | 32.6 |
| 21.9 | C | 42.1 |

ALL ACTIVITIES COMBINED

A LEVEL – MINIMUM TRAINING REQUIRED TO PERFORM TASKS; E.G. VISION TESTING, OBTAINING VITAL SIGNS.

B LEVEL – INTERMEDIATE LEVEL TASKS; E.G. PAP SMEAR, CHANGING ASEPTIC DRESSING. IN COMMUNICATION, OBTAINING MINIMAL MEDICAL INFORMATION.

C LEVEL – TASKS REQUIRING SOME INDEPENDENT JUDGMENT OR MODERATELY COMPLEX MANUAL SKILLS; E.G. PARTIAL OR COMPLETE PHYSICAL EXAMINATION, DENVER DEVELOPMENTAL EXAMINATION. IN COMMUNICATION, OBTAINING INTERPRETIVE INTERVIEW MATERIAL.

*Figure 9B.1. Comparison of public health nurses in health department role and at health center: professional level of activity (percentages of time).*

senior personnel within the health department who were willing to explore new organizational arrangements.

Again, there have been problems within this generally successful area. First, other health centers in Rochester have not incorporated this model

wholly into their programs. To a large degree this reflects funding constraints. Many of the outreach and follow-up services of health department
nurses are not reimbursable from Medicaid, and health centers are reluctant to invest staff positions in non-income-generating functions. Since the
Monroe County Health Department continues to provide these services
within the community, albeit at a much reduced level, other centers have
chosen to take what "free" services are available and to hire other nurses
for their programs, essentially returning to the separated system that
existed in the past. A second concern involves the nurse-physician communication problems engendered by this new coprofessional relationship.
Although the nurses are far more challenged and productive in this integrated relationship, there remain important and unresolved issues of
status and changed roles within the primary care team.

### The Health Center as an Employer in the Area

At present approximately 50 residents from the immediate neighborhood
are employed full time at the RNHC. Thus the center has become a major
employer of local people and, in this way, has contributed to the economic
development of the community. Moreover, a number of these employees
have gone on to higher administrative and nursing positions elsewhere
and hence have benefited from their experience at the neighborhood
health center. In this regard the RNHC is very much a "citizen of the
community"—providing salaries, dignified work, and a potential for career growth for many for whom this would not otherwise have been possible. This employment aspect is often overlooked in assessing OEO
programs, but observation of how it has operated in this case qualifies its
listing as a definite success. The center cannot help but add to the stability
and growth of the depressed community it serves.

### Mixed Notices

#### The Value of Outreach and "Patient Pursuit"

One of the stated goals of the RNHC at its inception was the involvement
of personnel (public health nurses and family health workers) in an effort
to provide intensive outreach identification of and follow-up for those
most needing care. The center aimed, in a sense, to make up for the lack of
medical sophistication of many of its clients by bringing services to them.
This remains an important philosophical commitment at the neighborhood health center but is listed as an unproved outcome for two reasons.
    First, no evidence has been provided by the RNHC that this approach

has been fruitful. It is entirely possible that the outreach efforts of the health center have been very successful, enabling multiproblem families to utilize health facilities more effectively and to obtain more stability and productivity in their life situations. There are abundant anecdotal indications that the task has been a difficult one to sustain. Evaluation techniques of sufficient sensitivity have not been devised to answer the question adequately.

Second, the new centers in the Rochester Health Network declined to incorporate significant outreach services in their programs. This refusal can, in part, be attributed to financial constraints—such services are not reimbursable. It also reflects, however, the attitudes of the medical staff in these programs that such services have not demonstrated their effectiveness. Indeed, as the numbers of patients at the neighborhood health centers have grown, the ability to provide outreach and follow-up has been progressively constricted to those deemed in most dire need.

A central obligation of the program remains to demonstrate that these enormous efforts of time and professional skill have proved worthwhile. The burden rests with the evaluators to develop techniques of patient assessment that will help to answer this question. Although dear to the hearts of "comprehensive careniks," this element of the program becomes increasingly difficult to sustain on faith alone.

### The Value of Team Care

A central precept of the RNHC was that care provided by nurses, health assistants, and physicians *in a team* would be better than the isolated services provided by each separately. Evidence was presented earlier that the nurses have been able to expand their professional role, possibly in part because of this team care. On balance, however, the team concept remains unproven. It is safe to say that most of the physicians at the health center, particularly those in internal medicine and obstetrics, have not developed sufficient enthusiasm or even understanding of team care and remain unconvinced of its efficacy. Even among the pediatricians, the most committed group, the roles of the family health worker and the nurse have not always been understood, and enormous problems of communications remain.

In this connection, a study conducted by anthropologist Lucy Russo (1970) documented serious communication problems among health assistants, nurses, and doctors. Although important changes and improvements have taken place since then, actualizing the concept of coprofessional planning for the social, psychological, and medical needs of patients remains a difficult task, and the price paid in time spent in intrateam communication has been a heavy one.

A uniformly successful model for team meetings and team communication is needed. There are many impressive and even inspiring anecdotes to support such an approach, reflecting enthusiasm of individual workers for the team model. But, five years after its inception, the question "How well does the team function?" remains an unresolved and perplexing one at the center. Care has been taken not to list this as a failure of the program because the team organization remains the policy and pattern here. Its failure to be incorporated in like fashion by other health centers, however, and the continued appearance of such questions as "What do the health assistants really do anyway?" and "Where does the nurse's role end and the doctor's begin?" attest to the unresolved status of this concept.

### The Integration of Dentistry and Medicine at the Team Level

The dental program at the RNHC has, in general, been a successful one providing high-quality dental services for patients. Despite five years of effort, however, it is difficult to conclude that medicine and dentistry are, in fact, integrated at the team level in any way. Team meetings involving dental personnel usually result in medical problems being discussed with bored dentists paying scant attention; occasionally, dental problems are considered while doctors barely listen. Perhaps, indeed, there is no great rationale for integration, and a "separate but equal" doctrine may be more appropriate. This in no way is meant to demean the value of dental services; indeed, in many ways, they are at least as high a health priority for the community as are medical services. Nevertheless, there is little evidence that having dentists and doctors in one organizational unit provides better care than having them reasonably close and in easy communication with one another. For the patient, for whom the RNHC exists, however, there are obvious benefits of physical proximity, much as in one-stop shopping in the supermarket.

### Community Control

Community participants in the initial development of the RNHC were much chagrined to find that they were, in reality, an "advisory body" and had no real power. Neither the OEO nor the University of Rochester had expressed interest in vesting full authority in a group without the assumption of responsibility by that group. The experience of those involved in the program, however, suggests that the advisory council concept is a fallacious one. Those with actual authority will take the advice they choose to hear and ignore any other kind, if at all possible. Naturally, talented and vigorous community members were not anxious to play such a menial role in the program.

The development of a representative community board has indeed been slow. An election held in 1972 for positions on the community board had the relatively small voter turnout typical of most OEO community elections—a small interested group both ran for office and voted. Nevertheless, one cannot be uniformly negative about the experience. The community board has now assumed de facto charge of the program, and, as part of the Rochester Health Network, has a growing voice in how the center is run. It is evident that, if a health program is placed in a community without that community's initiative and responsibility, its evolvement will be a slow and difficult process. A study of 10 such centers, with varying degrees of consumer control, failed to show striking differences in the types of services offered (Cunningham, 1972).

## Failures

### The Health Center as a Major Agent for Social Action

For a variety of reasons the RNHC has not really played a role as an agent for social change in this community; it has not evolved into a political or social force on almost any issue. Although there has been some involvement in welfare rights, issues involving lead poisoning, sickle cell screening, and services for the mentally retarded, on the whole the center has played down these aspects. Some would argue that it would be the height of paternalism for a health center managed by non-resident professionals to dictate to a community what its social action effort should be, and that such involvement would overstep the legitimate definition of the medical role. Others have pointed out that the health needs of the community are so interwoven with its social, political, and economic needs that a center can have no serious impact on the community without such involvement.

That the RNHC has not succeeded in this area is listed as a failure. But, in truth, it has not tried very hard. It might be contended that only now, when the center is established as an institution and is increasingly coming under community control, can its role in this regard begin. Again, a look at the situation five years hence may yield a different conclusion.

### The Center as a Focal Point for Social Services

It was hoped that the RNHC's establishment of a continuing, ongoing relationship with patients and their families would provide a logical basis for a coordination of social services. The myriad of social agencies in the community—welfare, family support, psychological services—touch only certain families at certain times. Moreover, each is constrained by some limitation on its involvement and some concern with delineated circumstances under which it may provide service (e.g., only those with defined incomes or only those with two or more major chronic diseases). Each agency is as concerned with what it will *not* do, or when it will *withdraw* services, as with when and how it will provide them.

The neutral stance of health services and the longitudinal commitment they make to patients would seem to provide a natural focus for social services as well, but clearly this has not occurred. The RNHC has not developed innovative or imaginative social services for its clientele and has no better relations with the social agencies than does any other health facility. Most interchange is based on case conferences dealing with individual problems at specific times. Rather than replacing or coordinating social services, the center has acted as another agency that provides them.

## The Integration of Pediatric and Internal Medicine to Provide Family Care

It was hoped that coordinated planning for family care between internists and pediatricians would occur because of a common record system, team organization, and close physical proximity. Unlike many multispecialty group practices which have no integration of services for adults and children, the RNHC hoped to be different. In large part, however, pediatricians and internists operate independently. (Where coordination does occur, it is accomplished by the nurse or health assistant.) In fact, there is less coordination than might be provided by a family practitioner. Moreover, there seems to be no advantage over having these specialists work in more isolated fashion. This mention of lack of integration is not considered a criticism of the specific medical care itself, but rather an acknowledgment that the pediatrician-internist "team" has not become a reality.

*Summary*

In summary, then, the RNHC's success is demonstrated by its continued growth and replication. It attracts capable new trainees, has generally engaged the patient population of the community, employs area residents, and has increasingly come under community control. It provides medical services in dignified and pleasant surroundings, a far cry from what existed previously. Indeed it is a source of no small satisfaction that the poorest people in the community are now provided with primary medical care in comfortable and pleasant physical surroundings in their own neighborhood. Moreover, the quality of this care is likely to be equal to that available to the nonpoverty population in the area.

If the RNHC has not been a vigorous spokesman for social action within the neighborhood, it has proved a potent force within the medical and planning agencies. Prepaid health plans and financial intermediaries have been obliged to consider the health center programs in their estimates. Medicaid pays for about half of the operational costs of the health centers. Relationships with physicians in private practice are generally good. The health center movement is seen by most practitioners not as a threat but as an ally in the provision of quality health services. In short, it would be hard to visualize the health system of Monroe County today without the health centers. Not only are they a very real and central part of health care for a major portion of the community, but also they are an accepted facet of medical practice today and present a growing force to be reckoned with in the future.

## REFERENCES

CHARNEY, EVAN, and MECHABER, JUDY

1972 *Public Health Nurses: Professional Level of Performance in a Neighborhood Health Center Compared with a Health Department* (mimeograph).

CUNNINGHAM, MERLE

1972 "Community Control and the Neighborhood Health Center: Beyond the Rhetoric." Honors Thesis, University of Rochester School of Medicine and Dentistry.

HILLMAN, BRUCE, and CHARNEY, EVAN

1972 "A Neighborhood Health Center: What the Patients Know and Think of Its Operation." *Medical Care*, 10:336-344.

NADER, PHILIP, EMMEL, ANNE, and CHARNEY, EVAN

1972 "The School Health Service: A New Model." *Pediatrics*, 49(6):805-813.

RUSSO, LUCY

1970 *Participant Observation Research: The Health Team* (mimeograph).

C. THE IMPACT ON THE UTILIZATION OF EMERGENCY
ROOM SERVICES

KLAUS J. ROGHMANN AND EVAN CHARNEY

Between 1960 and 1970 visits to the emergency rooms (ER) of the six
largest hospitals in Monroe County more than doubled (93,500 to 214,-
250). The average yearly increase was 8.7%, compared with a county population growth rate of only 2%. There is agreement that this increase
reflected not a true growth in emergencies, but rather a deficiency of our
medical care system. The rapid increase of the inner city black population, to whom other care facilities were neither available nor accessible,
was one pertinent factor. Emergency room use for minor illnesses indicates an overflow of demand not met by the private sector. The hospitals
in the community are centrally located and reasonably accessible (within
30 to 45 minutes by car or public transportation) to all segments of the
population. But such emergency care is costly and, by its very nature,
episodic and limited to sick care.

One of the primary goals of the Rochester Neighborhood Health Center
(RNHC) was, therefore, to provide available and accessible care to a poverty group in the inner city that previously had to rely on hospital emergency rooms for its sick care. If the RNHC has been successful in reaching
its target population and providing continuous family centered care, both
preventive and illness related, the use of ER services for minor sickness
should be reduced for the target population. Also, the continuous care
provided by the health team should replace the previous fragmentation
of care.

## Methods

Our first study of emergency room utilization for children, carried out by
Hochheiser et al. (1971), was specifically aimed at determining whether
there was any evidence that ER visits by target area residents declined
after the RNHC opened. Data from Strong Memorial Hospital for 1967
and 1969 were already available from an earlier project done as part of
the Rochester Child Health Studies (RCHS). Dense sampling of ER visits
(33%) for a limited time (five weeks, covering the last week of February and all weeks of March) had been used as a compromise to reduce
the amount of fieldwork. This project was expanded by adding data from

Genesee, Rochester General, and St. Mary's hospitals,[1] and by adding the March 1970 period as a third point in time.

A series of studies carried out collaboratively by the RCHS and the Genesee Region Health Planning Council provided data for 1968, 1970, and 1972 from all seven hospitals and covered the adult population as well. Every 100th emergency visit was selected out of all visits reported by the hospitals for 1968 and 1970. The ER logs of the seven hospitals in the community served as the sampling frame. The medical record for each person making the sample visit was requested, and data were abstracted as to age, sex, residence, diagnosis, procedures, time of arrival, mode of arrival, insurance status, source of referral, and disposition. Residence was coded by the 142 census tracts in the community. Results for the 1968 survey are reported elsewhere (Jacobs et al., 1971); some of the results for the 1970 survey were presented and circulated locally in mimeographed form (Wersinger, 1971).

A higher sampling fraction was used in the 1972 study conducted under the auspices of the Genesee Region Health Planning Council ($n = 2492$), and the data collection form differed from that of the earlier studies. Though not completely comparable, the value of having a third point in time seemed to outweigh these methodological reservations.

Knowledge of the ER utilization pattern from the household surveys, an independent study of dental emergencies (Roghmann and Goldberg, 1974), analysis of Medicaid payment files (Roghmann, 1974), and the RNHC fiscal report helped to quantify our expectations as to the maximum impact that the health center could have.

## Hypotheses

Since most visits to the ER are for accidents or acute infections for which no effective preventive measures are available, the health services (mostly preventive) of the RNHC should not immediately affect the utilization of emergency rooms. Pediatricians had about 10,000 patient encounters per year at the center. In fiscal year 1971, for example, the RNHC reported 10,300 child/physician visits, of which 4300 were for preventive care or long-term care management. Thus 6000 visits for episodic care is the maximum ER visit reduction to be expected for chil-

---

[1] Data for 1967 could no longer be retrieved for St. Mary's Hospital. For parts of the analysis we assumed no change between 1967 and 1969 for this hospital, estimating 1967 figures to be the same as those for 1969. The remaining three hospitals (Park Avenue, Highland, and Lakeside) did not serve a significant number of children from the community's poverty areas and therefore were ignored.

dren. Internists provided about 9500 visits to adults per year, of which half were for episodic care. Accordingly, the maximum reduction for adults would be 4750 visits.

Since ER utilization is 100% walk-in (no appointment), and since the RNHC operates for the most part on an appointment system, only the walk-in visits to the RNHC should diminish the demand for ER services. About 25% of the center's episodic care visits were reported as "walk-in." Short-term appointments for sick care are also available. The expected minimum reduction is, therefore, 25% of present episodic care, that is, about 1500 child visits and 1200 adult visits. The hypotheses are:

1.  About 20,000 ER visits were made by residents of the health center target area in 1968, with 8500 by children and 11,500 by adults. For children, therefore, a minimum reduction of 18% (1500 of 8500) and a maximum reduction of 70% (6000 of 8500) may be expected. For adults the minimum reduction should be 10% (1200 of 11,500) and the maximum, 40% (4750 of 11,500).

2.  The hospitals in the community should be affected according to the previous utilization patterns of target area residents. The largest decline, therefore, should be at Strong Memorial Hospital and the second largest at Genesee Hospital, with no decline at St. Mary's Hospital.

3.  About 60% of all RNHC patients are under 15 years of age. Of those 15 years and older, 75% are women. It is for these groups that effects should be expected. The pattern for male adults should change less than that for women or children.

4.  The utilization pattern of residents from other areas of Monroe County will be determined by other factors such as population growth and changes in the care structure (e.g., effects of Medicaid legislation, and the opening of new facilities or group practices). The analysis will present before-after comparisons by the sociopolitical areas described in Section 1A.


*Results for Children Under Age 15*

The basic findings regarding ER visits by children under 15 years by sociopolitical area are summarized in Table 9C.1. The most remarkable finding is that, in contrast to the steady increase in general ER utilization, the total number of ER visits by children remained the same. Also, the net change for the county was negligible. There were, however, considerable shifts in the composition of pediatric ER visits. The increase from the suburban areas was constant, reaching about 9% per year. Visits from the inner city, however, decreased rapidly, by about the same *volume* as the suburban visits increased. The decrease was most marked for the

*Table 9C.1.  Changes in Pediatric Emergency Room Visits by Sociopolitical area, for Patients under 15 Years of Age Only*

| | Third Ward | Seventh Ward | Subtotal | Rest of City | Suburban Areas | Total |
|---|---|---|---|---|---|---|
| *Sample[a]* | | | | | | |
| 1967[b] | 205 | 208 | 413 | 611 | 377 | 1401 |
| 1969 | 200 | 149 | 349 | 665 | 417 | 1431 |
| 1970 | 170 | 125 | 295 | 598 | 479 | 1373 |
| *Percentage Change* | | | | | | |
| 1967–69 | −2 | −28 | −16 | +9 | +11 | +2 |
| 1969–70 | −15 | −16 | −16 | −10 | +15 | −4 |
| 1967–70 | −17 | −40 | −29 | +2 | +27 | −2 |

[a] 33% sample over a five-week period, or 3.2% sample over one year (use weight factor of 31 for annual estimates).
[b] St. Mary's estimated with 1969 figures.

Seventh Ward, in which the RNHC is located. Its overall decrease between 1967 and 1970 was 40%. For the Third Ward, the comparison area without a health center until 1972, the decrease was much slower, amounting to only about 17% over the three years. Visits from the rest of the city actually remained constant. The change was greatest from 1969 to 1970, but this differed largely by area.

There are only three possible explanations for these findings: changes in the illness level in the three years studied, changes in the population in the areas, or changes in the medical care system. Changes in the illness level might have occurred in the four sampled weeks each year, but changes should have applied to the same extent to all areas in the county since the same time periods were sampled. Although changes in illness cannot explain the increase from the suburban areas and the decrease from the city area, population shifts can account for some of the findings. The suburban child population increased by about 5% per year over the period studied, thus explaining about half of the suburban increase. Population change cannot, however, account for the decrease in inner city visits because the child population of the inner city remained basically stable. It is probably true that the total population of the inner city decreased but only because of a decline in the adult population. There was, however, a moderate change in the age composition of the child population in the inner city: the number of live births was declining by about 4% per year. It is the newborns in their first two years who contribute most to the demand for ER services, and their proportion in the child population of the inner city decreased slightly (ignoring in-migration).

The changing age composition of the inner city children may account for most of the decrease in the Third Ward. Some of the target area (Seventh Ward) decrease can also be accounted for by this change, but certainly not all. Accordingly, it appears that at least half of the decrease can be attributed to the neighborhood health center. In absolute terms there was a reduction of about 2500 visits for children up to age 15, of which some 1500 were due to the RNHC. This is about what was expected as the minimum reduction for children.

Additional support for this conclusion comes from checking the other hypotheses listed. At what hospital did the changes occur, for which medical conditions was the reduction most pronounced, was payment status a factor, and is there any indication of changes in the age composition of ER users?

Strong Memorial Hospital, as predicted, was most affected by the reduction in pediatric ER visitors. The reduction in inner city pediatric visits was not matched for this hospital by an increase in suburban visitors; therefore an overall reduction in pediatric visits occurred. Genesee and

Rochester General Hospitals also showed a large reduction in Seventh Ward visits; but, as residents of this area never formed a large proportion of all ER patients, this reduction was more than balanced by an increase in visits by suburban residents. The pediatric visits to these two hospitals increased over the period studied. Genesee Hospital showed the largest increase over the three years, nearly doubling its suburban patient load. The new ER facilities opened at Genesee in 1968 had a definite effect on the utilization pattern.

Evidence for an effect of the RNHC on ER utilization comes also from the reduction of infectious conditions (from 63% to 44% of all visits) in pediatric patients from the Seventh Ward. No such reduction could be observed in Third Ward patients. Nevertheless, the utilization pattern for the inner city (about 50% infectious conditions, 25% accidents) remained very different from that for the suburbs (25% infectious conditions, 50% accidents).

The distribution by insurance categories did not change significantly over the three years. On the whole there was a decrease in the proportion of pediatric Medicaid patients from 35% in 1967 to 29% in 1970, but this is only a reflection of the shift toward a higher proportion of suburban patients and a lower proportion of those from the inner city. For inner city patients the payment status did not change (about 57% of all were covered by Medicaid, and about 30% by Blue Cross; 7% reported self-payment), nor was there a significant change for suburban patients (7% covered by Medicaid, 86% by Blue Cross, 7% self-payment).

The age composition of the inner city pediatric patients came closer to that of suburban patients, but not to the extent that had been expected. Inner city patients using the ER were typically in the 0–2 year bracket (about 37%); suburban patients, in the 10–14 year group (about 40%).

To summarize, the RNHC had a measurable effect on pediatric ER usage between 1967 and 1970. The reduction was in the order of 2500 visits annually from the target area, of which about 1500 can be attributed to the RNHC. The size of the reduction, however, was closer to the minimum than the maximum expected decrease. Compared to the large annual increases in total ER utilization, this reduction only helped to slow down the previous trend and was probably not even noticed by the medical directors of these facilities.

### Results from the Collaborative Studies

According to the collaborative research, visits by Monroe County residents of all age groups to the ER increased by 8.4% (from 187,100 to

202,800) from 1968 to 1970, but only by 1.2% (to 205,300) for 1972. Most of this increase was due to population increase; the per capita rate increased a moderate 3.3% from 1968 to 1970, and actually decreased from 1970 to 1972. But the figures hide a remarkable shift in age distribution. Visits by patients under 18 dropped both in absolute numbers and per capita; adult visits increased from 1968 to 1972 by nearly 20% in absolute numbers and 9% per capita. The age differential in ER utilization rates, with children having higher rates, still existed in 1968, but disappeared completely by 1970 and 1972.

Differences in the utilization rate by area of residence, however, persisted (see Figure 9C.1). The black poverty areas continued to have a rate of about one ER visit per person per year, though the RNHC area had a slight reduction in absolute volume of ER visits as well as in rate in 1970, and a major reduction in 1972. The suburban ER utilization rate (0.165 in 1970) continued to be only about one sixth of the inner city rate.

The RNHC area was the only area showing a persistent decrease in ER visits, from 19,800 in 1968 to 19,200 in 1970 and 15,700 in 1972. The initial reduction was unexpectedly small; the later reduction, unexpectedly large.

A breakdown by age groups, as suggested by the hypotheses, helps to clarify the picture (see Table 9C.2). Emergency room visits from RNHC area adults increased 17% over the first two years, whereas visits by children (under 18) decreased 29%. For the next two years child visits dropped even further (36% below the 1968 level), and adult visits also decreased (9% below 1968 level). The second poverty area (our comparison group) showed a different development with a small initial decrease followed by a moderate increase. The early and later decreases in Seventh Ward children's utilization can be attributed largely to the health center; for adults,

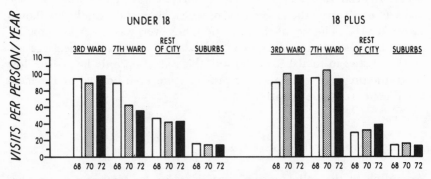

*Figure 9C.1. Emergency room utilization rates by Monroe County residents, 1968, 1970, 1972, by area of residence.*

however, there seems to have been a delayed impact. This different impact on adults and children makes sense if it is remembered that about two thirds of all children in the RNHC area were registered, compared with only one third of all adults. Families with children more easily meet the criteria for Medicaid and for OEO eligibility; more medical facilities are available for children; and children are more accustomed to clinic visits.

The number of ER visits of children from the RNHC area decreased from about 8500 in 1968 to approximately 6000 in 1970 and 5400 in 1972. Only about 2000 of the 6000 ER visits in 1970 were judged to require ER facilities and staff; 4000 could have been handled at the RNHC. Nor was the reduction of ER visits, though impressive, as large as it could have been; in fact it was halfway between the expected minimum and the expected maximum reductions. Furthermore, the development in the comparison area indicates that some of the reduction was probably due to changes in age composition. On the other hand, a much larger reduction than the volume of walk-ins treated in 1970 at the RNHC should not be expected.

The question remains whether all of the possible reduction in ER utilization has already been achieved, or whether a more flexible appointment system or an extension of hours of service might lead to further reductions. It is true that about 15% of all pediatric ER visits occur after 10 P.M. and before 9 A.M., but this percentage is about the same for the suburbs as for the inner city, and did not change between the two study years. It is also true that about 30% of all pediatric ER visits are made on Saturday and Sunday, but, again, this percentage is the same for the suburbs as for the inner city, and did not change significantly between the study years. The number of ER night and weekend visits from the RNHC area dropped between the two years at about the same rate as did weekday and daytime visits. Thus different hours of service would probably not reduce ER usage much further, though more services for "walk-in" sick care probably would. It should be noted that the RNHC operates a 24-hour telephone answering service, but there have been many problems in encouraging its use by registrants.

To summarize, two independent studies demonstrated a major effect of the RNHC on ER visits. The findings of the Hochheiser study on pediatric ER utilization could be replicated, although the time periods (1967, 1969, and 1970 in the first study; 1968, 1970, and 1972 in the second), methods, and definitions ("under 15" in the first study, "under 18" in the second) of the two studies were different. The remarkable additional finding about the longer lag period before impact on adult ER utilization still needs explanation. Chapter 7 provides part of the answer. The increase in the welfare population in 1969 (see Figure 1, Chapter 7) mostly af-

*Table 9C.2. Changes in Emergency Room Visits by Age and Sociopolitical Area*

| | Third Ward | Seventh Ward | Subtotal | Rest of City | Suburban Areas | Total |
|---|---|---|---|---|---|---|
| Sample [a] | | | | | | |
| | | | *Under 18 Years* | | | |
| 1968 | 95 | 85 | 180 | 329 | 232 | 741 |
| 1970 | 91 | 60 | 151 | 308 | 234 | 693 |
| 1972 | 101 | 54 | 155 | 313 | 235 | 703 |
| Change (%) | | | | | | |
| 1968-70 | -4 | -29 | -16 | -6 | +1 | -6 |
| 1968-72 | +6 | -36 | -14 | -5 | +1 | -5 |
| Sample [a] | | | | | | |
| | | | *18 Years Plus* | | | |
| 1968 | 145 | 113 | 258 | 511 | 361 | 1130 |
| 1970 | 166 | 132 | 298 | 585 | 452 | 1335 |
| 1972 | 151 | 103 | 254 | 688 | 408 | 1350 |
| Change (%) | | | | | | |
| 1968-70 | +14 | +17 | +16 | +14 | +26 | +18 |
| 1968-72 | +4 | -9 | -2 | +35 | +13 | +19 |

[a] 1% sample over 12-month period, all community hospitals (use weight factor of 100 for annual estimates).

fected the adult rather than the child population. At the same time private doctors, because of the 20% fee cut, reduced their services to Medicaid patients. As a result the number of adult Medicaid patients seen in the ER doubled between the two years studied. From a statistical point of view this explanation may satisfy, but substantively it disappoints for it suggests that the RNHC is perceived as being oriented more toward child and maternal care than family care.

## Discussion

One feature that has improved significantly is communication between hospital staff and RNHC personnel. Pediatric patients are frequently routed back to the health center after an ER visit, and certainly after a return visit to the clinic, particularly at Strong Memorial Hospital (the university hospital). Unfortunately a similar pattern for adult users of the center has not been observed, and it is our distinct impression that they have been brought into the new care system to a much smaller extent.

Patients continue to use multiple sources of health care to some degree. As prepayment plans evolve, they may have a major effect on this "shopping" pattern by the simple expedient of not paying for care if patients go outside their primary systems without being referred. What is evident at the present time is that the provision of good quality, easily available care in the community, including evening hours and 24-hour coverage, does not, by itself, entirely solve the multiple-site utilization pattern that has developed over the past several decades in our community. In short, the "carrot" has produced as much improvement as is practicable, and further change may now require some application of the "stick." If it is assumed (and not all do) that utilization of multiple resources is not a good thing for patients or their providers, this pattern will have to be changed by some further alteration of the payment mechanism. To be specific, a patient whose total medical care is covered by third-party sources (e.g., Medicaid) has no major deterrent to the use of ER or other hospital services as he wishes. As patients enroll with one primary care provider, however, payment barriers will be erected against their using ERs, and this may be the next necessary step. Some would argue that the existing situation should be accepted, with reliance on the interchange of medical records and on close communication between hospitals and health centers to ensure rational planning for patient care. This area remains to be studied over the next several years. At any rate, the stated goal of the RNHC to reverse the pattern of multiple and uncoordinated use of primary care resources has been only partially achieved. According to the threefold classification of Section 9B, this outcome should be reported under "mixed notices."

Those who work at a new health center or clinic sometimes have a tendency to overrate its impact on the target population. Large numbers of visits are being made to the health center, and those working there find it hard to believe that any patients in their target area are using other facilities.

Without some kind of evaluation research, it is difficult to see the impact of the health center in the proper perspective. If experimental designs are not possible, a range of comparison areas may be used to assess the before-after changes that do indeed occur. Fortunately, in these studies, such a comparison area was used. The RNHC did have an impact, though a limited one. In Chapter 7 it was demonstrated how the health center managed to slow the increasing reliance on the ER after the change in Medicaid regulations. Such data show the distance still to go before health centers serve the entire needs of their target populations.

## REFERENCES

HOCHHEISER, L.I., WOODWARD, K., and CHARNEY, E.

    1971   "Effect of the Neighborhood Health Center on the Use of Pediatric Emergency Departments in Rochester, New York." *New England Journal of Medicine,* 285(3):148–152.

JACOBS, A.R., GAVETT, J.W., and WERSINGER, R.

    1971   "Emergency Department Utilization in an Urban Community." *Journal of the American Medical Association,* 216(2):307–312.

ROGHMANN, K.J.

    1974   "Use of the Medicaid Payment Files for Medical Care Research." *Medical Care,* 12(2):131–137.

ROGHMANN, K.J., and GOLDBERG, H.J.V.

    1974   "Effect of RNHC on Hospital Dental Emergencies." *Medical Care,* 12(3):251–259.

WERSINGER, R.

    1971   *Emergency Department Utilization in Monroe County, New York: A Two-Year Comparison, 1968 and 1970.* Rochester, New York: Genesee Region Health Planning Council.

# D. THE IMPACT ON THE HOSPITALIZATION OF CHILDREN[1]

MICHAEL KLEIN, KLAUS J. ROGHMANN, AND EVAN CHARNEY

To our knowledge only two other studies have assessed the effect of a neighborhood health center on hospitalization (Bellin et al., 1969; James, 1971). In both, large reductions in admissions were reported. In neither study, however, were comparison groups utilized, nor rates computed, and that of James failed to deal with possible shifts in hospital admission patterns. This section attempts to deal with the limitations of these earlier studies.

## Materials and Methods

Because a stated objective of the Rochester Neighborhood Health Center was to reduce hospitalizations of children through comprehensive pediatric care, outreach, and home visiting by public health nurses and family health assistants, a set of related hypotheses was developed.

1. The health center will change the number and pattern of target area child admissions. Whereas child admissions for respiratory and infectious diseases will decrease, those for elective surgical and restorative procedures will increase.
2. The pattern of both admissions and diagnostic categories will remain unchanged for the control area and for nonusers in the target area.
3. Children who are patients of the neighborhood health center will spend fewer days in hospitals than those of the control area or the target area nonusers.

The basic research design called for a detailed analysis of the hospital admissions of children from the census tracts of the target and comparison areas. (The two areas were described in detail in Section 1A—see Figure 1A.1). A pilot study indicated that approximately two thirds of the target area child admissions were at Strong Memorial Hospital (the university hospital); the bulk of the remainder were at the Genesee Hospital, a university-affiliated community hospital. The other area hospitals admitted less than 10% of comparison and target area children. For pur-

---

[1] An earlier version of this section appeared in *Pediatrics* (Klein et al., 1973a).

poses of economy, then, the admissions to these two hospitals were taken to represent the total hospitalization experience in the two areas.

The target area primary care system included only the RNHC. The comparison area had five general practitioners and a health department funded center that delivered care from 9 A.M. to 5 P.M., Monday through Friday, using largely part-time physicians and operating without outreach. In addition, the comparison area contained two traditional well-child conferences.

This study tests the three hypotheses given above through a before-after comparison of the patterns of the two areas. Though the research design is not strictly experimental, since no random allocation of patients was possible, differences in hospitalization patterns of the two areas may reasonably be attributed to the different care facilities available to their residents, especially considering the "before" data baseline.

## Hospital Data

Records for the three study years—fiscal 1968 as the base year and fiscal 1969 and 1970 as the first two operational years—were available at Strong Memorial and Genesee Hospitals. All admissions of children under 16 years of age, excluding newborns and admissions to the obstetrical and gynecological service, were selected and described according to standard variables. The computer based data from Strong Memorial Hospital represent the total hospital experience, while some sampling was necessary for Genesee Hospital.[2]

In addition, for patients from the comparison and target areas, a de-

---

[2] Since the records at Genesee Hospital were not computerized, we were unable to replicate the detailed studies done at Strong Memorial Hospital. We were, however, able to obtain a discharge data file on all *medical* pediatric patients, and we hand-coded each admission by census tract, diagnostic category, and health center user status.

Since we had no way of obtaining the same detailed data on pediatric surgical cases at Genesee Hospital, certain estimates had to be made. We knew the total number of medical and surgical pediatric discharges and computed the percentage of all pediatric medical admissions for each fiscal year accounted for by the target and control areas. We assumed that this proportion would also apply for surgical admissions from these areas and thus derived an estimate of the number of surgical admissions.

The length of hospitalization was noted, and total hospital days by area were computed for *medical* pediatric patients only. The number of surgical days is an estimated figure based on the mean number of days for a surgical stay at Strong Memorial Hospital by fiscal year times the estimated number of surgical admissions by area at Genesee Hospital. Although we recognized that these methods of estimation might be faulty, we presumed that they would be equally faulty for each of the three fiscal years and hence would not affect changes uncovered in actual hospitalization patterns.

tailed analysis was undertaken in which the reason for admission was coded according to five diagnostic categories: (1) general medical; (2) respiratory/infectious; (3) surgical/elective; (4) surgical/traumatic; and (5) surgical/other.

The record of each target area admitted patient was reviewed against the RNHC files to see whether he was a health center patient. If so, his health center chart was examined to see whether he had had a visit with a physician *before* the date of his hospital admission (hereafter, such patients are called "users"), and, if so, whether he had been referred for admission by the health center (hereafter called "referred users"), or whether he had been referred by some source other than the health center, or was self-referred (hereafter called "leakers").

The population data required to compute rates are based on the 1964 and 1970 census with interpolations for the three intermediate fiscal years (Table 9D.1).

## The Rochester Neighborhood Health Center Data Base

The basic data on the number of children cared for by the RNHC during the midpoint in each of the two operating fiscal years were taken from the quarterly report of the center. It soon became obvious that some registered patients were receiving care elsewhere. This is explained by the fact that the center had registered large numbers of patients by door-to-door outreach and agency referrals. Since such registration in the first two years did not necessarily imply intention to use the center, registered patients at the RNHC cannot be compared to "enrolled" patients in other studies.

It was necessary, therefore, to do a substudy to determine the percentage of children who were registered and were actual users of the center. For this purpose a 5% random sample (250 charts) was drawn. Users in fiscal 1969 were defined as registered children who had had a visit in fiscal 1969, while users in fiscal 1970 were defined as registered children who had had a visit in either fiscal 1969 or fiscal 1970. Thus, although there were 2642 registered children in fiscal 1969, only 56% were users. By fiscal 1970, the effect of the initial outreach effort and agency referrals was wearing off, and 76% of 4347 registered children were users. The estimates for target area users and nonusers in Table 9D.2 are directly derived from the substudy results applied to area child census figures.

Moore (1973) has pointed out that the number of health center users in 1970 may be inflated because most fee-for-service group practices do not delete from their patient files those persons who have moved. This leads, over a number of years, to a grossly inflated figure of patients served by them. Had we done the same, our "user" estimate would be similarly

Table 9D.1. *Socioeconomic Characteristics of the Target and Comparison Areas, 1968–1970[a,b]*

| Characteristic | Target Area | Comparison Area |
|---|---|---|
| Child population under 16 years | | |
| 1968 | 8246 | 7604 |
| 1969 | 8138 | 7370 |
| 1970 | 8030 | 7136 |
| Percent of children in population | | |
| 1968 | 45 | 38 |
| 1969 | 45 | 39 |
| 1970 | 46 | 40 |
| Percent of nonwhites in population | | |
| 1968 | 63 | 71 |
| 1969 | 66 | 75 |
| 1970 | 70 | 81 |
| Percent of illegitimate births | | |
| 1968 | 44 | 41 |
| 1969 | 44 | 43 |
| 1970 | 44 | 45 |
| Median income (dollars) | | |
| 1968 | 6413 | 6601 |
| 1969 | 6668 | 6710 |
| 1970 | 6945 | 6862 |
| Number of housing units | | |
| 1960 | 7307 | 9982 |
| 1970 | 6318 | 8174 |
| Percent of Medicaid enrolled children in | | |
| 1970 | 63 | 55 |

[a] From Klein et al. (1973a), p. 834.
[b] Based on census data with some estimation through interpolation. These figures differ slightly from those presented in other sections of this book because of the different age definition (below 16 instead of below 18) and the exclusion of one census tract in the comparison area (programming error).

inflated and the "nonuser" estimate deflated, resulting in false denominators for admission rates. To avoid this problem we did not use registered patients, but only active patients as described above, and thus avoided the problem mentioned by Moore. However, the definition of "active" was less restrictive for fiscal 1970 (a visit either in fiscal year 1969 or fiscal year 1970) than for fiscal 1969 (a visit only in the one preceding year). This wider definition may have slightly inflated the user estimate

Table 9D.2.  Population Data by Residence, by Year, and by Rochester Neighborhood Health Center User Status[a]

|  | 1968 | 1969 | 1970 |
|---|---|---|---|
| Child population, Comparison area | 7604 | 7370 | 7136 |
| Child population, Target area | 8246 | 8138 | 8030 |
| Target area RNHC users | — | 1477 | 3286 |
| Target area RNHC non-users | — | 6641 | 4744 |
| Percent of RNHC child users on Medicaid | — | 79.0 | 82.3 |

[a] From Klein et al. (1973a), p. 834.

and deflated the nonuser estimate. The possible error due to this has been estimated in our reply to Moore (Klein et al., 1973b) and does not affect our main conclusion.

Another study (Hillman and Charney, 1972) at the RNHC showed that only 74% of randomly selected households registered more than six months before the interview identified the center as their primary source of medical care, thus supporting the results of the substudy.

## Results

### Admission Rates

Data for the admissions of children to the two hospitals, by area, are presented in Table 9D.3. The total number of hospital admissions by area was remarkably constant over the three fiscal years. The low admission rate per thousand from the comparison area also remained constant—and unexplained.

Further analysis of target area admissions by *user* status at the RNHC, however, yielded more information. In fiscal 1970 the target area users had a rate of 33 admissions/1000, while the target area nonusers had a rate of 67 admissions/1000. Even a reduced user estimate to consider the possibly inflated original estimate (see discussion above) does not change the basic finding.

### Hospital Days

Mean length of hospital stay in days is reported in Table 9D.4. Of particular note is the figure of 5.6 days/1000 for 1970 health center users,

*Table 9D.3.   Child Admissions to Strong Memorial and Genesee Hospitals by Residence, Fiscal Year, and Rochester Neighborhood Health Center User Status*[a]

|                                        | 1968 | 1969 | 1970 |
|----------------------------------------|------|------|------|
| Number of admissions,                  |      |      |      |
| Comparison area                        | 277  | 298  | 277  |
| Target area                            | 419  | 473  | 424  |
| Target area RNHC users                 | —    | 73   | 108  |
| Target area RNHC nonusers              | —    | 400  | 316  |
| Number of admissions per 1000,         |      |      |      |
| Comparison area                        | 36.4 | 40.4 | 38.8 |
| Target area                            | 50.8 | 58.6 | 52.8 |
| Target area RNHC users                 | —    | 49.4 ◄— b —►32.8 ⌉ |      |
| Target area RNHC nonusers              | —    | 60.2 | 66.8 ⌋ c |

[a] From Klein et al. (1973a), p. 836.
[b] $p < .02$.
[c] $p < .001$.

compared to 7.6/1000 for target area nonusers and 8.4/1000 for the comparison area.

The marked decrease (from 346 to 184) in hospital days per thousand among the target area health center users was due to both a reduction in the number of admissions and fewer days per admission. The marked fall in hospital days per thousand is seen more dramatically in Figure 9D.1, where these changes are displayed in graphic form. Again, employing a reduced user estimate does not affect this conclusion (Klein et al., 1973b).

### Diagnostic Categories at Strong Memorial Hospital

The first hypothesis stated that child admissions for respiratory/infectious illnesses would decrease, while those for elective/surgical or restorative procedures would increase. This was confirmed only for patients who were directly referred for admission by health center physicians: the percentage of such children admitted for respiratory/infectious illnesses went from 33% in 1969 to 19% in 1970; for elective/surgical or restorative, from 30% to 46%. Patients who were users of the health center but were not referred for admission (the "leakers") were frequently admitted for respiratory/infectious illnesses (57% of the time in 1970), and were almost never (11% of the time in 1970) admitted for surgical/elective reasons. These figures, however, had to be limited to the experience at Strong Memorial Hospital (see footnote 2), since the pediatricians at the RNHC

Table 9D.4.  Length of Hospital Use by Residence, Fiscal Year, and
Rochester Neighborhood Health Center User Status[a,b]

|  | 1968 | 1969 | 1970 |
|---|---|---|---|
|  |  | Days |  |
| Mean length of hospital stay, |  |  |  |
| Comparison area  (SMH only) | 5.4 | 7.6 | 8.4 |
| Target area  (SMH only) | 5.8 | 8.0 | 6.9[c] |
| Target area RNHC users | — | 7.0 | 5.6 |
| Target area RNHC nonusers | — | 8.2 | 7.6[d] |
| Number of hospital-days (SMH and TGH[e]) |  |  |  |
| Comparison area | 1496 | 2264 | 2327 |
| Target area | 2430 | 3784 | 2926 |
| Target area RNHC users | — | 511 | 604 |
| Target area RNHC nonusers | — | 3280 | 2402 |
| Number of hospital-days |  |  |  |
| per 1000 (SMH and TGH[e]) |  |  |  |
| Comparison area | 197 | 307 | 326 |
| Target area | 295 | 469 | 364 |
| Target area RNHC users | — | 346 | 184 |
| Target area RNHC nonusers | — | 497 | 489 |

[a] From Klein et al. (1973a), p. 836.
[b] SMH = Strong Memorial Hospital; TGH = The Genesee Hospital.
[c] $p < .02$.
[d] $p < .08$.
[e] Based on SMH mean hospital days.

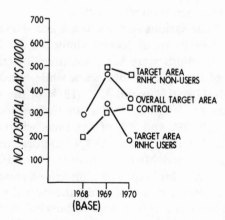

Figure 9D.1.  Child hospital days/1000 (SMH and TGH) by residence, by year, by
Rochester Neighborhood Health Center user or control status (Klein et al., 1973a).

are on staff at this hospital and admit almost all of their patients there. The results by diagnostic categories limited to Strong Memorial Hospital are, therefore, inconclusive.

Medicaid Admissions (Strong Memorial Hospital)

Analysis of RNHC user admissions to Strong Memorial Hospital in the two fiscal years showed a surprisingly large number in the non-Medicaid category. Since approximately 80% of the center's child users were receiving Medicaid assistance (Table 9D.2), it was expected that at least an equal percentage would be found in the hospitalized group, especially since hospitalization was often the event that prompted Medicaid enrollment. It would have been preferable to analyze all admissions by Medicaid status, but necessary estimations for the Genesee Hospital were not possible. Therefore only the Strong Memorial Hospital (the major hospital, where two thirds of both the referred and "leaking" users are admitted) data were analyzed by Medicaid status. The admissions are presented in Table 9D.5. Whereas the total number of Medicaid admissions remained constant, the number of user Medicaid admissions doubled from 1969 to 1970, reflecting a doubling in the general user population. No such change was seen in the non-Medicaid group of health center users.

The "Leakers" (Strong Memorial Hospital)

Although the percentage of "leakers" remained relatively constant (39% and 35% of users in 1969 and 1970), the Medicaid proportion increased from about 40% to approximately 80%. The proportion of non-Medicaid leakers, however, decreased from 60% to 20%!

The reasons for these various admissions are also shown in Table 9D.5, which presents a breakdown of leaker admissions by Medicaid status. Medicaid leaker admissions were for respiratory/infectious reasons approximately 70% of the time in both years, while non-Medicaid leakers were admitted only 17% (1969) and 33% (1971) of the time for respiratory/infectious reasons. Surgical/elective admissions took place among Medicaid leakers only 0% and 9% of the time, whereas non-Medicaid leakers were admitted to this category 33% of the time in both years.

As expected, the referred Medicaid patients were admitted approximately 50% of the time for respiratory/infectious reasons in 1969 and 33% in 1970. The referred non-Medicaid patients had only 0% and 5% admissions respectively, in this category. Surgical/elective admissions among the Medicaid referred group rose from 15% to 39%, while the non-Medicaid referred group decreased from 60% to 47% over the two years.

Table 9D.5.   *Target Area Pediatric Admissions to Strong Memorial Hospital by Rochester Neighborhood Health Center User Status, Medicaid Status, and Reason for Admission*

|  | 1968 | 1969 | 1970 |
|---|---|---|---|
| Total | 239 | 240 | 221 |
| User Status |  |  |  |
| Nonusers | 239 | 191 | 141 |
| Users | — | 49 | 80 |
| "Leakers" | — | 19 | 28 |
| Referrals | — | 30 | 52 |
| Medicaid Status |  |  |  |
| Medicaid | 131 | 130 | 117 |
| Non-Medicaid | 108 | 110 | 104 |
| Users by Medicaid Status |  |  |  |
| and Reasons for Admission |  |  |  |
| Medicaid users | — | 27 | 55 |
| Non-Medicaid users | — | 22 | 25 |
|  |  |  |  |
| "Leakers" |  |  |  |
| Medicaid | — | 7 | 22 |
| Respiratory/infectious | — | 5 | 14 |
| Elective/surgical | — | 0 | 2 |
| Non-Medicaid | — | 12 | 6 |
| Respiratory/infestious | — | 2 | 2 |
| Elective/surgical | — | 4 | 2 |
| Referrals |  |  |  |
| Medicaid | — | 20 | 33 |
| Respiratory/infestious | — | 10 | 9 |
| Elective/surgical | — | 3 | 13 |
| Non-Medicaid | — | 10 | 19 |
| Respiratory/infestious | — | 0 | 1 |
| Elective/surgical | — | 6 | 9 |

## Discussion

Much of this section has had to be devoted to methodology. It was hoped that questions left unanswered by the Bellin et al. (1969) and James (1971) studies would be resolved. With respect to our first and second hypotheses, it was not shown that the RNHC changed the number or pattern of child admissions for the entire target area child population, or that no changes occurred in the comparison area. There appear to be differences, however, for the two groups referred to as the target area users and nonusers. That these represent an effect of the health center cannot be proved, for there is the possibility that the population referred to as health center users was basically at low risk for hospitalization.

A firm statement can be made only with respect to the third hypothesis. The health center patients spent fewer days in hospitals than those of the comparison area or the target area nonusers. This difference was due to both fewer admissions and shorter average stays. But again it is difficult to judge to what extent this, in turn, is due to the care provided and to the self-selection of patients.

It should be noted that the major part of this study at Strong Memorial Hospital was relatively simple and accurate because of the availability of the admission data on computer tape. Sampling was not necessary; the total admitted population was studied. By contrast, obtaining additional information from other hospitals in the area was difficult, time consuming, and subject to error due to necessary estimating, hand sorting, and sampling. It is questionable whether such studies can be carried out in the future unless all hospitals convert to computerized data processing.

The diagnostic classification was chosen to approach the "selection" of a low-risk population of the target area. It should be realized, however, that, though we have been speaking of admission patterns by diagnostic category, we may actually be describing referral patterns of physicians rather than admission patterns of patients. The user admission data in Table 9D.5 suggest that in 1969 the non-Medicaid group was overrepresented and was admitted disproportionately for elective surgery. The Medicaid group, on the other hand, was admitted excessively for respiratory and infectious reasons. When the Medicaid group "leaked," it did so almost exclusively for respiratory and infectious illnesses. The non-Medicaid group also leaked often, but in this group much of the leaking was due to surgical/elective procedures.

By 1970 69% of user admissions were paid for by Medicaid, thus more closely reflecting the percentages both of target area children on Medicaid (63%) and of health center children on Medicaid (82%). The Medicaid group was admitted less often for respiratory/infectious reasons and more often for surgical/elective procedures. Of the Medicaid leakers, however, 70% still leaked for respiratory/infectious reasons. Although the interpretation of these figures is difficult, a pattern appeared to emerge. In the first year of the program the admissions were unrepresentative of the target area population and of the health center user group with respect to Medicaid status. Apparently the users with private hospital insurance (Blue Cross) were preferably admitted, largely for surgical/elective procedures, because of their payment status. Even when they leaked, they did so for surgical/elective as opposed to respiratory/infectious reasons.

In both years the Medicaid group was the most difficult to care for in terms of encouraging appropriate hospital utilization. Medicaid leakers increased as a proportion of all users, while non-Medicaid leakers decreased. Medicaid leakers for respiratory and infectious illness remained high. The outreach and patient-center communication was apparently most effective for the lower-risk group—users with private hospital insurance utilized the services so effectively that they made a major contribution to lowering the overall hospitalization rate for the user group. The question of the extent to which the low-risk populations of the target area, both Medicaid and non-Medicaid, became the initial health center users remains unanswered, and a separate study should focus on this question. The phenomenon of the leakers also merits a study of its own.

Certain key methodological points warrant restatement.

1. Hospital admission studies that ignore the question of possible shifting hospitalization patterns may yield data that are difficult to interpret.

2. Though an actual control population is difficult to obtain, an appropriately drawn comparison population covers a multitude of methodological sins.

3. Any study that is not attuned to identify leakers will yield artificially good results.

4. Hospital admission studies must be designed with reference to a population at risk. When this is done, rates can be computed.

5. The category "user" had to be specifically defined for this study. Careful distinctions have to be made between registrants, enrollees, and users. One needs to look separately at the registrants who use and those who do not use the health center, and special attention must be given to the "compliant" users versus the so-called "leakers."

6. The creation of the diagnostic categories, particularly respiratory/infectious and surgical/elective, may have raised more questions than were answered, but it presents an interesting model that may have utility in determining whether a program is meeting acute medical crises, as opposed to its ability to deal with previously unmet needs.

To summarize, the Rochester Neighborhood Health Center was used more by target area residents at low risk for hospitalization than by those at high risk. The admission rate of users was lower in the second year than in the first year of operation and lower than the comparison area population. The length of hospital stays was also reduced. Health center users were admitted less for respiratory/infectious and more for surgical/elective reasons.

A conservative conclusion as to the effect of the health center appears justified: for patients who were attracted to the center and became users, hospitalization rates and days declined. This is what was hoped to be the effect of the center. There remains, however, a group of children, not using the center although eligible, who continue to have high hospitalization rates. As is true of much of the evaluation of the RNHC, hospitalization outcomes are "mixed notices."

## REFERENCES

BELLIN, SEYMOUR, GEIGER, H. JACK, and GIBSON, COUNT

1969    "Impact of Ambulatory Health Care Services on the Demand for Hospital Beds." *New England Journal of Medicine*, 280:808–812.

HILLMAN, BRUCE, and CHARNEY, EVAN

1972    "A Neighborhood Health Center: What the Patients Know and Think of Its Operation." *Medical Care*, 10(4):336–344.

JAMES, DAVID H.

1971    "The Impact of a Children and Youth Project on the Need for In-Patient Hospital Care." Ambulatory Pediatric Association, Eleventh Annual Meeting, Program and Abstract (April 27–28) p. 19.

KLEIN, MICHAEL, ROGHMANN, KLAUS, WOODWARD, KENNETH, and CHARNEY, EVAN

1973a    "The Impact of the Rochester Neighborhood Health Center on Hospitalization of Children, 1968–1970." *Pediatrics*, 51:833–839.

KLEIN, MICHAEL, ROGHMANN, KLAUS, WOODWARD, KENNETH, and CHARNEY, EVAN

1973b    Letter to the Editor. *Pediatrics*, 52(5):755.

MOORE, GORDON T.

1973    Letter to the Editor. *Pediatrics*, 52(5):754.

# CHAPTER TEN

# The Migrant
# Health Project:
# Care or Conflict?

ROBERT J. HAGGERTY

The migrant health project was initiated in 1964 with a grant from the U.S. Public Health Service. The objective was to provide medical services to seasonal agricultural migrants who were not receiving such care. Although the program in Rochester was not born in controversy, conflict soon became a major element in its day-to-day activities. To discuss the role of conflict in social change (Coser, 1956), the story must first be told. This chapter is, therefore, largely descriptive. No formal evaluation of the migrant health program has been attempted. The poignancy of the problems, the energy expended on their solution, and the political lessons learned persuaded us to present an analysis of this project despite the lack of a major research component.

## The Migrant Agricultural System

There are an estimated 1.0–1.5 million migratory farm workers and their families in the United States. The eastern stream workers winter primarily in Florida, but also in other southern states and Puerto Rico, and then come north to harvest various crops.

Monroe County has generally flat, rich agricultural glacial land. Although now considered a highly industrialized metropolitan area, the county has large farm acreage, especially west of the Genesee River. Farm crops are varied: sweet and sour cherries are harvested in the early summer, followed by tomatoes, cucumbers, beans, and, late in the season, sugar beets, potatoes, apples, and, finally, cabbages. Some farms have large peach and plum crops. The short period wherein these crops can be picked emphasizes the need for outside hired help.

Of the about 10,000 migrants in the state only some 700 come to Monroe County. Neighboring Wayne County has over 4000 migrants per year, and Orleans County (where the current clinic is located), about 2000 per year. The rest are in other surrounding counties.

Most farms are small—at most only a few hundred acres—and can employ only a few to a maximum of about 100 migrant workers each. Thus camps of migrants are small and scattered. Increasing numbers (probably one fourth to one third) of workers are Puerto Rican and Chicano, while the remainder are southern blacks, largely from South Carolina and Florida. Generally several hundred children accompany their parents during the summer (Genesee Region Health Planning Council, 1971:D6–D7).

The crew boss system continues in force—the workers are recruited by a crew boss, usually black, who contracts with farmers to deliver a specified number of workers. The crew boss provides transportation, usually in old school buses or trucks. The majority of migrant agricultural workers arrive in late June or early July. At peak times farmers also employ "day-haul" workers from the city to harvest crops. There is considerable friction between these groups, not least because of different pay schedules. The day-haul groups are paid a total daily wage, whereas the migrant has a certain amount withheld by the grower to ensure his remaining until the end of the season.

Housing is provided on the farms and in many cases is rudimentary—tiny, crowded shacks with unsafe cooking facilities, open latrines, and contaminated drinking water. Violations of existing sanitary codes are frequent, but rarely reported. The single-spigot water supply for one whole camp (located in western New York State) of over 60 people, shown in Figure 10.1, was found to be contaminated with intestinal bacteria over the entire summer, because of the old public health menace of open-pit latrines too near the water supply.

Fires have taken several lives in these camps over the past few years. Heaping insult upon injury, high rents are charged for these uninhabitable quarters. The health departments have had inadequate staff to properly inspect camps and to close offending ones. In addition, they face several social and political dilemmas: for example, if they close the camp of a prominent grower who is also a county legislator, they may endanger the next year's entire health department budget.

Pay for the migrant is low (in the past, unprotected by the minimal wage law; current laws are frequently ignored) and is garnisheed for housing, food, and recreation (a "company store" on the farm often provides beer and liquor and a place for recreation at high prices).

The migrants' lot, then, is a sorry, depressing one, depicted over a decade ago in a classic documentary film by Edward R. Morrow (1960) and

*Figure 10.1. Single-spigot water source for migrant camp (living quarters in background).*

in numerous books (e.g., Coles, 1972). It has changed all too little since these accounts were presented.

Some of the causes of problems are evident: the crew boss—little supervised in his handling of workers; the farmer—tolerant of the crew boss, sometimes unwilling to improve living conditions, and himself caught in a competitive industry where to do differently would reduce already small incomes; and the health department—understaffed and unable to enforce sanitary regulations. When a rural community is inundated by a transient population such as migrant laborers, it does not have the resources for assistance that even a deficient urban poverty area has. Not only are there few physicians, but also hospitals are small and lack organized outpatient departments and emergency rooms. Thus, in addition to social and cultural antagonisms, the migrant adds a temporary burden to the already overloaded rural medical care system.

Though the migratory farm worker travels long distances, he is far from mobile when he arrives at his destination. Since the crew boss provides the long-distance transportation, the worker has no car of his own in the North, and cannot leave the camp except with transportation provided by the farm or at a high fee by someone with a car. In short, the migrant cannot get medical care unless it is available at the camp or transportation is provided to a more central facility.

## The Health Problems

Migrants' health problems are mainly of the acute type—injuries caused by accidents or violence, skin infections, and respiratory disorders—which they often neglect because to take time off from work during the day of harvesting means loss of income. In addition, a heavy burden of neglected chronic disease is also present—serious tooth problems, hypertension, diabetes, and alcoholism. Many cases of gonorrhea and obesity are also seen in the clinic serving these workers. The most seriously dysfunctional chronic diseases are not present in large numbers, however, because persons so afflicted cannot do the demanding physical work or travel the long distances required of a migrant.

Medical and dental care have been very scanty in the past. Our own dental team surveyed several thousand children in both the urban slums and the migrant program and found the rates of decayed and missing teeth to be equally high in the two groups; however, only 0.4% of teeth of migrant children had fillings, while the rate was 7.8% for the urban poor. This is one indication of the lack of dental care received by migrants in the past.

The health problems of the migrant worker, however, are not very different from those seen in general practice. What is different is the accompanying social, economic, and cultural setting in which they occur.

## The Program

Public Health Service (PHS) grant support for migrant health programs has been awarded on the basis of competitive grant applications with nearly full funding, that is, only small matching funds have been required by the PHS. The amounts appropriated, although increasing in recent years, have never been large. Starting at 7 million dollars per year in 1964, they increased to 15 million per year in 1971 for the entire United States. Our grant was for $41,381 in 1967, rising to $171,493 in 1968 and to $185,929 in 1971–1972. (The large jump occurring in 1968 was due to the addition of an adjacent county, with about 2000 seasonal agricultural migrants, to the program.)

The clinics have almost all been held at night to accommodate the workers' schedules. Moreover, since a large cadre of volunteers helps to staff the clinics, nighttime has been more convenient for the providers as well. Several sites have been used over the years: small camps, in very crowded unsatisfactory areas; a small house provided by a farmer; a college dispensary; a local hospital clinic; a private doctor's office; and, finally, a renovated store. At first an attempt was made to ensure access by having multiple clinics at the camps where the migrants lived, on the assumption that, at the end of a fatiguing day, these workers would be in no mood to travel far for medical care. But the makeshift physical facilities of the clinics that such a policy mandated were felt to be a greater handicap than inadequate transportation. A single clinic is now operated in a nicely renovated store in the major small trading city of the farm area, and transportation is provided for the migrant from his camp to the clinic. Both the migrant worker and the provider seem to prefer this pleasant medical care setting, which is similar to settings used by other populations.

The staff has consisted of a project nurse, trained in public health; one or two staff nurses; 15–20 physicians per year, each working only a few of the clinic sessions; dentists and their assistants; a health educator; health assistants (recruited from the migrant or ex-migrant population); and large numbers of other volunteers (as many as 50 per year).

Health education and certain screening tests are done in the camps, and well-child checks are conducted in schools where Head Start programs are in progress. Home visits are made, especially by the health educator and public health nurse, but most personal health services are provided in the clinic.

Dentistry has been a large and important part of the services provided—often the first dental care patients have received. As a result, a dental visit often consists of tooth removal rather than preventive or restorative care.

Among the related activities of the migrant health project have been health education, sanitation inspection, housing inspection, working with cooperating groups—Head Start, day care, VISTA—and attempts to alert the community (the health department, the medical society, the hospitals, the growers, the legislators, and the general public) to the plight of the migrant.

Exposure of health personnel—faculty, students, and some local physicians—to the problems of the migrant was perhaps the project's greatest accomplishment.

## Consumer Participation

Over the years we have been impressed by the great degree of apathy to medical care expressed by many migrants, but even more by their powerlessness. This program seemed, therefore, to offer a classic setting for developing consumer participation.

In 1969 a coalition of migrant workers was formed which, it was hoped, would eventually become the management corporation for the program. All the problems that have plagued urban neighborhood health center community boards have been experienced by this coalition, plus the added problem of planning for the clinic in the winter and spring before any migrants have arrived. There were a few ex-migrants who stayed north to live, to whom we turned to form such a board, but, in general, the leadership of the board and most of its members have been nonmigrants—by no means uninterested or ineffective advocates, but, nonetheless, neither migrants nor consumers.

The role of the coalition has been difficult to develop. It was hoped that the group would become incorporated and assume a management role, but to date it has not.[1] The members have selected personnel and advised on clinic settings, but large amounts of time have been spent on arguments over their own organization and control of the clinic—a feature of many such councils. They have yet to become organized to the point where they would take over the clinic. On the other hand, provider groups in the community would like to run the clinic but without any consumer voice. The university, as the sponsor, has been caught between the coalition and the local health establishment, and remains a reluctant manager until a representative group from the community can be developed.

## Politics and Conflict

No description of this program can ignore the political aspects, and no description by a participant can be objective. Our bias is that of the sponsor of the clinic. Arrayed against the clinic were often the farmers, the physicians in the rural areas, the hospitals in the small rural community, and the health department. The reasons for tension and conflict are not hard to understand: an outside group (the university, which is regarded with some suspicion anyway) sponsors a medical care program in somewhat isolated, small, conservative communities. This in itself implies that the "locals" cannot do the job (always a threatening gesture). Furthermore, the clinic expanded the boundaries of health care to include the championing of better housing and higher wages for the migrant. The implicit danger here was that this would encourage his rebellion against a system already threatened from many other directions as well.

It must be admitted that tact was not used in entering the communities,

1 During 1973–1974 the coalition was organized and became incorporated, and by the summer of 1974 it was the recipient of the grant. The program has moved to another location and has expanded its services to the agricultural poor to cover the entire year.

nor were local power groups properly enlisted early in the venture. Legitimate complaints were voiced by local physicians who were unhappy because the clinic was open only in the evenings. When a patient to whom the clinic had given initial treatment needed daytime, night, or weekend care, he had to turn to the local physicians, who had no medical record and felt dissatisfied with providing just off-hour back-up services.

In spite of these concerns a study of a random sample of physicians in the area (Dean et al., 1971) suggested that attitudes, in general, toward migrant care programs were reasonably receptive. The study compared attitudes toward the medical care of migrant farm workers with those toward the care of the elderly and of crippled children. Although, on the whole, viewpoints expressed by the sample of 55 physicians interviewed were less favorable with respect to the care of migrants than of the other groups, many of the responses were quite positive. For example, 81% agreed that migrant workers have a unique set of health needs, and 67% recognized that the care they receive is inadequate. Similarly, 75% thought that most or all of the care of migrants should be handled by local physicians with outside assistance, that is, support for their expenses being provided in large measure by the government.

Only a minority (4%) of the physicians interviewed agreed with the statement that "a major drawback to government programs for migrants is that they restrain freedom of the physician," and a majority thought that such programs should be continued (30%) or even expanded (52%). The investigators recognized that publicly expressed attitudes such as these may be misleading, but concluded, nevertheless, as follows:

> The principal implication of these findings is that those in charge of future government programs should be more sensitive to the contributions of local practitioners if programs are to be efficient and effective. Most rural physicians are not opposed to government involvement in medical care. Rather, they object to those programs which encroach upon what they feel is their domain of responsibility without adequate consultation (p. 2200).

There is no question that a major effect of the program stemmed from the political issues. The staff learned that excessive zeal and pressure often result only in increased resistance. But hundreds of young medical students, nurses, residents, and other volunteers became aware of the appalling shame of our society, which permits such human degradation and then hides it. They learned of the petty, racist attitudes of some of our citizens, and they discovered that medicine cannot be separated from the underlying social problems. How much the migrant himself benefited from these health services and other social intervention is less clear. No doubt some illnesses were treated that otherwise would not have been. But, to date, the program has not moved beyond an episodic type of patch-up medical care. Until a comprehensive rural health program can be developed into which the migrant can fit, this program will meet neither our goals nor his needs.

## The Role of Controversy

Controversy between growers, practicing physicians, the health departments and hospitals in rural areas, the program personnel, and the migrant coalition can be viewed as a weakness—an ineffective, wheel-spinning exercise. But others have seen, or at least rationalized, such controversy as necessary to produce social change, as did Coser (1956) in his seminal work. The issue, in his view, is whether the conflict is "realistic" with functional alternatives to achieve desired results. Some of the conflicts of the migrant project may have been "nonrealistic," due not to rival ends of the antagonists, but to problems unrelated to the migrant project. If this is the case, the conflict can become dysfunctional. Coser's thesis is that rigid social systems foster such dysfunctional conflict; our experience supports the thesis. One of our hopes for the migrant project was to reduce some of the rigidities in the relations between the various elements of the social systems that have come into conflict: the university, the personnel of the project, the rural communities, and the consumers. This has not been achieved. Better health will come to the migrant only when he is organized and has better housing and recreational programs, and when the economic system in which he is forced to compete rewards him adequately in money and dignity. A migrant program such as ours can offer only small assistance to this needed national effort.

What are the credits and debits of this program being administered by pediatrics, a university clinical department? It is the only one in the country to be so administered. Most are run either by local health departments or hospitals or by consumer groups. This question cannot be answered without addressing the larger problem of the role of a clinical department in the community; that will be discussed in the concluding chapter.

If we were to start over, we would incorporate more political science expertise to examine the process of conflict. When the program was started, it was not known how to study the conflicts and politics surrounding health care, nor could expert help in this area be obtained when the need for it was recognized.

In the future removing the barriers to the organization of health care for the disadvantaged—urban and rural—will need to proceed from mere organization of care to a study of the political process involved. Hopefully this can be done with enough scientific rigor to make the knowledge of health politics cumulative and not merely a collection of case histories.

## REFERENCES

COLES, ROBERT

   1972 *Migrants, Share Croppers, Mountaineers.* Boston: Atlantic-Little Brown.

COSER, LEWIS

   1956 *The Functions of Social Conflict.* New York: Free Press.

DEAN, T., BORKAN, E., and PLESS, I. BARRY

   1971 "Attitudes of Rural Physicians toward the Medical Care of Migrant Farm Workers, Crippled Children, and the Elderly." *American Journal of Public Health,* 61(11):2195–2200.

GENESEE REGION HEALTH PLANNING COUNCIL/ROCHESTER REGIONAL MEDICAL PROGRAM

   1971 *Health Data Resource Book.* Rochester, New York.

MORROW, EDWARD R.

   1960 "Harvest of Shame," CBS Report. Copyright November 25, 1960.

CHAPTER ELEVEN

# New Manpower Programs

## A. THE PEDIATRIC NURSE PRACTITIONER

ROBERT A. HOEKELMAN, HARRIET KITZMAN, AND EVAN CHARNEY

T he causes of the current deficiencies in medical care included, in the
past, a growing population; a decrease in the relative number of physicians delivering primary health care; a maldistribution of physicians,
leaving inner cities and rural areas underserved; a change in the needs of
the patient population due to an expansion of medical knowledge; and
an ineffective utilization of existing health manpower (Fein, 1967; Blasingame, 1968).

One of the most attractive means of improving health care is by increasing the efficiency of physicians through the use of allied health professionals (Lewis and Resnik, 1967; Yankauer, 1968). Since 1965 over 100
programs have been established throughout the United States to train a
variety of physician assistants; many more are under development.

We believe that the professional nurse is the most logical person to join
the physician, share the responsibilities for direct patient care, and thus
provide increased care. Accordingly, a program similar to that of Silver
et al. (1967, 1968) to enable nurses to assume expanded roles in ambulatory patient care was developed at the University of Rochester. Throughout there has been a concern for a careful evaluation of the new roles for
the nurse in order to make the findings applicable to child health care
generally.

*University of Rochester Program*

The development of expanded, collegial roles for nurses in ambulatory
child care at the University of Rochester began in the pediatric residents'
continuity clinic during 1966 and 1967. During that period the nurse provided the services in approximately two thirds of the well-child visits. She
was contacted about minor illnesses and managed these by phone, unless
a home or clinic visit was considered necessary for a more definitive diagnosis. The nurse also provided counseling when patterns of day-to-day liv-

ing were upsetting family balance or were inhibiting individual or family growth or both. It was believed that, for the team concept to be successful, the combined efforts of a nurse and a physician must produce better results than the sum of their individual efforts.

### Development of the First Curriculum

With this experience as a guide, the curriculum for the first pediatric nurse practitioner (PNP) training program at the University of Rochester was developed to prepare nurses to share the care of children under 2 years of age with physicians in private practice. The selection of nurses was facilitated because there was a large inactive group interested in returning to work. The intent was to recruit largely from those who had children of their own in order to add this mothering experience and skill to that of the professional nursing role. It was planned that many would work only part time to fit their home schedules into those of private pediatric practices and to make possible the use of nurses who otherwise could not work.

Discussions with four practicing pediatricians determined the services they considered essential for children under 2 years of age. This provided a base for defining standards and components of care within the practices. The potential responsibilities of the nurse practitioners within the private practice setting included hospital newborn visits, home visits, one half of the well-child visits, and telephone management of day-to-day health problems and minor illness. A four-month course of study was designed to build on the assumed skills of the entering nurses and enable each to reach the objectives defined.

Attitudes regarding role realignments and professional identity were recognized as a major consideration in the preparation of these PNPs. Discussions with physicians and nurses allowed each group to retain its identity, strengthen its own area of expertise, and join with the other in mutual support with coordinated patient care as the primary goal.

In subsequent years the objectives and curriculum were expanded since nursing students were being prepared to function in health care settings where a broader range of patient-physician and psychosocial needs existed than in private pediatricians' offices.

### Analysis of Trainee Characteristics

With recognition of the need for a large number of trained professionals to fill the gaps in delivery of child health care, and in view of the large pool of inactive nurses, applicants were sought from graduates of diploma and associate degree nursing programs as well as from baccalaureate and master degree programs. Licensure as a registered nurse (RN) was the only training prerequisite.

A second prerequisite for admission to the training program, however, was that the applicant must have a firm offer of employment in a practice setting, either private office or public clinic, to begin after completing her PNP course of study. This was required in order that those in the practice setting could be informed about the concept and role of the PNP.

By the end of 1973, 60 nurses had completed the program; 21 were graduates of diploma schools, 2 of an associate degree program, 24 of baccalaureate degree programs in nursing, and 13 of master's degree programs. Table 11A.1 shows the age distribution of the trainees, their activities before training, and their places of practice after training. Only 25 had mothering experience; thus the initial intent of attracting chiefly nonworking mothers back into the health care field was not achieved.

Not all nurses can function equally well in all of the settings in need of PNPs. Our experience suggests that public clinics and comprehensive

*Table 11A.1. Characteristics of University of Rochester Pediatric Nurse Practitioner Trainees, 1967–1973*

*Age Distribution*

| | |
|---|---|
| 20–25 years | 5 |
| 26–30 years | 16 |
| 31–35 years | 16 |
| 36–40 years | 16 |
| 41+ years | 7 |

*Nursing Activity before Training*

| | |
|---|---|
| Teaching | 8 |
| Active | |
| Pediatrics | 16 |
| General | 26 |
| Inactive | 10 |

*Practice Setting after Training*

| | |
|---|---|
| Private practice | 17 |
| Hospital clinic | 15 |
| Health center | 14 |
| Public health nursing, including well-child clinic | 9 |
| Teaching | 5 |

health care programs for indigent population groups present medical, social, and cultural problems of such complexity that only nurses with a high level of education or with pretraining and experience, and also those able to make a full-time physical, intellectual, and emotional commitment, can function successfully in those difficult settings. Nurses working in well-child conferences and in private office settings, where their activities are restricted to well-child care and screening and management of minor acute illnesses, function well without the commitment required of nurses working at more complex levels.

Valid conclusions concerning personality characteristics, preparation, and placement factors that need to be considered in making decisions concerning the training and utilization of PNPs cannot be drawn from a retrospective evaluation of our small groups of trainees. We are now engaged in a large-scale prospective study to evaluate these important issues.

### Curriculum Content

The curriculum used for training these nurses for an expanded role has evolved since the program began. Initially there were no pediatric nurse practitioner models to study or any of these professionals to help in the actual training process. Currently, however, models exist for each of the practice settings, and most of the educational input is provided by faculty who have gone through the training process and continue to function as PNPs.

Any curriculum must include a definition of the prerequisites for entering students (beginning behaviors) and of the educational goals, expressed in terms of knowledge, skills, and attitudes (end point behaviors). When each of these is fixed, determination of the educational process required to move the trainee from entering levels to end points of competency is a relatively simple matter. If, however, the entering skills of trainees vary and the educational goals also vary, depending on where the PNP is to practice, as is the case with our program, it is impossible to design a single curriculum that will meet the needs of all trainees. Under these circumstances it is necessary to set general minimal educational objectives with different levels of end behaviors and to provide a flexible curriculum to meet the needs of the specific level at which each student must be able to perform upon completion.

### Description of the Training Program

The *general objective* of this pediatric nurse practitioner educational program is to prepare the nurse to share with other members of the health team the responsibility for the care of children and their families. Upon completion of the course, the nurse will have skills in (1) providing health assessment of children from birth to adolescence; (2) providing individual, preventive, and therapeutic care and counseling to children and their families, as well as promoting habilitation and rehabilitation; and (3) providing preventive, diagnostic, and therapeutic services for specific conditions and illnesses of childhood.

The program spans a 16-week period. Students spend 10 hours per week in formal class work (160 hours) and four to six half-days per week in clinical tutorial teaching sessions (245 hours). The balance of the student's time is spent in independent study.

Seven units of study form the basis for the formal class presentations:

1. Growth and Development (23 hours).
2. Interviewing and Counseling (18 hours).
3. Family Dynamics (25 hours).
4. Health Maintenance (49 hours).
5. Childhood Illnesses (29 hours).
6. Community Resources (5 hours).
7. Family/Nurse/M.D. Relationships (11 hours).

These units of study correspond with those recommended in "Guidelines on Short-Term Continuing Education Programs for Pediatric Nurse Associates," prepared by the American Nurses' Association (ANA) and the American Academy of Pediatrics (AAP).

After completing the 16-week training program, the PNPs meet formally while they are at work in practice settings, initially at weekly intervals, to (1) familiarize themselves with newer developments and concepts in the management of well and ill children; (2) acquire understanding of new developments and concepts in nursing care; (3) gain additional self-appraisal skills of their effectiveness in providing patient care; (4) critically evaluate their contribution to the physician-nurse team, and bring to the group problems that have arisen in their practice; (5) formulate their career objectives and obtain information on the most appropriate method of pursuit; and (6) develop research that contributes to the advancement of new concepts in ambulatory nursing care. This mechanism, as well as consultation with the physicians who work with the PNPs, provides feedback to determine what changes are needed in the curriculum to improve graduate performance.

*Rochester Studies Concerning Pediatric Nurse Practitioners*

The growth of training programs and the resultant increase in the number of nurses prepared as pediatric nurse practitioners have stimulated several evaluation efforts throughout the United States. These studies have dealt with the performance and acceptability of PNPs and the changes brought about in practice settings by their utilization (Hoekelman, 1972). The conclusions drawn from these investigations are amazingly uniform in each area studied.

In the area of *performance* the PNPs studied provided all aspects of well-child care. In addition, they screened for acute illnesses and provided treatment for minor illnesses. Care in these areas rendered by the PNP working in collaboration with the pediatrician was more effective in terms of continuity, comprehensiveness, and compliance than that rendered by the pediatrician alone.

In the area of *acceptability* all studies indicated that parents were satisfied with the care the pediatric nurse practitioner-pediatrician team provided, and that this care was equal or superior to that rendered by the pediatrician alone.

In the area of *practice setting change* the utilization of PNPs resulted in a rise in physician productivity and an increase in the number of children cared for. Employment of PNPs was economically advantageous—to the employer, resulting in an increased net income, to the PNP in the form of increased wages, and to the recipients of care in terms of reduced costs.

Studies of PNPs completed or currently in progress at the University of Rochester are concerned with performance, acceptability, and practice change, as were those summarized above; in addition, they investigate the quality of performance and the changes in the level of well-baby care within a specific population brought about by the utilization of PNPs.

Private Practice Study

While experimentation with physician-nurse teams was occurring in the pediatric residents' continuity clinic, a study begun in private practices in the community provided data about physician activities. This study indicated that 56% of the private pediatricians' time was spent on well-child care, more than half of it with children under 2 years of age (Hercules and Charney, 1969).

As a result of the satisfaction with nurses providing a portion of the well-child care in the continuity program, and documentation of the amount of pediatricians' time that might be freed if well-child care could be shared, a controlled study was designed to examine the efficacy of physician-nurse care in private pediatric settings (Charney and Kitzman, 1971). The study aimed at testing the following hypotheses:

1.  Care by a child health nurse (PNP)-pediatrician team is as acceptable to patients as is care by the pediatrician alone.
2.  With such teams, well-child visits to the physician in the first two years of life are reduced by half, with no increase in illness visits, and no change in number or kind of diagnoses made or consultant referrals arranged.
3.  This type of care is acceptable to the physician and child health nurse.
4.  The program is economically feasible for office practice.

METHODS AND RESULTS.    During the calendar year 1969 all newborns in the four participating pediatric practices were enrolled in the study and assigned in alternate fashion to either the nurse-physician team or to the physician alone. Hospital newborn visits were made by the physician and the nurse at different times, and home visits were made by the nurse to most primiparous mothers in the experimental group during the first two weeks of infancy. After the neonatal period well-child visits in the experimental group were alternated between physician and nurse for a total of six in the first year and three in the second year of life. In the control group the same number of visits were made to the physician alone. All illness visits in both groups were made to the pediatrician. Parents in the experimental group were encouraged to call the nurse at a specified telephone hour for general guidance and advice, and to call either pediatrician or nurse for illness during the day, and the pediatrician in the evening and night.

At the end of 1969 a total of 1220 children was enrolled in the study: 703 in the experimental group and 517 in the control group. (In two of the practices, two study patients were enrolled for every control patient to increase the nurses' case loads more rapidly.) Of the patients initially enrolled, 78% remained active in the study, with roughly equal numbers of dropouts occurring in the experimental and control groups.

An office record review was conducted after the child was 1 year of age to determine the frequency and the nature of office visits and outside referrals. No difference was found in the total numbers of visits made by the children in the two groups. There was also no difference in the referral pattern between study groups.

An analysis of incoming telephone calls showed that experimental patients made 1.4 times as many calls per patient as control patients (268 to 140 calls during the one-week periods surveyed at approximately three-month intervals). However, the majority of these calls were to the nurse; calls to the pediatrician were reduced by about 21%. The majority of increased calls from the experimental group were generated in the first few months of the child's life. The nurses were able to manage 97% of the calls without immediate referral to the physician, reflecting both their level of confidence and the less serious medical nature of most of the calls.

Parents' acceptance of the program was measured by a mailed questionnaire to both experimental and control parents when the child was 8–9 months of age. The overall return rate after one mailing was 73%.

Mothers did not feel that their relationship with the doctor was compromised by seeing him less often or by their involvement with the nurse. When asked who provided various aspects of the child care (the doctor, the nurse, both, or no one), experimental families responded "both" in almost all instances, indicating that they perceived the shared nature of the relationship. There was only one question on which experimental and control families differed: experimental families were somewhat more satisfied with the child's growth and development assessment and counseling than were controls. Within the experimental group the nurse was perceived as displaying more interest in and concern for the family than the pediatrician, but parents expressed more confidence in the professional ability of the doctor than of the nurse. Although these differences were statistically significant, they all fell within the range of high satisfaction in both groups. It is clear that parents considered the level of child care to be enhanced by the nurse-pediatrician arrangement.

Satisfaction with the program by both pediatricians and nurses ranged from moderate to extreme, and currently (three years later) all of the nurses are still employed in the original offices. The nurses, however, stressed the importance of communication by regularly scheduled conferences more than did the doctors. In one office this was done over lunch several times weekly and was felt to be ideal by both. At the other extreme were instances in which patients were hospitalized or referred without the nurse's knowledge, an action that she felt reflected a diminished view of the importance of her role on the part of the pediatrician.

The average cost of each patient visit was calculated on the basis of a detailed accounting of office expenses and overhead. During the study the office overhead did not rise because of the nurse since she used equipment and space that would have been otherwise unoccupied.

SUMMARY.   Although all of the four hypotheses stated earlier can be accepted, with the exception that physicians saw the patients for somewhat more than half of the well-child visits, several logical extensions to the study might be considered:

1. Is the training described for the nurse appropriate to her role? (No comparison is available with nurses prepared by other methods.)

2. Can nurses be equally effective in behavioral problem counseling and chronic disease management?

3. Is well-child care the most effective measure to assess the service that the nurse can provide in ambulatory care?

4. Do the addition of the teaching and care emphasis by the nurse in well-child care and her availability during parent-child crises decrease the risk of long-range problems such as maternal deprivation, parent-child conflict, and school failure?

Only appropriate longitudinal studies can provide answers to these questions.

What is apparent from the results of this study is that patients, nurses and physicians receive satisfaction from the physician-PNP pattern of care delivery, and that, to the extent that this study was able to measure the quality of care, it appeared to be equal if not superior to that provided in the traditional way.

### Adequate Well-Baby Care Study

The controlled studies comparing results obtained by pediatric nurse practitioners in circumscribed areas of patient care with those obtained by pediatricians provided an indication of the quality of care rendered by the PNP as measured against a known standard. But further questions about the most effective use of available manpower remain.

"What Constitutes Adequate Well-Baby Care" was a study to further evaluate the care rendered by PNPs to well babies during the first year of life compared with that supplied by pediatricians; in addition, it examined the feasibility of *reducing* the number of well-baby visits made during the first year without reducing the quality of care.

RATIONALE FOR STUDY. Health supervision of young children, or well-child care, has long been advocated by medical and public health leaders in this country. The objectives of well-child care, perhaps best expressed at an American Public Health Association (APHA) Conference on Health Supervision of Young Children held in 1955 (American Public Health Association, 1955), are "to keep the well child well and promote the highest possible level of his complete well-being."

In order to reach this level of complete well-being during the baby's first year, the American Academy of Pediatrics and government administrators have advocated periodic health appraisals as often as every four to six weeks (American Academy of Pediatrics, 1967; N.Y. State Department of Health, 1967). Society has mandated medical care for all children (Cohen, 1967), and this includes well-baby visits conducted as frequently as recommended by these official bodies. If all babies were seen this often, however, the entire medical profession would have time for little else! We are committed to providing services for all children in our community; yet such a goal is obviously impossible if these recommendations are followed. What, then, are the alternatives? We could continue with current practices and provide optimum well-baby care for a few, and less than optimum care for the rest. We could train others to conduct well-baby visits, as was demonstrated in the PNP program, or we could schedule visits less frequently than recommended. The first alternative is not acceptable to us, but the second and third are worthy of consideration and are addressed in this study. We need to know whether others can be trained to carry out child health supervision and to achieve results equal to those obtained by physicians. And we need to determine whether it is necessary to examine all babies and counsel mothers as frequently as has been the custom.

DESCRIPTION OF STUDY.  The study was a three-way controlled trial to examine the relative efficacy of the presently recommended schedule of visits, compared to less frequent well-baby visits during the first year of life conducted by physicians as opposed to nurse practitioners. The use of nurse practitioners in well-baby care has been and is being studied by us and others (Ford et al., 1966; Silver et al., 1967, 1968; Charney and Kitzman, 1971; Hoekelman et al., 1973).

These studies, however, substitute the nurse practitioner for a certain percentage of scheduled well-baby visits, with the physician being involved exclusively in some of the visits and partially in others. In this part of the study, the effects of almost exclusive use of the nurse practitioner in the routine care of babies and of a drastic reduction in the number of well-baby visits in the first year of life were evaluated.

The study tests the "radical" hypothesis that the well-baby care delivered on an abbreviated schedule during the first year of life by a PNP is as adequate as that provided by a pediatrician using the currently advocated schedule.

METHODS.  For their first year 116 clinic and 130 private full-term, first-born well babies were randomly assigned to receive care in one of four ways: six visits conducted by an M.D.; three visits by an M.D.; six visits by a PNP, or three visits by a PNP.

The adequacy of care rendered was assessed by the amount of gain in maternal knowledge, important for competence in child rearing; by the attainment of the health supervision planned; by the degree of maternal compliance; and by the level of maternal satisfaction. These end points were subjected to two- and three-way analyses of variance to determine whether there were differences across the setting, provider, or schedule variables.

RESULTS. No significant differences were found between settings, except that clinic subjects attained higher than planned levels of health supervision ($p = .001$), and private practice subjects scored higher in maternal competence ($p < .001$) and maternal compliance ($p < .001$). In the clinic setting PNPs attained higher compliance scores than M.D.s ($p < .001$), and in the private practice setting mothers of babies on the reduced M.D. schedule (three visits), although highly satisfied, were less so than those on the more traditional M.D. six-visit schedule ($p < .004$). No significant differences were observed in the end points measured within settings between providers of care (M.D.s compared to PNPs), between visit schedules (six versus three visits), or between any of the provider-visit schedule combinations!

Thus well-baby care during the first year delivered by PNPs is as adequate as that provided by physicians, and the use of abbreviated visit schedules by either professional does not reduce the adequacy of care, as measured by the end points used in this study, for either private practice or clinic patients.

IMPLICATIONS. Even though this study and future ones may prove that PNPs and other specially trained health professionals can provide well-baby care equal or superior to that provided by physicians, it will be difficult to train enough of them in the near future to meet the need for such care if the presently recommended frequency of visits is continued.

If the demand and needs are to be met, we must be assured that all babies do not need such frequent examinations, nor all mothers such frequent counseling, as is currently being advocated. We need to substantiate Fuchs's (1969) premise: "Better medical care is not synonymous with more care." If drastic changes are to be made in routine well-child care, it must be established that such changes are not detrimental to the health of the child and the family. We believe that this study demonstrates a feasible way to deliver well-child care to children by substituting PNP for pediatrician visits, and by reducing the number of visits in the first year of life for well-child care.

It would seem obvious, but should be mentioned, that some children need more than the average number of visits. The purpose of this study was to show that a reduced number of visits is adequate for most, not that all children can do without the traditional number. With such a reduced average visit schedule and the use of PNPs, more manpower could now become available in this area for the few who need more care.

Rural Study

Two nurses trained as pediatric nurse practitioners were introduced into the health care system in a rural community without pediatricians (Hornell, New York) in an attempt to improve the level of well-baby care within that community. The levels of well-baby care attained in the year preceding and the year following the introduction of the nurses were determined. Some indirect measures of the quality of care rendered by PNPs and general practitioners were applied to the sample of babies studied. The attitudes of the public and of the physicians practicing in the community concerning the utilization of nurse practitioners in the delivery of health care were determined before the nurses began practice and again 15 months later.

Quantitative and qualitative changes occurred in the levels of well-baby care toward improvement from the first year to the second. The attitude of the public toward PNPs was positive in both years, and moved toward approval of greater involvement of these professionals in the delivery of primary health care. The attitude of physicians practicing in the community, however, was mixed, although more were favorable to the PNP concept than were against it. This situation had not changed appreciably after 15 months of pediatric nurse practice.

The specifics of the methodologies used and the results obtained in this study are reported elsewhere (Hoekelman et al., 1973).

Evaluation of Pediatric Nurse Practitioner Training

Since the introduction of the concept of the pediatric nurse practitioner and the establishment of the first training program (Silver et al., 1967), many institutions have developed continuing education programs to prepare nurses to assume expanded roles in child care (American Academy of Pediatrics, 1971). Some institutions have incorporated this training into master's degree educational programs, while others have considered it as becoming a part of undergraduate nursing education (Chioni and Panicucci, 1970). Difficulties are encountered in attempting to prepare nurses of diverse backgrounds for different levels of competence and performance within a single curriculum in a short-term continuing education program.

The "Guidelines on Short-Term Continuing Education Programs for Pediatric Nurse Associates" drawn up by the ANA and AAP (Joint Committee, 1971) attempt to resolve the confusion by making recommendations concerning student prerequisites, course content, faculty, facilities, and duration of training. These recommendations were based on the opinions of the members of the joint ANA-AAP committee who drew up the guidelines. It is of interest to note that the directors of four established PNP training programs were members of that committee; and, when one compares the curriculum contents of these programs (at the time the guidelines were promulgated), in terms of hours devoted to each of the instructional units recommended in the guidelines, marked differences are evident (Table 11A.2).

With standardization of the definition of "pediatric nurse practitioner" and of qualifications for a minimal level of acceptable performance, accreditation of educational programs and certification of graduates will become possible. This "credentialism" is of prime importance to the nurse, the physician working with her in a practice setting, the recipients of care, and the third-party payers for that care.

Although there are problems in credentialism, most new roles must eventually become standardized, and competence certified. The dangers of rigidity can be recognized and, it is hoped, avoided. At present, more evaluation of the range of behaviors needed and the best way to educate for them is required.

The experience with PNPs in Rochester to date has been excellent. Of the 60 who have been trained, 27 are working in Monroe County with schedules varying from 16 to 40 hours per week. They represent the equivalent of about 11 full-time pediatricians in the county, which has the equivalent of approximately 65 full-time pediatricians. These PNPs represent the largest single addition of pediatric manpower in the past

Table 11A.2.  Variation in Pediatric Nurse Practitioner Course Content: Four Different 16-Week Programs

| Instructional Unit | Four Programs: Hours Devoted to Training | | | |
| --- | --- | --- | --- | --- |
| | A | B | C | D |
| Growth and Development | 24 | 12 | 8 | 20 |
| Interviewing and Counseling | 8 | 16 | 8 | 23 |
| Family Dynamics | 8 | 11 | 7 | 24 |
| Health Maintenance | 24 | 16 | 8 | 37 |
| Childhood Illnesses | 11 | 12 | 12 | 34 |
| Community Resources | 7 | 8 | 7 | 7 |
| Family/Nurse/M.D. Relationships | 0 | 5 | 2 | 6 |
| Clinical Experience | 64 | 80 | 120 | 105 |
| Total hours | 146 | 160 | 172 | 256 |

five years in this county. The child health scene today is vastly different than it was eight years ago, in large part because of the introduction of this new and effective source of care.

## REFERENCES

AMERICAN ACADEMY OF PEDIATRICS

1967 *Standards of Child Health Care.* Evanston, Illinois: Council on Pediatric Practice, p. 18.

AMERICAN ACADEMY OF PEDIATRICS

1971 *Directory of Current Programs for the Training of Pediatric Nurse Associates, Assistants and Aides.* Evanston, Illinois: Council of Pediatric Practice.

AMERICAN PUBLIC HEALTH ASSOCIATION

1955 *Health Supervision of Young Children.* New York: Committee on Child Health, pp. 18–19.

BLASINGAME, F.J.L.

1968 "Physicians and the Marketplace." *Journal of the American Medical Association,* 204:143–146.

CHARNEY, EVAN and KITZMAN, HARRIET

1971 "The Child Health Nurse (Pediatric Nurse Practitioner) in Private Practice." *New England Journal of Medicine,* 285:1353–1358.

CHIONI, ROSE MARIE and PANICUCCI, CAROL

1970 "Tomorrow's Nurse Practitioners." *Nursing Outlook,* 18:32–35.

COHEN, WILBUR

1967 "Health Care of the Nation's Children." Paper presented to the American Academy of Pediatrics Conference, Washington, D.C., October 21, 1967.

FEIN, RASHI

1967 *The Doctor Shortage: An Economic Diagnosis.* Washington, D.C.: The Brookings Institute.

FORD, PATRICIA A., SEACAT, MILVOY S., and SILVER, GEORGE A.

1966 "The Relative Roles of the Public Health Nurse and the Physician in Prenatal and Infant Supervision." *American Journal of Public Health,* 56:1097-1103.

FUCHS, VICTOR

1969 "Improving the Delivery of Health Services." Address to the 36th Annual Meeting, American Academy of Orthopedic Surgeons, New York City, January 22.

HERCULES, COSTAS, and CHARNEY, EVAN

1969 "Availability and Attentiveness: Are These Compatible in Pediatric Practice?" *Clinical Pediatrics,* 8:381–388.

HOEKELMAN, ROBERT A.

1972  "Evaluation of Pediatric Nurse Associates." In *Proceedings of the Eastern
       Regional Workshop on Pediatric Nurse Associates.* New York: American
       Nurses' Association, pp. 66–71.

HOEKELMAN, ROBERT A., ZIMMER, ANNE W., and KITZMAN, HARRIET

1973  "Pediatric Nurse Practitioners and Well-Baby Care in a Small Rural Com-
       munity." In *ANA Clinical Sessions, 1972.* Englewood Cliffs, N.J.: Appleton-
       Century-Crofts, Publishing Division of Prentice-Hall.

JOINT COMMITTEE OF AMERICAN NURSES' ASSOCIATION AND AMERICAN ACADEMY OF PEDIATRICS

1971  "Guidelines on Short-term Continuing Education Programs for Pediatric
       Nurse Associates." *Pediatrics,* 47:1075–1079.

LEWIS, CHARLES E., and RESNIK, BARBARA A.

1967  "Nurse Clinics and Progressive Ambulatory Patient Care." *New England
       Journal of Medicine,* 227:1236–1241.

NEW YORK STATE DEPARTMENT OF HEALTH

1967  *N.Y. State Medical Handbook: Policies and Standards of Child Health Ser-
       vices.* Albany, New York, p. 2.

SILVER, HENRY K., FORD, LORETTA C., and STEARLY, SUSAN G.

1967  "Program to Increase Health Care for Children—Pediatric Nurse Practitioner
       Program." *Pediatrics,* 39:756–760.

SILVER, HENRY K., FORD, LORETTA C., and DAY, LEWIS R.

1968  "The Pediatric Nurse Practitioner Program." *Journal of the American
       Medical Association,* 240:298–302.

YANKAUER, ALFRED

1968  "Allied Health Workers in Pediatrics." *Pediatrics,* 41:1031–1032.

## B. THE FAMILY COUNSELOR

IVAN B. PLESS AND BETTY B. SATTERWHITE

In the search for new manpower to assist the physician in caring for more
children more adequately, most efforts have focused on modifying the
roles of existing professionals such as nurses, or on supplementing the
training of paraprofessionals such as medics, so that they will be able to
assume some of the responsibilities of the doctor. These programs are
based on the belief that sufficient training of good quality will enable the
recipient to reach the required level of competence. When the competence involved is chiefly "technical," the rationale makes sense.

In spite of the heavy emphasis that has been placed on the upgrading and retraining of health professionals, many nontechnical health needs can be met adequately by relying chiefly on the personality attributes of the workers. Such qualities are as plentiful among nonprofessionals—lay persons—as they are among physicians, nurses, and social workers. The potential manpower resource that exists outside the professional world, therefore, must be examined carefully.

This section describes one example of how this pool of human resources has been tapped to help in the care of children with chronic illnesses. Because this experiment has been so successful, we are now convinced that there are many similar jobs that women and men like these can do equally well. Our experience has led us to conclude that for many tasks training is of much less importance than personal characteristics. If we can develop the means whereby these characteristics (personality, temperament, intelligence, sensitivity, etc.) can be recognized reliably, and if we can find some method of paying for these services, there are endless ways in which nonprofessional men and women can help improve our system of health care.

## Family Counselors for the Chronically Ill

The results of the studies described in Part I dealing with chronic illness showed that many of these children have problems over and above those of their physical disorders. They experience difficulties of an emotional, social, and educational nature more frequently than do their peers. Similarly, their parents, brothers, and sisters experience problems of many kinds that are related to the presence of a handicapped child in the family. Many of these problems lie at the boundaries of medical care; few of them are "medical" in the traditional sense. As a result many physicians are unable or unwilling to handle them independently and either fail to recognize them or refer them to others when possible.

The kinds of help needed vary greatly: in one case it is simply a matter of providing a mother with a compassionate listener; in another it is the more mundane challenge of getting a wheelchair ramp built. There are times when advice is needed, others when the family requires more detailed explanations of the child's condition, and still others when the child himself needs counseling to help him identify and develop his special strengths and abilities. Few of these are tasks that the busy doctor can do, or would be inclined to undertake even if he had the time. Nevertheless, they are an integral part of what comprehensive health care must include, and can be as important in the life of the child and his family as is the medical treatment itself.

Problems like those mentioned exist in abundance, but because they are not central to medical care they are rarely dealt with by physicians. When help is provided, it is usually given by social workers who may be attached to specialty clinics or, if the problem is severe, by referral to psychologists and psychiatrists. But good health care must respond to problems as early as possible, and to meet this requirement assistance must be available to primary care physicians. With few exceptions, neither general practitioners, family doctors, nor pediatricians have social workers or public health nurses available who can deal with these aspects of care in the home. These considerations led to the development of a program designed to provide assistance for such problems by nonprofessional women who receive a minimum of training and guidance (Pless and Satterwhite, 1972).

*Selection and Training*

The first group of "family counselors" was selected in the summer of 1969. Letters describing the job in general terms and the qualifications desired were sent to agencies and individuals throughout Monroe County. The letter announced that a stipend of $1000 per year plus travel expenses would be paid for a part-time job to help in the care of children with chronic illnesses. Because of the limited remuneration, coupled with the need for flexibility and the availability of a car, the only group of women who expressed interest after the initial interview were of middle-class backgrounds.

All applicants had, in effect, been recommended by someone else with some sort of experience in the "helping" field. By comparison it is interesting to speculate on the number and kind of applicants who would have responded to a conventional newspaper advertisement. As it was, the degree of screening helped to narrow the selection, and the final choices were made after a lengthy interview. Each candidate also completed a standard personality profile—the 16 Personality Factor Scale (16PF) (Cattell and Bice, 1962)—but the results were not taken into consideration for selection purposes initially. (The test did, however, become a selection tool, along with the interview, in succeeding years.) No rigid criteria were applied for selection—two or more of the project staff who understood the kind of person wanted offered their impressions after interviews with applicants. Decisions were made when consensus was reached.

The same procedure was followed in the succeeding years with the added screening dimension of a letter submitted by the applicant describing why she was interested in the job and why she thought she would be good at it. An analysis of the successful applicants' social characteristics and, more importantly, the 16 PF profiles (see Figure 11B.1) offer several important clues to assist others who wish to recruit family counselors.

## Social and Psychological Characteristics

Table 11B.1 shows the demographic characteristics of 21 family counselors employed during the four years of the program. All were married and had raised families. All had graduated from high school, and most had some college education although, as a matter of policy, none with professional qualifications was considered. It was assumed that the demands on the counselors would be diverse and would cut across many disciplinary boundaries that persons with professional training would be more reluctant to cross than those without such training. Flexibility—willingness to play, in equal degrees, the roles of public health nurse, social worker, chauffeur, teacher, marriage counselor, and patient advocate—was thought to be more important than expert training. The average age of 43 years reflected our decision to consider only women who had been through the

STANDARD TEN SCORE (STEN)

| | 1 | 2 | 3 | 4 | 5 | 6 | 7 | 8 | 9 | 10 | |
|---|---|---|---|---|---|---|---|---|---|---|---|
| RESERVED | • | • | • | • | • | ———□——— | | | • | | OUTGOING |
| LESS INTELLIGENT | • | • | • | • | • | ——□—— | | | • | | MORE INTELLIGENT |
| AFFECTED BY FEELINGS | • | • | • | • | • | ———□—— | | | • | | EMOTIONALLY STABLE |
| HUMBLE | • | • | • | • | ———□——— | | | | | | ASSERTIVE |
| SOBER | • | • | • | • | • | ———□—— | | | • | | HAPPY-GO-LUCKY |
| EXPEDIENT | • | ———————□—— | | | | | • | • | • | • | CONSCIENTIOUS |
| SHY | • | • | • | • | • | • | ———□——— | | | • | VENTURESOME |
| TOUGH-MINDED | • | • | • | • | • | ——□—— | | | • | | TENDER-MINDED |
| TRUSTING | • | • | ——————□—— | | | | • | • | • | | SUSPICIOUS |
| PRACTICAL | • | • | • | • | ———□—— | | • | • | • | | IMAGINATIVE |
| FORTHRIGHT | • | • | • | • | ———□—— | | • | • | • | | SHREWD |
| PLACID | • | • | ——□—— | | • | • | • | • | | | APPREHENSIVE |
| CONSERVATIVE | • | • | • | • | • | • | ———□— | | • | | EXPERIMENTING |
| GROUP-DEPENDENT | • | • | • | ———□—— | | • | • | • | | | SELF-SUFFICIENT |
| SELF-CONFLICT | • | • | • | ————□——— | | | | • | • | | CONTROLLED |
| RELAXED | • | • | ——□—— | | • | • | • | • | • | | TENSE |

*EACH •——□——•REPRESENTS THE MEAN AND STANDARD DEVIATION OF SCORES ON THE IPAT 16 PERSONALITY FACTOR TEST. THE TEST IS STANDARDIZED FOR WOMEN WITH A MEAN AGE OF 36 YEARS SO THAT 68 PER CENT HAVE SCORES BETWEEN THE 4TH AND 7TH STENS.

Figure 11B.1. Distribution of counselor scores on 16 PF test profile* (n = 21).

Table 11B.1.  Demographic Characteristics of Family Counselors,
1969–1973 (N=21)

| Characteristic | N | Characteristic | N |
|---|---|---|---|
| Age (years) | | Occupation of Husband | |
| 31–40 | 8 | Professional | 9 |
| 41–50 | 8 | Business-industry | 8 |
| 51–55 | 5 | Technical-sales | 3 |
| | | Deceased | 1 |
| Education | | Number of Children | |
| College graduate | 7 | 1–2 | 6 |
| 1-3 years of college | 9 | 3–4 | 9 |
| High school graduate | 5 | 5–6 | 6 |
| | | Number of Volunteer | |
| Religion | | Activities | |
| Protestant | 15 | 1–2 | 5 |
| Jewish | 5 | 3–4 | 10 |
| Catholic | 1 | 5–6 | 6 |

process of child rearing, who had found it enjoyable, and who considered themselves successful. It also reflected the greater freedom of women whose children were currently in school or had completed it.

The personality profile (16PF) indicates that the counselors tended to be significantly "more venturesome, intelligent, outgoing, emotionally stable, sensitive, and experimenting" than the average woman of similar age. At first the profile was used primarily to validate our subjective judgments; but when an individual profile differed in any important respect from that of our "ideal" counselor, it served to alert us to the possibility that our judgment might be at fault. However, by the end of the third year, the project staff was in remarkably close agreement about all prospective candidates on the basis of the interviews alone.

The process of selection has been described in some detail because it is a key part of the novel concept being presented. Most physicians in practice and specialists in clinics, agencies, or health departments could succeed equally well in selecting a group of family counselors (or any similar nonprofessional assistants) by relying on judgments about their personal attributes, rather than on formal training.

## Training

The training that was provided never amounted to more than 20 hours initially, with, thereafter, monthly meetings of about 2 hours each. It was

obviously not long enough or detailed enough to produce technical competence, nor was it intended to do so. The sessions touched on such matters as the biology of some of the more common chronic diseases, health
education, resource materials, and principles of counseling. In no instance
was it suggested that the subject had been covered exhaustively or even
adequately. Instead, reliance was placed on the women's intelligence,
conscientiousness, and resourcefulness to determine for themselves what
more they needed to know or how they could go about learning it when
the need arose. Indeed, the real purpose of the training was to impress
on them that there was a job to be done and that they already possessed
the most important resources for doing it well. We tried to instill confidence in them and in their judgment, and to help them develop a strategy
for attacking certain types of problems. Throughout it was stressed that
no one was likely to know better than they what should be done or how
it should be done in any particular case. In short, they were told what
the goals were, but were not offered detailed plans on how to reach them.

*Patterns of Work*

During the first three years of the program's existence, each counselor was
assigned to eight families in which there was at least one child with a
chronic physical disorder. In the subsequent years the case load was more
open-ended, averaging 8–12 families at any one time.

The diagnoses of the children in each year's program are shown in
Table 11B.2. In the first year, when the program was being evaluated
experimentally, the children were randomly selected from the survey population, described in Section 3C. A group of children with similar social
characteristics and similar illnesses was also selected to serve as controls.
The object of the experiment was to see what effect, if any, one year with
the counselor might have on the children's mental health as reflected in
their psychological test scores. Thus some of the tests which had been given
to all children in the original survey were repeated for this group of
experimental and control children at the end of one year of counseling.

To help describe the program, the counselors were instructed to keep
detailed logs of all their daily activities related to the program. In addition they kept records of all their transactions with each family, and copies
of the monthly reports were sent to the child's doctor. From these sources
it was learned that each counselor spent an average of 8–10 hours a week
in work connected with the program. The total amount of time varied
from month to month and from family to family. Most of it—about 60%
in the first year and a higher percentage in later years—was spent in direct

Table 11B.2.  Diagnosis of Children in Family Counselor Program,
by Year

| Diagnosis | 1969 | 1970 | 1971 | 1972 | 1973 | Total |
|---|---|---|---|---|---|---|
| Endocrine and Metabolic | | | | | | |
| Diabetes mellitus | | 4 | 2 | | 6 | 12 |
| Other—AGS, FTT[a] | | | | | 4 | 4 |
| Blood | | | | | | |
| Sickle cell disease | | 3 | | 3 | | 6 |
| Hemophilia | | | | | 1 | 1 |
| Other—ITP[b], spherocystosis, neutropenia | 1 | | | 4 | | 5 |
| Nervous System | | | | | | |
| Epilepsy | 1 | 2 | 2 | 17 | 3 | 25 |
| Spina bifida/hydrocephalus | | | | 8 | 1 | 9 |
| Cerebral palsy | 1 | 4 | 7 | 3 | 4 | 19 |
| Blindness | 3 | 1 | 1 | | | 5 |
| Deafness | 5 | 1 | 2 | | 2 | 10 |
| Speech | 4 | 3 | 1 | | | 8 |
| Other—mongolism, learning disabilities, tumor | 1 | 1 | 1 | 10 | 1 | 14 |
| Circulatory System | | | | | | |
| Congenital heart disease | 1 | 2 | 5 | | 3 | 11 |
| Rheumatic fever | | 1 | 2 | | 2 | 5 |
| Respiratory System | | | | | | |
| Asthma | 4 | 19 | 7 | 6 | 4 | 40 |
| Hay fever, other allergies | 19 | 4 | 1 | 5 | 1 | 30 |
| Cystic fibrosis | | 5 | 2 | | 2 | 9 |

contact with the family. The rest was devoted to meetings, work with resources, or writing reports. A small percentage (11%) of time spent with families was on the telephone. The rest was in face-to-face contact with some family member, usually the mother or the child, virtually all of these contacts taking place in the patient's home.

It is difficult to quantify or classify activities during this time because there was so much overlapping. Broadly, a little more than half of the time (55%) was spent in some kind of verbal exchange—that is, with the mother talking about her problems and the counselor listening, or the reverse, with the counselor playing the active role and giving advice, information, or instructions. The remaining time (45%) was devoted to providing services of many kinds to the child and his family. These included transporting the child to clinics, tutoring, taking the family on outings, serving as an advocate, coordinating the plans of the child's

*Table 11B.2. (cont.)*

| Diagnosis | 1969 | 1970 | 1971 | 1972 | 1973 | Total |
|---|---|---|---|---|---|---|
| Digestive System | | | | | | |
| Ulcer | | 1 | | 1 | | 2 |
| Other—e.g., ulcerative colitis | 2 | 1 | | | 1 | 4 |
| Genitourinary System | | | | | | |
| Pyelonephritis | 3 | 7 | 2 | | 2 | 14 |
| Cystitis | 2 | 1 | | | | 3 |
| Skin and Subcutaneous | | | | | | |
| Acne | 4 | | | | | 4 |
| Eczema | 2 | 1 | | | | 3 |
| Musculoskeletal and Connective | | | | | | |
| Rheumatoid arthritis | 1 | 9 | | 6 | 2 | 18 |
| Legge-Perthes | | 2 | 1 | 1 | | 4 |
| Muscular dystrophy | | | | 2 | | 2 |
| Other—scoliosis, dermatomyositis | 1 | 4 | 4 | | | 9 |
| Congenital and Accidental | | | | | | |
| PKU[c] | | | | 2 | | 2 |
| Sturge-Weber | | | | 1 | | 1 |
| Harelip and cleft palate | 1 | 1 | | | | 2 |
| Achondroplasia | | | | | 1 | 1 |
| Other—e.g., accidents | | 4 | 3 | | 2 | 9 |
| Total | 56 | 81 | 43 | 64 | 47 | 291 |

[a] AGS: Adrenogenital Syndrome; FTT: Failure to thrive:
[b] ITP: Idiopathic thrombocytopenic purpura.
[c] PKU: Phenylketonuria.

doctors, teaching new skills, and distributing health education literature. Much attention was focused on the family's problems, as well as on the child himself. This was necessary because parents were frequently unable to pay attention to the specific needs of the child until their own problems were recognized and dealt with. The counselors were always encouraged to do what seemed most important or most relevant, even if it appeared to be tangential to the child's needs. Doing something concrete, however mundane, was stressed as opposed to becoming involved in a psychotherapeutic relationship. As a result, problems relating to housing, finances, clothing, schooling, and architectural accessibility for children in wheelchairs, were all handled with varying degrees of success.

For the parent, however, the most valuable aspects of the counselor's role were, first, her availability as a sympathetic listener, and, second, her

*Figure 11B.2. Family counselor and patient off on an outing.*

ability to serve as a source of information about the child's disorder. Her role as advocate, helping, for example, to get doctors to agree on the best course of action when the parents had received conflicting advice, was also important. For the child the frequent attempts the counselor made to help him see himself as someone of value in spite of his illness were of benefit. This was accomplished on some occasions through discussion, and on others by reinforcing the child's talents in specific areas such as art or dressmaking.

### Evaluation of the Program

#### Effectiveness with Parents and Children

At the end of the first year a formal evaluation of the program was carried out. All 56 parents were interviewed by persons not connected with the project to obtain an assessment of the counselors themselves and the services they provided. The effect of the program on the children was evaluated by comparing the results of the psychological tests given before and after the year of the program for those who were counseled with the results for their matched, noncounseled controls.

Most parents approved of the way the program was conducted and valued the services they received, particularly for themselves. They thought highly of the counselors as people and judged that the attributes ideally most important for this job were well represented in their own counselors. Although the evaluation interviews were obviously subject to bias, every effort was made to persuade parents to be objective, critical, and honest, and the many spontaneous comments were an indication of the extent to which this aim was achieved. Similarly, the parents' choice to continue in the program for another year and their willingness to contribute toward the cost of the service, if this was necessary, offer further validity to their acceptance of the program.

The tests used to evaluate the child's emotional status and, in particular, his self-concept included the California Test of Personality (Thorpe et al., 1953), Coopersmith's Self-Esteem Inventory (1959), and the Children's Manifest Anxiety Scale (Castaneda et al., 1956). The scores were compared and compiled in the form of an overall index. Of the 56 children in the counseled group, 33 (60%) showed improvement in psychological status, compared with only 17 (41%) of 42 controls who were not counseled. Conversely, only 33% of the study children showed a worsening in scores, compared with 52% of the controls.

These results are statistically significant ($p < .05$). Thus the counselors' efforts appear to have had a measurable effect on the psychological well-being of the children themselves, in spite of the relatively small amount of attention paid to them.

## Acceptability to Referring Physicians

In addition to the evaluation by parents and the assessment of the psychological status of the children, an attempt was made to evaluate the program systematically from the viewpoints of the physicians involved. The 1970 program included a total of 65 families referred by 19 private practitioners as appropriate candidates for counselor intervention. These physicians were interviewed to obtain their appraisal of the program's benefits and of the counselors as individuals.

BENEFIT TO PATIENTS, FAMILIES, AND PHYSICIANS. Of the 19 doctors, 17 observed some direct benefit from the program to families and were able to cite specific examples: improved relationships within the family, more regular attendance at appointments, greater compliance with instructions, and closer links with the school or other community agencies.

In addition, 17 physicians noted some benefits to themselves. Twelve felt that they had saved time on the telephone since the counselor answered many simple questions formerly addressed to the physician. Two physicians, however, felt that they spent *more* time with families because the program offered them a new modality of therapy and exposed more social problems. Fifteen doctors received information from the counselors that was of benefit in caring for the child; 17 thought the program gave them a more complete understanding of the child's problems.

OPINIONS REGARDING COUNSELORS. Fourteen physicians had nothing but praise for their counselors, commenting on their sensitivity, outgoing manner, perceptivity, and supportiveness. Apart from their strengths in personal relations, however, an equal emphasis was placed on their "action orientation" and on their concrete accomplishments. As one physician said, "The counselor extended herself as a person but didn't get so involved that it interfered with her getting results in terms of action." One criticism came from a specialist who felt the counselor had overstepped her bounds in supporting the family's decision to leave another physician with whom they were dissatisfied.

Monthly letters were sent to the physicians to report on activities and findings. Seventeen doctors considered them helpful, but many, nonetheless, thought that more direct communications, either by phone or in person, would have been preferable. (In succeeding years closer rapport with physicians via telephone and regularly scheduled conferences has been encouraged.)

THE FUTURE OF THE PROGRAM. Whereas 17 physicians thought that the program was a viable concept, 2 had some reservations. One felt that it was "good for clinics, but not for private practice." The other thought the program would be acceptable only if the counselor were trained to deal with physical as well as psychosocial problems. All but one would continue using a counselor if they could do so *without* any cost to themselves.

Eight doctors stated that they could not employ a counselor themselves because it would be financially prohibitive or because there would not be enough for her to do unless she were utilized "in a dual role." Six said they might be interested, and five expressed definite interest if they could find the necessary finances.

Several possible arrangements were suggested for the employment of a counselor: two would charge the patient directly; six would incorporate the cost in their overhead; two thought it possible that insurance would cover this type of service; five felt that state, federal or foundation funds should be obtained; and two stated that the service should be provided by specialty clinics.

There were many suggestions for the future of the program. Of the 17 doctors, 10 expressed hope for its continuation and expansion, and offered to write letters in support of it. Three suggestions were made about locations where counselors might operate, for example, the neighborhood health centers or specialty clinics. One physician advocated a formal team approach to care for chronically ill children in which the family counselor would be included.

### Acceptability to Nonreferring Physicians and Other Health Professionals

In addition to the physicians who referred families to the 1970–1971 program, 40 others (33 physicians; 7 other health professionals) involved in the children's care answered a postal questionnaire asking their views regarding the program. Of the physicians who responded, all but 1 felt that the program had merit, and many expressed the hope that it would continue and expand. Negative responses regarding the employment of a counselor revolved around funding problems rather than lack of interest. Of the other 7 professionals who responded, all thought the program worthwhile and the letters helpful. Social workers felt that counselors supplemented and updated information for them, thus helping to determine the need for further social work or medical intervention. The counselors were seen by them as able to devote time to some specific areas of family problems that the social workers themselves were not able to cover intensively.

### Counselors' Evaluation of the Program

A final aspect of evaluation tapped the opinions of the counselors themselves. All felt that the training sessions were helpful, particularly in removing initial feelings of inadequacy. It was agreed that future training programs should include more time to become familiar with the hospitals and other community resources and more emphasis on counseling techniques. (In succeeding programs this has been done.) They generally favored monthly sessions dealing with basic medical information about specific chronic illnesses, behavior modification, adolescent problems, and counseling techniques. Most considered the monthly report to physicians to be a valuable summary, but also thought that it was not a substitute for more direct communication with the physician, particularly at times of crisis.

The present method of recruitment and selection was judged to be effective, and it was generally agreed that a large pool of people is available for this counseling role. The kind of person best suited was aptly described by one counselor as a "calm, sympathetic, friendly 'activist,' neither intimidated by red tape nor shocked by circumstances of illness or environment, who recognizes her own strengths and limitations."

Many counselors saw the program as a valuable personal experience. Their enthusiasm for the challenge presented by the experimental nature of the program spilled over into a wider awareness of the extent and implications of chronic illness in children. The value of the program to the counselors themselves is reflected to some degree in the following comment:

Contact with the project has been a source of satisfaction. I am certainly more aware of problems existing in health care, and of inequities and injustices in the community. I am also aware that affluent people have problems too. I think I am beginning to see things as they are, not as they appear. I have increased my skills in interpersonal relationships and have gained friends I would not have encountered otherwise. The project has taught me to keep asking myself (and encouraging families to do likewise), What is important and what is not?

## Current Programs

Because of the success of the program, the Regional Medical Program in 1971 provided funds for its expansion, on a demonstration basis, into nine predominantly rural counties for a two-year period. A similar evaluation of the 1972 program produced equally enthusiastic reports.

During 1973 counselors were utilized in six pediatric specialty clinics at Strong Memorial Hospital, where they proved their worth as valid members of health care teams. In this setting they had the opportunity to focus on the special problems associated with particular physical disorders, and to demonstrate their ability to successfully fill gaps in comprehensive health care to which the professional members of the health care team do not have time to address themselves adequately.

## Discussion

In summary, it appears that this program is effective. It can be launched without excessive difficulty, operates economically, and is accepted and approved of by most parents and physicians. Furthermore, it provides direct, measurable benefits to chronically ill children and to their families. In the final analysis, however, the effectiveness of this program in meeting some of the widespread and grave shortcomings that exist in the health care provided for children with chronic disorders is still open to doubt. Even if family counselors on a wide scale proved to constitute the best possible solution to these problems, there are few means available for continued financial support.[1] Although some parents are willing to pay a certain amount for the service, these contributions alone are inadequate, and, as with so many other services, those who most require assistance are often least able to pay for it. None of the prepayment programs is at present willing to consider reimbursement. Perhaps a large-scale study showing that such a program significantly reduces hospitalization rates and the utilization of emergency rooms, or diminishes the need for mental health services, would persuade insurance companies of its cost effectiveness.[2] Some physicians may be willing to try incorporating the cost of a counselor into their office overhead. Departments of social work might include counselors as a line item on their budget, as they now do with case aides.

The issue of how such services can be paid for highlights a major dilemma in providing services for this and other boundary areas of child health care. It seems clear that attractive possibilities exist for meeting these needs by tapping the large pool of talented middle-class women. Many of these women already play valuable roles in staffing voluntary services that make essential contributions to our present medical care system. Such contributions, however, because they are voluntary, are often taken for granted. The work of hospital visitors, "candy-stripers," ambulance drivers, librarians, and the like is all too often ignored or downgraded, although many of those who perform these services are the wives (or husbands) of professional and semiprofessional wage earners. Many have college or university degrees and, after leaving the working world temporarily to raise their children, seek to return to play new, active roles in society. Unfortunately, many women in this group are sensitive to the

[1] Financial support for family counselor services has thus far come from local sources, including the John F. Wegman Foundation, the Emmet Blakeney Gleason Memorial Fund, the Rochester Female Charitable Organization, the Teen League of Rochester, the Fasco Corporation, and several philanthropic individuals. Grateful acknowledgment is made to these organizations and individuals.
[2] The actual cost of the program per family per year is estimated to be approximately $185. This figure is based on the starting stipend of $1000 for the care of 8-10 families over a one-year period. The average number of hours worked per year is about 400, giving an hourly wage of approximately $2.50. This figure includes all time spent in training and door-to-door travel, and all incidental expenses. One full-time counselor-equivalent in an average practice could provide services to at least 50 families (about one third of all those with chronic physical disorders) for an annual cost of not more than $7000. This is equivalent to an additional charge of $1.00 per visit for each family in the average practice.

charge of becoming "do-gooders"; they want to do something of proven value and to have their services recognized concretely. Although most women who are attracted to work of the kind described in this section may not need much in the way of financial compensation, we are convinced that programs such as this cannot (and should not) operate on a voluntary or semi-voluntary basis.

It seems clear that these and other boundary areas of health care are of central importance in improving the quality of health services, but it is also obvious that neither insurance companies nor patients themselves are prepared to pay much, if anything, for them. From a strict economic viewpoint this suggests that their true market value is minimal. We believe that, in time, this evaluation can be shown to be false; but, for the moment, to pay more or, for that matter, even to continue to pay as little as we have for these services does not appear to be feasible. We are also in the unusual position of knowing that because the women who are able to work in this program are not financially needy, and because they find the work interesting and challenging and the hours attractive, we can continue to recruit adequate numbers to the program at the present relatively low levels of reimbursement. To continue to do so, however, smacks of exploitation and may, in some respects, be depriving others who are needy of a source of income. Not to do so, conversely, entails a risk that some children and their families will be deprived of services that we believe they urgently require.

As with so much of medical care today, we face difficult dilemmas over the relations between cost, effectiveness, and the ultimate responsibility for payment. In contrast to many unproven forms of widely utilized treatment over which there is no difficulty with payment (e.g., tonsillectomy and adenoidectomy), however, this program has been shown to be efficacious and deserves widespread implementation.

*REFERENCES*

CASTANEDA, A., MC CANDLESS, B.R., and PALERMO, D.S.

1956  "The Children's Form of the Manifest Anxiety Scale." *Child Development,* 27:317–326.

CATTELL, R.B., and BICE, G.F.

1962  *The 16 Personality Factor Scale.* The Institute for Personality and Ability Testing. 1602 Coronado Drive, Champaign, Illinois 61820.

COOPERSMITH, STANLEY

1959  "A Method for Determining Self-Esteem." *Journal of Abnormal and Social Psychology,* 59:87–94.

PLESS, IVAN B., and SATTERWHITE, BETTY
   1972 "Chronic Illness in Childhood: Selection, Activities and Evaluation of Non-professional Family Counselors." *Clinical Pediatrics*, 11:403–410.

THORPE, L.P., CLARK, W.W., and TIEGS, E.W.
   1953 California Test of Personality, 1953 Revision. California Test Bureau, Monterey, California.

## C. THE PSYCHODIAGNOSTIC ASSISTANT

JAMES T. HERIOT

Patients seen for diagnosis and treatment of learning problems by pediatricians, pediatric neurologists, and child psychologists represent a large "diagnostic" category of children. Most studies estimate that 20% of the school age population have some such problem. In most instances a complete evaluation of these children should include a psychological appraisal, but actually the majority are not adequately studied. The present work load already strains the capacities of the disciplines involved.

The training of psychometric assistants is based on the thesis that professionals participate in many more facets of the diagnostic and treatment process than is necessary. They act as *data generators, data interpreters, data managers,* and *data implementers,* but need not do so if others with lesser training can perform some of these functions adequately.

As a solution to this kind of manpower deficit a number of professions are exploring the use of assistants and, in varying degrees, biomedically oriented computerized information systems. For example, radiology utilizes x-ray technicians to generate data and is investigating the use of computers to assist in the diagnostic process (Barnard and Dockray, 1970). Dentists employ dental hygienists and dental technicians to generate data and provide some aspects of dental treatment. The Medex program uses ex-corpsmen as doctors' assistants in private and public medical practice for aspects of routine screening and treatment (Smith, 1970). Industry has long employed the professional's aide or administrative assistant for many of the more routine daily activities.

Clinical psychology has made some use of sub-master's-degree-level psychometrists, but has very little experience in the application of computerized information systems. The psychologist at the M.A. or Ph.D. level has traditionally performed his own psychometric evaluations. Standard psychological testing, report preparation, and communication with referral sources for one patient can consume more than eight working hours. Delays in the preparation and delivery of reports, combined with excessive pressures for service, lead to lengthy waiting lists. Six months may be required for the completion of testing and for the preparation and dissemination of reports. Such delays have obvious repercussions when dealing with children who have school difficulties, behavioral problems, or emotional crises.

## The Psychodiagnostic Laboratory

A psychodiagnostic laboratory was established in the fall of 1969 to explore the use of paraprofessional psychometrists [psychodiagnostic assistants (PAs)] as data generators and to examine the feasibility of automated report writing. It is a part of the Developmental Pediatric Program and the Department of Psychiatry's Division of Psychology.

The organization of the laboratory is focused on the reduction of the professional's psychometric activities. A doctoral level psychologist serves as research and clinical director; a PA who has advanced to the technical associate level is the administrator and training director and assumes responsibility for most of the daily operations. Thus this former PA serves as office coordinator, supervises PA training, and acts as liaison between staff activities and the clinical and research director.

The major goals of the psychodiagnostic laboratory are as follows:

- A reduction in the amount of professional time involved in psychological testing and clerical work.
- A decrement in total man-hours spent in test administration.
- A reduction in waiting lists and in the duration between test administration and report dissemination.
- The development of paraprofessional job "ladders" and job descriptions that are attractive enough to recruit nonprofessional but highly competent staff members.
- The generation of research concerning consumer and professional acceptance of paraprofessional diagnosticians and computerized report writing.
- The adaptation of a tested theoretical model, and the development of procedures to replace the use of inappropriate and time-consuming full-scale psychological test batteries.
- The enhancement of the ability of the laboratory staff to service children and families who, because of lack of finances, geographic location, or transportation problems, cannot visit an office.
- The rendering of laboratory staff activities more flexible in terms of medical training and education requirements.

*Psychodiagnostic Assistant Characteristics*

A core staff of three PAs, ranging in age from 20 to 28 years, was recruited in 1969. None of them had bachelor's degrees, although two were part-time college students, nor did any of the three have experience directly related to psychometrics, although all had worked with children in some capacity. Their socioeconomic levels varied widely. They were recruited by word of mouth; no formal advertising was necessary.

*Psychodiagnostic Assistant Job Ladders:*
*Manpower and Career Considerations*

The PA training takes approximately one month, beginning with participant observation and moving rapidly into supervised test administration. There is possible progression from trainee status to "technical associate," a rank that, at the University of Rochester, qualifies the holder as professional staff.

The three initial PAs, after making important contributions to the laboratory's activities, have gone on to other career situations. One PA, without a bachelor's degree, has become executive director of mental health services in a large tri-city area in southern New England. Another earned his bachelor's degree and is now attending medical school. The third PA (who did not finish high school) has become a key staff member in a local OEO agency. As the staff "turned over," 19 more PAs have been trained: two were trained in Washington, D.C., for a day care evaluation project in that city (Block and Heriot, 1972); two were specifically trained to provide screening for a learning disorders clinic at Strong Memorial Hospital; and four more were trained for program and private referral evaluations. Four graduate students (trained PAs) are currently applying the laboratory's procedures in scholarly research. Four PAs have been trained for testing a severe to profoundly deaf population. Seven PAs have been promoted to the technical associate rank with increased responsibilities and rewards. In addition, the PAs have trained more than 20 volunteers who perform specialized testing and research services in local school districts.

*Test Characteristics*

Fourteen dimensions or variables are studied for each patient (see Table 11C.1). Two of the 14 dimensions (parental estimate of development[1] and

---

[1] The Parental Estimate of Development Scale (PEDS) was developed at the psychodiagnostic laboratory of the University of Rochester.

social maturity) are generated from the parent intake interview. After this interview the psychologist delivers his portion of the data to the PA and observes the child briefly in the test situation. The psychologist is then free to go on to other activities, but remains available by phone or direct communication for questions about procedures.

The testing of patients and the training of new technicians take place in testing rooms. All paper work and materials required for test administration are packaged in age-specific kits.

## Report Content

Administration of the test battery takes from one to one and one-half hours, which is about one third to one fourth of the time normally required for psychological test battery administration. In fact, an experienced PA can perform the entire battery in the time normally required for administration of one full-scale IQ test, such as the Stanford Binet or one of the Wechsler tests.

*Table 11C.1.  Test Variables and Examples of Types of Measures*

| Variables | Measures for a School-Age Child |
|---|---|
| Parental estimate of development | PEDS |
| Social maturity | Vineland |
| Spatial organization | Wechsler or Hiskey Blocks or Spatial Reasoning |
| Long-term visual retention and closure | Wechsler |
| Continuous attention | Knox Cubes |
| Visual memory | Hiskey or ITPA[a] |
| Coding-decoding | Wechsler |
| Spoken vocabulary | Wechsler or Binet |
| Auditory comprehension | Wechsler |
| Auditory memory: immediate recall | Digits, Sentences |
| Immediate recall with reuse | Digits, Backwards |
| Reading (single-word recognition) | Wide Range Achievement Test, Gates-Macginitie, and special adaption of Peabody Picture Vocabulary |
| Reading comprehension | Gates |
| Arithmetic | Wide Range Achievement Test |

[a] Illinois Test of Psycholinguistic Abilities.

On completion of testing, the results are ready for the psychologist to interpret to parents and professionals. If specifically requested by the referring source, the automated information system[2] can be used to prepare and print a final copy of the report on the day of testing.

The report consists of a narrative description of the patient's performance in the 14 test dimensions, a data profile sheet, and a section that is a combination of the PA's observations and the psychologist's comments and recommendations.

"Same-day" parental intake, administration of tests, and interpretation of results offer obvious advantages, particularly for parents who must travel long distances or for whom travel is difficult. The advantages are also clear in terms of training medical and graduate students. They can follow the entire intake, test, and data interpretation process in a relatively short time.

*Professional Acceptance of Psychodiagnostic Assistants and Psychodiagnostic Laboratory Procedures*

Professional acceptance of the reports has been favorable. An initial 270 "first-time" report readers were asked to compare our reports to standard psychometric reports in 11 dimensions. Typical dimensions along which the reports were judged were relevance, specificity, precision, and success in identifying etiological factors. The results of this study are reported more fully elsewhere (Heriot 1972).

*Patient and Consumer Follow-Up*

Phone or interview follow-up with the first 100 patients seen by the laboratory yielded parental estimates of improvement in the majority of the children seen and generally favorable consumer reactions to the procedures and personnel. No objective appraisal of efficacy has yet been made.

*Extendability of Psychodiagnostic Laboratory Services*

Traditionally, psychologists work only in their own offices. An important benefit derived from using PAs as test administrators is the ability of the laboratory to extend its services into the field. For instance, PAs are ad-

[2] Computer Consoles, Inc., Model CCI 520 724 Information System, Rochester, New York.

ministering the battery to children at the Rochester Neighborhood Health Center (now the Anthony L. Jordan Health Center), at the Rochester School for the Deaf, in collaboration with the School Health Program in several school districts of Monroe County, and in the learning disorders clinic, the diagnostic clinic for developmental disorders, and the adolescent clinic at Strong Memorial Hospital. This extension of the laboratory's procedures to other care settings allows the staff to serve a population that often has great difficulty in keeping its clinic appointments. Mobility permits psychometric staff to take procedures *to* medical students, house staff, and fellows for training purposes. Taking procedures to the patient also allows the laboratory staff to engage and collaborate in research that would not otherwise be possible. Furthermore, testing can be carried on concurrently at multiple sites. Although such mobility is mechanically possible with traditional psychological services, cost/benefit considerations render it impractical.

*Increases in Training and Service Volume*

The psychodiagnostic laboratory has performed more than 2500 full evaluations since mid-1970 to the end of 1973. This volume of clinical service would be unmanageable for one Ph.D.-level psychologist doing the usual battery of psychological tests. Moreover, the PA training process could easily be expanded. Depending on the availability of funds to support salaries, a large and effective staff can be developed in a rather short period of time. Generally service income can be generated to meet these costs. The limiting feature with traditional psychologists' services is lack of personnel, who take a long period to train, as well as lack of resources. This program overcomes one of these limitations—the lack of Ph.D. psychologists.

*The Psychodiagnostic Screening Battery:*
*Theoretical Model and Rationale*

The psychodiagnostic laboratory's procedures are tied to a theoretical model developed by Mark (1962), from which many of the procedures used and the manner in which results are interpreted are derived. This model operates on the philosophy that cognitive abilities develop unevenly, particularly in persons suspected of behavioral or learning aberrations. For instance, less than 1% of the patients seen by the laboratory reveal an even distribution of test scores. This variability within a patient population is an argument against the use of global IQ tests. If full-scale IQ tests are required for legal decisions or placement alternatives, the laboratory reports a prorated IQ based on three subtests that have been found to be highly correlated with a full-length IQ test.

The testing process is free of technician decision-making in that the technicians follow predetermined flow charts in deciding what test to use, how to interpret scores, and what optimizing techniques to attempt. It is this decision-free nature of test administration, scoring, and interpretation that enables the laboratory to use nonprofessional personnel.

A battery of the 14 test dimensions thought to discriminate most successfully between achievers, underachievers, and overachievers was assembled. Research reporting on the battery's discriminatory capabilities has been documented (Heriot, 1973). The measures utilized to test for these were extracted from previously standardized tests and subtests (see Table 11C.1).

Scores in all 14 dimensions are compared against a patient-specific standard. This standard is an attempt to express what the patient can achieve when his performance is enhanced by a favorable environment, such as one-to-one teaching. Significant variations of scores from these standards are followed by further limit testing or the use of optimizing techniques. The purpose of limit testing is to rule out various etiological factors. If optimizing is successful (i.e., if the deviant score is elevated significantly), it automatically generates a prescription for teachers and other persons working with the patient to use the same optimizing technique.

## A Case Study: Differential Diagnosis of Learning Disabilities

The psychodiagnostic laboratory operationally defines a learning disability as a major (1 standard deviation) discrepancy between academic achievement and general intellectual capabilities. In addition, the psychodiagnostic laboratory model requires that the student be underachieving with respect to peer instructional norms. Such an operational definition minimizes false positives, but is defensible statistically in terms of minimizing false negatives. An example of the utility of the system is presented in the form of a case study.

M.C. was a 6½-year-old boy referred for congenital ophthalmalplegia, diagnosed and confirmed as Moebius syndrome (Stebbins et al., 1975). The referral, made by the Anthony Jordan Health Center, was for hyperactivity, school learning difficulties, peer problems, and cosmetic difficulties associated with Moebius syndrome. The question of the presence or absence of a learning disability was specifically posed, and the test battery was administered twice in conjunction with complete physical and neurological studies. Intellectually, M.C. was found to be in the borderline to dull-normal range. He indeed did display visual motor difficulty, particularly in form reproduction. However, on final testing, his academic achievement was either in line with his intellectual capability or exceeded it. The diagnosis of learning disability was rejected, and his parents and teachers were counseled to lower their expectations, not because of learning disabilities, but because of mildly reduced intelligence. The decrease in pressure for performance and the accompanying rewards for achieving at a more realistic level were accompanied by a marked decline in hyperactivity and immediate improvement in peer relationships and general school adjustment.

The precision and specificity of the measures and the fact that they derive from a rational model permitted a differential diagnosis, the results of which could be communicated to parents, teachers, and referring physicians with confidence and efficiency.

## Summary

The psychodiagnostic laboratory has expanded the number of psychological test services performed through the use of nonprofessional testers, the selection of a battery of subtests to measure various components of intellectual functionings, and the utilization of an automated information system to speed up reports. It is highly acceptable to families and physicians and provides a career ladder for the psychodiagnostic assistants. The laboratory is another example of health manpower expansion through the use of nonprofessionals, one of the most significant trends in health services delivery today.

## REFERENCES

BARNARD, H.J., and DOCKRAY, K.T.

1970  "Computerized Operation in the Diagnostic Radiology Department." *American Journal of Roentgenology, Radium Therapy and Nuclear Medicine,* 109(3):628–635.

BLOCK, A.H., and HERIOT, J.T.

1972  "An Evaluation of ITA and Traditional Orthography as Early Reading Techniques." *Improving Human Performance: A Research Quarterly,* 1(2): 17–50.

HERIOT, JAMES T.

1972 "Pediatric Acceptance of a Psycho-Educational Screening Instrument Using Paraprofessional Examiners and Computer Supported Report Writing" (mimeograph).

HERIOT, JAMES T.

1973 "Memory/Attention versus Visual/Perceptual Correlates of Learning Disorders in a Pediatric Population" (mimeograph).

MARK, H. J.

1962 "Elementary Thinking and the Classification of Behavior." *Science*, 135:75–87.

SMITH, R. A.

1970 "Medex." *Journal of the American Medical Association*, 211(11):1843–1845.

STEBBINS, W.C., EMMEL, A., HERIOT, J.T., and ROCKOWITZ, R.

1975 "Severe Visual Motor Difficulty and School Achievement: Moebius Syndrome (a replication)." *Developmental Medicine and Child Neurology* (in press).

# SUMMARY
# AND
# IMPLICATIONS:
## Where Do We Stand?

*When we talk about evaluation studies leading to verdicts of "success" or "failure,"*
*it should be recognized that we are greatly simplifying and abbreviating the*
*typical results. Most social action programs are so complex in the variety of*
*inputs and the multiplicity of objectives, that simple overall judgments are not*
*likely to lead to quick decisions. . . .*

Cain and Hollister, 1969:50

Biomedical research differs from sociomedical research in that biomedical
experiments, using classical designs, frequently result in clear-cut answers
to well-formulated questions. Answers to sociomedical research problems,
in contrast, are rarely clear-cut and may lie in the political rather than
the "scientific" sphere.

Our program in child health falls between these two categories of
research and blends them. We have defined the problems, and searched
for answers. We used control groups when possible and comparison groups
when not, and attempted to find solutions to the many problems studied.
Empirical studies result only in diagnoses, not in therapy. We live in a
"political" environment; our job is incomplete with only a diagnosis.
Our task includes implementing changes that will inprove children's
health. Combining empirical research with innovative programs is a
feature that distinguishes our approach.

In this final chapter we review our goals, achievements, and limitations;
summarize the basic findings of our research; and discuss a number of
unresolved issues. We describe our efforts in community pediatrics in the
hope that others will consider embarking on similar programs in their
communities.

### Community Child Health: Philosophy

Community child health is a philosophy that should pervade university
pediatric departments. It combines the traditional research, education,
and service programs with a concern for all children in a defined geographic area, not only those who receive care. Care is provided within the

social networks of the family and the community, not only to individual children. For us, the ultimate goal in the program described here, is to improve child health in our community and to develop models that are applicable elsewhere.

This book does not cover the total field; rather it presents a case study of one department's engagement in community child health. As a case report it has, in our view, greater general usefulness than if we had attempted to cover the entire field. We have presented herein only that portion of the department's work with the community in which there has been research or evaluation programs or both.

A program in community child health research should include the following essentials: (1) a geographically defined population; (2) an ongoing data system to monitor this population and define needs; (3) new programs to meet specific demonstrated needs; and (4) evaluation of these programs. With one such problem solved, the circle begins again: new needs are identified, and new or modified programs are implemented, followed by their evaluation.

A facilitating goal, and indeed the primary one for a university department, is the education of personnel. Only if medical students, pediatric house staff, practitioners, nurses, and other health personnel are involved in a program continuously pervaded by the basic elements stated above, will their education be complete. Education without involvement in the organization and provision of health services, however, is not sufficient preparation for tomorrow's health care personnel. Child health problems involve in their cause and cure a large component of social factors. Therefore any community child health group must devote considerable energy to the creation and staffing of services that take these factors into account. Research in this area should not be isolated from an involvement in services.

An additional aspect of this department's research activities within the concept of "community" has included the integration of some biomedical investigations with health services studies. To illustrate, over the course of the past several years, the random sample survey has been used as a sampling base for determining the prevalence of $\alpha$-1-antitrypsin deficiency in the community, the prevalence of antibodies to *Hemophilus influenzae* in different age groups, and the prevalence of epilepsy (in preparation for a comprehensive care program), as well as providing normal "controls" for several studies of chronic disease.

Most of the research reported in this book is action-oriented, although certain more theoretical sections on health and illness behavior are also included. In our view, action includes implementation; researchers in health services, more than in other fields, must be committed to the application of their findings as well as to the creation of new knowledge.

314     Summary and Implications

Accordingly this program in community child health has involved its investigators in active participation in community health planning, in health delivery systems, and in the process of implementation.

Since most children receive their health care in private offices, we have not limited our research to the public sector or the poor, although this is where many of the most pressing problems exist. In addition, conducting research with practitioners in both the public and private sectors is one effective way to rapidly implement the conclusions of the research. For instance, the controlled trial study of pediatric nurse practitioners was done in pediatricians' offices. When the experiment was completed, all participating pediatricians continued to employ nurse practitioners; no additional time and effort were needed to "sell" the research findings. This linking of health services research to the clinical delivery arm is one of the major justifications for a clinical department's involvement in these activities. Although many research studies in health services can be done only on much larger populations, or can (with considerable effort) be sold to the practicing community by nonclinicians, the task is easier if the research and service are linked.

Though we always aim at conducting our studies in an objective way, we do not claim that our sociomedical research is value-free. Both the selection of research topics and the use of research findings are influenced by value judgments. The research itself, however, can only clarify factual relationships—what happens under certain circumstances in given settings. In this book, we try to convince other researchers of the objectivity of our procedures and the conclusiveness of our findings. There will be those who will disagree with our values and with what we select to study or teach. Such disagreements cannot be resolved in scientific terms. We try to keep clear the distinction between values and the objective study of programs.

Disagreement arises when our convictions as citizens are implied in some of our discussions. Like others, we have our views about Medicaid legislation and the statewide abortion law. We believe that health care is the right of every individual regardless of age, sex, income, or race. Unfortunately, the proportion of the gross national product that can be claimed for medical care is limited; other needs such as national security compete with health care for the federal dollar. The old controversy about whether a capitalistic free market system is the most efficient mechanism for allocating scarce resources to health care needs, or whether health should be treated as a public utility like national security, is still open for discussion. Such broad issues will remain subjects on which honorable men will disagree for some time to come.

Change itself is ofttimes difficult, especially when interests differ. For instance, conflict is likely when a new organization of services is introduced into areas where traditional medical practices prevail. Many of the broad goals on which there is consensus, however, can often be reached only by exceeding traditional limits of professional behavior and by becoming actively involved as an advocate for children. Our dedication to the values of community pediatrics may bring us into conflict with other providers or even with parents or community groups. Indeed, any engaged professional who believes in the value of his work will sooner or later become involved in politics within or beyond the boundaries of his profession.

Social institutions are constantly changing and need continuous self-renewal. Untested radical changes are as prone to failure as are the frequent proposals to return to "the good old days." Many of our own programs are replete with compromise. In spite of the compromises, however, we have committed ourselves to finding the best answers, or to illuminating the options and effects by experiments, once a basic political decision has been made. For example, we reject the charity approach of care for handicapped children and consider that these patients have a right to care by professionals, but we are willing to compromise and accept volunteer services until such time as these children can obtain their "rights." We train part-time counselors to work with families of children with chronic illnesses, but pay these counselors poorly. We train nurse practitioners to perform many of the same services as doctors, but pay them at a significantly lower rate. We did so initially in both cases because there were too few existing professionals to meet these needs. What begins as a compromise, however, often appears in time to provide an equal or a better way to meet certain needs more efficiently. The basis for these compromises was often our desire for immediate solutions to pressing problems. By means of innovations such as those described, we avoided delaying the provision of needed services simply because we could not afford to pay the "going rate" for these services when supplied by the most highly qualified professionals.

It might appear from this discussion that we have been excessively concerned with cost/benefit considerations and with issues of credentialism and licensing. The whole question of credentialism is a complex one. On the one hand, some evidence of basic competence is needed to protect the public; in exchange, the public must be prepared to pay more for those who can provide such evidence. On the other hand, we believe that in many areas of health care credentials can be misleading, as, for example, when personality attributes are of greater importance than technical skill, or when highly trained persons are used for work that can be done as well by others lacking such skills. Similarly, it is clear that the benefits of many human services will never be demonstrated in economic terms. More cost/benefit studies are premature in a field in which outcomes of any kind are so difficult to measure. Moreover, because such "hard-nosed" economic comparisons are not central to our concern for meeting basic human needs and attending humanely to less basic human needs, we choose to leave them for others to study.

## The Basic Findings

### The "New Morbidity" (Part I)

The major health problems of children today are different from those that prevailed when pediatrics came into existence a century ago. Death now is a rare occurrence except in the newborn, making even more tragic the fatalities that do occur. We do not belittle the importance of dealing with the complex illnesses that continue to plague children—leukemia, tumors, genetic and congenital problems, and occasional life-threatening infections, as well as accidents. But even augmenting our ability to treat and someday prevent these problems will not suffice to make most children function more effectively in society.

There is considerable anxiety for short periods of time when children have acute infectious disease. It is clear from our surveys, however, that the current major health problems of children, as seen by the community, are those that would have barely been mentioned a generation ago. Learning difficulties and school problems, behavioral disturbances, allergies, speech difficulties, visual problems, and the problems of adolescents in coping and adjusting are today the most common concerns about children. In addition family social problems and the management and handling of everyday life stresses are major concerns requiring attention.

To improve child health, this new morbidity must be addressed by the health professions, as well as others, with the same energy and dedication they previously devoted to life-threatening problems. The new morbidity rarely kills, although the hazards of accidents in adolescence and the complex sociomedical problems of the battered child are two examples in which death is still a very real possibility. The basic nature of the new morbidity is different: its causes lie in the complex interaction of biological, social, and cultural factors, and its solutions will require extension of the pediatrician into the community in collaboration with representatives of many other disciplines.

The studies reported in this book document the heavy burden placed on families by the new morbidity. These data, in turn, have guided the implementation of programs aimed at solving such problems. It is our conviction that departments of pediatrics interested in improving the health of children in the community and in training personnel for the future must engage in a scholarly study of the problems of the new morbidity.

## Health and Illness Behavior (Part II)

There are two reasons for our interest in why people use health services when they do, in why they take certain preventive measures, and in what the barriers are to both preventive care (health behavior) and sick care (illness behavior). First, even after eliminating financial barriers and inaccessibility of medical care, there remain sizable differences in the rates with which different groups use health services. Generally those who have the greatest need (e.g., those in the lowest socioeconomic group) use these services least. Second, there is also much variation in the manner in which people live and in the measures they take to prevent illness, such as participation in direct preventive programs (e.g., immunization) or the observance of indirect preventive measures such as adequate exercise, proper nutrition, the intelligent use of tobacco, alcohol, and drugs, the adoption of reasonable risk-taking behavior, and the development of successful measures for coping with stress.

Our studies, based on household interviews and the more detailed diary approach, provide only moderate support for present theories of health and illness behavior. Though certain general tendencies can be recognized, there will always remain considerable differences in the ways people react, depending on the specific illnesses, specific health objectives, and specific life histories of the persons involved. Explanations based on general health beliefs and attitudes can account for only a small part of the variance. The major variation for both health and illness behavior is related to demographic and social status factors, that is, social class, race, education, sex, and age. Except for education, these factors are not easily changed. More promising is the study of short-term decision-making. Our data show that family stress, on a day-to-day basis, is related both to the frequency of illness and to the way people use health services. Further investigation into the development of coping mechanisms for handling stress is, therefore, a major item for child health research in the future.

These findings pose several problems for those responsible for health services; each category or patient, in regard to behavioral objectives, must be approached individually. Even then, there are no simple short cuts via general belief or attitude modifications.

It is often said, in deprecation, that sociomedical research only documents the obvious. True, these detailed analyses reaffirm that the poor and the black receive less medical care than the average citizen. But these analyses also show that poverty is more important than race with respect to health. Indeed, poor whites report more illness than poor blacks, modifying the stereotype that blacks experience more illness. Dental care is easier to defer and, accordingly, shows even sharper patterns by social class. There is much lower use by the poor, and little improvement was seen over the first years of new programs intended to meet this need. Well-child care for the indigent is not very good in this community. Again, social factors other than race, especially parity and income, were found to be crucial to receiving adequate care. Surprisingly, we found that young unwed mothers actually entered the system of well-baby care more regularly than older, multiparous, low-income mothers. In this particular study, public health nurses were able to get mothers into well-baby care, but the level of care was not improved. This is a sobering thought for those who argue that most of health services research is simple common sense: "Add a public health nurse, and you are bound to get improvement in care"; "Add a postcard reminder system, and people will keep their appointments."

Solutions are clearly not as simple as statements such as these suggest. Some things do not work that might be expected to, while others work unpredictably or vary with the circumstances. It is these "circumstances" that health services research seeks to identify whenever possible. For example, health supervision was better at neighborhood well-baby clinics than at university hospital clinics, suggesting that these hospitals, reputed paragons of quality, may not be the best places to deliver well-child care.

Although we could not confirm any of the proposed sociopsychological theories of health and illness behavior, we gathered sufficient information to reject some popular views. One stereotype often found in the popular press, and even among professionals, is that some people will never use health services even if free; another stereotype is that if humane, easily available health services are provided, people will use them appropriately. As with so many other aspects of life, the truth lies somewhere between. For some people, certain basic attitudes are important barriers to the use of medical care, regardless of all other factors. For others, all that is required to change a nonuser into a user is to provide reasonable accessibility without a financial barrier. This is not to imply that we believe it is necessary only to remove these barriers. Additional understanding of the consumer's behavior is needed before we can develop a more effective and efficient health services system.

Equally important is the lack of consensus on what constitutes "appropriate" health or sick care. It remains difficult to demonstrate precisely what types of preventive services (other than immunizations) result in measurable benefits to health; it will be even more difficult to prove that medical care is beneficial in the area of the new morbidity. Patients want help for problems that are not always defined in such a way that the provider views them as his responsibility. The efficacy of health services must be demonstrated, and the "boundary" areas outside the field traditionally defined as medicine must be explored. These, alongside the overriding issue of costs, may well be the most important problems facing health services research today.

## Service Programs (Part III)

Several new programs described in Part III of our book should be of great interest to most readers. Developments of major national importance such as Medicaid, the New York State abortion law, the emergence of neighborhood health centers, migrant projects, and several new manpower programs are examples of some of the measures intended to improve health services. They have emerged in more or less similar fashion throughout the country. Our study documents the successes and failures of these programs in more detail than often is possible on a national basis. Although not all such programs throughout the country have had the same successes or failures, they can all be evaluated similarly, and, to the extent that like conditions exist, similar results can be expected.

Our four main study objects—the Medicaid program, the abortion law, the Rochester Neighborhood Health Center, and new manpower programs—had both anticipated and unanticipated effects. The Medicaid program failed in its officially stated goal of integrating the health care for the poor and the nonpoor. But it succeeded administratively in enrolling the "eligibles" into the program and in providing secure funding for their care. The institutions that always provided medical care for the poor, and the new ones such as health centers are now in a better position to compete for scarce health manpower. Although the indigent have benefited from the resulting redistribution of medical services, the dual system of care for the poor and the nonpoor remains.

Passage of the liberalized abortion law found the medical care system prepared to provide abortion services to all, as shown in the stable number of abortions performed over the first three years, and in the equal abortion rates for the poor and the nonpoor. However, an unintended consequence is that most projections of future population development and of manpower needs for pediatric care and for elementary education have had to be drastically lowered. The prevention of unwanted births, together with a reduction in ideal family size, may be providing an automatic solution to the medical care crisis for children.

The Rochester Neighborhood Health Center achieved most of its stated goals. Reliance on the emergency room for regular sick care declined for target area residents; the hospitalization pattern of children changed; and previously unmet needs were served. Less predictable was the development of the health center as an institution different from the private group practice model, as well as from hospital clinics. Further analysis of this new institution is needed to determine the advantages and disadvantages of each of these different models.

Finally, most of the manpower programs were successful in that they demonstrated the feasibility of using new health care workers. The quality of their work and the satisfaction of the patients clearly show that new forms of health manpower are possible in American society. The old two-class system of health care workers (M.D.s and non-M.D.s) has become less clear-cut. Intermediate positions have been created, giving rise to new occupations or professions in general—and to new questions. Will there be equal pay and equal status for equal work? Will these persons be licensed? Will new liability insurance be needed? The impact of the new manpower on the social stratification system in health occupations has not yet been determined.

The total effect of these service programs is difficult to assess. The health of children, in terms of outcome variables like mortality, is only slightly improved. In general, however, these programs have not aimed at reducing mortality or even at reducing the traditional morbidity. In terms of our original model, the goal has been to increase and redistribute the volume of health services, because rendering health services generally considered beneficial where they were not previously available is seen as worthwhile in and of itself.

Throughout history man has turned to some type of healer; we believe that access to modern healers is a right of contemporary man. Although not all health needs of children have been met (e.g., there remain significant numbers of children who have not been immunized against diseases such as pertussis), most of the barriers to access in this community have now been eliminated. The next step is to determine what components of these services affect health, and then to provide these in an optimum fashion.

A significant finding, and one not previously documented anywhere in the nation, is the decline in this community in the utilization of health services per child over a 6 year period, in spite of an expanding manpower supply and a lowering of financial barriers to such services. This reflects, in our view, a decreasing need for traditional health services. It suggests the beginning of an "epidemic of wellness"—a goal to which all those in child health have aspired.

One characteristic of our studies has been an attempt to carry out comparison studies or controlled trials where possible. The evaluations of pediatric nurse practitioners and family counselors demonstrated that controlled trials, even in private practices, are possible. The Rochester Neighborhood Health Center studies showed that similar areas in a community can be selected for comparison. In other instances, such as the impact of Medicaid or the abortion law, only studies at several points in time, yielding data on trends, furnish explanatory information. In the case of the migrant health project, we relied on description alone. With effort and skill researchers can and should move closer to the ideal of controlled trials, even in community service programs. Notwithstanding, we also believe that certain aspects of health services delivery, such as the right of a population to medical care, represent sociopolitical decisions that can be little affected by research. The role of research is to define what works and how it works, and to modify programs once the basic goals have been achieved.

## Unresolved Issues

Many issues raised in the course of our studies or implied in our general work with children in the community indicate a series of unresolved problems to be studied in the future.

### Segregation or Integration of Different Health Services

Most of us favor integration of the various components of health care, as we do of many other facets of life, yet there are difficulties in putting this concept into practice.

Theoretically, at least, we believe that children's services should be part of an integrated system of health care for people of all ages. One reason is that hospital services for children, as part of the functioning of a general hospital, would seem to offer many advantages in terms of shared use of expensive facilities such as x-ray and laboratories. Another reason is that many problems of children have their origins in family life stress; thus it would seem more efficient and effective to deal with them by caring for an entire family in one setting, making general medical services for children (now called primary health care) a part of total family care. It was for this reason that we chose the "family type" care with funding from the Office of Economic Opportunity Neighborhood Health Center Program rather than the "children only" programs sponsored by the Children and Youth Projects of the Maternal and Child Health Division.

But in practice we admit considerable ambivalence on these matters. The sorry fact is that children often end up as "poor relations" in integrated programs; they represent a decreasing proportion of the total population, a group with considerably less pressing demands than those of the aged (witnessed by the fact that, in 1970, the health expenditures per person paid for from public funds were 16 times higher for those "65 and over" than for those "under 19"—(Cooper and McGee, 1971), and receive a smaller slice of the budget. Local examples include our difficulty in establishing a children's intensive care unit in a general hospital, or special laboratory facilities, or the near impossibility of obtaining adequate funding for the ambulatory "people-oriented" services needed for children today, compared to the in-hospital technological laboratory-oriented services made available and paid for by insurance for the elderly. We still hold to our view that the ideal is integration, but at times we yearn for the "separate but equal" rather than the present integrated but unequal services we often have to accept for children.

Another facet of integration involves the care of the handicapped child. We believe that the ideal would be for all care, even of the severely handicapped, to be coordinated by the primary care team, rather than each disease group being cared for by subspecialists. But, in fact, neither system is working ideally in most places. Primary care physicians (pediatricians or family physicians) often are unwilling to provide even general care for the child with severe handicaps (e.g., patients with spina bifida), yet subspecialty clinics, usually well set up for technical care, do not ordinarily provide preventive services, nor do they take responsibility for 24-hour-a-day comprehensive care. We seek to educate health workers and to organize systems of care that will eliminate these gaps by integrating services and by keeping the central focus of care in the generalists' (and the families') hands. As a result of several recent studies of patients in specialty clinics, we are more aware, however, of how far we have yet to go in achieving this goal. Unfortunately, there are few data to prove which method of care organization is more effective and more acceptable to parents and providers.

Still another question of integration concerns the mental health field. We believe that this very important component of care should be given as part of general child health services. In the Rochester Neighborhood Health Center this works better than we have seen anywhere else, yet there is still definite room for improvement. Elsewhere it has been more difficult to achieve, because of a scarcity of consultants in psychiatry and psychology to work intimately as members of general health teams, inadequate financing of mental health services when given by generalists, and problems in communications. Data presented from our studies (and others) on the very large role that family life stress and crises play in causing illness and in determining when people seek care support our view that more attention to behavioral and social factors must be a part of general health care for children, not a separate subspecialty of the system.

In all these areas effective integration lies somewhere in the future; it is, however, an issue of high priority for health services researchers to undertake.

Where Are the Boundaries of Health Care?

A related problem is the issue of the boundaries between health and other problems of human life. Should medicine only heal wounds or also struggle to prevent them? Because low family income or the parental loss of a job is associated with higher rates of illness in children, health care workers ought to have some influence on such issues as guaranteed annual income and general employment policies. Because children who live in inner city areas or in old housing have a high incidence of lead poisoning, health care workers ought to have some influence on housing policy. Because one of the major problems of parents relates to schooling, health care workers ought to have some influence on education. Because a marital dispute may trigger a child's visit to a physician for a minor illness, the child health worker ought to have some influence in dealing with marital difficulties. The question, of course, is not whether pediatrics has a mandate in these broader issues, but how much of a mandate it has, and in what way, and how effective such activity might ultimately be in relation to the more restricted, traditional goals of pediatrics.

In general, we view with alarm the possibility that highly paid, skilled health workers might become involved in building houses, creating cooperatives, unionizing workers, or providing marriage counseling—not because these activities are unimportant, but rather because they are so important they should not be left to the health worker, an amateur in these fields. On the other hand, we believe strongly that the health worker must be a part of a system of human services in which these problems receive adequate, skilled attention no matter what part of the system identifies them. It is certainly part of our future agenda to determine how best to combine such human services.

Dependency or Initiative?

We believe current health practices foster too much dependency and not enough independence. The more we learn about the causes of ill health, the clearer it becomes that, aside from genetics, the major determinant of a person's health is his way of life—how he eats, sleeps, exercises, smokes, uses drugs, relates to other human beings, and copes with stress. These activities are all learned, but the health care system does little to try to modify the learning process. This is so in part because we know little about what messages to give, and, in part, because we know little about how to change human behavior. The future of child health lies in the area of helping people to learn how to care for themselves—how to take preventive actions and how to use health services appropriately—rather than in continuing to do things to and for people.

## How Are Financing and Administration Affected?

One of the most controversial issues of the past several years relates to the financing of health care. We remain uncertain about the effects of pre-payment versus fee for service. Should general tax revenues or social security insurance be used as a major funding source? Should national, state, local, or private insurance groups act as administering agents? At what level should there be coinsurance, copayments, and deductibles, or should insurance be limited to catastrophic illnesses? All these questions are of paramount importance. We have not addressed them in these studies because our priorities were of a different order. We would be remiss, how-ever, if we did not state our philosophy toward financing—which, inci-dentally, is based on our values rather than on any body of facts.

We believe that adequate health services must be guaranteed to every child; neither poverty of the parents nor their attitudes and values should stand in the way of his receiving adequate care. There could be several mechanisms of financing to achieve this goal. But within this con-cept of universal access and equity, we also recognize that incentives need to be developed to stimulate the individual to learn how to keep himself healthy.

We have also ignored the issue of the administration of health services. We are concerned about the impersonal nature of care that characterizes large institutions, whether they be hospitals, neighborhood health centers, or multispecialty group practices. Because we believe the humane, per-sonal approach to be essential for good medical care, we are convinced that small units are necessary at the actual point of delivery of health care. To effect economies of size, however, such units must have access to expensive, but rarely used, equipment and laboratory resources. This means that they must be part of a larger system or network.

The adequate financing and administration of health services are prob-lems of major importance for which, with the expansion of health center networks and the emergence of different forms of organizing and paying for medical care, studies can be designed to provide answers.

## What Is the Future of Pediatrics?

The future of child health in the community hinges to a large extent on the future of the primary care pediatrician. Here a number of forces, many of which have been described in this book, are at work; when taken together, they are likely to change the nature of pediatric training and practice in the near future. These have been described in some detail elsewhere (Pless, 1974; Haggerty, 1972) and will only be summarized in the following paragraphs.

Basically, three forces are at work. One is the result of the combined influence of a number of factors that are rapidly changing the traditional pattern of pediatric practice. In the past the bulk of child health care consisted of the supervision of normal infants. But we have shown that there is a rapidly declining birthrate and that most healthy infants can be supervised adequately by nonphysicians (e.g., pediatric nurse practitioners). Moreover, it has been suggested that the previously accepted standards for health supervision can be reduced to about 50% the number of visits currently recommended. Thus the care of newborns and healthy infants could be removed almost entirely from the direct service of the primary pediatrician, if such a course were chosen. Another large section of pediatric practice has dealt with children who have minor, acute illnesses, usually infectious respiratory or gastrointestinal disorders. But it is now clear that most of the important communicable diseases have been reduced dramatically; and, as new vaccines for the more common respiratory viruses and other methods of prevention of some of the remaining bacterial infections are developed, this decline will continue. This is not to say that no problems remain. Impoverished children from urban, ghetto, and rural areas still receive little of this "traditional" care, and screening and care for many chronic problems leave much to be desired. But the trend is clear: there is less need for traditional well-child care and management of acute illness in children.

The second force at work is a manifestation of several converging trends in health manpower development. One is the increasing number of physicians being graduated as a result of the impetus provided by the recommendations of the Carnegie Commission on Higher Education (1970) and by state and federal subsidies. Although this trend may soon be reversed by direct government action, the target set for 1978 was 16,400 first-year enrollments, compared with 7973 in 1968. The importance of this increase for child health care depends on the percentage of physicians recruited into pediatrics and family medicine. Alongside this rapid growth in physician manpower, there has been a parallel rise in the number and apparent capabilities of allied health workers, much of which has been aimed at child health in particular (Silver and Ott, 1973). It is clear from our own description of the pediatric nurse practitioner that they can absorb much of the pediatrician's traditional work load without any demonstrable loss in quality or patient satisfaction. Finally, the growing popularity of family medicine as a specialty needs to be taken into consideration. It is too soon to predict for how long this growth will continue (from 50 family medicine residents in 1969 to more than 2000 in 1973), but the prospect of family practice is an attractive one for many entering medical students. In our view the likelihood of its survival is directly related to the ability of family medicine training programs to fulfill the promise of "specialist" qualifications. This requires an intense emphasis on the unique features of illness in the family unit and necessitates, in turn, more comprehensive training about the family as a social unit, based not only on the experience of family doctors, but also on the more theoretical perspective of the social sciences. The chief import of the growing popularity of family medicine, as far as pediatrics is concerned, arises from the likelihood that the presumed "total family orientation" will emerge; hence their insistence on child health care as a desirable and indeed necessary part of the total package. Thus, if family medicine survives and flourishes, and child care is included among the family doctor's capabilities, there will be major implications for primary pediatrics.

In addition to the changes in child health needs and in manpower developments, a third, at present minor, force is at work that could become important in the future. It consists of an apparently growing desire of people at large to "demystify" medicine, to have more control over their own care, to treat more illness without recourse to doctors, and to gain more influence over how medical care is organized and delivered. Some of this appears to be an outgrowth of "consumerism"; some of it merely reflects the spin-offs of various health fads; and some may be the result of subtle but potent health education processes.

Taken together, these forces must inevitably reduce the pediatrician's work load if it is defined exclusively in traditional terms. He could respond in various ways to this crucial threat to his survival. For example, he could move to a geographical area of greater need—in effect, redistributing pediatric manpower and thus, in the short run, serving the purposes of society and himself; or he could choose to abandon primary pediatrics and attempt to practice only as a consultant to other physicians, presumably family doctors for the most part. This latter step could be accomplished either by subspecializing (i.e., by becoming doubly qualified in both pediatrics and an "organ specialty" such as cardiology, neurology, or rheumatology), or by retaining his general expertise, but functioning as a first-line consultant to other primary physicians, as in the British model. In effect, either of these latter options would largely remove the pediatrician from primary care.

Another option is to expand the scope of primary pediatrics by accepting responsibility for many of the boundary areas that have been highlighted throughout this book. Although we sense a growing awareness among pediatricians of the "new morbidity," there is also considerable uneasiness, stemming from their recognition that many of the problems represent areas for which they are inadequately prepared. This suggests a reluctance to move into these areas of unmet need because the pediatricians sense that the job will be done badly, and that they will derive little reward from it.

There are two deep issues that may delay or prevent acceptance of the new morbidity as a future responsibility for primary pediatrics. The first is the implicit diminution of professional status and prestige that accompanies a shift from technical expertise toward expertise of an interpersonal, managerial nature. The second is the important question of whether the value society places on these problems is such that pediatricians will be compensated adequately for their services. As was pointed out in the discussion of the family counselor, there is real doubt whether this will ever be the case within the existing conceptual framework of health services. In the struggle to control the costs of medical care for the "old morbidity," most of which is a reflection of spiraling hospital costs (the quintessence of the old morbidity), a climate of opinion is being created that may, at least in the short run, prevent any part of the medical care dollar from being spent on these "marginal" areas.

It is difficult to see where reasonable solutions to this dilemma lie. A complete redefinition of medical care toward a totally comprehensive conceptualization seems unlikely until, perhaps, it can be shown conclusively that such an overall approach reduces, in the long run, basic medical care needs. Thus counselors, case aides, health educators, and even social workers may become acceptable medical expenses only if it can be demonstrated that they reduce hospitalization, emergency room utilization, doctor visits, or institutional care.

As was stated previously, this constitutes a "hard-nosed" view toward the financing of health care services. Increasingly, however, it represents the position adopted by officials in government, by politicians, and by insurance program administrators. It is certainly the position held by some, if not most, health economists. Many health service researchers accept the practical realities of this argument, at the same time acknowledging that any outcomes, let alone those that can be measured in economic terms, are hard to come by.

What, then, are some alternatives to these views? Are there not societies that attempt to provide truly comprehensive health and social services for their citizens whether or not the "benefits" of such programs can be proved? Examples are seen in varying degrees in the Scandinavian countries, in Britain and other European nations, and, in our own hemisphere, in Cuba and Canada. For some, these examples simply represent one manifestation of "socialized medicine." This is partly true, but they are equally an expression of philosophies of government with enlightened social welfare policies operating within some form of socialized economy. The most outstanding current example is the People's Republic of China. The amazing strides made there in the provision of a full range of health and social services since the Revolution may be viewed as constituting simply a very wise, well-calculated investment in the future. But to other observers they represent the response of the Chinese to what Gunnar Myrdal has termed a "moral imperative." In his book *Asian Drama* (1968), Myrdal explored the health problems of the developing nations. According to Wray (1974), "It is clear from his [Myrdal's] thorough review of the scanty data available for developing countries that it is difficult to justify the necessary investments in decent health care on purely economic grounds." However, Myrdal points out that "there is a value premise, operating in public policy . . . , that is in fact a *moral imperative*" (Wray, 1974).

Though in the past this imperative has been accepted "to combat disease and prevent premature death" (Wray, 1974), it now has to be extended to cover the new problems or the new morbidity discussed in this book. If it is not extended, one alternative would be to remove the "boundary area" entirely from the sphere of medicine, placing it, instead, within the realm of social welfare. Such a path has been initiated in some European countries and may be followed here, to the detriment, in our view, of medical care in general.

In summary, if pediatrics is viewed as a medical discipline that treats only traditional children's diseases (the old morbidity), our attempt to sketch a picture of child health in the community may have little significance. Conversely, if pediatrics is viewed more broadly as truly encompassing all of "child health," that is, preventive, mental, emotional, social, and educational elements, as well as the treatment of organic disease, and if it is accepted that the most important determinants of these broader aspects of the health of children lie in the context of the community, then we believe that the message of this book is of great potential significance.

With substantial assistance from improved sanitation, better and more abundant food supplies, vaccines, a higher level of housing, and general economic development, medicine has successfully overcome many of the diseases that plagued children a generation ago. The pediatrician of the future must be prepared to move into the several new boundary areas not now considered a part of medical care. Medicine's special contribution is to understand the biological components of health, to meld this knowledge with social and behavioral components, to develop new services and test their efficacy, and to assist in ensuring their universal implementation.

The changing nature of the family in our society—more working mothers, fewer children, more single-parent families, more frequent adoptions, more biracial families, more communal living—all affect child health. Likewise, the structure of the community, the way decisions are made, the provision of recreational and school facilities, and the opportunities for employment are also of relevance for the future of pediatrics. For a university department of pediatrics, moving to become a department of child health in name as well as in deed, we have tried to demonstrate some of the benefits of engaging in the real world of the family and community.

To move pediatrics toward this future, more departments of the medical school and the university must engage in the direct provision and evaluation of health services. This will result in advancing our knowledge of the field and will enable new doctors and other health workers to learn how to deliver health services more effectively. We recognize the dangers of overengagement, of having too little energy or time left to evaluate critically what one is doing, to ask questions, and to doubt the current wisdom. We recognize an even greater danger, however, in the all too easy detachment of academicians from the field and their withdrawal to the ivory towers of their disciplines.

Though child health has improved rapidly, there are still many problems to be solved. It is especially important not to lose sight of the basic health needs of children; they are relatively simple—prenatal care, proper nutrition, immunizations, access to care when sick, and a loving family. Simple as these needs are, for many children in our society today they are not yet met. In many cases it is insufficient merely to make services available and accessible without financial barriers; an advocate such as a visiting public health nurse will have to be given the right of access to children to determine their progress and to intervene when appropriate. We have addressed this issue inadequately in this book, but we want to reaffirm our belief that one task of child health services is to see that simple and effective health care is provided to all and that excessive involvement in "precious" add-ons does not lead to the neglect of basic needs. Actually many of the remaining basic problems result from the isolation of academic departments of pediatrics, medicine, and even community medicine from events of the real world.

We hope to have demonstrated, with this account of our work, what one department can do to engage itself in the community, develop and evaluate new programs, teach the young physician, expand the boundaries of pediatrics, and, it is hoped, as a consequence of all this, move steadily toward the goal of better health for all children.

## REFERENCES

CAIN, GLEN G., and HOLLISTER, ROBINSON G.

1969 *The Methodology of Evaluating Social Action Programs.* Institute for Research on Poverty Discussion Papers, The University of Wisconsin, Madison.

CARNEGIE COMMISSION ON HIGHER EDUCATION

1970   Higher Education and the Nation's Health: A Special Report and Recommendations. New York: McGraw-Hill Book Company.

COOPER, BARBARA S., and MC GEE, MARY F.

1971   "Medical Care Outlays for Three Age Groups: Young, Intermediate, and Aged." Social Security Bulletin, May, pp. 3,7.

HAGGERTY, ROBERT J.

1972   "Do We Really Need More Pediatricians?" Pediatrics, 50(5):681–683.

MYRDAL, GUNNAR

1968   Asian Drama: An Inquiry into the Poverty of Nations, Vols. I-III. New York: Pantheon.

PLESS, IVAN B.

1974   "The Changing Face of Primary Pediatrics." Pediatric Clinics of North America, 21(1):223–244.

SILVER, H.K., and OTT, J.E.

1973   "The Child Health Associate: A New Health Professional." Pediatrics, 51(1):1–7.

WRAY, JOE D.

1974   Health and Nutritional Factors in Early Childhood Development in the People's Republic of China (mimeograph).

# Research Methods

# Sample Design
# and Fieldwork

his appendix describes the manner in which many of the data presented in the book were collected. The quality of sampling and fieldwork determines the validity of the data and hence the conclusions that can be drawn from them. Some demographic characteristics of the samples are reported. To the extent that these characteristics are known from other sources (e.g., census), they have been checked to determine the agreement with other reports. This appendix concludes with some remarks about the advantages and disadvantages of survey research in a clinical department.

*Designs and Procedures*

When the work was organized initially in 1966, there was no local survey group that could provide sampling frames, lists of streets by census tracts, or lists of physicians and dentists by specialty. In addition, interviewers and coders had to be hired and trained, questionnaires developed and tested, coding schemes devised, and their reliability established. Special procedures were used that were later dropped; for example, interviews were transcribed onto code sheets to allow for editing, double coding, and training of personnel. There was no computer "software" for analyzing the results, and access to data processing machinery was limited to evenings and weekends (Haggerty and Roghmann, 1970; Roghmann and Haggerty, 1970). By the end of the study period, however, a smoothly functioning and efficient field team was in operation. A keypunch and a computer terminal were available in the survey office, and advanced software packages were in general use.

The goal of the first survey was to study a sample of 1000 randomly selected families (about 1% of all children) in order to describe their medical care needs and the health services they received. The data were intended to serve as a baseline to measure changes over subsequent years. A smaller, midterm survey was included in 1969 to test existing models of health behavior and to examine the role of stress in the utilization of care. Finally, another 1200-family survey was conducted in 1971 to examine the changes that had occurred in between.

Sampling and Fieldwork for the 1967 Survey

The design of the Rochester Child Health Main Survey (1967) was determined by the availability of sampling frames for the child population and by the feasibility of the fieldwork. As there was no listing of families with children, or of children themselves, substitute sampling frames were used. The annual school census—a house-to-house survey of children for planning educational facilities—was conducted only in the 17 suburban districts. For the city we were left with no other choice but to construct a list of the approximately 100,000 households from which to draw our sample. Four sequential samples (Samples 1, 2, 3, and 4) were drawn for the city, using every 3000th address as a starting point of a 10-residence segment.[1] The sample residences had to be visited to see whether any children were present. This procedure yielded an unbiased family sample. The suburban school district lists were pooled into one list of suburban children, from which every 200th child was selected for an unbiased child sample (Sample 5). Table A.1 gives proportions, refusals, and successful interviews for each of the five subsamples.

During the pretests we found that, after determining the demographic and social characteristics of the household and the mother's health care patterns, the desired information about the health of the children could be obtained only for a maximum of two children in each family within a reasonable period of time. Administering one "household questionnaire," one "mother questionnaire," and two "child questionnaires" required about one and one-quarter hours—the maximum time a respondent and an interviewer could work together effectively. To continue the interview in a second session would have increased the dropout rate. Furthermore, interviewing about additional children produced little new information, since subsequent children were likely to show a utilization pattern similar to the patterns for the two about whom data had already been obtained. Accordingly it was decided to select only two children at random from all those listed for each family. Thus we were *sampling children within families*, and the sampling fraction varied from family to family, depending on the number of children in each.

---

[1] The initial design called for a one-stage cluster sample of housing units, using a systematic selection of starting points for clusters of 10 housing units. A cluster or segment was defined as 10 neighboring units on a block. The latest block statistics and the city directory were used for the listing of units. The enumeration of units and the definition of starting and end points of segments were done by the supervisor in the field. Out of each segment of 10 units we expected six households with no children, three households with children, and one dropout (no contact or a refusal). The resulting clusters of families were of unequal size and fairly heterogeneous. A sequential sample typically consisted of 34 segments of 10 units each and yielded about 120 families. The sampling fraction of one such sample was 0.3%.

334 Sample Design and Fieldwork

Table A.1. Samples Drawn for 1967 Main Survey

| | City Samples[a] | | | | Total City Samples | Suburban Sample[b] |
|---|---|---|---|---|---|---|
| | 1 | 2 | 3 | 4 | | 5 |
| Addresses | 352 | 351 | 346 | 345 | 1394 | 558 |
| Vacant or demolished | 12 | 12 | 16 | 11 | 51 | — |
| Occupied houses | 340 | 339 | 330 | 334 | 1343 | 558 |
| No children | 214 | 188 | 216 | 226 | 844 | — |
| Families | 126 | 151 | 114 | 108 | 499 | 558 |
| Refusals | 3 | 5 | 9 | 8 | 25 | 24 |
| No contact or incomplete | 8 | 8 | 7 | — | 23 | 2 |
| Completed interviews | 115 | 138 | 98 | 100 | 451 | 532 |
| Percent with children | 37 | 44 | 35 | 32 | 37 | 100 |
| Percent completion rate | 91 | 91 | 86 | 93 | 90 | 95 |

[a] Household samples.
[b] Child sample.

Although the decision to use unequal sampling fractions within families was justified by fieldwork limitations, it led to biased child samples in which children from small families were overrepresented. To correct for this bias we made use of "within family" homogeneity and "weighted" the data about the children who were interviewed.[2] Thus 70% of the results from the city child samples are based on original interviews, and the remaining 30% are best estimates for the "missed" children.

A second problem arose from mixing different sampling frames to arrive at representative cross sections of the child population. Using a family sample (as done in the city samples), we would have to interview about all children; using child samples, we should interview only about the one child selected. The different sampling approaches really required different interviewing approaches, yet we were working with the same group of newly trained interviewers at the same time in both city and suburbs. Rather than complicate the fieldwork further, we decided instead to complicate the analysis to correct for any bias. Thus we continued to interview up to two children even in the suburban areas, fully realizing that children from large families were thus oversampled. A spe-

[2] Because sibling groups have fairly homogeneous medical care patterns, data about two children permit a prediction of these patterns in the remaining ones. An intraclass correlation coefficient ($rho_i$), computed as a measure of homogeneity (Kerlinger, 1966:196), showed that homogeneity is highest for medical care patterns (about 81%) and relatively high for the time of the last doctor visit (about 60%). (See Tables 1 and 2 in Roghmann and Haggerty, 1970, for further details.)

cial weight factor was used to correct for this bias in the suburban sample. To summarize, our 1967 procedures introduced two biases that needed correcting in the analysis. The first one was due to the fieldwork (only up to two child interviews per family) and affected *all* household interviews. The second one was due to using different sampling frames; a correction had to be applied to the household interviews from the suburban areas tc make them compatible with those from the city. This double correction for the suburban interviews sounds more complicated than it is in fact; the two weight factors are simply multiplied to give a final weight factor. Furthermore, as the first correction is for oversampling children from small families and the second for oversampling children from large families, the two largely cancel each other; the final weight factor is only slightly greater than 1.00 (see Table 3 in Roghmann and Haggerty, 1970, for further details).

The fieldwork covered a 12-month period, starting in the fall of 1966 and continuing into the fall of 1967 in order to determine seasonal variations. The address listing for the city had 4% vacant houses. In another 1% no contact could be established in spite of frequent visits. Sixty-one percent of the households had no children. Of the 483 valid addresses contacted for city households with children, interviews were completed in 451 or 93%.

Of the 558 suburban addresses, all with children, completed interviews numbered 532 or 95%. The total fieldwork cost (mileage, part-time interviewers, part-time coders) was about $10,000 or $10 per completed interview.

### Sampling and Fieldwork for the 1969 Survey

A random sample of $\frac{1}{2}$% of all families with children aged 17 or younger was the goal for our midpoint survey. The indigent population was oversampled (1%) to provide sufficient inner city families for detailed analyses. Because of the earlier difficulty in obtaining a proper sampling frame for children, a new approach was chosen for the 1969 survey.

The monthly updated family contract list of the leading health insurance company (local Blue Cross) and the list of families on Medicaid were combined to yield one sampling frame. This covered about 95% of all families in the county. For the remaining 5% a frame was constructed by listing all pediatric admissions (including newborns) to the Strong Memorial Hospital over the last three years who were covered neither by Blue Cross nor by Medicaid. Systematic random samples were then chosen from each of these lists, with the Medicaid population being oversampled for analytical reasons. Pretest cases, randomly selected from the clinic population, were added as a subfile. The total sample of 512 families described in Table A.2 is, therefore, intentionally biased toward lower-class patients.

To arrive at generalizations about all families in Monroe County, the pretest cases were excluded and correction factors, computed on the basis of hospital insurance coverage,[3] were applied to the remaining cases. The weighting corrects for the intentional oversampling of the Medicaid population and excludes the pretest cases.

Because a shorter "child questionnaire" was used in 1969, and return interview visits were possible, information was obtained on *all* children in the family. The sample was, therefore, representative of *both* children and families. In addition, the mother was asked to keep a health calendar for a 28-day period to provide information on minor events such as stress, medications, and symptoms which are easily forgotten and therefore cannot reliably be learned by interview.

The fieldwork was again conducted over a 12-month period to avoid any seasonal bias in reported illnesses. Eighty-two percent of the household interviews were completed. There was no correlation of "dropouts" with socioeconomic status, but they were related to age. For Blue Cross "family contract holders under 55 years old" the completion rate was 85%, whereas for those 55 years and older it was only 72%. Refusal was the main reason for noncompletion. Other reasons were death, jailing, and lack of contact in spite of seven visits. The lower completion rate in 1969 was due mainly to the greater respondent cooperation required for completing the health calendar for 28 days (Roghmann and Haggerty, 1972).

On the average, 2.6 personal visits involving approximately 50 miles of travel by the interviewer and 2.5 phone calls were required to complete the interview and the calendar. Each complete set of family data required about seven hours of interviewers' and coders' time. Because of the intensive fieldwork involved, the costs were high: about $3000 for local travel, $10,000 for part-time interviewers and coders, and $5000 for paying respondents. Keypunching and verifying cost nearly $2000. The average cost per interview, therefore, excluding fixed costs for office rental, full-time office staff, and computer analysis, was $40.

## Sampling and Fieldwork for the 1971 Survey

The 1971 survey was designed to be as similar to the 1967 study as possible. The use of the shortened 1969 questionnaire avoided the problem

---

[3] After recoding missing values into the modal group, the following weights were assigned: covered by Medicaid and Blue Cross, 0.7; covered by Blue Cross only, 2.1; covered by Medicaid only, 1.0; covered by neither Medicaid nor Blue Cross, 3.0; pre-test cases, 0.

Table A.2.  Samples Drawn for 1969 Main Survey[a]

| Sampling Frame | Addresses Drawn | No Children | Invalid Addresses | Sample Cases | Refusals | Other Dropouts | Completed Cases |
|---|---|---|---|---|---|---|---|
| Pretest | | | | | | | |
| Clinic population (Medical center outpatient and emergency room visitors) | 48 | — | 2 | 46 | 8 | 1 | 37 (80%) |
| Main Sample | | | | | | | |
| 1. Blue Cross list (June 1969 drawing) | | | | | | | |
| a. Family contracts, holders <55 years | 432 | 51 | 49 | 332 | 40 | 10 | 282 (85%) |
| b. Family contracts, holders 55-64 years | 268 | 118 | 24 | 126 | 26 | 9 | 91 (72%) |
| Total | 700 | 169 | 73 | 458 | 66 | 19 | 373 (81%) |
| 2. Medicaid list | | | | | | | |
| May 1969 drawing | 54 | — | 4 | 50 | 2 | 5 | 43 |
| November 1969 drawing | 59 | — | 5 | 54 | 7 | 5 | 42 |
| Total | 113 | — | 9 | 104 | 9 | 10 | 85 (82%) |
| 3. Hospital list (neither Blue Cross nor Medicaid) | 25 | 1 | 4 | 20 | 2 | 1 | 17 (85%) |
| All cases in file | 886 | 170 | 88 | 628 (100%) | 85 (13%) | 31 (5%) | 512 (82%) |

[a] From Roghmann and Haggerty (1972), p. 148.

of sampling within families because all children would be included. Also, the results from the 1970 census were available, thus providing a detailed listing of housing units by block for the entire county. (The 1960 census had block data only for city census tracts, not for suburban areas.)

A list of all 228,339 housing units in the 765 block groups of Monroe County was constructed. Five "1 per 1000" systematic random samples were drawn, using randomly selected numbers as starting points for small clusters. These were defined as the "sample point" addresses, and they and the neighbors to the right and left were included in the sample. Five sequential samples were selected instead of four (as in 1967) because of an anticipated higher refusal rate; we wanted to be certain that there would be at least 1000 families for analysis. Table A.3 gives the sample design.[4]

To keep costs down, the actual addresses were identified by using the computerized file of a local public utility company instead of "in the field" enumeration. Sample addresses were put on computer tape, and sets of gummed labels were produced to stick on the household questionnaire and letters of introduction.

The completion rate of interviews varied by sample and averaged about 82%. Noncompletion was due chiefly to refusals, the rate of which was again higher in the city than in the suburbs. Altogether 1216 families with 2952 children were successfully interviewed. The average number of children per family was 2.4; the average number of individuals in a family, 4.6. The fieldwork cost totaled $16,000 ($3000 for mileage and $13,000 for interviewers) or $13 per family. About 3500 households were contacted to identify the 1216 families finally included in the sample (Roghmann et al., 1973).

*Comparison of Demographic Characteristics
in Sample and in Census Data*

Comparisons of sample statistics with population parameters known from the census have been described for the 1967 data (Haggerty and Roghmann, 1970:70). There were only minor differences (e.g., 8.4% nonwhite in sample vs. 8.8% nonwhite in census), and these were within the expected limits of sampling error.

A comparison of 1971 survey results with 1970 census figures for sex and age is presented in Table A.4. The 2952 children in the sample repre-

[4] Each sequential sample would yield a 0.3% sample of addresses (about 685); the pooled samples would cover 1.5% of all addresses (about 3425). Even if only 40% of the addresses had households with children, and if only 80% of these could be interviewed, this should still give us over 1000 families for analysis.

*Table A.3.* *Samples Drawn for 1971 Surveys*

| Sequential Samples | City | | Suburbs | | Total | |
|---|---|---|---|---|---|---|
| | Clusters | Addresses | Clusters | Addresses | Clusters | Addresses |
| 1 | 106 | 318 | 123 | 369 | 229 | 687 |
| 2 | 106 | 318 | 123 | 369 | 229 | 687 |
| 3 | 105 | 315 | 123 | 369 | 228 | 684 |
| 4 | 105 | 315 | 123 | 369 | 228 | 684 |
| 5 | 105 | 315 | 123 | 369 | 228 | 684 |
| Pooled sample | 527 | 1581 | 615 | 1845 | 1142 | 3426 |
| Sampling fraction (%) | | 1.5 | | 1.5 | | 1.5 |

339

sented 1.2% of all children in the county. The age breakdown in the sample is similar to that in the population. For girls the percentages differ, on the average, only 0.4 point; for boys the difference averages 1.4 points. The greatest difference was in the"under 5" group, where the sample had considerably lower proportions than the population. This probably reflects the falling birthrate as well as sampling error.

Another important comparison, by ethnicity and sociopolitical area, is presented in Table A.5. The results show a good representation of the population in our sample. Differences reflect post-census changes (urban renewal in the two inner city areas), the fact that we only sample individuals in families with children under 18, and sampling error.

### Survey Research in a Clinical Department

A commitment to community pediatrics underlies the type of research described in this book. However, clinical departments are equipped for clinical research, not for sociomedical studies. The commitment to a series of surveys over a six-year time span prevented a "one-shot" approach; thus we set up a small survey research group of our own.

Our experience is that a minimum of two full-time staff members is

*Table A.4. Comparison of Selected Sample Statistics with Known Population Parameters for the 1971 Survey, Monroe County, New York*

| Age (years) | Sample 1971 | | | Census 1970 | | |
|---|---|---|---|---|---|---|
| | Boys | Girls | Total | Boys | Girls | Total |
| | A. Absolute Figures | | | | | |
| Under 5 | 369 | 379 | 748 | 33,129 | 31,485 | 64,614 |
| 5–9 | 417 | 434 | 851 | 36,122 | 34,574 | 70,696 |
| 10–14 | 456 | 421 | 877 | 35,869 | 34,456 | 70,325 |
| 15–17 | 244 | 232 | 476 | 19,405 | 18,857 | 38,262 |
| Total | 1486 | 1466 | 2952 | 124,525 | 119,372 | 243,897 |

Sampling fraction: 1.21%

| Age (years) | Boys | Girls | Total | Boys | Girls | Total |
|---|---|---|---|---|---|---|
| | B. Column Percentages | | | | | |
| Under 5 | 24.8 | 25.6 | 25.3 | 26.6 | 26.4 | 26.5 |
| 5–9 | 28.1 | 29.6 | 28.8 | 29.0 | 29.0 | 29.0 |
| 10–14 | 30.7 | 28.7 | 29.7 | 28.8 | 28.9 | 28.8 |
| 15–17 | 16.4 | 15.8 | 16.1 | 15.6 | 15.8 | 15.7 |
| Total | 100.0 | 99.7 | 99.9 | 100.0 | 100.1 | 100.0 |

Table A.5. *Ethnicity and Residential Area, Monroe County, New York*

| | Sample 1971 | | | | Census 1970 | | |
|---|---|---|---|---|---|---|---|
| Area | White | Black | Puerto Rican | Total | White | Nonwhite | Total |
| **A. Absolute Figures** | | | | | | | |
| Third ward | 33 | 185 | — | 218 | 5,118 | 20,078 | 25,196 |
| Seventh ward | 20 | 134 | 18 | 172 | 6,773 | 14,309 | 21,082 |
| Rest of city | 1482 | 316 | 54 | 1852 | 232,203 | 17,718 | 249,921 |
| Suburbs | 3311 | 13 | — | 3324 | 411,603 | 4,081 | 415,684 |
| Total | 4846 | 648 | 72 | 5566 | 655,697 | 56,186 | 711,883 |
| **B. Column Percentages** | | | | | | | |
| Third ward | 0.7 | 28.5 | — | 3.9 | 0.8 | 35.7 | 3.5 |
| Seventh ward | 0.4 | 20.7 | 25 | 3.1 | 1.0 | 25.5 | 3.0 |
| Rest of city | 30.6 | 48.8 | 75 | 33.3 | 35.4 | 31.5 | 35.1 |
| Suburbs | 68.3 | 2.0 | — | 59.7 | 62.8 | 7.3 | 58.4 |
| Total | 100.0 | 100.0 | 100 | 100.0 | 100.0 | 100.0 | 100.0 |

required: a survey supervisor to organize and direct the fieldwork, and a programmer to plan the editing and coding, analyze the data, and prepare basic reports. The need for a full-time programmer must be emphasized. Most university computing centers operate on a self-service basis, and extensive preparations are required to adjust files and to prepare specialized library programs. The survey supervisor should have extensive keypunch experience and some programming skills. This reduces the risk of accumulating data that are not easily accessible for answering questions quickly. Full-time staff members should be thoroughly acquainted with the research requirements; continuity of the staff is of extreme importance for this type of research.

Our survey group has continuously used from 5 to 10 part-time interviewers, most of whom were housewives 30 years of age or older with children of their own. Their educational and social status was usually above that of most of the respondents.

Community pediatric fellows spent part of their time in the offices of the survey group and conducted a number of spin-off studies with the help of the survey staff. There were constant consultations between project directors and staff and frequent group presentations to maintain a high quality of the research. Peer reviews were conducted before new grants were submitted or papers presented.

It is difficult to state what is required as a minimum for a community research group, or even what size and organization structure are optimal. It is clear, however, that a small core of professionals with research as their main commitment is essential.

## REFERENCES

HAGGERTY, ROBERT J., and ROGHMANN, KLAUS J.

    1970  "Rochester Child Health Surveys." *Proceedings of the 5th International Scientific Meeting of the International Epidemiological Association, Primosten, Yugoslavia, August 25–31, 1968.* Belgrade, pp. 55–73.

KERLINGER, FRED

    1966  *Foundations of Behavioral Research.* New York: Holt, Rinehart and Winston.

ROGHMANN, KLAUS J., and HAGGERTY, ROBERT J.

    1970  "Rochester Child Health Surveys. I: Objectives, Organization and Methods." *Medical Care,* 8:47–59.

ROGHMANN, KLAUS, J., and HAGGERTY, ROBERT J.

    1972  "The Diary as a Research Instrument in the Study of Health and Illness Behavior." *Medical Care,* 10:143–163.

ROGHMANN, KLAUS J., HECHT, P., and HAGGERTY, ROBERT J.

    1973  "Family Coping with Everyday Illness: Self-Reports from a Household Survey." *Journal of Comparative Family Studies,* IV(1):49–62.

# Family Functioning and Family Problems

### Reliability and Validity of Family Functioning Index

Evidence of the reliability and validity of any new measure is desirable before it is used as a basis for conclusions or testing hypotheses. This was accomplished in several ways. A first test was obtained by comparing the scores for this random sample of families against those of a group of families known to have major problems. To do so the original Family Functioning Index (FFI) was adapted for self-administration, and parallel forms were designed for husband and wife (Pless and Satterwhite, 1973). These questionnaires were then given to all new registrants at three professional family service agencies. Husbands and wives attending these agencies for counseling were asked to complete the questionnaire independently ($n = 43$). The average index score of the wives attending the agencies was compared with the average score for the families in the random sample studied in 1968. The mean score for the agency sample, 19.1 (SE = .99), was significantly lower than that for the random sample, 25.4 (SE = .26), ($p < .001$), indicating that the agency families' troubles are reflected in this measure.

A second indication of the validity of the FFI was obtained by asking case workers at the agency to rate the functioning of families assigned to them on a five-point scale designed to reflect the content of the index. Since all but one of the case workers at the agency submitting the majority of completed questionnaires held master's degrees in social work, it was assumed that their ratings could be regarded as a standard against which the FFI could be validated. The correlation between the total FFI scores of mothers attending the agency and the ratings of the case workers was $r = .48$.[1] Between case worker ratings and the fathers' Index scores, the correlation was $r = .35$.[1] These results provide further evidence that the index is valid even within a group with reduced variance and closely reflects disturbed family functioning as judged by experienced social workers.

A third and similar validation was provided by obtaining independent

---

[1] With $n = 43$, a correlation coefficient of .393 is significant at $p = .01$; a coefficient of .304 is significant at $p = .05$.

ratings by lay family counselors assigned to work with the families of 65 children with chronic disorders (see Section 11B). In each instance the counselor had known the family for at least one year. The mother's FFI score, as obtained from the original household interview, was compared with the counselor's independent rating, using the five-point scale described above. The correlation obtained was $r = .39$.[2]

The reliability of a test may be estimated in a number of ways. Two common methods are to compare scores from different observers (interobserver reliability) and to compare scores at different points in time (test-retest reliability). In the case of the family service agency study it was possible to compare the index scores obtained from husbands and wives independently; the correlation between these was $r = .72$.[1]

To assess the stability of the index over time, 30 families were selected for repeat assessment in 1973, five years after the administration of the initial interview (Satterwhite et al., 1974). The families selected were chosen according to their original FFI scores in such a way that three were in Group I (scores between 0 and 18), six in Group II (scores between 19 and 23), 12 in Group III (scores between 24 and 28), six in Group IV (scores between 29 and 30), and three in Group V (scores between 31 and 35). For the purposes of the retest, one-parent families and those who had received family therapy were excluded. An interviewer who had no knowledge of the previous FFI scores repeated the questions comprising the index. The correlation between the FFI scores obtained in 1968 with those for 1972 was $r = .83$,[3] indicating a remarkable degree of stability over time.

[2] With $n = 65$, a correlation coefficient of .325 is significant at $p = .01$.
[3] With $n = 30$, a correlation coefficient of .463 is significant at $p = .01$.

## REFERENCES

PLESS, I. BARRY, and SATTERWHITE, BETTY

1973   "A Measure of Family Functioning and Its Application." *Social Science and Medicine*, 7:613–621.

SATTERWHITE, BETTY, ZWEIG, SUSAN, and PLESS, I. BARRY

1974   "Test-Retest Reliability of the Family Functioning Index and Significance for Use in Pediatric Practice" (mimeograph).

APPFNDIX TO SECTION 3C

# Chronic Illness

*1. Study Design for Chronic Illness Survey*

In each of the random sample household surveys (1967, 1969, and 1971) questions were asked about symptoms of chronic illnesses among children in the household, regardless of their ages. The parent was also asked to assess the seriousness of any observed symptom and, for those judged to be "very serious" or "somewhat serious," to describe what action, if any, had been taken in response to the symptom or condition (e.g., contacted a doctor or treated it alone).

In the 1969 survey, the same interview procedure was followed as in 1967. However, in this survey and in the one conducted in 1971, three symptoms of low frequency were eliminated: anemia, seizures, and paralysis. From each of these studies point prevalence estimates of symptoms were calculated, as shown in Table A.6, for the universe of children from birth to 17 years of age who were residents of Monroe County.

In 1968 a series of special studies was begun to establish the prevalence of chronic disorders among children of school age and to examine the relationship between these conditions and subsequent psychological, social, and educational problems that might affect the child's functioning. The sample for the special study was drawn from children aged 6–17 years in 1967. By 1968 this group of children was a year older, and hence the age range of those actually studied was 7–18 years. The decision was made to restrict this investigation to school age children because psychological tests involving reading and writing skills were to be used along with information from parents and the schools about the child's behavior and performance.

It was hypothesized that psychological and other such problems are significantly more frequent among children with chronic disorders than among their healthy peers, and, furthermore, that the nature of the family unit influences the development of these difficulties. The studies also sought to evaluate the provision of care for these children in relation to the full range of medical and psychosocial needs.

The "universe" of those surveyed in 1967—ages 6–17 years ($n = 1520$)— was checked for those who had reported symptoms of chronic illnesses judged to be "serious" or "somewhat serious." As shown in Figure A.1, 364 children fell into this "presumptively ill" category. From the remaining (presumably healthy) children in the 1967 sample, a control group was

345

Table A.6. *Frequency of Symptoms of Chronic Conditions, Both Sexes, 0–17 Years, Monroe County, New York*

| Symptom Reported | 1967 (n = 2311) | | 1969 (n = 2465) | | 1971 (n = 2950) | |
|---|---|---|---|---|---|---|
| | Number Observed | Rate/1000 | Number Observed | Rate/1000 | Number Observed | Rate/1000 |
| Asthma | 74 | 32.1 | 98 | 39.8 | 100 | 33.9 |
| Hay fever | 153 | 66.5 | 174 | 70.6 | 252 | 85.4 |
| Other allergies | 375 | 162.9 | 389 | 158.0 | —d | — |
| Hard to understanda | 134 | 60.1 | 135 | 54.8 | 146 | 49.5 |
| Difficulty seeingb | 211 | 91.8 | 80 | 32.5 | 90 | 30.5 |
| Difficulty hearing | 82 | 35.6 | 70 | 28.4 | 79 | 26.8 |
| Joint pains | 172 | 75.4 | 161 | 65.4 | 156 | 52.9 |
| Sinus trouble | 127 | 55.4 | 113 | 45.8 | 159 | 53.9 |
| Heart trouble | 65 | 28.3 | 56 | 22.7 | 45 | 15.3 |
| Kidney troublec | 58 | 25.2 | 36 | 14.6 | 33 | 11.2 |
| Rashes | 284 | 124.1 | —d | — | 380 | 128.8 |
| Cross-eyed | 89 | 39.1 | — | — | — | — |
| Anemia | 33 | 14.4 | — | — | — | — |
| Seizures | 10 | 4.4 | — | — | — | — |
| Paralysis | 5 | 2.2 | — | — | — | — |

a 1969, 1971 wording: "Trouble speaking—stammering, lisping, or hard to understand."
b 1969, 1971 wording: "Difficulty seeing even with glasses."
c 1969, 1971 wording: "Chronic kidney trouble."
d Not asked in this year.

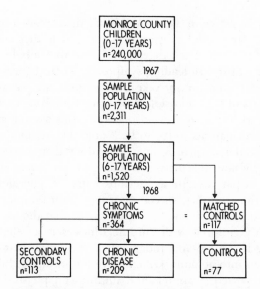

*Figure A.1.   Chronic illness survey, 1968: sampling and case selection.*

drawn by matching healthy children with sick children according to age, sex, socioeconomic area of residence, and race, so that for approximately every three children with symptoms of chronic illness one healthy child with the same combination of social characteristics was selected. Of the 117 original controls chosen, 77 participated in the subsequent stages of the investigation. Of the missing 40, 15 were found to have a chronic disorder on subsequent interview, 9 could not be located, and 6 had left home. The remaining 10 were outright refusals.

Both the group of 364 "presumed" cases and the matched controls were interviewed a second time in 1968 to obtain sufficient information to establish with reasonable certainty whether a child had a chronic illness. Interviewers were not informed about the categories in which the children had been placed, and they administered the interview in identical fashion to all parents. The first section identified the presence of a chronic illness, using lists of "impairments" and "chronic conditions" similar to those used by the National Health Interview Survey (Wilder, 1965). The duration of the symptoms was then established; and, if a diagnosis had existed for at least three months before the interview, subsequent sections were followed to obtain a detailed medical history and to measure the level of disability and the impact on child and family. A series of questions designed to ascertain the level of family functioning was included for all parents (see Section 2A).

One question of methodological interest is whether symptoms alone provide a reliable indication of the frequency of established cases of chronic illness. As shown in Table A.6, in all three years a high degree of consistency was obtained for symptoms for which the wording of the questions was unaltered. The range of variation was only between 10 and 20 per 1000 for 8 of the 10 leading symptoms. These figures represent *all* observed symptoms and do *not* take into account the parents' judgment of the seriousness of the condition. Subsequent analyses show that symptoms can be divided into two groups based on this assessment: those that more than 60% of parents judge to be "somewhat serious" or "very serious," that is, paralysis, seizures, anemia, kidney trouble, strabismus, impaired hearing, vision difficulties, asthma, and hay fever; and those that less than 50% of parents rate as "serious," that is, allergies (other than hay fever or asthma), rashes, speech disorders, joint symptoms, sinus conditions, and disorders of the heart. This suggests that the use of symptoms alone to identify children with chronic illnesses is a reliable screening procedure *only* if the parents' judgment of the seriousness of the symptom is also taken into account. Others have found only a limited association between reported symptoms and findings on physical examination (Roberts, 1973).

It is also of interest to note that the combination of the two questions listing chronic "conditions" and "impairments" correctly identified 91.8% of those with chronic illness and 81.8% of those ultimately judged to be healthy.

Methodological considerations make it difficult to draw firm conclusions about causal relationships between chronic illness and psychosocial disturbances. A "cause and effect" association can be established only by comparing the situation before and after the onset of illness, as well as comparing those who have illnesses and those who do not. Although the former is possible only in a longitudinal study of considerable scope and duration, we were able to compare the status of children having chronic illnesses with that of a matched comparison group of healthy children (controls). Such comparisons have their limitations, however, because it is impossible to sensibly ask some questions of parents with healthy children. Accordingly, in the analyses of impact, some of the results compare the experiences of the sick and the well, whereas others contrast children with moderate or severe disabilities and children with only mild disabilities.

## 2. Psychological Tests in Chronic Illness Survey

The psychological and social functioning measures were chosen with a full awareness of their limitations. Emphasis was placed on tests of self-concept, but various appraisals were also obtained from the child's parents, teachers, and peers.

All tests were administered by someone other than the interviewer to avoid any subtle influence on the child's responses by an examiner who was aware of the child's condition, that is, whether he had a chronic illness or was a healthy control. The logistics of testing were formidable, involving many visits over a six-month period to homes, schools, or the research offices. Tests were administered orally to all children under age 11 to avoid bias in favor of those brighter or more adept at reading. In each instance the tester attempted to establish good rapport with the child before beginning and tried to motivate him to respond as honestly and completely as possible by assuring that his replies would be entirely confidential.

The complete test battery included a measure of intelligence (Ammons and Ammons, 1962); the Children's Self-Social Constructs Test (Long et al., 1967); the Children's Manifest Anxiety Scale (Castenada et al., 1956); the California Test of Personality (Thorpe et al., 1953); a "draw-a-person" test; a series of sentence completions (Cruickshank, 1963); the Self-Esteem Inventory (Coopersmith, 1959); and the self-tests (Bower, 1969) with the special forms for children of younger ages. In addition, the Lambert and Bower (Bower, 1969) sociometric procedure was used in the classrooms of all children in grades kindergarten to nine, and teachers completed a behavior symptom rating scale and personality description scale designed by Cowen et al. (1963). Parents also completed a Behavior Symptom Questionnaire (Kearsley et al., 1962).

## REFERENCES

AMMONS, R.B., and AMMONS, C.H.

1962 *The Quick Test (QT)*. Provisional Manual, Psychological Reports Monograph Supplement I-VII.

BOWER, E.

1969 *Early Identification of Emotionally Handicapped Children in School*. Springfield, Illinois: Charles C Thomas.

CASTANADA, ALFRED, MC CANDLESS, BOYD, and PALERMO, DAVID

1956 "The Children's Form of the Manifest Anxiety Scale." *Child Development*, 27:317–326.

COOPERSMITH, S.

1959 "A Method for Determining Self-Esteem." *Journal of Abnormal and Social Psychology*, 59(1):87–94.

COWEN, E.L., IZZO, L.D., MILES, H., TELSCHOW, E.F., TROST, M.A. and ZAX, M.

1963   "A Preventive Mental Health Program in the School Setting: Description and Evaluation." *Journal of Psychology*, 56:307–356.

CRUICKSHANK, WILLIAM

1963   *Psychology of Exceptional Children and Youth.* Englewood Cliffs, New Jersey: Prentice-Hall. pp. 311–368.

KEARSLEY, R., SNIDER, M., RICHIE, R., CRAWFORD, J., TALBOT, N.

1962   "Study of Relations between Psychologic Environment and Child Behavior—Pediatric Procedure." *American Journal Diseases of Children*, 104:12–20.

LONG, BARBARA, HENDERSON, EDMUND, and ZILLER, ROBERT

1967   "Developmental Changes in Self-Concept during Middle Childhood." *Merrill Palmer Quarterly*, 13(3):201–215.

ROBERTS, JEAN

1973   *Examination and Health History Findings among Children and Youth, 6–17 Years: United States.* Vital and Health Statistics, Series 11, No. 129. Data from the National Health Survey, Department of Health, Education and Welfare, Public Health Service. Washington, D.C.: Government Printing Office.

THORPE, L.P., CLARK, W.W., and TIEGS, E.W.

1953   California Test of Personality, 1953 Revision. California Test Bureau, Monterey, California.

WILDER, CHARLES S.

1965   *Chronic Conditions and Activity Limitation: United States, July 1961–June 1963.* Vital and Health Statistics, Series 10, No. 17. Data from the National Health Survey, Department of Health, Education and Welfare, Public Health Service. Washington, D.C.: Government Printing Office.

# The "New Morbidity"

## 1. Behavioral Problems of Preschoolers (R. W. Chamberlin)

• Measuring Childrearing Patterns

Two data sets shed light on some of the questions regarding behavioral problems of preschoolers. One is the 1969 countrywide survey, described in the Appendix to Chapter 1, which contains a representative sample of families having a preschool child (the "R" sample). Although information on preschool behavioral problems is limited, this survey provides an overview that is useful in interpreting the more detailed, but nonrepresentative, second set. Data from the latter ("S") sample were obtained by home interview (Chamberlin, 1969) with mothers of a selected group of intact middle-class families, each having a healthy 2-year-old child and receiving care from either of two groups of pediatricians located in the suburbs of Rochester. At the time of their 2-year-old well-child visits, mothers whose children met the sample requirements (e.g., healthy 2-year-old), who had intact families, and who varied in their childrearing approaches were invited to participate in the study. Equal numbers of boys and girls were necessary for the design. Out of 244 families invited, 198 (81%) agreed to take part. The demographic characteristics of these samples are outlined in Table A.7.

In the "S" sample interview items describing the parent's behavior were factor analyzed (Chamberlin, 1972). The mother's patterns were as follows:

*Use of negative contact:* ordering, scolding, use of physical punishment and yelling.

*Use of positive contact:* praising, hugging, playing with the child, explaining things to him.

*Use of protection and compliance:* feeding with a spoon, restricting peer contact, avoiding daytime separations, staying with the child at bedtime, giving in to temper tantrums and nagging.

The following patterns of child behavior emerged from factor analysis of mother ratings:

*Aggressive-resistant:* disobedient, hits others, shows temper, stubborn, whining.

*Table A.7.  Sample Characteristics of the Two Rochester Studies*

| Characteristic | Representative ("R") Sample, Monroe County (weighted $n$ = 474) | Selected ("S") Sample, Suburban Rochester ($n$ = 198) |
|---|---|---|
| 1. Age of Child (years) | 2–5 | 2 |
| 2. Percent **Male** | 54 | 46 |
| 3. Percent **White** | 82 | 99.5 |
| 4. Percent of Homes with both Parents Present | 90 | 100 |
| 5. Percent of Mothers working Full Time | 11 | 0 |
| 6. Mother's Education | | |
| Not a high school graduate (%) | 26 | 3 |
| High school graduate (%) | 46 | 25 |
| 1–3 years' college (%) | 15 | 32 |
| College graduate (4 years) (%) | 11 | 40 |
| 7. Mother's Religion | | |
| Catholic (%) | 58 | 40 |
| Protestant (%) | 36 | 48 |
| Jewish (%) | 3 | 8 |
| None or other (%) | 3 | 4 |

*Table A.8.  Relationships between Mother and Child Behavioral Patterns[a] ($n$ = 198)*

| Child Behavioral Pattern | Mother Childrearing Pattern | | |
|---|---|---|---|
| | Negative Contact | Positive Contact | Protection and Compliance |
| Aggressive-resistant | .37[b] | .10 | .14 |
| Dependent-inhibited | −.01 | .04 | .40[b] |
| Friendly-outgoing | −.10 | .28[b] | .04 |

[a] Product moment correlations
[b] $p < .01$

*Dependent-inhibited:* clings to mother, fearful, easily upset, seeks attention, shy.

*Friendly-outgoing:* cheerful, curious, talkative, friendly, likes to be held.

Intercorrelations between these measures are shown in Table A.8.

## 2. The Frequency and Nature of School Problems (P. R. Nader)

• Coding Parental Responses to the Open-Ended Question on School Problems

Parental responses to interview questions were recorded verbatim. To develop coding categories, the responses from the earlier surveys were listed and a mutually exclusive system was developed to categorize the reasons given for the problems reported. Responses were placed in the category that seemed most appropriate, allowing a first and a second "diagnosis." Initial interjudge agreement on category assignment was no less than 89% and often approached 98%. Conflicts in initial assignment were resolved and led to further clarification of coding instructions for the 1971 survey.

Coding reliability was high enough to be excluded as a major source of error. But the reliability of the mother's initial reporting was another matter. To obtain an estimate of this, results were examined from the follow-up of children who had participated in the special repeat 1967 home interview survey (see Section 3C) and for whom the standard school questions had been asked in the initial interview. A reinterview of the mother, plus standardized achievement and ability test results obtained from the schools, was used to assess response reliability, possible changes over time, and validity.

Children were grouped by the highest ($n = 66$) and lowest ($n = 26$) school achievement ratings as defined by achievement and ability tests, and these results were compared with the mothers' reports on the original interview data. The response reliability was fairly high, but differed for the "high" and the "low" achievers. For the "ever held back" question, the agreement was 82% for low achievers and 98% for high achievers; for "trouble with schoolwork," the agreement was 71% for low achievers and 94% for high achievers. The high reliability of the better achievers was to be expected since only one child had been held back for illness and only four had experienced learning problems. For the low achievers there was more chance for disagreements, with over half having reported school problems, and nearly 50% of these having been held back a year.

This generally high reliability in response to the school questions should not lead to the conclusion that parental perception necessarily yields a correct picture of a child's school functioning. For example, only 55% of the mothers of *tested* low achievers reported that their children had trouble with schoolwork. Therefore these figures are probably an underestimate of actual school problems if "underachievement" measured in this way is accepted as the best objective indication of school difficulties.

Developing a practical coding system for the reasons for school problems was not as difficult as anticipated. Responses to questions seeking the reason for a school problem such as "not completing work because of talking" or "skipping school" seemed to fall naturally into the *discipline* category. *Academic* problems implicit in responses such as "poor in arithmetic," "can't spell," and "failed math" were also easily identified. A "reading" subcode was specified for academic problems.

Responses reflecting behavioral or emotional difficulties fell into four categories: (1) motivational: "won't try," "lazy," "underachiever"; (2) emotional: "a mother problem," "daydreaming," "disturbed"; (3) hyperactive: "short attention span," "can't sit still"; and (4) immature: "immaturity," "too young." For this analysis these were combined into a single *behavioral-emotional* category.

Other self-evident categories included teacher-pupil interaction ("teacher was mentally sick," "trouble with teacher," "teacher later fired"); language problem (could only speak Spanish); physical handicap (subcode sensory: "vision," "hearing," or subcode motor: "crippled," "cerebral palsy"); and mobility ("moved in March, slowed up at new school"). Chronic illness ("allergy," "asthma," "diabetes," "seizures"), when noted, occurred frequently in combination with absenteeism ("absent a great deal").

## REFERENCES

CHAMBERLIN, ROBERT W.

1969  "A Study of an Interview Method for Identifying Family Authority Patterns." *Genetic Psychology Monographs*, 80:129–148.

CHAMBERLIN, ROBERT W.

1972  "Early Patterns of Parent and Child Behavior: Can We Identify High Risk Combinations?" (mimeograph).

# Available Models

*Variables Used to Assess Suchman Model*

1. Knowledge about Disease
   (Knowledge of Disease: Andersen)

Now here is something a bit different. We are interested in what you think about health and health care. I will first read a few statements on symptoms and disease to you and ask you if you agree, disagree, or are undecided about each statement.

| | Agree | Undecided | Disagree | | |
|---|---|---|---|---|---|
| • Shortness of breath after light exercise may be a sign of cancer. | 1 | 2 | 3 | VAR299 | F |
| • Shortness of breath after light exercise may be a sign of heart disease. | 3 | 2 | 1 | VAR300 | T |
| • Coughing or spitting up blood may be a sign of tuberculosis. | 3 | 2 | 1 | VAR301 | T |
| • Coughing or spitting up blood may be a sign of diabetes. | 1 | 2 | 3 | VAR302 | F |
| • Open sores or ulcers that do not heal may be a sign of cancer. | 3 | 2 | 1 | VAR303 | T |
| • Open sores or ulcers that do not heal may be a sign of heart disease. | 1 | 2 | 3 | VAR304 | F |
| • Unexplained loss of weight may be a sign of tuberculosis. | 3 | 2 | 1 | VAR305 | T |
| • Unexplained loss of weight may be a sign of diabetes. | 3 | 2 | 1 | VAR306 | T |
| • Pains in the chest may be a sign of heart disease. | 3 | 2 | 1 | VAR307 | T |

- Pains in the chest may be
  a sign of tuberculosis.              1        2        3      VAR308   F


KNOWDIS = VAR299 + VAR300 + VAR301 + VAR302 + VAR303 +
         VAR304 + VAR305 + VAR306 + VAR307 + VAR308 − 10
RECODE  KNOWDIS  (0  THRU  10 = 10)  (11,13 = 12)  (15 = 14)
                 (18  THRU  20 = 18)
INTERPRETATION:  The higher the score, the better the knowledge.


2. Skepticism of Medical Care
   (Attitude toward Health Services: Andersen)

The next statements are on health care as available now. I would like you to tell me again if you agree, disagree, or feel undecided about each statement.

|  | Agree | Undecided | Disagree |  |  |
|---|---|---|---|---|---|
| • Most illness could be prevented if all people received medical care. | 3 | 2 | 1 | VAR321 | Pos |
| • Most doctors are more interested in their incomes than in making sure everyone receives adequate medical care. | 1 | 2 | 3 | VAR324 | Neg |
| • Modern medicine can cure almost any illness. | 3 | 2 | 1 | VAR326 | Pos |
| • A person understands his own health better than most doctors do. | 1 | 2 | 3 | VAR327 | Neg |
| • The drugs doctors prescribe are not much better than home remedies. | 1 | 2 | 3 | VAR328 | Neg |
| • If you wait long enough, you can get over almost any illness without medical aid. | 1 | 2 | 3 | VAR329 | Neg |
| • Nowadays, doctors can prevent most serious diseases. | 3 | 2 | 1 | VAR330 | Pos |
| • All people have health problems; there is not much you can do about it. | 1 | 2 | 3 | VAR331 | Neg |

SKEPTIC = VAR321 + VAR324 + VAR326 + VAR327 + VAR328 +
VAR329 + VAR330 + VAR331
RECODE SKEPTIC (8 THRU 16 = 1) (17,18 = 2) (19,20 = 3) (21,22 = 4)
(23,24 = 5)
INTERPRETATION: Low score = low trust in medical care
High score = high trust in medical care
*Note:* The index really measures trust or PERCEIVED BENEFITS of
care.

3. Dependency in Illness

The following statements are more about how you experience illness.
Please tell me again if you agree, disagree, or feel undecided about each
statement.

|  | Agree | Undecided | Disagree |  |  |
|---|---|---|---|---|---|
| • When I think I am getting sick, I find it comforting to talk to someone about it. | 1 | 2 | 3 | VAR332 | Pos |
| • When I start getting well, it is hard to give up having people do things for me. | 1 | 2 | 3 | VAR333 | Pos |

DEPEND = VAR332 + VAR333
RECODE DEPEND (2,4 = 3)
INTERPRETATION: Low score = low dependency
High score = high dependency

4. Friendship Solidarity

• Would you say that most of your present friends are people you grew up
with?

No, none . . . 0
Yes, some . . . 1 ⎱ 1 (Recoded)      VAR386   Pos
Yes, most . . . 2 ⎰
• Are most of your friends of the same religion as you?
No . . . 0
Yes . . . 1                           VAR409   Pos
• Would you say that most of your close friends are also friends with each
other?
No . . . 0
Yes . . . 1                           VAR410   Pos
GROUP = VAR386 + VAR409 + VAR410

INTERPRETATION:  Low score = low solidarity
                 High score = high solidarity

5. Group Support

How about your neighbors:
  • Do you get along well with them?        No . . . 0
                                            Yes . . . 1        VAR398   Pos
  • Do you help each other sometimes,
    for instance, with babysitting?         No . . . 0
                                            Yes . . . 1        VAR399   Pos
How about your relatives:
  • Do you have any relatives living
    in the area? (Greater Rochester)        No . . . 0
                                            Yes . . . 1        VAR401   Pos
  • Would they come and help you if
    you asked them?                         No . . . 0
                                            Yes . . . 1        VAR402   Pos

SUPPORT = VAR398 + VAR399 + VAR401 + VAR402
INTERPRETATION:  Low score = low support
                 High score = high support

*Variables Used to Assess Rosenstock Model*

1. Readiness to Act

  *a.* Perceived vulnerability or susceptibility (not measured).
  *b.* Perceived consequences or *seriousness* of sickness.

|  | Agree | Undecided | Disagree | | |
|---|---|---|---|---|---|
| • Once you get some serious illness, other troubles such as unemployment are sure to follow. | 3 | 2 | 1 | VAR322 | Pos |
| • The most important thing in life is to be in good health. | 3 | 2 | 1 | VAR323 | Pos |
| • If you are in poor health, it is difficult to get or hold good jobs. | 3 | 2 | 1 | VAR325 | Pos |

SERIOUS = VAR322 + VAR323 + 325
RECODE SERIOUS  (0,1,3 = 2)  (4,5 = 3)  (6,7 = 4)  (8,9 = 5)
                (10 THRU 14 = 6)

INTERPRETATION: Low score = no serious consequences
High score = very serious consequences

2. Perceived Benefits (see "Skepticism of Medical Care")
3. Perceived Barriers

There are many reasons why people do not see a doctor as often as they should. Here are some of them. For each reason, please tell me if you agree, disagree, or feel undecided about it.

|  | Agree | Undecided | Disagree |  |  |
|---|---|---|---|---|---|
| • People don't like going to the doctor. | 3 | 2 | 1 | VAR315 | Pos |
| • Fees and medications are too expensive. | 3 | 2 | 1 | VAR316 | Pos |
| • There are not enough doctors available. | 3 | 2 | 1 | VAR317 | Pos |
| • It is too difficult finding a doctor or getting an appointment. | 3 | 2 | 1 | VAR318 | Pos |
| • It is too difficult finding a baby-sitter or transportation. | 3 | 2 | 1 | VAR319 | Pos |
| • Too much time is required getting there or waiting. | 3 | 2 | 1 | VAR320 | Pos |

BARRIER = VAR315 + VAR316 + VAR317 + VAR318 + VAR319 + VAR320 − 6
RECODE BARRIER (0=1) (3=2) (4,5=3) (6,7=4) (8,9=5)
(10 THRU 14=6)
INTERPRETATION: Low score = no barriers perceived
High score = many barriers seen

4. Readiness to Seek Care
(Attitude toward Physician Use: Andersen)

Next I have some statements on when to see a doctor. Some people say you should go to a doctor at the first signs of trouble; others believe that most symptoms usually go away and you should wait until you are sure there is something wrong. For each of the following symptoms, would you agree or disagree that you should see or telephone a doctor?

|  | Agree | Undecided | Disagree |  |  |
|---|---|---|---|---|---|
| • Sore throat or running nose for a couple of days, but no fever. | 1 | 2 | 3 | VAR309 | Pos |

• Sore throat or running nose
with a fever as high as 100°F
for two days or more.                  1        2        3        VAR310    Pos
• Diarrhea (loose bowel
movements) for about a
week.                                  1        2        3        VAR311    Pos
• Feeling tired for several
weeks for no special reason.           1        2        3        VAR312    Pos
• Unexplained loss of over
10 pounds of weight.                   1        2        3        VAR313    Pos
• Severe shortness of breath
after light exercise.                  1        2        3        VAR314    Pos

THRESH = VAR309 + VAR310 + VAR311 + VAR312 + VAR313 +
         VAR314 − 6
RECODE  THRESH  (0=1)  (3=2)  (4,5=3)  (6,7=4)  (8,9=5)
                (10 THRU 14=6)
INTERPRETATION:  Low score = low threshold/fast use of physician
                 High score = high threshold/slow use of physician

# The Stress Model for Illness Behavior

*Variables Used to Assess Stress Model*

1. Feeling Confined by Child Care

| | Agree | Undecided | Disagree | |
|---|---|---|---|---|
| • Having to be with children all the time gives a woman the feeling her wings have been clipped. | 3 | 2 | 1 | VAR334 |
| • One of the worst things about taking care of a home is that a woman feels she can't get out. | 3 | 2 | 1 | VAR336 |

CONFINED = VAR334 + VAR336 − 2
RECODE CONFINED (0 = 1) (2 = 3)
INTERPRETATION: Low score = not confined
High score = feeling confined

2. Working under Tension

| | Agree | Undecided | Disagree | |
|---|---|---|---|---|
| • Most of the time, I am working under a great deal of strain. | 3 | 2 | 1 | VAR335 |
| • I get pretty nervous and tired during the day. | 3 | 2 | 1 | VAR337 |
| • I often feel like I am losing control over things. | 3 | 2 | 1 | VAR338 |

TENSION = VAR335 + VAR337 + VAR338 − 3
RECODE TENSION (1 = 2) (3 = 4) (5 = 6)
INTERPRETATION: Low score = no tension
High score = high tension

3. Perceived Difficulty in Coping

• Most people have the problem of matching income and expenses. Which
  of the following statements describes your situation best?
  Usually have money left over for investment...4
  Have long-term savings deposits
  (education of children) ....................4
  Have short-term savings deposits
  (holidays, etc.)..........................3          VAR356
  Just get along with income.................2
  Have trouble making ends meet.............1
• When there is a serious illness in the family, how difficult is it for you to
  take the situation in hand and do what needs to be done?
  Very difficult .............................1
  Somewhat ................................2
  A little ..................................3          VAR419
  Not at all difficult .......................4
• How about other troubles: how difficult is it for you to handle them?
  Very difficult .............................1
  Somewhat ................................2
  A little ..................................3          VAR420
  Not at all difficult .......................4


COPING = 12 − (VAR356 + VAR419 + VAR420)
RECODE COPING (0 = 1) (3 = 4) (5 = 6) (8 THRU HIGHEST = 7)
INTERPRETATION:  Low score = no difficulty
                          High score = very difficult


4. Family Functioning

• All marriages have times when things go wrong. Would you say that your
  own marriage was . . .
  Very smooth with little trouble .............1
  Smooth with occasional trouble .............2
  Frequently upset by troubles ................3          VAR343
  Most of the time upset ....................4
• How about the weekends and evenings? Does your husband spend a lot
  of his time with you and the children together, some of his time, or is he
  usually too tired or too busy with other things?
  A lot of his time ..........................1
  Some of his time ..........................2
  Too tired ................................3          VAR344
  Too busy with other things ................4

• Would you say, all in all, that your family is happier than most others you know, about the same, or less happy?

Happier ................................. 1
About the same .......................... 2          VAR345
Less happy ............................... 4

UNHAPPY = VAR343 + VAR344 + VAR345
IF   (UNHAPPY LE 4) FAMTYP = 4 (Happy)
IF   (UNHAPPY EQ 5 or 6) FAMTYP = 3 (Mixed)
IF   (UNHAPPY GE 7) FAMTYP = 2 (Unhappy)
IF   UNMARRIED FAMTYP = 1 (Unmarried)

5. Stress Scoring (The following areas were probed for stressful events; coders assigned stress weights ranging from 1 to 3.)

• Thinking about when you had your children, did you have them when you wanted them or would you rather have had them earlier or later? (Open-ended question.)          VAR342

*If renting*

• Did you have any problems with your landlord over the last 12 months?
No ... 0
Yes ... 1     IF YES: What was it?          VAR391

*If owning*

• Did you have any problems with your house over the last 12 months?
No ... 0
Yes ... 1     IF YES: What was it?          VAR392

• Thinking about your housing situation in general, do you think it is satisfactory the way it is or would you rather move?
Satisfactory .... 1
Would move ... 2     WHY?          VAR397

• How about the schools in this neighborhood: do you like your children going to the schools or would you rather have them go somewhere else?
Like schools ........... 1
Rather somewhere else ... 2     WHY?          VAR404

• Over the past 12 months, did anyone in your or your husband's family die, such as grandfather or uncle?
No ....... 0
Yes, one ... 1
Yes, two ... 2     IF YES: Who?          VAR412

• Were there any accidents in the car, at work, in the home or elsewhere over the last year?
No ....... 0
Yes, one ... 1
Yes, two ... 2     IF YES: What happened?          VAR414

*Table A.9. Medical Care Utilization as a Function of Stress Exposure and Coping Skills*

| | Utilization | | Last Doctor Visit | | |
| --- | --- | --- | --- | --- | --- |
| | Percent in Last 2 Weeks | Rate over Last 12 Months | For Preventive Care | At Private Physician | N |
| **Stress Exposure** | | | | | |
| 0 No stress | 12.4 | 2.30 | 51.6 | 80.7 | 436 |
| 1 | 13.7 | 2.06 | 51.2 | 80.4 | 424 |
| 2 | 13.1 | 2.25 | 47.8 | 77.9 | 571 |
| 3 | 12.2 | 2.25 | 44.3 | 73.3 | 442 |
| 4 | 14.8 | 1.95 | 48.3 | 74.5 | 325 |
| 5 | 13.6 | 2.22 | 45.6 | 66.8 | 250 |
| 6 | 13.6 | 2.36 | 52.3 | 65.3 | 176 |
| 7 | 12.1 | 2.44 | 41.1 | 59.6 | 141 |
| 8 Highest | 13.9 | 2.71 | 31.6 | 57.8 | 187 |
| | n.s. | n.s. | $p<.05$ | $p<.01$ | |
| **Family Type** | | | | | |
| 1 Incomplete | 11.2 | 1.95 | 38.8 | 40.2 | 336 |
| 2 Married: unhappy | 14.1 | 2.55 | 43.1 | 70.4 | 297 |
| 3 Married: mixed | 12.7 | 2.16 | 47.1 | 77.8 | 1130 |
| 4 Married: happy | 14.2 | 2.34 | 50.8 | 81.4 | 1159 |
| | n.s. | n.s. | n.s. | $p<.01$ | |
| **Group Support** (See Table 4A.1) | n.s. | n.s. | n.s. | $p<.05$ | |

| | | | | | |
|---|---|---|---|---|---|
| **Coping Ability** | | | | | |
| 0  Not difficult | 11.1 | 2.52 | 48.1 | 83.3 | 486 |
| 1 | 15.2 | 2.61 | 50.0 | 87.9 | 348 |
| 2 | 13.8 | 1.92 | 49.3 | 74.1 | 710 |
| 3 | 13.2 | 1.89 | 47.3 | 63.8 | 469 |
| 4 | 15.2 | 2.23 | 42.1 | 75.1 | 382 |
| 5 | 11.5 | 2.51 | 38.1 | 70.8 | 226 |
| 6 | 10.2 | 2.66 | 47.3 | 67.3 | 205 |
| 7  Very difficult | 14.3 | 2.07 | 53.2 | 45.2 | 126 |
| | n.s. | $p<.05$ | n.s. | $p<.01$ | |
| **Feeling Confined** | | | | | |
| 0  No | 12.7 | 2.16 | 48.9 | 74.2 | 1647 |
| 1 | 12.7 | 2.87 | 49.4 | 78.5 | 158 |
| 2 | 13.2 | 2.16 | 44.4 | 73.7 | 666 |
| 3 | 6.8 | 2.67 | 44.6 | 77.0 | 74 |
| 4  Yes | 16.7 | 2.36 | 43.7 | 69.8 | 407 |
| | n.s. | n.s. | n.s. | n.s. | |
| **Tension** | | | | | |
| 0  None | 13.3 | 2.03 | 50.0 | 77.9 | 1477 |
| 1 | 17.1 | 2.63 | 46.5 | 79.4 | 170 |
| 2 | 13.1 | 2.13 | 46.7 | 80.5 | 497 |
| 3 | 14.1 | 2.56 | 38.3 | 71.1 | 128 |
| 4 | 12.5 | 2.39 | 41.3 | 58.2 | 385 |
| 5 | 17.3 | 2.54 | 53.8 | 61.5 | 52 |
| 6  Lot | 9.9 | 2.99 | 43.6 | 60.1 | 243 |
| | n.s. | $p<.05$ | n.s. | $p<.01$ | |

Table A.10. Probabilities of Transitions from Combined Variable States for Mothers and Youngest Children

| This Day | | | Next Day | | | | | | | | | N |
|---|---|---|---|---|---|---|---|---|---|---|---|---|
| Stress: | | | No | No | No | No | Yes | Yes | Yes | Yes | | |
| Illness: | | | No | No | Yes | Yes | No | No | Yes | Yes | | |
| Stress | Illness | Utilization: Utilization | No | Yes | No | Yes | No | Yes | No | Yes | | |
| No | No | No | .761 | .005 | .061 | .004 | .131 | .001 | .036 | .002 | 1.000 | 15,740 |
| No | No | Yes | .627 | .040 | .087 | .008 | .190 | .008 | .032 | .008 | 1.000 | 126 |
| No | Yes | No | .344 | .003 | .431 | .022 | .072 | .001 | .118 | .009 | 1.000 | 3,084 |
| No | Yes | Yes | .311 | .015 | .429 | .077 | .036 | .000 | .117 | .015 | 1.000 | 196 |
| Yes | No | No | .358 | .004 | .040 | .003 | .504 | .005 | .084 | .003 | 1.000 | 5,899 |
| Yes | No | Yes | .214 | .000 | .054 | .000 | .554 | .018 | .143 | .018 | 1.000 | 56 |
| Yes | Yes | No | .237 | .004 | .171 | .010 | .204 | .002 | .349 | .023 | 1.000 | 2,393 |
| Yes | Yes | Yes | .097 | .000 | .260 | .058 | .149 | .000 | .364 | .071 | 1.000 | 154 |

• Were there any other events or problems over the last year that gave you a lot of trouble or worries (such as separation, divorce, unwanted pregnancy, courts, or police)?

No . . . . . . . 0
Yes, one . . . 1
Yes, two . . . 2     IF YES:    What was it?                         VAR416

STRESS = VAR342 + VAR391 + VAR394 + VAR397 +
         VAR404 + VAR412 + VAR414 + VAR416
RECODE STRESS (0 = 1) (3 = 4) (6 = 7) (8 THRU HIGHEST = 8)

# Ambulatory Care: Decreasing Utilization Rates

## 1. Estimating the Volume of Ambulatory Services from Provider Studies

A number of assumptions underlie these supplier estimates. No agency keeps separate records on visits for the specific age group under study, but several studies on pediatricians' practices (Hessel and Haggerty, 1968; Hercules and Charney, 1969; Breese et al., 1966),[1] family medicine (Riley et al., 1969),[2] emergency room use (Jacobs et al., 1971; Kluge et al., 1965; Roghmann, 1973)[3] and outpatient department (OPD) visits[4] permit reasonable estimates.[5] In 1969, 28% of all OPD visits in Monroe County were for children. The proportion of child visits among all emergency room visits has decreased, from about 40% in 1967 to about 37% in 1969 and 34% in 1971. The equivalent of 59 full-time pediatricians delivered

---

[1] The findings from these three studies are rather consistent and suggest that a pediatrician in full-time private practice has, on the average, about 255 patient contacts outside the hospital per week, of which 115 are office visits, 15 are house calls, and 125 are patient phone calls. National figures confirm these findings, except for house calls (3.3 per week). (See Balfe et al., 1971:50; Jackson, 1971:31.) We estimated an average of 7 house calls a week.

[2] This study indicates that general practitioners have about 197 patient contacts a week, of which 140 are office visits, 7 are house calls, and 50 are patient phone calls.

[3] In addition to these studies, yearly statistics for all hospitals in the county from 1960 to 1970 were made available by the Genesee Region Health Planning Council.

[4] Only one study of a pediatric outpatient clinic from the community was available: Haggerty, R.J. and Taylor, H.: "Patients in a Pediatric Out-Patient Department: Implications for Organization of Services." Mimeographed manuscript, 1966.
In addition, yearly statistics for all hospitals in the county from 1960 to 1970 were made available by the Genesee Region Health Planning Council. For an estimate of the age breakdown of these patients, the Data Processing Department of the University of Rochester Medical Center, which provides 75% of all outpatient visits in the community, analyzed the age composition for a typical week in 1971.

[5] We found no accurate data on "other clinic" visits and on school health appraisals. Information was obtained from major suppliers (ABC clinics, the Rochester Neighborhood Health Center, city school district), but for other sources we had to make educated guesses.

services in private practice in 1967, 59 in 1969, and 62 in 1971.[6] There was a considerable turnover of pediatricians during the time span analyzed, and a large number of them had half- or quarter-time commitments. We assumed that each pediatrician worked about 48 weeks a year (Balfe et al., 1971:50). According to our household surveys, the proportion of all private office visits to pediatricians increased from 47% in 1967 to 53% in 1969 and to 60% in 1971. Most of the remaining private sector visits were to general practitioners.

Some of the studies quoted were from an earlier date, and some of the findings, especially those relating to the relatively large number of house calls made, were probably no longer applicable for the study period. Possible errors are discussed in Section 6A. A physician survey conducted in 1973 indicated that the estimate in Table 6A.1, the latest of which amounted to 1.35 million medical care encounters, or 5.42 per child per year, cannot have been far off. About 87% of these were provided in the private sector, and 11% in the public sector. The expansion of the public sector was due to two new health centers (Roghmann and Lawrence, 1973).

## 2. Estimating the Volume of Ambulatory Services from Consumer Studies

For each of the estimates presented some error is involved. (Another estimate, based on a health calendar kept for 28 days, is available only for the 1969 survey.[7]) Random samples were used for all three surveys, though the 1969 sample was only half the size of the 1967 and 1971 samples and involved a different sampling frame.

The two-week and the 12-month recall questions make different demands on the respondents' memories, but the 12-month estimate is also biased (as explained below) toward a healthy or low-care-utilization child population. Places for well-child care such as schools and nonhospital "well-child" clinics yield higher 12-month than two-week proportions of

---

[6] The numbers of pediatricians in full-time private practice in our community in 1967, 1969, and 1971 were established by expert judgment. A list of every pediatrician in the medical directory with an office in the community was prepared and updated each time a coder encountered a new pediatrician's name in any interview. This list was given to a panel of five pediatricians, knowledgeable of the community during the study years, to rate each pediatrician as to the percentage of a full work load of private practice that he delivered in each year. The 87 pediatricians on the list were equivalent to 59 full-time private practitioners in 1967, to 59 full-time private practitioners in 1969, and to 62 full-time practitioners in 1971.

[7] The health calendar led to an estimate of 250,000 phone calls, 800,000 office visits, 69,000 emergency room visits, 80,000 outpatient visits, and 65,000 other clinic visits in 1969.

visits, both absolutely and relatively. Telephone consultations or emergency room visits have lower proportions for the same reason.

The 12-month estimates of yearly utilization rates for 1967 and 1971 were obtained by excluding children who reported a doctor consultation in the preceding two weeks, and by adding all the visits reported by the rest of the sample for a 12-month period. Rates are computed by dividing this sum over the number of respondents, excluding the "two-week positive" cases. Not only is the relative sampling error for this estimate low (about 3% in the survey), but also more detailed estimates by source of care are possible.

A bias is introduced, however, because of the skewed distribution of children and of visits per child per year (see Figure A.2). The mean number of visits deviates greatly from the modal number. A small percentage of children—those with major chronic illnesses or those who happen to have serious illness in the year under study—accounts for a disproportionately high percentage of all doctor visits in that year. The estimate based on our 12-month frequency question describes a child population in which these high utilizers are underrepresented. To assess the error and to compute a correction factor, data for a group of children with distributions even more skewed than those of Figure A.2 were used. With a skewed distribution such as that of Figure A.2, the 12-month estimate would be only 7% below the unbiased estimate. For an extremely skewed distribution like that encountered for a poverty group (Roghmann and Haggerty, 1974), the 12-month estimate was 20% below the unbiased estimate. Compared with the size of the measurement error, this known design effect is rather moderate and can be considered in any estimation.

No other studies have been found in which two-week and 12-month estimates are combined, and hence no figures are available to compare to these data. For the fiscal year 1967, the National Health Interview used a 12-month recall period instead of the two-week period. The estimate

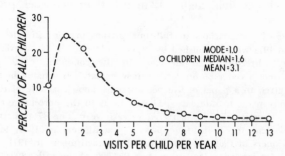

*Figure A.2. Distribution of children by utilization rate (last 12 months, excluding last 2 weeks), Rochester metropolitan area, 1967.*

proved to be 76.8% of the preceding year's estimate, which was based on the two-week question (Jackson, 1971:31), and the difference was attributed to memory bias. The findings reported here indicate that a more differentiated approach can be made by combining the two questions. For some sources, however, the first estimate would be better, whereas for others the second is preferable. From the measurement point of view, the two-week recall question is better, as the recall of doctor visits for the two weeks preceding the interview is probably more reliable than the recall over a 12-month period. The term "recall" is used here as signifying the balance between overreporting (false positives) and underreporting (false negatives). For short-term measures the overreporting is greater; for long-term measures, the underreporting.

## REFERENCES

BALFE, B.E., LORANT, J.H., and TODD, C. (Eds.)
1971 "Reference Data on the Profile of Medical Practice." Center for Health Services Research and Development, American Medical Association.

BREESE, B.B., DISNEY, F.A., and TALPEY, W.
1966 "The Nature of a Small Pediatric Group Practice." *Pediatrics*, 38:264–275.

HAGGERTY, ROBERT J., and TAYLOR, H.
1966 *Patients in a Pediatric Out-Patient Department: Implications for Organization of Services* (mimeograph).

HERCULES, C., and CHARNEY, E.
1969 "Availability and Attentiveness: Are these Compatible in Pediatric Practice?" *Clinical Pediatrics* 8:381–388.

HESSEL, S.J., and HAGGERTY, R.J.
1968 "General Pediatrics: A Study of Practice in the Mid-60's." *Journal of Pediatrics* 73:271–279.

JACKSON, ANN L.
1971 *Children and Youth: Selected Health Characteristics, U.S., 1958 and 1968.* National Center for Health Statistics, Department of Health, Education, and Welfare, Series 10, No. 62. Washington, D.C.: Government Printing Office.

JACOBS, A.R., GAVETT, J.W., and WERSINGER, R.
1971 "Emergency Department Utilization in an Urban Community." *Journal of the American Medical Association*, 216:307–312.

KLUGE, D.N., WEGRYN, R.L., and LEMLEY, B.R.
1965 "The Expanding Emergency Department." *Journal of the American Medical Association*, 191(10):97–101.

RILEY, G.J., WILLE, C.R., and HAGGERTY, ROBERT J.

1969 "A Study of Family Medicine in Upstate New York." *Journal of the American Medical Association*, 20S:2307.

ROGHMANN, KLAUS J.

1973 "The National Center for Health Statistics: A Research Resource for Pediatricians." *American Journal of Diseases of Children*, 126:439–440.

ROGHMANN, KLAUS J., and LAWRENCE, RUTH

1973 "The Volume of Private Practice Care in Monroe County, New York." *Working Papers in Health Services Research and Evaluation*, No. 10, University of Rochester Department of Pediatrics (mimeograph).

ROGHMANN, KLAUS J., and HAGGERTY, ROBERT J.

1974 "Measuring the Use of Health Services by Household Interviews: A Comparison of Procedures Used in Three Child Health Surveys." *International Journal of Epidemiology*, 3:(1):71–81.

# The Impact of Medicaid

## 1. Using Medicaid Payment Files for Research

The local Medicaid payment data system is maintained by the County of Monroe Department of Social Services.[1] A record of all payments made to providers of medical and dental care is stored on computer tapes, with each payment record identifying the client and his birthdate, the provider, the dollar volume, the date of payment, the type of service, and the date it was delivered. The total payments made in a given year require five computer tapes for storage. Two sets of such tapes, those for 1968 and those for 1970, were requested for this research.[2] The selection of the years followed a parallel before-after design of our surveys.

There are three main methodological problems to be considered in the analysis: the time lag between service and payment, the coding of the client's residence by census tract, and the determination of the population covered by Medicaid.

Bills are paid, on the average, some three months after the services are delivered, but this lag varies by vendor and time of year. Whenever there are major differences between the payment files of two years, it is important to check whether the service periods covered are comparable.

The second problem involves the coding by census tract. The original payment records contain Medicaid number and name, but not the address or census tract of the client. However, a Medicaid enrollment tape exists that contains both Medicaid number and address. By allocating census tract numbers via automated address coding to the Medicaid number, a matching file was created that permitted coding of most records. The coding by census tract is needed to distinguish between services delivered to residents of the Rochester Neighborhood Health Center and services delivered to a second poverty area and the rest of the community.

The third problem is the need to check for changes in the base population. To compute utilization rates of Medicaid clients in the target and

[1] Though Medicaid (Title XIX) is a statewide program with the same regulations applying to all New York State counties, its administration, including data processing forms and procedures, is handled independently by each county.

[2] Note that the request is not for confidential *medical* records, but for *administrative* records. Nevertheless, their use for research purposes has to be cleared by the director of the department or his deputy. The same safeguards to guarantee anonymity apply as for interview data, that is, only authorized study personnel are given access to the data, and only for the previously stated and approved research objectives.

the comparison area, data on Medicaid enrollees by census tract are needed as a denominator. There are monthly updated membership lists with Medicaid number, family composition, and address that can be used for this purpose. This was not necessary for the present study, however, as our interest was limited to children, for whom the enrollment figures changed little between the two years.[3]

## 2. Checking for Errors in the Payment Files

This exploratory study uncovered a few previously unknown character-istics of the local Medicaid payment files. Although it was known that one claim might cover several visits to a private practitioner, it was also found that one visit might generate several claims. Another finding was that indi-vidual claims for hospital stays were not permitted to exceed $999 per claim. If an admission led to larger bills, several such claims had to be presented. Before an analysis of hospitalization claims can be attempted, such double reporting has to be eliminated.

Another previously unknown detail was revealed when comparisons against interview data identified frequent clerical errors such as wrong birthdates. Birthdates were being used to identify different children in a family; the wrong birthdate on a claim card leads the computer to "detect" an "additional" child.

Thus the in-depth analysis of about 100 families gave us further insight into the validity of the data, as well as some clues about the continuity of care (number of vendors used by each family) and the variation in costs and utilization rates by individuals and by families. However, this sample was too small to try to make any detailed comparisons by service areas or special groups of patients, for example, health center registered patients versus nonregistered patients in the target area. Even with the minor errors discovered, this study showed that reliable medical care research is possible on the basis of Medicaid payment files.

[3] The total Medicaid case load in the service time span covered by the 1970 payments file was about 45,800, that is, 12,500 less than in 1968. The number on "basic as-sistance" increased from an average of 23,400 to 31,200, but this increase was more than balanced by a sharp drop in the "medical assistance" group, specifically in those 18–65 years old. Members of this age group were excluded from eligibility, un-less disabled, by the changes of 1969. The child population on Medicaid remained, in our estimate, about the same: 31,000 in 1968 and 30,000 in 1970. However, the child population on Medicaid was economically worse off in 1970 than in 1968. In 1970 about 68% (20,400) were on welfare; in 1968, only 55% (17,050). The children on medical assistance frequently have Blue Cross coverage as well, because of the em-ployment of one of the parents. Those on basic assistance, however, have no other coverage, nor do they have the financial means to use health services outside Medicaid.

# PART FOUR

# Update 20 Years Later

M uch has changed in the care of children in the community. The Rochester area, like the nation as a whole, has had good news and bad news about child health. Our knowledge about how to improve the health of children has increased dramatically, yet we continue to struggle to make needed services available in a more restrictive political and economic environment. Manpower shortages have eased and many newly created institutions, like health centers, have survived, but new problems have emerged. State agencies have increased their influence where federal agencies retreated. Despite all these changes we will argue that the philosophy of community pediatrics as described 20 years ago is as valid now as it was then.

Community pediatrics was previously defined as "a commitment to organize health services for *all* children in a defined geographical area rather than only for those who find their way to existing services." This commitment requires a dual approach—a community focus as well as an individual focus. Although, by nature, services are individual, to reach *all* children one must first understand the social structure of the community. However, as readers of the original edition will have learned, this operationalization of community pediatrics only in terms of access and availability provides an excessively narrow definition. Our discussion of health planning, public health issues, insurance coverage, demographic changes, changes in family structure, etc. expressed professional and personal concerns about the health of children, bordering on child advocacy and political activism. We stopped short of endorsing specific political ideologies or organizational principles, such as government regulation, market mechanism or voluntaristic community efforts. While we see this as a necessary step, it has become clearer that health services alone are not the major contributor to improved child health. Rather, their integration with other community services and, more important, the whole social cultural environment in which children and their families live, is the major determination of health.

Effective professional leadership must transcend daily political alignments, yet be based on a solid understanding of the political and social processes that affect child health. Neither longing for an older and simpler way of life nor a hope for futuristic solutions based on new technologies should mislead us. The broader definition of community pediatrics as expressed here includes professional and community leadership to enhance the physical and social environment of children. It also includes the use of social science knowledge and methods. To realize its objective, namely the improvement of health for all children, community pediatrics requires different forums and methods in the 1990s than it did in the 1960s and 1970s. This is so in part because much has changed in the social environment for families and children, and a documentation and analysis of these changes from the perspective of community pediatrics makes an update of the earlier edition essential.

*Child Health and the Community* was a community study. Sociologists have always focused on communities—their neighborhoods, schools, parks, politics, and social structures. Communities are easier to understand and more manageable when planning for services and interventions. Pediatricians work in urban and suburban practices, or health centers. Children grow up in families, neighborhoods, and schools. This is the level where individuals are active in associations, committees, and social movements, and where their involvement has visible effects. But academic departments have a tendency to isolate themselves from their local community. They see themselves as having a national orientation. They train professionals who make frequent geographic moves as part of their career development. Medical professionals are oriented toward national societies and toward the national network of medical schools and hospitals where their careers unfold. Social scientists prefer a focus on theory rather than applied local research. Local roots can be dysfunctional for both medical and social scientists.

The philosophy of community pediatrics attempted to overcome such withdrawal into the traditional professional roles, although not to ignore national roles. It implied a commitment to local involvement and leadership. If improvement of child health for all is the final goal, we have to get involved; to reach out into the community; and to develop local roots. This attitude also implies reaching out across disciplinary boundaries and forming alliances with nursing, social work, and all the basic, social science disciplines that are exploring new ways to serve children. A community study of such efforts is necessarily a case study. Its purpose is to illustrate some principles and trends as a basis for advocacy and education.

The intended audience for this book has not changed. It is written for pediatric practitioners, public health staff, nurses, social workers, health planners and administrators—in short, for all who share an interest in children and the professions and institutions serving children. Much of the material is descriptive. The presentation has a wide theoretical perspective: demographic changes, economic trends, institutional and organizational innovations, and professional developments are each presented. The focus is on change, however, especially the survival of new institutions despite changing political environments and the development of new professions and services aimed at helping children.

# CHAPTER TWELVE

# Facts and Figures: The Setting and the Problems

Rochester in the 1970s and 1980s has remained in a relatively privileged position of socioeconomic stability, but has also experienced the nation's population shifts. The baby boom cohorts joined the labor force and formed families, and the echo boom strained the hospitals' obstetric capabilities in the 1980s. The echo boom is about over and a steady decline in live births can be predicted far into the next century. The need for abortions continued and has been unaffected by the current political controversies. Should there be a return to a restricted abortion law, a new "unwanted baby" boom would result and create an acute crisis in the obstetric care facilities. Poor black mothers and white teenagers would be affected most.

Infant mortality declines have been dramatic, but celebration of this success has been muted. Major socioeconomic differences persist and continue to receive more attention than the observed reductions. Although the measurement and interpretation of racial/ethnic differences poses major problems, as with abortion services, scientific and political assessments are often difficult to separate.

Finally, we take a new look at medical service structures. Rochester's hospital bed supply and physician manpower closely mirrors the national average, rather than the high rates that characterize the Northeast. The hospital bed supply has been kept low, in large part due to successful health planning, while physician manpower supply has increased dramatically. Anecdotal evidence suggests that the demand for physician services has not yet been saturated.

The Rochester community, a 5-county standard metropolitan area in upstate New York, with a population of one million and a single tertiary care center, has remained a microcosm of American society, and reflects well changes occurring throughout the nation.

## A. THE NEW POPULATION PROFILE: SOCIOECONOMIC STABILITY, BUT MAJOR POPULATION SHIFTS

KLAUS J. ROGHMANN

In the past twenty years, Rochester has not experienced any major economic or social upheavals. Large companies like Eastman Kodak and

Xerox still dominate Rochester's industry, but there are a large number of small companies whose employments balance the ups and downs of the large multinational corporations. The community continues to enjoy high employment levels and a strong cooperative spirit among its members. The gradual decline of manufacturing has been compensated for by a steady expansion of the service sector. The city's newspapers and television stations have remained constants. Certainly, outside observers would stress continuity in the city's development, rather than change.

A few statistics will help to illustrate this profile of relative socioeconomic stability. Table 12A.1 presents mobility and unemployment data for the 5-county Rochester Standard metropolitan area (SMA) in comparison to New York State and the national average. Nationally, 5-year *mobility* across county lines in 1980 was 21.4%. The New York State rate was 15.8%, the Rochester SMA rate was 14.9%, and the urban Monroe County rate 13.5%. Comparable 1960 rates were lower across the board, but the pattern was the same. The *unemployment* figures also show consistently lower rates for urban Monroe County since 1960 than for the SMA as a whole, and usually lower SMA rates than both the state and the national average (table 12A.1). Eastman Kodak and Xerox followed the national pattern of frequent restructuring, including early retirement plans and even layoffs, but in relative terms, the 1970s and 1980s were good decades for the community.

The median family income and the median house values (Table 12A.2) also reflect the same picture. For 1960, 1970, and 1980, family

*Table 12A.1. Mobility and Unemployment in Rochester SMA, 1960, 1970, 1980*

| County | Moved from Outside County in Last 5 Years | | Unemployment* Civilian Labor Force (BLS) | | | |
|---|---|---|---|---|---|---|
| | 1960 | 1980 | 1960 | 1970 | 1982 | 1986 |
| Livingston | 16.9 | 23.2 | 5.0 | 3.9 | 6.9 | 7.1 |
| Monroe | 9.6 | 13.5 | 4.6 | 3.1 | 5.7 | 5.0 |
| Ontario | 15.7 | 19.7 | 6.4 | 4.4 | 6.8 | 6.7 |
| Orleans | 14.0 | 15.2 | 9.4 | 6.7 | 12.7 | 8.5 |
| Wayne | 13.6 | 16.1 | 7.6 | 5.2 | 7.9 | 8.1 |
| SMA* | 11.3 | 14.9 | 5.1 | 3.6 | 6.3 | 5.7 |
| NY State | 13.7 | 15.8 | 5.2 | 4.0 | 7.1 | 6.3 |
| U.S. | 17.4 | 21.4 | 5.1 | 4.4 | 6.5 | 7.0 |

*Average of counties weighted by population.

income in Monroe County was the highest in the SMA. It, in turn, had a higher average value than all of New York State, which itself was above the national average. Actually, Monroe County's median family income was always more than 20% above the national average. House values, a good indicator of local costs of living, tend to be lower than the state average, and in 1980, even lower than the national average. Housing values during the 1970s had not increased in upstate New York as much as they have nationally.

Other socioeconomic indicators for 1980 (Table 12A.3), like the percent of families below the poverty line, the percent of families with a female head of household, and the average years of education show a population slightly better off than other SMAs. There is less poverty and fewer families have a female head of household.

Overall, the Rochester SMA generally appears to be very close to the typical U.S. SMA, although a little better educated and with slightly higher median incomes.

*Table 12A.2. Median Family Income and House Value in Rochester SMA 1960, 1970, 1980*

| County | Median Family Income ($) | | | Median House Value ($) | | |
|---|---|---|---|---|---|---|
|  | 1960 | 1970 | 1980 | 1960 | 1970 | 1980 |
| Livingston | 5,607 | 10,520 | 19,596 | 9,900 | 16,913 | 38,200 |
| Monroe | 7,147 | 12,420 | 24,256 | 14,900 | 21,835 | 44,200 |
| Ontario | 5,734 | 10,511 | 20,514 | 10,700 | 15,279 | 39,100 |
| Orleans | 5,608 | 10,118 | 20,356 | 9,100 | 13,175 | 31,700 |
| Wayne | 5,667 | 10,488 | 20,385 | 10,100 | 15,489 | 35,300 |
| SMA | 6,744 | 11,885 | 23,106 | 13,601 | 20,126 | 42,035 |
| NY State | 6,371 | 10,609 | 20,180 | 15,300 | 22,599 | 45,900 |
| U.S. | 5,660 | 9,586 | 19,917 | 11,900 | 17,130 | 47,300 |

*Average of counties weighted by population.

*Table 12A.3   Socioeconomic Indicators, 1980*

|  | Monroe County | Rochester SMA | All U.S. SMAs |
|---|---|---|---|
| % Families below poverty | 6.5 | 6.5 | 8.7 |
| % Families, female head of household | 15.4 | 14.2 | 15.3 |
| % Education, 16 years + | 21.3 | 19.1 | 17.9 |

The population structure has changed markedly in the last 20 years, although this transformation occurred slowly and was not highly visible. In terms of maternal and child health, there have been three developments of special significance: the "community's" expansion beyond the old south and southeast county boundaries; a reduced child population; and increased ethnic and racial diversity. None of these are peculiar to the Rochester region; they represent national trends.

Table 12A.4 shows the population development of the 5 counties now listed by the Census Bureau under the Rochester "Standard Metropolitan Area," (SMA) with a population of about one million people. In the surrounding 4 counties of Livingston, Ontario, Orleans, and Wayne, the population has grown steadily over the past 25 years. Actually, Monroe County's suburbs spread into the surrounding areas, specifically into Livingston, Ontario and part of Wayne County, all of which experienced a population growth of over 30% over the last 30 years. To the west, Orleans County remained largely rural and benefitted less from the expansion of the Rochester SMA. Within Monroe County, the total population has remained stable since 1970, but a further shift out of the city and into the surrounding suburbs took place. Between 1970 and 1980 alone, the city population decreased from nearly 300,000 to just over 240,000. Preliminary census data for 1990 indicate a further decline to 232,000. Minority populations continue to reside in the city, representing about 40% of the population: the black population in the city for 1990 was 73,000, the Hispanic population was 20,000, and the Asian population was just over 5,000. By comparison, only 5% of the suburban population was nonwhite: the black population in the suburban towns in 1990 was 12,000, the Hispanic population was 6,400, and the Asian population was 8,600. The racial and ethnic differences are described further below. Figure 12A.1 is a map of the SMA, showing the important differences between the surrounding counties, the suburbs and the city of Rochester.

This population shift within the Rochester SMA is important to understand shifts in health care needs. It is the young population that moved across county lines into new residential developments in the neighboring counties. These people still work in Monroe County and they still seek health care in Monroe County. Hence, if service needs are only projected on the basis of Monroe County population data, major underestimates will result. For example, the number of deliveries in Monroe County by nonresidents between 1980 and 1989 increased from 1,400 to 2,400.

Figure 12A.2 and Figure 12A.3 describe the changing age structure of the community. While in 1960 children under 5 represented 11.1% of the total population, this proportion was down to 7.6% in 1990. Most

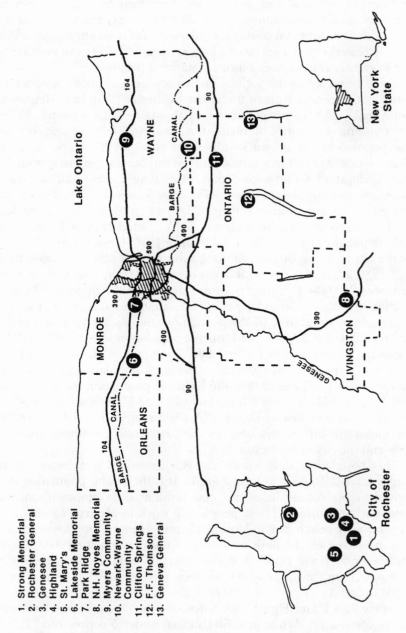

Figure 12A.1.    Rochester Standard Metropolitan Area

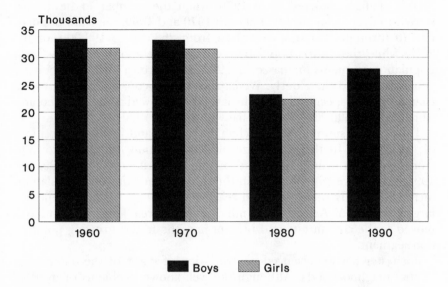

*Figure 12A.2.   Child Population under Age 5*
*Monroe County Population*

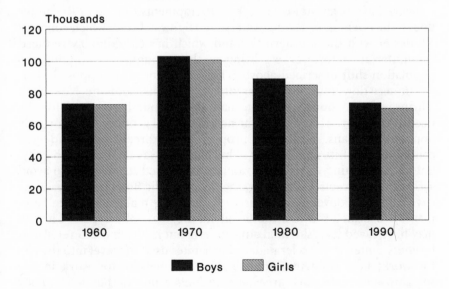

*Figure 12A.3.   Child Population from 5 to 19 Years*
*Monroe County Population*

of this change occurred since 1970, when the number of newborns started to drop dramatically. Between 1970 and 1990, the child population (0 through 19 years) decreased from 268,000 to 198,000, or by 26%, while the entire population remained at about 712,000. Two population segments increased: the 20–44 age group (the "baby boom" generation), and the elderly. We expand on the consequences of these changes below, specifically how the late 1980s showed a mini baby boom, which will be followed by a mini baby bust in the 1990s.

Table 12A.5 summarizes the changing ethnic and racial composition of the county. In the 1960s, the black population doubled, growing from 24,000 to over 52,000, and in the 1970s, it grew to 71,000. By 1990, there were 85,000 blacks in the county. The Hispanic population increased rapidly since 1970 and reached 26,500 by 1990. In addition, large numbers of Asians from India, China, Korea, and Vietnam have moved to the community and present now the fastest growing population segment.

Rochester has experienced gentrification of many of the older residential neighborhoods. Although the well-known problems of insufficient funding for education and health care for minorities are certainly still present, no one grievance dominates the local political debate. As in all of New York State, and many other states in the Northeast, the Rochester community suffered from cutbacks in state and federal funding affecting human services, especially for education.

There have been, however, a few developments unique to Rochester due to the opening in 1980 of Interstate Highway I-390, which connects Rochester with the southern tier and which has considerably reduced commuter time for workers living in these counties, prompting the population shift described above. The city of Rochester opposed plans to connect downtown Rochester directly to I-390 and the New York Thruway, even though the state had already purchased land for the needed corridor. According to the neighborhood groups who vigorously opposed the plans, the freeway proposal was a threat to the residential community and its atmosphere. This highway was built up to the city, but not connecting with it. Exit ramps were placed strategically to avoid access to city streets. As a result, the major traffic flows now bypass the city. All newly developing areas with shopping malls and office complexes are located south of the city along the new I-390 bypass. The city may have saved its residential atmosphere, but its decline as a retail and business center was accelerated. Suburbanites used to travel into the city for work; now residents increasingly leave the city for work in the suburbs. The new work areas are no longer on city bus lines. They require independent means of transportation, resulting in a new form of segregation for city residents.

*Table 12A.4  Population Development 1960–1990: Rochester Standard Metropolitan Area*

| County | 1960 | 1970 | 1980 | 1990 | % Change 1960–90 | Racial/Ethnic Composition | | | |
|---|---|---|---|---|---|---|---|---|---|
| | | | | | | % Black | | % Hispanic | |
| | | | | | | 1980 | 1990 | 1980 | 1990 |
| Livingston | 44,053 | 54,041 | 57,006 | 62,372 | +41.6 | 1.17 | 2.42 | .61 | 1.56 |
| Ontario | 68,070 | 78,849 | 88,909 | 95,101 | +39.7 | 1.64 | 1.81 | 1.08 | 1.33 |
| Orleans | 34,159 | 37,305 | 38,496 | 41,846 | +22.5 | 5.16 | 6.58 | 1.05 | 2.46 |
| Wayne | 67,989 | 79,404 | 84,581 | 89,123 | +31.1 | 3.23 | 3.13 | 1.04 | 1.70 |
| Monroe | 586,387 | 711,917 | 702,238 | 713,968 | +21.8 | 10.12 | 11.91 | 2.38 | 3.70 |
| Total | 800,658 | 961,516 | 971,230 | 1,002,410 | +25.2 | 8.02 | 9.35 | 1.99 | 3.12 |

*Table 12A.5.   Distribution of Monroe County Population by Race and Ethnicity*

| Race/<br>Ethnicity | 1960 | 1970 | 1980 | 1990 |
|---|---|---|---|---|
| White | 561,556 | 655,821 | 613,525 | 600,328 |
| Black | 24,184 | 52,218 | 71,041 | 5,041 |
| Other | 883 | 3,878 | 17,672 ** | 28,599** |
| Total | 586,623 | 711,917 | 702,238 | 713,968 |
| Hispanic*** | 2,101† | 5,792† | 16,538‡ | 26,450‡ |

†Born in Puerto Rico of Puerto Rican Parentage.
‡Includes Puerto Ricans plus Mexican, Cuban, and other Hispanic. Puerto
Ricans represent about 70% of total.
**Includes the following:

|  | 1980 | 1990 |
|---|---|---|
| American Indians | 1,633 | 1,982 |
| Chinese | 1,436 | 3,015 |
| Japanese | 435 | 657 |
| Asian Indians | 1,696 | 2,827 |
| Korean | 720 | 1,879 |
| Vietnamese | 653 | 1,401 |

***Racial breakdown in 1980 was 42.3% white, 6.6% black, and 51.1% other.
Racial breakdown in 1990 was 40.1% white, 8.2% black, and 51.7% other.

*B. THE CHILD POPULATION IN 1988: THE AGING OF MOTHERHOOD
AND THE COMING BABY "BUST"*

KLAUS J. ROGHMANN
AND
RALPH R. SELL

Sociologists focus on fashionable swings in public values like preferences
for large or small families, or for early or late childbearing during the
life cycle. Such swings produce the well-known fluctuations in live births
referred to as "booms" or "busts" that can have highly disruptive ripple
effects on other segments of society. These cycles affect the demand for
health services, educational resources, and labor markets when large or
small cohorts finish school and look for jobs. If fertility patterns do not
change to compensate for such fluctuations, there are "echo booms"
and "echo busts" one generation later.

The Rochester community had a baby boom during the 1960s and a baby bust during the 1970s. These are described in the first edition of *Child Health and the Community*. The 1980s had a mini echo boom. Will the 1990s bring an echo bust? Figure 12B.1 presents the development of live births over a 20-year period, by race and area in Monroe County. It shows the peak of the baby boom in 1970 (13,563 newborns) and the bottom of the baby bust in 1976 (8,966 newborns), but then indicates a stabilization of births at around 10–11,000 per year. These fluctuations did not have a large impact on nonwhite births, but they strongly affected white births. As a result, the trend in the city (Figure 12B.2) is not as marked as in the suburbs (Figure 12B.3). Suburban births decreased from about 6,700 in 1970 to 3,450 in 1974, a nearly 50% decline. This change resulted from a true decline in fertility, rather than fewer women of childbearing age. More effective family planning, with backup through easy access to abortions, greater occupational opportunities for women, later childbearing, and a change in public attitudes, all contributed to the reduction. However, there is considerable evidence that this reduction in fertility has ended.

Figure 12B.4 shows the observed later childbearing. During the 15 years between 1974 and 1988, childbearing decreased over 15% in the 20–24 age group, but increased by nearly 15% in the 25–29 age group; it doubled in the 30–34 age range, and tripled in the 35–39 age range.

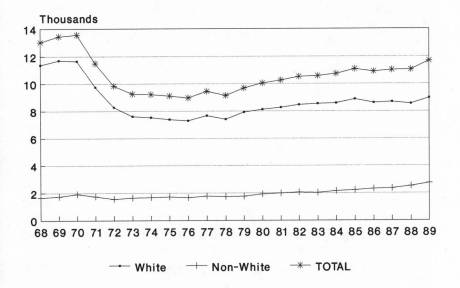

*Figure 12B.1. Newborns by Race, 1968–1989*
*Residents, Monroe County, NY*

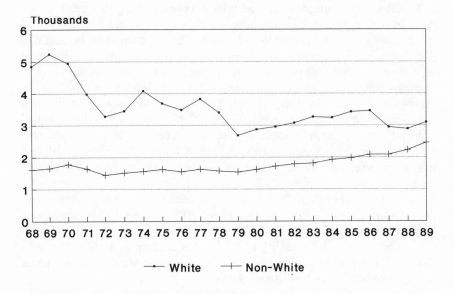

*Figure 12B.2.   Newborns by Race, 1968–1989
Residents, City of Rochester, NY*

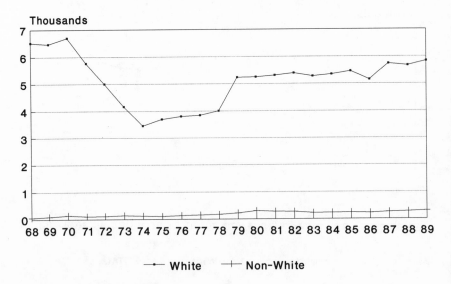

*Figure 12B.3.   Newborns by Race, 1968–1989
Residents, Suburbs of Monroe County, NY*

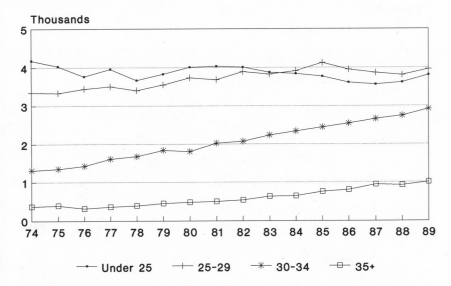

*Figure 12B.4.   Newborns by Age of Mother*
*Residents, Monroe County, 1974–1989*

Such trends towards postponed childbearing can lead to quick declines, but later lead to more live births when many women try to "catch up." Thus, while the total number of newborns stabilized again at a higher level, the average age of the mother was markedly higher. We anticipate that this shift toward later fertility will be permanent, reflecting the changed role of women in American society. It certainly moderated the expected "echo baby boom" of the 1980s.

Unless an upsurge in fertility occurs, or a return toward younger childbearing begins, we cannot expect a similar compensation for the expected "echo baby bust" in the mid-1990s and early 2000s. By "aging" the cohorts of women recorded at the 1990 census for Monroe County and applying 1989 age-specific fertility rates from 1989 to them, we predict a peak of about 12,000 newborns by Monroe County residents in 1990, then a yearly decline of 200 during the 1990s to reach 9,800 by the year 2000 (Sell, 1991). Figure 12B.5 describes the trend for all age groups, Figure 12B.6 has the projections for the younger age groups, and Figure 12B.7 for the older age groups. Figure 12B.5 also shows how out-of-county births will compensate for some of the baby bust of the residents' births.

The current stabilization of newborn cohorts for Monroe County residents and the higher average age of mothers should be positive factors for child health. However, two important factors moderate these

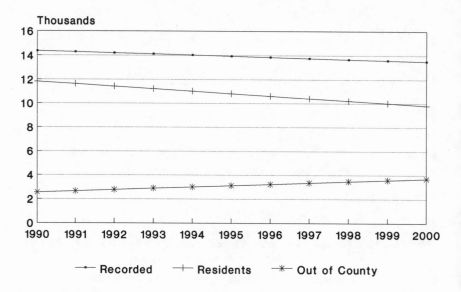

Figure 12B.5.  Projection of Newborns 1990–2000
Monroe County, NY

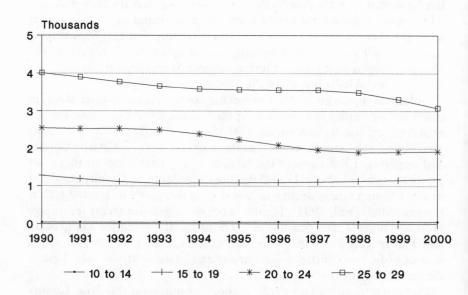

Figure 12B.6.  Birth Projection 1990–2000
Residents, Monroe County, NY

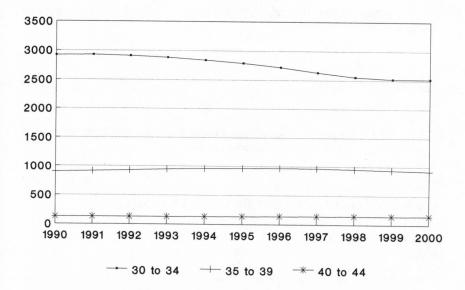

**———•——— 30 to 34    ——+—— 35 to 39    ——*—— 40 to 44**

*Figure 12B.7.  Birth Projection 1990–2000
Residents, Monroe County, NY*

trends. First, they have affected mostly white, suburban women, and not the city's minority women, who did not experience a parallel increase in career opportunities and the change toward an older age at child-bearing. Social cleavages have increased—national trends indicate that minority childbearing is predominantly nonmarital and heavily concentrated in the teen years. A second aspect of importance for health planning is that the above observations only hold for the residents of Monroe County. Rochester hospitals experienced more of a baby boom than these charts indicate. The reason is the increased population in the surrounding counties. Newborns from surrounding counties dramatically increased in the 1980s as rural hospitals closed and fewer physicians in these counties provided obstetric care. While we are confident about the projected decline of live births for Monroe County residents, there is no basis for the same confidence in making projections for the neighboring counties. If the increase from adjacent counties is only a spillover from former Rochester residents moving into these newly developing counties, we could plan for the trend easily. If the increase is due to further reduction of obstetric services in these counties, the change cannot be predicted. Hospitals in Rochester may not see much of a decline in deliveries, but schools will begin to see a decline in enrollments in the mid-1990s. Individual hospitals will be differentially affected by the projected decline in newborns, depending on their service areas. Those serving Monroe County suburbs will notice the decline most.

*REFERENCE*

SELL, R.
1991   "Live Birth Projection for Monroe County Residents, 1990–2000." Rochester, New York: Center for Governmental Research.

## C. INDUCED ABORTIONS: CONTROVERSIES UNRESOLVED

KLAUS J. ROGHMANN

On July 1, 1970, New York State liberalized laws to allow abortions upon request. When federal funds for Medicaid abortions were withdrawn, the state compensated with its own funds. Abortions are reported to the State Office of Vital Statistics on fetal death certificates and allow easy monitoring. Annual reports from the State Office of Vital Statistics include abortion figures. These data (Figure 12C.1) are remarkable in their stability over this nearly 20-year period.

The annual number of abortions quickly reached over 3,000 (1972) and remained at that level with only minor changes. During the baby bust years, the level reached 3,500, and during the economic recession of 1981–82 it reached nearly 3,800. For most of the 20-year period, services were provided in a supportive environment in spite of the ongoing political debate in which fundamental differences were vehemently aired without resolution. The normal political process aimed at reaching compromise apparently does not work in this debate. More recently, a militant antiabortion faction has opted for civil disobedience and patient harassment as their strategies. There will be no end to this debate until a more fundamental decision through a referendum or constitutional amendment is reached.

An additional problem that recently arose is that abortions are no longer available to Medicaid patients. Medicaid fees are so low that physicians in Monroe County no longer accept Medicaid patients. Medicaid patients now have to be referred to Buffalo for abortions, but few teenagers follow through on those referrals.

Although live births are divided about 50:50 between city and sub-

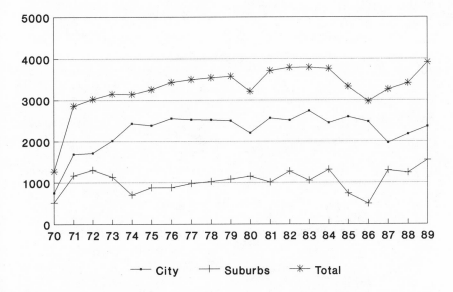

      —•— City      —+— Suburbs      —*— Total

*Figure 12C.1.   Induced Abortions since July 1, 1970*
*Residents, Monroe County, NY*

urbs, reported abortions are divided 66:33, reflecting the younger, poorer, and different ethnic composition of the city. Some of these observed differences may be due to the quality of reporting, with suburban providers underreporting their caseload. Nevertheless, if we examine the geographic distribution of abortions in relation to all pregnancies (live births plus abortions), about 30% of all pregnancies are terminated in the city, but only 15% in the suburbs (Figure 12C.2).

A closer examination by age in city and suburbs (Figure 12C.3) suggests that age is the major determinant of the abortion decision: pregnancies too early or too late in the life cycle are more likely to be terminated, both in the city and the suburbs, although this pattern is much more pronounced for the suburbs than for the city.

The lowest termination rate is in the 30–34 year age range, and the highest in the 10–14 year age group. These low rates reflect more experienced and more sophisticated family planning in the 25–34 year olds, which is in turn, a function of age and health care accessibility.

The more moderate curvilinear pattern for the city is due to a more complex pattern for nonwhites. First, their fertility at younger ages is a multiple of that observed for whites. For pregnancies among women under 15 years of age, nonwhites make up 72% of all live births in the county and nearly 80% of all abortions, although nonwhites only make up 17% of the total population in this age group. Second, most of the

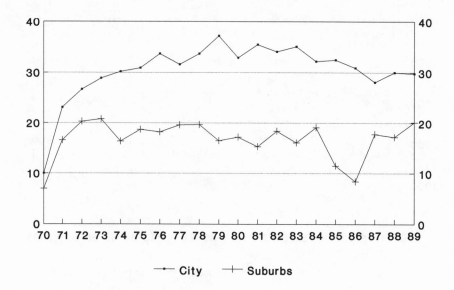

*Figure 12C.2.  Pregnancy Termination Rates*
*Residents, Monroe County, NY*

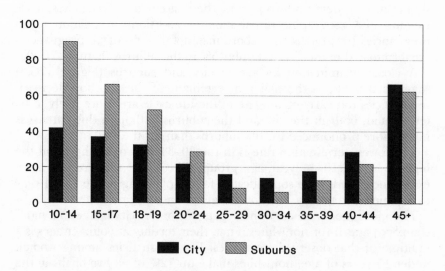

*Figure 12C.3.  Pregnancy Termination Rates by Age and Area of Residence*
*Monroe County, NY 1986 and 1987*

nonwhite pregnancies in the 15–17 year age group are considered desirable, that is, carried to term, in the city population. Only 22% of nonwhite pregnancies of 15–17 year olds in the city are terminated, compared to 66% of all pregnancies occurring among suburban whites in this age group. As a result, there is not the same curvilinear relationship with age as is observed in the white population (Figure 12C.4). Up to age 19, whites have higher termination rates than nonwhites; from age 20 up nonwhites have higher rates.

Elimination of the abortion option would above all increase white teenage childbearing. If effectively eliminated for all, it would immediately restore us to the baby boom years of the 1960s. Hospitals would have to expand their obstetric units. Medical schools would have to increase their training of obstetricians greatly. Given the current shortage of obstetricians and obstetric beds, a crisis in obstetric services would be the immediate result. However, nobody expects such a scenario. History suggests a more frightful alternative, namely that safe and legal abortions would be replaced by unsafe and illegal abortions. A major setback for maternal and child health would be the result.


## D. INFANT MORTALITY: MAJOR SOCIOECONOMIC DIFFERENCES REMAIN

KLAUS J. ROGHMANN


Public policy debates primarily rely on infant mortality as a key indicator of child health. Figure 12D.1 presents the number of infant deaths per 1,000 live births in the city and suburbs of the Rochester community over a 20-year period.

While the figure shows a clear downward trend, there are also a few reservations and concerns to observe. First, even with annual birth cohorts above 10,000, the data show erratic fluctuations from year to year that demonstrate the multicausal nature of infant mortality. Factors like the economy, weather, long-term trends, and pure chance, affect these yearly rates, as do access, availability, and quality of health services. There are "good" years and "bad" years for infant mortality that are difficult to explain. Nineteen eighty-five was a very good year. Nineteen eighty-three was a bad year. Such difficulties become more pronounced when racial or ethnic subgroups are examined. Most analyses, therefore, limit themselves to white and nonwhite differences.

Second, in spite of all reservations about the data, infant deaths in the

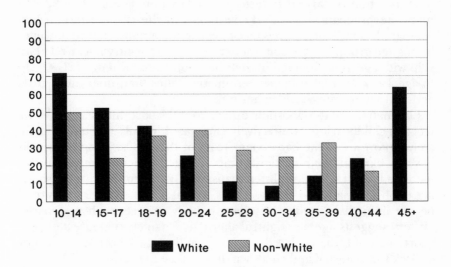

*Figure 12C.4.   Pregnancy Termination Rates by Age and Race
Monroe County, NY 1986 and 1987*

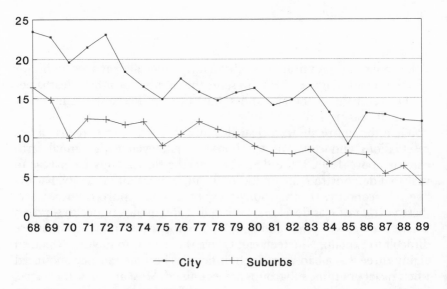

*Figure 12D.1.   Infant Mortality since 1968
Monroe County, NY*

county dropped from over 250 in the late 1960s to about 100 in the late 1980s, or by about 60%. Even considering the smaller number of live births in the later years, the decline was still about 50% and occurred both in the suburbs and the city. Comparing the trends for both areas, it appears that city rates followed suburban rates with a lag of about 10 years. Separate figures for whites and nonwhites by area of residence for longer periods are hard to obtain, which makes it difficult to separate socioeconomic from racial trends.

In order to estimate the racial component in city/suburbs comparison, we aggregated the data for 1986 through 1988 for greater stability, and computed city and suburban rates for both whites and non-whites (Table 12D.1).

City residents experienced a twofold higher infant mortality (12.3/6.6) than suburban residents, and nonwhites experienced a twofold higher infant mortality (15.8/7.5) than whites. However, there also was an interaction effect between race and area of residence. In the suburbs, nonwhites had a *lower* infant mortality, whereas in the city, nonwhites had a *higher* infant mortality.

The extremely low infant mortality of 5.3 for suburban nonwhites may be due to the selective migration of the healthiest nonwhites to the suburbs, to a different ethnic composition of nonwhites in the suburbs, or simply to random fluctuation in such small numbers. If we only compare cells with reasonably large numbers, the effect of living in the city is a 36% increase in infant mortality for whites (9.1 versus 6.7). City dwelling nonwhites show a 87% increase over city dwelling whites (17.0 versus 9.1). As a result, the cumulative effect of living in the city *and* being nonwhite is a 153% increase, that is, the rate for nonwhite city

*Table 12D.1. Infant Mortality by Race and Area of Residence, Monroe County, 1986–1988*

|         |              | Whites | NonWhites | Total  |
|---------|--------------|--------|-----------|--------|
| City    | Live births  | 9,264  | 6,395     | 15,659 |
|         | Infant deaths| 84     | 109       | 193    |
|         | Rate         | 9.1    | 17.0      | 12.3   |
| Suburbs | Live births  | 16,566 | 749       | 17,315 |
|         | Infant deaths| 111    | 4         | 115    |
|         | Rate         | 6.7    | 5.3       | 6.6    |
| Total   | Live births  | 25,830 | 7,144     | 32,974 |
|         | Infant deaths| 195    | 113       | 308    |
|         | Rate         | 7.5    | 15.8      | 9.3    |

398 Facts and Figures: The Setting and the Problems

dwellers (17.0/1000) is 2.53 larger than for white suburbanites (6.7/1000).

Given the restriction to a single community and a 3-year period, the above comparisons are difficult to interpret. First, blacks in Rochester are the largest group of nonwhites (85%), but in the suburbs, they comprise only 51% of all nonwhites. Second, the city-suburb distinction mostly reflects socioeconomic differences, yet does not measure this difference well. The calculated rates mostly reflect the arbitrary nature of the categories selected, rather than inherent properties of citydwelling or being nonwhite. Not surprisingly then, the success story of a greatly reduced infant mortality has not received much attention. Rather, attention has continued to be focused on the remaining differences. Racial and ethnic differences remain and continue to be difficult to evaluate. The community level remains the best place to attack these problems, yet from an epidemiological point, they also remain the most difficult to study.

## E. FACILITIES AND MANPOWER: FEWER HOSPITAL BEDS, BUT MORE DOCTORS

KLAUS J. ROGHMANN

Statistics on health facilities and health manpower are usually presented to describe the structure of a health care market, but can be misleading. Rates per population, computed on a county basis, ignore that hospital service areas and the areas covered by county boundaries are not identical. The available figures for the Rochester community reflect well national trends toward continuously fewer hospital beds per population and a greater supply of physicians. Rochester is actually ahead of these national trends, with a bed/population ratio below the national average and far below the high ratio of New York State and the Northeast.

Table 12E.1 presents official hospital statistics from 1960 to 1985, with the 1960 and 1970 figures only pertaining to Rochester City (which then included all hospitals located in the county). Smaller hospitals disappeared, usually through merger with larger ones. The number of beds in Monroe County declined 40%, from 6,830 in 1960 to 4,128 in 1985, in spite of an increasing population. The 1985 rate of 588 beds per 100,000 population compares well with the national average of 544, and was well below the average of 646 for all New York State SMAs. The historical Monroe County data, however, ignore the difficult issue

*Table 12E.1    Hospital Beds in Rochester SMA*

| County | Year | Hospitals | Beds | Beds/100,000 |
|--------|------|-----------|------|--------------|
| Monroe | 1960 | 12 | 6,830 | 1,165 |
|  | 1970 | 10 | 6,250 | 878 |
|  | 1980 | 10 | 4,319 | 615 |
|  | 1985 | 9 | 4,128 | 588 |
| Livingston | 1980 | 1 | 85 | 149 |
|  | 1985 | 1 | 85 | 146 |
| Ontario* | 1980 | 3 | 786 | 811 |
|  | 1985 | 3 | 696 | 753 |
| Orleans | 1980 | 2 | 179 | 465 |
|  | 1985 | 2 | 179 | 458 |
| Wayne | 1980 | 2 | 258 | 305 |
|  | 1985 | 2 | 258 | 295 |
| Total SMA* | 1980 | 19 | 6,425 | 579 |
|  | 1985 | 18 | 6,146 | 545 |
| NY State | 1980 | 351 | 127,818 | 728 |
|  | 1985 | 328 | 114,928 | 646 |
| U.S. | 1980 | 7,123 | 1,383,789 | 611 |
|  | 1985 | 7,024 | 1,322,149 | 544 |

*Source:* County and City Data Book, 1962, 1972, 1983, 1988 (Washington, DC: U.S. Department of Commerce, Bureau of the Census).
*Excluding the VA hospital for long-term psychiatric patients

of population denominators referred to above. Rochester hospitals serve a much larger population than just urban Monroe County, and the true rate is even lower.

The hospitals and beds of the 5 adjacent counties included in the census definition of the Rochester SMA are also presented, both for 1980 and 1985. The great variation of county rates reflects the incongruence of county and service populations. Excluding the 800-bed VA hospital from the statistics results in a lower rate for the SMA than quoted above for Monroe County. The SMA rate in 1985 was only 545 beds/100,000, about the same as the national average of 544 and far below the New York State average of 646. Rochester, in terms of the bed/population ratio, reflects the national average rather than that of the Northeast of the country.

Aggregate figures on facilities only provide a good comparative background. Individual admissions or discharge data, by place of service and patient origin are needed for a service assessment of a community. In the original edition, we depended on Blue Cross claims data for such assessments because Blue Cross covered some 90% of all children, thus providing good denominator and numerator data. In the 1980s this was no longer true, due to the expansion of HMOs and IPAs, but another data source became available in 1980. The State Planning and Research Cooperative System (SPARCS) was established to keep track of all inpatient services in New York, independent of payer. Table 12E.2 gives the statistics on all pediatric admissions by hospital in the Rochester SMA based on this source.

Pediatric discharges (Table 12E.2) cover all patients 14 years or younger exclusive of nursery discharges, obstetrical discharges, and psychiatric services. Pediatric discharges were defined by patient age, not clinical service. Many hospitals provide surgical care, like ear/nose/throat or eye surgery, as well as emergency care for children in Rochester. But actual pediatric care is concentrated at Strong Memorial and Rochester General Hospitals in the urban county, and at the community hospitals in the rural counties. Strong Memorial Hospital provided about 42% of all inpatient care days in the SMA, followed by Rochester General Hospital with another 15%. The two are the University of Rochester clinical centers serving the area.

The analysis by patient origin is equally important. The SMA's hospitals generated 11,265 pediatric discharges, but SMA's residents only consumed 10,300; that is, nearly 1,000 admissions were to children living outside its borders. The analysis by individual counties shows even greater discrepancies. Monroe County produced 7,334 pediatric inpatient services, but consumed only 5,728. Monroe County has not only one of the lowest bed/population ratios, it also uses many of them to serve surrounding counties: 22% of its discharges in the pediatric age group were for residents of neighboring counties. The SPARCS files have opened up a data source of much greater detail and relevance than anything that was available 20 years ago. Comparative analyses with other areas in the country are now possible (Perrin et al., 1989). Knowledge of population denominators, together with data on patient flows, allow detailed epidemiological studies that were not possible 20 years ago.

Data on ambulatory services are more difficult to obtain, but data on physician supply is a rough substitute. There are two sources for historical data on physician supply for the SMA—first the New York

*Table 12E.2. Pediatric\* Discharges, Rochester, SMA, 1980 (by patient origin and location of hospital)*

| Location of Hospital | Patient Origin | | | | | |
|---|---|---|---|---|---|---|
| | Livingston | Monroe | Ontario | Orleans | Wayne | Non-SMA |
| *Livingston* | | | | | | |
| Noyes | 193 | — | — | — | — | 126 |
| *Monroe* | | | | | | |
| Highland | 41 | 307 | 14 | 2 | 4 | 30 |
| Lakeside | — | 114 | — | 30 | — | 9 |
| Park Ridge | 1 | 123 | — | — | 3 | 24 |
| Rochester Gen. | 32 | 1,816 | 53 | 34 | 156 | 44 |
| St. Mary's | 6 | 325 | 5 | 1 | 5 | 7 |
| Strong Medical | 161 | 1,982 | 160 | 49 | 208 | 331 |
| Genesee | 61 | 1,038 | 34 | 11 | 69 | 47 |
| *Ontario* | | | | | | |
| Clifton Springs | — | — | 68 | — | 101 | 14 |
| F.F. Thompson | 25 | — | 319 | — | 42 | 39 |
| Geneva General | — | — | 327 | — | 73 | 639 |
| *Orleans* | | | | | | |
| Arnold Gregory | — | — | — | 309 | — | 11 |
| Medina | — | — | — | 297 | — | 70 |
| *Wayne* | | | | | | |
| Myers | — | — | — | — | 178 | 7 |
| Newark | — | — | 52 | — | 1,014 | 79 |
| Non-SMA | 204 | 113 | 20 | 159 | 5 | N/A |
| Total | 724 | 5,728 | 1,052 | 892 | 1,904 | 1,477 |

\*All patients, age 14 years and younger, excluding newborn, obstetrical, or psychiatric categories

State reports on licensed physicians, and second, the AMA Physician Masterfile kept by the AMA since 1906 (Table 12E.3).

Licensed physicians increased in the SMA from 1,487 in 1969 to 1,950 in 1979, and to 2,747 in 1988. Most (87% in 1988) of the physicians reside in Monroe County, where the number of licensed MDs nearly doubled over the past 20 years. The AMA Masterfile, however, is more relevant for our purposes. It excludes federal physicians (like those staffing the VA hospital) and only counts active physicians, by address of practice, rather than all licensed physicians. As Table 12E.3 shows, physician supply in the SMA, and especially for urban Monroe County, is generous and above the national average. In 1985, the SMA rate was 257/100,000, compared to 197/100,000 for the total United States and 286/100,000 for New York State, putting the community above the national rate, but below the high rate typical for the Northeast of the country.

In short, Rochester has experienced a major shift over the last 20 years from reliance on inpatient care to reliance on outpatient care.

*REFERENCES*

PERRIN, J.M., HOLMER, C.J., BERWICK, D.M., WOLF, A.D., FREEMAN, J.L., and WENNBERG, J.E.
  1989  "Variations in Rates of Hospitalization of Children in Three Urban Communities." *NEJM*, 320 (18):1183–1187.

*Table 12E.3.  Active, Non-Federal Physicians in Rochester SMA, 1980, 1985*

| County | 1980 | | 1985 | |
|---|---|---|---|---|
| | Number | Rate/100,000 | Number | Rate/100,000 |
| Livingston | 43 | 75 | 42 | 72 |
| Monroe | 2,039 | 290 | 2,253 | 320 |
| Ontario | 123 | 138 | 127 | 137 |
| Orleans | 28 | 73 | 33 | 84 |
| Wayne | 69 | 82 | 69 | 79 |
| Total SMA | 2,302 | 237 | 2,524 | 257 |
| N.Y. State | 43,413 | 247 | 50,943 | 286 |
| U.S. | 393,407 | 174 | 470,434 | 197 |

*Source:* County and City Data Book, 1983, 1988 (Washington, DC: U.S. Department of Commerce, Bureau of the Census).

403

# CHAPTER THIRTEEN

# The New Health Care Market: Health Services for Children

This chapter spells out some of the major changes that occurred in our orientation toward the analysis of utilization data. Section 13A spells out how the academic orientation imported from medical sociology has shifted toward a practical orientation in terms of local health planning and evaluation research. Our focus has changed. Maximizing explained variance in patient behavior is no longer our goal. Nor is it crucial to generalize to national populations. A precise understanding of events on the local level in relation to new health plans or new services has taken priority.

Section 13B gives an example in the field of ambulatory pediatrics, where managed care under the Independent Practitioner Association (IPA) auspices has led to a marked increase in services in spite of the official goal to reduce costs. Section 13C gives an example of using local databases to evaluate a new medical service—neonatal intensive care—in terms of later excess utilization for inpatient care. Both show how the local community can be used as a laboratory for health services research to better understand services to children. We see this research as extensions of our earlier work, enhanced by a better understanding of our goals.

## A. MODELS OF HEALTH AND ILLNESS BEHAVIOR: FROM MEDICAL SOCIOLOGY TO CLINICAL EPIDEMIOLOGY

KLAUS J. ROGHMANN

The 1975 report on community child health was mostly descriptive. We used a "model" (p. 8) of a local health care market as a checklist to ensure that we had not overlooked any major components. This model also helped structure the narrative and label the various segments of the book. It was a very pragmatic use of the term "model."

At that time, there was an increasing emphasis in the academic literature on two other uses of the term "model." The first was prevalent in medical sociology, where the term was used to encompass theoretical frameworks of health and illness behavior. These models were typically given the names of their proponents, such as the Rosenstock model (Rosenstock, 1966), the Suchman model (Suchman, 1965; 1967) or the Andersen model (Andersen, 1968; Andersen and Newman, 1973). They incorporated sociologic insights and were based on intensive, qualitative studies of a few cases, or careful studies by participant or nonparticipant observers. They were strongly influenced by social psychology and social anthropology. These models provided better insights, perspectives, and understanding, and clarified social science terms like "health and illness behavior."

The second use of the term "model" came from statistics and was increasingly used in survey and econometric analysis. Political scientists, sociologists, and economists incorporated multivariate analysis into their quantitative approach to extensive studies of large samples. In this context, the term "model" stood for an equation relating a dependent variable to a set of independent variables. Models were developed by adding or dropping variables on the basis of statistical evaluations and were evaluated according to the proportion of variance they accounted for. Researchers were concerned with confounding, and masking effects, as well as with mediating and interaction effects. Low explained variance was attributed both to measurement error and errors in prediction. This statistical approach finally led to systems of equations to represent underlying causal processes and pathways.

During the 1960s, the obvious challenge was to bring the qualitative and quantitative approaches together to quantify what had been learned from qualitative studies. We responded to the challenge by attempting to operationalize most of the sociological variables, and to link them to four measures of physician utilization as dependent variables: at least 1 doctor visit in last 2 weeks; any doctor visit over the last 12 months; type of doctor visit—preventive; and type of doctor visit—private. Few significant correlations were found, and no summary models were presented. Hence we concluded, "There is considerable doubt . . . about how to interpret results from high-level analysis when low-level analysis fail to" (p. 140) confirm the component relationships. True, clear relationships with "enabling" factors like socioeconomic status and illness were found, but this hardly warranted a new model for the utilization of pediatric services beyond our simple pragmatic use of the term. It was more appropriate to relinquish the attempt to quantify the existing sociological models and retreat to our pragmatic use of the term for health planning and program evaluation.

This response to these negative findings now appears to have a larger following. One key article (Mechanic, 1979), to be referred to again in the chapters that follow, examined similar early negative findings. For example, Andersen et al. (1975) had used their model in a 1971 survey of 3,880 families, with 11,822 people, but even with many predictors in the equation, they were only able to explain 16% to 25% of the variance in health care utilization. In 1975, a replication using a 7,787-person sample explained 22% of the variance (Andersen and Aday, 1978). Not surprisingly, in both cases the best predictors of use were indicators of bad health. An international collaborative study (Kohn and White, 1976) used 21 predictor variables but only explained 4% to 10% of the variance in physician utilization by adults. Using 1971–1973 National Health Interview Survey data, Wolinsky (1978) explained between 9% and 12% of the utilization variance, and again, most was attributed to recent morbidity. Mechanic reluctantly concluded that attempts to explain illness behavior with multivariate analyses of large samples have failed. Although some (e.g., Rundall, 1981), argued that there has been an incomplete translation of theory into statistical testing (interactions vs. main effect), few further research efforts to translate sociological models into quantitative equations have been attempted.

Early attempts to translate general explanations of patient behavior, like physician utilization, into statistical models have failed. It appears to be more appropriate to treat the previous general models as paradigms for the development of more specific models explaining specific behaviors like use of preventive dental care, the management of hypertension, or use of birth control by teenagers. Because these health behaviors have different determinants, any "one model fits all" approach is bound to fail. Nevertheless, the "classic" formulations still provide guidance in the development of specific theories (Glanz and Lewis et al., 1990).

An alternative response to the negative findings is to abandon the notion that fairly stable personal characteristics, like attitudes, are key determinants of physician utilization. Instead, microprocesses in illness behaviors (processual approach) such as stressful daily events, illness circumstances, and individual coping resources were conceptualized as more important. Data from daily diary entries were therefore analyzed for dynamic processes. It soon became evident that standard statistical procedures were insufficient to capture the wealth of diary information. Even when better statistical procedures were adopted, the complexities of the analyses did not lend themselves to publication in journal articles. It appears that the richness of our understanding of ongoing social processes, as exhibited in classic sociological readings, as well as in the case descriptions of clinicians, is still beyond the statistical modeling techniques and psychometric assessment tools currently available. However, the challenge still remains to bridge these gaps and arrive at approaches that overcome these limitations.

What we called the "stress model" of utilization behavior in the original edition pointed in that direction. The explosion of research on stress and health, with emphasis on modifiers like social support and individual coping skills, are seen as support for that interpretation. The model emphasizes links between stress and physiological processes such as antibody levels, hormone response, dietary intake, or weight gain. It also focuses on specific outcomes in specific situations, such as a stress model of teenage pregnancy. Laying the groundwork for the typical modern survey with repeated follow-ups and record cross-linkages, such a model offers a compromise between the cross-sectional survey and the detailed 4-week daily diary entry.

A few points further elaborated in the utilization section are worth mentioning. National survey designs and public access file availability have revolutionized opportunities in medical care research. Instead of individual researchers only studying their own small databases, national user groups now exist for most national surveys, such as the National Longitudinal Survey of Youth or the annual National Health Interview Survey, with its many supplements. National databases are available at minimal cost on CD-ROM. Local data bases (like those kept in the General Pediatric Research Unit in Rochester) include communitywide hospital data, cumulative birth certificate files, and computerized medical records covering child visits since birth for selected high-risk groups or selected practices. Survey data are linked with utilization histories as captured in data systems such as the Medicaid Medical Information System. Physician utilization is well measured, and the determinants are much better understood. Our earlier attempts to qualify sociological models may have been overly ambitious, but today's "successes" would not have been possible without understanding the "failures" of the past. More important, our goals have also shifted. We no longer focus on such abstract terms as patient behaviors but on specific types of patient and provider behaviors in localized markets where interventions are feasible.

*REFERENCES*

ANDERSON, RONALD
 1968   *A Behavioral Model of Families. Use of Health Services*, Research Series No. 25. Chicago: Center for Health Administration Studies. University of Chicago.

ANDERSEN, R., and NEWMAN, J. F.
  1973  "Societal and Individual Determinants of Medical Care Utilization in the United
         States." *Milbank Memorial Fund Quarterly*, 51:95–124.

ANDERSEN, R. KRAVITZ, J., and ANDERSON, O. W.
  1975  *Equity in Health Services: Empirical Analysis in Social Policy.* Cambridge: Ballinger.

ANDERSEN, R., and ADAY, L. A.
  1978  "Access to Medical Care in the U.S.: Realized and Potential." *Medical Care*,
         16:533–46.

GLANZ, K., LEWIS, F. M., and RIMER, B. K. (Editors)
  1990  "Health Behavior and Health Education." San Francisco: Jossey-Bass Publica-
         tions.

KOHN, R. and WHITE, K. L. (Ed.)
  1976  "Health Care—An International Study: Report of the World Health Organiza-
         tion/International Study of Medical Care Utilization." London: Oxford Univer-
         sity Press.

MECHANIC, DAVID
  1979  "Correlates of Physician Utilization: Why do Major Multivariate Studies of
         Physician Utilization Find Trivial Psychosocial and Organizational Effects?"
         *Journal of Health and Social Behavior*, 20:387–396.

ROSENSTOCK, IRWIN M.
  1966  "Why People Use Health Services." *Milbank Memorial Fund Quarterly*, 2, 44:94–
         127.

RUNDALL, THOMAS G.
  1981  "Suggestions for Improving the Behavioral Model of Physician Utilization."
         *Journal of Health and Social Behavior*, 22:103–104.

SUCHMAN, EDWARD A.
  1965  "Social Patterns of Illness and Medical Care." *Journal of Health and Human
         Behavior*, 6:2–16.

SUCHMAN, EDWARD A.
  1967  "Preventive Health Behavior: A Model for Research on Community Health
         Campaigns." *Journal of Health and Human Behavior*, 8:197–209.

WOLINSKY, F. D.
  1978  "Assessing the Effects of Predisposing, Enabling, and Illness-Morbidity Charac-
         teristics on Health Service Utilization." *Journal of Health and Social Behavior*,
         19:384–396.

## B. THE UTILIZATION OF HEALTH SERVICES—AMBULATORY CARE: FROM THE STUDY OF PATIENT BEHAVIOR TO THE STUDY OF SYSTEM IMPACT

KLAUS J. ROGHMANN
AND
PETER G. SZILAGYI

From our current vantage point, this approach toward measuring utilization in the earlier studies may appear trivial or naive. True, we used

multiple points in time to detect trends. Patient diaries and personal interviews served to provide information. At that time, private, fee-for-service practice dominated the ambulatory-care sector. Physician surveys gave provider data on ambulatory care. Blue Cross and Medicaid together covered nearly all hospital services and thus yielded solid inpatient data. There were, however, large differences in the estimates derived from the supplier and consumer responses, leaving no illusion about their accuracy. Yet the sources of error were easy to locate and adjustments could be made.

Some trends were clearly visible: Children were becoming healthier; the manpower crunch was over. The ever increasing use of the emergency room for acute care by inner-city children had stopped largely due to the development of a network of health centers. Our focus on the community, where practitioners and families interact in the "health services market," kept things in perspective. In spite of the crisis atmosphere of those years, our diagnosis was optimistic.

As in most such assessments, we were both right and wrong. Inpatient services had become concentrated in the medical center and were required less often for common acute problems. Medicaid continued to expand to address the health problems of the poor. While some problems, like teenage pregnancy, continued to be a major focus, several completely new concerns arose that demanded attention. Twenty years ago, intensive care for newborns was in its infancy, University Affiliated Programs for Developmental Disorders (UAPDDs) were still to come, and prenatal diagnosis of birth defects was not yet feasible. The involvement of the federal government in the care of handicapped children (PL 94-142) was still a decade away. The insurance industry had not yet begun to expand into the health care field through managed care in an effort to contain costs. Consequently, the trends that we documented at that time were only intermediate stages of what was to follow.

In medical sociology, general optimism prevailed. It was believed that a better understanding of patient behavior was imminent and would contribute to improving the organization of health care. Concepts of health and illness behavior, including utilization behavior, received increased attention. Yet the hoped-for "breakthrough" never came.

In its title, David Mechanic's classic article "Correlates of Physician Utilization: Why Do Major Multivariate Studies of Physician Utilization Find Trivial Psychosocial and Organizational Effects" (1979) reflects the disappointment. A follow-up review "Medical Sociology: Some Tensions Among Theory, Method and Substance" (Mechanic, 1989) continued the debate, and demonstrated that the issue is still alive. While quantitative and qualitative researchers produce divergent findings, quantitative studies dominate. What can be done to solve these problems? The imprecision of measurement of utilization behavior, so vividly experienced in our work 20 years ago, is a major stumbling block. Retaining the consumer perspective, Mechanic (1989) proposes a triangulation of methods, with diary data serving as the bridge between the qualitative and quantitative information, as one solution. While the different methodologies for studying utilization behavior pose a clear difficulty, these obstacles should not prevent taking a stand on the issue. Changing to provider data gives more precision but contributes little to explaining patient behavior.

Our view during the early research, reconfirmed during later work, was that the conceptual frameworks available at that time were too nonspecific to provide more than an analytic paradigm. They provided a way to think about phenomena that had to be further specified with concrete theories during actual work on a problem (see Section A. "Models of Health and Illness Behavior"). For different components of the paradigm to be activated, specific research has to define them. Utilization behavior under different payment mechanisms must be considered in relation to economic factors, including consumer and provider incentives. Explaining acceptance of a prenatal diagnosis of a birth defect has to focus on patients' strategies for coping with uncertainty about rare, but disastrous events, or with the possibility of aborting a defective fetus. What we know about physician behavior under uncertainty may not provide a good paradigm for predicting patient behavior under such conditions. The more medicine expands into a broader mosaic of human services, the less a simple paradigm about a diffuse illness or health concept can be applicable and the more illness-specific theories will be needed.

This view has, of course, major implications for measurement needs. For the identification of major trends in the aggregate, even the rough methods from 20 years ago are sufficient. Much greater precision is needed for predictions at the individual level. For example, we must know *what* services were utilized, not just *that* services were utilized. There are clearly different predictors for well child visits than for acute illness visits. Severity is a key predictor for most illness visits, while distress is the main factor for the timing of visits. Will respondents, in later interviews, recall the circumstances, including their feelings of distress, of their doctor visits? Survey research quickly reaches its limit when recording and analyzing such details. Diaries go much further in capturing the sequencing of important events. Qualitative research goes into still greater detail. The statistical methods for testing the details of qualitative analysis are still undeveloped. What can be recommended?

Some developments over the last 2 decades may contain part of the answer, but they may not yet be fully recognized or reflected in the structure of our academic institutions. The old type of utilization survey conducted with students from social science departments is probably dead. We do not anticipate a replication of the Rochester Child Health Surveys done 20 years ago. Detailed home interviews with random samples of households have become prohibitively expensive. Secondary data analysis will largely replace much of this type of research. "It is now not uncommon to find talented researchers in mid-career who have never had the experience of designing their own study or gathering new data" (Mechanic, 1989:147).

The National Health Interview Survey, for example, with its various supplements, provides excellent raw data for the academic community to analyze. Data files are well documented and easily accessible. Furthermore, academic advisory committees provide input for the surveys conducted by the National Center for Health Statistics. The result has been a split into 2 styles of research: one dominated by independent, specialized studies of small samples, using group interviews, or other qualitative methods; the other using mail or telephone surveys of large samples rather than detailed personal interviews, with obvious limitations on what is obtainable. Questionnaires have been replaced by program modules for use in telephone surveys, or on lap-top computers for the few large-scale personal interviews still conducted by the federal government.

Utilization data—specific counts of events like admissions or doctors visits—are now mostly studied using existing data bases. This can be done by data abstraction from medical charts, direct access to computerized files of birth and death certificates, or the analysis of hospital claims to insurance firms. Group practices, Health Maintenance Organizations (HMOs), Independent Practice Associations (IPAs), and insurance companies maintain encounter files for administrative purposes. None of these files include the attitudinal and detailed demographic measures that the sociologist often uses as explanatory variables. But in terms of details about the actual number of services, costs, and diagnoses, they are better and more reliable than what a retrospective survey, limited by patient recall, can provide.

With the change in methodology has also come a change in the status of researchers. It is more likely that the health care researcher is now part of a team in a medical center than an academic scholar in a liberal arts institution. The sociologist has become a social epidemiologist, in charge of specific research projects, collaborating with clinical faculty, and training postdoctoral fellows in research techniques. The PhD in medical school departments will always remain in a "staff" position and may never have the same "line" authority as the clinical physician. Yet the demand for his/her skills offers opportunities to create a new and important role and career path for the academic medical sociologist.

Whether this new role will become institutionalized and receive explicit recognition is still uncertain. If sociologists fail to meet the need for collaborative researchers, academic physicians will acquire basic social science research skills during their fellowship years or develop research programs with sociologically trained assistants. The openness of the Department of Pediatrics at the University of Rochester toward sociologists and other social scientists has been one of its greatest strengths. Community pediatrics, with its multidisciplinary orientation, can be seen as a professional philosophy, operating in a clinical department that fosters medical care research with a community orientation.

There are two examples of current ambulatory utilization studies in Rochester that illuminate collaborative research using precise data to answer specific questions. The first is an evaluation of the impact of prepaid ambulatory care, and the second is the long-term effect of perinatal morbidity.

## IPA Effects

In the 1980s, one of the most dramatic changes in the Rochester health care market, and in the nation, was the rapid expansion of prepaid ambulatory care plans, especially Independent Practitioners Associations (IPAs). In contrast to the staff-model HMOs with a closed panel of physicians, patients sign up with doctors in private practice. As these IPA panels include over 80% of all providers, they usually include the patient's current provider, whom they will continue to see, but the IPA patient no longer receives that doctor's bill. Instead, the bill is sent directly to the IPA, which pays member physicians on a fee-for-service (FFS) basis. The provider functions as a patient care manager—one who, together with the other physicians on the panel, is at financial risk for overutilization. Should the FFS payments to member physicians exceed premium intakes, the deficit has to be shared. The IPA doctor is thus supposed to optimize (reduce) care to contain costs. The assumption is that patient behavior does not change.

An alternative argument is that such prepaid plans remove the price barriers that normally regulate demand, with patient behavior changing in the direction of increasing demand. Physician behavior may continue in the old principle of "provide generously what creates no out-of-pocket expenses" for the patient, rather than maximizing plan goals from which the provider profits only indirectly. The validity of these opposing arguments was tested through utilization research of the new kind (Szilagyi et al., 1990).

We selected a large suburban group practice of five pediatricians serving about 14,000 children. The only major change in the practice over the last 10 years had been the gradual increase of prepaid ambulatory care during the 1980s. The IPAs constantly monitor the utilization behavior of their panel of physicians to achieve compliance with plan objectives. One of the IPAs, with permission of the practitioners, released some basic utilization data on the 5 pediatricians of this group practice (1987—Medical Utilization Profile). Within this plan, the group cared for nearly 2,600 children who received 11,000 primary care visits and 3,100 specialty care visits from them in 1987. These children also made 148 emergency room visits and had 125 hospital admissions in 1987. Of the 82 pediatricians on the IPA panel, this group was close to the middle of the cost distribution.

A retrospective cohort study was designed to assess the effects of IPA enrollment in this practice. All children switching from self pay on fee-for-service basis for ambulatory care to prepaid ambulatory care in an IPA between 1980 and 1987 qualified. For each patient who switched to prepaid care, a matched control who remained on self pay was selected from the patient registration file. Matching was based on age (within 3 months), sex of the child, and zip code. Zip code areas are reasonably homogeneous in terms of neighborhood socioeconomic status and substituted for individual matching on socioeconomic status.

There were 902 possible pairs, but complete final data could only be obtained on 640 pairs. Note that whenever one member of a pair dropped out for any reason, its counterpart also had to be discarded. For the 1,280 children in the study, all utilization over a 2-year period was obtained. For cases (IPA enrollees) chart abstraction was for 1 year before the switch and 1 year after the switch. For controls, the parallel 2-year period was selected. The children were an average age of 8.5 years and averaged 1.5 sibs. About 8.7% of the children had a chronic illness, as did about 6.1% of their sibs. Only one significant difference could be found between IPA and self pay patients before the switch: 15% of IPA patients had ongoing referrals, while only 8.4% of self pay patients had ongoing referrals. Self selection of patients on the basis of illness therefore was not controlled.

*Table 13B.1* summarizes the findings of this study. IPA patients had significantly more acute and weekend visits, even before joining the plan. They also had more chronic illness visits, laboratory services, and referrals than the controls, but the differences did not reach significance using standard formulas for random samples for these types of utilization. This finding provided reasonable evidence that those with a higher propensity to seek care are more likely to join prepayment plans (self selection process in open-enrollment markets). After joining the IPA, cases dramatically increased their utilization further, while the self pay

Table 13B.1    Mean Utilization Rates: Number of Visits or Services per Patient
per Year for the IPA Group Before and After Enrollment Compared with those
of Controls (N = 640 matched pairs)

| | Before[1] | | After[2] | | IPA Effect[3] |
|---|---|---|---|---|---|
| | pre-IPA | FFS | IPA | FFS | |
| Acute | 2.05 | 1.72** | 2.16 | 1.53*** | +0.25 |
| Well-child | 0.70 | 0.70 | 0.67 | 0.56*** | +0.06 |
| Chronic | 0.16 | 0.10 | 0.25 | 0.13* | +0.04 |
| (Total) | 2.90 | 2.52* | 3.09 | 2.22*** | +0.35 |
| After-hours | 0.68 | 0.70 | 0.82 | 0.64* | +0.09 |
| Weekend | 0.34 | 0.25* | 0.38 | 0.25*** | +0.06 |
| Laboratory in | 0.66 | 0.58 | 0.82 | 0.65 | +0.07 |
| Laboratory out | 0.10 | 0.07 | 0.22 | 0.08** | +0.07 |
| Referrals | 0.10 | 0.07 | 0.16 | 0.09** | +0.03 |

[1]Comparison for **before** year: Correlated 2-tailed t-test.
[2]Comparison for **after** year: ANCOVA, using **before** as covariate (df = 639)
[3]IPA Effect: Additional utilization rate per patient per year due to IPA, controlling for baseline utilization, from ANCOVA model (Multiple Classification Analysis)
*p < 0.05
**p < 0.01
***p ≤ 0.001

controls slightly dropped their utilization as expected, due to their increasing ages. (All patients were 1 year older in the second year, and pediatric utilization decreases with age.) The increase for the IPA patients was significant, controlling for higher previous utilization, for all categories of utilization except in-office lab studies. We concluded that a significant IPA effect, over and above the selection effect, had occurred. Since ambulatory care costs represent about 80% of all pediatric care costs, it is doubtful that prepaid ambulatory care through IPA plans had the desired effect of cost containment.

We did not interview subscribers about their reasons for joining the IPA plan or about the number of visits. We did not interview physicians about their cost containment efforts. Our conclusions are, therefore, indirect. But the precision with which we managed to measure utilization, in combination with the study design, suggests strong IPA effects, even if the mechanism for this phenomenon was not directly exposed. This IPA study is a good example of the new utilization studies now prevailing.

*NICU Effects*

Neonatal intensive care units (NICUs) were one of the key developments of pediatrics in the 1970s. Morbidities in the perinatal period were previously seen as something not within the reach of the pediatrician; custodial care was the predominant mode of treatment. Once the notion became established that perinatal morbidities are much like later morbidities, and should be addressed in an aggressive way, the long-term sequelae of the early morbidities had to be considered. What type of morbidities are they? Are these morbidities that follow a chronic, "permanent damage" model, or do they follow the "greater hardiness" model often observed when children emerge from acute illness with better immunity and resistance than if they had not experienced the earlier attack?

Major permanent damages, like birth defects, are sequelae that are easy to detect. But what about excessive attack rates by normally occurring acute childhood diseases? It was decided to follow ambulatory care utilization of children who were discharged from a NICU and of healthy control babies through the preschool years to see whether more morbidities would be brought to the pediatrician's attention. The cumulative history of morbidities registered in medical charts was used to form a "health status index" to address this question. Expanding the function of utilization data to serve as a *morbidity index* far exceeded their previous use.

A Neonatal Tracking Program was created at the University of Rochester in the early 1980s to follow graduates of the NICU, through both parent questionnaires and pediatrician reporting. This allowed us to trace the children's morbidity experience through their preschool years. Four sites with divergent patient populations were selected for detailed study: a suburban private group practice, a group model HMO, a low-income outpatient clinic, and a city practice serving both poor and working-class patients. Up to 2 matched healthy newborns were selected as controls at each site to assure that cases and controls would be comparable on biologic and socioeconomic variables and that any differences remaining would be attributable to the morbidity observed in cases at birth.

At the suburban group practice site, 295 charts qualified for study—

about one-third cases and two-thirds controls. Chart abstractions produced 8,089 visits over a 5-year period: some children under observation for the full-time span, others for only 1 year. The visits were made during 1,164 child years, including some incomplete years (less than 12 months, but more than 10 months). Incomplete years were included with an adjustment if only 2 months were missing. Sometimes only 1 control could be found. A set of sib controls was also added.

*Table 13B.2* presents utilization rates by age of patient for the suburban group practice. No matter what set of comparisons is chosen, matched triplets (1 case, 2 controls), matched pairs (1 case, 1 control), or sib pairs, we observe the same finding. There is an initial excess utilization in the first and second year of life for graduates of the NICU, in the order of 20% higher utilization, but the difference becomes minor by the third year of life and even reverses itself by the fifth and sixth year. Clearly, this pattern is most consistent with "The Greater Hardiness" model, i.e., a pattern of acute illness from which a complete recovery has been achieved. Our data are consistent with those of other researchers (McCormick, Shapiro, and Starfield, 1980).

The analysis for the group model HMO showed similar findings, although the number of cases identified was smaller, and an outlier distorted results for the fourth year. For the first year of life, cases showed 1.4 more visits than matched controls, 4.5 more visits than sib controls and 2.8 more visits than random controls. These differences become smaller in the second and third years.

Utilization analyses for the low-income outpatient clinic and the working-class practice were inconclusive. No different patterns were seen, but it was unclear whether this was due to an absence of different morbidity patterns, a different threshold for seeking care in these populations, or inadequate sampling frames for selecting controls. The utilization data available through these chart abstractions far exceed the quality of data obtainable through retrospective interviews. An interview with the parents about perceptions of their children's health may have added a new dimension, but was not crucial for our purpose. Utilization data obtained from provider records gave a more persuasive answer.

*REFERENCES*

MCCORMICK, M.C., SHAPIRO, S., STARFIELD, B.H.:

1980   "Rehospitalization in the First Year of Life for High Risk Survivors." *Pediatrics*, 66:1991.

Table 13B.2.  Ambulatory Care Utilization: NICU–Graduates versus Matched Controls

| Year Of Life | Cases | | | Controls | | | Difference in Means |
|---|---|---|---|---|---|---|---|
| | n | Means | SEM** | n | Mean | SEM | |
| *A. Analysis of matched triplets (two controls)* | | | | | | | |
| 1st | 81 | 11.85 | .62 | 154 | 9.71 | .40 | 2.14 |
| 2nd | 81 | 10.16 | .65 | 148 | 7.94 | .49 | 2.22 |
| 3rd | 64 | 6.05 | .56 | 118 | 5.32 | .38 | .73 |
| 4th | 43 | 6.10 | .75 | 80 | 5.53 | .65 | .57 |
| 5th | 25 | 6.21 | .92 | 53 | 5.64 | .55 | .57 |
| 6th | 10 | 2.86 | .36 | 29 | 5.76 | .76 | −2.90 |
| Total* | 307 | 8.57 | .33 | 582 | 7.22 | .22 | 1.35 |
| *B. Analysis of matched pairs (one control only)* | | | | | | | |
| 1st | 19 | 9.36 | .88 | 18 | 8.87 | .94 | .49 |
| 2nd | 19 | 7.86 | 1.33 | 17 | 7.35 | .66 | .51 |
| 3rd | 14 | 4.83 | 1.13 | 14 | 4.70 | .88 | .13 |
| 4th | 11 | 3.03 | .52 | 10 | 2.70 | .54 | .33 |
| 5th | 10 | 3.58 | .58 | 9 | 4.71 | 1.08 | −1.13 |
| 6th | 5 | 3.96 | .70 | 4 | 5.35 | 2.60 | −1.39 |
| Total* | 78 | 6.31 | .53 | 73 | 6.08 | .45 | .23 |
| *C. Analysis of sib pairs**** | | | | | | | |
| 1st | 31 | 12.16 | .94 | 31 | 10.06 | .80 | 2.10 |
| 2nd | 31 | 10.52 | 1.19 | 29 | 9.12 | 1.43 | 1.40 |
| 3rd | 22 | 6.51 | 1.09 | 25 | 5.83 | .92 | .68 |
| 4th | 12 | 4.58 | 1.18 | 21 | 5.35 | 1.39 | −.77 |
| 5th | 8 | 3.13 | .60 | 13 | 5.27 | 1.03 | −2.14 |
| 6th | 3 | 2.88 | .44 | 5 | 8.26 | 1.75 | −5.38 |
| Total* | 108 | 8.71 | .59 | 124 | 7.61 | .53 | 1.10 |

*Total may include visits from an unlisted seventh year
**Standard error of the mean
***Cases in the sib pairs are also listed in the previous groups

MECHANIC, DAVID

1979 "Correlates of Physician Utilization: Why Do Major Multivariate Studies of Physician Utilization find trivial Psychosocial and Organizational Effects?" *Journal of Health and Social Behavior*, 20:387–396.

ROGHMANN, K.J.

1989 "Follow-up Care for NICU Graduates: Report on a Research Program 1985–1988." School of Medicine and Dentistry, Rochester, N.Y.: Department of Pediatrics.

SZILAGYI, P.G., ROGHMANN, K.J., FOYE, H.R., PARKS, C., MCWHINNEY, J., MILLER, R., MCINERNY, T., KLEIN, S.

1990 "The effect of IPA Plans on Pediatric Ambulatory Care Utilization in One Group Practice." *JAMA*, 263:2198–2203.

## C. THE UTILIZATION OF HEALTH SERVICES—INPATIENT CARE: THE COMMUNITY AS THE LABORATORY FOR HEALTH SERVICES RESEARCH

KLAUS J. ROGHMANN

AND

RALPH R. SELL

Inpatient utilization has rarely received the same attention by sociologists as has physician utilization. After all, admissions are not initiated by the patient, and access to inpatient care is less subject to special barriers than is ambulatory care. Referring physicians or emergency room staff decide about admissions to the floor; physicians in the delivery room decide about admission to the NICU. Decision making is concentrated in fewer "players" in the health care market. Physicians remain the gatekeepers for inpatient care, although hospital administrators, insurance representatives, and state regulatory bodies determine the financial environment in which inpatient care is delivered.

Pediatric care costs do not include a large inpatient component. The analysis of pediatric inpatient claims has to recognize two factors: first, most pediatric claims are for nursery admissions; and second, the cost distribution for nursery claims is extremely skewed. Most nursery claims are for a few hundred dollars for 3–4 days in the newborn nursery, but some are for long stays in the intensive care unit, costing several hundred thousand dollars.

Table 13C.1 gives the average IPA payments per member/month for an average group practice of five pediatricians in 1987, each seeing

*Table 13C.1. Payments Made per Patient per Month, IPA Plan (1987— Medical Utilization Profile, in dollars)*

| MD | Type of Care | Excluding Outliers | | Including Outliers | |
|---|---|---|---|---|---|
| | | Self | Peers | Self | Peers |
| A: | Ambulatory | 18.90 | 23.02 | 18.79 | 26.84 |
| | inpatient | 3.31 | 4.11 | 3.31 | 6.78 |
| B: | Ambulatory | 22.57 | 22.52 | 39.27 | 26.30 |
| | inpatient | 1.94 | 3.94 | 13.90 | 6.53 |
| C: | Ambulatory | 18.55 | 23.57 | 25.16 | 27.92 |
| | inpatient | 2.97 | 4.39 | 7.71 | 7.40 |
| D: | Ambulatory | 24.51 | 21.71 | 24.45 | 24.85 |
| | inpatient | 5.52 | 3.42 | 5.54 | 5.60 |
| E: | Ambulatory | 17.62 | 22.14 | 26.25 | 25.25 |
| | inpatient | 1.98 | 3.59 | 9.13 | 6.03 |

about 500 children covered by prepayment. Ambulatory costs averaged about $20/month, compared to $3/month for inpatient care. Inpatient costs are much more affected by outliers and represent the typical situation for which insurance was designed: rare, but expensive events. Normal costs/member/month covered by the IPA were about $24. Including outliers, the average payments were about $31. If we were to take the IPA patients as typical, in a community like Rochester with nearly 200,000 children under 18, pediatric care costs would amount to about $6.14 million per month (excluding the $4–$5 copayments by patients).

Studies of inpatient utilization, apart from utilization reviews conducted by health plans, are now largely based on secondary data analysis. The National Center for Health Statistics provides natality files for population studies and birth/death certificate linked files to study perinatal deaths. The Hospital Discharge Survey provides national hospital data on a large sample basis. States like New York keep their own hospitalization files for planning purposes (SPARCS). Though these large data bases permit good monitoring of the nation's health in terms of "inpatient morbidity," they rarely permit detailed epidemiological studies that can follow individuals over time. Unique patient identifiers, such as social security numbers, are only used within the Medicare system or other government financed care plans. While no such system is generally available for children, selected populations like AFDC children can be followed through the Medicaid system for limited periods. Special research projects, however, can be designed for local markets to follow cases over time. A summary of the methodology and findings for one such project is presented here to demonstrate that in-house data bases within one community can be used for studies that might be impossible on the national level.

## NICU Inpatient Follow-Up

The concerns that led to long-term follow-up of graduates of NICUs have been described above. One response is the creation of a Neonatal Tracking Programs (NTP) at some tertiary care facilities to serve as both a service and research facility. Few doubts exist about the value of NTPs as a service facility for children with a history of perinatal morbidity, but their value as a research facility is still debated for two reasons: the high follow-up losses due to difficulties in tracking children from a predominantly low socioeconomic background; and the need for matched controls. Infants admitted to NICUs are often the result of high-risk pregnancies, both in terms of medical risks and socioeconomic disadvantages. Such infants receive care in underfunded inner-city clinics that cannot provide sufficient outreach. If NICU graduates from such environments have excess admissions during their preschool years, does this reflect differences in medical care and socioeconomic background, or does it reflect the consequences of perinatal morbidity?

The data bases used to study this question in the Rochester community were the following: (1) Rochester Area Hospital Corporation (RAHC) cumulative admission files, (2) Birth certificate (BC) files, and (3) the Perinatal Data Registry (PDR). The RAHC files include all admissions, but few variables for each one. Recorded variables include a few demographic characteristics, hospital specific identifiers and admission data such as date of admission, diagnosis, length of stay (LOS), and charges. The birth certificate files match nursery admissions and add detailed demographic information and a short pregnancy history. The PDR files include the medical details of the pregnancies and of infants delivered at the tertiary center, plus the transports from other hospitals to the tertiary center. All files are computerized without confidential identifiers such as names or addresses. All data are based on in-house clinical records. When linked, they provide a detailed data set with demographic, medical, and financial information. Human subject review committees approve research projects as consistent or not consistent with the purposes of the linked files.

There are three methodological steps in this research project: record linkage, casetype classification, and child year aggregation.

Record Linkage

The three files described above were all organized by calendar year, and linkage proceeded by calendar year. An example is the linkage program of PDR and birth certificates (BC) for the tertiary center, for 1980 through 1983. First, the PDR files had to be reduced by eliminating records not belonging in the live born BC files, e.g., stillborn babies. Of the remainder, the PDR had 11,479 records, the BC files had 11,476 records. Five linking criteria were used: date of birth (DOB), sex and race of the infant, maternal age in years, and birth weight (BWT) in grams. A perfect match on all 5 criteria was achieved for 71% of all records. The matching accuracy was then relaxed in steps. For example, maternal age is often recorded during a prenatal visit months before the baby is born, making it one year lower in the PDR file than on the birth certificate. Allowing maternal age to vary by one year permitted another 6.8% of records to be linked.

Next birth weight was allowed to vary by 100 grams, because infants are weighed several times after birth, and weight is recorded with different levels of precision. This relaxation allowed another 11.2% of records to be linked. Race designations, if Hispanic is a different category than white, often vary from record to record. Relaxing perfect race matching allowed 2.6% more cases to be linked. After 7 such iterations, machine linkage of 95.7% of all records was achieved. The remaining 4.3% could be "hand" linked. Clerical errors during data entry (2,300 grams instead of 3,200 grams, age 23 years instead of 32 years) are easily spotted when all other criteria are correct (although it often remains unclear which entry is correct). Overall, linkage of over 99% was achieved.

Casetype Classification

All infants were classified into one of the following 7 categories: (1) "cases" (having perinatal morbidity requiring NICU admission); (2) delivery room, nursery or postneonatal deaths because they obviously cannot be followed; (3) infant transports; (4) maternal transports (controls for transports should be drawn from hospital of origin); (5) morbidity exclusions; and (6) potential controls. Potential controls can be further classified as "best" or "other" controls. For some cases no satisfactory controls may be identifiable. The casetype classification is achieved through matching programs, that is, programs to find best matching controls for cases. (We use the term "linkage" to link records *from different files* for the same infants, and the term "matching" for finding other infants as controls to match cases.

Casetype classification is a cumulative process used to arrive at mutually exclusive categories. First, infant deaths, infant transports, and maternal transports are coded; second, morbidity exclusions are identified. Very stringent criteria were applied in the first phase (1980–1983) to ensure that only perfectly healthy infants would qualify as controls (gestational age of 37 weeks or higher, birth weight of 2500 grams or higher, Apgar score of 8 or higher at both 1 and 5 minutes). The potential controls were sorted by both "required" and "desirable" matching criteria. Required criteria were comparable obstetric and pediatric care, same sex, same race, and same parity. Desirable criteria were initially only socioeconomic variables such as maternal age and education (later marital status and insurance coverage). Table 13C.2 gives the summary of the casetype classification for 1980 through 1983, and for 1984 through 1986 using less stringent morbidity exclusions.

Child Year Aggregation

Once all records had been linked and all infants classified, subfiles for each infant were created from the RAHC files to contain the original nursery claim and all readmissions of that infant over the preschool years, sorted by date of admission. The hospital specific personal identifiers (infant unit numbers) were crucial for this step. The date of the first admission was set equal to the date of birth and assigned to all readmissions, allowing a precise "age at admission" calculation for later admissions. Aggregation of all admissions in the subfiles gave the sum of all lifetime inpatient care per child for the time period screened. Lifetime inpatient care was further divided into first year of life care, second year of life care, etc.

The study followed 7 annual cohorts in 2 phases, 4 for the 1980–1983 phase and 3 for the 1984–1986 phase. All 7 cohorts were observed for the "calendar year of birth" and the "calendar years after birth" up to 1987 inclusive. Seven cohorts were observed for the "second calendar year"; 6 cohorts were observed for the "third calendar year after birth"; 5 for the "fourth calendar year of birth," etc. If we consider the midpoint of the year as the average "date of birth," the first cohort was observed for an average of 7.5 years, the second cohort for 6.5 years, etc., with the seventh cohort observed for only 1.5 years. Altogether, 31.5 cohort years were studied. As the number of readmissions and precise age of readmission are easily established, the only remaining task is to calculate the number of children "at risk" for readmission for each year from the original linked files.

*Table 13C.2. Casetype Classification for Study Period*

| | Phase 1 Cohorts | | | | Phase 2 Cohorts | | |
|---|---|---|---|---|---|---|---|
| | 1980 | 1981 | 1982 | 1983 | 1984* | 1985 | 1986 |
| Cases | 312 | 360 | 397 | 371 | 274 | 388 | 438 |
| Best controls | 583 | 641 | 689 | 620 | 534 | 642 | 803 |
| Other controls | 978 | 907 | 913 | 1,007 | 1,369 | 1,615 | 1,585 |
| Morbidity exclusions | 638 | 696 | 758 | 823 | 321 | 383 | 379 |
| Infant transports | 199 | 227 | 203 | 205 | 230 | 259 | 259 |
| Mother transports | 136 | 134 | 154 | 91 | 155 | 141 | 141 |
| Deaths | 47 | 48 | 47 | 70 | 48 | 49 | 48 |
| Total | 2,904 | 2,987 | 3,165 | 3,248 | 2,842 | 3,462 | 3,653 |

*Only births by residents of the metropolitan county, not births by delivery sites in the metropolitan county.

*Findings*

Excess Utilization

Table 13C.3 gives a summary of the utilization findings for all pediatric admissions, including nursery claims, of the 21,045 children observed for 81,642 patient years. During this observation period, 3,654 readmissions to the same hospital where the children were born were observed. The overall readmission rate per year was 44.8/1000, with marked differences by casetype. Remember that "best controls" were equal to cases in terms of socioeconomic background and medical care received. The readmissions for best controls were only 46.0% of the rate for cases. "Other controls," that is, healthy newborns that usually had a better socioeconomic background and better care, had only 40.8% as many readmissions as cases. Infant and maternal transports, usually with greater morbidity than inborn admissions to the NICU, had readmission rates of 14.0% and 32.4% higher than cases, respectively.

The direction of these differences had been expected, but the size of the differences, on a population basis, were unknown. The great surprise was the small difference between best controls and other controls, and the small difference between best controls and "morbidity exclusions." We had expected a greater influence of both intitial morbidities and the socioeconomic factors separating "best" and "other" controls.

Length of Excess Utilization

The next question concerns the length for which NICU graduates may be at increased risk. Table 13C.4 provides a first approximation. A fairly clear pattern emerges, but some inconsistencies from the fourth year of follow-up onward, remain. (The number of readmissions per casetype per year frequently dropped below 10, and the base for calculating rates fell below 500 observation years. We believe that these inconsistencies are mostly due to sampling error.) Considering the best controls as our standard for relative risk calculations, cases had about 150% higher admission ratios than controls for the first 3 years of life, about 70% higher for the fourth and fifth years, and equal or even better rates from then onward.

Other controls had readmission rates about 80% of those of the best controls, independent of age. Morbidity exclusions showed a crossover phenomenon compared with best controls: they had higher rates in the first 4 years of life, but lower rates for the next 3 years. Infants and maternal transports were similar to cases, but they required 1 year

*Table 13C.3. Study Population, Years under Observation and Readmissions*

| Casetype | Base | Years under Observation | Readmissions | Rate/1000 |
|---|---|---|---|---|
| Cases | 2,486 | 9,683 | 738 | 76.2 |
| Best controls | 4,452 | 17,355 | 620 | 35.7 |
| Other controls | 8,254 | 29,454 | 916 | 31.1 |
| Morbidity exclusions | 3,958 | 17,675 | 678 | 38.4 |
| Infant transports | 966 | 3,729 | 324 | 86.9 |
| Maternal transports | 926 | 3,746 | 378 | 100.9 |
| Total | 21,045 | 81,642 | 3,654 | 44.8 |

*Table 13C.4. Excess Inpatient Utilization by Age and Casetype*

A. Readmission Rates by Age and Casetype

| Age of Readmission | Cases | Best Controls | Other Controls | Morbidity Exclus. | Infant Trans. | Mother Trans. |
|---|---|---|---|---|---|---|
| 2–12th month | 142.3 | 57.0 | 43.9 | 67.9 | 180.1 | 237.8 |
| 2nd year | 81.2 | 30.5 | 23.4 | 34.9 | 78.3 | 90.5 |
| 3rd year | 51.5 | 20.4 | 14.8 | 22.8 | 56.1 | 46.5 |
| 4th year | 23.3 | 13.6 | 14.1 | 20.4 | 24.9 | 23.4 |
| 5th year | 22.9 | 13.2 | 10.8 | 9.6 | 22.7 | 34.6 |
| 6th year | 13.6 | 15.7 | 12.4 | 11.3 | 27.8 | 22.0 |
| 7th year* | 12.9 | (31.2) | (18.6) | (26.9) | (31.5) | (35.2) |
|  | 76.2 | 35.7 | 31.1 | 38.4 | 86.9 | 100.9 |

B. Relative Risks in Relation to Best Controls

| Age of Readmission | Cases | Best Controls | Other Controls | Morbidity Exclus. | Infant Trans. | Mother Trans. |
|---|---|---|---|---|---|---|
| 2–12th month | 2.50 | 1.00 | .77 | 1.19 | 3.16 | 4.17 |
| 2nd year | 2.66 | 1.00 | .77 | 1.14 | 2.57 | 2.97 |
| 3rd year | 2.52 | 1.00 | .73 | 1.12 | 2.75 | 2.28 |
| 4th year | 1.71 | 1.00 | 1.04 | 1.50 | 1.83 | 1.72 |
| 5th year | 1.73 | 1.00 | .82 | .73 | 1.72 | 2.62 |
| 6th year | .87 | 1.00 | .79 | .72 | 1.77 | 1.40 |
| 7th year | .41 | 1.00 | .60 | .86 | 1.01 | 1.13 |
|  | 2.13 | 1.00 | .87 | 1.08 | 2.43 | 2.83 |

*Partly includes readmissions of eighth year (average of 7.5 years).

longer—until the seventh year of life—for differences from the best controls to disappear.

### Financial Impact

The final question examined is the financial impact of these cumulative morbidities. Table 13C.5 gives the average charges for all preschool admissions, including the initial nursery admission, by casetype. The cost differences are much larger than a simple comparison of admission rates would suggest, primarily due to the cost of the initial NICU admission. In relation to costs of care in later years, these averages do not appear excessive.

### Discussion

Chapter 12 only provides background parameters for a study such as this. Chapter 13 described health care delivery issues against this background. Pediatric care is one of the key determinants of child health, but not the only one. Our basic argument, presented 20 years ago, was that medicine alone cannot claim credit for all improvements, nor should it take sole responsibility for all deteriorations, in child health. It is an awareness of changes in society and the local community, and collaboration with these outside forces in the interest of improved child health, that count most. Our openness to such general trends, in addition to leadership in the areas for which we shoulder the main

*Table 13C.5. Average Charges and Length of Stay by Casetype*

|  | Average | | Relative Risks | |
|---|---|---|---|---|
|  | Charges ($) | LOS (days) | Charges ($) | LOS (days) |
| *Normal Births* |  |  |  |  |
| Best controls | 753 | 3.4 | 1.00 | 1.00 |
| Other controls | 560 | 3.0 | .74 | .88 |
| Morbidity excl. | 687 | 3.7 | .93 | 1.09 |
| *Special Risks* |  |  |  |  |
| Cases inborn | 5,884 | 9.7 | 7.81 | 2.85 |
| Infant transp. | 12,362 | 12.6 | 16.42 | 3.71 |
| Maternal transp. | 16,670 | 20.2 | 22.14 | 5.94 |
| *Deaths* |  |  |  |  |
| Dead | 12,406 | 7.4 | 16.42 | 3.71 |

responsibility, characterized Rochester's approach to community pediatrics.

## Specific Utilization

The example of our utilization research was presented to demonstrate the methodologic and theoretical progress made in the last decades. Utilization is measured with greater precision using available records to answer increasingly precise questions. How important are the losses to follow-up of NICU graduates? How important are social factors? How important is the care environment? Can we evaluate the relationship between ambulatory and inpatient utilization, or consider their relation to adult utilization? What regional differences may exist (Perrin et al., 1989)? The examples presented here from ongoing projects clearly show the continued relevance of constant utilization monitoring.

## Medical Sociology

In 1979, David Mechanic correctly assessed the cul-de-sac in the sociological studies of physician utilization. It appeared that any nonspecific focus on the patient, with attitudes and social factors considered as distinct independent variables and response to morbidities as vague dependent variables, did not and would not pay off.

There are three responses to Mechanic's conclusions. The first is to urge that there be a greater specificity in morbidities or preventive behaviors. The focus on perinatal morbidities is one example. Determining which type of doctor visit is more price sensitive than others in the context of IPA plans is another example. The second response is to encourage a greater focus on professions, with emphasis on the development of subspecialties and their recent growth. Medical care is at the heart of the human services industry: it is the fastest growing segment of our economy. What is the role of new technologies and knowledge in the expansion of clinical departments? How do they relate to the growth of basic science departments? A redirection of efforts from patients to providers may better help us understand "progress" toward better health in our society. A third response is to urge more emphasis on organizational factors operating in the community, such as insurance plans, state regulations, economic trends, and their growing impact on child health.

In short, what has happened over the last 2 decades should help allocate more pertinence to certain factors. It may also help direct our attention in the future.

Child Health Impact

The famous "bottom line," of course, is how all the various factors contribute to the level of child health in the community. Will public health measures or privte practice effectiveness be more important in determining child health? What community factors are especially important in child health? Can we find better measures than infant mortality as an index of health status? What issues should be addressed in the future?

While we do not claim to have answers to all these questions, we emphasize that the various processes and issues presented here are small, but progressive steps in the direction of our larger goal—the improvement of child health.

*REFERENCE*

PERRIN, J.M., HOLMER, C.J., BERWICK, D.M., WOLF, A.D., FREEMAN, J.L., WENNBERG, J.E.

1989  "Variations in Rates of Hospitalization of Children in Three Urban Communities." *NEJM*, 320(18): 1183–1187.

CHAPTER FOURTEEN

# Analysis and Assessment: New Institutions and New Professions

The program in community pediatrics at the University of Roches-ter, which began in 1964, was based on the premise that only by taking a population approach and organizing services to meet the needs of all the children in the community could one improve the health of children significantly. This led to several actions: the consolidation of hospital pediatric services to provide a critical mass of patients and to organize high-quality services; involvement of all pediatricians with clinical appointments at the university hospital; establishment of house-hold surveys to determine needs and measure progress; the develop-ment of collaborative research with practicing pediatricians; and im-proving health services for the underserved. Considerable successes were achieved, as reported in the first edition of this book, especially in shifting acute care from hospital emergency rooms to neighborhood health centers.

We had more difficulty showing a dramatic improvement in the health status of children. We held what now seems a peculiarly naive notion—that providing health care alone would have a significant effect on children's health. Genetic endowment, social and physical environment, and health habits, undoubtedly account for a good deal more of the variance in the health status of children than does whether or not they receive good medical care. On the other hand, health care is not without its tangible benefits. Prenatal care, followed by good care in infancy, does reduce infant mortality. Immunizations do prevent infectious diseases. Lead poisoning detection and community control programs do reduce the burden of lead poisoning. And the receipt of medical care is perceived by most of the public as a right, or at least as a social good. Hence we make no apologies for organizing health services at the community level in an attempt to deliver first-class general pediatric care to all children and as a way to improve child health.

A second philosophic basis for the community child health program was that only by involving the community in the organization of services could we effectively change health care. This, too, proved to be a relatively naive assumption, for several reasons. First, our understanding of the political process was limited, and we were only one of many players. Second, community organizations, such as the community board of the health center, had relatively little direct impact on health care. However, some of the organizations that were created as a result of the community approach have persisted and have experienced a dramatic increase in volunteer participation. For example, the section on the family counselor program below documents how it grew into an extensive volunteer program for the Department of Pediatrics at Rochester. In addition, there are several anecdotes that describe how members of the original community health center boards and their families have come to occupy important public positions. Empowerment through the community health programs may very well have led to these achievements.

Finally, as an academic and research institution, we believed that the education of a new breed of pediatrician could best occur in a setting where services were organized on a population basis. In addition, we felt that such studies as those relating to effectiveness of these services would create a new area of research. They would legitimize research other than traditional biomedical and clinical research, namely epidemiologic, health services, and behavioral research. All of these were predicated on a geographically determined population base, rather than on samples based on referrals, and therefore potentially biased. The educational format has continued to be broader than in most pediatric residency training programs, and the research continues, although with diminished funding from federal sources, the volume has diminished.

The first edition of *Child Health and the Community* dealt with how we tried to improve the health of children in a community through research, development of new service programs, and education of a new breed of providers. This update continues that tradition, and assesses to what degree the pieces put in place 20 years ago have survived and how they have grown.

The Rochester community, like the rest of the country, has changed during the last 2 decades. The political climate is more conservative. Most of the original team members have left to meet challenges elsewhere. Some are still in the same community, but in different positions. The "spirit" of the team and of the book, however, is still alive: our individual and collective commitment to the advancement of child health, the constant assessment of efforts to reach that goal, and concern about the future strategies required to fulfill these common objectives, remains. It is this spirit that has brought us to a critical review of that period. What has happened to the new institutions, the innovative manpower programs, the promising theoretical concepts, and the various community initiatives?

We knew that poverty would not disappear, that the problems of migrant workers would persist, that teenage pregnancies would not be avoided, and that behavior problems would not become a thing of the past. But community child health programs were developed to ameliorate the effects of these problems. Many of these new institutions were born in conflict and grew up in controversy. Some programs did not survive the harsh world of confrontational politics, and some became political footballs, or were redefined. This review tries to identify trends, patterns, and themes so that we may improve our understanding of these events and learn for the future.

## A. THE CONCEPTUAL FRAMEWORK: THE GROWTH OF PROFESSIONS AND INSTITUTIONS

Our review again uses a sociological framework. The development of the medical profession, and of medical institutions, is as much driven by scientific advances and new technologies as by social and economic forces. Pediatrics has grown in distinct phases (Halpern, 1988) linked to the growth of hospitals, medical schools, and social reform movements in the larger society. These phases follow a distinct pattern of professional differentiation. Amelioration, social betterment, and social problem orientation have played a major role in the development of pediatrics, in contrast to organ-based or technology-based medical specialties. Within the specialty of pediatrics, general and community-oriented pediatricians are a self-selected group who see themselves both as advocates for child health and as defenders of their own economic self-interests within narrow disciplinary boundaries. They take the holistic view that the whole child, in the context of family and community, is "the patient."

Historically, leaders in the field of child care have been known for running free dispensaries, donating time to hospitals, and advocating new services that only later gained public recognition and provided financial rewards. Their commitment to charity and volunteerism has always been strong. Compassion for the sick and disadvantaged is a special part of pediatric's cultural heritage. Furthermore, with a strong focus on maternal and child health and a concern for all children, pediatrics has always been deeply connected to the public health movement. Pediatricians recognize the close association of social factors such as poverty, discrimination, and living in violence-ridden ghettos as directly related to many physical and mental health problems of children. They see solutions both in terms of individual services and social reform. Certainly liberal ideas characterize pediatricians. Psychosocially oriented pediatricians, and their Ambulatory Pediatric Association, were most receptive to the social reforms of the 1960s. These pediatricians admire books like *Within Our Reach* (Schorr, 1988) and *Adolescents at Risk* (Dryfoos, 1990), but are appalled by books like *Losing Ground: American Social Policy 1950–1980* (Murray, 1984). The growth of community pediatrics cannot be understood without acknowledging its strong ties to social betterment. As in the even more political public health field, all of this emphasizes the need for extreme care so that scientific evidence is not biased by excessive child health advocacy.

Within sociological theory, the sociology of professions and organizations is the most helpful approach for our analysis. Both professions and formal organizations are seen as basic social structures created to perform complex tasks. Markets and primary groups, such as the extended family, are similar basic structures. The goal of pediatric care is supposed to be the production of child health, but all too often it has equally served to promote the profession. The American Academy of Pediatrics, among other professional organizations, has as its primary goal the improvement of the health of its clients—children—not the promotion of the profession. A number of theorists (Arrow, 1974; Williamson, 1975) contrast the benefits and costs of basic social structures to help understand the emergence and survival of specific institutions. Their perspective allows a developmental conceptualization in terms of the structural differentiation of institutions or professions, that is, development to more complex forms with little possibility of returning to simpler forms or earlier states.

Organizational sociology also offers assessments of technology with its implications for organizational structures: long-linked technologies versus intensive technology (Thompson, 1967); the number of routine and exceptional cases and levels of problem-solving activities (Perrow, 1970); tight and loose coupling of organizational structures (Meyer and Rowan, 1977); and concerns for effectiveness in human service industries.

As we have argued elsewhere (Roghmann, 1988), the technology of health care delivery is only "loosely coupled" to health outcomes, and this allows for great flexibility of institutional and organizational forms. Even within a single country, practice styles differ widely from area to area (Wennberg, 1982). Health outcomes are remarkably independent of organizational forms and reflect, primarily, the health of the underlying social infrastructure. The state of the family, community, schools, and economy are key factors determining the health of children.

The poor performance of the United States in international comparisons of child health primarily reflects the deterioration of the social infrastructure, and not deficiencies in medical technology, the quality of care, or even access to care, as important as this is. Meetings of concerned pediatricians reviewing the current state of child health are usually depressing because the speakers recognize the deplorable state of child health but know that the key determinants are outside their control. Medical care, if broadened in concept, may improve health (Starfield, 1985), but it is not the entire answer. This fact has encouraged those in community child health to extend the boundaries of medicine to incorporate family, schools, community environment, and socioeconomic factors. These, then, are the conceptual tools that arise from the organizational perspective.

Some additional concepts come from new advances in the sociology of professions. Professions used to be seen as static, ideal-type configurations with certain characteristics clearly distinguishing them from other occupational structures. These characteristics included a special body of knowledge, long periods of training in professional schools, certification for practice, professional organizations, an established body of ethics, and some form of self governance. Responses to the proliferation of medical specialization in the form of a primary care movement were discussed (Kunitz, 1986).

More recent conceptualizations, especially the one formulated by Halpern (1988), view professionalization as a dynamic social process and part of general historical trends toward occupational specialization within trends toward greater societal complexities. While the previous traditional viewpoint uses a rational systems approach (Scott, 1981) to show why certain configurations of occupational groups are best for solving complex problems, the new approach has an open systems perspective (Scott, 1981) combined with a natural systems or developmental orientation. Halpern focuses on the social environment, with its patterns of occupational structures and organizational forms, and examines how market forces and scientific or technological factors lead to the emergence of new structures in this environment. Particularly, she focuses on 4 aspects of this configuration. These are described briefly to introduce terms that will be used in the later analysis.

First, the continuing *division of labor* leads to changing work patterns and career opportunities to which the current occupational collectivity must react. These changes may be due to new technology; social reform movements; government reactions; increased demand (because of demographic changes, such as local migration patterns); or to changes in work settings, such as the creation of dispensaries, asylums, clinics, wards, hospitals, or new departmental divisions in medical schools.

These new work settings present opportunities to learn, research, train, and establish reputations for expertise. Such reputations may then attract outside consulting incomes for those working in the new settings.

For pediatrics, the establishment of dispensaries in the 1880s attracted elite physicians who later formed the first pediatric society. In the 1900s, hospitals with special children's wards proliferated and offered opportunities for hospital care and teaching, while also facilitating patient recruitment for private practice. As a result, pediatric departments in medical schools were founded. In the 1920s and 1930s, the social reform movement resulted in infant-welfare centers, child guidance clinics, and child hygiene measures. These helped generate a large demand for well child contacts, which in turn resulted in widespread proliferation of private practices that did not require affiliation with a medical school.

In the post–World War II period, dedicated pediatricians created many new positions, such as the directorships of outpatient departments and emergency rooms. New institutions, such as health centers and health maintenance organizations, generated additional positions. While previously many of these tasks were accomplished by part-time physicians who donated their services, most of the new positions required full-time commitments, partly due to new state regulations. Physicians in these settings had to codify the emergent patterns of their work into new organizational structures.

Second, what may appear as an ideal-type combination of characteristics that flourished because of their optimal structure may have been only a kind of *isomorphism with the prevailing social structures* at the time of their emergence. Stinchcomb (1965) observed that certain economic structures emerge in waves: savings banks in the 1830s, railroads and steel companies in the 1850s and 1870s, mail order houses in the 1870s, the automobile industry in the 1920s, and, finally, computer companies in the 1970s. These cohorts of organizations reflect some basic common characteristics prevailing at the time of their founding and appear to have maintained these structures into the present. Similarly, the development of medical specialties and subspecialties has resulted both from new technology and from social pressure to follow prevailing patterns of professional development.

Third, *organizational innovations* may play a role similar to technical innovations or market forces. New institutions, such as neighborhood health centers, infant-welfare centers, intensive care units, faculty practice groups, school health clinics, or divisions in academic departments, are all social inventions that may thrive and expand or falter and disappear, depending on what needs they serve and what resources they can mobilize.

Finally, there are feedback mechanisms or *symbiotic relationships* between professional and organizational institutions. Hospitals may encourage subspecialty proliferation to gain recognition for quality of services; departments may urge members to gain national visibility as scholars and to attain grants and prizes because this helps attract residents and students. Universities like to delegate some control functions to academic committees, but maintain strict control over budgets, insist on indirect cost allocations, and use faculty for their own purposes.

The new approach to the analysis of the development of formal medical disciplines like pediatrics as the interplay of professions and organizations in modern societies, proposed by Halpern, although a remarkable advancement over previous sociological analyses, remains retrospective. Survival and success can easily be explained in hindsight; both are far more difficult to predict. Failed institutions get as little attention as failed companies or disapproved grants or manuscripts. Accordingly we supplement Halpern's analysis with a life-history approach to institutions—one that focuses as much on failures and restraints to growth as on successes. The retrospective approach fails to address normative issues and "missed opportunities." Why are so many obvious solutions bound to fail? Why can't we deliver effective preventive health services for children at school, or for adults at the work place? What about those institutions that are continually kept at the brink of bankruptcy, yet never allowed to fail? Inner-city schools, neighborhood health centers, Medicaid programs—in short, the whole range of service institutions for the poor—are financially starved and kept ineffectual, yet they are not allowed to disappear. This "underclass of institutions," intentionally kept "financially fragile," must be understood if we are to serve all children in a community. If the technology to reduce infant mortality, increase educational achievements, and lower teenage pregnancy rates is available, why do we put up with such "rotten outcomes" (Schorr, 1988)? There appears to be a "nonfatal pathology" in many of our institutions that has not yet been explained and that is absent in other modern societies. We appear to have succeeded in creating new institutions, such as health maintenance organizations, independent practitioner associations, Head Start or school clinics, but have still failed to solve such basic problems as ensuring access to health services.

Our approach to the analysis of these phenomena emphasizes the social and political environment in which most organizations function. In the original edition of this book, we emphasized social and environmental changes, such as the introduction of Medicaid, the impact of the New York State abortion law, and the federal requirements for neighborhood health centers. Markets for services can be intentionally structured so that the players are bound to remain weak, permanently fighting budget cuts unrelated to their organizational performance, and requiring grass-roots politics or public confrontations to capture needed resources. Understanding semipublic, health care delivery institutions requires political science concepts and cross-national analyses. This examination should include both the evaluation of local political processes and the comparison of different national structures. For example, Japanese or European approaches to primary education, welfare programs, and family policies emphasize consensus building and entitlement programs for the poor; their successes may elucidate our own organizational failures, which have emerged from the economic environment of the 1980s.

In the following sections, we present our analyses under two headings—institutional shifts and conceptual shifts. The first reviews actual organizational structures, such as departmental divisions, occupational careers, and formal programs. The second reviews concepts of illness, utilization behavior, and organizational accountability. The presentation of our arguments also changes and relies increasingly on interview data with leaders and knowledgeables in the field.

## REFERENCES

AAROW, KENNETH J.

1974   *The Limits of Organization.* New York: W.W. Norton Company.

DRYFOOS, J.G.

1990   *Adolescents at Risk: Prevalence and Prevention.* Oxford: Oxford University Press.

HALPERN, SIDNEY A.

1988   *American Pediatrics—The Social Dynamics of Professionalism, 1880–1980.* Berkeley, California: University of California Press.

KUNITZ, S.J.

1986   *"The Training of Primary Physicians."* Lanham, Md: University Press of America.

MEYER, JOHN W. and ROWAN, BRIAN

1977   "Institutionalized Organizations: Formal Structure as Myth and Ceremony." *American Journal of Sociology,* 83:340–363.

MURRAY, CHARLES

1984   *Losing Ground: American Social Policy 1950–1980.* New York: Basic Books.

PERROW, CHARLES

1970   *Organizational Analysis: A Sociological View.* Belmont, California: Wadsworth.

ROGHMANN, KLAUS
1988  "The Evolution of the U.S. and West German Health Care Systems: Contrasts and Challenges," Chap. 3 in *Health and Illness in America and Germany*, edited by G. Lueschen, W. C. Cockerham, and G. Kunz. Munich: Oldenbourg Publishers.

SCHORR, LISBETH B.
1988  *Within Our Reach—Breaking the Cycle of Disadvantage.* New York: Doubleday Anchor Press.

SCOTT, W. RICHARD
1981  *Organisations. Rational, Natural, and Open Systems.* Englewood Cliffs, NJ: Prentice Hall.

STARFIELD, BARBARA
1985  *The Effectiveness of Medical Care: Validating Clinial Wisdom.* Baltimore: Johns Hopkins University Press.

STINCHCOMBE, ARTHUR, L.
1965  "Social Structure and Organization." In *Handbook of Organizations*, edited by James A. Mark, pp. 142–193. Chicago: Rand McNally.

THOMPSON, JAMES D.
1967  *Organizations in Action.* New York: McGraw-Hill.

WENNBERG, J.E. and GITTELSON, A.
1982  "Variations in Medical Care Among Small Areas." *Scientific American*, 246:120–134.

WILLIAMSON, OLIVER E.
1975  *Markets and Hierarchies: Analysis and Antitrust Implications.* New York: Free Press.

*B. PROFESSIONAL GROWTH AND INSTITUTIONAL SHIFTS: SUBSPECIALIZATION, NEW PROFESSIONAL IDENTITIES AND MARGINAL INSTITUTIONS*

*The Capture and Transformation of Psychosocial Pediatrics: Primary Care and the Development of General Pediatrics*

KLAUS J. ROGHMANN

Over the past 20 years pediatrics has expanded rapidly. For example, academic pediatrics in Rochester experienced a fourfold growth in staffing and budget. However, earlier psychosocial programs, such as school health, behavioral pediatrics, and community pediatrics have not grown into separate formal structures. Instead, they have been merged with continuity clinics, pediatric emergency services, and other "ambulatory" initiatives into a General Pediatrics Division. General pediatrics has become yet another of a dozen such new divisions. Its growth was not due to its "psychosocial" components, but to the new, stronger position of ambulatory care. It came about as a consequence of new state requirements for emergency room services, stronger training requirements in primary care, upgrading of hospital and medical school positions in ambulatory care, and expanded fellowship training programs—notably The Robert Wood Johnson General Pediatrics Academic Fellowship Program.

The new growth of general pediatrics followed old growth patterns. Innovative services expanded into new areas (e.g., free dispensaries, hospital services as charities, well-child clinics as public services) until these services became well established, accepted, demanded, and finally incorporated into occupational and professional structures with their own training programs, associations, certifications, and journals. The leaders in the new field now write grant proposals, give seminars on grant and abstract writing, present papers, and set the climate for junior faculty. In short, they are actively building a new institution. Kunitz (1986) has described much of these developments in Rochester, and the details are not presented here. The danger for these new programs remains that without a large clinical income, they may stay at that initial level and remain marginal to their discipline. The main threat to their survival is that most of these programs must depend exclusively on outside financial support. Interdisciplinary research introduces further complexities when PhD faculty from social science disciplines become members of clinical departments with expectation of 100% salary recovery through grants. Such dependence creates instability. The return to primary care, as a counter movement to strong historical trends toward specialization, is one of most fascinating phenomena of the last two decades.

## The Pediatric Nurse Practitioner: A Transition in the Development of Nursing

KLAUS J. ROGHMANN AND HARRIET KITZMAN

The development of nursing as a profession has not been characterized by as many phases as the development of medicine, but similar patterns are evident. In the 10-year period following 1965, nursing used the manpower shortage as a unique opportunity to undergo rapid development, especially for the nurse practitioner. The country was ready for social reforms and the federal government was vigorously pushing new manpower programs. In brief, the time was ripe: "There was need. We were ready to work together to get all of this going. Short term, continuing education model programs developed the role of nurses in a way that enabled graduates to find positions with new, expanded responsibilities" (HK).

The initial continuing education model was not what the nursing leadership had been seeking. The profession itself, however, was badly divided among services, administration, and academic training. There were only weak graduate programs to prepare future leaders. When the interdisciplinary collaborative programs to expand the nursing role and nurse practitioners started, they were mostly located in medical schools, hospitals, and colleges, rather than in schools of nursing. Some 140 programs were initiated and about $12 million budgeted annually (LF). Research was conducted in conjunction with medical faculty, and by the end of the decade approximately 1000 publications showed the acceptance and effectiveness of nursing in the new expanded role. Pediatric nurse practitioners found a home in pediatric associations like the Ambulatory Pediatric Association. Most new practitioners easily found employment in the private sector or in clinics and health centers. The "fast fixes, such as continuing education" (HK) had worked, but would they last?

After the first decade of celebrated successes, the climate quickly changed. "Until the nurse practitioner began to be perceived by physicians as a threat, she was encouraged to pursue these higher goals. Once she had achieved a more lofty status, physicians began to show signs of regret and withdrew their encouragement and support. As the partnership deteriorated into conflict, it became necessary for the law to intervene" (Studner and Hirsh, 1986). The doctor shortage disappeared, and the first forecasts of physician oversupply appeared. Spitzer (1984), a physician, predicted "the slow death of the nurse practitioner movement" (Molde and Diers, 1985). The federal government, after supporting nurse practitioner training generously, "failed to follow through with policies for their utilization. In nursing homes, they say that nurse practitioners can be reimbursed. It is ridiculous to spend all that money, and then not insure the institutionalization in the delivery system" (LF). Presentations about nurse practitioner roles began to disappear from pediatric meetings, as did even the term "nurse practitioner." What had happened?

A literature search of the 5 years since 1983 found 859 new publications on nurse practitioners or equivalent roles—not exactly a decline. However, the journals in which these publications appeared have changed: *Pediatric Nursing, Nursing Management, Nurse Practitioner, Public Health Nursing, Nursing Research, Nursing Outlook, Annual Review of Nursing Research* became the main outlets. Presentations were still made at annual meetings, but no longer to physician audiences.

We started with peds and ob/gyn. Next week, I will be speaking before the pediatric oncology nurse practitioner's association. All these new associations, professional groups, councils, and conferences have been formed, both regional and national. Mostly they have been formed by practitioners who are moving into specialty areas. They are coming out of a combination of nurse practitioner and clinical specialist programs. (LF)

Nurse practitioner training disappeared from medical schools. "It is interesting to listen to you say that we don't have a nurse practitioner program and that we no longer have the continuing education model. In reality, there are more nurse practitioners prepared at the University of Rochester now than there were in 1972" (HK). The new role did not vanish; it became part of the established collegiate nursing programs. "When the first nurse practitioner program started in Colorado, Loretta Ford wanted very much for this to be a master's program in community health. This was to be the clinical role for the master's level clinical specialist in community health" (HK). But the schools of nursing were not quite ready at that point. Interdisciplinary programs filled the void until a new generation of nursing faculty, many coming right out of nurse practitioner programs, emerged to develop new curricula and offer advanced training. The 4-month training programs were turned into two-year master's programs, with 60 credit units. The original community health model evolved into the Family Health Nurse Clinician, and, more recently, into the Primary Care Clinician, with younger and older patient tracks. Within these tracks, specialty fields were added.

How long can this expansion of the nursing role continue? Will the market soon be saturated? "These are very interesting questions because there was this big flurry when there were projections of an oversupply of physicians. . . . There was a lot of concern among the students who were starting at that time. Interestingly enough, however, the demand has probably increased, rather than decreased" (HK). Where do all the new master's trained clinicians go? "Many drift into private practice to work as physician substitutes, where they handle routine tasks like well-child visits and telephone management. About half stay in the local area, and the others leave for all over the country. A fair number still join MDs in private practice, but they move into many other settings as well—settings that used to be regarded as too complex for them. The number of nurse practitioners at HMOs and Neighborhood Health Centers has remained relatively constant. At the Anthony Jordan Health Center and the alcoholism clinic, there are two master's prepared nurses. One is a psychiatry/mental health person and the other is responsible for health assessments and the coordination of clinical care. These are good examples of roles that would not have been present ten years ago."

What emerges from these interviews is the rapid further profession-alization and specialization of nursing. The old nurse practitioner pro-gram described in the first edition of this book served only as a transi-tional phase. There is a rapid proliferation of new journals and associations, with subspecialty development and increased activity over a large range of health care institutions. The "copying" of structures from the medical profession comes as no surprise, because it enables nursing to escape supervision from medicine. Independent practice by nurse practitioners exists, but has not evolved as successfully as have the many salaried positions in health care organizations. Case management, coordination of care, and management positions appear to be the expanding sectors, while private practice does not have the same appeal for nurses as it has for physicians. Wherever nurse practitioners are in a private practice setting, office billing for services prevails. All of this indicates the successful adjustment of the profession to the rapidly changing health care system—an adjustment that may fit the new environment better than the old, private practice model of care.

What is the outlook for the future? New PhD programs in nursing started about 10 years ago. Before then, faculty in the colleges of nursing did not need PhDs. If they had advanced degrees, they usually came from the social sciences and education. The new graduates go mostly into teaching, research, and administrative positions. At the same time, nursing has been incorporating the clinical practice and decision-making model, which has gradually replaced the passive nursing model of "just following physician's orders." There are clear expectations that nurses will develop to still higher level of clinical decision-making skills. This is true not only for the master's level nurse practitioner, but also for the "old" clinical specialist. "As I look at what is happening in the rest of the country, I think the next step won't be a Ph.D., but a D.N.S. (Doctor of Nursing Science). Yes, there will be a clinical doctorate for people involved in practice rather than teaching" (HK). At the same time, clinicians in the master's track may no longer be required to complete a 60 credit program with a full thesis and independent research. Instead, these programs will have reduced credit requirements and become comparable to other university master's programs. Further innovations on the horizon for nursing appear to be yet another new model—the liberal arts graduate degree for nursing—rather than a medical school program that lacks master's level training. The model may be more like the advanced training in schools of education than physician training. The Master in Business Administration program may be still another model. Clearly, nursing does not see its advanced position as substitute doctor in private practice, nor by and large as researcher, but as middle manager in health care institutions. Graduates will be managers and "professionals within organizations" rather than professionals in private practice. Growth potentials will be limited by the organizations they work for, but these organizations appear to be in a growth market. Professionalization is rapidly advancing, but following a model different from that of physicians and lawyers.

## REFERENCES

FELDMAN, MARY JANE, VENTURA, MARLENE R., and CROSBY, FRANCES
1987 "Studies of Nurse Practitioner Effectiveness." *Nursing Research*, 36:303–308.

FORD, LORETTA (LF)
1988 Interview with Klaus Roghmann. Rochester, New York.

KITZMAN, HARRIET (HK)
1988 Interview with Klaus Roghmann. Rochester, New York.

KUNITZ, STEPHEN J.
1986 *The Training of Primary Care Physicians.* Lanham, Md.: University Press of America.

MOLDE, SUSAN, and DIERS, DONNA
1985 "Nurse Practitioner Research: Selected Literature Review and Research Agenda." *Nursing Research*, 34:362–267.

SHAMANSKY, SHERRY L.
1985 "Nurse Practitioners and Primary Care Research: Promises and Pitfalls." *Annual Review of Nursing Research*, 3:107–125.

STUDNER, JON M., and HIRSH, HAROLD L.
1986 "Nurse Practitioners: Functions, Legal Status and Legislative Control." *Medicine and Law*, 5:61–75.

SPITZER, WALTER O.
1984 "The Nurse Practitioner Revisited: Slow Death of a Good Idea." *New England Journal of Medicine*, 310:1049–1051.

*Family Counselors: The Role of Community Work in the Modern Health Care World*

KLAUS J. ROGHMANN AND I. BARRY PLESS

In the original edition of this book, the family counselor was described as a competent helper for families struggling to cope with a child's chronic illness. But such a limited definition misses a crucial element that requires as much attention as the manpower issue, namely the "professionalization" of community work. Since the earliest description of American communities by Alexis de Tocqueville there have always been volunteers in schools, neighborhoods, and churches to help people in times of need. We no longer talk about "charity," but about "community services." These bridge the realities of modern industrialization and high-technology medicine and humanize the lives around us. Family counselors were recruited from the ranks of nonprofessional women partly to overcome manpower shortages in social services and to create new career paths, but also to tap the tradition of volunteerism. Family counselors were women who had successfully raised families and had attributes like "maturity, warmth, empathy, concern." They had flexible work hours and provided their own transportation. They were trained according to a "continuing education" model, that is, a number of short training sessions and monthly meetings at which they exchanged experiences and updated their knowledge (Pless et al., 1976; Rice et al., 1976–77). Certainly, the counselors helped families with chronically ill children at no charge to the families, but the essential characteristic of the counselor role was more that of a volunteer community worker than of a professional. Two competing models of "helping" coexisted.

In retrospect, to describe the original counselor program as an example of volunteerism seems misleading. The initial program emerged out of set of research questions dealing with better ways to help children with chronic disorders. Because of the research constraints, it was decided that a token sum ought to be paid to help persuade the women that they were "not simply volunteers," but participants in a scholarly undertaking. This, in turn, entailed added expectations, including record keeping, logging, and so on, to which they had to conform.

It may be that this token payment was a mistake because it raised expectations or altered self-perceptions. Indeed, one of the reasons the program ultimately floundered, in spite of the 4 subsequent iterations and in spite of imbedding it in the Social Work Department, may well have been that these women did not feel comfortable seeing themselves as volunteers. They knew they had a number of special, often distinctive skills, and believed these should be recognized in several ways, including monetary.

In this sense, then, there are some interesting analogues to the description of the evolution of nursing and nurse practitioners in the preceding section.

The transition from the counselor program to the Child Health Advisory Group, and other such "official" expressions of volunteerism is really the history of one energetic and talented woman who served as project director for the family counselor program.

The leaders of the 5 separate programs that developed in Rochester over a 5-year period addressed parallel tasks in the same spirit, expanding the family counselor role. Thus, a community newsletter was started, a logo was adopted, and the Child Health Advisory Group was created to bring the university and community together. Communication gaps were addressed by special symposia. One was a semiannual symposium with school personnel. Another was the Janice Lynn Cohn Memorial Symposium, which brought local clergy and pediatricians together. The Sarah Davidson Library was created in the same spirit, to help parents of sick children by making a variety of reference works on children's diseases easily accessible. All of these were shoestring operations with no departmental funding, but they served as models for hundreds of other communities who wrote requesting curricula or book lists. They were "successes" in terms of meeting needs and receiving national visibility, but "failures" because they were never institutionalized and thus received no hard money support. It is difficult to evaluate such efforts scientifically, but it is evident that they improved community relations. They may even serve as a model for private initiatives, such as the "thousand points of light" programs. What happened to these early community initiatives? Are they still valid at a time of competitive cost containment?

A conceptual framework is needed to help understand the various aspects of the family counselor program. Social problem orientation and individual leadership were the decisive characteristics in this approach, rather than professional or institutional leadership. New leadership brought new management styles. The family counselor program, which in a clinical trial in 1973 had shown positive effects for children, expired formally, but informally, many relationships between counselors and physicians continued. A survey in 1979 showed mixed results (Son, 1979): all of the family counselors had profited from the program; 13 of the 21 said helping families was their prime motivation for entering the program. Eighteen were still active in volunteer work. Half decided to return to school and several entered social work. However, the same number regarded the compensation as inadequate and felt "slighted" or demeaned when comparing themselves with others doing the "same work," for example, social workers. Others considered the program only as a temporary learning experience. For them the pay was incidental. Positive comments usually referred to their personal growth, while negative comments reflected concerns about their acceptance by other professionals. Their personal missions were to get "more participation by physicians," "to sensitize doctors who seem to feel that only poor patients need our help." Many felt there was inadequate understanding of their role.

The same lack of appreciation was also expressed about the other tasks that grew out of the program. Volunteers were just volunteers and were not given the same respect as salaried professionals. Fund-raising, only incidental to the earlier programs, was taken away from these volunteers and assigned to a new professional public relations staff. Many felt disenchanted with the limited possibilities of the volunteer's contribution and frustrated by the department's apparent indifference toward them: "In terms of departmental power, forget volunteers"; "It is all fund-raising now. Forget cultivating the community."

The old Community Advisory Board became Strong Children's Medical Center (SCMC) Advisory Board, and a professional community affairs staff was hired. Public awareness activities, such as the Telethon, Radiothon, dinners, and marathons are now organized. "We are different today than we were fifteen years ago when Bob Haggerty launched the Child Health Advisory Group . . . or ten years ago, when David Smith established the department's Office of Community Liaison, with a full-time staff . . . or five years ago, when the SCMC received permission from the University to form an advisory board" (Hoekelman, 1988). Indeed, professional fund-raising allocated over $400,000 to the department's 1988 budget of $16.4 million. "I challenge you to think big because we are big and we are growing bigger every day" (Hoekelman, 1988). Indeed, no matter what standard is applied, a metamorphosis had occurred that must be regarded as a success. The early family counselor program was a critical stepping-stone in this development. However, the community service aspects of the original new manpower program grew by adding new programs and began to dominate. When fund-raising efforts were associated with the program, the original mission clearly disappeared into the background, new staff was added, and a completely new mission developed. In retrospect, it is difficult to separate the effects of personnel, programs, and principles on the development of this initial manpower program.

*REFERENCES*

HOEKELMAN, ROBERT A.

1988   "Chairman's Report, Strong Children's Medical Center, Annual Report 1987–88" (unpublished manuscript).

PLESS, I.B., SATTERWHITE, B., and VANVECHTEN, D.

1976   "Chronic Illness in Childhood: A Regional Survey of Care." *Pediatrics*, 58:37–46.

RICE, N., SATTERWHITE, B., and PLESS, I.B.

1976–77   "Family Counselors in a Pediatric Speciality Clinic Setting." *Social Work in Health Care*, 2:193–203.

SON, LINDA H.

1979   "A Follow-Up Study on Family Counselors. Independent Study Research Project" (unpublished paper).

## School Health: From Medical Model to Educational Model

KLAUS J. ROGHMANN AND PHILIP R. NADER

School health used to follow a traditional medical model, with emphasis on annual physicals, immunizations, and a school nurse to attend to minor illnesses or to send children home when ill. When more serious conditions were identified or suspected, referrals were made. There was a clear understanding, however, that no primary care was to be delivered at the school.

The school health program in Rochester started to change this model. First, Yankauer and Lawrence (1955, 1957) demonstrated that annual physical examinations yielded little benefit. This led to a widespread reduction in these "ritual" services. Second, in the 1960s, Nader documented that the main problems of schoolchildren were learning difficulties, behavior problems, and developmental issues (Nader, 1975). Attending to these "new morbidities" required a new focus (Nader, Roy, and Ailman, 1981). Local community aides, supervised by public health nurses, were recruited to make referrals and provide counseling (Nader, Emmel, and Charney, 1972). Nader also expanded the role of the school nurse and doctor to provide comprehensive health services in conjunction with an adjacent neighborhood health center. This expanded "new model" used local health aides and links to health centers to deliver 24-hour, 7-day-a-week medical services.

At the same time, schools in the community were seen as another training site for pediatric residents to get more involved in health care. This was an extension of our community pediatrics orientation.

What happened to these innovations? The answers depend on who is interviewed. Residents no longer train in schools and the "comprehensive medical model" for providing health care has disappeared. The integration of services from aides, through public health nurses to medical director/health centers has disappeared (Nader, 1989). The comprehensive medical model has been largely replaced by an "educational model" in which psychologists and health educators run school health programs. Indeed, the dominant themes in most school health programs now are health promotion, disease prevention, and the implementation of Public Law 94-142 to identify and insure as normal an environment as possible for handicapped children. The old Committees on the Handicapped (now Committees on Special Education) have become important new educational institutions with minimal medical input. Many new health education topics, such as AIDS and drug education, are mandated by states, and many of the institutional structures are products of new legislative actions. Most of the "new morbidities" are handled without pediatric input.

A community pediatrician with over 20 years of experience as a school doctor (McInerney, 1989) gives the following description of the current local system:

The City School District contracts with the County Department of Health to provide medical services to the city's schools. The Health Department in turn hires six pediatricians to act as consultants to school nurses, who are also provided by the Health Department. Generally, the pediatricians spend one-half day (3–4 hours) per week to provide several services: athletic physicals (fortunately, the coordinator of these services has won approval for a program of "every other year" physicals, supplemented by a preparticipation interview by the school nurse—a model the whole community should adopt); advice on how a student's chronic medical problem may impact on his or her ability to function in school; liaison between the school and the student's physician (this is especially important when subspecialists are involved because communication between specialty clinics and school nurses is still poor); assistance to the pupil personnel team with learning and behavioral problems; provision of expanded neurologic exams, or advice on emotional problems that can be helped with program modification or counseling. Other functions are health education, provided either directly or by helping the school nurse. These include AIDS education and parenting courses for adolescent mothers, and being a member of the Committee on the Handicapped (this is usually effective in name only because the physician's attendance is only required if the parents request it). The job also includes inspecting the school for safety problems, and consulting with cafeteria personnel regarding the nutritional value of school lunches.

In the suburban districts the situation is different. Each district still hires its own school physician who is not always a pediatrician. They still perform health appraisals as prescribed by New York State. While most students have these done by their own physicians, some 10–20% still have to be seen. Some districts are utilizing school nurse practitioners, under the supervision of the school physician, to assist with the task. In summary, little has changed for school physicians in the suburbs. They increasingly provide consultation to school personnel as they attempt to structure appropriate education for children with chronic illness, handicapping conditions, or developmental disabilities. The number of special education classes has skyrocketed over the past 15 years. One suburban district has 10% of its students identified as having a handicapping condition, while the city is struggling with a rate in excess of 25%! (TM)

The innovative school health service described by Nader, Emmel, and Charney (1972), which was linked to the health center, no longer operates. However, for the past 7 years, a new program—the Anthony Jordan Health Center (AJHC) School Health Program, funded by the New York State Department of Health, Bureau of Child Health—has operated as part of a statewide school health demonstration project (MB). Services for the high school are subcontracted to Threshold, Center for Alternative Youth Services, another agency specializing in adolescent health. Dental services are subcontracted to the Eastman Dental Center.

Thus, the school health program has moved away from the "strict medical model" to one that responds to changing needs. It now has 3 components: health education, mental health counseling, and linkage to existing medical and dental services. The reason given for the elimination of the comprehensive medical model was "not having a full-time staff member available for direct primary care on site, and the linking of families to existing medical services which already provide continuity of care." There is still a health assistant on this team, but her role is to assist families without a primary care physician to gain entry into the local health care system. The main staff members are a health educator who also serves as project manager (full-time), a certified social worker (half-time), a psychologist (1 day a week), and a health assistant. A physician preceptor is involved 2 hours a week to oversee the program and provide medical services.

This new model has moved toward a retrenchment of medical services from the schools as a site for delivering medical care. Instead, there are more bridges between agencies in the community through subcontracting medical and dental services, or replacing direct services with referral staff. The structures that have emerged are those negotiated by administrators and local politicians who direct their various educational and health institutions to collaborate with each other. This new environment does not allow much room for professional role expansion.

Much like pediatrics, nursing has also been affected by this transformation in the schools.

There really has not been the movement (in nursing) that I projected in the public schools. The model available for school health—a combination of graduate education with the pediatric nurse practitioner—should match the needs of schools. Some of our graduates have been successful, but, when budgets are so tight, no one wants to expand health care services because those costs are seen as the responsibility of another sector of society. There's just no room in the school budget to add another highly paid (as they see it) employee. It is much easier for the schools to get nurses at minimum wages because of the hours. They are picking up RNs who have kids in the school, whereas someone who is really in a career mode would compete with a teacher's salary. There is little acceptance of pediatric nurse practitioners in the school system. (HK)

There has been at least 1 national development that deviates from this picture and that has received much attention. The Robert Wood Johnson Foundation funded a multisite, school-based nurse practitioner program to provide health services, modeled loosely on the Cambridge, Massachusetts primary health program (Porter and Butler, 1987). The other major new program for personal health services in schools is the school-based clinic for adolescents. Both models are highly effective, especially for underserved areas and for emancipated or alienated youths, but they appear not to be viable structures in the current health care environment. Funds for them are only available through philanthropy. Professional societies reject them because they cannot replace good comprehensive services with links to secondary and tertiary care. No matter how effective, such programs are extremely volatile and only feasible with the support of isolated agencies and professionals. Once the seed money from foundations is gone, the programs close.

REFERENCES

BARLOW, MATHEW J.
    1989   Interview by Philip R. Nader.

KITZMAN, HARRIET
    1988   Interview by Klaus J. Roghmann.

MCINERNY, THOMAS
    1989   Interview by Philip R. Nader.

NADER, PHILIP R.
    1975   "The Frequency and Nature of School Problems." In *Child Health and the Community*, edited by Robert J. Haggerty, Klaus J. Roghmann, and Ivan B. pless, pp. 101–105. New York: John Wiley.
    1988   "School Health Services." In *Maternal and Child Health Practices*, edited by Helen M. Wallace, George Ryan Jr., Allan C. Oglesby, pp. 463–482. Oakland, California: Third Party Publishing Company.
    1989   Interview by Robert J. Haggerty.

NADER, PHILIP R., EMMEL, ANNE, and CHARNEY, EVAN
    1972   "The School Health Service: A New Model." *Pediatrics*, 49:805–813.

NADER, PHILIP R., ROY, L., and AILMAN S.
    1981   "The New Morbidity: Use of School and Community Health Care Resources for Behavioral, Educational and Social-Family problems." *Pediatrics*, 67(1):53.

PORTER, P.J., and BUTLER, J.C.

1987 "Healthy Children; an Assessment of Community-Based Primary Care Health Programs for Children and Their Impact on Access, Cost, and Quality." *Adv-Pediatr.*, 34:379–409.

YANKAUER, A. and LAWRENCE, R.

1955 "A Study of Periodic School Examinations." *American Journal of Public Health*, 45:71.

1957 "A Study of Periodic School Examinations." *American Journal of Public Health*, 45:1421.

## Adolescent Health Care: A Continuing Challenge

KLAUS J. ROGHMANN AND ROBERT J. HAGGERTY

In the original edition of this book we addressed many areas of concern under the heading "new morbidity." The three we focused on include behavioral problems of preschoolers, problems of school-age children, and those of adolescents. Recognizing a problem and finding a solution, however, are quite different challenges. Pediatricians still handle most preschool problems adequately, although the conferences and counseling sessions require extra time and special scheduling. Some school issues are handled increasingly, and generally well, through mental health counselors within schools. Problems of adolescents, however, continue to pose great challenges.

Addressing these newly recognized problems required new social structures. Originated through the volunteer efforts of faculty and staff, the adolescent program of the University of Rochester originally met twice a week in an outpatient setting, and one of these was on Saturday morning. When this format proved inadequate, outreach efforts were established with outside funding. The university, however, insisted on high indirect costs, even for such off-site services. In this difficult environment a number of institutions emerged that have passed the test of time.

The adolescent clinic was organized by a behavioral pediatrician, an adolescent psychiatrist, and a clinical psychologist. Two extensions into the community soon developed—Threshold and the Rochester Adolescent Maternity Project (RAMP). Threshold was initially developed as a drug treatment program by a community health services resident (Martin Wasserman), but it did not receive state funding. When it changed to a general adolescent care program, the state approved funding, but the university did not because only 10% in indirect cost was allocated at a time when the university was demanding 53%. The state eventually agreed to pay in order to get the service running.

Threshold has since provided health care in a store-front clinic in downtown Rochester for 3,500 inner-city youth per year. It represents a model of a much needed, yet financially unstable, organizational structure—one that was never allowed to flourish and never allowed to fail. The university unloaded the program at the first opportunity, but in crisis situations when all other support fails, it resumes Threshold's management. At present, Threshold is again run by the university. Local charities and social services have raised operating funds, but only for short periods. Having served the community for some 20 years now, Threshold will always be needed to fill the gaps in health care for adolescents, yet it continues to be characterized as "crass politics of the lowest form. . . . Interest groups . . . use such services, and the social problems they present, as political footballs in scrimmages for needed resources" (Salancik, 1981). Health care to poor adolescents includes a large amount of family planning services not "morally" supported by the public. Like abortion, these services are a source of continuous conflict with no solution in sight.

The other program, Rochester Adolescent Maternity Program (RAMP), was a purposeful extension of the original adolescent program to deal with pregnant adolescents who could not get the special attention they require in general obstetric/gynecology clinics. The first application to the State Division of Youth was voted down by an unsympathetic board. After much work by local minority organizations and local industry, a second application was approved. For some 20 years now, RAMP has provided services for the most difficult third of all teenage pregnant mothers in the Rochester community.

The adolescent clinic also attracted residents and fellows to work in schools. This later developed into the new comprehensive school health model described above. RAMP tried many innovative ideas, such as hiring ex-patients to be assistants or outreach workers. Patients received a joint workup by medical and nursing students, and the setting stimulated a variety of interdisciplinary research.

As with the school health program, the adolescent program suffered greatly when its innovators left, although the community organization that was spawned has survived. This organizational pattern is now familiar. With volunteer work and enthusiasm, a small core of innovators prepare the infrastructure. Then, in collaboration with state or federal agencies, new outread programs are created to address previously identified needs. This often happens only after overcoming opposition from within the university or other established institutions, such as the youth board or school board.

While 20 years ago the area of adolescent medicine was hardly accepted as a division of pediatrics, the issues confronting the field are now quite different. They include the potential fragmentation of adolescent medicine into subspecialties, such as eating disorders, chronic illness, and cancer. Shortages persist, now as before, in the availability of support from psychiatry and other mental health professionals. Insurance coverage remains a basic problem because, although some patients have insurance through their parents, most psychosocial services are excluded. In summary, while service structures and academic specialties have developed, the social infrastructure for their delivery remains weak.

## REFERENCES

FRIEDMAN, STANFORD B.
1989    Interview by Robert J. Haggerty.

SALANCIK, G.R.
1981    "The Effectiveness of Ineffective Social Service Systems." In *Organization and the Human Services*, edited by H.D. Stein, pp. 142–150. Philadelphia: Temple University Press.

*Neighborhood Health Centers: Survival in a Hostile Environment*

KLAUS J. ROGHMANN

In a recent presentation, Milton Roemer (1988) reviewed the history of neighborhood health centers under the title "Resistance to Change: The Case of The Community Health Centers." He concluded that "throughout most of the world—both developing and industrialized, free-market and socialist—the community health center, in which primary health care (preventive and curative) is provided by interdisciplinary teams, is increasingly becoming a conventional facility. In Scandinavian countries, it is the major resource for ambulatory service, as it is in all the socialist countries. . . . The technological and economic value of health care organization, long appreciated in hospitals, has at last come to be recognized for ambulatory services." In short, Roemer sees health centers as a generic organizational form for the delivery of health services, like hospitals or private practices. Although these centers have appeared in many different cultural settings over the past 350 years, they have become well established only recently and prosper only in supportive environments. Wherever this generic form provided care only for a poor constituency, it remained a volatile institution. Wherever it became incorporated into the mainstream of medical care, the health center became a leading delivery site for ambulatory services in the same way that hospitals, also originally planned for the poor, became the leading delivery sites for inpatient care. Health centers appeared under various names; first, they were known as dispensaries, then polyclinics, and more recently as neighborhood and now community health centers. Center sponsorship also varies among institutions. Usually, they were originated by a concerned physician and only later were they supported by government or professional societies. A few historical milestones will illustrate this point.

In 1632, Renandot opened a consultation center in Paris where he offered the poor free advice and made referrals to physicians, surgeons, and apothecaries who offered to treat the poor without charge. When his center flourished, the medical dean at the University of Paris took legal action to stop his work and successfully closed his center. At the same time, the court ordered the medical school to set up a charitable consultation system for the poor. By 1707 such dispensaries were so well established in France that every medical faculty offered one.

In England, the Royal College of Physicians opened a dispensary for the poor in London in 1697, and it operated until 1725. A philanthropic layman opened a new dispensary in 1746, and from 1770 onward, the idea was so well established that 15 more dispensaries followed rapidly. In addition, some hospitals started to see outpatients. In 1769, Dr. George Armstrong established a special "Dispensary for Poor Infants" in London, where he provided services at his own expense. During the eighteenth century, including the period of Enlightenment in Europe, these ideas met little resistance and spread quickly. "Doctors, merchants, clergymen, and other middle class citizens acquired a sense of responsibility for the welfare of the poor" (Roemer, 1988:1236). Indeed, many inspirations from these times fueled the new developments in the 1960s. The "George Armstrong Lecture" is still the highlight of the Ambulatory Pediatric Association's annual meetings.

The nineteenth century, with its rapid urbanization and industrialization and accompanying large migrations within and between countries, brought a new need for public health measures and greater emphasis on sanitation and housing rather than on individual health care. The explosion of medical knowledge started with bacteriology and the implications for better hygiene. Hospitals expanded rapidly, adding outpatient departments at the same time. In Germany, Bismarck started his social security legislation, which included illness insurance through employment-related sickness funds that contracted with private physicians for the care of their enrollees. The social security model for the delivery of medical care found wide acceptance in Europe and Latin America. In the United States, dispensaries were established throughout the nineteenth century. Rochester, New York, as an industrial city in which entrepreneurs like George Eastman built their production facilities with the help of immigrant manpower, also opened a dispensary at one of its settlement houses.

For the ethnic neighborhoods in northeast Rochester, the Baden Street Settlement House provided many social services, including a dispensary with a TB clinic, a VD clinic, a dental clinic, and a well-child clinic. During the 1920s, this dispensary provided for 40,000 visits per year. It was on this very site that the Rochester Neighborhood Health Center was opened in 1968, as described in the earlier edition of this book. By 1987, the center was providing for 85,000 visits per year. No longer of Italian or Eastern European extraction, the area's population has become mostly black and Hispanic. In light of the neighborhood's cultural changes, the health center maintains a historical perspective on its constituency: "One thing that all neighborhood health centers have to be aware of is the different type of population, culturally, than they were treating twenty years ago. . . . For example, 25% of our patients are now Hispanic. . . . We have to have bilingual capabilities. We have to be culturally sensitive to particular medical and social points of view" (MB).

In 1964, Evan Charney started a continuity clinic in the medical center to teach residents primary care. Nurse practitioners were involved, and a team approach was developed. Outreach efforts were made, but these proved to be difficult. Most patients lived some 5 miles away and had to change buses to reach the clinic. Because clinics were separated by patients age, a comprehensive family approach was not possible. During this time, Kenneth Woodward, a previous chief resident in pediatrics and now a leading black physician in the community, was appointed medical coordinator of the Baden Street Health Center. Many of the special clinic functions of the old Baden Street Dispensary had been transferred to health department clinics, so it was reorganized as a family-oriented, comprehensive community health center—an obvious place for an extension of the continuity clinic. A coalition soon emerged between Action for a Better Community (ABC), the local agency for the "war on poverty" programs, the Monroe Health Department, which was staffing many of the clinics for the poor, and the University of Rochester. To operate the Neighborhood Health Center, Charney and Woodward applied for a grant from the Office of Economic Opportunity (OEO), the medical center provided physicians, the health department placed 14 public health nurses at the center, and

ABC endorsed the collaboration. On July 1, 1968, the Rochester Neighborhood Health Center started operations in basement clinics at a public housing project near the old Baden Street Settlement House. Although originally opposed, the university eventually accepted responsibility for administering the grant from OEO.

Five years later, the Anthony Jordan Health Center Corporation (AJHC) was founded with a 25-member local board and took over the operation of the center. The health department continued to provide up to 16 public health nurses to the center. Federal support continued through the Rochester Health Network (RHN), which had been created by Neighborhood Health Centers of Monroe County, Inc. (NHCMC) to operate a network of health centers. Later, 4 other health centers were established in other areas of the city and in a western rural area. After separating from RHN in 1981, AJHC became a direct grantee of federal funds under Section 330. AJHC also hired its own staff of nurses to replace the health department's public health nurses who had been withdrawn during a period of severe budget restriction. In April 1982, AJHC was designated a Comprehensive Health Center by the United States Public Health Service. In October 1984, the Comprehensive Outpatient Alcoholism Center officially opened. AJHC was awarded 3-year accreditation from the Joint Commission on Accreditation of Health Care Organization in May 1988. The center now operates a teen center with funding from The Robert Wood Johnson Foundation, as well as a Women, Infants, and Children (WIC) program; and it has applied for mental health certification. The statistics provided in Table 14B.1 indicate the volume of services it delivers, and the declining support from federal agencies.

Between July 1985 and July 1987, AJHC participated in MediCap, a managed care experiment for Medicaid patients to be described later, and suffered heavy losses, resulting in major layoffs.

Despite all evidence of organizational growth, the evaluations by key

Table 14B.1.  Provision of Services by the AJHC during the 1980s

| Year | Visits | Expense ($) | % Direct Federal Support |
|------|--------|-------------|--------------------------|
| 1981 | 74,762 | 4,248,000   | 27.7 |
| 1982 | 72,891 | 4,532,000   | 24.7 |
| 1983 | 75,924 | 5,058,000   | 26.6 |
| 1984 | 73,511 | 5,404,000   | 26.1 |
| 1985 | 80,144 | 6,318,000   | 26.1 |
| 1986 | 85,332 | 6,291,000   | 19.4 |
| 1987 | 82,997 | 6,258,000   | 17.0 |

people remain mixed. The business manager calls the center "financially fragile"; Evan Charney (EC) also stresses its "anemic funding." "With major funding from Medicaid now limited to strictly medical services (and it is inadequate even for these), the innovative community outreach and sociopsychological services were discontinued early. The lack of a patient population of mixed social classes also deprived the center of financial and public support" (EC). Indeed, the excessive reliance of the center on Medicaid payments put it at great financial risk. Medicaid funds are determined on a year to year basis, competing with other budget items. There is no possibility of cross-subsidies from other payment sources.

Two other issues were brought up in the interviews. First, acceptance of community centers by the traditional medical establishment is important. Because the Rochester center was university operated for the first 5 years, "physicians in the health centers were linked to teaching hospitals, and this allowed them to admit patients and play a role in teaching pediatric residents. But they were received with reluctance by the medical leaders" (EC). When the health center board refused to have the center serve as a teaching site, the university's interest in the health center also declined. Second, administrative leadership and control within the health center setting had been restrained. HMOs can recruit high-powered business managers to expand services, raise premiums, enroll target populations, and establish sound financial reserves. In their "business" environment, neighborhood health center administrators are only allowed minimal leadership roles as public service administrators. Their options are highly restricted. In an atmosphere of limited and fragmented power, management functions become relatively weak.

If survival is the main criterion for success, the health centers of Monroe County have certainly been successful. If level of functioning, quality of care, and financial stability are the main criteria, however, the verdict is different. Those concerned with care to the poor have already planned a reassessment: the Monroe County government (Department of Social Services) is reviewing services to the Medicaid population in the post-MediCap environment; the Health Department has completed a state-mandated health assessment; the Finger Lakes Health System Agency (FLHSA) released a Primary Care and Preventive Services Plan; Health Futures, a Blue Cross-backed consulting firm, organized a citizen's committee to look at the uninsured population; and MetroAct, a local concerned citizen's group, has stated their worries about the provision of care to the poor. All of these initiatives raise serious questions about the central role of health centers, and as a result the

FLHSA has established a task force on health centers to address the following three questions:

1. Has the environment (funding sources, third-party payments, regulations, etc.) in which the centers operate changed?
2. How have the centers responded to these changes? Are these transitory difficulties only, or will the service structure to the poor be permanently affected?
3. If changes are to be made, can they be made by the centers on their own or are changes in the larger medical care environment needed?

The creation of a task force reflects the recognition that the health centers are operating in a new environment. They no longer carry out programs directed by the federal government, such as improving access to care or helping the poor to develop a political infrastructure. In the future, they must survive without federal support. Brecher and Forman (1981) argue that changes in reimbursement policies and management are needed to establish financial stability. Ginzberg and Ostow (1985) evaluated the Robert Wood Johnson Foundation's Municipal Health Services Program (1978–1984), and also emphasized the rapidly changing social environment, such as a decline in the inner-city population and the increase in physician supply. They also called attention to the need of the federal government to constrain future outlays for both Medicare and Medicaid and the efforts of states to constrain Medicaid expenses, and the withdrawal of local government from the delivery of care through community hospitals. At the same time, competitive cost containment efforts, like Diagnosis Related Groups, Health Maintenance Organizations, and preferred provider arrangements, have made it increasingly difficult for hospitals to subsidize charity cases.

Rochester has managed to establish a network of 5 federally subsidized inner-city health centers, compared to only 2 in Buffalo, and 1 each in Syracuse and Albany. In 1985–86, the federal grant paid for 33% of the expenses of the Rochester network; in 1986–87, the amount was down to 17.5%. Services were cut, resulting in the initiatives discussed above. To avoid further deterioration, local government may have to subsidize the network. However nobody expects the health centers to disappear. The community recognizes that the centers do a good job providing health care to the poor, and a return to pre–health center conditions is unimaginable. While hopes are expressed that with a decreasing inner-city population and an increasing physician supply, new private practices will spring up in areas previously abandoned by practitioners, there is no sign of such developments in Rochester.

Ginzberg and Ostow (1985) also suggested that private third-party payers and local leadership explore "all payer systems" to cooperate in the care of the poor and uninsured. This would generate a supportive environment for the health care system, enabling it to thrive much as it does in Scandinavia and other welfare states. But without federal incentives or support, it is unlikely that such a system will emerge in the near future. For this to occur, a major change in the health care environment would be required. This change would have to include universal health insurance and a recognition of the growing needs of the urban poor. Instead, a more likely scenario is the continuation of crisis management for institutions that we can no longer live without.

This assessment of the development of the neighborhood health center movement in one community is quite different from a recent national review of its success. In her book *The U.S. Experiment in Social Medicine* (1988), Alice Sardell implies that the neighborhood health center is part of a "failed" experiment. She argues that the health center movement incorporated ideas that had been advocated by health care reformers for decades, including comprehensive care, community participation, and "social medicine." Health center advocates, according to her analysis, saw the institution not just as a way to provide quality health care to low-income populations, but also as "a model for the reorganization of health care services for the entire U.S. population" (Sardell, 1988: 4). This view links health care reformers to broader concerns for programmatic social innovations, such as the war on poverty. But these health care reformers never became part of the established health policy networks in Congress or the administration, and their movement failed.

Rochester's experience, however, offers a different perspective. The question we addressed was not how political processes define national objectives, but how local constituents react to national opportunities. There are many anecdotes about how new power structures emerged or crystallized around new institutions in poverty areas and how they affected local politics. The Rochester experience was one of cooptation from many sides: academic pediatricians developed and evaluated new programs for these settings, applying for grants, publishing research findings, and developing their discipline on new frontiers; private practitioners came to the center for a half-day of community service; hospitals found relief for their crowded outpatient and emergency services. As a whole, the community welcomed federal funding to the areas of greatest need. Local supporters of the new centers had no hidden agenda to "create a model for the reorganization of health care for all," and were surprised by occasional opposition to their involvement. The Rochester health center advocates may never have heard of social medicine, but they sensed that they had witnessed the creation of a new kind of institution—one that filled a niche in the existing service spectrum. The health center is still an emerging institution in Rochester. In no way can it be considered a "failed" experiment.

## REFERENCES

BARLOW, MATHEW J.

1989  Interview by Klaus J. Roghmann.

BRECHER, C., and FORMAN, M.

1981  "Financial Viability of Community Health Centers." *Journal of Health Politics, Policy and Law*, 5(4):742–768.

CHARNEY, EVAN

1989  Interview by Klaus J. Roghmann.

GINZBERG, ELI, and OSTOW, MIRIAM

1985  "The Community Health Care Center: Current Status and Future Directions." *Journal of Health Politics, Policy and Law*, 10:283–298.

MERSHA, TIGINEH

1985  "The Failure of the Group Model: A Case Study." *Health Care Management Review*, 10:73–80.

QUINTANA, RUBEN

1988  "Meeting the Unmet Needs of the Poor, Uninsured and Underserved of Monroe County: A Proposal to the Local, State and Federal Governments of Support of Rochester's Inner-City Health Centers" (unpublished manuscript). Rochester: Health Care Coalition.

ROEMER, MILTON I.

1988  "Resistance to Innovations: The Case of the Community Health Center." *American Journal of Public Health*, 78:1234–1239.

SARDELL, ALICE

1988  *The U.S. Experiment in Social Medicine. The Community Health Center Program 1965–1986.* Pittsburgh: University of Pittsburgh Press.

SCHORR, L.B., and ENGLISH, J.T.

1968  "Background, Context and Significant Issues in Neighborhood Health Center Programs." *Milbank Memorial Fund Quarterly*, 66:289–296.

WOOD, J.B., HUGHES, R.G., and ESTES, C.L.

1986  "Community Health Centers and the Elderly: A Potential News Alliance." *Journal of Community Health*, 11:137–146.

## C. CONCEPTUAL SHIFTS: THE NEW MORBITITY AND CHRONIC ILLNESS

Our 1975 report on "Child Health and the Community" used a simple paradigm. We analyzed the problems that children faced and the service structures required to address these problems. In the period during and following our study, the social environment of children changed rapidly, as did their health needs. To address the "new" morbidities of childhood, "new" services were required. During this time, our thinking also changed. New concepts and theoretical frameworks emerged that are more difficult to trace than the fate of new organizations or professions. This section examines the development and current status of several new concepts that were defined in our previous analysis, and determines which have stood the test of time, and which have been redefined.

### The New Morbidity Redefined as Psychopathology

KLAUS J. ROGHMANN

A generic term coined to address two aspects of the modern childhood environment, "new morbidity," has been both accepted and redefined in the years since our original study. First, the term acknowledged that children were at an increased risk for certain problems because of changing physical and social environments. There are many modern health hazards—pollution, car safety, toy safety, hi-rise living, urban decay, and lead paint. Each requires constant vigilance and legislative action. In addition to physical issues, children also face a deteriorating social environment, including a predominance of out-of-wedlock child rearing in the lower social classes, an increasing number of the poor and homeless, a reduction of social programs, and neglect of public school systems in the inner cities. The middle class experienced increased geographical mobility and family instability. More recently, two-income families have become the rule without necessarily raising the standard of living. Child care centers increasingly replace key functions of the traditional family. Fast-food chains relieve the disappearing homemaker of some household tasks like shopping and cooking. Television has become a babysitter and educator. The effects of these changes on child growth and development are still unknown.

While the old health problems may have less impact, they still remain.

Access to primary care has been reduced, with more and more children in poor areas becoming underimmunized. Adolescents continue to use inappropriate coping mechanisms, such as alcohol and drugs. Sexually transmitted diseases still take their toll, and new infections, like AIDS, have emerged. Children are exposed to these problems earlier and experience fewer social controls to help them deal with such issues. When adolescents enter the job market, they find that modern technologies have created an economic environment in which only those workers with intensive and extended training are successful. Those without such education face a bleak future. Some reason that as there is nothing to lose, they might as well have out-of-wedlock children, and many turn to drugs and delinquency.

Seen as maladaptations of children to these new environments, the concept of "new morbidities" challenged professional leaders to respond with new services. We looked at the development of preschoolers, school functioning in later years, and the special problems of adolescents (without explicitly addressing teenage sexuality and childbearing). This broad conceptualization, of course, was too vague and required redefinition, preferably, with a precision adequate for disease coding manuals. One such redefinition of "new morbidity" was psychopathology in children. This stimulated the discussion about the pediatrician's role in the delivery of mental health services to children (Costello, 1986; Costello and Pantino, 1987). Rochester was the site for two large surveys of the prevalence of psychopathology in children as determined by their pediatricians (Goldberg et al., 1979; Goldberg et al., 1984). The first covered 3,742 children in a feasibility study; the second followed up with a study of 18,351 children in 30 practices. Estimates of period and lifetime prevalence were obtained; risk factors were established (Weiland, Pless, and Roghmann, 1992), and current treatment modes and referral patterns were identified.

There is now general agreement that some 13% to 20% of children in the general population have one or more clinically significant emotional or behavioral problem. Behavioral problems, such as attention deficits or conduct disorders, are more frequent than emotional problems like depression and anxiety. Boys exhibit more behavioral, and girls more emotional problems. These studies emphasize that only some of these problems come to the attention of pediatricians. Costello et al. (1988) report a 16% prevalence of emotional and behavioral problems in a HMO population of 7 to 11 year olds. The pediatricians seeing these children, however, only reported the presence of a problem in 5.6% of the children using an ICD-9 classification. The two Rochester studies, using a younger population, reported 5.0% and 5.1% current prevalence rates. Hence there is good evidence that only one third of all psychopathology is recognized by pediatricians, leading Costello et al. to call these problems "the new hidden morbidity."

Such findings raise other questions, including the long-term sequelae of neglected psychopathology, and the training of primary care pediatricians to recognize such pathology and to either treat or refer affected children. Both the training of pediatricians, and the training of child psychiatrists or other qualified mental health specialists, however, has, in our view, not advanced much over the past 20 years except for a few institutions with vigorous behavioral pediatrics programs. Because counseling is time consuming and does not easily fit into the 15-minute schedule of busy pediatricians, double time slots have to be provided for conference visits, and health insurance coverage has to be extended to compensate for these consultations adequately. Accessibility to such services is likely to remain a problem for many years. Furthermore, parental perceptions about what constitutes a "medical" problem versus a disciplinary/individual problem, need to be addressed. Similarly, more attention must be given to pediatricians' perceptions about which treatments are effective and appropriate.

The specification of the "new morbidity" as psychopathology is helpful because it focuses on some of the problems, but it should not prevent us from recognizing other dysfunctional behaviors or inadequate environments. School problems were discussed earlier. Failure to give many adolescents an acceptable education and the opportunity for economic self-sufficiency (William T. Grant Commission on Work, Family and Citizenship, 1988), or to make teenage childbearing a less attractive alternative for poor adolescents, is still considered a part of the "new morbidity." We may not have medical answers for coping with the consequences of the new social environment but we should, nonetheless, recognize their "health" effects and address them with innovative research and programs.

*REFERENCES*

COSTELLO, ELIZABETH J.
  1986  "Primary Care Pediatrics and Child Psychopathology: A Review of Diagnostic Treatment, and Referral Practices." *Pediatrics,* 78:1044–1051.

COSTELLO, ELIZABETH J., and PANTINO, THOMAS
  1987  "The New Morbidity: Who Should Treat It?" *Developmental and Behavioral Pediatrics,* 8:288–291.

COSTELLO, E. J., COSTELLO, A. J., EDELBROCK, C., BURUS, B. J., DULCAN, M.K., BRENT, D., and JANISZEWSKI, S.
  1988  "Psychiatric Disorders in Pediatric Primary Care." *Archives of General Psychiatry,* 45:1107–1116.

GOLDBERG, I. D., REGIER, D. A., MCINERNY, T. K., PLESS, I. B., and ROGHMANN, K. J.

 1979  "The role of the Pediatrician in the Delivery of Mental Health Services to Children." *Pediatrics,* 63:898–909.

GOLDBERG, I. D., ROGHMANN, K. J., MCINERNY, T. K., and BURK, J. D.

 1984  "Mental Health Problems among Children Seen in Pediatric Practice." *Pediatrics,* 73:278–293.

WEILAND, S. K., PLESS, I. B., and ROGHMANN, K. J.

 1992  "Chronic Illness and Mental Health Problems in Pediatric Practice: Results from a Survey of Primary Care Providers." *Pediatrics* 89: 445–449.

WILLIAM T. GRANT COMMISSION ON WORK, FAMILY AND CITIZENSHIP

 1988  The Forgotten Half: Pathways to Success for America's Youth and Young Families. Washington DC: Youth and America's Future.

*Preschool Behavior Problems: From the Identification of High-Risk Families to Preventive Community Programs*

I BARRY PLESS AND ROBERT W. CHAMBERLIN

A promising lead in the early Rochester studies was the study of child-rearing styles and child behavior patterns (Chamberlin, 1984). What happened to these problems? Are they still there, and how are they treated?

   Yes, they are still very frequent but appear to be of little predictive value. The diagnosis is still very fuzzy and what matters more depends on the degree and duration of the problem. Most can, however, be treated with any of a variety of brief intervention approaches. The major change in the period since is an abandonment of the theory of high risk, which was a premise for many earlier planned and targeted interventions. The major departure since the original work is a move away from the high-risk concept because we constantly found a pattern of shifting sands. Behaviors in early childhood fail to predict later functioning, either over time or across settings. As a result you really could not identify a high-risk group for intervention with any accuracy.

   The shift among researchers has been toward a community-wide approach involving parent education and support, rather than trying to target specific families. Specific families can be targeted for specific programs but only on a community-wide basis. The data clearly support this, particularly longitudinal studies that have tried to identify high-risk groups. This has lead to a greater acceptance of Sameroff's transactional model of child development.

   Behavior problems and particularly those related to preschool children are taught about more frequently and the entire behavioral and developmental focus within ambulatory pediatrics has received more emphasis. However the programs themselves generally fall outside of the traditional clinical settings.(RWC)

A major implication of this shift is the reduced involvement of primary care providers and a greater focus on prevention.

The prevention of behavior problems along with a host of other similar difficulties are problems related to family dysfunction of one sort or another, such as low birth weight, child abuse and neglect, school failure, etc., and hospitalizations of children under age 1. Instruments to detect high-risk children have been refined, but they are mostly used in research rather than in clinical practice.

Certainly these types of problems are commonly encountered by pediatricians in private practice. As a result of our experience, it appears that screening is of limited value for the reasons I have suggested—there are too many variables involved. For example, if you identify a group of children with problems at one point in time and then repeat the screen 6 months later, you may come up with an entirely different sample. (RWC)

What about the prevention of these problems through parent education?

We've become much more sophisticated in how to do that now. I see the coming community model for interventions similar to the Stanford Heart Disease Program, where you come in and do community organization to bring diverse groups together; you use social marketing techniques and have multiple programs targeted for multiple segments of the population. Hence the general thrust of the original observations in *Child Health and the Community* were on the right track, focusing on families and the community, and not simply on individual children. But we have become far more sophisticated in how to do this since 1975.

It is important to recognize, however, that community interventions take a long time to be effective and a short period of programatic support is unlikely to see positive results. In terms of evaluating the outcomes we must look at effects on the family and community and not simply those focused on the child. Another aspect of community intervention is clearly that one needs something like home visitors to reach the highly stressed families and those that do not use traditional clinic-based services. These would be targets for parent education and support, but would an intervention go into a family with a view to detecting behavior problems or approach the problem more generally? (RWC)

In this sense then, would behavior problems in the preschool child only be one segment of a more general pattern of dysfunction?

This is true of the delivery of preventive services in general. However, home visiting cannot be relied on alone—it's one of an array or programs such as parent drop-in centers, preschool education programs, developments promoting day care programs, and work-related matters, such as paid leave for pregnancies and time off for child care. To clarify, the outreach worker would be used to target particular programs to particular segments that may be viewed as high risk but one cannot rely on one specific program as a way to impact the community as a whole. It all goes back to the bell-shaped curve—there are many more medium-risk families ready to take the place of high-risk ones when their life circumstances change, than there are high-risk families who are going to be cured by some sort of intervention. Therefore, if one concentrates all resources on the high-risk group, one never catches up.(RWC)

The other striking change from the original study is the demographic shift in family structures and composition. When the earlier edition of this book was published, 11% of mothers were working full time. Now that figure approaches 60%. There are an increasing numbers of single parents, higher divorce rates, and more births out-of-wedlock. Clearly, day care and other preschool programs should be part of a community strategy. This places much of the responsibility outside of the private practice setting and onto the community as a whole. It includes public health, political and social agencies, as well as educators.

Nonetheless some private practitioners have become involved in this approach. For example, 2 former Rochester residents who are in practice in Norway, Maine, have added a day care center, a parent drop-in center, and an early intervention program in combination with their primary care pediatric practice. There is another medical center that has gone well beyond the delivery of primary care to try to impact the schools and other community agencies through the use of home visitors. This closely approximates the Scandinavian model. The primary care physician who simply tends to address the clinical symptoms of the stressed family coming to his office is not going to be very effective if he attempts to intervene alone. He must be aware of what is available in the community to help families cope.

Two examples of this that were present during the period when the book was being written were the Neighborhood Health Centers and to a lesser extent, the use of family counselors.

The principle link regarding behavior problems, especially in the preschool age, has become with clinical and developmental psychology rather than psychiatry, which was where the emphasis was when the earlier edition of this book was written.

## REFERENCES

CHAMBERLIN, ROBERT W.

1984 "How Well Do Early Childrearing Styles and Child Behavior Patterns Predict Later Home and School Functioning?" Chapter 21 in *Handbook of Longitudinal Research*, vol I, edited by S.A. Mednick, et al.

1989 Interview by I. Barry Pless

## Chronic Illness as a Generic Concept

I BARRY PLESS

Ten years before *Child Health and the Community* was written, the fact that children with chronic disorders required special consideration beyond the care for their specific disease had just begun to be recognized. What was becoming increasingly clear was that there were generic problems related to how services are best organized to meet the broad range of their clinical needs. The shift in perception of a wide array of health care providers arose from a growing number of studies suggesting that the care of these children is far more complex than had been appreciated previously. In particular, the frequency with which they, or their families, experienced secondary psychosocial problems was highlighted by these reports. The services needed to address these problems adequately, both from a preventive and curative perspective, required changes at the clinical and community level. What gradually emerged was a recognition that somehow the two had to be better integrated and that some new services, or levels of organization, were needed to do so.

In retrospect, our work appeared to catalyze this process. The momentum had already begun, but the rate of change was accelerated by the work of the Rochester team. The most important contribution may well have been simply to solidify the notion that chronic disorders needed to be considered from a noncategorical rather than specific disease perspective. It was repeatedly emphasized that the chronicity of the condition mattered most, rather than the specific diagnosis. Our early work accomplished this by making chronic illness one of the specific foci of the first of the three Rochester Child Health Surveys. As a result, the prevalence of chronic disorders was established with some precision, and the findings were frequently cited in subsequent papers on the subject. A second focus of the original survey was to examine the extent to which these illnesses were associated with secondary morbidity of a psychosocial nature. Although these analyses were not very sophisticated, they proved to be an important contribution to a growing body of literature drawing attention to this phenomenon.

In addition to defining the problem more precisely, our work included an attempt to try to address it from a preventive perspective. To this end the family counselor program was established and formally evaluated. The results were extremely encouraging, and as a consequence this program expanded from Monroe County to the surrounding Genesee region. Various combinations of attachment of family counselors to physicians were tried, and in the end they fell under the aegis of social work at Strong Memorial Hospital. Although this proved to be a successful arrangement, tolerated surprisingly well by both the counselors and their social worker colleagues and supervisors, serious difficulties were soon encountered. These arose when requests were made to fund the program through the hospital budget. The family counselors were, in a sense, volunteer community workers, but it was always felt that it was important to pay them a stipend, however meager. But even this proved too great an obstacle for the hospital to accept in view of the unconventional nature of the service being provided. In a few, isolated instances, specialists insisted that such counselors were essential to their patients. In these cases other means were found to provide the necessary reimbursement and to cover basic costs. But this was the exception rather than the rule, and as time went on, the program died out.

It did not disappear, however, without leaving its mark on the national scene. In Colorado a similar program was established to provide assistance to low-income families in an attempt to prevent child abuse and other unfavorable developments. The Rochester program also appears to have had an important influence on the shape of the Pediatric Ambulatory Care team trial conducted at Jacobi Hospital (Stein and Jessop 1991), although the staffing in this case was essentially provided by nursing.

Perhaps the most important by-product of the Rochester experience in this area was the impact it had on those responsible for the Vanderbilt Public Policy Studies. The late Professor Nicholas Hobbs was impressed with our view of the problems of children with chronic illness and their families. Much of the thinking of the team he gathered to examine the public policy implications in this was similarly affected by our example. After several years of hard work, the Vanderbilt group produced 2 volumes addressing the needs of these children in precisely the fashion being put forward by us (Hobbs and Perrin, 1985a; 1985b). Subsequently, similar themes were echoed in the work of the American Academy of Pediatrics' Committee on Handicap, and was extended by the creation of the Research Consortium on Chronic Illness, established under the auspices of the William T. Grant Foundation. As a result, there is an ongoing and growing body of work that continues to address the problems originally identified by us.

REFERENCES

HOBBS, N., AND PERRIN, J.M.
    1985a  *Issues in the Care of Children with Chronic Illness.* San Francisco: Jossey-Bass.

HOBBS, N., AND PERRIN, J.M.
    1985b  *Chronically Ill Children and Their Families: Problems, Prospects and Proposals from the Vanderbilt Study.* San Francisco: Jossey-Bass.

STEIN, R.E.K., AND JESSOP, D.J.
    1991  "Long-Term Mental Health Effects of a Pediatric Home Care Program." *Pediatrics* 88:490–496.

## D. A NEW ENVIRONMENT FOR HEALTH CARE COST CONTAINMENT, MEDICAID AND IPAs

*Hospital Cost Containment:*
*A Local Success Story for the 1980s*

KLAUS J. ROGHMANN

Based in part on a 1972 interview with a former secretary of health, education, and welfare, Marion Folsom, the first edition of this book reviewed the early health planning efforts in the Rochester community. Out of the Health Division of the Council of Social Agencies and the Health Council of Monroe County (created in 1966), the Genesee Region Health Planning Council (GRHPC) was formed in 1969 to function as the "B" agency of comprehensive health planning. GRHPC had the local review function for hospital and health facility construction and later turned into a regional health systems agency, known as the Finger Lakes Health Systems Agency (FLHSA). In the 1980s, federal policy changed again—the federal government pulled back from health planning and state governments assumed these responsibilities. In spite of the continued dismantling of health planning agencies across the country, the FLHSA was able to rely on local funding and remained a powerful mediating agency in the community. The spirit of local initiative persisted through the 1980s. Seeking exemptions from outside regulation wherever possible, the community took responsibility for identifying problems and developing solutions. In a true cooperative spirit, self-planning, self-regulation, and "self-policy" were seen as more effective in dealing with local problems than reliance on outside regulation.

Hospital planning, of course, is always at the heart of most health planning efforts. When health care costs began to escalate, various cost containment options were discussed, and several forms of managed care were initiated in 1973 (see below). By 1989, the majority of the population was covered by some HMO-type plan in an attempt to control health care costs.

Maxicap was the first local attempt to control inpatient care costs (Sorensen, Saward, and Stewart, 1982). The Hospital Experimental Program (HEP) was the second attempt and has shown itself successful year after year (Block, Regenstreif, and Griner, 1987). Administered by the Rochester Area Hospital Corporation (RAHC), the HEP program was a local prospective hospital payment system that has taken over many hospital planning functions. It allocated funds for expansions and technological improvements, reviewed the sharing of charity and bad debt burdens, and made adjustments for case-mix and severity ratings, as well as the costs of medical education. When the program was established, Medicare patients were exempted from DRG payments. The Social Security Administration agreed to accept Medicare rates as determined on the basis of local historical data and small yearly increments, and the New York State Social Services Department similarly agreed to accept local rates for Medicaid patients. Local third-party payers, such as Blue Cross and Health Maintenance Organizations, joined this prospective payment plan. All of these payers made predetermined weekly payments to the hospitals, instead of payments based on utilization. Claims were still generated, but they were only used for internal management and research purposes. To perform needed analyses of this shared data base, a local data management subsidiary was created.

HEP was based on 4 management principles. First, incentives work better than penalties and sanctions. Second, rewards should be allocated according to outcome rather than input. Third, accountability should be restricted to those cost increases that are under the control of the hospitals. Fourth, long-term stability in revenue and cash flow improves management. In contrast to payments based on DRGs, there was no incentive to fill beds. If a procedure could be performed on an outpatient basis, this saved money for all, and the hospital avoided the costs of an admission. During their first 5 years (1980–1984) in the program, Rochester hospitals actually managed to achieve an operating margin of 2.6% and thus increase their reserves. No other region in New York showed a surplus for the same period (Block, Regenstreif, and Griner, 1987). Admissions per 1,000 population decreased from 135 to 124, while New York State as a whole had only a minor decrease in rates, from 149 to 148. In New England, admissions declined during this period from 148 to 141. Audits for inappropriate admissions and length of stay showed lower rates than elsewhere. Quality of care was monitored through the number of observed complications and showed no change from 1980 through 1984.

The second HEP contract ran from 1985 to 1987, the third contract started in 1988 and ended in 1990. In 1991 Rochester hospitals returned to the statewide care-payment system called New York Prospective Hospital Reimbursement Methodology. Everybody agrees that health care cost will increase more without the cooperative than with it (Beau, 1991).

The success of the decade-long HEP program would not have been possible had there not been a tradition of trust and cooperation in the community and an environment favorable to the hospitals. Successful hospital planning had reduced the bed to population ratio to 3.4 per 1,000, compared to 4.4 per 1,000 for New York State. Blue Cross of Rochester could always offer community rating to local employers who favored sharing the community burden rather than insisting on short-term advantages through the experience ratings offered by other carriers. Local physicians are used to second opinions, utilization reviews, and other efforts to minimize inpatient care. Although the Rochester community spirit cannot easily be exported to other communities, it showed that alternative cooperative arrangements can be preferable to regulation and price competition. Alternative forms of cooperation, based on enlightened self-interest, community initiative, and professional leadership, are still feasible. The demise of HEP in 1991 was greeted with great sadness by most. "It is sad and it's troubling, because it speaks to how wide the gulf has become" (John Urban, president of Preferred Care).

REFERENCES

BEAU, CHRISTINA LE,

1991   "Area Hospital Pact Pronounced Dead." *Rochester Business Journal*, March 25–31.

BLOCK, J., REGENSTREIF, D., and SHUTE, L.

1981   "Experimental Payment Program: It's Working for Rochester Area Hospitals." *Hospital Financial Management*: 10–20.

BLOCK, J.A., REGENSTREIF, D.I., and GRINER, P.F.
  1987   "A Community Hospital Payment Experiment Outperforms National Experience: The Hospital Experimental Payment Programs in Rochester, NY." *JAMA*,
257:193–197.

SORENSEN, A., SAWARD, E., and STEWART, D.
  1982   "Hospital Cost Containment in Rochester: From Maxicap to the Hospital Experimental Payments Program." *Inquiry*, 19:327–336.

## The Local Medicaid Program 10 Years Later: The MediCap Experiment

KLAUS J. ROGHMANN

Looking back over the last few decades, it is clear that the 2 most
important changes in the U.S. medical care environment took place in
the mid-1960s. Medicare, the federal entitlement program for the
elderly, and Medicaid, the state/local medical assistance plan for the
poor, were introduced. Medical care costs had increased excessively by
then, and the organizational structures for care delivery had become
too complex to leave the care of the poor to individual acts of charity or
to local welfare departments. The elderly no longer had access to
employment-based insurance and needed a national program. But the
2 programs were given completely different structures, and this significantly influenced their later developments. As a national federal program with its own trust fund, Medicare is assured of its continued
existence. Providers integrate enrollees into the mainstream of care, and
the Medicare card is as welcome as any other insurance card. Much
research and development went into the program's organization, with
strong cooperation from providers and insurers.

Medicaid, in contrast, is administered by county social service departments according to state regulations. Somewhat smaller than the Medicare program, Medicaid's enrollees are about 75% of Medicare's, and its
total expenditures are about 60%. Yet, the fragmentation of state
programs, the need for local means testing, and the lack of political
power among the poor prevents Medicaid from developing stable and
efficient organizational and financial structures for the delivery of
needed medical services. Providers have tried to accommodate the
constant changes that local and state governments impose on these
programs by fixing eligibility criteria, benefit structures, and provider
fees. The Medicaid program competes with educational, highway, and
other local expenses in yearly budget battles. Unless Medicaid is pro-
tected through a separate and stable long-term budget, even the most

dedicated and energetic efforts to integrate health care for the poor into the mainstream of American medicine will be bound to fail.

In the early 1970s, there was a Medicaid population of 50,000 in categorical programs (cash payments) and 10,000 in the medically indigent program in Monroe County. In the mid 1980s, the figures were 41,000 categorical Medicaid patients and 7,500 medically indigent. The program was first administered locally, with research collaboration between the university's medical center and the local program as described in the 1975 edition of this book. Private physicians were paid customary and usual fees and accepted the poor as patients. After the first state-mandated fee cut for physicians, many stopped taking new medicaid patients. The rejected enrollees turned to more expensive hospital facilities, which increased costs for ambulatory care by 31% in 1969. The cost data reported for those early years have long been obsolete. By 1984, the cost per adult Aid for Dependent Children (AFDC) patient/month had increased to $75, and the cost per Home Relief (HR) patient had increased to $103 per month.

Even 20 years ago, local program administrators and legislators were concerned about rising costs and discussed ways of enrolling the Medicaid population in health maintenance organizations. Rochester had started 3 HMOs in 1973, and some form of managed care for the poor was an obvious choice. After a decade of negotiations, the local Medicaid program was given the go-ahead to respond to a new initiative by the Health Care Financing Administration. It received funding ($700,000) for a Medicaid capitation demonstration project (June 1982–April 1988) in cooperative agreement with the New York Department of Social Services. A nonprofit organization (MediCap Plan, Inc.), with a local 15-member board, was established to plan and administer the project. MediCap Inc. contracted with a local HMO, the Rochester Health Network (RHN), to provide the services. RHN, in turn, signed up the community's 10 major providers of health care for the poor. Enrollments in 1986 are given in Table 14D.1

A network HMO, RHN provided prepaid services at a number of affiliated health centers and through its affiliate Independent Practitioners' Association (IPA), the Monroe Plan. In September 1986 a group model HMO, the Genesee Valley Group Health Association (GVGHA), also signed up with MediCap. Initially, MediCap was to enroll all 42,000 Aid for Dependent Children and Home Relief members over a 3-year period, then integrate the 7,500 Medical Assistance members, and finally, incorporate the Supplemental Security Income (SSI) and disabled population. The capitated rate was to equal 95% of fee-for-service (FFS) costs based on previous expenditures. The Medicaid administration developed actuarial rates to reimburse the 10 provider groups. The

*Table 14D.1.　MediCap Enrollments by Major Providers, 1986*

| Health Centers | |
| --- | --- |
| A. Jordan Health Center | 7,255 |
| Genesee* Health Services | 4,625 |
| Westside Health Center | 4,274 |
| Northeast Health Center | 1,469 |
| Oak Orchard Health Center | 210 |
| | 17,833 |

| Hospital Outpatient Departments | |
| --- | --- |
| Strong Memorial Hospital | 4,507 |
| Rochester General Hospital | 2,906 |
| St. Mary's Hospital | 1,967 |
| Highland Hospital | 1,723 |
| | 11,103 |

| Private Practitioners (Organized as an Independent Practitioners' Association) | |
| --- | --- |
| Monroe Plan | 6,626 |
| | 35,562 |

*Located at the Genesee Hospital and often listed under hospital.

FFS costs listed above ($75 for AFDC adults, $103 for HR adults) were similar to prevailing local rates for simple health insurance contracts in 1988 (Blue Choice, $71.06; Group Health, $69.43; Blue Cross/Blue Shield, $78.41; Preferred Care, $66.57). These rates, therefore, appeared economically feasible.

Enrollment began in July 1985 and was complete for Phase I in May 1986. The program had mandatory enrollment (subject to "good cause" exemption), with open provider selection; enrollees were then locked into their choice for a period of 6 months (subject to grievance). Under this benefit package, all medical care was provided, directly or through referral, by the enrollee's primary care physician.

During the first year of operation, the agreed-upon 95% of previous FFS costs were provided, that is, a 5% cost reduction was anticipated. For the second year, the state cut that allowance by 20% to profit from the alleged cost savings of managed care. According to local providers, however, such savings never materialized. In January 1987, an intensive process of rate negotiation started for the third year of the program. Providers had become increasingly dissatisfied with the plan's management, and had suffered substantial losses. The large providers claimed they were charged for services that were outside the agreement. Furthermore, subjects who should have been covered by other payers, like SSI, were enrolled and assigned to them. When severe delays occurred in processing claims, lawsuits resulted. The local newspapers covered these disagreements in detail, as negotiations turned to political debate. By April 1987, it became obvious that the program was in deep trouble. Making data available to the public, RHN demonstrated a loss of $2.8 million, for which the 10 providers were at risk. The Anthony Jordan Health Center had to cut services drastically and requested help from the Public Health Service. Providers demanded that part of the 20% cut should be restored retroactively and that a substantial rate increase for year 3 was needed. When the New York State negotiators disagreed, most providers withdrew from the program at the end of year 2. Some 8,000 subscribers continued on a voluntary basis for a few more months, but eventually MediCap Plan, Inc. was dissolved, RHN went out of business, and Medicaid patients returned to FFS status along the previous guidelines. Clearly, a local experiment had failed.

No formal evaluation of the reasons for the failure of this program is available. Three consumer surveys obtained information from potential or actual enrollees. Secondary data analysis of the Medicaid Medical Information System (MMIS) files was done to propose detailed rate settings. With funds provided by the local Department of Social Services (Temkin-Greener, 1986; Temkin-Greener and Winchell, 1991), the first survey was conducted between May and July 1984, aiming for a 10% sample of the AFDC population. The final sample consisted of 495 heads of households with information on 479 children and 495 adults. The survey population was 60% black, 29% white, 9% Hispanic, and the rest Asian/Native Americans.

In contrast to many national surveys, only 4% reported not having a regular source of care (the excellent access to care in Rochester has been observed by others [Singer, Butler, and Palfrey, 1986]). Of those with a regular care source, 56% went to hospital clinics, 35% to free-standing health centers, and 8% to private practice physicians. Proximity was the predominant reason given for selecting a health center ("It's close to where I live"), and quality of care as the motivation for selecting a hospital clinic ("I get good care there"). Asked where they would go if they could go "anywhere," only 38% indicated they would switch. When asked to actually select a specific place or doctor, only 13% chose a different place. The survey showed that few Medicaid patients would actually switch if they were offered a choice, and that the MediCap plan would not significantly change the provider selection.

The second survey was taken using a self-administered questionnaire (English and Spanish versions available), during the second quarter of enrollment (Roghmann, Zastowny, and Temkin-Greener, 1988). Three sites were included, giving a total sample of 2,622. Three attitude domains were studied: health beliefs (folk vs. modern medicine), readiness to seek care (for children and self), and satisfaction with care. Through a search of the MMIS files, linkage with prior utilization was possible: attitudes and utilization were not strongly related, but demographics and utilization were. Home Relief enrollees had higher costs than Aid for Dependent Children enrollees. Utilization did not correlate strongly between years (1984 vs. 1985) for Aid for Dependent Children enrollees ($r = .161$), but did for Home Relief enrollees ($r = .786$), that is, past high utilization predicted high future utilization for Home Relief patients, but not for Aid for Dependent Children patients. Although such "between years" correlation is necessary for adverse selection, which can significantly affect prepayment plans, patient differences for 4 major providers were examined, but no evidence for adverse selection was found. The results showed that for Aid for Dependent Children enrollees, at least, prepayment should not have favored any one source. Subjects had low folk medicine and high modern medicine orientations, and expressed generally high satisfaction with the care received.

The third and final survey was conducted from October 1986 to December 1986, after about 1½ years of MediCap experience (Temkin-Greener and Winchell, 1991), using a sample of 788 AFDC and HR members. Questions about care satisfaction taken from the first survey were asked. Due to the IPA plan in the MediCap package, access to private practice physicians had increased from 7.6% to 18%. For blacks, the increase was from 6.6% to 11.7% and for whites, from 11.6% to 30.6%. Twenty-three percent of the respondents had changed their source of care, again giving proximity most often as their reason. Satisfaction with the care received increased, and people appreciated having both greater access to private doctors and a primary care physician in charge of their care. Only 5.8% mentioned dissatisfaction with restricted emergency room access, or that approval was required for specialist referral.

No survey of providers was taken, and no chart reviews were performed to assess differences in quality of care under prepayment. A local research proposal for such a study was not funded and a federally funded evaluation was terminated when the experiment failed.

Newspaper reports quoted local providers as criticizing the arbitrary, repeated rate cuts at a time when yearly cost increases were above 10%. State negotiators claimed local mismanagement and excessive layers of local administrative staff. Indeed, the largest local health center was without a medical director for over a year; the claims processing expertise and computer facilities were inadequate; and payments to providers were greatly delayed. Furthermore, private HMOs and MediCap handled unauthorized emergency room claims differently. High charges for alcoholism and drug treatment and mental health services had not been anticipated. The effectiveness of some primary care managers (residents in hospital outpatient departments) was debated. But these management problems could have been solved with proper attention. They appeared minor compared to the volatility introduced by the instability of funding. Control for this experiment had shifted to state administrators, and local mechanisms to resolve conflicts no longer worked. Normal market mechanisms, like enrollment and disenrollment choices of consumers in prepayment plans, had become irrelevant. The organizational structure of Medicaid and the local organization of medical services proved to be incompatible.

Other states have also tried programs like MediCap and most have failed. Establishing needed changes in state regulations, reimbursement mechanisms, and case-management techniques has been much more complex than anticipated. It has been argued that these plans failed to attract the high-level management skills retained by private HMOs or commercial health insurers. Rather than blaming the victim, it is more persuasive to argue that it is exactly the organizational rigidity and the financial restrictions of Medicaid that prevent local leadership and management to find solutions. Unless a separate program with independent funding for Medicaid is established, we do not anticipate any major changes in the current system.

## REFERENCES

ROGHMANN, K.J., ZASTOWNY, T.R., and TEMKIN-GREENER, H.

    1988    Utilization of Services and Satisfaction with Care: The Relevance of Health Beliefs in a Medicaid Population (unpublished manuscript).

SINGER, J.D., BUTLER, J.A., and PALFREY, J.S.

    1986    "Health Care Access and Use among Handicapped in Five Public School Systems." *Medical Care*, 24:1–13.

TEMKIN-GREENER, H.

    1986    "Medicaid Families under Managed Care: Anticipated Behavior." *Medical Care*, 24(8):721–732.

TEMKIN-GREENER, H. and WINCHELL, M.

    1991    "Medicaid Beneficiaries under Managed Care: Provider Choice and Satisfaction." *Health Services Research*, 26: 509–529.

A New Form of Managed Care: The IPAs Take Over

KLAUS J. ROGHMANN

The professionalization of pediatrics through various stages of development has already been referred to (Halpern, 1988). The last stage capitalized on the psychosocial aspects of a social problem-oriented discipline and can be called the "coming of age in general pediatrics" (Green, 1983). Community pediatricians have always realized that free market mechanisms in the delivery of health services do not benefit all members of society equally. Patients in greatest need benefit least, and charity and professional ethics are not sufficient to balance such market inequities. To deliver a more equitable provision of services to all children, new organizational forms are needed. Continuity clinics, emergency services, health centers, school clinics, health department clinics, and "alternative" health care delivery sites, filled the gaps left by the predominant private practice organization of services. The development of high-technology, high-cost medicine, with its reliance on hospital care, further aggravates the situation. The open-ended medical care market, with no caps imposed on resource utilization, made what some judge to be excessive claims on the gross national product. Clearly, the country needed a new way to manage health care services. In Rochester, this took the form of health maintenance organizations (HMO). The University of Rochester recruited Ernest Saward as dean of community affairs. A coalition of the health insurance industry, local employers, and the medical center led the way.

The growth of HMOs came in two waves. The first started on July 1, 1973, too late to be covered in the 1975 edition of this book. Three HMOs were marketed simultaneously: a group model HMO, with its own newly constructed health center; a network HMO, using several city health centers that also served a large Medicaid population; and an independent practitioners' association (IPA) sponsored by the local medical society. They went under the trade names Group Health (Genesee Valley Group Health Association), RHN (Rochester Health Network) and HealthWatch, respectively. At the end of 1974, HealthWatch was the clear winner in enrollments, with 20,167 enrollees compared to 10,397 at Group Health and 3,500 at RHN. HealthWatch was also, however, the one HMO that had seriously underestimated the administrative controls needed to run an IPA. It suffered from adverse selection and was terminated after 3 years. The remaining HMOs doubled their enrollments in the third year to 20,631 and 7,743 respectively, but from then on only grew slowly to reach 36,732 and 18,345 enrollees respectively by the end of 1979, capturing 7.7% of the total county population of about 700,000. These two HMOs managed to lower health care costs by reducing hospitalization, but their market penetration was too low to have a major impact on overall costs. Their premiums remained significantly higher than the rate for traditional Blue Cross, due to their more extensive benefits.

As a result of their failure to have a major impact on overall costs, the local health systems agency established a task force on HMOs to review previous developments and make recommendations for future actions. There was concern that other community actions, like the successful history of constraining hospital construction and the HEP program described above, had already reduced Rochester's medical care expenses to a level at which few additional savings were possible. There was also concern that the existing HMOs were not aggressive enough to expand further. RHN was more concerned about access than cost containment, especially for the city's Medicaid and Medicare populations. Group Health was concerned about cost containment, but as a group practice HMO with its own facilities, expansion was only possible by building costly satellite health centers. While still in the planning stage, a new IPA, Preferred Care, was welcomed by the task force because it would use existing private practitioners' offices and would have neither Group Health's physical constraints, nor RHN's social objectives. The task force recommended more aggressive marketing through industry and local government, further Medicaid capitation efforts (see MediCap section above), and a special low Blue Cross rate for the working poor. On January 1, 1989, Blue Cross introduced ValuMed for low-income individuals (less than $10,000/year) and families (less than $20,000/year).

The new IPA, Preferred Care, proved successful in enrollment and effective in management. Within 3 years it had enrolled more members than either RHN and Group Health. Within 5 years its enrollment was equal to the sum of both earlier HMOs. The need for an IPA-type HMO was clearly established, but the limit of further enrollments remained unknown. In 1985 Blue Cross, still the predominant Health insurer, created its own IPA, called Blue Choice, to stem the continued loss of its members to Preferred Care. The premium differential between traditional Blue Cross and the IPAs narrowed. Rate competition proved to be the key to successful enrollment campaigns. Within 2 years, Blue Choice surpassed Preferred Care in enrollment. By the end of 1988, the combined HMO enrollments reached 435,000 in a county of then 710,000. For the child population, the penetration was estimated at 65%. (Exact penetration figures are difficult to establish because all insurers draw from neighboring counties as well. Similarly, local denominators cannot be determined with precision because only the employed population qualifies for membership, and only to the extent that their employers offer health insurance.)

There had been strong competition for enrollment especially since 1985, mostly on the basis of premium rates. As a result, all insurers suffered heavy losses. Price increases on January 1, 1989 averaged 19.9% for single contracts and 19.2% for family contracts. RHN, which had contracted with MediCap Inc. to enroll all Medicaid members and suffered heavy losses in that experiment, merged with Preferred Care. The two remaining IPAs became the community's dominant insurers. Next to the Minneapolis community and the San Francisco Bay area, Rochester now has one of the highest HMO penetration rates. If a second attempt to integrate Medicaid patients into this system were to be made, a fairly uniform practice environment for all children in the community would be achieved. If this had happened, we would have achieved one of the primary goals of community pediatrics—"a medical home" for *all* children. Nevertheless, through these insurance plans, clear responsibilities for the care of at least the enrolled child populations in the community have been established. Access to care and financial barriers are no longer key issues.

*Analysis*

There are two levels of analysis that can be applied to these changes in the health care market. First, there is the analytical approach, which dissects events in terms of functions fulfilled by the various players in a market. Second, there is the empirical analysis of the actual changes in utilization patterns, health, costs, and the effects of these changes. We will use both levels.

Economists first look at the basic difference between the health care market and other markets, and then at the structures that evolve as a result of these differences. Services are typically restricted to space-time coordinates that permit vast differentiation and limit competition. Services can neither be imported nor stored for later use, but are locally produced and consumed at times that are frequently beyond the control of either the provider or the consumer. Before the arrival of the hospital, minimal capital investment and long training periods were involved, and private practices were the main production units. The practitioner was both the business executive who ran the practice, and the clinician who produced the services. As in the past, medical education and the medical profession today are primarily concerned with excellence in clinical service. Running practices or hospitals is delegated to administrators who raise the needed capital, recruit support staff, and create the environment in which the clinician operates. Markets assume that needs are limitless and that price mechanisms are required to allocate resources to the highest bidder. Market imperfections can arise from local monopolies, the removal of price constraints through third-party payments, excessive regulations, or the use of health care facilities for symbolic purposes, for example, local pride manifested by an insistence on separate ambulance and hospital services. The explosion of medical care costs since the 1970s is seen as one indication of these market imperfections.

Creating HMOs to increase health care market efficiency can work through several mechanisms. First, HMOs can free doctors from their dual responsibility of running a business and providing clinical services. If the HMO provides a patient base, a referral system, a fee collection service, the physical plant, and the necessary insurance, physicians can concentrate on their clinical activities. The routine deduction of insurance premiums through employers eliminates collection costs for premiums payments. Guaranteed insurer payments to providers save fee-collection costs for providers. Second, HMOs can have greater bargaining power against hospitals, specialists, pharmacists, and other allied providers. By guaranteeing a certain volume of services, they can negotiate discounts for their members. Marketing expenses and opportunities to exploit consumer ignorance in crisis situations are reduced. Preferred provider organizations (PPOs) are the typical forms used by employers, insurers, or HMOs to achieve such market powers and balance monopolistic provider situations. Third, HMOs can change the practice styles of clinicians by establishing uniform protocols for certain situations in which previous uncertainty about treatments may have lead to overutilization of resources. (Clinicians don't want to be "bothered" by considering the economic implications of their decisions and would rather provide "the best" for their patients.) Fourth, patients too, tend to "overutilize" services in an attempt to provide the "best" for themselves and their children, but they lack the clinical knowledge that would enable them to know what the best is. Inappropriate use of ambulances, emergency rooms, and "second opinions" are likely if no direct costs to the user are imposed (although this argument remains debatable). "Managed" care restrains excessive use by consumers in the same way as preadmission reviews, second opinions for surgery, and peer review mechanisms restrain unreasonable resource use by providers.

HMOs will improve health care delivery to the extent that inefficiencies previously existed in given markets. This, of course, is an empirical question that has to be investigated by actual studies of ongoing systems. If no excessive resource use previously existed, and additional paperwork is created as well as new layers of bureaucracy, resource use will increase. Aggregate costs for a community can remain unaffected even when some parts of the community benefit from new organizations. If marketing efforts are successful in selectively recruiting low-risk enrollees, one plan may benefit, but overall community costs will remain the same. Experience rating versus community rating has such an effect. The Rochester community felt that experience rating would not lower aggregate costs but simply shift them and possibly add administrative costs. Rochester Blue Cross has always taken pride in its low administrative costs, although it may have tolerated some excessive clinical costs. Again, an empirical analysis is required to determine when the two balance and when aggregate costs reach a minimum. Clinical costs will become excessive if no administrative controls are applied, yet no one wants to invest in administrative costs beyond what can be saved through reduction of excessive clinical costs.

Finally, we may want to impose certain ceilings and floors on a market system, based on noneconomic considerations. HMOs take on the responsibility for defined populations, with all enrollees having equal access, and all having a primary care source. With financial barriers eliminated, service use is primarily determined by need. A floor is set that was lacking in the old system, and a ceiling is imposed by the plan's financial viability. Insurance for catastrophic illness reduces this ceiling effect. But it is clear that there may be costs and benefits beyond what can be expressed in aggregate costs. Community values will determine what floors and ceilings we accept.

There are also situations when ceilings are set too low, as may be seen in the failed MediCap experiment. Professionalization led to an increase in the power of the care providers, which was not balanced by a corresponding increase in the power of clients and society. HMOs return power to society and to clients as purchasers of professional services. State government continues to try to force down "excessive" growth of the medical sector. The result is a cap on provider control: opportunities for clinicians to achieve very high incomes are restricted and professional power is held in check by organizational restraints. It will be up to community pediatrics to provide organization, leadership, and training for working in this new complex environment.

Actual research on the effects of HMOs is less frequent than the analytical reasoning as to why HMOs should succeed, or journalistic reports on enrollment figures, or financial successes, or losses. Using data from a randomized controlled trial taken over a 5-year period, Manning, Wells, and Benjamin, (1987) reported on mental health service use under HMO versus FFS coverage. They found equal mean utilization rates in the 2 populations, but a more even spread of services in the HMO population than in the FFS population. Demographic factors have slightly different effects in the 2 settings, while age and education have more pronounced effects (Wells, Manning, and Benjamin, 1986). Health status does not seem to differ between HMO enrollees and FFS patients (McFarland, 1986). Since concern has been focused on whether high utilizers, like chronic illness patients, are underserved in HMO settings, Yelin, Shearn, and Epstein (1986) examined patients with rheumatoid arthritis under both FFS and HMO care. Prepaid patients received similar amounts and kinds of health care as FFS patients and had similar outcomes. If anything, FFS reported poorer overall health status for its group. The results indicate that concerns about reduced care or lower-care quality under prepayment are unfounded, but constant vigilance is still needed.

Rochester research on capitation effects followed 3 phases. First, under the leadership of the Department of Preventive Medicine, and in collaboration with pediatrics and Blue Cross, a number of studies focused on enrollment choices for HMOs and their effects on inpatient care. The enrollment studies indicated that 7% market penetration was about the ceiling under the initial rate structure for the group and network model HMOs that prevailed during the 1970s. Inpatient care studies demonstrated the selection effects of different enrollment strategies, both in terms of age and health status, and in terms of inpatient admissions controls (Wersinger et al., 1976). A second phase focused on capitated Medicaid, care satisfaction, and utilization rate stability over time. Concerns over adverse selection are misplaced if utilization does not correlate over time, that is, if high utilizers stay high utilizers, and low utilizers stay low utilizers. As reported above, there was little "stability" of utilization for the Aid for Dependent Children population, but much over time correlation for the Home Relief population. In terms of readiness to seek care, or faith in folk medicine, health beliefs played only a minor role in explaining overall utilization (Roghmann, Zastowny, and Temkin-Greener, 1988). Third, studies were conducted in a large suburban pediatric group practice to assess the effects of IPA enrollment on various forms of utilization (see utilization section above). Both a selection and an IPA effect were found (Szilagyi et al., 1990). High utilizers tended to select IPA insurance, and once covered, their utilization increased further. A subset of children with chronic illness, those coming for hyposensitization shots, were also examined (Szilagyi et al., 1992). Before IPA enrollment, such children were underutilizers of regular care; after enrollment, they came up to normal rates. These last studies are important as they focus on children rather than adults, IPAs rather than group model HMOs, and use ambulatory visits rather than inpatient care.

Overall, our evaluation of managed care is positive. Access to care is improved, and underutilization is eliminated. Our reservations concern cost containment efforts which appear excessive and may be unnecessary if the administrative costs involved in managing such complex systems can be reduced as most countries with national health insurance have done. While prepayment coverage increases ambulatory care for children in the community, aggregate costs will most likely increase as well.

## REFERENCES

GREEN, MORRIS
  1983   "Coming of Age in General Pediatrics" *Pediatrics* 72:275-82.

HALPERN, SIDNEY A.
  1988   *American Pediatrics—The Social Dynamics of Professionalism 1880–1980* Berkeley, Calif.: University of California Press.

MCFARLAND, B.H., FREEBORN D.K., MULLOOLY, J.P., POPE, C.R.
  1986   "Utilization Patterns and Mortality of HMO Enrollees." *Medical Care,* 24:208–208.

MANNING, W.G., WELLS, K.B., and BENJAMIN, B.
  1987   "Use of Outpatient Mental Health Services over Time in a Health Maintenance Organization and Fee-for-Service Plans." *American Journal of Psychiatry,* 144:283–287.

ROGHMANN, K.J., ZASTOWNY, T.R., and TEMKIN-GREENER, H.
  1988   "Utilization of Services and Satisfaction with Care: The Relevance of Health Beliefs in a Medicaid Population" (unpublished manuscript).

SZILAGYI, P.G., ROGHMANN, K.J., FOYE, H.R., PARKS, C., MCWHINNEY, J., MILLER, R., MCINERNY, T., KLEIN, S.
  1990   "The effect of IPA Plans on Pediatric Ambulatory Care Utilization in One Group Practice." *JAMA,* 263:2198–2203.

SZILAGYI, P.G., ROGHMANN, K.J., FOYE, H.R., PARKS, C., MCWHINNEY, J., MCINERNY, T., KLEIN, S.
  1992   "Increased Ambulatory Utilization in Independent Practice Association Plans Among Children Receiving Hyposensitization Therapy." *Inquiry* (in press).

WELLS, K.B., MANNING, W.G., and BENJAMIN, B.
  1986   "A Comparison of the Effects of Demographic Factors and Health Status on Use of Outpatient Mental Health Services in HMO and Fee-for-Service Plans." *Medical Care,* 24:949–960.

WERSINGER, R., ROGHMANN, K.J., GAVETT, J.W., and WELLS, S.M.
  1976   "Inpatient Hospital Utilization in Three Prepaid Comprehensive Health Care Plans Compared to a Retular Blue Cross Plan" *Medical Care,* 14(9):721–732.

YELIN, E.H., SHEARN, M.A., and EPSTEIN, W.V.
  1986   "Health Outcomes for a Chronic Disease in Prepaid Group Practice and Fee for Service Settings." *Medical Care,* 24:236–247.

YELIN, E.H., SHEARN, M.A., and EPSTEIN, W.V.

1986   "Health Outcomes for a Chronic Disease in Prepaid Group Practice and Fee for Service Settings." *Medical Care,* 24:236–247.

# "Summary and Implications" Revisited

ROBERT J. HAGGERTY,
KLAUS J. ROGHMANN,
AND
I. BARRY PLESS

> Plus ca change,
> plus c'est la meme chose
>
> Alphonse Karr, *Les Guepes*

O f all the segments of the 1975 edition of this book, this segment on trends, principles, and values needs the least revision. The basic trends have continued and our principles and values remain the same. Most of the previously unresolved issues are still unresolved.

Social trends such as the change in family structure and the economic change toward low-paying service industries have continued. There were no major political changes or initiatives in the health care sector comparable to Medicaid, Neighborhood Health Centers, or the abortion law in the period following the original volume.

However, issues like health planning have regressed or disappeared in the prevailing conservative political climate. The community spirit of voluntarism and emphasis on local leadership has also suffered. State regulation and market mechanism are now fallback positions. Little progress was made on controversial issues like abortion and birth control for teenagers. Many of the changes have been toward a further hardening of positions and a refusal to compromise. The management of the Medicaid program has increasingly antagonized the private sector. Care for the poor has been taken even more out of the mainstream of American medicine and relegated to public clinics.

Input from the social sciences toward a better understanding of these situations has also decreased. At the University of Rochester, the Department of Sociology was closed altogether and former faculty now work as applied social scientists in other settings.

In terms of changing disease patterns, we may have been too optimistic. We predicted a further decrease in old morbidities and a greater redirection of attention toward the new morbidities. Although there has certainly been a decline in mortality and major morbidity, the old morbidities linked to poverty have not disappeared. On the contrary, new diseases like AIDS and drug-dependent infants have emerged, and nationally there is growing concern about a resurgence of old diseases like measles and rubella.

In terms of mainstream medicine, much progress was made, however. Neonatal intensive care has seen major advances and developmental problems are dealt with more aggressively. Child abuse is addressed more openly. Genetics has progressed and is now a clinical division in most medical centers. There are new vaccines against infections and new treatments for cancer. Medical centers have strengthened their role and within pediatrics, general pediatrics has become the largest subspecialty.

In the marketplace the development of HMOs and IPAs have made access to primary care easier for those with health insurance. Primary care has also had a revival as general pediatrics and family practice have grown stronger. Our concern with manpower problems, in terms of oversupply has proven unfounded. The demand for clinical services appears to be limitless. Even with the anticipated reduction of newborns in the mid-1990s, we are no longer concerned about manpower oversupply.

As to the "new morbidities," we failed to accurately forecast many of the recent developments. Psychologists and educators now attend to special-needs children more often than do pediatricians or psychiatrists. State mandates for early intervention structure services, but in educational rather than medical institutions. Problems underlying the new morbidities have increased, but we have not yet learned to deal with them more effectively. Hence, all our earlier remarks about the boundaries of medical care remain as true now as they were 15 years ago.


COMMUNITY CHILD HEALTH: PHILOSOPHY


When *Child Health and the Community* was published in the mid-1970s, we ended the volume with a chapter called "Where Do We Stand?" It is interesting to compare some 15 years later, what is still valid and what has changed.

Community child health grew out of two streams: one was *ambulatory pediatrics,* which in the mid-1970s was already some 20 years old. The other was traditional *public health,* which had at least a century of tradition. One new element of ambulatory pediatrics in the 1960s was the combination of preventive and curative care at one delivery site; but such services were usually provided only to those who could find their way there. In contrast, public health services were concerned with prevention and with reaching all the population in an area. Combining these 2 aspects, and combining them with a research and training program of a clinical department constituted our operational definition of "community pediatrics." Although this still holds true, we now want to emphasize a third component—the physical and social environment in which children grow up.

Over the past 15 years, ambulatory pediatrics evolved in most teaching institutions into academic general pediatrics (Haggerty, 1992). This was certainly true at Rochester, which became one of 6 such training sites for academic general pediatrics, but largely with new faculty. Many of the original faculty in the community child health program at Rochester moved on to leadership positions in academic general pediatrics in other settings, and some into the leadership of pediatric departments. In contrast, the public health component of community child health services has not received much emphasis during the last 15 years. It may even be fair to state that it has evolved very little over that period. Few, if any of the faculty have moved into public health positions. It is still the case that a well-defined population is a necessity for community pediatric services. Only with a known population and a well-understood social environment can we organize services so that they reach all children. In addition, it has become evident that an integration of medical services with other human services in the community is highly desirable.

One can speculate why there is still less integration of services than is desirable. One reason for the lack of a public health component in most pediatric services today is the diminished role of public health nursing. In most cities in the past 15 years, public health nursing services, which have traditionally had a geographical base in which they operate, have been reduced. Even in the neighborhood (now called "community") health centers in Rochester there has been a diminished emphasis on population-based health care, and more on only servicing enrollees. Another component of the community child health program was the involvement of the public in advisory committees and advocacy. This too has diminished, in Rochester and throughout the nation.

Another reason may be more fundamental, namely, the often adversarial roles of the public and private sector, each operating on different principles. The public sector receives a fixed budget and has limited funds with which to expand services. The private sector operates in a free market, where prices and services follow different rules. In spite of the failure of development of many of the community aspects of community child health, we stand today where we did in the 1970s, convinced that services should be population-based, that the community must have a voice in them, and that medicine should take an active leadership role to ensure that good health care is delivered equitably.


## THE FUTURE OF COMMUNITY PEDIATRICS


The philosophy of community pediatrics is not shared by all. Some see it as wishful thinking—as a longing for simpler times when extended families lived in small, tightly knit communities and the family doctor knew all his patients and their families intimately. They remind us that the clock cannot be turned back. Others see community pediatrics as an idea that is incompatible with modern economics and political processes and one that may do more harm than good. Brown and McLaughlin (1990) would argue that our views are "thoroughly mistaken," and "that the communitarian, voluntaristic faith must be shaken and reformed if policy is to move beyond ever more elaborate labyrinths of cost shifting." We do not share these views. The delivery of human services such as medical care should always be affected by local voluntary and coopera-tive efforts, including active health planning and collaboration between the public and private sectors. Community activism is part of American culture. It is part of our role as citizens and professionals and determines the quality of life in our communities. It should be part of the value system that we pass on in medical education.


## THE NEW MORBIDITY


We coined this term, "new morbidity" in the early 1970s as a shorthand way of indicating that the nature of pediatric practice had changed radically, and that the traditional concern with infectious diseases was being superseded by a number of social and behavioral problems. On the one hand, it is gratifying that the term has taken hold and is used widely today; on the other hand, it is disturbing that so little progress has been made in reducing the burden of the new morbidity upon our youth. True, the relation of behavior and health is high on the public's agenda today among the middle class and in the business world. Health promotion through behavior change has achieved a high visibility in these groups. But within the disadvantaged community, socioeconomic barriers preclude much attention to health-promoting activities. Struggling with mere survival precludes most families in disadvantaged communities from paying much attention to healthy diet and appropriate exercise. Smoking and alcohol and substance abuse remain high among these populations. The emphasis in most health promotion programs is on individual motivation to achieve behavior change. But it is clear that socioeconomic factors are major deterrents to behavior change among this group. Only social changes, better jobs, less poverty, and less social disorganization in the community will allow disadvantaged people to pursue healthier lives.

In the 1970s we did not give such high priority to socioeconomic factors as causes of illness and barriers to good health as we do today. At the time we put more emphasis on the use of health services as the way to improve health. Today we believe that the use of these services is a necessary but not sufficient factor for ensuring the health of all children. Much more is needed.

## CHILD HEALTH SERVICES IN THE LAST DECADE OF THE TWENTIETH CENTURY

Fifteen years ago, Americans thought that universal health insurance was just around the corner, but were concerned that financial access to traditional health services would not be enough. Much energy was spent organizing comprehensive services and educating health personnel to provide high-quality service. But the movement to health insurance for all was derailed in the 1980s. We still believe that organization and training are important for good health services, but we are now more inclined to be incrementalists; we accept that the removal of financial barriers is the first stage in the movement to universal access.

As we write, leading industrialists, the American Academy of Pediatrics, and the New York State Health Department are all pushing for universal financial access to health care in America. Perhaps its time will finally come in the 1990s. But it must be accompanied by the 4 principles we enunciated two decades ago: (1) service to defined populations; (2) a system that monitors achievements and evaluates effectiveness; (3) initiatives to develop new service programs to meet unmet needs; and (4) training of appropriate personnel to meet these needs.

These are the essential characteristics of a health service that can meet the community's needs well. As noted, a truly good health service must be married to other broader community developments to ensure health. Another of our goals was to educate health personnel in settings where these characteristics were in place. This is still far from being achieved. Indeed, we are seeing something of a falloff in recruitment to primary care and community programs, largely as a result of increasing financial incentives for training in the subspecialties and a lack of exciting opportunities for providers of primary care.

## A VISION FOR THE FUTURE OF CHILD HEALTH AND THE COMMUNITY

Our new vision of child health in the community comprises 3 parts:

1. A *program* that gives every child access to a primary care provider or group of providers who know the child's name, can meet the majority of the child's health needs, both preventive and curative, and can provide services without financial barriers;

2. An organized system of care for *children with chronic illness* that provides not only early diagnosis, family education, counseling, and the majority of the physical health care within the primary care setting, but also enables easy access to subspecialist care when appropriate. It must also be one that emphasizes the improvement of the functioning of the child in everyday living, rather than the diagnosis and treatment of the physical disorder;

3. A *social environment* that gives young people a sense that their future will include both a meaningful job that will enable them to establish and maintain a stable family, and also a responsible role as a citizen. This will require first, the cooperation of business and the educational system in providing such jobs and the training necessary to fill them; and second, opportunity for young people to serve their community and thus develop their role as citizens in later adult life.

Our new vision of child health in the community thus involves an effective linkage of the health, welfare, education, and business communities. The goal of each community should be to provide a great place for children to grow up; a place where children count and become part of the community's agenda even if they fail to be part of the national agenda.

Rochester has achieved reasonable success in meeting the primary care needs of all its children, although (as is true for the nation as a whole) it still lacks a financing mechanism that guarantees access without financial barriers. Considerable strides have been made toward providing generic care for children with chronic illness, including early diagnosis, but it is fair to say that to date, most of their care is still provided by the subspecialist, and there has not been an institutionalization of generic approaches such as the family counselor program, as noted earlier. Finally, Rochester, like most communities, has a long way to go to integrate the health, welfare, education, and business communities in a meaningful way. Until this happens, many young people will continue to be deprived of a sense of a bright future. It is our hope and dream that the next generation of those who pursue the improvement of child health in the community will seek to advance all 3 of these domains.

## CHILD HEALTH: THE ULTIMATE GOAL

This review of developments in organizing and monitoring child health, which began in one community through one pediatric department, updated 15 years after the original presentation, must not be taken as the end result or goal of the program. The goal of community child health is to improve children's health. Children's health today is far more broadly defined than merely their physical health. The ultimate criterion for success of any program in child health must be how well all of the children in the community succeed in achieving their full potential, whether the impediment to be removed is physical illness, problem behaviors, school difficulties, or other problems. The boundaries of health, especially when one deals with the new morbidity, overlap with education, welfare, housing, employment, environmental concerns, and indeed, even with the moral climate of the community. Children and their families must have reasons to hope that a better life lies ahead of them, and society needs to do its share to encourage that hope. We have lived through a decade of "social Darwinism" during which children have been neglected. As a result, hope for the future, especially among our disadvantaged, has been reduced sharply. The challenge of community child health in the 1990s is to replace selfish "me-ism" with a commitment by the community to promote the optimal functioning of all its children. Only then will our goal of community child health as conceived in the 1970s be fully achieved.

## REFERENCES

BROWN, L.D., and MCLAUGHLIN, C.
1990    "Constraining Costs at the Community Level: A Critique." *Health Affairs,* pp. 6–
        33.

HAGGERTY, R.J.
1992    "Academic General Pediatrics: An Endangered Species?" *Pediatrics* (in press).

# Author Index

# Subject Index

AAP, *see* American Academy of Pediatrics
Abortion law, description of, 210
  implications for pediatric manpower, 319
Abortion ratio, definition of, 211
  by legitimacy, 213-214
  by maternal age, 214
  by pregnancy history, 214
  by race, 212-214
Accessibility, 199-201
Action for a Better Community, 225
Acute care, facilities, 28-29
  of migrants, 268
Acute illness, accidents as cause of, 74
  changing patterns of, 78
  classification of, 74
  consultations for, 72
  definition of, 73
  disability days due to, 76
  infections as cause of, 74
  needs, 325
  organ disorders as cause of, 74
  reason for seeking care, 76
Admissions, *see* Hospital admissions
Adolescent medicine, need for, 105, 107, 109-110
Adolescents, behavioral problems of, 106-107
  chronic illness in, 106-107, 109
  births to, 217
  hospitalizations of, 105-107
  use of alcohol by, 107
  use of drugs by, 107
  and parents, 108-109
Aggregate analysis of abortions, 211
Alinsky, Saul, 18
Ambulatory health services, estimating volume from, consumer studies, 369-371
  provider studies, 368-369
  types of, 29-30

utilization of, 169-175
volume and rate of, 169-170, 174-175
Ambulatory medical care, volume of contacts, 169-171, 174-176
American Academy of Pediatrics, recommended health supervision levels, 188-189, 192
ANA-AAP joint committee, 286
Andersen model, of health services utilization, 120, 127, 136-139
  and medication usage, 162-165
  variables used, 142, 154
Anthony Jordan Health Center, *see* Rochester Neighborhood Health Center
Availability, 199-201

Baden Street Dispensary, description of, 222
Baden Street Health Center, description of, 221-222
  services provided by, 227
Behavioral patterns, relationship of mother to, 353
Behavioral problems, and adolescents, 106-107
  doctor consultations for, 72
  etiology of, 99-101
  mothers' reports of, 96-97
  physicians' criteria for, 97-99
  prevalence among preschoolers, 95-96, 99
  prevention of, 110
  and the primary physician, 96, 99
  screening for, 111
  and trouble with schoolwork, 103, 107
Births, decline in, 210-211, 214, 216
  by race and legitimacy, 210-211
  to teenage mothers, 217
Birthrate, by locale, 68
  decrease in, 211

501

# Index to Part Four